Y0-CDL-149

ANNUAL REVIEW OF ANTHROPOLOGY

EDITORIAL COMMITTEE (1976)

A. R. BEALS
R. BURLING
K. V. FLANNERY
R. M. NETTING
B. J. SIEGEL
R. T. SMITH
J. N. SPUHLER
S. A. TYLER

Responsible for organization of Volume 5
(Editorial Committee, 1974)

A. R. BEALS
J. W. BENNETT
R. BURLING
M. S. EDMONSON
K. V. FLANNERY
B. J. SIEGEL
J. N. SPUHLER
S. A. TYLER

Assistant Editor   J. HEAVENER
Indexing Coordinator   M. A. GLASS
Subject Indexer   B. D. OZAKI

ANNUAL REVIEW OF ANTHROPOLOGY

BERNARD J. SIEGEL, *Editor*
Stanford University

ALAN R. BEALS, *Associate Editor*
University of California, Riverside

STEPHEN A. TYLER, *Associate Editor*
Rice University

VOLUME 5

1976

ANNUAL REVIEWS INC.   4139 EL CAMINO WAY   PALO ALTO, CALIFORNIA 94306

ANNUAL REVIEWS INC.
Palo Alto, California, USA

COPYRIGHT© 1976 BY ANNUAL REVIEWS INC., PALO ALTO, CALIFORNIA
ALL RIGHTS RESERVED. No part of this book may be reproduced in any form
or by any means without permission in writing from the publisher.

International Standard Book Number: 0-8243-1905-2
Library of Congress Catalog Card Number: 72-82136

Annual Reviews Inc. and the Editors of its publications assume no
responsibility for the statements expressed by the contributors to this
Review.

REPRINTS

The conspicuous number aligned in the margin with the title of each article in this
volume is a key for use in ordering reprints. Available reprints are priced at the
uniform rate of $1 each postpaid. The minimum acceptable reprint order is 10
reprints and/or $10.00, prepaid. A quantity discount is available.

PRINTED AND BOUND IN THE UNITED STATES OF AMERICA

PREFACE

With this volume we complete the first five years of the Annual Review of Anthropology. During this period the editors have sought to identify the major output in the numerous subfields of the discipline, new and old. By and large we have tried to include in each volume reviews of work on delimited problems or geographic regions that appear to merit timely evaluation of current research. At the same time we have provided representation of published work in all major fields of anthropology—physical, linguistic, archaeological, social, and cultural —although the relative coverage of the subdisciplines has varied from year to year. By concentrating on problems rather than subdisciplines we have preserved flexibility in chapter length and have been able whenever possible to integrate the contribution of more than one specialty. Chapters on nutrition, human ecology, and work of archaeologists and ethnologists in the American Southwest are cases in point. For this reason the volumes are not divided into conventional sections. The cumulative index at the end of each volume is meant to provide the reader with a ready means of identifying reviews of the same or related topic categories over the years.

Occasionally we have invited essays that address themselves to a certain uneasiness felt by some of our colleagues about what it is that remains to our discipline, as its subject matter comes to embrace, for example, complex modern societies, and as it draws upon the theoretical and conceptual contributions of other behavioral sciences. The chapter on culture theory (Volume 3) is one such. Whether any one claim for the shape of the anthropology of the future will prevail over others is probably as moot as that of the "new anthropology" of a generation ago. Certain paradigms, by virtue of the care and persuasiveness with which they are presented, may indeed attract a substantial amount of future research, but the range of interests reflected in the work of younger and older anthropologists alike—even occasional changes in direction during the course of a single career—make it unlikely that any single body of theory or subject matter will dominate the discipline or any of its parts. Current debates, such as those over the "proper study" of economic anthropology, ethnicity, human ecology, and universals, for example, have stimulated work in a number of interesting directions. In any event, the efforts of protagonists for one view or another are of intrinsic interest, and we shall seek reviews of these debates and of empirical studies which support them in succeeding volumes.

The editors always welcome suggestions for review topics, and qualified authors for them, from colleagues who perceive a need not covered in volumes already published. The response to this enterprise in scientific communication has been very positive, and the assistance of our colleagues in this respect has played a useful role. We wish at this time also to thank our contributors, past and future, for preparing critical reviews of high quality.

Finally, we call attention to chapters that appear in the Annual Reviews of Ecology and Systematics, Sociology, and Psychology that may provide related coverage for those of our readers with interests in these disciplines.

THE EDITORS

CONTENTS

ANNUAL REVIEWS INC. is a nonprofit corporation established to promote the advancement of the sciences. Beginning in 1932 with the *Annual Review of Biochemistry*, the Company has pursued as its principal function the publication of high quality, reasonably priced Annual Review volumes. The volumes are organized by Editors and Editorial Committees who invite qualified authors to contribute critical articles reviewing significant developments within each major discipline.

Annual Reviews Inc. is administered by a Board of Directors whose members serve without compensation.

BOARD OF DIRECTORS
1976

Dr. J. Murray Luck
Founder Emeritus, Annual Reviews Inc.
Department of Chemistry
Stanford University

Dr. Esmond E. Snell
President, Annual Reviews Inc.
Department of Biochemistry
University of California, Berkeley

Dr. Joshua Lederberg
Vice President, Annual Reviews Inc.
Department of Genetics
Stanford University Medical School

Dr. William O. Baker
President
Bell Telephone Laboratories

Dr. James E. Howell
Graduate School of Business
Stanford University

Dr. William D. McElroy
Chancellor
University of California, San Diego

Dr. Wolfgang K. H. Panofsky
Director
Stanford Linear Accelerator Center

Dr. John Pappenheimer
Department of Physiology
Harvard Medical School

Dr. Colin S. Pittendrigh
Department of Biological Sciences
Stanford University

Dr. Alvin M. Weinberg
Director, Institute for Energy Analysis
Oak Ridge Associated Universities

Dr. Harriet Zuckerman
Department of Sociology
Columbia University

Annual Reviews are published in the following sciences: Anthropology, Astronomy and Astrophysics, Biochemistry, Biophysics and Bioengineering, Earth and Planetary Sciences, Ecology and Systematics, Energy, Entomology, Fluid Mechanics, Genetics, Materials Science, Medicine, Microbiology, Nuclear Science, Pharmacology and Toxicology, Physical Chemistry, Physiology, Phytopathology, Plant Physiology, Psychology, and Sociology. In addition, two special volumes have been published by Annual Reviews Inc.: *History of Entomology* (1973) and *The Excitement and Fascination of Science* (1965).

Wilton Marion Krogman

Ann. Rev. Anthropol. 1976. 5:1-14
Copyright © 1976 by Annual Reviews Inc. All rights reserved

FIFTY YEARS OF PHYSICAL ANTHROPOLOGY: The Men, the Material, the Concepts, the Methods

♦ 9567

Wilton Marion Krogman
Emeritus Professor, School of Medicine,
University of Pennsylvania, Philadelphia, Pennsylvania 19104

There is a saying that "when a man hits his mid-60's he moves into his anecdotage." This isn't really so. What he does do is draw upon experience, evaluate achievement, and reflect upon the historical perspectives in his chosen field of endeavor. Oh, I know that there is a temptation to say "Ichabod, Ichabod, thy glory hath departed," or to bewail that "there hath arisen in Egypt a generation that knoweth not Joseph." Stated more cogently we may query, "Where are the giants of yesteryear?" That's what I shall write about.

I gave my first lectures in physical anthropology and did my first research paper in the spring of 1925, half a century ago. I was then a course assistant to Professor Fay-Cooper Cole at the University of Chicago. It was in that year that Dr. Cole assigned me a term paper subject that determined my entire professional career. He said, "Bill, I want you to write on the anthropology of the teeth." That did it! Teeth led to jaws, jaws to face, face to head, head to body; in other words, a coordinated whole. But, more than that, it led from statics to the dynamics of age progress. Thus was my life-work in growth and development, comparative and human, launched.

In the preparation of the term paper I read all I could of the published work of three men: William King Gregory, paleontologist; Milo Hellman, orthodontist; T. Wingate Todd, anatomist and physical anthropologist. In the summer of '25 I drove with my family to New York City. I took my term paper with me and went to see Hellman at 57 W. 57th Street. He looked it over and suggested I recast it a bit and submit it for the Morris L. Chaim Prize ($250) of the First District Dental Society of New York City. I followed his advice and won the prize.

However, this event involved an incredible and far-reaching circumstance: Gregory and Todd were the judges. Sometime later Todd stopped off in Chicago to see the lad who, while he showed immaturity, also showed promise. I told him I would like to do graduate work with him. In 1928–29 Todd arranged a Cleveland Foundation Fellowship in anatomy for me, and I wrote my doctoral dissertation under his direction. In 1929–30 I was an instructor at the University of Chicago. In 1930–31 I was a National Research Council Foreign Fellow with Sir Arthur Keith at the Hunterian Museum of the Royal College of Surgeons, London. In 1931 I joined Todd as his colleague, associate Professor of Anatomy and Physical Anthropology. Todd's department was a magnet for the physical anthropologists of the 1930's, and it was there and then that I met most of the current leaders in the field.

I think I can leave the autobiographical motif now and turn to some of the men I met and admired.

First and foremost was Todd, one of the most inspirational men I ever knew. He was a human dynamo, 6 feet tall, sturdily built, literally exuding vitality. In the halls of the department of anatomy at Western Reserve University his stride rang with a staccato beat—he did not walk, he strode, he loped. He was vigorous in action and speech. He had a strong will, but tempered it with an innate kindness and consideration and a ready wit.[1] In his department he ran a tight ship, believe me. He was a magnificent speaker with a beautiful command of the English language. He was a Scotsman with a burr that he could turn on and off at will. His writings were clear, logical, and with an almost lyrical tone. His ability to coin a phrase or an apt slogan or motto was unsurpassed.

Todd attended Owen's College and Victoria University, Manchester, England where he received the M.B. and the Ch.B. Later he achieved the M.R.C.S., the L.R.C.P., and the F.R.C.S. In 1912 he came to Western Reserve University, Cleveland, as Henry Wilson Payne Professor of Anatomy and Chairman of the Department. He announced as his goal to take Anatomy "from the charnel house to the realm of the dynamics of the living human body." I paraphrase: from bones to body, from skeleton to tissues, from death to life, from ultimate status to the urgency of age-time, age-progress.

In 1939 I evaluated Todd's contributions to anatomy and physical anthropology and in 1951 his catalytic role in the field of growth and development.

For the '39 article I annotated 191 of Todd's published papers and books. His contributions may be classified as follows:

I. Anatomy
   1. "Cervical" ribs
   2. The nerve supply of arteries
   3. Comparative anatomy of peripheral nerves
   4. The gastro-intestinal tract

---

[1]Todd enjoyed a good laugh, even though it was at his expense. I gave him this limerick:
  There was a man named Todd,
  Whose behavior was exceedingly odd.
  He spelled, if you please,
  His name with two d's
  When one is enough for God.
He often repeated it, poking fun at himself.

5. The growth of bone
6. Respiratory system, heart, muscles, nasopharynx

I would like to summarize at this point as follows:

Todd was interested in 'pure' anatomy, i.e., morphology, as well as in 'applied' anatomy, i.e., growth and repair. In the analysis of his contributions the former stands as basic. It is only after morphology is mastered that the interpretations of growth can begin. The one the foundation, the other the edifice, forever tenanted by the vital spirit that reared it.

Published communications attest to research ability, but nothing save personal contact may attest to ability as a teacher. In Todd's hands anatomy gained life, took on promise, held out hope. A vivid imagery, a marvellous command of words, a wealth of comparative and anecdotal reference, combined to transmute dissecting-room knowledge into living interpretation. As aids to teaching there were built up collections of human and mammalion osteology. Stereoscopic slide projection brought depth, fluoroscopy brought movement. The 'normal' of the textbook was subordinated to the physiological range of harmonious function.

II. Physical Anthropology
   1. Prehistory, Egyptology, American Indian
   2. Craniometric studies and the problem of shrinkage in dry bone
   3. Body size and proportions in American Whites and Negroes
   4. Skin color
   5. Suture closure
   6. Age-changes in the pubic symphysis

Todd's contributions to physical anthropology—apart from the applied anthropology of growth—have centered about the analysis of age changes in the skeleton, the recognition of sex- and stock-linked characters in the human body, and the translation of measurements on the dead in terms of similar measurements on the living. Throughout, his insistence upon scientific accuracy, standardization of technique and conservatism of interpretation and conclusion have contributed in no small degree to the advance of physical anthropology, not only in America but in the world. His laboratory was a Mecca for research men, his publications were—and are— basic.

III. Growth
   1. Ossification: rate and sequence, human and mammalian
   2. Age changes, progressive
   3. Growth and development: longitudinal
   4. Craniofacial growth, human and comparative
   5. Miscellaneous: Brush Foundation booklets; "popular" articles

Todd's essential contribution to the study of growth and development of the child may be summarized in one word: completeness. Some idea of the thoroughness of his approach may be gained from the following brief statement of the routine schedule of examination: 1) anthropometric: stature; weight; body proportions; muscular strength; 2) X-ray: stage of physical development or maturity; mineral reserves of the body; staying power of muscles; proper utilization of foodstuffs; scorings and scars of previous illness; response of the constitution to health vicissitudes which menace or retard development; 3) jaw and tooth development: dental calcification and eruption; cranio-facio-dental growth; 4) gymnasium tests: skill; speed of movement; grace; strength; accuracy; 5) psychological examination: ability, latent or expressed, both in pure intellect and practical intelligence; powers of analysis, attention, concentration, synthesis; 6) cultural tests: interests and latent talent; 7) personality examination: increasing capacity for full responsibilities of citizenship.

It is almost academic to try to name Todd's *magnum opus*, yet I shall point to his Atlas of the ossification patterns of hand and wrist, which established the basic pattern for all succeeding hand-wrist atlases.[2]

In final analysis I think it is Todd's stimulation of anatomical research in medicine and dentistry that is his enduring contribution: the effect of amputation upon bone development; the osteology, myology, vascularity, and surgical anatomy of hand and foot; the manifestations of congenital defects and age-changes in the vertebral column; the role of allergy in naso-pharyngeal growth; calcification and bone repair; pre- and post-natal skeletal ossification in human, anthropoid, ape, mammalian; tissue respiration and the ovulatory cycle; brain waves and the growth of the cerebral cortex; comparative craniofacial growth in human, anthropoid, ape, mammalian; dental calcification and eruption and growth of the bony jaws; the correlated physical and behavioral growth of Cleveland white children, and the physical growth of Cleveland Negro children. All of these researches were under Todd's inspirational direction.

These were days before federal largesse. The work was financed via university funds plus two private patrons: The Charles Brush Foundation, under Todd, monitored general bio-behavioral development; the Chester and Frances Bolton Fund, under B. Holly Broadbent, D.D.S., monitored growth of head, face, jaws, and teeth. The Brush and Bolton series were both longitudinal on the same samples of Cleveland children. It was in Todd's laboratory that the Broadbent-Bolton Roentgenographic Cephalometer was originated, the principles of which today are basic to craniofacial growth research the world over.

Todd built up at Western Reserve four remarkable collections. The best known is the series of complete human adult skeletons, male and female: 2000 American white, 1300 American Negro. They were all carefully documented from hospital/institutional/morgue records, but each was measured and assessed for racial, sex, and age data by Todd and his colleagues (I was responsible for about 600). Each individual had passed thru the gross dissection laboratory; heads were cut in sagittal section and study of orbital contents and middle ear was done without any bone destruction whatsoever.[3] With the financial aid of Dr. Carl Hamann, professor of surgery, Todd built up two lesser known collections: mammalian skeletons, and horns and antlers. In each category there was one or more of most of the major genera and species of the mammalian class—two magnificent synoptic series. When I taught mammalian osteology and the selective development of horns and antlers, I brought to class unparalleled

---

[2]Later, Todd's X-ray data yielded similar atlases for knee and foot.

illustrative material as demonstration. The collection of anthropoid skeletons was so much a part of Todd's interests that at one time, based upon an inventory I made, about 75% of all known gorilla and chimp skulls and skeltons were at Reserve in Todd's department.

I first met Ales Hrdlicka in 1924. He came to the University of Chicago to give some lectures, and Dr. Cole asked me to sort of "take him in tow." I had heard of him, of course, and had seen a bust-size photo of him. That magnificent leonine head gave me an impression of a very large man. When I met him (he was about 5'7") I realized that he was, literally and figuratively, a "little giant" (a la Stephen A. Douglas). Stature did not count—the man did! Hrdlicka was the founding father of American Physical Anthropology.

Hrdlicka, born in Bohemia, came to New York in 1882 at the age of 13. He worked as a cigar maker and went to night school. At 19 he had typhoid; his physician, a former rabbi, urged him to study medicine. In 1892 he was graduated from the Eclectic Medical College of New York City, and in 1894 from the New York Homeopathic College. Soon thereafter he passed his state board examination in allopathy in Maryland. Of interest is the fact that he took an internship in the New York Homeopathic Hospital for Insane, resulting in an 1895 publication on the somatometry of 1000 adult patients grouped by type of insanity. In 1897–98 at the College of Physicians and Surgeons, New York City, he cooperated with Huntington in the study of "normal" bodies and skeletons.

In 1896 Hrdlicka had studied with Manouvrier in Paris and here received his grounding in what may be termed 'traditional' physical anthropology, i.e. the quantitative measurement of skulls and bones, heads and bodies (though basically the former). To my knowledge, no one—in the United States at least—has measured more skulls and bones than did Hrdlicka.

In 1899–1902, from the American Museum of Natural History, he made the first of many field trips, to the Indians of the southwestern United States and of northern Mexico, and (later) South America. In 1903 he signed on with the Division of Physical Anthropology of the U.S. National Museum, becoming its curator in 1910. Hrdlicka was a world traveler; for example, he went to South Africa in 1926 and became one of the first authorities to back Raymond Dart in his designation of *Australopithecus africanus* as a hominid. In this same year he began the first of nine trips to Alaska; as a result, he published definitive studies of the Eskimos and the Aleuts.

But we honor Hrdlicka for two enduring achievements: the establishment of the American Association of Physical Anthropologists in 1928 (I was in London at the time, but Todd registered me as a charter member at the first AAPA meeting in Charlottesville, 1930), and the establishment of the American Journal of Physical Anthropology in 1918 (he continued as editor through Volume 29, December 1942).

There were three main objectives in Hrdlicka's professional life: 1. the study

[3]Orbit and middle ear were taught via demonstration dissections on a baker's dozen or so of selected cadavera.

of normal variability in the body, the skeleton, the teeth, in terms of race, sex, and age-change; 2. the tabulation of somatic differences in American whites and Negroes, American Indians, and Eskimos; 3. tabulation and phylogenetic evaluation of the skeletal remains of fossil man. In these endeavors he was a tireless, devoted, self-effacing worker. He lived moderately, even frugally, but was very generous where physical anthropology was concerned.[4] On several occasions he bailed out the *American Journal of Physical Anthropology* when, on an annual basis, it ran in the red. He set up in Prague the Ales and Marie Hrdlicka Foundation for anthropological research. Hrdlicka was loyal to physical anthropology, loyal to friends, and loyal to his own ideas. Adolph Schultz observed that "in regard to his own conclusions Hrdlicka seems to have been rarely plagued by doubts."

Hrdlicka clung to the idea of the relatively recent migration of man to America. Hooton once said he was like Horatio, standing at the (Aleutian) bridge and holding back the advance of early hordes. He looked at statistics askance, for his morphology and morphometry told him the whole story. Constitutionalism was also suspect, even though his 1895 study of the somatometry of the insane was later cited as pioneer by the Kretschmerian school. Under his editorship, publications on morphology predominated rather than studies of function.

Hrdlicka had his own ideas, certainly, but he listened to others. He and Todd and I had many a productive pro-and-con discussion. We knew where he stood, he knew where we stood, and both foundations were accepted on even terms. In his discussions of papers at meetings I never heard him say a malicious or iconoclastic word. He might say of a given statement, "this is what I think," or "this is the way I would have done it," and so on. With Hrdlicka physical anthropology was a way of life . . . and he lived accordingly.

I met Franz Boas at AAPA meetings and had the privilege of several personal conferences at his Columbia University office. However, his professional stature so overwhelmed me that I never have presumed to say that we were "friends"; "colleague's"? yes; for his early work in growth and development was not only well known to me, but it was inherent in Todd's growth-research design as well. Todd felt that Boas's work in the field of growth was incisively innovative. I have never surrendered my opinion that Boas was the "compleat anthropologist," with Kroeber and possibly Wissler as runners-up. "Papa" Boas inspired many great cultural anthropologists of the first half-century, and well into the second. Himself great. he evoked greatness in others.

Boas was trained with a major in physics and in a minor in geography, and at the age of 24–25 years did his first field work in these areas in Greenland. He was

---

[4] I attest to his generous nature by a personal note. At the 1938 A.A.P.A. meeting in Philadelphia he took me aside. He had heard I was leaving Reserve to go to Chicago. He said that the Midwest should have a medically trained physical anthropologist. Did I have an M.D.? I said, "no, but I have course credit for the first two didactic years at Chicago." He then offered to defray my medical education were I to so enroll. I declined his generous offer with grateful thanks.

educated at Heidelberg, Bonn, and Kiel. His doctoral dissertation was on the color of H_2O, and this work he brought to bear years later to a problem in the psycho-cultural view of race; it was the *idea* of color (pigmentation) held by a people, not the color itself that mattered. In a similar vein I once heard Redfield declare, "there *are* no races—there are only socially supposed races," i.e. races are what people think they are. Here then is an attempted resolution of the biology (genetics) of race and the sociology (attitudes) toward race.

I am not going to go into Boas's magnificent ethnological and linguistic studies of the Indians of the northwest coast. I do not feel that I am a competent judge. In physical anthropology he stresses three major themes: 1. the nature of the physical and behavioral differences between peoples (races);[5] 2. the physical growth and development of the child; 3. the role of biometrics in areas 1 and 2.

In my student days at Chicago I was literally weaned on "The Mind of Primitive Man," his address in 1900 to the American Folklore Society (published as a book in 1911). Here were stressed two factors: initial isolation and then contact between peoples, resulting in one species, *Homo sapiens*. These processes, however, hold for all domesticated animals; hence man must partake of the instability of type and the extreme variability in form that characterizes domesticated forms. In sum, plasticity not stability is the keynote in the understanding of our own kind. And the evidence? the 1912 *Changes in the Bodily Form of the Descendants of Immigrants*.

In the 1930s Boas visited Todd in Cleveland several times, and also during that time we had the opportunity to meet with him at American Anthropological Association meetings. It was during this time that I began my studies of protohistoric and early historic crania from Asia Minor. It is true that I was then influenced by a conventional cranial typology, but I was far less rigid than I might have been had I not read Boas's 1911–12 works.

However, it was in the growth field that I owed most to Boas's pioneer work. In 1888–92 he taught at Clark University, Worcester, Mass. His studies were, of course, cross-sectional. Nevertheless, his height-weight tables of Worcester children were for many years accepted as physical growth standards. Additionally, he took other somatometric measurements.

The result of Boas' studies in anthropometrics and genetics is summarized by:

$$\sigma_{pop} = \sqrt{\sigma_{fam}^2 + \sigma_{fr}^2}$$

where σ_{pop} = gross variation of a given population, s^2fam = average difference between families, and s^2fr = average variability within these families. As a result, Todd fit this into his "family-line patterns of growth," i.e. tall, average, and short lines.

Personally, I gained far more of a *viewpoint* from Boas—both from his writings and from listening to him and talking with him—than I did any meth-

---

[5]In 1894, in his AAAS vice-presidential address, he spoke on "Human Faculty as Determined by Race."

odological principles or procedural design. There is no such thing as racial heredity in a behavior-cultural sense; there is only the liberalizing effect of human interaction where one accords the other the dignity of individuality, either grouped or singly. I came to think of "The Mind of Primitive Man" more as "The Spirit of Mankind," a sort of bill-of-rights of human values. Certainly, Boas exemplified this in his espousal of liberal causes and organization.[6]

Charles B. Davenport, after professorships at Harvard (1888–99) and at Chicago (1899–1924), came to the Carnegie Institution of Washington as Director of Experimental Evolution. His interests were genetically oriented and he interpreted his racial studies in this light.

Davenport worked in two major fields: growth-changes and racial classification and characteristics. In his growth studies he was concerned with age-changes in body build, based on the index W/H^2. He developed curves of infant growth; his studies on the growth of the head, the nose, arms and legs, and the foot are still useful in terms of their basic (cross-sectional) nature.

It is in the area of his racial studies that Davenport is best known (and in my opinion unfairly labeled as "racist"). In 1929 he and Morris Steggerda published *Race Crossing in Jamaica*, and it is this work I want to comment upon briefly. The study was set up originally to include 100 adult "full-blooded" Negroes (black), 100 Europeans (white), and 100 crosses of the two (brown). "The three racial or color groups were to be selected from about the same social status." In each group of 100 there were to be 50 male, 50 female. The actual total was 370: black (54 M, 51 F); brown (93 M, 72 F); white (50 M, 50 F).

There is no doubt that Davenport felt that "there are differences in sensory and intellectual fields between the races of mankind." But in some ways he was surprisingly naive. For example, he explained racial variability in his Jamaican material as due to "frequent mutations," engendered in the case of blacks and whites, as separate groups, to the impact of a "new environment," and in the case of the browns to the effects of intermixture ("hybridization"). Finally, he really had no idea of the impact of what he called "social status" upon individual or group performance. In following, as he did, the results of Army Alpha tests in blacks, browns, and whites he was following the bent of his time, with no idea that such tests were *not* measuring innate capacity and ability.

[6] I have told this story to a few friends, and I repeat it here. In 1933 I became a consultant in skeletal identification to the FBI, and in 1938 I wrote a "Guide," published in the FBI Law Enforcement Bulletin. During World War II, I was in the Washington office of the FBI and an agent approached me and asked me if I knew a Professor Franz Boas, and what did I know about him? I asked why. He told me that Boas was under investigation, and was to be brought up for interrogation because of personal identification with so many "un-American" and "pinko" groups. I told him in no uncertain terms of the personal integrity of the man, adding that so sincere was he in his liberal views that I was quite sure that his name on an organizational letterhead meant most often that he "lent" his name in sympathy rather than in 100% endorsement. Hoover called off his "birddogs."

In one of his papers Davenport said that "what a man shall do in his world depends largely upon the instincts and special capacities with which he was born: these are *family characteristics*" (emphasis W. M. K.)

Davenport published some 3273 pages on Army Anthropometry ("I fixed it so that the uniforms would fit in the next war"). He published on heredity of skin, hair, and eye color; stature; longevity; twin births; congenital mental inadequacy and bone defects; goiter, otosclerosis, pellagra, albinism. He emphasized the necessity of laboratory procedures and field work in the teaching of physical anthropology ("teaching anthropology without a laboratory is like teaching baseball without a baseball diamond").

I know Charles Davenport and Morris Steggerda well, especially Morris. As we discussed race and race "differences" in the '20s and '30s, we were pretty well influenced by the current slavish adherence to the Army Alpha "evidence." In the '40s, when Davenport died, and the '50s, when Steggerda died, the two men had begun to question—and in a measure repudiate—the idea of genetically entrenched intellectual endowment. But, as we still know today, that kind of prejudice dies hard.

I must mention Steggerda for his early critical viewpoint concerning the universal application of the standards of height and weight growth. The standards of the early 1900s were, of course, based on middle-class American white children. Steggerda said that the routine use of such standards might be unfair where there are racial or ethnic factors, as well as environmental, to be considered. Hence he constructed H-W tables for Maya children, for Navajo children, and even for Holland (Michigan) Dutch children. He advised similar H-W tables for American Negro children, but did not live to construct them.

Next to Ales Hrdlicka, Earnest Hooton stamped American physical anthropology not only with his researches, but with his influence and personality. He was a great, inspiring teacher; under him Harvard became the center of training in physical anthropology and his students also became leaders in the field. Hooton was not basically trained in biology, but rather in a broad liberal arts direction. In 1911 he received his doctorate at the University of Wisconsin. In 1912, at Oxford University, he received the Diploma in Anthropology under R. R. Marett. In 1913 he joined the Harvard anthropology department.

In his approach to the study of *H. sapiens,* Hooton brought a Boasian approach, i.e. he was concerned with variation *within* a human population in terms of its origins and its adaptational responses. Such population groups were plastic and mutable.

Hooton was a prodigious worker, inspiring students to a like pitch of achievement, and organizing large-scaled studies. The studies of living populations embraced European peoples and the survey of the peoples of Ireland, the peoples of the Canary Islands, the Riffians, the Australian Aborigines, and the hybrids of the "Bounty." The interest in biobehavioral studies embraced constitutional typology (the Grant study) and criminal behavior types ("Crime and the Man"). Under Hooton an early study in human engineering was undertaken for the Pennsylvania railroad, to standardize seat sizes. A chair-measuring apparatus was set up in the Pennsy station in New York City, measuring buttock spread and buttock-knee projected length. Naturally, the study became known as the HFS—the "Harvard Fanny Study."

Hooton felt that medicine and dentistry, in their repair of congenital or acquired defects, were adding to man's genetic load. I remember his castigation of the orthodontist: "You take a girl or boy with malaligned jaws or teeth, haul 'em around with your wires, make 'em look pretty, and then they marry, beget kids, and you've produced for yourselves another generation of patients. In a way you've, at microevolutionary level, circumvented natural and sexual selection."

Hooton's *Indians of Pecos* is one of the most thorough craniological studies of prehistoric American Indians ever done. Today we may not agree with his typological identifications, but the study is a model of its kind. In a roundabout way I too benefitted by Kidder's thorough archeological methods: the skeletal material recovered included a fine series of children's skulls. These and the adult skulls were studied by orthodontist Milo Hellman, and it was on this series that Hellman set up the dental stages I–VIII that in a cranial series permitted the study of facio-dental development and age-changes from birth through old age. I have used this in my own growth researches.

One last word about Hooton: when his *Up from the Ape* was published I said time and again to my students, "I'd give my right arm to have written as fine a book as this." I still hold that opinion.

I'd like to wind this up with two charts: I, Physical Anthropology: Yesterday; and II, Physical Anthropology: Today.

Chart I is what I taught at Reserve, at Chicago, at Penn. I won't claim for one minute that I did areas I–VI with equal authority. In I, I leaned on Gregory, Lull, Schultz, Wilder. In II and III I was pretty thoroughly Martin's "Lehrbuch." In IV I leaned on Todd, Hellman, Scammon, and my own work. For V I turned to Newman, Snyder, Alexander Weiner, and the German School under von Verschuer. The last area, VI, was within my own bailiwick, for I taught Gross Dissection and Neuroanatomy. For skin, hair, and eyes I turned to Danforth, Davenport, and Hrdlicka.

In Chart I, I have tried to show the ways in which I interrelated and integrated the six main areas. In those days—at least I felt that way—physical anthropology had its main import in its relation not only to biological man but to cultural man as well.

Now look at Chart II, which I'm sure is a *tour de force,* for so particularate has physical anthropology become that I unabashedly confess that not all areas of detail are known to me. However, for the sake of comparability I have kept the same six captions (even though slightly renamed).

Human paleontology and its methods of dating has made tremendous strides. When I first taught a course on "The Evolution of Man," nearly 75% of the evidence was based on teeth and jaws. Today we can knowledgeably demonstrate the evolution of bipedalism and the emergence of the hand as a tool user and tool maker. *Pari passu,* primatology, in structure, in function, and in behavior, has burgeoned, the more so because primates are now recognized as basic to much of medical research.

Craniometry, osteometry, somatometry are less and less measured for their own sakes, i.e. as relatively isolated techniques. They are now part and parcel of occupation anthropology ("human engineering"), medical anthropology, dental anthropology, and forensic anthropology. Measurement of bone and body is nuclear to studies in growth and development, and in this area Hoobler introduced chemical anthropology, i.e. the biochemistry of nutrition.

In genetics advances have been almost incredible: the DNA-RNA code and the development of karyotyping have lead to insight into, and newer interpretation of, basic Mendelian heredity. The annectant areas of microbiology have brought added insight.

The area listed as VI has remained fundamentally unchanged, save as details of form and function have been highlighted in studies of growth and development and of genetics.

At the bottom of Chart II I record my feeling that physical anthropology is a biobehavioral science more or less in and of itself. It may be that it is I who am out of touch, yet in recent years I have gained the impression that physical anthropology and cultural anthropology—both in broad context—exist side by side rather than integratively.

I want to round out this half century of memories by paying tribute to my three great teachers: Fay-Cooper Cole of Chicago, who taught me the joy of the sharing of knowledge, the stimulation of young minds, and the warmth of the teacher-student realtionship; Sir Arthur Keith, who taught me perspective and a life philosophy in my own work and thinking; T. Wingate Todd, who underpinned my professional career.

Finally, let me summarize the role of each of the men I have studied with, directly or indirectly:

BOAS: the breadth of knowledge of one trained in the rigorous laws of the universe.

DAVENPORT: the endeavors of one who worked with and for the comprehension of natural law.

HOOTON: the rules of variability were his guide, the urge to better understand his own species was his goal.

HRDLICKA: the uncompromising energy of a dedicated man who unselfishly worked for physical anthropology throughout the entire world.

STEGGERDA: the human values of a teacher who nourished mind and spirit alike.

TODD: the demanding comparative approach of one who recognized the dynamics of time-change in Nature.

To me these men—and others I've not referred to—were giants. This is not to imply there are no giants today. Remember, with eventide shadows lengthen

PHYSICAL ANTHROPOLOGY: YESTERDAY

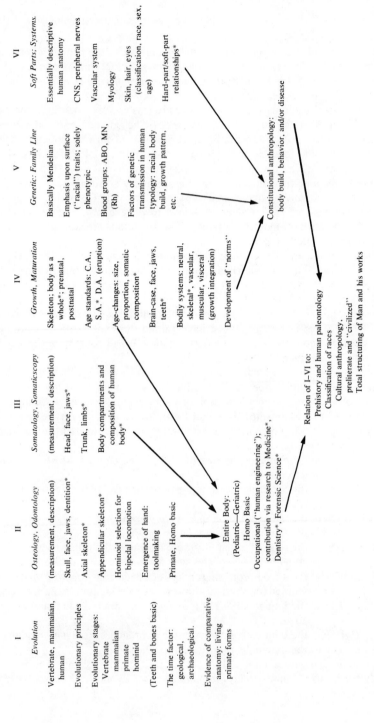

I	II	III	IV	V	VI
Evolution	*Osteology, Odontology*	*Somatology, Somaticscopy*	*Growth, Maturation*	*Genetic: Family Line*	*Soft Parts: Systems.*
Vertebrate, mammalian, human	(measurement, description)	(measurement, description)	Skeleton; body as a whole*; prenatal, postnatal	Basically Mendelian	Essentially descriptive human anatomy
Evolutionary principles	Skull, face, jaws, dentition*	Head, face, jaws*	Age standards: C.A., S.A.*, D.A. (eruption)	Emphasis upon surface ("racial") traits; solely phenotypic	CNS, peripheral nerves
Evolutionary stages: Vertebrate mammalian primate hominid	Axial skeleton*	Trunk, limbs*	Age-changes: size, proportion, somatic composition*	Blood groups: ABO, MN, (Rh)	Vascular system
(Teeth and bones basic)	Appendicular skeleton*	Body compartments and composition of human body*	Brain-case, face, jaws, teeth*	Factors of genetic transmission in human typology: racial, body build, growth pattern, etc.	Myology
The time factor: geological, archaeological.	Hominoid selection for bipedal locomotion		Bodily systems: neural, skeletal*, vascular, muscular, visceral (growth integration)		Skin, hair, eyes (classification, race, sex, age)
Evidence of comparative anatomy: living primate forms	Emergence of hand: toolmaking		Development of "norms"		Hard-part/soft-part relationships*
	Primate, Homo basic				

Entire Body:
(Pediatric—Geriatric)
Homo Basic
Occupational ("human engineering"); contribution via research to Medicine*, Dentistry*, Forensic Science*

Constitutional anthropology: body build, behavior, and/or disease

Relation of I–VI to:
Prehistory and human paleontology
Classification of races
Cultural anthropology, preliterate and "civilized"
Total structuring of Man and his works

*x-ray techniques employed

PHYSICAL ANTHROPOLOGY: TODAY

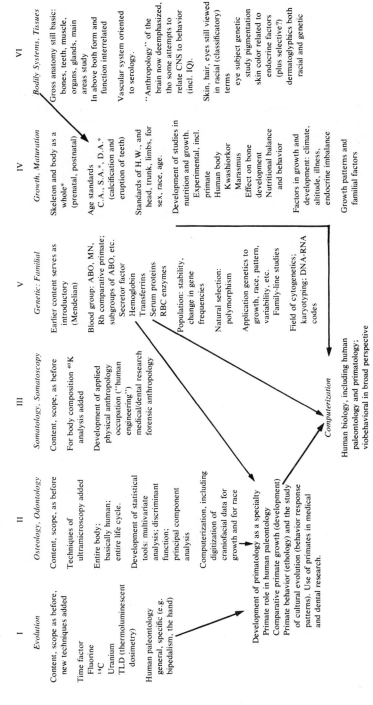

I Evolution

Content, scope as before, new techniques added

Time factor
Fluorine
^{14}C
Uranium
TLD (thermoluminescent dosimetry)

Human paleontology general, specific (e.g. bipedalism, the hand)

Development of primatology as a specialty
Primate role in human paleontology
Comparative primate growth (development)
Primate behavior (ethology) and the study of cultural evolution (behavior response patterns). Use of primates in medical and dental research.

II Osteology, Odontology

Content, scope, as before

Techniques of ultramicroscopy added

Entire body; basically human; entire life cycle.

Development of statistical tools: multivariate analysis; discriminant function; principal component analysis

Computerization, including digitization of craniofacial data for growth and for race

III Somatology, Somatoscopy

Content, scope, as before

For body composition ^{40}K analysis added

Development of applied physical anthropology occupation ("human engineering") medical/dental research forensic anthropology

IV Growth, Maturation

Skeleton and body as a whole* (prenatal, postnatal)

Age standards C.A., S.A.*, D.A.* (calcification and eruption of teeth)

Standards of H.W., and head, trunk, limbs, for sex, race, age.

Development of studies in nutrition and growth. Experimental, incl. primate
Human body
Kwashiorkor
Marasmus
Effect on bone development
Nutritional balance and behavior

Factors in growth and development: climate, altitude, illness, endocrine imbalance

Growth patterns and familial factors

V Genetic: Familial

Earlier content serves as introductory (Mendelian)

Blood group: ABO, MN, Rh comparative primate; subgroups of ABO, etc.
Secretor factor
Hemoglobin
Transferrins
Serum proteins
RBC enzymes

Population: stability, change in gene frequencies

Natural selection: polymorphism

Application genetics to growth, race, pattern, variability, etc. Family-line studies

Field of cytogenetics; karyotyping; DNA-RNA codes

VI Bodily Systems, Tissues

Gross anatomy still basic: bones, teeth, muscle, organs, glands, main areas study

In above both form and function interrelated

Vascular system oriented to serology.

"Anthropology" of the brain now deemphasized, tho some attempts to relate CNS to behavior (incl. IQ).

Skin, hair, eyes still viewed in racial (classificatory) terms
eye subject genetic study pigmentation skin color related to endocrine factors (plus selective?)
dermatoglyphics both racial and genetic

Computerization

Human biology, including human paleontology and primatology; viobehavioral in broad perspective

*x-ray techniques employed

13

and stature increases by projection. More, there is a diffusion, a diminution of clarity, even a halo effect. So it is with the perspective of time: memory shadows, impression lengthens, outline dims.

Even so, American physical anthropology was blessed with early greatness, embodied in men of ability and vision—men who, at, and for their times, were truly giants. They were frontiersmen. If today we work, relatively removed from nuclear, "traditional" physical anthropology, it is because they dared to take the initial forward and outward steps. We follow, but we also advance!

Ann. Rev. Anthropol. 1976. 5:15–34
Copyright © 1976 by Annual Reviews Inc. All rights reserved

PROBLEMS IN ANTHROPOLOGICAL BIBLIOGRAPHY

♦ 9568

Margaret Currier
Honorary Associate in the Bibliography of Anthropology, Peabody Museum
of Archaeology and Ethnology, Harvard University, Cambridge, Massachusetts 02138

INTRODUCTION

The problems of keeping up with the literature are not new. This paper begins with a sketch of the state of anthropology, libraries, and bibliographical problems 100 years ago. Since that time librarians, publishers, and professional associations have all contributed solutions to the problem of bibliographical control, particularly in access to the periodical literature. Recent technological developments are revolutionizing the compilation and publishing of bibliographies and reshaping the library scene. Forecasts for the future will have regional, national, and international aspects.

This article is limited to trends in the bibliography of anthropology. Lack of space precludes listing the monographic bibliographies and more than a small percentage of available reference tools. However, these have been described in some detail by Beckham (4), Frantz (8), Hoselitz (9), White (28), Winchell and Sheehy (29), and Wynar (30).

BACKGROUND

Anthropology in 1876

Imagine for a few moments the state of anthropology and its literature 100 years ago, in 1876. Darwin's theories were influencing the discussions of European prehistorians on man as toolmaker at the eighth session of the Congrès International d' Anthropologie et d'Archéologie Préhistoriques in Budapest (3). In France Topinard's *L'Anthropologie* (26) was just off the press, and he was collaborating with Broca in editing the *Revue d'Anthropologie*. In England they were also discussing Tylor's *Primitive Culture* (26a) published in 1871 and the first volume of Spencer's *Descriptive Sociology* (23). Their American counterparts might have been attending meetings of the American Ethnological Society, the American Philosophical Society, or the National Academy of Sciences, publishing articles in the *American Naturalist,* or presenting papers to the American Association for the Advancement of Science, of which Section 6

15

was the "Permanent Subsection of Anthropology" and featured in 1876 O. T. Mason (12), J. W. Powell (18), and L. H. Morgan (13). Under the auspices of the Smithsonian Institution, which, according to Fewkes (7, p. 746), "has been to the American anthropologist a foster parent of original research," archaeologists were studying the Potomac and Trenton gravels, and shell-heaps from Maine to Florida. Moreover, 670 American Indian vocabularies had been collected.

Formal instruction in anthropology as such was not yet possible at universities in the United States. In museums, artifacts and some skeletal material were being brought together from natural history collections. At Harvard University a separate building was being constructed for the Peabody Museum of American Archaeology and Ethnology, originally intended as a center for research on the aborigines and antiquities of the New World. For 10 years its collections had been housed in the Museum of Comparative Anatomy, under the curatorship of the eminent natural scientists, Jeffries Wyman and Asa Gray. Frederick Ward Putnam, who became curator in 1875, had been a student of Louis Agassiz. Consequently nonzoological specimens collected by Louis and his son, Alexander Agassiz, soon became part of the Peabody collection. The Peabody Museum Library, probably the first devoted specifically to anthropology, owned less than 1000 books and pamphlets, in comparison with 130,000 in 1975.

Libraries in 1876

In library circles 100 years ago, Melvil Dewey was promulgating his revolutionary ideas for arranging books in the stacks by numbers representing the subjects with which they dealt, rather than on consecutively numbered shelves in a fixed location.

The centennial year of 1876 is also historically significant for a conference of librarians in Philadelphia which resulted in the American Library Association. What was discussed in those meetings?

James G. Barnwell, of the Philadelphia Mercantile Library, proposed a "universal catalogue" with the following arguments:

> He who enables us to accomplish any useful purpose in less time than was previously possible, is so far a public benefactor; and if this remark is correct in regard to its most usual application—namely, to the abridgment of the amount of physical labor resulting from improved machinery—how much more strongly is it applicable to contrivances for similarly abridging the labor of the intellect. . . . If an index to a single volume or the catalogue of a single library is of such value that we are accustomed to consider it indispensable, surely the publication of a catalogue to include the literary stores of every existing or possible library would be an object worthy of a nation's enterprise (2, pp. 54–55).

Barnwell suggested that if other government aid was not forthcoming, this would be considered within the functions of the Smithsonian Institution, established "for the increase and diffusion of knowledge among men".

PERIODICAL INDEXING AND ABSTRACTING

General Indexes

Already scholars were up against difficulties in keeping up with the wealth of printed matter, especially in the periodical literature. At this same 1876 conference of librarians in Philadelphia, Thomas H. Rogers from the Warren County Library in Monmouth, Illinois, proposed a cooperative index for public libraries providing a subject index to periodical literature, to miscellaneous collections, and to standard works in history, science, and the arts. This he envisioned in one volume, with monthly indexes cumulating into annual supplements (19).

William Frederick Poole's *Index to Periodicals,* "an alphabetical index to subjects located in the reviews and other periodicals to which no indexes have been published," had been in existence since 1802. This was in such demand by other libraries that later editions were issued, and it was continued in supplements until 1907, when its place was taken by the *Annual Magazine Subject Index.*

But Poole's index covered only the subject approach to periodical articles. What about the author approach? Other librarians went to work to remedy the deficiency: Ezra Abbot, for example, Assistant Librarian in the Harvard College Library. As early as 1861 the card catalogue, handwritten in a round library script by young ladies who were paid 6 or 8 cents an hour,[1] was in two sections. The Author Catalogue listed not only books and pamphlets, but also important papers in the memoirs and transactions of learned societies and in periodicals, an innovation in American libraries.

The British were working at the problem in this same period, for in 1867 the Royal Society of London issued its famous *Catalogue of Scientific Papers,* covering the years 1800–1863, "an index to the titles and dates of scientific papers contained in the transactions of societies, journals and other periodical works." The preface gives credit to Dr. Joseph Henry, secretary of the Smithsonian Institution for the idea, but the work was done by the Royal Society and it was published at public expense by the Queen's printers. It is a monumental accomplishment, arranged alphabetically by authors, and includes papers from all the European countries and the USA. It was continued in four series to cover papers through the year 1900.

The Germans, with characteristic devotion to bibliographic detail, began in 1896 a semiannual *Bibliographie der deutschen Zeitschriftenliteratur, mit Einschluss von Sammelwerken* and in 1911 the international *Bibliographie der fremdsprachigen Zeitschriftenliteratur,* arranged according to key words (*Schlagworten*) and supplied since 1925 with author indexes. The first volume in 1911 indexed the *American Anthropologist* and the *AAA Proceedings,* the *Archives d'Anthropologie Criminelle, Folklore* (published in London), and the *Indian Antiquary.* The same firm, Felix Dietrich Verlag, long in Leipzig but now

---

[1] See Currier's *Cataloguing at Harvard in the Sixties* (6, pp. 70–72).

in Osnabrück, combined these two periodical indexes in 1965 under the title *Internationale Bibliographie der Zeitschriftenliteratur,* of which they had been series A and B. It now issues a four-volume subject index and two-volume author index each year. The list of journals indexed now takes up 120 pages in triple columns, and appears to include all important anthropology journals on a worldwide basis.

In the twentieth century, special index publishers came onto the scene in America. H. W. Wilson Co. produced the *Readers' Guide to Periodical Literature* which first appeared in 1901, indexing according to both authors and subjects back to 1900, and it was issued at intervals during the year, with annual and two- to five-year cumulations. Available in all libraries large and small, it provided a key to the popular magazines.

So successful was it that Wilson produced in 1907 a supplement, known from volume 3 as the *International Index to Periodicals,* "devoted chiefly to the humanities and science." This is still appearing, albeit in a different guise, for in 1965/66 it became the *Social Sciences and Humanities Index,* and in 1974/75 split into two separate publications, *Social Sciences Index* and *Humanities Index.* The former now includes general anthropology, geography, law, medical sciences, political science, and sociology, and indexes *African Studies, American Anthropologist, American Journal of Physical Anthropology, Anthropos,* etc. *Humanities Index* concerns itself with archaeology, folklore, history, languages and literature, performing arts, philosophy, and religion. Here one finds citations from *American Antiquity, American Journal of Archaeology, Antiquity,* etc. H. W. Wilson went on in 1929 to special subject indexes such as the *Art Index, Education Index,* and at one time considered an index to anthropology.

In England the Royal Society of London's *Catalogue of Scientific Papers* was superseded by its *International Catalogue of Scientific Literature,* an annual bibliography of books and articles, published between 1902 and 1919, each issue consisting of 17 volumes. Anthropology is section P. In 1919 the Library Association commenced its *Subject Index to Periodicals,* which in 1962 separated into the *British Humanities Index* and the *British Technology Index.*

Anthropology Indexes

What has been done specifically for anthropology? Just as the important periodicals were made accessible to readers by the large libraries before the advent of regularly published indexes, so was it with anthropology. The library of the Peabody Museum of Archaeology and Ethnology at Harvard University had been indexing journal articles and incorporating them into its separate author and subject catalogues since Professor Roland B. Dixon became librarian early in this century. But not until 1963 was this cataloguing and indexing available to the large scholarly libraries, and hence to the world at large, when G. K. Hall & Co. in Boston photographed and published the *Author* and *Subject Catalogues* in 54 volumes, to which three supplements have now been issued.

Also in 1963 the Royal Anthropological Institute in London issued the first volume of its quarterly *Index to Current Periodicals in the Library*. These two publications are helpful in different ways: The Peabody Museum *Catalogue* is a detailed retrospective list of books, pamphlets, serials, and periodical articles indexed by author (personal or corporate) and by subject on a geographical and topical basis. The Royal Anthropological Institute *Index*, on the other hand, is a current awareness tool, listing the recent literature according to geographical areas subdivided into broad categories: General, Physical Anthropology, Archaeology, Cultural Anthropology, Ethnography, and Linguistics. Only since 1972 have annual author indexes appeared, but there are indications that a cumulative author index will be published.

What about indexing in the subfields of anthropology? A few examples will be discussed below.

The prehistorians have the *Bibliographie Annuelle de l'Age de la Pierre Taillée* issued in Paris by the Bureau de Recherches Géologiques et Minières since 1958, covering the years 1955/56 to date. This is a continuation of the *Old World Bibliographies* from 1948–55 issued by the American School of Prehistoric Research and compiled by Hallam H. Movius Jr.

About the same time the Council for Old World Archaeology was formed to make available news on research in progress, together with bibliographies of work done in 22 areas of the world by prehistorians, classical and historical archaeologists. The *COWA Surveys and Bibliographies,* available to subscribers either as complete sets or for individual areas, have been compiled by volunteer area editors and were edited first by Lauriston Ward and since 1957 by Donald F. Brown. Publication has now been suspended.

The most systematic and comprehensive indexing tool for the social anthropologists is "IBSCA," the *International Bibliography for Social and Cultural Anthropology* which consists of annual volumes covering the literature since 1955. This is part of a Unesco-inspired attempt at bibliographical control in all of the social sciences. In 1950 an International Committee for Social Science Documentation considered that its main task was to supply each social science discipline with the basic bibliographical instruments essential to it, whatever the country of origin or language. Books, reports, and government publications are listed, but it is included here because the bulk of the entries are articles from journals.

IBSCA has an impressive list of 518 journals indexed, which is misleading if one takes this figure to be the approximate number of important journals devoted to social and cultural anthropology. Actually it is a list of journals indexed for the four publications prepared under the overall title *International Bibliography of the Social Sciences:* the *International Bibliography of Economics*, the *International Bibliography of Political Science*, the *International Bibliography of Sociology*, and the *International Bibliography of Social and Cultural Anthropology*. Articles from these journals are cited in whichever bibliography is most pertinent, in a classified subject arrangement, with author indexes and specific topical indexes (in English and French) at the ends of the volumes.

IBSCA is produced under the aegis of a standing advisory committee appointed by the International Congress of Anthropological and Ethnological Sciences. It is a valuable key to the literature, albeit frustrating for two reasons. Its publication date, for understandable editorial reasons, is two years after the publications listed. And now after 18 volumes, one feels the need of a cumulative index.

Anthropology being by its nature a geographically oriented discipline, the various regional bibliographies and indexes are often fully as valuable as topical tools.

The French societies based at the Musée de l'Homme in Paris can be counted on to supply good coverage. The annual *Bibliographie Africaniste* commenced in 1931 in the *Journal de la Société des Africanistes,* and has included journal articles since 1957. The *Bibliographie Américaniste,* which appeared annually in the *Journal de la Société des Américanistes,* became a separate publication in 1965. *The Bibliographie de l'Océanie,* although compiled at the University of Hawaii, is still published in Paris in the *Journal de la Société des Océanistes.*

Since 1925 Africanists have had from Belgium the *Bibliographie Ethnographique de l'Afrique Sud-Saharienne,* published through 1959 as the *Bibliographie Ethnographique du Congo Belge et des Régions Avoisinantes,* emanating from the former Musée Royal du Congo Belge in Tervuren, now the Musée Royal de l'Afrique Centrale.

And the bibliographies listed since 1929 in the journal *Africa,* published by the International African Institute in London, have appeared separately beginning in 1971 as the *International African Bibliography.* Since 1972 it has been prepared at the School of Oriental and African Studies. Those bibliographies from 1929–72 were published under the title *Cumulative Bibliography of African Studies* by G K. Hall & Co. in 1973 as a two-volume *Author Catalogue* and a three-volume *Classified Catalogue.*

Although also not entirely anthropological, the annual *Handbook* of *Latin American Studies* deserves special mention as an area index. Started in 1935 as an interdisciplinary project with the backing of the American Council of Learned Societies and the Social Science Research Council, it has always given good coverage to anthropology. Alfred M. Tozzer and Robert Redfield supplied 168 references on 18 pages in the first volume, while the 35th volume in 1973 devotes 136 pages to anthropological references supplied by 12 editors. It has proved its worth for identifying citations to articles in journals and compilations as well as to monographic volumes.

The Association for Asian Studies now publishes separately the annual *Bibliography of Asian Studies* (covering East, Southeast, and South Asia) which formerly appeared in the *Journal of Asian Studies,* earlier issued as the *Far Eastern Quarterly.* This bibliography also has been made more accessible through the publication by G K. Hall & Co. in 1969–70 of the *Cumulative Bibliography of Asian Studies, 1941–1965* in eight volumes, supplemented by a 1966–1970 cumulation in six volumes published in 1972–73.

A different approach to keeping abreast of the periodical literature is the reproduction of tables of contents, done regularly in the issues of *Current Anthropology* from 1961–69. This has also been done systematically on a larger scale by the Institute for Scientific Information which issues weekly *Current Contents* in six broad scientific fields. *Social and Behavioral Sciences* and *Life Sciences* are the two series which embrace the field of anthropology. Each issue contains a subject index based on key words in the titles of the articles. It also supplies an author index and address directory for use in applying for reprints.

Abstracts

While the indexing of periodical articles was instituted largely by librarians and publishers, it was the professions, logically enough, which went one step further with the preparation of abstracts.

In 1897 the French produced *L'Année Biologique,* edited by Yves Delage of the Sorbonne, abstracting periodical publications from the year 1895. In the United States the early part of the twentieth century saw the appearance of *Chemical Abstracts* in 1907 (sponsored by the American Chemical Society), *Biological Abstracts* in 1926 (Union of American Biological Societies), superseding earlier *Abstracts of Bacteriology* and *Botanical Abstracts. Psychological Abstracts* (American Psychological Association) and *Child Development Abstracts* (National Research Council's Committee on Child Development) appeared in 1927.

The next phase was the breaking down of abstracting services into narrower subject fields. In 1939 *Biological Abstracts* began to issue its sections separately: A, *Abstracts of General Biology;* B, *Abstracts of Basic Medical Sciences;* and by 1946 H, *Abstracts of Human Biology.*

By 1947 *Excerpta Medica* was making its appearance in Amsterdam, aiming to abstract every article from every medical journal in the world. Its 15 (now 22) sections could and can be purchased separately. Section 1 still covers Anatomy, Anthropology, Embryology, and Histology; section 22, Human Genetics.

In Paris the 1940s saw the beginning of an outstanding international abstracting service, the *Bulletin Signalétique* (called at first *Bulletin Analytique*) published by the Centre National de la Recherche Scientifique. Periodicals, congress proceedings, colloquia, composite volumes, reports, etc are abstracted by experts with worldwide coverage. In the 1960s the *Bulletin* was rearranged in sections. Anthropology comes under Sciences Humaines, and since 1970 appears in sections 521: Sociologie & Ethnologie; 524: Sciences du langage; 525: Préhistoire; 526: Art et archéologie (Proche Orient, Asie, Amérique); 527: Sciences religieuses.

1950 saw the appearance of *African Abstracts* issued by the International African Institute in London, and *Sociological Abstracts* began to appear in 1952.

Abstracts of Folklore Studies (American Folklore Society) commenced in 1963; *America: History and Life,* edited by American historians, in 1964/65; and *British Archaeological Abstracts* (Council for British Archaeology) in 1968.

Now in the 1970s new ones are still appearing. Of particular interest is *Abstracts in Anthropology.* Its attempts to cover archaeology, ethnology, linguistics, and physical anthropology on an international basis are laudable. In spite of a good editorial advisory board, the first three volumes published by Greenwood Periodicals in Westport, Connecticut, were disappointing. However, since 1973 when it appeared under new editorship in the Department of Anthropology at New York University, backed up by expert advisory editors who are specialists in specific geographical areas and subjects, it has shown great improvement.

In 1975 *Abstracts in Human Evolution* first appeared in loose-leaf format, a product of BiblioGraphicS Information Resources in Los Angeles.

This by no means is a complete list of useful indexing and abstracting publications. So numerous are the possibilities for locating periodical articles that in 1974 a two-volume (920-page) *Index to Abstracting and Indexing Services* was published by Chicorel (5), devoted entirely to Humanities and the Social Sciences. This could be a useful reference tool, for it is an alphabetical list of journals recording under each the abstracting or indexing publications in which its contents will be found

Computer Indexing and Abstracting

Indexing and abstracting—in fact, the publishing industry and the organization of libraries—took a new turn in the 1960s and 1970s. Phenomenal advances in technology have made bibliographies into "data bases," librarians into "information specialists," and as one information processing specialist, H. D. Sedgwick, put it, the publishing slogan became "Goodbye, hot metal, hello, cool tape" (20). Linguistics took on a new dimension when it became necessary to learn how to converse with computers, and some university graduate schools began to accept statistical techniques or ability to program in an appropriate language as substitutes for one foreign language in requirements for advanced degrees, according to Sessions (21). This trend began in the sciences, notably in research and development divisions of industry, but soon gained general acceptance and has more recently spread to the social and behavioral sciences, a phenomenon which cannot be overlooked.

This is also the period of the acronym explosion.

BIOSIS The Bio-Science Information Service of *Biological Abstracts* in Philadelphia began to supply the *Abstracts* with cumulative indexes, not only in print, but on microfilm and microfiche, and more recently "on-line" to be consulted through a terminal in a library or laboratory for references to a given topic or combination of keywords. The citations may appear on a television-type screen, printed out, or be mailed for a given fee.

MEDLINE Medical Literature Analysis and Retrieval System On-line, a product of the National Library of Medicine in Bethesda, Maryland, now offers 60 percent of the material from its *Index Medicus,* the citations in 3000 journals in the biomedical field for the current year and two previous years, on a subject basis, using any of the 12,000 medical subject headings in its controlled vocabulary list (MESH). Citations may be printed out at the user's terminal or, if lengthy, mailed from the computer centers in Albany, NY, or Bethesda, Md. Moreover, MEDLINE is just one of a family of data bases available from the National Library of Medicine. Anthropologists are not so likely to make use of CANCERLINE or TOXLINE (Toxicology Information Service). However, they may find it profitable to consult CATLINE (books and serials catalogued since 1965), SERLINE (serial records from 1969), or SDILINE, a current awareness service listing citations to be included in the forthcoming issue of *Index Medicus*.

NTIS   The National Technical Information Service of the US Department of Commerce, is another government-sponsored collector of data bases. This is the supplier from which one purchases copies of research reports of US government-sponsored research, available on paper or microfiche. But it also produces the *NTIS Bibliographic Data File* on magnetic tape, including published and nonpublished abstracts of research projects. From its long list of services, the following have potential value for anthropologists:
1. Census data on microfilm or microfiche.
2. *Weekly Government Abstracts;* technical report summaries in printed newsletter form, available for 25 subject areas, such as Behavior & Society, Medicine & Biology, etc.
3. *Government Reports Announcements* and *Government Reports Index,* issued weekly in print, or on magnetic tape available for lease.

SSIE   The Smithsonian Science Information Exchange tends to be associated by anthropologists with research done by their colleagues in the Smithsonian Institution. However, this is a very different, albeit important and useful tool, recording and reporting scientific research in progress by US government agencies, state and local organizations, foundations, associations, and universities. Custom searches are available quarterly or monthly for updates of *Research Information Packages* on subjects of high current interest, such as Cultural Anthropology.

ERIC   The Educational Resources Information Center, developed by the US Office of Education, is a multifaceted enterprise of enormous benefit to the education field and pertinent to anthropologists for child development, languages and linguistics, as well as for American Indian materials. Its information is collected by clearing houses located in various parts of the USA (Early Childhood at the University of Illinois in Urbana, Social Studies in Boulder, Colorado, and Information Resources at Stanford University in California). Effective access to ERIC necessitates the use of several keys: the *Thesaurus of ERIC Descriptors* for precision in selecting the topics to be researched (i.e. American Indians, Canadian Indians, Eskimo) and *Resources in Education* (before 1975, *Research in Education*) which has abstracted and indexed 10,000 documents, reports, and scholarly papers annually since 1966. Full texts of the documents are available on microfiche in many libraries, or can be ordered in print or microfiche from the ERIC Document Reproduction Service in Bethesda. ERIC's *Current Index to Journals in Education* is a monthly index to US and foreign education journals, with semiannual and annual cumulations. Also available are *ERIC Educational Documents Abstracts* and *ERIC Educational Documents Index*. The bibliographies can be used manually, or the service may be consulted on-line. In addition, personalized Current Awareness and Retrospective Search services can be purchased.

ISI   The Institute for Scientific Information in Philadelphia is a member of the private sector of the information industry and has different approaches to bibliographical control of the world's scientific and technical journal literature. It is the publisher of *Current Contents,* discussed earlier, but it also produces citation indexes which give bibliographical references, not only to each article in the journals indexed, but to each name or topic cited either in the article or in the bibliography at the end, be it book, journal article, book review, or unpublished material. This concept goes back to *Shepard's Citations,* a key to American legal decisions in use since 1873, but is periodical indexing with a new dimension. *Science Citation Index,* published by ISI, first appeared in 1963, covering journal literature back to 1961. Since 1972 *Social Sciences Citation Index* (SSCI) has been available, covering journals back to 1970. Anthropologists cannot afford to ignore it, even though the title gives no indication that it embraces archaeology and physical anthropology as well as social and cultural anthropology. The coverage is increasingly international as time goes on. The January 1975 list of *Source Publications* includes journals from 46 countries, and the anthropology coverage is significantly comprehensive. Here an anthropologist can find not only who has cited his own previous publications, and in what context, but also who, if anyone, is doing research on a given topic. Graduate students looking for dissertation topics now find this a good supplement to *Dissertation Abstracts International* and *the Comprehensive Dissertation Index*. SSCI is now available in book form in most research libraries. It is difficult to use at first, since one must handle the quarterly and annual issues of the *Citation Index* itself, the *Source Index* giving the full bibliographical reference, perhaps the *Corporate Address Index* and the *Permuterm Subject Index*. It is worth the manual effort at least for trial runs. However, the entire cumulated *SSCI* is also now available on-line, and most colleges and universities now have terminals providing access by computer. For in-depth searches, the cost of computer time is probably a good investment. The Institute for Scientific Information also offers various auxiliary services:

1. ASCA (Automatic Subject Citation Alert) which will supply weekly individualized computer-produced current citations under specific keywords or topics in accordance with the subscriber's "profile."
2. ASCATOPICS (Automatic Subject Citation Alert) which will supply

weekly individualized computer-produced citations in nearly 500 selected research areas, such as Behavior Genetics and Human Genetics in the "Life Sciences" or Anthropology, Cross-cultural Comparisons, Anthropological Linguistics, Mythology & Folklore, Sex Roles, Status of Women, etc in the "Social and Behavioral Sciences" series.

3. *Index to Scientific Reviews* such as these in *Annual Review of Anthropology.*

4. OATS (Original Article Tear Sheet) service whereby one may order full copies of any article cited in all ISI publications, to be mailed out within 24 hours.

The foregoing are examples of the kind of computer-produced services in the United States, but one should not have the impression that only here are such services available. One excellent European example is the Centre de Documentation Sciences Humaines of the Centre National de la Recherche Scientifique (C.N.R.S.), publisher of the *Bulletin Signalétique* mentioned above. The Centre offers retrospective searches or subscriptions to current awareness searches eight times a year, according to one's profile based upon key words (*mots clés*) kept on file in its Paris office. Citations are mailed out in sheet form or on slips (fiches). In Amsterdam *Excerpta Medica* has a similar data bank back to 1969.

COMPILATION AND PUBLISHING OF BIBLIOGRAPHIES

Due to the impossibility of achieving adequate coverage, individual books and monographic bibliographies are not listed in this article, but mention should be made of tools for locating them and trends in publishing. Aside from library card catalogues, trade and national bibliographies, and the book reviews and lists of new publications featured in most of the professional journals, there are the multivolume printed catalogues of the world's large and important libraries. University libraries have for years expanded their shelf space to make room for the giant sets: the Library of Congress author and subject catalogues, those of the British Museum, the Bibliothèque Nationale, and others. Since the early 1960s university, college, and special research libraries have also been making way for the products of an inventive and visionary publisher, the late Garrison K. Hall.

G. K. Hall & Co.

In the 1940s and 1950s Hall was producing bound custom-made photographic reproductions of individual books and set up the Micro-Photography Company in the small town of West Newbury, Massachusetts. As technological advances in microfilm technology took place, he foresaw a market for published card catalogues and special indexes available hitherto only by traveling to consult the originals. Now G K. Hall & Co. in Boston has become a publisher whose usually tall and brightly bound sets are to be found in the reference sections of research libraries around the world.

In the early 1960s came the *Dictionary Catalog of the Edward E. Ayer*

Collection of Americana and American Indians at the Newberry Library in Chicago; then the library catalogues of the School of Oriental and African Studies in London, the Peabody Museum at Harvard University, the Bishop Museum in Honolulu, and the Colonial Office in London. As library reference shelves continued to sag with the weight of these multivolume sets, the demand grew as scholars and librarians welcomed these keys to obscure or new citations to the literature of special subjects or areas. In the late 1960s came the *Biographical and Historical Index of American Indians and Persons involved in Indian Affairs* and the *Dictionary Catalog* of the Library of the US Department of the Interior, the catalogues of the Mitchell Library in Sydney, Australia, and the Deutsches Archaeologisches Institut's library in Rome. For the Latin Americanists G K. Hall made available the Pan American Union's *Index to Latin American Periodical Literature, 1929–1960* and *1961–1965*, and the *Catalog of the Latin American Collection of the University of Texas Library* in Austin, followed in 1970 by the *Catalog of the Latin American Library* at Tulane University in New Orleans (known until 1962 as the Middle American Research Institute Library). The *Catálogo de la Biblioteca Nacional de Antropología e Historia* in Mexico appeared in 1972.

In the 1970s G K. Hall & Co. has ventured in other directions with the cumulated bibliographies of Asian and African studies already noted. The firm is also producing in its "Series Seventy" for the most part single-volume bibliographies, such as the *Catalogue of the C M. Doke Collection on African Languages in the Library of the University of Rhodesia; Ghana: an Annotated Bibliography of Academic Theses;* and Hans Schlüter's *Index Libycus, 1957–1969.* It is also publishing in 1976 *Ethnomusicology and Oral Data,* a phonography from the Archives of Traditional Music from the Folklore Institute at Indiana University. Still another venture into the translation field in 1974 promises English versions of the Russian *Itogi Nauki,* review volumes issued by VINITI (Vsesoiuznyii Institut Nauchnoi i Tekhnicheskoi Informatsii). Volume I (1973) of the *Human Genetics* series appeared in 1974. The latest pertinent 1975 publication is the *Catalog to Manuscripts* at the National Anthropological Archives at the National Museum of Natural History in Washington (known to many as the Bureau of American Ethnology Archives at the Smithsonian Institution).

Human Relations Area Files

In the 1930s, when Professor George P. Murdock conceived and created the Human Relations Area Files under the aegis of the Institute of Human Relations at the Yale University Medical School, a unique project came into being. Key sources on a variety of cultures were selected, and each paragraph of the complete texts was indexed and reproduced on sheets to be filed under every appropriate subject category. These were not bibliographical citations, like those appearing in library card catalogues, but sections of the actual texts. Perhaps Murdock did, but probably no one else dreamed that by 1975 the

Human Relations Area Files Inc., with headquarters still in New Haven, would be jointly sponsored and controlled by 24 universities and research institutions, would have handled 4300 sources, and be available either on paper or microfiche in nearly 250 institutions from New Haven to New Zealand and Nigeria. Nowadays few anthropology students have not heard of HRAF, and some are required to make use of the files, not to mention Murdock's *Outline of Cultural Materials* (15) and *Outline of World Cultures* (16), together with the eight-volume subject index and HRAF *Source Bibliography*.

HRAF continues to be innovative in the use of computers for compiling and publishing. The Human Relations Area Files Automated Bibliographic System (HABS) has in the past 10 years under the direction of Hesung C. Koh (11) added a new dimension to automated bibliographical control. It is not limited by classification scheme or language, like the Library of Congress MARC (Machine Readable Cataloging) system which is becoming a standard for library cataloguing. It was originally designed for Koh's Korean bibliography project and has been refined for use in the preparation of HRAF bibliographies. One special feature incorporated in the HABS system is an evaluation of each citation to provide data quality control. Each item is coded for the author's nationality, sex, discipline, date, length and type of field work, language facility, use of primary and secondary sources, as well as precise subjects discussed, precise geographical area studies, and time period covered. Thus, having amassed a list of citations, one can distinguish which sources would presumably be most reliable and pertinent to one's own research. An excellent example of the use of data quality control, is the two-volume *Lapps Ethnographic Bibliography* compiled by O'Leary & Steffens (17), which contains in the Introduction and Guide to Citations explanations of the system. HRAF staff members have been involved in international conferences on bibliographical control, and future developments will be watched with interest.

Two Individual Bibliographies

MURDOCK & O'LEARY'S *ETHNOGRAPHIC BIBLIOGRAPHY OF NORTH AMERICA* (14) The fourth revised edition of Murdock's *Ethnographic Bibliography of North America,* prepared under the direction of Timothy J. O'Leary, published by HRAF Press in 1976 in the *Behavior Science Bibliographies* series, is a product of the HRAF Automated Bibliographic System. The third edition published in 1960 contained 17,300 entries, all of which have now been put into machine-readable form. Another 28,000 entries have been added, representing published books and articles relating to the Native Peoples of North America issued between 1959 and 1972. The result is a five-volume work with much fuller citations and broader coverage as to subjects and areas. It includes additional groups, particularly in northern Mexico, corresponding to those described in the *Handbook of North American Indians* being prepared at the same time under the editorship of William C. Sturtevant for publication by the Smithsonian Institution Press commencing in 1976.

This new *Ethnographic Bibliography of North America* was actually computer printed. There were no galleys to be proofread, since the editing had been done at an earlier stage in data-processing the citations. In other ways the computer has revolutionized the publishing process for reference books because all of the data is now stored on tape. Special bibliographies can be printed out. New material can be added for later editions, and by changing the programming of the computer, they can be issued in a different format. The compiler has prepared a lengthy introduction which not only describes the scope and preparation of this work, but discusses in detail other bibliographical sources on the Native Peoples of North America.

SKINNER'S *MODERN CHINESE SOCIETY* (22)   Another extraordinary work which could have been produced in no other way than by computer is *Modern Chinese Society*, an analytical bibliography prepared under the editorship of G. William Skinner and published by Stanford University Press in 1973 in three volumes, covering citations in Western, Chinese, and Japanese languages. This enterprise was 10 years in the making, having been sponsored by a special subcommittee of the Social Science Research Council and by the American Council of Learned Societies. Work was done simultaneously at Cornell, Columbia, Harvard, the University of Tokyo, and Stanford.

Some 90,000 titles of books, articles, etc were collected, then evaluated for scope and scholarly value; bibliographical citations were prepared or emended, and encoded annotations of contents were provided by 120 trained annotators, mostly graduate students. The entire publishing operation was by computer with automatic typesetting and printing, using SABS, the Stanford Automated Bibliography System (like its counterpart HABS) including data quality control. The first volume, *Publications in Western languages, 1644-1972*, contains 802 pages, comprising an introduction detailing the method of compilation and production, the citations themselves, and no less than six indexes, making it possible to retrieve references by historical period, geographical area, specific local area, and personal or corporate author.

Modern Chinese Society and the *Ethnographic Bibliography of North America* are monumental achievements demonstrating what can be done when dedicated scholars harness the computer to achieve specific bibliographic goals.

THE BIBLIOGRAPHICAL PRESENT

Now that we are faced not only with a tremendous worldwide increase in publications, but also with a proliferation of keys to their identification and retrieval, how is bibliographical control to be achieved? Obviously a simple card file in an anthropologist's office, subscriptions to the best journals, communication with colleagues in one's special field, supplemented by the nearest research library, will no longer guarantee access to all the pertinent literature. The problems are not totally insoluble, however, and they are being attacked on several fronts by individual librarians, anthropologists, professional associations, foundations, and the information industry.

The United States and Canada

On a local level a group of concerned and energetic librarians and anthropologists in Chicago formed in 1971 the Library Anthropology Resource Group (LARG) which holds monthly meetings and has taken steps to ease their own burdens and those of their colleagues elsewhere. Their first project, a list of journals and series available in libraries of the Chicago area, has been published in preliminary form as *Serial Publications in Anthropology* edited by Tax & Grollig (25), which, in an enlarged edition can become a bibliography of use to the profession at large. A bibliography of anthropological bibliographies is now in process. Their compilation of the *Fifth International Directory of Anthropologists* appeared in 1975.

A national library-oriented group which may be expected to participate in efforts toward bibliographical control is the Anthropology Section of the Association of College and Research Libraries, a division of the American Library Association with which it holds annual meetings. Its 1975/76 program calls for the preparation of subject and area bibliographies and the encouragement of the use of computer bibliography.

Library networks are springing up in all parts of the USA and Canada and in other parts of the world as well. At first formed primarily to avoid duplication and keep down costs in the acquisition and cataloguing of books, they are increasingly valuable in locating materials for interlibrary loan. Linked by telephone or teletype, they are becoming increasingly sophisticated in the use of computers. Terminals are being set up in strategic spots, usually in the reference areas of college and university libraries where one or more information specialists are on hand.

As time goes on, American library users will become familiar with the acronyms for their regional networks, such as CLASS (California Library Authority for Systems and Services), MIDLNET (Middlewest Regional Library Network), NELINET (New England Library Information Network), OCLC (Ohio College Library Center), SOLINET (Southeastern Library Network), or CAN/SDI (Canadian Selective Dissemination of Information). These systems in turn are members of CCLN (Council for Computerized Library Networks). A somewhat different type of consortium is the Research Libraries Group (RLG). The libraries of Harvard, Yale, and Columbia Universities and the New York Public Library have organized to promote more economical collection development, cataloguing, and use of their combined resources. A computer-based joint catalogue of their holdings is one of the first priorities.

ASIS (the American Society for Information Science) is another source of activity. Founded in 1937 as the American Documentation Institute, it has now expanded to a membership of 4000 with 24 local chapters. Its annual meetings and publications provide an exchange of information between communications experts, computer and data processing specialists, manufacturers of equipment, publishers, and librarians.

In 1975 the National Science Foundation, the National Commission on Libraries and Information Science, and the Council on Library Resources established an ADVISORY GROUP ON NATIONAL BIBLIOGRAPHIC CONTROL in order to coordinate their programs and to recommend priorities for action. All three organizations have interests in libraries, abstracting and indexing services, publishing and information delivery, and will set up joint work groups in each area.

The US National Commission on Libraries and Information Science (NCLIS), established by law in 1971, devoted several years of intensive research and discussion before publishing its findings and proposals in 1975 in a document entitled *Toward a National Program for Library and Information Services.* Here are spelled out the problems and possible solutions, some of which are bound to come to pass. Two of the assumptions on which this National Program is based are:

> that the total library and information resource in the United States is a national resource which should be developed, strengthened, organized and made available to the maximum degree possible in the public interest . . . and that with the help of new technology and with national resolve, the disparate and discrete collections of recorded information in the United States can become, in due course, an integrated nationwide network (27, p.x).

As one librarian, R C. Swank (24), has so aptly stated:

> No society can advance beyond a certain point without effective access to its collective memory of record, or conversely, an advanced society that loses control of the record will regress.

The NCLIS report strongly recommends a coordinated system of intrastate, interstate, and national library networks, linked by telephone, teletype, computers or telecommunication to provide aid in acquisitions, cataloguing, storage, location, and dissemination of information, and leading eventually to link-ups with a worldwide system.

This is definitely within the realm of possibility, since the present state of technology promises potential two-way communication of both picture and sound, facsimile transmission service, and access to data processing. Some of the problems to be conquered are: standardization of equipment, solution of copyright problems, and the ironing out of areas of conflict between government or privately funded abstracting and indexing services and those produced by the profit-making information industry publishers.

The International Scene

An entire review article could be written on international efforts towards the gathering, processing, storage, retrieval, and dissemination of information. I shall limit myself here to three examples which represent different approaches: UNISIST, a Unesco Science project; UBC, a plan of the International Federation of Library Associations; and the Commission on Documentation in the Anthropological Sciences.

UNISIST   In October 1971 Unesco held an Intergovernmental Conference for the Establishment of a World Science Information System (UNISIST) (10).

This was the outcome of a joint study with the International Council of Scientific Unions (ICSU) of the needs of scientists for information, of the existing facilities and resources in the field of science information, and of the economic aspects of a worldwide system of science information networks. While any such plans will not come to immediate fruition, a few steps have been taken. For example, there is already in operation an International Serials Data System and in Paris an International Center for the Registration of Serials. Most significant for anthropologists is the recent expansion of UNISIST to include the social sciences.

UBC   Universal Bibliographic Control (UBC) is a concept for the promotion of a worldwide system for the control and exchange of bibliographic information. It was formally presented by IFLA (International Federation of Library Associations) to the Unesco Intergovernmental Conference on the Planning of National Overall Documentation, Library and Archives Infrastructures in September 1974. Its purpose is to make universally and promptly available, in a form which is internationally acceptable, basic bibliographic data on all publications issued in all countries, as reported by D. Anderson (1). Ideally the project will involve the acquisition by national libraries of all publications produced in their countries and the prompt preparation and publication of national bibliographies, according to international standards and applicable to both manual and mechanized systems. Cataloguers have long been working towards standardized forms of entries. IFLA has already worked out an International Standard Bibliographic Description for Monographs [ISBD (M)] which has been generally adopted since 1972.

COMMISSION ON DOCUMENTATION IN THE ANTHROPOLOGICAL SCIENCES
Another potential source of collaborative effort towards bibliographical control is the Commission on Documentation in the Anthropological Sciences. In August 1973 37 librarians, documentalists, and anthropologists met in Chicago to discuss problems prior to the Ninth International Congress of Anthropological and Ethnological Sciences. Thirty were from the United States and Canada, but Australia, Czechoslovakia, England, Nigeria, Switzerland, and Yugoslavia were also represented. Their first accomplishment was a successful petition to the Permanent Council of the Congress for status as a Commission, with the following objectives:

> We are concerned that scholars have maximum access to the basic extant sources of anthropological and ethnological data, both written and non-written. We should like to strive toward standardization in bibliographical style and compatibility of information systems, both within the discipline of anthropology and beyond. We are concerned in furthering rational and economical approaches to the preservation, analysis and dissemination of the wide range of materials, including oral literature, of concern to anthropologists.[2]

[2]From unpublished report of meetings, Aug. 28–Sept. 8, 1973, distributed to attendees and others.

Hans E. Panofsky, Curator of the Melville Herskovits Library at Northwestern University, presented the petition and was elected the first chairman. Two ongoing committees were named. The Committee on the Adequacy of Anthropological Resources, under the chairmanship of Polly Grimshaw of the Indiana University Libraries, aims to examine and evaluate all relevant anthropological bibliographical resources in the four major fields of anthropology —physical anthropology, archaeology, social/cultural anthropology, and linguistics. These will also include resources from all geographical areas and in all languages. Types of relevant resources to be covered will be: (*a*) published and unpublished research materials; (*b*) government publications; (*c*) audio-visual materials, including films, photographs, sound recordings, artifacts, maps, human biological materials, and those resources which cover other types of material culture; (*d*) archival material; (*e*) machine-readable data. Committee members are now at work evaluating the existing published abstracts and indexes.

The Committee on Bibliographic Standards, under the chairmanship of Robert O. Lagacé of the Human Relations Area Files, has as its objectives: (*a*) to define and/or specify the requirements of a bibliographic system which will meet the basic bibliographic information needs of scholars and students in the anthropological and ethnological sciences, while being both capable of implementation on an international, cooperative basis, and economically feasible; (*b*) to devise such a system as efficiently and rapidly as possible, utilizing whenever appropriate previous work in this field so as to minimize the required labor and costs.

The opportunities for effective collaboration among practicing anthropologists, librarians, and information scientists on an international level are vast. Although the beginnings have been disappointingly slow, it is hoped that the Commission will have at least laid the groundwork for real progress by the Tenth International Congress of Anthropological and Ethnological Sciences, scheduled for Delhi in 1978.

THE BIBLIOGRAPHICAL FUTURE

What does the future hold in store? Surely the number of anthropologists is not decreasing. Anthropology has never been a discipline with distinct boundaries, and now the interdisciplinary combinations seem almost limitless. Consequently the results of more research are being published. The problem of becoming aware of, not to mention reading, the pertinent literature will be a perennial burden or obstacle to be overcome.

As has been indicated, help will be forthcoming from concerned anthropologists, librarians, publishers, and from the information industry. Libraries and research institutions will undoubtedly be linked in local, regional, national, and international networks, with a terminal in every library, if not in every office. It will be possible to identify and locate research material useful for one's particular research project and easier to identify and contact others working along the same line, thus avoiding some duplication of effort and waste of time, energy, and funds.

Books and reports will for some time to come be available on interlibrary loan, but experiments indicate the possibility of viewing texts on a screen at one's desk. The growth of reader-printers for microfilm and microfiche makes print-outs from such transmitted material more than an idle dream. For some time to come the cost of computer equipment and services will limit their extensive use to the larger libraries and institutions.

Thirty or 40 years ago the technologists were predicting the condensation of our great university libraries into microfilms in cans and microcards in catalogue card trays. Most libraries will continue to maintain their card catalogues for a few years at least, but the New York Public Library stopped adding new cards on December 31, 1971. Since that date it has issued *The Dictionary Catalog of the Research Libraries*, a cumulative list of authors, titles, and subjects representing books and book-like materials added to the collections since January 1, 1971. Monthly cumulations or supplements are issued, so that one does not need to search in more than two alphabets. The catalogues of many special collections of the New York Public Library have already been published, either by G K. Hall & Co. or by the Library itself. The Library of Congress expects to close its card catalogues in 1979. Certainly more and more catalogues will be computer-produced now that photocomposition is a reality. Another example of an automated catalogue is the *Australian National Bibliography*. The 1972 annual volume was actually published in February of 1973, whereas the 1971 volume did not appear until late November of 1972 (1).

The average student will still need to go to the library for his materials, even though more of them may be collections of select readings made up for individual courses, or microform reproductions. The individual anthropologist will continue his subscriptions to journals and purchase basic books which he can handle in his office, and will run down to the library to verify references without having to pay for computer time. The great desideratum in technological development is the expansion of the 24-hour day, allowing time for reading the references retrieved!

ACKNOWLEDGMENTS
Grateful acknowledgments are due to librarians, anthropologists, and others who have given of their time and stores of information; I am particularly grateful to Diane Baden, Polly Grimshaw, Carol F. Ishimoto, Hesung C. Koh, Marie Lannon, Timothy J. O'Leary, Hans E. Panofsky, Jutta Woltereck Reed, Antonio Rodriguez Buckingham, and Helen F. Rogers.

Literature Cited

1. Anderson, D. 1974. *Universal Bibliographic Control.* Pullach/München: Verlag Dokumentation. 87 pp.
2. Barnwell, J. G. 1876. A universal catalogue: its necessity and practicability. *Libr. J.* 1:54–58
3. Baye, J. de 1876. Congrès International d'Anthropologie et d'Archéologie Préhistoriques, 8.ses-

sion à Budapest. *Bull. Monumental* 7:19

4. Beckham, R. S., Comp. 1963. A basic list of books and periodicals for college libraries. In *Resources for the Teaching of Anthropology*, ed. D. G. Mandelbaum, G. W. Lasker, E. M. Albert, 77–316. Berkeley: Univ. California Press. 316 pp.

5. Chicorel, M. 1974. *Chicorel Index to Abstracting and Indexing Services, 11–11a: Periodicals in Humanities and the Social Sciences.* New York: Chicorel Libr. Publ. Corp. 2 vols. 920 pp.

6. Currier, M. 1942. Cataloguing at Harvard in the Sixties. *Harvard Univ. Libr. Notes* 32:67–73

7. Fewkes, J. W. 1897. Anthropology. In *The Smithsonian Institution, 1846–1896*, ed. G. B. Goode, 745–72. Washington: De Vinne Press. 856 pp.

8. Frantz, C. 1972. *The Student Anthropologist's Handbook.* Cambridge, Mass.: Schenkman. 228 pp.

9. Hoselitz, B. F., Ed. 1970. *A Reader's Guide to the Social Sciences.* New York: Free Press. 425 pp. Rev. ed.

10. Intergovernmental Conference for the Establishment of a World Science Information System, Paris, 4–8 October 1971. *UNISIST; Final Rep.* Paris: Unesco. 60 pp.

11. Koh, H. C. 1973. HABS: a research tool for social science and area studies. *Behav. Sci. Notes* 8:169–99

12. Mason, O. T. 1877. The antiquities of Porto Rico. *Proc. Am. Assoc. Adv. Sci. 25th, Buffalo, 1876:* 294–99

13. Morgan, L. H. 1877. Four papers on the Iroquois to be published in his *Ancient Society. Proc. Am. Assoc. Adv. Sci. 25th, Buffalo, 1876:* 340

14. Murdock, G. P., O'Leary, T. J. 1976. *Ethnographic Bibliography of North America.* New Haven: HRAF. 5 vols. 4th ed.

15. Murdock, G. P. 1971. *Outline of Cultural Materials.* New Haven: HRAF. 164 pp. 4th rev. ed.

16. Murdock, G. P. 1975. *Outline of World Cultures.* New Haven: HRAF. 256 pp. 5th rev. ed.

17. O'Leary, T. J., Steffens, J.,

Comps. 1975. *Lapps Ethnographic Bibliography.* New Haven: HRAFlex Book EP04-001. 2 vols. 499 pp.

18. Powell, J. W. 1877. On the mythology of the North American Indians. *Proc. Am. Assoc. Adv. Sci. 25th, Buffalo, 1876:* 340

19. Rogers, T. H. 1876. A co-operative index for public libraries. *Libr. J.* 1:62–63

20. Sedgwick, H. D. 1970. Goodbye hot metal, hello cool tape. *Datamation* 16 (16):32–35

21. Sessions, V. S., Ed. 1974. *Directory of Data Bases in the Social and Behavioral Sciences.* New York: Science Assoc. Int. 300 pp.

22. Skinner, G. W., Ed. 1973. *Modern Chinese Society: an Analytical Bibliography.* Stanford Univ. Press. 3 vols.

23. Spencer, H. 1873–1934. *Descriptive Sociology.* London: Williams & Norgate. 19 parts

24. Swank, R. C. 1971. Interlibrary co-operation, interlibrary communications, and information networks. In *Proc. Conf. Interlibrary Communications and Information Networks*, ed. J. Becker. Chicago: Am. Libr. Assoc. 347 pp.

25. Tax, S., Grollig, F. X., Eds. 1973. *Serial Publications in Anthropology*, comp. Library-Anthropology Resource Group. Univ. Chicago Press. 91 pp.

26. Topinard, P. 1876. *L'Anthropologie.* Paris: Reinwald. 574 pp.

26a. Tylor, E. B. 1871. *Primitive Culture.* London: Murray. 2 vols. 972 pp.

27. U. S. National Commission on Libraries and Information Science 1975. *Toward a National Program for Library and Information Services: Goals for Action.* Washington DC: G.P.O. 106 pp.

28. White, C. M. et al 1973. *Sources of Information in the Social Sciences; A Guide to the Literature.* Chicago: Am. Libr. Assoc. 702 pp. 2nd ed.

29. Winchell, C. M. 1967. *Guide to Reference Books.* Chicago: Am. Libr. Assoc. 741 pp. 8th ed. Supplements by Sheehy, E. P., 1968 to date

30. Wynar, B. S., Ed. 1970 to date. *American Reference Books Annual.* Littleton, Colo: Libraries Unlimited

Ann. Rev. Anthropol. 1976. 5:35–67
Copyright © 1976 by Annual Reviews Inc. All rights reserved

THE ORIGINS OF
MESOAMERICAN WRITING

◆ 9569

Joyce Marcus[1]
Department and Museum of Anthropology,
University of Michigan, Ann Arbor, Michigan 48109

> The demarcation line between iconographic symbolism and writing is faint at times, faint enough at least for Olmec enthusiasts to leap over it and proclaim as writing what in other cultures would pass as depiction of attributes on body or clothing, a claim which would embrace everything from painted teepees to mediaeval heraldry.
>
> J. Eric S. Thompson (59, p. 205)

Ancient writing systems which remain undeciphered have had an unusual capacity to arouse excitement in both professionals and amateurs. In the New World, the scholarly study of Mesoamerican writing systems has been undertaken for only 100 years. This short period of investigation, conducted by a relatively small number of investigators, has nevertheless led to some major breakthroughs; but most scholars would agree that we are still unable to transcribe, interpret, or "read" entire texts. We are frequently able to obtain the gist of various passages, but we cannot read them in the spoken language as the Indian speakers might have.

In 1865 a German scholar, Dr. Ernst Förstemann, accepted the position of head librarian at the Royal Public Library in Dresden. This move resulted in a great advance for the field of Maya writing. The Royal Library in Dresden had long contained a fiber-cloth manuscript labeled "an invaluable Mexican book with hieroglyphic figures" (60, p. 153). To Förstemann we owe a considerable debt for his initial elucidation and publication of the entire Dresden Codex in 1880. This Postclassic Maya book probably dates to A.D. 1200–1250, though some scholars feel it is a copy of a much earlier book. Förstemann then began a study of the two other extant codices currently found in the cities which provide their names, the Codex Madrid and Codex Paris. Later Förstemann turned his

[1] Part of the research for this paper was facilitated by Grant RO-21433-75-460 from the National Endowment for the Humanities, whose generous support is gratefully acknowledged. In addition, Jeremy A. Sabloff provided me with hard-to-get publications without which I could not have completed the paper. Figures 1, 3–11, and 14 were drawn by Jane Mariouw, while Mark Orsen drew Figures 2 and 12. Very special thanks to Mary Hodge, who typed the entire manuscript and prepared Figure 13.

attention to the inscriptions in stone from Classic Maya archaeological sites (A.D. 250–910). By 1894 it was possible to read the dates on these Maya monuments—to identify the period glyphs and their relationship to one another. In only 14 years, by studying both codices and stelae, Förstemann had discovered how the Maya calendar operated.

In 1905 J. Thompson Goodman, owner and editor of the *Territorial Enterprise* of Virginia City, Nevada (the newspaperman who gave Mark Twain his start) also made important contributions to Maya studies. Goodman published a paper in which he offered the first correlation of the Maya and European calendars (26). In 1926 Juan Martínez Hernández reaffirmed the correlation (36), while J. Eric S. Thompson tested it in 1927 with lunar and Venus-cycle data (54). Their combined efforts are called the Goodman-Martínez-Thompson correlation, which is now widely accepted.

The atmosphere of the field changed dramatically in 1949, for it was in that year that the Mexican scholar Alfonso Caso was able to establish a correlation between Mixtec dates and Christian dates and link the ancient Indian dynasties of Teozacoalco and Tilantongo, Oaxaca (6). For the Mixtec manuscripts, various scholars had previously suggested that the content was largely historical. In 1902, Zelia Nuttall had suggested that the codex which now bears her name contained historical data (39). James Cooper Clark in 1912 had reported the story of a famous Mixtec ruler named 8 Deer "Tiger Claw" (8). In 1935 Herbert Spinden discussed a group of Mixtec manuscripts and declared that the content was primarily devoted to genealogies and sequences of political events (51). Thus, studies had already shifted from an astronomical to an historical perspective within the field of Mixtec writing; the "door to history" opened in 1949.

In the field of Maya hieroglyphic writing, it was not until 1958 that the attention of scholars turned to the noncalendric information. Heinrich Berlin (1) opened up a new frontier by discovering that each major Maya center had a particular glyph used many times in its texts, but infrequently employed outside of that site. Berlin termed these "emblem glyphs," and suggested they were site names, dynastic names, or perhaps the names of tutelar deities. We now feel that these glyphs do indeed represent geographical referents. Following this breakthrough, Tatiana Proskouriakoff (43) was able to demonstrate that many Maya monuments recorded local history—births, accessions to the throne, and other feats involving local rulers. By combining the work of Berlin and Proskouriakoff we are now able to establish territorial units, personal names of rulers, their births, accessions, conquests, royal marriages, and deaths. Just as Caso opened the door to the Mixtec dynasties and their history, Proskouriakoff opened the historical door for the Maya field.

At least four major systems of writing arose in Mesoamerica: the Zapotec and Maya systems, which began with hieroglyphic texts on stone; and the Mixtec and Aztec systems, which featured pictorial manuscripts on hide or paper. All other regional systems seem to be variants of one of these four major types. In this paper I will address myself only to the origin and early evolution of Mesoamerican writing, from roughly 600 B.C. to A.D. 900—a period dominated by hieroglyphic systems of the Zapotec and Maya types. The later pictographic systems of the Mixtec and Aztec (A.D. 900–1600), which really deserve an article of equivalent length, will not be discussed here.

THE EVOLUTIONARY CONTEXT OF EARLY WRITING

It is now clear that Mesoamerican hieroglyphic writing began in a pre-State evolutionary context, among societies with intensive agriculture and hereditary social ranking, but prior to true social stratification or political centralization. Let us briefly discuss early Mesoamerican writing in the light of ancient writing systems in general.

Although many Old World scholars and epigraphers have claimed that the writing of the New World Indians cannot be compared with achievements in the Near East, they frequently reveal either personal prejudice or lack of information:

> Would it not be surprising, somebody may ask, if the pre-Columbian Indians, who produced a culture frequently compared with the fully developed cultures of the ancient Near East, did not have a writing of the same stature as the systems found in the Orient? The answer I could give is that the Amerindian cultures cannot properly be compared with the cultures of the Near East (Gelb 25, pp. 57–58).

First of all, the functions and the origins of writing in the Old and New Worlds appear to be quite different. The earliest writing of the "Protoliterate" period in the Near East occurs on clay tablets and apparently deals with economic transactions. Much of this early writing had as its content the number of foodstuffs, goods, or animals to be transferred, as well as the personal names of the principals. One function was to keep accurate economic records.

For the New World, the earliest writing is closely associated with the calendar: historical events are set within a chronological framework. The content of Classic Mesoamerican writing is primarily genealogical, dynastic, and militaristic. We are provided with personal names of rulers, their births, marriages, and conquests. One of the functions seems to be to legitimize each ruler's right to accede to the throne. Some of the differences between early writing in the New and Old Worlds are therefore functional, and have nothing to do with levels of "cultural achievement" in the two areas.

The evolution of writing has been delineated by Gelb as proceeding from

(*a*) *pictography* (pictures as signs; pictograms) to
(*b*) *logography* (a sign stands for a word; logograms) to
(*c*) *syllabary* (a sign stands for one or more syllables) to
(*d*) *alphabet* (a sign stands for one or more phonemes)

Although many writing systems have a pictorial character in their earliest stages, there are almost always some signs that evolved out of arbitrary conventions. Thus one could reasonably argue that none of Gelb's four proposed stages are "pure." Each stage preserves some of the signs from earlier stages; hence, we see heterogeneous systems employing pictograms, ideograms, and some phonograms at the same time. Therefore, it is somewhat difficult to classify writing systems except perhaps by the relative percentages of pictograms, ideograms, logograms, phonograms, and so forth.

Various definitions of writing have been suggested by scholars. For Gelb (25, p. 12), writing is "a system of human intercommunication by means of conventional visible marks." For our purposes this definition is far too broad, for it would include petroglyphs, some Mesoamerican mural painting, and the heraldry referred to by Thompson at the start of this paper. Diringer (20, p. 13) has defined writing as the "graphic counterpart of speech, the 'fixing' of spoken language in a permanent or semi-permanent form." For Diringer there are four stages of *true* writing:

1. *Pictography.*
2. *Ideographic writing:* This is the first step in rendering a script capable of conveying abstractions and multiple associations. Thus, whereas in pictography a circle may stand for the sun, in an ideographic writing system, it might also mean heat, light, a god associated with the sun, the words "day" or "time." Also, animals may be ideographically depicted, using the head alone, or a paw (i.e., a part stands for the whole).
2a. *Analytic transitional scripts:* The basic units are words. This form of writing is intermediate between ideographic and pure phonetic writing.
3. *Phonetic scripts:* A sign stands for a sound. The convention of using symbols to represent syllables arose in many parts of the world at different times, but few scripts ever shed completely the ideograms of earlier stages.
4. *Alphabetic writing:* Individual letters represent single sounds, both vowels and consonants.

The four major Mesoamerican writing systems (Zapotec, Maya, Mixtec, and Aztec) were all heterogeneous systems—partly pictographic, ideographic, and phonetic. The only type of writing not represented was the alphabetic system, which seems to be a rare development and is frequently considered by many Old World scholars to be the "highest" form of writing.

A DEFINITION OF WRITING

Because I do not feel that petroglyphs, iconographic motifs, and heraldic symbols qualify as writing, I will begin with a definition of early writing in general and proceed to a discussion of early Mesoamerican texts in particular.

1. Writing is recognizable by its format; even when we are unable to read or interpret certain examples of writing, we are able to infer that a certain text is writing by its organization.
2. More than 90 percent of all early writing has a linear format, either in *rows* (as in the case of Mesopotamia and Egypt) or *columns* (as in the case of China and the Maya region).

3. This linear format implies the order of reading, either:
   (a) left to right, or right to left;
   (b) top to bottom, or bottom to top.
4. There is some degree of relationship to the spoken language.
5. There is a limited set of conventionalized signs that combine according to specific rules, i.e. "grammar."

As for early Mesoamerican texts, they typically have three or more signs or hieroglyphs in a column (in this paper, isolated hieroglyphs are not considered to be examples of "texts"). The column seems to be the essential organizing principle for Mesoamerican writing. In the beginning come single-column texts; later, paired columns are common; and finally, there are paired columns that are to be read together from left to right and from top to bottom.

MESOAMERICAN CALENDRIC SYSTEMS

Because the earliest examples of Mesoamerican writing are inextricably linked to the pre-Columbian calendar, a brief description of the workings of this calendar is necessary before proceeding to the earliest texts. All Mesoamerican peoples made use of a vigesimal system for most of their counting functions. The vigesimal system is based on multiples of 20, rather than the decimal system we use. Most Mesoamerican Indians had two principal elements to express their numerals: the dot, which had the numerical value of 1, and the bar, which had the numerical value of 5. By various combinations of these two elements, all the numerals from 1 to 19 could be expressed. After the number 19, the zero was reached, which was than followed by 1, 2, and so on. Numbers were also recorded positionally in a manner similar to our 10s, 100s, and 1,000s—1, 20, 400, 8,000, and 160,000 were the vigesimal equivalents. In other words, 20 units of the first order made one unit of the second order, and so forth.

One of the most important elements of the Mesoamerican calendar was the cycle of 260 days. A series of 20 differently named days were combined with the numbers from 1 through 13. Thus the combination of a number (or numerical coefficient) and a day name formed a unit. The same combination of name and numerical coefficient cannot recur until 260 days have elapsed; the 261st day will then have the same designation as the first day of the cycle. This 260-day cycle has been called the Sacred Round.

The various combinations of day names and numbers exerted tremendous influence over the lives of Mesoamerican Indians, both noble and commoner. The benevolence and the malevolence of each day name and number determined when maize should be planted or harvested, and so forth. This system of augury affected every individual, because the influences of the day of one's birth were felt to mold and shape one's whole life. Among the Zapotec, Mixtec, and other peoples, it was common for individuals to be named after the day of their birth. Thus individuals had names like 8 Deer, 5 Flower, and 13 Crocodile. According to Antonio de Herrera, Mixtec men and women could not marry if their calendric names included the same numerical coefficient, such as 1 Reed and 1 Wind; the numerical coefficient of the man's name was ideally supposed to be higher than that of the woman's name (Herrera 29, p. 320; Smith 50, p. 29).

For the yearly round of mundane events, however, this cycle of 260 days would not suffice; for other purposes, the Indians also had a year of 365 days. This year was divided into 18 "months" of 20 days each, and there was an extra period of 5 "unlucky" days at the end of the year. This 365-day unit is often called the Vague Year, because the true year is 365 days and 6 hours long. Each of the "months" of the Vague Year also had a series of positions numbered from 0 to 19.

When we combine the 260-day Sacred Round and the 365-day Vague Year we have a Calendar Round cycle. This permutation of 2 cycles resulted in a 52-year calendar of 18,980 differently designated numbers-plus-days, and numbers-plus-months. If, for instance, we take the first day of the Maya year 2 Ik 0 Pop ("2 Ik" is a day in the 260-day cycle; "0 Pop" is a position in the month Pop within the Vague Year), the question arises: How many revolutions will each cycle have to make before the day 2 Ik again returns to the position 0 in the month Pop? Since the day 2 Ik cannot return to its position until 260 days have elapsed, and since the position 0 Pop cannot return to its position until 365 days have passed, it should be clear that 2 Ik 0 Pop cannot recur until a number of days have passed which is equal to the multiple of these cycles:

$$\frac{260}{5} \times \frac{365}{5} \times \frac{5}{1} = 52 \times 73 \times 5 = 18{,}980 \text{ days}$$

In other words, the day 2 Ik 0 Pop will recur after 52 Vague Years of 365 days, or 73 Sacred Rounds of 260 days each.

THE MAYA INITIAL SERIES OR "LONG COUNT"

Some time during the first century before Christ, the Indians of southern Mesoamerica devised a system of numeration by position, involving the establishment of the mathematical concept of zero. By position-value notation, they were able to record five different orders of time.

The lowest unit of this calendar was the day or *kin*. The second order of units, consisting of 20 *kins*, was called the *uinal* or "month." In a pure vigesimal system of numeration, the third order should have been 400, but at this point a variation was introduced for the calendar calculations. The third order, the *tun*, was composed of 18 *uinals* (not 20) or 360 *kins*, because this unit was a closer approximation to the length of the solar year. Above the third order was the *katun* or period of 20 *tuns*. The fifth order, the cycle or baktun, was composed of 20 *katuns* or 144,000 days.

Thus, in any inscription which contains an Initial Series date, we would expect to see the following five orders presented in descending order:

1 cycle or *baktun* = 20 *katuns* = 144,000 days
1 *katun* = 20 *tuns* = 7,200 days

1 *tun*	= 18 *uinals*	= 360 days
1 *uinal*	= 20 *kins*	= 20 days
1 *kin*		= 1 day

The *tun* or approximate year of 360 days appears to be the basis for most of these calculations (Thompson 57, p. 141). Were the day to have been the basis for the calendar, it would have been more logical to expect a normal vigesimal progression with a year of 400 days instead of 360. Also, as we shall see, the Introducing Glyph contains the *tun* or year sign as well.

The Initial Series Introducing Glyph is so called because it usually stands at the beginning of the inscription and serves as an indicator that an Initial Series date follows. This ISIG is frequently several times as large as the other glyphs in the inscription. The only part of the ISIG which varies is the central element, which is the glyph of the patron deity who rules the month in which the Initial Series date falls. The four constant elements are a trinary superfix (sometimes two scrolls flanking a central crescent), a pair of comblike elements, the *tun* sign, and a trinary subfix (three nubbin feet).

The starting point from which almost all Maya dates were reckoned was 13.0.0.0.0 4 Ahau 8 Cumku, a designation which means that exactly 13 *baktuns* have been completed, and the seating of *Baktun* 1 has just taken place. *Baktuns* then occur in groups or cycles of 13, with the next *baktun* carrying the numerical coefficient of 1, 2, 3, etc. The Maya were calculating units of *elapsed* time: that is, the number of days that had passed since the zero point of 13.0.0.0.0. The oldest Long Count dates known were recorded in *Baktun* (or Cycle) 7, approximately 3,000 years after the Maya zero point or base date (see below). Since they were speaking of elapsed time, a date such as 7.0.0.0.0 actually falls in *Baktun* 8, and is really the seating date of *Baktun* 8.

Since no month positions are given on Cycle 7 monuments, we cannot be sure that they were counted from the same 4 Ahau as the dates of the Classic Maya. However, there is evidence on Stela C at Tres Zapotes (see below) to suggest the base date was the same.

Had the Maya continued to record events by this Initial Series method up to the time of the Spanish Conquest in Yucatán, there would be little problem of correlation with our calendar today. According to the most widely accepted correlations (the Goodman-Martínez-Thompson and the Modified Thompson 2), the base date of the Maya calendar (13.0.0.0.0 4 Ahau 8 Cumku) fell on August 10, 3113 B.C. This date was selected as the base or zero point for the start of the calendar, perhaps at a much later time. We have Long Count dates for *Baktuns* or Cycles 7, 8, 9, and 10, spanning the years from 36 B.C. to A.D. 909.

FORMATIVE PERIOD TEXTS AND CALENDRICS

We may now proceed to a discussion of the earliest hieroglyphic inscriptions in Mesoamerica (see Figure 1). These early texts appeared on stone monuments in southern Mexico and Guatemala during the period 600 B.C. to A.D. 50. They

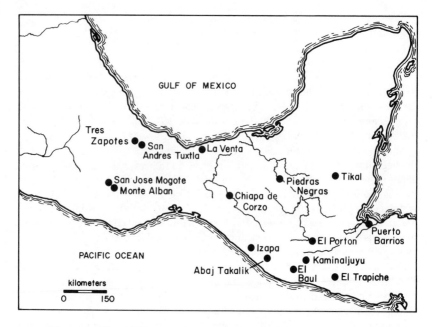

Figure 1   Map of Mesoamerica showing localities mentioned in the text.

include our oldest evidence for single-column texts and the 260-day calendar, followed soon after by double-column texts and the 365-day calendar. Not until the last century B.C. is there evidence for the "Long Count" dating of monuments, and Long Count dates do not appear in the lowland Maya region until after A.D. 200.

The Early Formative Period (1500–900 B.C.)

The Early Formative was a period of village societies with evidence for rapidly emerging differences in social rank. It was also a period of complex and elaborate iconography, with a variety of abstract symbols artistically expressed in stone sculpture, ceramics, and roller-stamps which may have been used for decorating textiles or human bodies. Many of the iconographic symbols of this period are so widespread as to be pan-Mesoamerican, although the style which has received the most attention is that of the Olmec people of Mexico's Gulf Coast (Coe 12, Joralemon 30). As the quotation from Thompson at the start of the paper indicates, Olmec iconography is so rich that many of its enthusiasts have "leapt over the demarcation line" and attributed the origins of Mesoamerican writing to the Olmec. A more restrained view has been taken by at least one leading Olmec scholar, Michael Coe (12, p. 756), who says, "Although it is often stated that the Olmec had hieroglyphic writing, the evidence for this is admittedly slim."

One of the most serious problems facing proponents of an Olmec origin for writing is chronological: the Olmec actually came along too soon. As Coe's recent work at San Lorenzo, Veracruz shows (14), the Olmec monumental carving style goes back to 1200 B.C. and had virtually run its course by 400 B.C. A decade ago, Coe (12, p. 769) had already argued that "With the destruction of La Venta [another important Olmec site, in Tabasco] around 400 B.C., the style ends at that site, and presumably throughout the climax region, since truly Olmec monuments elsewhere are almost indistinguishable in style from those at La Venta." The only Olmec monument of the period 1200–400 B.C. which can even remotely be construed as having a column of hieroglyphs is Monument 13 at La Venta; and (as discussed below) this monument appears to be no earlier than 500–400 B.C., by which time there are several hieroglyphic texts outside the Olmec region. Moreover, the most frequently cited Gulf Coast monument— Stela C at Tres Zapotes (also discussed below)—has a Long Count date of 31 B.C., and hence falls 400 years after the decline of the Olmec. The irony is that it is the Olmec enthusiasts themselves who have weakened the case for the Olmec; in their efforts to attribute to the Olmec "America's first great art style," they have pushed back the dates until the Olmec are now too early to be credited with inventing the Long Count.

A second objection to any theory of Olmec origins is the lack of congruity between Olmec iconographic symbols and early Mesoamerican hieroglyphs. None of the most common Olmec symbols—the St. Andrew's cross, the flame eyebrow, the U motif, and so on— were used as hieroglyphs in Middle or Late Formative texts; nor are any of Mesoamerica's earliest indisputable hieroglyphs common in Olmec art. What the Early Formative peoples did do in the way of "setting the stage" for what was to follow was (a) establish the use of stylized, nonrepresentational symbols which were of widespread intelligibility and meaning, and (b) work out sophisticated techniques of stone monument carving, which would later become the preferred medium for writing. However, they had not yet taken the next step to writing and calendrics. Their iconography was complex, but complex iconography—whether produced by the Olmec, the Kwakiutl, or the Maori—does not qualify as a writing system.

Perhaps the best way to summarize it is to say that Early Formative Mesoamerica was communicating a richness of cosmological, ritual, and perhaps even social information, but not political information. When writing began in the Middle Formative it was in the form of *political information set in a calendric framework*. This may in fact be our strongest clue to the original impetus for the earliest Mesoamerican writing.

The Middle Formative Period (900–400 B.C.)

It is during the second half of the Middle Formative period (perhaps as early as 600 B.C.) that our earliest demonstrable examples of hieroglyphic writing occur. As of 1976, hieroglyphic and calendric inscriptions of this period are limited to stone monuments in the Valley of Oaxaca (in the Zapotec region) and the site of La Venta (in the Olmec region).

1. MONUMENT 3, SAN JOSÉ MOGOTE, VALLEY OF OAXACA   Monument 3 (Figure 2) was discovered at San José Mogote (15 km north of the city of Oaxaca) in 1975 and is published here for the first time. It was discovered in situ serving as the threshold stone for a corridor between two large public buildings of the Rosario phase (600–500 B.C.) atop Mound 1 (Flannery & Marcus 24). Monument 3 was laid flat on a bed of stone slabs, so that anyone entering the corridor would tread on the body of the slain or sacrificed captive depicted in the carving. It is our oldest example of a type of carved stone traditionally (and erroneously)

Figure 2   Monument 3, San José Mogote, Valley of Oaxaca.

referred to as a *danzante*, of which more than 300 examples were previously known from the nearby site of Monte Albán (Caso 4,5). Elsewhere Coe (10) and I (34) have argued that the 300 *danzantes* at Monte Albán—all of which were evidently originally set in a single wall—represent a "gallery" of slain prisoners, as evidenced by their closed eyes, open mouths, and awkward position; their nudity; and the "flowery" scrolls which probably represent blood flowing from various parts of the body. The building in which the *danzantes* were originally set was believed by Caso to date to the Monte Albán IA period (500–400 B.C.).

Monument 3 at San José Mogote is significant because the figure has between his feet a short notation of two glyphs which can be read as "1 Earthquake" (the seventeenth day in the Zapotec list of 20 day names). This inscription is a date in the 260-day Sacred Round, our first documented use of that calendar. It may represent the day on which the victim was sacrificed or, in accord with Zapotec custom, his personal name (= day of birth).

As for the 300 *danzantes* at Monte Albán, a possible link between Zapotec monuments and the Zapotec spoken language may be concealed in the flowery "blood scrolls" which issue from the groin or genital area of some figures. According to Paddock (40, p. 118), the Zapotec word for flower is *gui*, the word for sexual organ *gui* plus the possessive prefix *x* or *sh*. Still another meaning for *gui* is given by Córdova (19) in his dictionary of sixteenth-century Zapotec: "that which is offered in sacrifice." The groin scrolls of the *danzantes* may therefore represent a triple pun, for "flower"-"sexual organ"-"sacrificial victim." Such scrolls do not constitute writing, but they serve to remind us that Mesoamerican writing systems featured a great deal of punning and rebus-writing which cannot be understood without reference to the spoken language.

2. STELAE 12–13, MONTE ALBÁN, VALLEY OF OAXACA   Stelae 12 and 13 (Figure 3) were discovered at the southern end of the so-called *danzante* gallery, which runs between System M and Mound L (the Building of the *danzantes*) in the southwestern sector of the main plaza at Monte Albán (Caso 3). The in situ position of Stelae 12 and 13 at the end of the *danzante* wall almost certainly places them in the phase Monte Albán IA (500–400 B.C.).

Stelae 12 and 13 constitute a pure text of approximately 8 separate hieroglyphs. The text includes hieroglyphs both with and without numerical coefficients; therefore, at least some of the hieroglyphs would seem to deal with calendric information. In fact, these stelae are often cited (Caso 3, 5, 7; Prem 41) as evidence for the antiquity of the 260-day calendar [*pije* or *piye* in the Zapotec language (Córdova 18)]. The day signs seem to be set apart by their inclusion within roughly circular cartouches. In Column A, Row 1 the year sign with the day "4 M" as the year bearer appears [in the Caso system (3), individual hieroglyphs are given a letter designation]. The next two hieroglyphs on Stela 12 are unknown in meaning, but they do not appear to include numerical coefficients. In Column A, Row 4 another apparent day sign appears with the numerical coefficient of 8 beneath the cartouche. Moving over to Stela 13, in Column B, Row 1 appears a jaguar glyph which is not surrounded by a car-

A   B

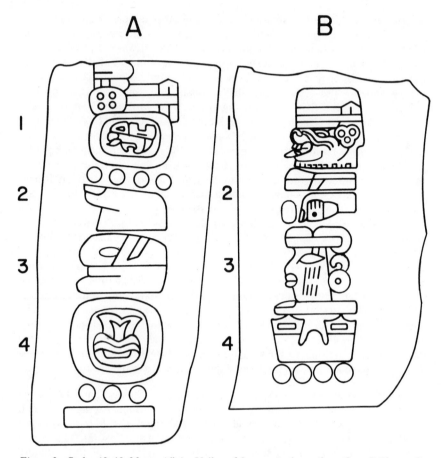

Figure 3   Stelae 12–13, Monte Albán, Valley of Oaxaca (redrawn from Caso 7, Figures 2, 3).

touche; this jaguar glyph is apparently subfixed by two bars, signifying 10. In Column B, Row 3 appears a profile head glyph with a digit or finger, which has in the past been variously interpreted as signifying "five," "first" (the ordinal number one), or perhaps having no numerical significance. Finally, in Column B, Row 4 there is a 4 subfixing an apparent month glyph.

I feel we should consider the possibility that these two stelae comprise a single continuous inscription which may have been read in pairs of hieroglyphs as were later inscriptions: e.g. A1-B1 from left to right, then A2-B2, and so on from top to bottom. Thus we might read this text as beginning with a year sign, with the year bearer as the day 4 M in the month 10 Jaguar; again at A4-B4, one sees the day 8 Z in the month 4 W. One reason for this suggestion is that the hieroglyph at B4 occurs with numerical coefficients larger than 13. In the 260-day calendar, day signs can *only* occur with numbers from 1 to 13; however, *months* can occur with numbers from 1 to 19. If both days and months are given, there is the possibility that even at this early date we have some evidence for the Calendar Round.

Thus these two stelae may constitute our most ancient evidence for the 260-day calendar, the year bearer, the year sign, and (possibly) the division of the 365-day year into "months" of 20 days each. The double-column format and the lack of a pictorial scene qualify these stelae as perhaps our oldest unambiguous evidence for writing. Since no example of a glyph with a numerical coefficient over 18 is known, one might also assume that we have some evidence for the typical Mesoamerican vigesimal system.

Additionally, during Monte Albán I at least 20 *danzantes* have short texts of from two to eight hieroglyphs. There are, however, no *danzantes* that show the association of a numerical coefficient and day sign. The usual interpretation for these short captions is that they represent personal names. There are some hieroglyphs that occur with more than one *danzante,* but no two combinations of hieroglyphs are identical. For Monte Albán I, I would estimate that we have some 30 monuments with an early form of writing. Most importantly, we have Stelae 12 and 13, which taken together constitute a text arranged in the typical Mesoamerican format of vertical columns.

3. MONUMENT 13, LA VENTA, TABASCO   Monument 13 at La Venta (Figure 4), discovered in 1943 by Drucker and Wedel (Drucker, Heizer & Squier 23), is a carved columnar basalt slab which depicts a standing figure carrying a pennant-like object; this has given the stone its nickname, "the Ambassador Monument" (Coe 15, p. 148; Drucker, Heizer & Squier 23, p. 40). It was found upright in the drift sand layer (Level a), which was the uppermost stratum of Mound A-2 in Complex A at La Venta.

> The placing of Monument 13 here clearly occurred after the (b-1) red clay was deposited. . . . Monument 13, therefore, in its present position dates from the very end of the La Venta site (23, p. 43).

This places Monument 13 in stratigraphic Phase IV at La Venta. Based on the following discussion of radiocarbon samples at the site, I would tentatively assign the monument to the period 500–400 B.C., making it roughly equivalent in time to Monte Albán IA.

> We are, however, in a position to provide an estimated date for Phase IV. . . . The arithmetic average of samples M-528 and M-533 is 2,265 years ago (309 B.C.). Using the method of determining the weighted average (Wauchope 62), we derive the figure 2,289± 195 years (B.C. 333 ± 195). . . . We therefore place the end of Phase IV as falling within the period 450 to 325 B.C., probably near the early part of that span. In round numbers, we have selected the date 400 B.C. as marking the termination of the use of the Ceremonial Court by its builders (23, p. 267).

Although no calendric glyphs (days, months, year bearers, etc) or numerical coefficients appear on Monument 13, there are three possible hieroglyphs in a

Figure 4   Monument 13, La Venta, Tabasco (redrawn from Drucker 22, Figure 61).

vertical column which appear to the right of the standing figure. The last hieroglyph seems to be the head of a bird, perhaps constituting part of the name of the individual depicted. To the left a footprint appears in isolation; this sign later became a common convention in Mesoamerica for "travel" or "journey."

This monument is crucial for those who maintain that the Olmec people invented writing. Three hieroglyphs is admittedly slim evidence, but they do constitute a column, which is the format for later Mesoamerican writing. Significantly, however, there are no corresponding calendric hieroglyphs or numerical coefficients on any Olmec stone monument of this period.

The Late Formative Period (400 B.C.–A.D. 50)

The Late Formative period saw major advances in both writing and calendrics, with double-column texts becoming common for the first time. Toward the end of the period appeared our first Long Count dates, including the concept of the base date as well as position-value notation (units of 1, 20, 360, 7,200, and 144,000 days). In conjunction with these calendric advancements, we can note greater complexity in the formation of glyphs—an increase in the number of noncalendric hieroglyphs and in the number of compound glyphs (main signs + affixes).

The geographic distribution of Late Formative monuments is also more extensive than was the Middle Formative distribution. Oaxaca and the Gulf Coast continued to be important areas, now joined by Chiapas and by the highlands and Pacific coast of Guatemala. Within a period of 50–70 years, at least four sites erected Long Count monuments in calendar Cycle 7—Chiapa de Corzo, Tres Zapotes, El Baúl, and Abaj Takalik. As of this writing, there are still no Cycle 7 monuments known from the lowland Maya region, which is so closely associated with the Long Count in most archaeologists' minds.

1. BUILDING J, MONTE ALBÁN, VALLEY OF OAXACA   During Period II at Monte Albán (perhaps as early as 200–100 B.C.), a curious public building with an arrowhead-shaped ground plan was erected in the Main Plaza. While this structure, Building J, has frequently been referred to in the literature as an "observatory," there is no solid evidence for such a functional interpretation. Rather, its most outstanding feature is a series of at least 40 carved stone slabs set in its façade, interpreted here as a record of places conquered or subjugated by Monte Albán (Marcus 35). These so-called "conquest slabs" were originally defined by Caso (5, p. 21) as including the following elements: (a) a "hill" sign, signifying "place"; (b) a human head, upside down, beneath and attached to the "hill" sign; (c) a compound glyph that represents the name of the place, appearing above the "hill" glyph; (d) a hieroglyphic text that in its most complete form includes the year sign, year-bearer, month, day, and an assortment of glyphs in columns (35). Some of these Mound J texts are arranged in the double-column format (Figure 5). There is an increase in the number of noncalendric signs, but we are still unable to derive much meaning from these inscriptions beyond the name of the place itself. However, given the large number of monuments with writing at Monte Albán during both Middle and Late Formative times, I have confidence that some progress will be made soon.

2. STELA 2, CHIAPA DE CORZO, CHIAPAS   Stela 2 (Figure 6) was one of eight broken stela fragments discovered in 1961 inside the fill on the surface of Mound 5b at Chiapa de Corzo. Lowe (33, p. 194) suggests that the fragments had been removed, already broken, from a place nearby, primarily because after a careful search he was unable to locate more fragments.

The carved stone is a single rectangular fragment of finely laminated white limestone with a prepared face (Lee 31, p. 105). The importance of this fragment is that it bears a series of bars and dots arranged horizontally, which indicate position-value notation. What can be read immediately from the stone are the following: part of a bar (5); another bar (5); three dots (3); two dots (2); two bars and three dots (13); a vertical bar and a dot (6).

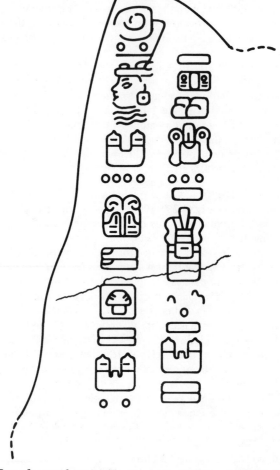

Figure 5 Part of a text from Lápida 14 set into Structure J, Monte Albán, Valley of Oaxaca (redrawn from Caso 7, Figure 12).

If we assume that this series of numbers represents a fragment of an Initial Series date, we then would be missing the Initial Series Introducing Glyph, the number of *baktuns,* and quite possibly part of the number referring to the *katuns,* since this is the place where the subsequent weathering begins on the stone. Since the number of *kins* is 13, we know that the day sign must be the thirteenth day of the 20 days in the 260-day calendar. This would be *Ben* (Maya name) or *Acatl* (Nahuatl or Aztec name). If we look at the day sign carefully we note that it most closely resembles the later Aztec day sign, *Acatl* or "reed," rather than the corresponding Maya sign. Thus, if our Initial Series reaches a day 6 *Acatl,*

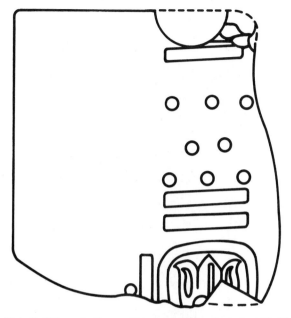

Figure 6   Stela 2, Chiapa de Corzo, Chiapas (redrawn from Lee 31, Figure 60).

and we assume that we are counting the number of days that have elapsed since 4 Ahau 8 Cumku (the base date used by the Maya), we would reconstruct the Stela 2 date as (7.16) 3.2.13 6 Acatl (16 Toxcatl) or 6 Ben (16 Xul). This Long Count date, the oldest presently known, would correspond to December 9, 36 B.C. (Coe 13, p. 59).

3. STELA C, TRES ZAPOTES, VERACRUZ   The site of Tres Zapotes includes approximately 50 mounds, stretching along the Arroyo Hueyapan for 3 km. The mounds are separated into 4 groups, each of which has a plaza; the easternmost has been designated Group C. The principal mound of this group is located on the highest point of the site terrace. Immediately in front of the south base of this high mound, Matthew Stirling in 1939 discovered the lower half of a broken monument, Stela C, with a flat stone altar set in front of it. On the front of Stela C was a "jaguar mask" panel, while on the back appeared a column of bars and dots (Stirling 52, p. 1; Figure 7).

This apparent Long Count date consists of a vertical column of bars and dots placed horizontally. The numbers are not accompanied by period glyphs (e.g. days, months, years, and so forth). However, on the basis of position-value notation, Stirling reconstructed the Long Count date as (7) .16.6.16.18. Having recovered only the lower half of Stela C in 1939, he inferred that if the top half should ever be found it would include the Initial Series Introducing Glyph and the number 7, for *Baktun* 7. His reconstruction has been confirmed by the recent

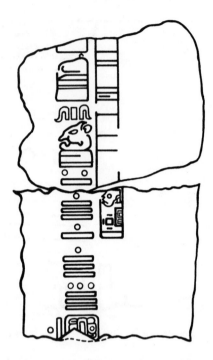

Figure 7   Back side of Stela C, Tres Zapotes, Veracruz (redrawn from Cohn 17, A8).

discovery of the top half of Stela C, which indeed includes both the Introducing Glyph and a (*Baktun*) 7 (Cohn 17; Figure 7).

The variable element in the Initial Series Introducing Glyph resembles a jaguar head, which is the patron of the month Pop. In the Petén or "Classic Maya" system, the month position would be 1 Uo; however, in the Campeche or "Puuc" system, it would be "completion of Pop." The ISIG variable element is either a jaguar (patron of Pop) or the jaguar sun (patron of Uo); thus, either the Campeche or Classic Maya system could have been employed. In either case, the patron god in the ISIG appears to strengthen the case that the same base date (3113 B.C.) was employed for both Cycle 7 and later Classic Maya texts.

Stirling, by analogy with later Maya monuments, assumed that the number 6 (which appears to the left of the last hieroglyph) represented the coefficient of the day. His complete reading was (7) .16.6.16.18 6 Etznab (1 Uo). From the Maya base date in the year 3113 B.C., one computes the number of days elapsed or 7 × 144,000; 16 × 7,200; 6 × 360; 16 × 20; 18 × 1, which then reaches a day 6 Etznab in the month 1 Uo. With a Gregorian calendar correlation, this date would fall in 31 B.C.

In summary, the important characteristics of Stela C, Tres Zapotes are the following:

1. Two columns of hieroglyphs.
2. An Initial Series Introducing Glyph.
3. A column of horizontally placed bars and dots.
4. A vertical coefficient and a day glyph.
5. No month coefficient or month glyph.

4. MONUMENT E, TRES ZAPOTES, VERACRUZ   Monument E at Tres Zapotes is carved into the bedrock floor of the Arroyo Hueyapan, just east of the "Burnt Mounds" group; the carving was found more than a meter below the surface of the stream at low water mark (53, p. 21). The monument bears a dot, a bar, and a third element which is either a second bar or an unknown glyph (Figure 8).

There has always been some question as to the chronological position of Monument E. On the basis of associated ceramics, Drucker (21, p. 118) felt that Monument E was associated with the Lower Horizon of Trench 26, or Tres Zapotes I. Coe (11, Table I) would assign Tres Zapotes I to the Late Formative period (300 B.C.–A.D. 1), making Monument E broadly contemporary with Stela C.

5. STELA 1, EL BAÚL, GUATEMALA   Stela 1, also known as the Herrera Stela, was discovered at the site of El Baúl in the Department of Escuintla on the Pacific piedmont of Guatemala (Waterman 64). Waterman (63, p. 351) photographed Stela 1 in 1923, and in 1924 reported that its location was on the flank of a "great structure."

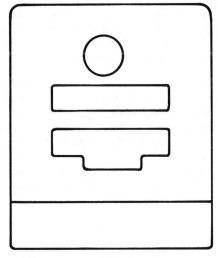

Figure 8   Monument E, Tres Zapotes, Veracruz (redrawn from Stirling 53, Figure 5).

Walter Lehmann (32, p. 175) was the first individual to suggest a reading of the inscription: 7.19.7.8.12 12 Eb (20 Kankin or 0 Muan). Since that time another reading has been offered by Michael Coe (9, p. 603) as 7.19.15.7.12 12 Eb (0 Ceh). Still another has been tentatively put forth by Tatiana Proskouriakoff as 7.18.14.8.12 12 Eb (5 Cumku). These readings would correspond to A.D. 29, 36, and 16, respectively.

We may look at the inscription (9, Figure 4) to see the merits of each reconstruction. The text (which appears on the left side of the monument) opens with an apparent day sign with a superfix of 12. The two dots and two bars appear above a fleshless jawbone, which is recognizable as the day Eb in the Maya calendar; but the presentation of the day sign before the Initial Series or Long Count date is most unusual. Four small hieroglyphs immediately follow the day 12 Eb, and they appear to be paired. Below these tiny hieroglyphs, we have a Long Count date without the Initial Series Introducing Glyph. Then there is a clear bar with two dots above it—Cycle (or *Baktun*) 7, according to all the proposed reconstructions. Because of the subsequent weathering of the stone, the next number is less clear; as Coe (9, p. 603) has indicated, it is either 18 or 19 (*katuns*). In photographs published by Burkitt (2, Figure 4), Proskouriakoff (42, Figure 110a), and Thompson (56, Figure 8d), the number of *katuns* appears to be 18. The next number should take up three lines, e.g. 14 or 15. The number of "months" or *uinals* could be either 8 or 7; it is very difficult to tell because of the weathering on the left side of the number. Finally, we have 12 *kins*—which would have to be there in order to connect back to the day sign Eb at the top of the inscription, since Eb is the 12th day of the 20 possible day names.

The two best reconstructions appear to be Coe's and the alternative suggested to me by Proskouriakoff: 7.19.15.7.12 12 Eb (0 Ceh) or 7.18.14.8.12 12 Eb (5 Cumku), respectively. The difference between the two dates is approximately 20 years, Coe's date corresponding to A.D. 36, while Proskouriakoff's corresponds to A.D. 16. Since there is no month coefficient or month sign, we are unable to determine which reconstruction is correct.

6. STELA 2, ABAJ TAKALIK, GUATEMALA   Numerous monuments have been discovered in the southeastern portion of the Department of Quezaltenango on the Pacific piedmont of Guatemala (Miles 37, Thompson 55). Spanning two adjacent *fincas* or ranches—Santa Margarita and San Isidro Piedra Parada— there lies a single extensive site. On the boundary line between the two *fincas*, and near one of the pre-Columbian mounds, stood Stelae 1 and 2 (9, p. 604).

In 1925, Lehmann excavated and recorded Stela 2, designating it the "Piedra Schlubach" (32, p. 176). Stela 1 at that time was referred to locally as the "Piedra Fuentes," and reported to be from San Isidro Piedra Parada; Stela 2 later came to be referred to as the monument from Santa Margarita (42, Figures 109a, b). Because of the confusion caused by the two *finca* names, Miles (37, p. 246) suggested that for convenience all of the local designations should be subsumed under the name Abaj Takalik ("Standing Stones"), which will hereafter be used to designate the site.

Stela 2 bears a hieroglyphic text arranged in a column. The first hieroglyph closely resembles the Initial Series Introducing Glyph of the later Maya. The trinary affix (three elements) appear above an effaced *tun* or year sign; below this glyph, there appear to be two dots above a bar. This horizontal 7 should therefore be considered to indicate a Cycle or *Baktun* 7, since it immediately follows the Initial Series Introducing Glyph. Unfortunately, the rest of the Initial Series date cannot be reconstructed, but given the evidence at present, I see no reason to question the fact that this monument records a contemporaneous *Baktun* 7 date.

7. KAMINALJUYÚ, GUATEMALA   The site of Kaminaljuyú in the highlands just west of Guatemala City has produced at least two Late Formative monuments with texts. Both Stela 10 (Miles 37, p. 255; see also Heath-Jones 28) and Altar 1 have been dated to the Miraflores phase (300 B.C.–A.D. 1). Stela 10 is a black basalt sculpture which includes day signs in cartouches accompanied by bar-and-dot numerals. Incised on this important monument are 4 columns of text, including at least 30 hieroglyphs which cannot as yet be read. Additionally, Altar 1 (37) includes a text in the double-column format. Typologically, the Kaminaljuyú texts still represent our most likely precursors for the later Maya hieroglyphic system.

8. OTHER MONUMENTS   One other monument with a text which could be assigned stylistically to the Late Formative is Monument 1 at El Portón in the Salamá Valley, northern Guatemalan highlands (Sharer & Sedat 48, p. 185). Unfortunately, its exact chronological placement is uncertain.

A Late Formative site whose monuments have received a great deal of attention is Izapa, on the Pacific Coast of Chiapas not far from the Guatemalan border (Quirarte 44). Izapa has frequently been described as a site whose stone monuments bridge the gap between the Formative Olmec and the Classic Maya (Coe 12, p. 773). This cannot be the case with regard to writing or calendrics, however, since not a single Izapa monument contains a hieroglyphic text or date.

TEXTS OF THE PROTO-CLASSIC PERIOD (A.D. 50–200)

The double-column format is even more developed and geographically widespread during this period, as evidenced by the El Trapiche monument from El Salvador. However, the most securely dated example of Proto-Classic writing is the Tuxtla Statuette from Mexico's Gulf Coast.

1. EL TRAPICHE, EL SALVADOR   The El Trapiche Mound Group is located 1 km northeast of Chalchuapa in western El Salvador. Buried at the base of 23 meter-high Mound 1 were battered fragments of three stone monuments, one of which shows an extensive hieroglyphic inscription with 8 columns, or 4 "paired" columns of text. Sharer (47) suggests that this stela dates somewhere

between 200 B.C. and A.D. 200, and on stylistic grounds a Proto-Classic assignment is reasonable. Unfortunately, only a few glyphs are uneroded, but they are already recognizable as Maya glyphs.

2. THE TUXTLA STATUETTE, VERACRUZ, MEXICO The jadeite Tuxtla Statuette was discovered in 1902 by a farmer plowing his fields in the district of San Andres Tuxtla, Veracruz, some 25 km from the site of Tres Zapotes (Washington 61, p. 1). Although there are approximately 50 hieroglyphs on the sides and back of the statuette, what will concern us here is the apparent Initial Series date on the front of the figure (Figure 9).

In most respects, the Initial Series on the Tuxtla Statuette is quite similar to that recorded on Stela C at Tres Zapotes. The Introducing Glyph carries a trinary superfix, in this case three scrolls. The Introducing Glyph is followed by a column of horizontally placed bar and dot numerals. If we again assume position-value notation, we would reconstruct this date as follows:

$$
\begin{array}{rcrcr}
8 \ (baktuns) & \times & 144{,}000 \ \text{days} & = & 1{,}152{,}000 \ \text{days} \\
6 \ (katuns). & \times & 7{,}200 \ \text{days} & = & 43{,}200 \ \text{days} \\
2 \ (tuns) & \times & 360 \ \text{days} & = & 720 \ \text{days} \\
4 \ (uinals) & \times & 20 \ \text{days} & = & 80 \ \text{days} \\
17 \ (kins) & \times & 1 \ \text{day} & = & \underline{17 \ \text{days}} \\
& & & & 1{,}196{,}017 \ \text{days} \\
& & & & \text{elapsed}
\end{array}
$$

If we assume that the above number of days elapsed is counted from the base 4 Ahau 8 Cumku, the Calendar Round to be reached is 8 Caban (0 Kankin). Looking at the last number in the column, we notice that there is indeed a vertical 8 as a coefficient to a day sign. Although the day does not look like Caban as written by the Maya, it should logically be Caban because that is the 17th day of the possible 20 day names; the month position and month are not given. The Initial Series date 8.6.2.4.17 8 Caban (0 Kankin) would correspond to A.D. 162 in our calendar.

THE ORIGINS OF CLASSIC MAYA WRITING

During the period A.D. 292–909, the Maya of northern Guatemala, eastern Mexico, and western Honduras achieved the maximum elaboration of Mesoamerican writing. Among the hundreds of Maya glyphs of this period are many which can be identified as verbs, nouns, adjectives, prepositions, and other parts of speech. The complexity of the system has been clearly underestimated by at least one noted Old World epigrapher, who tells us that "even a superficial knowledge of the inscriptions of the Aztecs and Mayas is enough to convince oneself that they could never have developed into real writing without foreign influence" (Gelb 25, p. 58).

The spoken language of the Maya is primarily monosyllabic, and the individual elements of Maya hieroglyphs also seem to be monosyllables. Compound

Figure 9   Text from the front side of the Tuxtla Statuette (redrawn from Satterthwaite 46, Figure 3).

glyphs (main signs plus affixes) are usually composed of nouns + adjectives, or verbal roots + tense. In this respect most scholars (Graham 27, Thompson 58) agree that, of all Mesoamerican writing systems, the Maya most closely reflects or corresponds to a spoken language. Maya writing does seem to exhibit greater complexity, flexibility, and capacity to record the nuances of the spoken words. Additionally, various written elements represent sounds, others represent objects, and others represent ideas. There are also determinatives, which serve to reduce ambiguity by specifying a particular meaning for the glyphs to which they are attached. The Maya system is partly phonetic, partly pictographic, and partly ideographic. Most of the recent epigraphic controversy has centered around the question: How phonetic or syllabic is it?—a question which cannot as yet be answered (Thompson 58, 59).

Classic Maya writing has plausible Late Formative antecedents, though knowledge of those antecedents would never have allowed one to predict the subsequent complexity of the period A.D. 292–909. In this section, I will confine

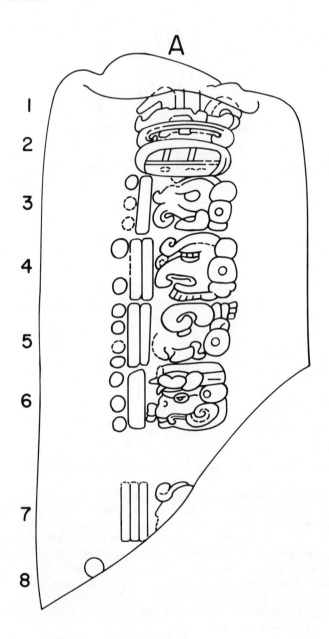

Figure 10   Back side of Stela 29, Tikal, Guatemala (redrawn from Shook 49, 33).

myself to a discussion of the two earliest known Classic Maya texts, and then give an example of how one of the better-known Late Classic monuments might be translated.

1. STELA 29, TIKAL, GUATEMALA   Tikal lies about 320 km north of Guatemala City, in the tropical rain forest of the Department of Petén. In 1959, one of the University of Pennsylvania's Tikal Project workmen, Marcos López, discovered a fragment of a stela some 200 meters west of the Great Plaza. This stela fragment lay face up, with the left edge of the front side partially exposed (Shook 49, p. 30). The fragment proved to be the upper half of a stela then designated Stela 29; it was located on the rear slope of a mound near a fragment of Altar 13. William R. Coe has characterized this location as "an ancient dump" (16, p. 92).

Although the front of Stela 29 portrays a Maya ruler in Early Classic style, what concerns us here is the appearance of the bar-and-dot glyphs (numerical coefficients) on the back of the monument (Figure 10). The text can be transcribed as follows:

A1-2	Initial Series Introducing Glyph
A3	8 *baktuns*
A4	12 *katuns*
A5	14 *tuns*
A6	8 *uinals*
A7	15 *kins*
A8	One dot (a fragment of the numerical coefficient of the day)

If we calculate the total number of days in the Long Count date 8.12.14.8.15, we can reconstruct the Calendar Round date as 13 Men 3 Zip. In the inscription we have one of the three dots of the numerical coefficient 13, but we are lacking the other two bars and the day sign Men. Additionally, we are missing the month position and month glyph.

For the first time, we have the bar and dot system of numeration set up vertically in order to serve as prefixes to the period glyphs. Satterthwaite (45, p. 37) has noted that the period glyphs for the *baktun, katun,* and *tun* are bird glyphs; the *uinal* glyph is the head of a frog, and the period glyph for the *kin* is largely missing, but by analogy with later monuments it should be the head of the "sun god." Thus, for the first time, the bars and dots appear vertically and act as coefficients for specified period glyphs which are of the "head-variant" type. According to the Goodman-Martínez-Thompson correlation, we can date this monument to July 6, A.D. 292.

2. THE LEYDEN PLAQUE, PUERTO BARRIOS, GUATEMALA   In 1864, canal excavators discovered the Leyden Plaque near the Río Graciosa, a few kilometers from Puerto Barrios on the north coast of Guatemala. The Dutch civil engineer, S. A. van Braam, later presented the pale green jadeite plaque to the Rijksmuseum voor Volkerkunde in Leyden, Netherlands, where it remains today (Morley & Morley 38, p. 5; Shook 49, p. 29).

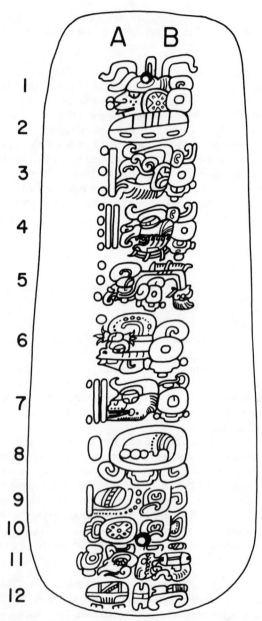

Figure 11 Back side of the Leyden Plaque, Puerto Barrios, Guatemala (redrawn from Shook 49, 34).

While the front of the plaque shows a high-status individual standing in front of a captive, what will concern us here is the inscription on the back of the plaque (Figure 11). This inscription can be transcribed as follows:

A1-B2	Initial Series Introducing Glyph with a variable central element, a *kin* or "sun god's" head, which is the patron for the month Yaxkin; see A10.
A3-B3	8 *baktuns*
A4-B4	14 *katuns*
A5-B5	3 *tuns*
A6-B6	1 *uinal*
A7-B7	12 *kins*
A8-B8	1 *Eb*
A9	Glyph G of the Supplementary Series (lunar series); this is the form for the fifth day.
B9	Meaning unknown; perhaps indicating seating (0 position) of the month.
A10	Yaxkin.
B10-B12	Perhaps the seating or accession of a lord.

The inscription on the Leyden Plaque is similar in most respects to the earlier Stela 29 from Tikal; both include "head-variant" period glyphs which are prefixed by vertical bar-and-dot coefficients. However, there are some very important differences:
1. The Leyden Plaque gives us our oldest complete example of an Initial Series Introducing Glyph which includes the patron god for the month to be reached by the Long Count date.
2. The Leyden Plaque includes (for the first time) some information about the lunar cycle.
3. The Leyden Plaque is the first text to include the month position and glyph.

According to the Goodman-Martínez-Thompson correlation, the date on the plaque (8.14.3.1.12) corresponds to September 15, A.D. 320—apparently carved some 28 years after the Tikal monument, Stela 29. Interestingly, Morley & Morley in 1938 (38) presented a strong argument that Tikal was the original place of manufacture for the Leyden Plaque.

3. STELA 3, PIEDRAS NEGRAS, GUATEMALA   Piedras Negras is a major Classic Maya ruin on the east bank of the Usumacinta River in the western Petén of Guatemala. Stela 3 from that site provides us with a good example of how a Late Classic Maya inscription might be read, since it has been more fully deciphered than most monuments of its time (Proskouriakoff 43, Thompson 58).

The front of the monument, although somewhat eroded now, portrays the male ruler of the site in A.D. 711. The back of the monument portrays his wife and daughter, who appear in the open space below the inscription in Figures 12 and 13. The inscription is read in paired columns, A1-B1, A2-B2, and so forth.

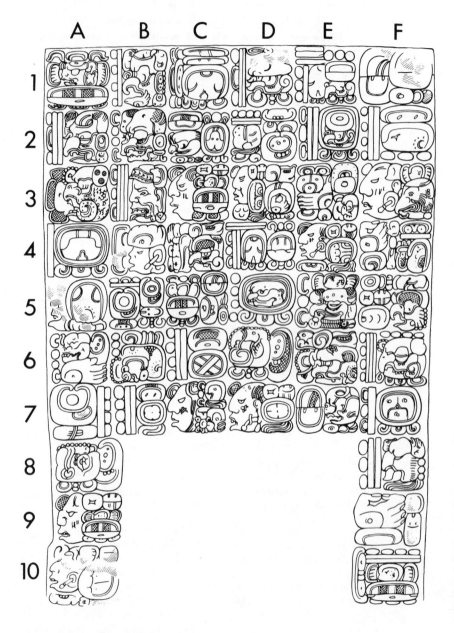

Figure 12   Back side of Stela 3, Piedras Negras, Guatemala (redrawn from Thompson 58, Figure 2).

	A	B	C	D	E	F
1	ISIG variable is sun god; patron of Yaxkin	9 baktuns	0 kins 10 uinals	12 tuns	15 kins 8 uinals (reversed positions) 3 katuns	Forward count to
2	12 katuns	2 tuns	Forward count to 1 Cib	14 Kankin	11 Imix	14 Yax
3	0 uinals	16 kins	Lady Ben-Ich "Katun"	Lady Akbal	Event	Lady "Katun" (vulture substitute)
4	5 Cib	7th lord of the night	Ruler's name	10 kins 11 uinals (reversed positions) 1 tun	Lady Akbal (Darkness)	Completion 5th haab
5	?	Moon age is 27 days	1 katun forward count to	4 Cimi	1 katun	Anniversary of accession to the throne
6	2 lunations	Glyph X	14 Uo	Was born	Ruler's name	19 kins 4 uinals
7	29-day moon	14 Yaxkin	Lady ?	Lady "Kin" (sunlight)	Forward count to	6 Ahau
8	Was born					13 Muan
9	Lady Ben-Ich "Katun"					Completion
10	Lady Akbal (Darkness)					14th katun

Figure 13 Glyph-by-glyph transcription of the back side of Stela 3, Piedras Negras, Guatemala.

When this stela was erected in A.D. 711, the ruler was 46 years old; his wife ("Lady Darkness") was 37; and their daughter ("Lady Sunlight") was 3. The text on the back of the stela begins with the date A.D. 674 (the birth date of the ruler's wife) and proceeds to A.D. 686, when the wife was involved in an event as yet untranslated. From there it proceeds to A.D. 707 (the birth date of their daughter); to A.D. 711 (the 25th anniversary of the ruler's accession to the throne, at which time the monument was erected); and finally to the completion of the 14th *katun,* 9.14.0.0.0. Figure 12 shows the original text on the back of Stela 3, while Figure 13 gives a plausible glyph-by-glyph translation.

SUMMARY AND CONCLUSIONS

On the basis of present evidence, hieroglyphic writing in Mesoamerica began during the second half of the Middle Formative period, some 600 to 400 years B.C. A major theme of early Mesoamerican writing seems to have been the presentation of political information in a calendrical framework. This suggests that political evolution and early writing were functionally linked in some way that remains to be worked out.

The format of early Mesoamerican writing was a vertical column of hieroglyphs; by Late Formative times, a double-column format had evolved. At the present state of our knowledge, it would be unwise to attribute the origins of this writing to any single ethnic group, for it may have emerged over a wide area. Our earliest columns of text come from Oaxaca and Tabasco, but they are soon followed by texts from Chiapas, Veracruz, and southern Guatemala (Figure 14).

Our oldest evidence for the 260-day ritual calendar comes from Middle Formative Oaxaca. By Late Formative times, this 260-day Sacred Round had been combined with the 365-day Vague Year to produce the 52-year Calendar Round. Ironically, although the Long Count (which made use of all the above) is popularly associated with the lowland Maya, our earliest examples of Cycle 7 Long Count monuments come from the Zoque region (Chiapa de Corzo), Veracruz, and the Guatemalan Pacific piedmont. Not until the third century A.D. was the earliest known dated stela erected in the Maya lowlands. However, it was in that region that Mesoamerican hieroglyphic writing was to achieve its maximum versatility, greatest complexity, and closest proximity to the spoken language.

Despite the breakthroughs described in the introduction to this paper, the study of Mesoamerican writing is still in its infancy. Tremendous strides have been made in calendrics and in the recovery of political information, but hundreds of glyphs dealing with other topics remain to be translated—for example, those apparently dealing with ritual activity and kinship. Beyond this frontier lies the equally intriguing question of why the early urban centers of the Zapotec and Maya were so concerned with writing and calendrics, while the great metropolis of Teotihuacán in the Valley of Mexico seems to have afforded it so little importance.

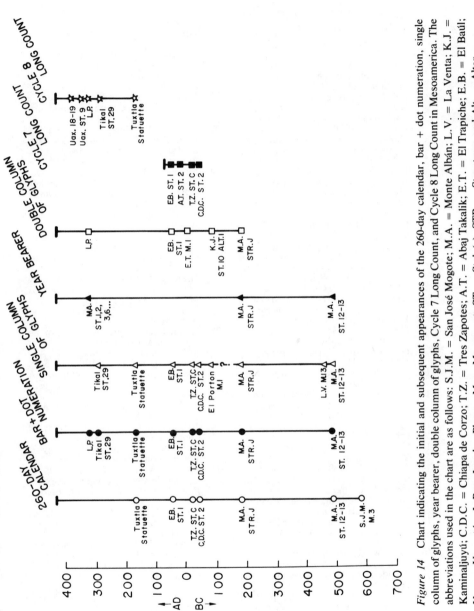

Figure 14 Chart indicating the initial and subsequent appearances of the 260-day calendar, bar + dot numeration, single column of glyphs, year bearer, double column of glyphs, Cycle 7 Long Count, and Cycle 8 Long Count in Mesoamerica. The abbreviations used in the chart are as follows: S.J.M. = San José Mogote; M.A. = Monte Albán; L.V. = La Venta; K.J. = Kaminaljuyú; C.D.C. = Chiapa de Corzo; T.Z. = Tres Zapotes; A.T. = Abaj Takalik; E.T. = El Trapiche; E.B. = El Baúl; Uax. = Uaxactún; L.P. = Leyden Plaque; M. = Monument; ST. = Stela(e); STR. = Structure; and Alt. = Altar.

Literature Cited

1. Berlin, H. 1958. El glifo "emblema" en las inscripciones mayas. *J. Soc. Am.* n.s. 47:111–19
2. Burkitt, R. 1933. Two stones in Guatemala. *Anthropos* 28:9–26, 781–82
3. Caso, A. 1928. *Las Estelas Zapotecas.* Publicaciones de la Secretaria de Educación Pública. Monografías del Museo Nacional de Arqueología, Historia y Etnografía. Mexico: Talleres Gráficas de la Nación
4. Caso, A. 1938. Exploraciones en Oaxaca, quinta y sexta temporadas 1936–37. *Inst. Panam. Geogr. His.* Publ. 34
5. Caso, A. 1947. Calendario y escritura de las antiguas culturas de Monte Albán. *Obras completas de Miguel Othón de Mendizábal* 1:5–102
6. Caso, A. 1949. El mapa de Teozacoalco. *Cuad. Am.* 8(5):145–81
7. Caso, A. 1965. Zapotec writing and calendar. In *Handbook of Middle American Indians,* ed. R. Wauchope, G. R. Willey, 3:931–47. Austin: Univ. Texas Press
8. Clark, J. C. 1912. *The Story of "Eight Deer"* in *Codex Colombino.* London: Taylor & Francis
9. Coe, M. D. 1957. Cycle 7 monuments in Middle America: a reconsideration. *Am. Anthropol.* 59(4):597–611
10. Coe, M. D. 1962. *Mexico.* New York: Praeger
11. Coe, M. D. 1965. Archaeological synthesis of southern Veracruz and Tabasco. See Ref. 7, 3:679–715
12. Ibid. The Olmec style and its distributions, 739–75
13. Coe, M. D. 1966. *The Maya.* New York: Praeger
14. Coe, M. D. 1968. San Lorenzo and the Olmec civilization. In *Dumbarton Oaks Conference on the Olmec,* ed. E. P. Benson, 41–78. Washington: Dumbarton Oaks
15. Coe, M. D. 1968. *America's First Civilization.* New York: Am. Heritage Publ.
16. Coe, W. R. 1967. *Tikal, A Handbook of the Ancient Maya Ruins.* Philadelphia: Univ. Museum, Univ. Pennsylvania
17. Cohn, V. 1972. Missing part of mystery tribe's calendar is found. *Washington Post,* Feb. 16, 1972
18. Córdova, J. de 1578. *Arte en lengua zapoteca.* Mexico: Balli

19. Córdova, J. de 1578. *Vocabulario en lengua zapoteca.* Mexico: Pedro Charte y Antonio Ricardo
20. Diringer, D. 1962. *Writing.* New York: Praeger
21. Drucker, P. 1943. Ceramic sequences from Tres Zapotes, Veracruz, Mexico. *Bur. Am. Ethnol. Bull. 140*
22. Ibid 1952. La Venta, Tabasco: a study of Olmec ceramics and art. *Bull. 153*
23. Drucker, P., Heizer, R. F., Squier, R. J. 1959. Excavations at La Venta, Tabasco, 1955. *Bur. Am. Ethnol. Bull. 170*
24. Flannery, K. V., Marcus, J. 1976. The evolution of the public building in formative Oaxaca. In *Continuity and Change in Prehistoric Cultures,* ed. C. Cleland, 205–21. New York: Academic
25. Gelb, I. J., Ed. 1974. *A Study of Writing.* Univ. Chicago Press
26. Goodman, J. T. 1905. Maya dates. *Am. Anthropol.* 7:642–47
27. Graham, J. 1971. Sobre la escritura Maya. *Desarrollo Cultural de Los Mayas,* ed. E. Z. Vogt, A. Ruz Lhuillier, 257–72. Mexico: Univ. Nac. Autón. Mex.
28. Heath-Jones 1959. Definition of an ancestral Maya civilization in Miraflores phase: Kaminaljuyú. *Abstracts of papers,* 24th ann. Soc. Am. Archaeol., ed. D. A. Suhm, 37
29. Herrera, A. de 1947. *Historia general de los hechos de los castellanos en las islas y tierra firme del Mar Océano* VI, Madrid
30. Joralemon, P. D. 1971. A study of Olmec iconography. *Studies in Pre-Columbian Art and Archaeology* 7. Washington: Dumbarton Oaks
31. Lee, T. A. 1969. The artifacts of Chiapa de Corzo, Chiapas, Mexico. *Pap. New World Archaeol. Found.* 26
32. Lehmann, W. 1926. Reisebrief aus Puerto Mexiko. *Z. Ethnol. Jahrg.* 58:171–77
33. Lowe, G. W. 1962. Algunos Resultados de la Temporada 1961 en Chiapa de Corzo, Chiapas. *Estud. Cult. Maya* 2:185–196
34. Marcus, J. 1974. The iconography of power among the Classic Maya. *World Archaeol.* 6(1):83–94
35. Marcus, J. 1976. The iconography of militarism at Monte Albán and neighboring sites in the Valley of

Oaxaca. In *The Origins of Religious Art and Iconography in Pre-Classic Mesoamerica,* ed. H. B. Nicholson, 123–39. Los Angeles: Univ. California, Latin American Center

36. Martínez Hernández, J. 1926. *Paralelismo entre los calendarios Maya y Azteca. Su correlación con el calendario Juliano.* Merida: Compañía Tipográfica Yucateca

37. Miles, S. W. 1965. Sculpture of the Guatemala-Chiapas highlands and Pacific slopes, and associated hieroglyphs. See Ref. 7, 2(10):237–75

38. Morley, F. R., Morley, S. G. 1938. The age and provenance of the Leyden Plate. *Carnegie Inst. Washington, Contrib. Am. Anthropol. Hist.* Publ. 509, Contrib. 24

39. Nuttall, Z. 1902. *Codex Nuttall, Facsimile of an Ancient Mexican Codex Belonging to Lord Zouche of Harynworth, England.* Cambridge: Peabody Museum, Harvard Univ.

40. Paddock, J. 1966. Monte Albán: ¿sede de imperio? *Rev. Mex. Estud. Antropol.* 20:117–46

41. Prem, H. J. 1971. Early calendrics and writing. Some aspects of the emergence of civilization in Mesoamerica, ed. R. F. Heizer, J. Graham. *Contrib. Univ. Calif. Archaeol. Res. Facil.* 11:112–32

42. Proskouriakoff, T. 1950. A study of Classic Maya sculpture. *Carnegie Inst. Washington,* Publ. 593

43. Proskouriakoff, T. 1960. Historical implications of a pattern of dates at Piedras Negras, Guatemala. *Am. Antiq.* 25:454–75

44. Quirarte, J. 1973. Izapan-style art: A study of its form and meaning. *Studies in Pre-Columbian Art and Archaeology 10.* Washington: Dumbarton Oaks

45. Satterthwaite, L. 1960. Maya "Long Count" numbers. *Expedition* 2(2):36–37

46. Satterthwaite, L. 1965. Calendrics of the Maya lowlands. See Ref. 7, 3:603–31

47. Sharer, R. J. 1969. Chalchuapa: Investigations at a Highland Maya ceremonial center. *Expedition* 11(2):36–38

48. Sharer, R. J., Sedat, D. W. 1973. Monument 1, El Portón, Guatemala and the development of Maya calendrical and writing systems. *Contrib. Univ. Calif. Archaeol. Res. Facil.* 18:177–94

49. Shook, E. M. 1960. Tikal Stela 29. *Expedition* 2(2):29–35

50. Smith, M. E. 1973. *Picture Writing from Ancient Southern Mexico: Mixtec Place Signs and Maps.* Norman: Univ. Oklahoma Press

51. Spinden, H. J. 1935. Indian manuscripts of southern Mexico. *Ann. Rep. Smithsonian Inst.* 1933: 429–51

52. Stirling, M. W. 1940. An initial series from Tres Zapotes, Vera Cruz, Mexico. *National Geographic Soc. Contrib. Tech. Pap. Mex. Archeol. Ser.* 1(1):1–15

53. Stirling, M. W. 1943. Stone monuments of southern Mexico. *Bur. Am. Ethnol. Bull.* 138

54. Thompson, J. E. S. 1927. A correlation of the Mayan and European calendars. *Field Mus. Nat. Hist., Anthropol. Ser.* 17(1)

55. Thompson, J. E. S. 1943. Some sculptures from southeastern Quezaltenango, Guatemala. *Carnegie Inst. Washington, Notes on Middle Am. Archaeol. Ethnol.* 17:100–12

56. Thompson, J. E. S. 1948. An archaeological reconnaissance in the Cotzumalhuapa region, Escuintla, Guatemala. *Carnegie Inst. Washington* Publ. 574, Contrib. 44

57. Thompson, J. E. S. 1950. Maya Hieroglyphic Writing: Introduction. *Carnegie Inst. Washington* Publ. 589

58. Thompson, J. E. S. 1972. *Maya Hieroglyphs Without Tears.* London: Trustees of the British Museum

59. Thompson, J. E. S. 1973. The Maya glyph for capture or conquest and an iconographic representation of Itzam Na on Yucatecan Façades. *Contrib. Univ. Calif. Archaeol. Res. Facil.* 18:203–7

60. Tozzer, A. M. 1907. Ernst Förstemann. *Am. Anthropol.* n.s. 9:153–59

61. Washington, H. S. 1922. The jade of the Tuxtla statuette. *Proc. US Nat. Mus.* 60(14):1–14

62. Wauchope, R. 1954. Implications of radiocarbon dates from Middle and South America. *Middle Am. Res. Rec. Tulane Univ.* 2(2):17–40

63. Waterman, T. T. 1924. On certain antiquities in western Guatemala. *Bull. Pan Am. Union* 58:341–61

64. Waterman, T. T. 1929. Is the Baúl Stela an Aztec imitation? *Art Archaeol.* 28(5):182–87

Ann. Rev. Anthropol. 1976. 5:69–91
Copyright © 1976 by Annual Reviews Inc. All rights reserved

DIFFERENT RATES IN   ◆ 9570
THE EVOLUTION OF PROTEINS
AND PHENOTYPES

R. H. Byles

Laboratory of Physical Anthropology,
University of California, Los Angeles, California 90024

A relatively new sort of geneticist has come into existence within the last two decades. He represents a kind of hybrid between the fields of molecular genetics and population genetics and studies what has come to be called molecular evolution. Today there is a journal dedicated to this subdiscipline and a large number of practitioners within both biology and physical anthropology. It is out of this area of study that the major subject of this review derives: the apparent paradox between the rates of molecular evolution and the history of phenotype evolution. This is not the only area of interest within the field of molecular evolution, but the idea of the molecular clock is of particular interest to the anthropologist, and an appreciation of the neutralist point of view is necessary to an understanding of it. For this reason these two topics will be the focus of this paper.

THE CENTRAL DOGMA

The biological community has long adhered to the idea that the primary function of some unit of inheritance, called a gene, was the manufacture of species-specific protein molecules. Species were dissimilar because they were dissimilar in terms of their protein metabolism. Since living organisms are systems of chemical interactions, and the materials of most importance in this process are the proteins, then evolution at its most basic level is change in the shared protein metabolism of the species.

There are two kinds of proteins which are generally recognized: structural proteins and enzymes. Structural proteins are the building materials of the organism. Such substances as melanin and albumin, the finished products of some metabolic processes, are structural proteins. Enzymes are proteins which do the work of metabolism. They are the components of the process itself. The enzymes enable the processes of metabolism to go forward.

A central dogma of biology states that it is the function of the genetic material to provide the "plans" for the manufacture of the proper enzymes and structural proteins and that the various species share a common set of "blueprints" for the manufacture of protein in distinction to members of other species for whom the blueprints are significantly different.

The protein molecules, in this view, are the unit of dissimilarity between the phenotypes of different organisms. While minor variation in protein metabolism can exist between different members of the same species, it is less significant than the differences which exist between members of different species.

The hereditary unit which determines the specific structure of a particular protein molecule is defined as a gene [adhering to the definitions proposed by Georgiev (6)]. By a process which is not completely understood, a unique sequence of base pairs in a DNA molecule results in the production of a protein molecule with a unique sequence of amino acids. The code has been broken, and the particular order of three nucleotides which produce a given amino acid is known.

This is the "one gene, one enzyme" hypothesis, and a central dogma of modern genetics. The unit of phenotypic evolution is the protein molecule which is determined by the basic unit of genotypic evolution, the gene.

EVOLUTION DEFINED

The definition of evolution which is accepted by modern population biologists is that evolution is change in a population of the frequency of a gene. This is effected by either mutation, selection, migration (gene flow), or genetic drift. These are inclusive and exhaustive causes of change in gene frequency.

Given these assertions, it is possible to give the evolution of the structure of the gene, and the frequencies of alternative genes, an operational definition. If the "one gene, one enzyme" hypothesis is true, then evolution in the structure of proteins must be the most direct possible reflection of the genes themselves. Since DNA is very inconvenient to study and proteins are very convenient to study, for a variety of technical reasons, the central dogma allows for an operational definition of evolution as changes in the structure and frequencies of alternative structures of protein molecules. Persons who exploit this operational definition are interested in molecular evolution.

The study of molecular evolution has some advantages over the study of evolution in other kinds of phenotypes. Molecules evolve in natural unitary increments and not continuously. The substitution of one amino acid for another is a basic unit of change. This allows the student of these changes to measure the degree of difference between the proteins of two individuals by using a natural integer scale. Conceptually this is a much more convenient situation than that enjoyed by those who study the "quantitative" phenotypes.

All of these characteristics have made the study of the evolution of proteins very attractive to the population biologist. As we shall see, however, this initial

Table 1 Translation of the genetic code

Triplet	Amino Acid	Triplet	Amino Acid
UUA		ACU	
UUG		ACC	
CUU		ACA	Threonine (thr)
CUC		ACG	
CUA	Leucine (leu)	GGU	
CUG		GGC	
UCU		GAA	Glycine (gly)
UCC		GCG	
UCA			
UCG		AUU	
AGU	Serine (ser)	AUC	Isoleucine
AGC		AUA	(ileu)
CGU		UUU	Phenylalanine
CGC		UUC	(phe)
CGA		UGU	Cysteine
CGG		UGC	(cys)
AGA	Arginine (arg)	UAU	Tyrosine
AGG		UAC	(try)
GUU			
GUC		CAU	Histidine
GUA	Valine (val)	CAC	(his)
GUG		CAA	Glutamine
CCU		CAG	(glu)
CCC		AAU	Asparagine
CCA	Proline (pro)	AAC	(asp)
CCG		AAA	Lysine
GCU		AAG	(lys)
GCC		GAU	Aspartic
GCA	Alanine (ala)	GAC	(asp)
CCG			
UAA		GAA	Glutamic
UAG	Chain termination	GAG	(glu)
UGA		UGG	Tryptophan
AUG	Methionine (met)		(tryp)

Note: Alterations in the last nucleotide are usually synonymous in effect.

convenience is not without its very real debits, for what this field has gained in conceptual simplicity has been lost in practical complexity. The result is that there is no agreement over even the most basic assumptions necessary to use this new tool in a genuinely productive way.

NEUTRALIST-SELECTIONIST PROBLEM

In 1969 a paper appeared in *Science* which was the benchmark in the evolution of the debate between those who sought to find the explanation for all evolution in the process of natural selection and those who saw a large role for the effects of genetic drift and other random phenomena. This is the famous "Non-Darwinian Evolution" paper of King & Jukes (10). They argued that the major forces in operation in the evolution of molecules were mutation and genetic drift. This is possible because environmental exigencies will only result in selection if different phenotypes which are highly correlated with particular genotypes produce different numbers of offspring. Therefore, selection cannot operate to change the relative frequencies of alleles which have no effect on the phenotype and, furthermore, will not produce changes if the alternative phenotypes have the same fitness. One of these two, particularly the former, is the rule and not the exception, according to King & Jukes.

Since biologists agree that evolution *is* the evolution of proteins, this point of view has serious repercussions for everyone. The argument remains unresolved.

The neutralists argue that there are a large number of mutations which cannot be subject to the forces of natural selection because they in no way affect the phenotype. Some kinds of these truly neutral mutations undoubtedly occur. The chart of the genetic code (Figure 1) demonstrates one way in which this is true. Observe that several different combinations of nucleotides are possible for the same amino acid. Obviously a mutation which alters the sequence of nucleotides such that it produces a different but synonymous message is a neutral mutation. If the combinations of nucleotides which produced synonymous messages were random, one could argue that this source of synonymy was trivial as the mutations which produce it must be rare. As King & Jukes have pointed out, however, of the 549 possible single nucleotide substitution mutations possible, 134 produce synonyms. Changes in the last nucleotide in the triplet are not as likely to produce a different message as alterations in the first two positions. Therefore, mutations affecting the final nucleotide in a codon have a high probability of neutrality. Alterations at the second position, with two exceptions, always code for a different amino acid. The first position is likewise restricted in the number of neutral changes. This kind of neutral mutation, in conjunction with the forces of genetic drift, can alter allele frequencies without the intervention of selection [for an opposing point of view, see Dobzhansky (4)].

Another potential for neutrality exists in the protein structure. This is the distinction between the so-called active and variable locations.

Consider the case of the protein cytochrome c. This is a critical enzyme in the respiration of cells, and any organism which does not have the correct genetic information to form a functioning cytochrome c molecule will not survive. The stabilizing selective forces acting upon this molecule are clearly rather intense. This is a relatively short molecule (accounting for the fact that it was among the first in which the exact sequence of amino acids was determined), having only 104 amino acids. Of these 104, 35 do not vary from organism to organism or from species to species. The remaining 69 are able to vary, and the different molecules which result appear not to differ in their ability to correctly perform their critical role in metabolism. Furthermore, the sites at which no variation can be tolerated are associated with the molecular interactions and activities of the molecule, in particular the binding site with the heme groups (10, 14). Thus there are parts of the molecule which, because of their function, are subject to intense stabilizing selection, and there are others where mutations can be tolerated with no effect on the ability of the molecule to play its role in metabolism. Therefore, neutral mutations are apparently possible in restricted areas of the enzyme.

The neutralists have pointed out that most of the evolution which has been observed to take place in the species studied has been primarily in those areas that are not affected by selection. Furthermore, the selection that is seen to occur is of the stabilizing sort. This is difficult to understand, as a significant proportion of evolution in gross phenotypes has apparent selective significance.

The argument eventually boils down to two issues. First, are the mutations and resulting variants pointed out by the neutralists really neutral, or do subtle differences exist between the reproductive potential of individuals with different alleles? In the second view, the apparent neutrality of the alleles is just the result of our inability to discern very subtle selective pressures. This argument has even been directed at synonymous codons, arguing that different transfer RNAs are required and that the availability of these at the metabolic site may enhance the efficiency of one allele or another in some subtle way (2). The problem is that the argument is difficult, if not impossible, to demonstrate. The operation of such subtle selective forces is easy to posit but difficult to find. This then begins to resemble an ad hoc effort, without philosophical respectability.

The second argument is that this evolution is simply trivial. Evolution which has no effect on phenotype is of no interest to the serious student of evolution, although it might be interesting to the pure theorist. If the interest of the population biologist is only in the evolutionary changes which occur as a result of the adaptive process, then this is again true by definition. It develops, however, that these neutral variants, assuming they exist, do have a real application to the world of the phylogeneticist. To the anthropologist, this usefulness has taken the form of the highly controversial molecular clock.

If it is assumed that two categories of events begin by containing the same elements, but that time allows elements to be altered or replaced by a limited set of alternative elements, then it can also be assumed that the rate of divergence of these two categories is relatively constant. The rate of change will be a function of the probabilities of replacement or alteration for each unit of time. The two collections of elements can be assumed to diverge from the common beginning so that the time since the process began can be calculated from half of the differences between the two sets. This set of logical propositions is familiar to anthropologists, as it has formed the basis of past analyses. Swadesh, for example, reasoned in precisely the same way in his development of the method of glottochronology. The arguments which form the foundation of various geophysical and geochemical methods of dating are very similar in their logic.

There is a difference between the divergence of molecules and the divergence of vocabulary in related languages, however. It is possible to assume that in language a change in the form of a vocabulary element is irreversible. The number of kinds of change which can take place is sufficiently large that it is unlikely that the precise reverse of any change will occur. In protein structure, however, this is not the case. An amino acid can only be replaced by another of a very limited set of alternatives (20), and furthermore, it appears that a change from one amino acid to another implies a high probability of reversion. This means that truly identical results can occur because of a large number of changes as well as no changes at all.

Early in the game it was realized that if it was possible to calculate a rate at which random amino acid substitutions occur, it would be possible to compare the proteins from members of different species of animals and estimate the time at which they diverged from their common ancestor (5, 14, 24, 25). Again the analogy with glottochronology is a good one. Zuckerkandl & Pauling were the first to show that, for the hemoglobin molecule, divergence in amino acid sequence among several species was a monotone function of the time of separation (25). Later they demonstrated that if there was a constant random replacement of amino acids—that is, a constant probability of replacement true at all amino acid sites in the molecule—and if the probabilities of reversion were assumed to be no better than the probabilities for any other replacement, then the amount of divergence between the parent and descendent molecules should be approximated by an exponential function (26). This conclusion was independently argued by Margoliash & Smith (14) and has been accepted by the majority of investigators subsequently.

Direct use of this logic unfortunately is limited by technical considerations. At the beginning, and to a large degree today, the sequencing of amino acids in a molecule is a complex, time-consuming, and expensive business. The direct comparison of the amino acid sequences for several proteins for a group of species, the obvious approach, is not practical. Simpler techniques for estimating these differences were needed and several were attempted. The two which are of most interest are the techniques of microcomplement fixation and electrophoresis.

Microcomplement fixation is a technique which estimates the differences in the antigenic properties of two molecules. As two molecules become more similar, a smaller concentration of the first is required to produce a significant reaction with antibodies against the second. This use of the extremely sensitive immune response of mammals is both fast and accurate. Indeed, the degree of reactivity between the antigen and antibody can be used to calculate the number of amino acid differences between two molecules (antigens) from different species (24).

The technique of electrophoresis takes advantage of the fact that different molecules differ in their size and electrical properties. An electric field is produced in a medium and the molecules to be compared are placed in the medium. The negatively charged molecules migrate toward the anode, and the positively charged ones toward the cathode. The speed of migration is a function of the surface charge of the molecule. Depending on the pore size of the medium, it is also possible to select circumstances in which the larger molecules travel more slowly than the smaller ones. This allows the investigator to distinguish on the basis of size and charge.

Unfortunately, it happens that molecules which are different in other respects have the same electrophoretic properties. Variants which are not detectable by means of electrophoresis are said to be "silent." Apparently there are often several silent variants of the same molecule; therefore it is usually the case that the method of electrophoresis underestimates the variability in a population, and often what appear to be monomorphic proteins are in fact polymorphic. King & Ohta have presented a particularly lucid explication of this bias in the method (9).

THE ALBUMIN CLOCK

By now everyone is aware of the attempt by Sarich & Wilson to use the technique of microcomplement fixation and the assumption of neutral evolution to fix the time of divergence of the major lines of the apes and Old World monkeys. This paper caused a terrific uproar among involved investigators, because the dates claimed for the divergence of the African apes and our own species were in conflict with the conclusions of the paleontologists. Indeed, the dates claimed by the proponents of the "molecular clock" were much too recent to be reconciled with the dates arrived at by the paleontologists and geologists.

Sarich & Wilson (22) combined the conclusions of Zuckerkandle & Pauling (26) with the technique of microcomplement fixation to arrive at these time estimates. The specifics of the ability to infer a genetic distance between species that is homologous with the number of amino acid differences for some protein is largely the result of the earlier work of Wilson et al (24).

These investigations derived the formula for the rate of immunologically detectable change between sibling species to be estimated by the functions:

$$ID = e^{kt} \qquad\qquad 1.$$

where ID is the index of dissimilarity experimentally determined by the technique of microcomplement fixation, t is the time since the species have diverged, and k is some constant. The value of k is estimated by application of this

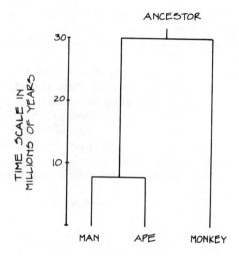

Figure 1   Divergence in the Anthropoidea.

technique to a pair of species for which the value of *t* is known. This research used the time of divergence of the Anthropoidea and Hominoidea as the baseline from which to estimate the value of *k*. Since this is an exponential function, some error in this value can be tolerated without unduly influencing the results. Having estimated a value of *k*, it is possible to apply the formula where *t* is unknown. The result of this application is the phylogeny of Figure 2.

The bone of contention from the first was the very late estimate for the divergence of man and the chimpanzee. Although this logic has undergone several replications over the years, the result is remarkably internally consistent and altogether inconsistent with the conclusions of paleontology.

A PARADOX

The argument which followed the publication of the Sarich & Wilson article was largely confined to a discussion of who had the correct time perspective for the evolution of the primate line. It appears to me, however, that a much larger and more important issue has been overlooked, at least in the anthropological literature. The disagreement about the actual date of divergence is not an issue of great importance except to a few. What is significant, however, is that there is an apparent paradox in which the rate of molecular evolution is slow in relation to phenotypic evolution, at least as it can be measured. The conservatism of meaningful molecular evolution is not surprising but it is troublesome. If molecules are the means by which phenotypes evolve, as well as the most direct expression of the genetic material, then phenotypes and molecules ought to evolve at the same rate. Either the clock is wrong, the time scale we have established for evolution is wrong, or the central dogma is wrong. This is the interesting question and the one which will be discussed here. There is, in general, an embarrassing lack of variation in the molecular structure of animals. Beginning with the demonstration that Histone IV, a critical molecule in the regulation of DNA transcription, was only trivially different in such remote species as the calf and the pea-plant, the absence of great variation in the species of animals has been disturbing (3). It is true that in most respects the metabolism of frogs and goats and flies and people is remarkably similar. The very recent data produced by the clock are only a single example of a much larger phenomenon. The expectation is that to the extent that phenotypes are the result of inheritance, they are the result of protein metabolism. Protein metabolism is directed by the base sequence in the DNA and this sequence is a code for a sequence of amino acids. Therefore, the evolution of proteins and the evolution of heritable phenotypes is the same evolution. That there should be an apparent paradox between the rates of protein evolution and the rates of phenotypic evolution is therefore troublesome.

Opponents of the dates estimated generated by the albumin clock of Sarich & Wilson, as well as the other attempts to calibrate the rate of molecular evolution before and after, have been addressing themselves indirectly to the more interesting paradox between the rates of molecular evolution and phenotypic evolution. This debate has been particularly visible to anthropologists, as the debate between Sarich and the paleontologists has been loud, acrimonious, and largely unproductive. We will discuss the arguments of the antagonists and protagonists as they relate to the paradox.

Furthermore, a number of molecular biologists have made observations in recent months which bear on this difficulty and these concepts will be reviewed as well.

Real or Artifact

In general, it is possible to divide those who have participated in this discussion into two groups: those who see the paradox between the rates of morphological and biochemical change as a *real* paradox, and have sought to explain the different rates; others have argued that the paradox is only *apparent* and an artifactual result of the way in which data have been collected and analyzed. The observations of this group are particularly interesting.

Changing Rates

Of those who argue that there are in fact differing rates for phenotypic and molecular evolution, the most interesting positions are assumed by M. Goodman et al (7) and B-J Williams (submitted for publication, 1975). The former argues that the rate of molecular evolution in the primate line has decreased due to changes in the structure of the placenta. The latter maintains that the rates of molecular evolution are not constant and that the conclusions of Zuckerkandle & Pauling, while accurate, are not applicable in the conventional sense in which they have been applied.

The Placentalization Hypotheses

The process of isolation and rejection which results from the introduction of foreign materials into the body requires that the "antigen" have several properties. In order to stimulate an immune response, the antigen must be an organic material, particularly fats and proteins, it must have large molecular weight (50,000), and it must not be isolated from the bloodstream by any mechanism. As the tissue of a fetus is "foreign" in the immunological sense of the word, it can stimulate an immune reaction in the mother resulting in rejection and expulsion. This will not occur if the fetus is not detectably different from the mother or does not meet one of the criteria stated above. In most animals, an offspring which would be detectably different from the mother escapes rejection because it is isolated from the bloodstream and therefore the immunological detection system of the mother. In most mammals, the placenta acts as this type of a barrier in that the fetus and the mother have completely separate circulatory systems.

Apes, humans, monkeys, and a few other mammals have a hemochorial placenta which allows exchange of chemical materials between the mother and developing fetus. The selective advantages of this kind of system are simply that it allows the "naive" infant to share the immunological benefits of the mother's disease experience. The major disadvantage of this system is that it allows the immune system of the mother contact with the tissues of the fetus, and if the proteins of the two are significantly different, the response of the maternal system will be rejection of the offspring. The classic example of this is Rh incompatibility, but there are others as well. It is Goodman's rather ingenious argument that this should result in a slowing of the rate of evolution in the primate line. Clearly any change in the structure of large molecules being produced by a developing fetus could trigger a response on the part of the mother which would result in death. Thus selection, acting through the maternal immune system, could act as a kind of governor on the rate at which molecular evolution could proceed.

The major difficulty with this point of view is that it predicts that there should be a slower rate of protein evolution in the Anthropoidea as compared to the Prosimiae. Unfortunately there is no evidence that this is the case; indeed, Sarich has argued for the reverse (21).

Furthermore, this hypothesis, while responsive to the particular case of the primates, cannot be argued for any other major grouping of animals involved in the difficulty and therefore cannot be considered to have solved the problem of different rates in general.

The argument put forward by Williams is more interesting. This argument recognizes the role of coadaptation in metabolism. It is not the case, as is almost always assumed, that the primary adaptation of genes for most proteins is the environment. Indeed the primary adaptation of most genes is to each other. In a metabolic system it is critical that the various components be able to interact in such a way as to produce an efficient metabolic system. It is this system which has direct adaptive significance. The selective meaning of any change in the activity of a protein must first be measured in terms of the other members of the system. Furthermore, proteins (tyrosine, for example) which are involved in a wide variety of metabolic pathways will have almost no latitude for change simply because of the myriad of metabolic neighbors with which they have to interact. Thus it is not proper to simply consider the rate at which a given molecule can evolve without understanding that the other molecules with which it is involved restrain the amount and direction of acceptable change.

Thus it is possible to envision a universe in which mutations occur at random, but in which the effects of these mutations are not neutral in terms of the metabolic neighbors of the affected molecule. Under these circumstances the rate of divergence between lineages which share a common ancestral species will accelerate as time goes by. In other words, for some time after a split between two closely related species, they will have the same shared coadaptive metabolic systems. Thus the constraints placed by the adaptation to other genes will be the same. As small and minor changes begin to accumulate and the lineages begin to diverge, one result is that the nature of the interactions between molecules will also begin to diverge. This divergence means that while both lines continue to contain coadapted complexes of genes, the precise nature of that coadaptation is altered. While the *constraints* on change remain equally rigid in both descendent groups, the *areas of latitude* slowly begin to separate and become different. Thus while the rate of change in the two groups remains equal, the degree to which this change can be divergent (as opposed to parallel) is increased. While the change in molecular structure which produces differences from the molecular ancestor is constant, and the number of differences between the parental and descendent lines is exponential [as shown by Pauling & Zuckerkandl (26)], it cannot be assumed that the same is true *between* the two *descendent* lines. The sister lineages diverge from the parent lineage at an exponential rate; they do not diverge from each other at an exponential rate.

Figure 3 demonstrates the difference between the analysis of Williams and the more conventional assumptions. Graph I, the conventional point of view, assumes that there will be no difference in rate due to coadaptation. Therefore, as the descendent lines X and Y diverge from common ancestor at an exponential rate, they diverge from each other at equal rates (b). Figure X shows the same process with the assumptions of Williams. The angle is determined by the degree of coadaptation in the molecules under investigation. Figure I is simply the special case in which the value is equal to 180°. As you can see, the degree of divergence, the biochemical distance, between X and Y is the joint product of the rate of divergence from the common ancestor and the degree of coadaptation.

The assumptions made by Williams are reasonable in terms of the models of metabolism proposed in recent years. Furthermore, the estimates which are produced for the separation of different lineages within the primate line will be more consonant with the evidence gathered by the paleontologists. The major difficulty with this point of view is in estimating the "degree of coadaptation"

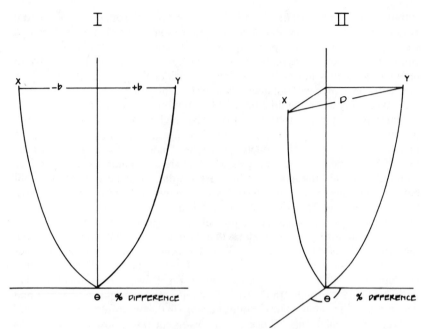

Figure 2   Protein divergence: D = 26 only where Θ = 180°.

I	II
Evolutionary differentiation of the proportion of amino acid sites in proteins X and Y. This assumes that if X and Y differ in 2b sites, they each differ from the ancestral protein in b sites.	Evolutionary differentiation of proteins X and Y which does not assume that the difference between X and Y is the sum of their differences from the ancestral protein.

characteristic of this or that molecule. Also this does not apply to the larger question of the conservation of molecular evolution as the distance D will become indistinguishable from that, assuming the θ equal 180° in time. The precise amount of time required for the predictions of the two models to become indistinguishable is a function of the quantity 180° − θ, but eventually it will occur. Thus the slow divergence of molecules in very divergent lines is not explained. This is an elegant and reasonable explanation for the difficulties with our understanding of evolution in recently diverged descendent groups, however, and therefore applies to the assumptions of the albumin clock.

EVOLUTION OF "CONTROLLER" DNA

The most commonly accepted model of gene function is that proposed by Georgiev. His use of the word "gene" corresponds to that used by most investigators in molecular evolution and the central dogma. The gene is defined as the information of transcription, that is, the order of base pairs responsible for the coding of a specific sequence of amino acids. This he defines as being only part of the "operon" which also includes the information of regulation.

In any cell the rate at which a given protein is produced is genetically and environmentally controlled. During development the order in which sites producing specific proteins become active and the rates at which they produce their products are controlled by mechanisms internal to the cell. These mechanisms are capable of responding to changes in internal variables (overabundance of product, for example) as well as external environmental realities. It is the ability of these controlling mechanisms to function which allows the cells in a developing fetus to differentiate into diverse tissues, although as descendants of the same fertilized egg they all share the same genetic information. Alterations in the order of events in the developing organism, as well as changes in the rates of production of critical proteins, must, perforce, be at the root of the major differences between different species of organisms. That the phenotypic differences are first and foremost expressed in the development process is a commonplace observation. That this must be due to the controlling mechanisms of metabolism to a greater degree than the infrastructure of the structural genes derives from the observations of the molecular evolutionists, particularly the observation that the order of amino acids in the active areas of enzymes is fixed. This could account for the paradox between the rates of evolution of structural genes and the evolution of phenotypes.

In response to the difficulties of the similarities between man and chimpanzee, King & Wilson (12) have invoked this point of view. They conclude that the major portion of divergent evolution between these species has occurred on the controlling regions of the DNA and not in the structural sequence (excepting synonyms). It is the way in which genetic changes alter phenotypes which count in adaptive evolution, and the number of detectable genetic differences between molecules is of little significance.

Beyond this limited application of the observations of the molecular biologists is the more general treatment of the problem by Jack Lester King (submitted for publication, 1975). To him the significance of the recognition of what he calls the "enormous gene," containing a small structural sequence and a huge regulating section, will result in several necessary conceptual revisions. Among the eight implications which he posits as significant for the population geneticists are several of significance to this problem. The first and major implication is that implied by King & Wilson, that the majority of evolution may be the result of changes on the controlling regions of genes and not the structural areas. If this is true, then we would expect the rate of evolutionary change which is reflected in the amino acid sequence of proteins to be conservative relative to the "invisible" changes taking place in the controlling regions. The irony is that these changes are only invisible through the microscopic vision of the molecular evolutionist; they are plainly visible as changes in phenotype through the macroscopic vision of the natural historian.

Secondly, King observes that if the model suggested by Georgiev is applied to evolutionary thinking, then it must be concluded that all variation is quantitative in nature. This is a relief to the population biologists who have become increasingly more annoyed as the simple two-allele systems we have talked about so blandly over the years turn out not to be so discrete, and show a range of expressions grouped into arbitrary categories. This is also a relief to those who were concerned that the result of the integration of molecular biology and evolutionary thinking was the conclusion that evolution is nearly impossible, at least very unlikely.

If genes are coadapted into blocks of interacting parts which are systematically related, and if changes are only trivial or drastic, then the only evolutionary change which is both significant and viable must result from the simultaneous and mutually harmonious mutation of many separate genes. The odds against such an event occurring are enormous. This view of the evolutionary process is clearly unacceptable, but if one only uses the information available about the nature of structural genes, then it is inescapable. The second implication of King solves this dilemma. If small changes are possible in the controlling areas which only quantitatively affect the metabolism of the organism, then gradual and orderly evolution is again conceptually possible.

Finally, the mutation rate in the combined controlling and structural area of the operon is greater than that of the structural area alone. This means that the mutation rate is much larger than expected on the basis of investigations of structural genes alone (as much as 50 times as great). Most of this change is invisible to the eye of electrophoresis or any of the other methods used to assess variation in enzymes. Thus the paradox of the clock only occurs because we are looking at the most conservative component in the metabolic system.

We will return to this point of view, in combination with that proposed by Williams, at the conclusion of this paper.

It is also possible to conceive of this paradox of rates as an "artifact" of the reasoning which lies behind the idea of a molecular clock, or the methods used to determine the variation among different species. Several persons have argued that this is the case, and it is useful to examine these arguments.

The most straightforward argument of this type is the assertion by Sarich that the time of divergence estimated from the geological evidence is simply in error (21). His argument concludes that it is the date of the split between the Apes and Man which has been poorly ascertained, as he assumes that the time ascribed to the divergence between the Anthropoidea and the Cercopithecoidea is essentially correct. In fact, due to the use of the logarithm in the calibration of the clock, this date can be in error to a substantial degree and affect the results very little.

This assertion met with angry, even defensive, response from the natural historical camp. Indeed, Sarich has hit a real nerve with this point since it is assumed by almost everyone to be in error, but can be definitively shown to be false by nobody. The status, even the reconstruction, of the critical Ramapithecus fossils remains dubious. The common ancestor of the chimpanzee and humans is not known, and therefore this is a ripe area for attack. Furthermore, the dates for the Miocene-Pliocene sites and their predecessors are obscure and uncertain. The provenience of the critical primate fossils with relation to the datable strata is often unclear. The result is that one can look at any single paleontological conclusion and find it lacking in sufficient data to be convincing. The fact that all of the information taken in toto seems to indicate a split between the chimpanzee and man earlier than 25 million years ago is not based on very solid evidence, but rather a preponderance of rather shaky evidence. Any assertion like Sarich's introduced into this kind of situation is bound to ruffle some feathers. Furthermore, Sarich has argued that the assumptions of the clock model are robust and the logic is firm. The information from the paleontologists is weak; therefore where contradictions exist, the nod must be given to the molecular evidence.

This point of view is largely uninteresting for two reasons. First, the robustness of the assumptions underlying the clock model are overestimated by Sarich. We have pointed out some serious questions in this regard and will see several more. Secondly, this argument does not address the larger question of the conservatism of molecular evolution in general. This is an empirical argument and will only be settled by the collection of firm phylogenetic and geologic data for the last 50 million years of primate evolution. When it is settled, it is unlikely to shed light on the more general picture.

A possible source of artifactual contradiction between the fossil record and the molecular data would arise if the assumptions and the derived functions used to estimate times of divergence from the raw molecular data were in error. Objections of this type range from rather naive curve fitting (20) to a very well reasoned and clear exposition (19).

The realization that a curve described by a log-log function applied to the molecular data produced dates which fit the fossil data better than the exponential assumptions of Sarich was properly dismissed by the proponents of the clock (21). Unless a function is proposed which both fits the assumptions required by our knowledge of the evolutionary process and fits the data better, it must be rejected. Sarich has convincingly argued that the log-log model proposed by Read & Lestrel fails on the basis of the first criterion. A subsequent analysis by Read, however, is cognizant of the constraints imposed by our understanding of molecular evolution. Read demonstrates that the simple exponential formula of Sarich & Wilson (22) does not fit the assumptions or the data of the molecular biologists (19). Firstly, the conclusion of Zuckerkandle & Pauling, that the rate of apparent mutation should be constant with reference to generations, is not borne out by the experimental data, although Ohta (17, 18) has argued that there is in fact no contradiction between the experimental data and the theory of neutral mutations (17).

Read suggests that the proper formulation is:

$$\text{ID} = a\,\text{D}^{b} \qquad\qquad 2.$$

where a and b are parameters to be estimated from the fossil data. It should be pointed out that this is anticipated by Nei (15, 16). Fitting a variety of parameters to a series of molecular phylogenies allows the estimation of the time of divergence between man and chimp to be brought into relative harmony with the fossil evidence. This argument is of little help for two reasons. First, it does not approach the more general problem. While Read's formula does reconcile the difficulties in the special case of the primates, it does not help us to understand the conservatism of molecular evolution in general. Since this is a general phenomenon, we must be wary of conclusions so limited in their application. Secondly, this argument still appears to me to be without biochemical foundation. Read's curve better fits the paleontological data, but its reference to what is known of the evolution of molecules is obscure. It is more than simple curve fitting, but falls to the same objection. A complete answer must reconcile what is known of molecular evolution as a process, as well as a body of data, with the fossil record.

King & Ohta (9, 11) have published what amounts to a critical review of estimates of variability based upon electrophoretic data. They have pointed out that this technique will inevitably result in the underestimation of the amount of real variation within and between populations. As we have discussed, the technique of electrophoresis will separate molecules which are different in their net electrical charge at a given pH. With some of the more sophisticated methods, it is also possible to sort molecules by size. This leads to the recognition of different "bands" of proteins which appear in the experimental gels. It has always been assumed that these were a single protein, and they are routinely referred to as alleles. Almost certainly this is an incorrect assumption. It is possible for different alleles to produce proteins which are different but which happen to be the same size and have the same charge. King & Ohta suggest that these bands should be understood as representative of different phenotypes, and they call them "electromorphs." A single electromorph may contain the metabolic products of one or many different genes.

Others (1, 23) investigating the variation in various proteins were able to show that members of the same electromorphic category were in fact different in their ability to withstand the effects of denaturing heat. Thus there were several categories of heat resistance within a single electromorphic category. These "hidden" variants cause an underestimation of variability where electrophoresis is used. The new technique of isoelectric focusing, electrophoresis through a pH gradient, also is able to detect variation not detected by simple electrophoresis.

A conclusion reached by King & Ohta is that the estimates of genetic variability based on electrophoretic data are underestimates. This bias would produce the illusion that protein evolution is much more conservative than it actually is. It is assumed that this objection is less applicable to immunological techniques since these methods are more sensitive to subtle differences in molecular structure. Any error which exists, however, is certainly in the direction of an underestimation of the real variability.

This difficulty is not immediately applicable to the problems with the dating of the primate phylogeny. It is, however, significant in terms of the comparisons which are routinely done between species by population biologists. Therefore, there may be a general bias toward conservatism in the literature that follows directly from electrophoretic research.

CONSTANCY OF RATE

The assumption that the rate of molecular evolution is constant is critical to the conclusions of those interested in the molecular clock as well as those investigating the more general questions of protein evolution. King (8) has indicated that the means by which these data are analyzed, particularly the application of the rule of parsimony, may bias the results in favor of a constant rate whether or not it actually exists. King's argument is as follows:

The simplest situation which can be analyzed is that in which one ancestral line produces two descendent lines. One of these in turn branches into two more, leaving a total of three descendent lines (Figure 3a).

It is only possible to investigate the sequence of amino acids in the proteins of the extant populations A, B, and C. The structure of the molecules typical of the ancestral population is not available except in rather special circumstances. If an amino acid site in some molecule is investigated, five possible results could be ascertained.

1. A different, B and C the same
2. B different, A and C the same
3. C different, A and B the same
4. all alike
5. all different

For obvious reasons it is necessary to assume that given any of these possible situations, we will accept the simplest explanation. Consider the case in which all three of the molecules are the same at the variable site. There are several possible ways in which this may have occurred. One is that there was no evolution at all, and this is the simplest and routinely accepted conclusion. This is a bias in favor of equal rates, however. Consider the case of "back mutation" (Figure 3b). In this case, there has been significant evolution in the line from D, the most recent point of divergence, and the contemporary A population. From the adaptive point of view, this is irrelevant evolution in that it produced no change, but it is a case in which one of the lines has evolved faster than the other two, and it will be scored as a case of constant evolutionary rate.

King points out that the most relevant cases for the test of the hypothesis of constancy are categories one and two diagrammed below (c, d, e). The most parsimonious conclusion is that a single evolutionary event has taken place (c), while the diagram shows that the same result could be achieved by multiple changes in a single line (d) or convergent evolution in the identical lines (e).

The most serious source of error pointed out by King, however, is the case in which all three sequences are different. This cannot be accomplished by less than two mutation events, although an unlimited number are possible. If we assume that the minimum number has occurred (a bias of significant proportions

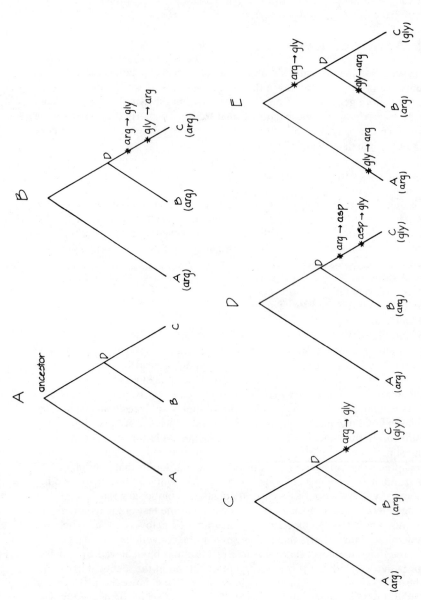

Figure 3 Sample cladograms showing "synonymous" results with different rates of evolution.

to begin with), then we are left with four possible ways in which this could occur. Only one of these is consistent with the constant rate hypothesis (I). However, the algoriths used to assess the differences between populations consistently assume that under these circumstances the number of changes since the divergence point D and the A and B population is the same. In other words, they assume that in these circumstances situation (I) has occurred. This bias is extreme.

The point which emerges is that the conclusions reached by some molecular evolutionists—that evidence has been found to support the hypothesis of constant rates—is based upon the biases present in the logic of the experiment itself, and therefore in a rather roundabout way the consequence has been affirmed. Constant rates would appear in the analysis in circumstances where they don't exist.

DISCUSSION

It was asserted early in the paper that the issues which directly emerge from the attempts to calibrate a molecular clock are issues of relatively minor biological importance. In fact, however, the discussion which developed from this point of view may well have pointed toward solutions to at least two very troublesome biological questions: (a) the conservatism of molecular evolution in general; and (b) the problems caused by the recognition of coadaptation as a reality of metabolism.

Before addressing these issues, however, it is perhaps necessary to make some statement about the state of the "clock" controversy per se. It is very clear that the assumptions which must be made by those attempting to assess the point of divergence of descendent lines by comparison of amino acid sequences in proteins are much too naive to withstand close scrutiny. The necessity of accepting the simplest model, in this case the smallest number of mutational events, produces a genuine bias in the analysis. The fact is that the logic which assumes that when two groups exponentially diverge from a common ancestor they diverge from each other by half as much is not defensible. Furthermore, it is argued that the assumptions of the clock do not fully reflect the theory or the data of the neutral mutation hypothesis upon which it is based, and indeed this hypothesis itself is open to question. The clock concept is probably a valid one, but the calibration process will be a much more difficult conceptual and practical problem than the original assumptions would have indicated. Therefore, it is not possible to assert dates of divergence based on this model at this time, although it is likely that revised and more sophisticated versions of these methods will produce interesting results. The assertions of its proponents notwithstanding, it appears that this method will become acceptable only as a result of a clear demonstration that it produces results consistent with those achieved by the paleontologists and geologists. The claims that the clock itself represents best evidence are at this time without foundation.

Attempts to explain this discrepancy between the conclusions of paleontologists and the biochemists have led to the statement of a very important point of view. The apparent conservatism of molecular evolution is not difficult to explain per se. Stabilizing selection will undoubtedly retard the accumulation of alterations in the critical active sites of enzymes. The relative rarity of these changes is now a matter of record. The fact that the less adaptively relevant parts of the molecule are more given to change is a score on the side of the neutralist theorists, but a thorn in the side of evolutionists in general. If the adaptively, indeed metabolically, insignificant parts of the genome are the only parts which evolve, or at least evolve with reasonable speed, then how does adaptive evolution occur at all? We are left with what is in essence an explanation for uninteresting evolution only (18).

This unfortunate state of affairs is compounded by the further effects of coadaptation of molecules. It is clear that for most, if not all, alleles, the focus of adaptation is on each other. Enzymes and structural proteins must be mutually coadapted to function. Slight alterations in the activity of one protein can simply terminate the development of critical metabolic materials. Furthermore, even if the pathway continues to function, its terminal product is required to interact with the terminal product of some other pathway and so on. Natural selection is able to apply *adaptive pressure* upon the result of the interaction of all of these coadapted systems of coadapted systems; *stabilizing selection* can act *directly* upon every allele at every locus. The result of this coadaptive selection appears to be the reduction of variation which further reduces the ability of adaptive pressures to cause change. If it is assumed that only one metabolic sequence is involved in some phenotype variable, the effect of coadaptation is to eliminate variation. In the simple case in which only two alleles are involved in a "pathway," but their relative fitness is mutually interdependent, the relative fitness values of the genotypes at a given locus are a function of the frequencies of alleles at the other locus:

Genotype:	$\bar{A}_1\bar{A}_1$	$\bar{A}_1\bar{A}_2$	$\bar{A}_1\bar{A}_1$
Frequency:	p^2	$2pq$	q^2
Relative fitness:	$1 - st^2$	1	$1 - sr^2$

where $\bar{A}_1 = p$, $\bar{A}_2 = q$, $\bar{B}_1 = r$, $\bar{B}_2 = t$.

From this it is clear that for a fixed allelic frequency r at the B_1, B_2 locus there is a heterotic equilibrium frequency p at the A_1, A_2 locus,

$$\hat{p} = s^2/(sr^2 + st^2) = r^2/(r^2 + t^2).$$

Similarly, for a fixed value of p,

$$\hat{r} = p^2/(p^2 + q^2).$$

In contrast to the more usual heterotic equilibria, however, these are not stable equilibria, because neither r nor p are in fact fixed, and they mutually interact. This can be seen by calculating the rate of change at one locus, Δp:

$$\Delta p = p' - p = (p - sp^2t^2)/(1 - sp^2t^2 - sp^2t^2 - sq^2r^2)$$
$$= (spq^2r^2 - sp^2t^2 + sp^3t^2)/(1 - sp^2t^2 - sq^2r^2)$$
$$= [spq^2r^2 - (1 - p)(sp^2t^2)]/(1 - sp^2t^2 - sq^2r^2)$$
$$= [spq/(1 - sp^2t^2 - sq^2r^2)](qr^2 - pt^2).$$

Let $K = spq/(1 - sp^2t^2 - sq^2r^2)$; let $p = 0.5 + \epsilon$; let $r = 0.5 + \phi$.

Then: $qr^2 = 0.125 + 0.5\phi + 0.5\phi^2 - 0.25\epsilon - \epsilon\phi - \epsilon\phi^2$;

$pt^2 = 0.125 - 0.5\phi + 0.5\phi^2 + 0.25\epsilon - \epsilon\phi + \epsilon\phi^2$.

From (3),

$$\Delta p = K(\phi - 0.5\epsilon - 2\phi^2\epsilon) \cong K(\phi - 0.5\epsilon)$$

and similarly,

$$\Delta r \cong K(\epsilon - 0.5\phi).$$

It can be seen from this that the equilibrium that exists at $p = r = 0.5$ is unstable:

(a) If ϕ and ϵ are both positive and $2\phi > \epsilon > 0.5\phi$, Δp and Δr will also be positive and both p and r will increase to fixation. Similarly, if both ϕ and ϵ are negative and $2\phi > \epsilon > 0.5$, p and r will both decrease to zero.

(b) If $\epsilon > 2\phi$, p will decrease and r will increase until $2\phi > \epsilon > 0.5$, in which case a then holds; similarly, for $\phi > 2\epsilon$, p and r will converge until $2\phi > 2 > 0.5\phi$, and subsequently both will continue either to fixation or loss.

(c) If ϕ and ϵ have opposite signs but are equal in value, p and r will theoretically converge toward the equilibrium value of $0.5(\phi = \epsilon = 0)$, but any random perturbations would be sufficient to send p and r either to fixation or loss.

Where there are more loci and more alleles, the effects of adaptive selection are simply swamped.

It is clear that there is something wrong with this logic as this line of reasoning leads to the conclusion that evolution cannot occur at all. This problem is also troublesome to the physical anthropologist, as much of our discipline is concerned with the adaptive evolution of present or past populations.

The discussion which derived from the difficulties generated by the molecular clock have provided a potential answer to this conundrum. The investigations of King & Wilson have used the evidence of Sarich et al to argue that it is the controlling section of Georgiev's "operon" which is evolving. This point of view, and the elaboration of its significance by King, solves the problems generated by the data discussed above. If it is rates and timing of metabolism which are primarily responsible for the production of the phenotype in development, and not the order of amino acids in the structural proteins, then the conservatism in the evolution of the active area of enzymes is no longer a problem. Furthermore, if the observation by King, that the variation for all genes is quantitative and that common mutations with minute effects are possible in the controlling regions of the DNA, then the creation of an "all or nothing" environment by coadaptation will no longer necessarily emasculate the effects of adaptive selection. Indeed, this derivation from the paradox of the molecular clock may well turn out to be one of the most significant conceptual points of the last 10 years of evolutionary studies.

CONCLUSION

The work in molecular evolution over the last few years has produced a series of problems. As Lewontin (13) articulately demonstrates, even very basic questions remain to be answered about the effect of genes in an adaptive context. The major disputes, neutralist versus selectionist, balanced versus classic, and others have been over issues which are surprisingly basic. These arguments have affected the thinking of population biologists in all disciplines, Physical Anthropology among them. Most of the gaps in our understanding of the evolutionary process have seemed at times to be growing rather than shrinking. As the tools of analysis become more precise, the data become less interpretable; at least it seems so in the more discouraging moments. The encouraging signs are that the arguments are beginning to produce the kind of clear paradox which usually precedes an improvement in understanding. The problems associated with the causes and rates of molecular evolution are a good example of this process, and the clear statement of the problems which have resulted from these controversies threaten to provide productive and hopefully conclusive lines of investigation.

Literature Cited

1. Bernstein, S. L., Throckmorton, L. H., Hubby, J. L. 1973. Still more genetic variability in natural populations. *Proc. Natl. Acad. Sci.* 70:3928–31
2. Caskey, C. T. A., Beaudet, A., Narenberg, M. 1968. RNA codons and protein synthesis. *J. Med. Biol.* 37:99–118
3. De Lange, R. J., Smith, E. L. 1971. Histones: structure and function. *Ann. Rev. Biochem.* 40:279–314
4. Dobzhansky, T. 1970. *Genetics of the Evolutionary Process.* New York: Columbia Univ. Press
5. Doolittle, R. F., Blombäck, B. 1964. Amino acid sequence investigations of fibrinopeptides from various mammals: Evolutionary implications. *Nature* 202:147–52
6. Georgiev, G. P. 1969. On the structural organization of operon and the regulation of RNA synthesis in animal cells. *J. Theor. Biol.* 25:473–90
7. Goodman, M., Moore, G. W., Farris, W., Poulik, E. 1970. The evidence from genetically informative macromolecules on the phylogenetic relationships of the chimpanzees. *Chimpanzee* 2:318–60
8. King, J. L. 1973. *Estimating relative evolutionary rates from triad sequence differences.* Presented at Workshop on Molecular Evolution, Montpellier, France
9. King, J. L. 1973. The probability of electrophoretic identity of proteins as a function of amino acid divergence. *J. Mol. Evol.* 2:317–22
10. King, J. L., Jukes, T. H. 1969. Non-Darwinian evolution. *Science* 164:788–98
11. King, J. L., Ohta, T. 1975. Polyallelic mutational equilibria. *Genetics* 79:681–91
12. King, M. C., Wilson, A. C. 1975. Evolution at two levels in humans and chimpanzees. *Science* 188: 107–15
13. Lewontin, R. C. 1974. *The Genetic Basis of Evolutionary Change.* New York: Columbia Univ. Press
14. Margoliash, E., Smith, E. L. 1965. Structural and functional aspects of cytochrome *c* in relation to evolution. In *Evolving Genes and Pro-*

teins, ed. J. Bryson, H. J. Vogel, 221–42. New York: Academic

15. Nei, M. 1971. Interspecific gene differences and evolutionary time estimated from electrophoretic data on protein identity. *Am. Nat.* 105:385

16. Nei, M., Chakraborty, R. 1973. Genetic distance and electrophoretic identity of proteins between taxa. *J. Mol. Evol.* 2:323–28

17. Ohta, T. 1972. Evolutionary rates of cistrons and DNA divergence. *J. Mol. Evol.* 1:150–57

18. Ohta, T. 1973. Slightly deleterious mutant substitutions in evolution. *Nature* 246:5978–89

19. Read, D. W. 1975. Primate phylogeny, neutral mutations, and molecular clocks. *Syst. Zoo.* 24:209–21

20. Read, D. W., Lestrel, P. E. 1970. Hominid phylogeny and immunology: a critical appraisal. *Science* 168:578–80

21. Sarich, V. M. 1972. Hominid origins revisited. In *Climbing Man's Family Tree,* ed. T. D. McCown, K. A. R. Kennedy, 450–60. New

Jersey: Prentice-Hall

22. Sarich, V. M., Wilson, A. C. 1967. Immunological time scale for hominid evolution. *Science* 158:1200–3

23. Singh, R. S., Hubby, J. L., Throckmorton, L. H. 1975. The study of genic variation by electrophoretic and heat denaturation techniques at the octanol dehydrogenase locus in members of the *Drosophila virilis* group. *Genetics* 80:637–50

24. Wilson, A. C., Kaplan, W. O., Levine, L., Pesce, E., Reichlin, M., Allison, W. J. 1964. Evolution of lactic dehydrogenases. *Fed. Proc.* 23:1258–66

25. Zuckerkandle, E., Pauling, L. 1962. Molecular disease, evolution, and genic heterogeneity. In *Horizons in Biochemistry,* ed. M. Kash, B. Pullman, 189–225. New York: Academic

26. Zuckerkandle, E., Pauling, L. 1964. In *Evolving Genes and Proteins,* ed. J. Bryon, H. J. Vogel, 97–166. New York: Academic

Ann. Rev. Anthropol. 1976. 5:93–106
Copyright © 1976 by Annual Reviews Inc. All rights reserved

THE STATE OF NON-STATE LINGUISTICS

◆ 9571

Charles-James N. Bailey
Technische Universität Berlin, Ernst-Reuter-Platz 7, Zi. 814,
1000 Berlin 10, Germany

During the past 5 to 10 years, there has grown up a framework of linguistic analysis which provides for the fact that language users possess the ability to shift styles and to understand speakers of vastly different social and regional backgrounds. Scholars working in this framework reject the reigning assumption of the structuralists (23) and transformationalists (28) that the only proper object of a linguistic formulation is an *idiolect*—what is heard from one speaker at a given moment in a given style. Limiting their work to such *monolectal* analyses has been a matter of principle for transformationalists, who are unwilling to admit the possibility that the study of variation can contribute to an understanding of linguistic competence, the object of their investigations. Everything temporal—change, nonrandom differences, and the like—belongs to *performance* and as such has no interest for the pure linguist.[1] It does not matter that variation is patterned, investigable, and part of one's linguistic ability; someone else should study it! Although many differences separate linguists working in the new framework, they agree in rejecting monolectal analyses in favor of *polylectal*[2] formulations which generate the patterned variants of a language.

The present review mentions essential developments in the study of variation, but ignores the work of many scholars who have treated the matter from within another discipline or at least without linguistic models. However, some pioneer work of prevariationist linguists deserves mention. Allen (1) showed statistically that "dialects" are gradient; Elliott, Legum & Thompson (33, 49) and Quirk (54) offer important anticipations of variation theory (cf 4); Ross's thesis (55) on

---

[1] It is now known that performance errors like slips of the tongue can be predicted with models of natural change.

[2] The term *pan-dialectal,* whose terms are mutually contradictory (contrast 6, pp. 26–27; cf 8, p. 27), has been criticized by several avid would-be critics of variation studies whose knowledge of what they criticize amounts to uninformed gossip. For reasons that are not clear to the present author, use of this term since the sixties has signaled ignorance of how theories are constructed, tested (and altered), and used.

variables in syntax will be discussed later. Kiparsky (41) made the very fruitful suggestion that instead of a feature [± foreign], one should recognize degrees of foreignness—in a pattern in which exemption from one rule implicates exemption from another, and so on (cf also 50). Short histories of the development of variation theory can be found in Bailey's work (7, 9, 14).

It is clear that a scholar setting out to investigate real language data is faced with two axiomatic frameworks. The *static paradigm* has prevailed since Saussure's views became widely accepted in the second quarter of this century. Even diachronic and dialectological studies have been pointlessly cramped into this procrustean bed; linguistic history had been viewed as a succession of *states* much earlier (cf 52). The Newtonian character of this framework is explicit in Katz's book (40, p. 115), cited and misquoted by Berdan (15, p. 13). That Chomskians accept the possibility of constructing universal theories on data that are not even universal in a room of 12 native speakers is testimony to the miraculous might and glory of preconceived notions, whose power is so lethiferous that this point of view has been accepted without qualm.

> But as soon as the theory was retracted from absolute homogeneity and dialect differences among speakers were accepted, the theory was powerless to determine whether observed variation resulted from differences among grammars or from the imperfect reflection of competence in performance. In other words, the theory could not determine in any principled way what were properly its data and what were not (15, pp. 52–53).

Such an axiomatic framework contrasts sharply with the *dynamic paradigm* (5), which is Einsteinian (to continue the trope) in accepting time as an inomissible factor in linguistic analysis.[3] The fact that innovations commence gradually, that young and old differ, that in Western societies women are often ahead of men in unmonitored speech and behind men in monitored styles,[4] and that a change begun in one class has reached others in progressively less advanced forms—all this requires time-based models in place of foot-dragging static models like phonemes, dialects,[5] and the like. Language is a millipede, not a monopode; it sings in several keys and demands a well-tempered clavier, not a pre-Bachian instrument that has to be retuned for each key! The old argument that this ideal may be true but cannot be realized for want of appropriate models is no longer valid (6, 8, 31, 45).

---

[3]The list of traits that distinguish the two paradigms (8, pp. 34–35) should be modified by deleting the words "Idiolects are not systematic," which the writer now knows to be wrong (see e.g. 61).

[4]But see (58), where in-group reversals of the feature [favored] are seen to upset the pattern in a predictable manner.

[5]The only interesting cases of isoglossic bundling are those separating castes (16). In contrast with this old conceptualization of dialects, which is easily falsifiable, is a new concept of a dialect as a constellation of implicational relationships (cf 6, p. 28; 8, p. 29). When tested out on ancient Greek (13), it agreed with the intuitions of the ancients in a way quite foreign to isoglossic findings (cf 12).

To see how languages pattern, consider Table 1. Here A, B, C, D may represent styles, social groupings, or regions, and similarly for I, II, III, and IV. Where age groupings of the two sexes are represented on one of the axes, the change will begin in a corner of the matrix. (For a matrix with linguistic variables, see Table 2 below.) Whatever the variables, the pattern stays fairly constant, but can be varied in predictable ways [e.g. by reweighting features (8, pp. 56, 83) or by a crossover principle (8, pp. 102, 108)]. What is a stylistic or age difference here is a class or areal difference there; grandfather's unmonitored style may be daughter's monitored style; or the unmonitored style of one class or ethnic group will be the monitored style of another. When a phenomenon is variable, it is usually more frequent in unmonitored style, where "natural" (10) changes begin; but hypercorrections, mostly rule inhibitions, begin in monitored styles. Many languages exhibit the phenomenon that speakers maintain in monitored styles vowel distinctions which they merge in unmonitored styles.

How does a grammar handle all this variation? The pattern shown in Table 1 might be more or less advanced in time if different parameters are used or in fact when the same parameters are used at a later time interval. What remains more or less constant is the pattern: if *d* is present, then so is *c;* if *c* is, so is *b;* and if *b* is,

Table 1   Spread of linguistic innovation from its origin in cell A-III across a matrix formed by two social or stylistic parameters [a]

	A	B	C	D
I	b	a		
II	c	b	a	
III	d	c	b	a
IV	c	b	a	

[a] The temporal order of the forms of the change is: d (most recent), c, b, a (oldest form of the change). Note that isolects having d have c; those having c have b; and those having b have a: $d \supset c \supset b \supset a$. Note further that the cell containing the most recent form of the change is presumed to be the point of origin of the innovation.

so is a.[6] How this pattern is assigned to the parameters of society is at issue among variationists. Perhaps it would be more revealing to say that what divides variationists is the issue of where one begins—with language or with geography and society. Those who begin with extralinguistic groupings in fact combine this procedure with a strictly statistical approach to the analysis of variation—thus their name *glottometrists*. Here belong Labov and his students, Cedergren, the Sankoffs, and others. Labov calls them *quantitativists, sociolinguists,* or *secularists* and refers to others as *scholastics* or *theorists*. These latter are often called *lectologists*.

As pointed out in (15), the quantitativists, no less than the transformationalists, have their own variety of *homogeneity myth*. They assume that the members of a particular area or social grouping are homogeneous. Put another way, they assume that lines (namely, *isoglosses*) can be drawn around speakers of a given area, class, sex, or age group, and that a given phenomenon (or its absence) will be found on one side of that line but not, or only variably, on the other. Glottometrists have not been deterred by the fact that such an assumption was proved incorrect in the earliest days of dialectology, by counterexamples like Nathan B. (44) or by the obvious fact that intralanguage patterns like $d \supset c \supset b \supset a$ are unaffected by whether the isoglossic approach is practical—or by whether isoglosses coincide in bundles (8, pp. 75–76). Nor has it mattered that Labov's early investigations of New York City English (44) revealed that, whereas socioeconomic differences best correlate with the inhibition of $\mathit{ə}$-deletion (the desulcalization rule), it is social differences (education and occupation apart from income) that best correlate with pronunciations of *th* in *these* and ethnic distinctions that best correlate with the raising of the vowels in *bad* and *off*. Labov's own reactions are recorded in (44, pp. 245–47). In general, glottometrists treat such facts as problems rather than as counterexamples, leaving theoretical issues to fend for themselves. They build sociological features into their rules, generally as conditions attached to the rules.[7]

The inclusion of sociological features in rules means that such rules can never serve as rules for entire *language communities,* but must be forever limited to individual *speech communities* like New York City (or some part of it), which are defined by them (8, p. 101). One may even question whether such rules are polylectal rules. To help the reader grasp what is at issue, it is necessary briefly to consider the different conceptions of polylectal rule among variationists. As employed by Bailey, a polylectal rule generates an implicational series of outputs which can then be assigned by *sociolinguistic algorithms* (8, pp. 107–8) to the social parameters of a given speech community. The validity of implicational

[6]Implicational patterns can be much more complex. The presence of q may implicate the absence of r, or conversely; or the co-occurrence of q (or not-q) and r (or not-r) may imply s or not-s. Other possibilities exist. (On resolving apparent deviations, cf 18.)

[7]See work by Cedergren and Sankoff (26, 27, 57). Labov has switched from the earlier variable-rule formulation (45) to this newer probabilistic formulation.

patterns has been discussed by many authors (3; 8, pp. 82–86; 29; 34; 36), as has the validity of the data-gathering procedures used in studying variation (15, 24, 38, 39). Such discussion can also be found in much of Labov's work and elsewhere. In contrast with dynamic (i.e. time-differentiated) outputs, the output of a rule in the quantitative framework is either a single one (that agreeing with the combination of input probabilities for a given set of social factors) or the various speech-community possibilities all at once (not in an implicational pattern). Either way, this is a static rule. This has not been understood by the glottometrists; and, like Berdan, they confuse *dynamic* with *historical,* or at least do not see that history exists here and now; Labov, however, is free of this last error.[8] Another way of employing *polylectal* rules has been proposed by Bickerton (19), where so-called polylectal rules link different systems (rather than subsystems) in a manner conjectured to be congruous with the internalized ability which language users in creole areas exhibit in switching from one variety of the language to a linguistically—and usually socially—adjacent one.[9] We do not know to what extent such polysystematic formulas and rules that generate subsystems are alike.[10]

There are several obvious problems with the glottometrists' approach, to which they have never satisfactorily addressed themselves.[11] To begin with, it is

---

[8]Strikingly, however, Labov (48, p. 37) admits that a certain figure which has appeared in most of his writings (it is the one with the stratification of r-fulness in New York) "shows us nothing about the change we know is in progress in New York City. . . ."

[9]Less astute scholars have treated this phenomenon in polyglott speakers as mere interference between systems. But polyglotts are obviously striving after an overall unity and succeeding only here and there in a systematic manner. When this striving occurs on an extensive scale, as in creoles, certain formal features of divergent systems have to be sacrificed in favor of a unified result. This is done in a systematic manner which, in Bickerton's view, is universal. These formal simplifications need not result in a simpler system, since inflectional loss (20) may be replaced by periphrastic (analytical) verbal systems which are semantactically even more complex than what went before. Since the large contribution of creole studies to variation theory and to recent linguistic theory in general is detailed by Bickerton (22) in this volume, it will not be discussed here.

[10]We do not know how to characterize linguistic systems, but their bounds obviously are gradient. [For the contrary, and erroneous, view, see Baily (6, footnote 7).] Compare "two-day, one-week" language differences in West Africa, for example, where the time referred to is that required by speakers of one variety to acquire working familiarity with another. Since certain varieties of English have more lexical vowels than others, it is easier for some speakers to understand others than conversely. Further, it is clear that lexicon and rules play different roles in mixture. While this is a truism in creole studies, it remains unknown to some would-be variationists.

[11]It is an idiosyncrasy of glottometrists that they have spent their words trying to convert transformationalist unbelievers while steadfastly sidestepping the problems raised by those variationists they regard as heretical. Their efforts to prove to the former that variation exists and is systematic will continue to frustrate them for reasons clearly set forth by Berdan (15, passim).

self-evident that group statistics may falsify the facts of individual speech (15, 17, 53), since individuals having a given phenomenon always present or always absent are lost in group statistics among the hordes whose uses of the phenomenon more obviously reflect the Great Bell Curve in the sky. This, of course, raises the issue of psychological justification, since what cannot be conceived of as learnable ought not to be proposed as an analytical reality, e.g. the internalization of statistics.[12] For the glottometrist who adheres to Labov's slogan, "Leave the brain alone!" the brain is a black box which can safely or provisionally be ignored, along with all questions of psychological justification. But there remains the locus of language ability. So far from feeling any compulsion to locate it in the brain of the individual, Labov (47, p. 83) can say in Saussurian language that "the vernacular is the property of the group, not the individual." This is an unexpectedly mystical position for a dyed-in-the-wool secularist!

Linguists of various persuasions (15, 17, 18, 21, 25, 37, 53, 61) believe that the seat of language ability is in the individual, and that correlations with social factors are an extrinsic analytical consideration. It must be clearly stated that no accumulation of statistics showing $d < c$ can *prove* that the pattern is $d \supset c$ (which, if it really exists, is what is psychologically real); such statistics may be useful, if rightly used, in discovering the inner linguistic pattern.[13]. Berdan is as far from seeing this point as any nonhybrid glottometrist, and it affects most of what he writes. In particular, he does not realize that what is *natural* can never be shown by statistics; only what is *normal* is amenable to this method-

---

[12]Sankoff has referred to materials purporting to show that children can learn probabilistic patterns; but these examples do not, so far as I know, cover anything remotely as complex as linguistic patterns actually are. Some writers have supposed that *relative* frequencies could be internalized in a way not credible for absolute frequencies. But Berdan (15, p. 66) says that "as long as . . . relative frequencies are viewed simply as descriptive of the [speech-community] corpus from which they were tabulated [,] they are of little utility [for] the construction of grammars." However, the universal nature of the Great Bell Curve in the sky does make probabilistic learning less unthinkable than other statistical learning.

[13]To the probabilistic types of rules put forth by Cedergren & Sankoff (27), Berdan (15, p. 233 and footnote 6) adds formulations with overall probabilities for rules as wholes, thus allowing for cases in which rule features are not independent. Like the transformationalists, Berdan speaks of language as though it were solely a matter of production rather than (much more so) a matter of understanding (cf 15, p. 222). Certain important misunderstandings of Bailey's position and errors of fact in (15) are discussed in (14). Other commentators fall far below Berdan's standard of conscientious reading of what he criticizes. One of these has widely propagated the notion that Bailey and others propose something so absurd that no one would propose it, namely, setting up new underlying segments for every variation (e.g. stylistic pronunciations of *coop, roof,* etc), as if the lexicon could not have variant entries! (see 8, p. 27). Most variationists have failed to grasp the essential difference between rules and lexicon (see footnote 10 above).

ology.[14] Statistics may be useful in discovering which of two possible analyses is to be preferred (15, p. 154). The problem of beginning with extralinguistic factors, as Bickerton (21, pp. 301–2) stresses, is that your charts may fail to pattern.

If we accept the fact that language variants do not fall into neat packages correlated with regions and social groupings (the isoglossic theory), and accept Bickerton's well-argued views that what the linguist is looking for is "what goes with what" (21, p. 306), how do we in practical terms arrive at our goal? Figure 1 exhibits a not untypical distribution of *isolects* (i.e. minimally different collocations of diverse phenomena) differentiated on the basis of which stage of a rule output is found in one of four linguistic environments. This schematization is based on a real example (8, p. 87). The reader is welcome to try to draw isoglosses around all examples of a/w, a/z, b/w, c/y, d/z, etc. A more rewarding procedure is that of collocating the isolects in such a way that minimally different ones are adjacent in a table like Table 2. The result is a purely linguistic pattern, made without regard to the areal pattern of Figure 1. A similar approach applies to social differences. The pattern in Table 2 can be generated with the following rule:

$$q \rightarrow a \rightarrow b \rightarrow c \rightarrow d\, /\!\!-\!\!-\; \begin{bmatrix} m\,F_i \\ m\,F_j \end{bmatrix} \qquad\qquad 1.$$

where the input segment is $//q//$, where feature F_i is more heavily weighted than F_j (written beneath instead of above F_i here), and where environment w in Table 2 is represented in Equation 1. The other environments are predicted by a metaprinciple of the theory (cf 8, p. 38), which ensures that they are generated in this sequence: after w there follows x: $[m\,F_i, u\,F_j]$, where m denotes a universally less expected, or marked, value of a feature, and u the most expected, or unmarked, value of a feature.[14] After x comes environment y: $[u\,F_i, m\,F_j]$; and finally comes z: $[u\,F_i, u\,F_j]$. The difference in the isolectal patterns to the left and right of 0, the isolect of origin, is provided for with general or specific *rate indexes* (8, p. 62) affecting various features in the rule, including those of input $//q//$, not shown in Equation 1. The approach just described has provided satisfactory analyses of patterns quite unamenable to isoglossic analysis. It does not adopt the homogeneity myth, and Nathan B. is of course no problem here. For those who do begin with extralinguistic parameters, it should be an inter-

---

[14]The positivism of Labov and his colleagues makes them immune to the force of arguments about natural directionality (e.g. 8, p. 49) and the like. Ockham rejected the idea of natures common to particulars. It is important to note here that it is not the world of "nature" in the modern sense which is at issue, but a conception of nature as the ideal realization of a thing's being; the *natural* is whatever accords with and fosters this. Thus, having colds every winter is normal but not natural, for it impedes the perfection of our nature.

[15]The mode of ascertaining these values is discussed in the Appendix of (11) and with greater detail in other writings cited there.

$$\frac{-12}{\begin{array}{l}a/w\\a/x\\a/y\\a/z\end{array}}$$

$$\frac{7}{\begin{array}{l}a/w\\a/x\\b/y\\c/z\end{array}}$$

$$\frac{-4}{\begin{array}{l}c/w\\c/x\\c/y\\c/z\end{array}}$$

$$\frac{-11}{\begin{array}{l}a/w\\a/x\\a/y\\b/z\end{array}}$$

$$\frac{1}{\begin{array}{l}b/w\\c/x\\d/y\\d/z\end{array}}$$

$$\frac{-6}{\begin{array}{l}b/w\\b/x\\c/y\\c/z\end{array}}$$

$$\frac{3}{\begin{array}{l}b/w\\b/x\\c/y\\d/z\end{array}}$$

$$\frac{-2}{\begin{array}{l}c/w\\c/x\\d/y\\d/z\end{array}}$$

$$\frac{0}{\begin{array}{l}d/w\\d/x\\d/y\\d/z\end{array}}$$

$$\frac{6}{\begin{array}{l}a/w\\b/x\\b/y\\c/z\end{array}}$$

$$\frac{-8}{\begin{array}{l}b/w\\b/x\\b/y\\b/z\end{array}}$$

$$\frac{4}{\begin{array}{l}a/w\\b/x\\c/y\\d/z\end{array}}$$

$$\frac{-1}{\begin{array}{l}c/w\\d/x\\d/y\\d/z\end{array}}$$

$$\frac{2}{\begin{array}{l}b/w\\c/x\\c/y\\d/z\end{array}}$$

$$\frac{5}{\begin{array}{l}a/w\\b/x\\c/y\\c/z\end{array}}$$

$$\frac{-9}{\begin{array}{l}a/w\\b/x\\b/y\\b/z\end{array}}$$

$$\frac{-10}{\begin{array}{l}a/w\\a/x\\b/y\\b/z\end{array}}$$

$$\frac{-3}{\begin{array}{l}c/w\\c/x\\c/y\\d/z\end{array}}$$

Figure 1 Schematized distribution of isolects (bundled phenomena) in social/geographical space. The values of a, b, c, and d are the same as in Table 2; the slant followed by w, x, y, z represents one of four environments in which the change occurs. Each isolect is numbered with an Arabic numeral, as in Table 2, with which this figure corresponds.

esting inquiry whether such social features can reweight. One presumes so, given that women delete *que* or //l// in Montreal more than men in some social classes, but less so in others.

Since for Labovians tabulations like Table 1 are, at least initially, matrices with social factors along each axis, they would agree, if I understand them, that the statistics found in such grids for desulcalization, vowel-raising, and *dh*

Table 2 Matrix of isolects[a]

Environ-ments	-12	-11	-10	-9	-8	-7*	-6	-5*	-4	-3	-2	-1	0	1	2	3	4	5	6	7
w	a	a	a	a	b	b	b	b	c	c	c	c	d	b	b	b	a	a	a	a
x	a	a	a	b	b	b	b	c	c	c	c	d	d	c	c	b	b	b	b	a
y	a	a	b	b	b	b	c	c	c	c	d	d	d	d	c	c	c	c	b	b
z	a	b	b	b	b	c	c	c	c	d	d	d	d	d	d	d	c	c	c	c

[a] No isolect violates the constituent principle that no later stage of a change (a is earliest, d is latest) is found in an earlier environment (w is earliest, z is latest) than any earlier stage of the change. The isolectal groups are numbered away from 0, where the changes are complete—the presumed origin of the change. The isolects in this table correspond to those in Figure 1. The asterisked isolects in this table are unattested in Figure 1, but predicted by the theory as possible isolects—ones to go looking for.

variation furnish the only way to discover patterns of variation in these instances and therefore to discover the directionality of the changes in question (but cf footnote 8). For this to be true, it would be necessary to show that other matrices employing only *linguistic* variants are not to be found. Those who find patterns entirely determined by linguistic variants in the data which they have examined do not believe that Labov has proved his case. His later studies of apical-stop-deletion do in fact emphasize linguistic environments.

No attempt has been made in this survey of variation studies to provide a complete bibliography, even of one's own writings, but the works referenced here provide additional references. One would like to discuss the ground-breaking article by Weinreich, Labov & Herzog (59), Parker's early utilization of the present approach in studying Quechua regional variants (51), DeCamp's early wave-like analysis of some related Anglo-Saxon changes (30),[16] as well as review in depth some of Labov's brilliant and significant studies (e.g. 45, 46, and analyses in 2, 56, and elsewhere). It is important at least to comment on the balance found in the work of Fasold and Wolfram. Cognizant of and apt at the statistical approach to gathering data, they nevertheless reject the theoretical anomalies of the glottometrists. Despite a number of errors of detail,[17] Wolfram

[16]What DeCamp (30) in 1958 treated as separate phenomena would now be regarded as instances of rule-reordering and rule-generalization. These latter are just as amenable to wave-like spreading as unconnected phenomena.

[17]Thus on pp. 62–63 it is implied that vernacular Black English *be* for *would be* is a phenomenon that is foreign to (even unmonitored styles of) standard pronunciation, even though it has been known at least since the time of Daniel Jones that standard //d// becomes /b/ before //b// (as in *tabpole, goob-bye,* and *I'b be* for *I'd be*). After this assimilation, /bb/ simplify to [b] in rapid pronunciation, leaving *be* for *'d be*. Confusion is occasionally caused in this book by failure to distinguish underlying from phonetic clusters. It is greatly to be hoped that a new edition would remove these defects.

& Fasold (62) provide the most informative, clear, and balanced introduction to variation studies for the beginner. The findings of Coleman (29) and Kucera (43), though interesting and important, suffer from ignorance of past work in the investigation of variation.[18]

Space will be taken to mention Ross's (55, p. 63) finding that (separable) verb particles like *down* in *run down* or *up* in *call up* are less easily separated from their verbs as the intervening material varies. Instead of Ross's analysis, an alternative one can now be proposed. Since smaller amounts of intervening material are more acceptable than larger amounts, and since a fixed amount is more acceptable in faster than in slower tempos, the whole process of particle-separation should be reducible to a temporal one in the new framework. In rule 2, $\underset{>}{Y}$ signifies that the rule operates more as the time taken to say Y is less:

$$X, V, \quad Particle \quad \underset{>}{Y}$$

$$\begin{array}{ccc} 1 & 2 & 3 \\ \Rightarrow 1, & 3 + 2, & \emptyset \end{array} \qquad 2.$$

Many rules—marked with > over the arrow—are more operative as the time factor is decreased; note that natural changes begin in unmonitored (including rapid) pronunciation.

All variationists agree on the causal role of society in linguistic change. Of course, one could not predict what changes are possible if universal principles and the form of an existing grammar did not conspire to predict possible types of natural change. But which of the possible changes gets propagated is socially determined, especially in the case of hypercorrections and borrowings. The timing of changes and their relative rates are certainly due to social factors. Whether all variation patterns are implicational (cf footnote 6) is not known, but this does not appear to be true. The existence of implicational patterns leads to the plausible hypothesis that the brain stores variation in some manner analogous to Venn diagrams.

Even to formulate such a hypothesis as the last is a violation of the dogmas of the Labovians. To understand the Labovian, readers are strongly urged to study Labov's latest homily (48), where he once again assembles oft-reiterated themes. Here we find an optimistic pre-Heisenbergian faith in the certainty that science can bring, at least if we quantify: "The pivotal point is the introduction of *measurement,* which converts our work from qualitative to quantitative, from iterative to cumulative, from argumentative to provable" (pp. 4–5, emphasis his). Others might wish to emphasize other aspects of what is "scientific" which are ignored by the Labovians. But in the end, one pays one's cash and takes

---

[18]A copy of the proceedings of the Second Colloquium on New Ways of Analyzing Variation (36a) arrived too late to be considered here, as it deserves to be. ʼne reader should look at the interesting articles there. Interestingly, implicational patterns have been found in the sign language of the deaf.

one's choice, for what one holds to be scientific is closely bound up with what one opts to regard as truly real.

We may lean most heavily on (static) universals, as Kiparsky (42) tends to in discussing Labov's findings, and as true-blue Chomskians apparently always do. At the opposite extreme, we may reject the whole idea of nature in linguistics and restrict our analyses to the statistical analysis of the essential flux of language in given speech communities. A third alternative is to avoid these extremes, to admit the reality and importance of this flux, but also to look for the universal relationships to which such fluctuation is subject.[19] This is what Kiparsky's general practice in fact is, and what the present writer has long advocated. The fourth possibility, eclecticism, is of no theoretical interest. The second, however, with its mechanistic view of grammar and its rejection of the principle that theory is underdetermined by data, leads to a confusion of function and form, of the normal (statistical) with the natural, and much else that might well be sidestepped. On the other hand, any predetermined choice of what data are admissable is hazardous, and more so for the theoretical-universalist approach than for the all-embracing empiricist approach.

To conclude, it seems proper for a survey of the present sort at least to mention some reasons for the recent decline of interest in variation studies and for the failure of institutes like the one held in Ann Arbor in the summer of 1973 to convert the linguistic public. It is the writer's belief that the antitheoretical posture of many variationists and the lack of theoretical ability on the part of all but a small number, as well as the frequent lack of adequate linguistic training, are responsible. Perhaps worst has been the number of investigators, including not a few epigones, who have uselessly repeated the important validations of Labov's New York research by Wolfram (60) and Fasold (35). Only a few have found much of interest. In addition, the doctrinaire definition of *data* advocated by glottometrists has been influential enough—if not among linguists, at least among those who affect linguists—to have at times given drones an edge over capable and creative scholars who reject the definition in question. The notion that the only true data are measured data may or may not win friends in the social sciences, but its effect on linguists has mostly been negative.

---

[19]It is easy to be distracted by the issue of whether implicational patterns should cut across different components of the grammar and lexicon and by the issue of whether implicational scales must be "more than an empirical accident" (15, p. 192; 32). Certainly it is true that lexical items are borrowed in patterns which are empirical accidents, for example, the introduction of new products at given times, or the use of a foreign word in a popular song. This does not prevent their forming implicational patterns with one another or with semantic, morphological, or phonological items.

Literature Cited

1. Allen, H. B. 1964 (1971). The primary dialect areas of the upper Midwest. In *Readings in American Dialectology,* ed. H. B. Allen, G. N. Underwood, 83–93. New York: Appleton-Century-Crofts. 584 pp.
2. Anderson, L. B. 1974. Distinct sources of fuzzy data: ways of integrating relatively discrete and gradient aspects of language, and explaining grammar on the basis of semantic fields. In *Towards Tomorrow's Linguistics,* ed. R. W. Shuy, C.-J. N. Bailey, 50–64. Washington DC: Georgetown Univ. Press. 351 pp.
3. Anshen, F. 1973. Some data which do not fit some models. In *New Ways of Analyzing Variation in English,* ed. C.-J. N. Bailey, R. W. Shuy, 62–68. Washington DC: Georgetown Univ. Press. 373 pp.
4. Bailey, C.-J. N. 1970. Using data variation to confirm, rather than undermine, the validity of abstract syntactic structures. *Univ. Hawaii Work. Pap. Ling.* 2/8:77–85
5. Bailey, C.-J. N. 1971. Trying to talk in the new paradigm. *Pap. Ling.* 4:312–38
6. Bailey, C.-J. N. 1972. The integration of linguistic theory: internal reconstruction and the comparative method in descriptive analysis. In *Linguistic Change and Generative Theory,* ed. R. P. Stockwell, R. K. S. Macaulay, 22–31. Bloomington: Indiana Univ. Press. 301 pp.
7. Bailey, C.-J. N. 1973. Introduction. See Ref. 3, xi–xv
8. Bailey, C.-J. N. 1973. *Variation and Linguistic Theory.* Arlington: Cent. Appl. Ling. 162 pp.
9. Bailey, C.-J. N. 1974. Contributions of the study of variation to the framework of the new linguistics. *Ling. Ber.* 29:1–10
10. Bailey, C.-J. N. 1974. Naturalness in historical reconstruction and changes that are not natural. In *Papers from the Parasession on Natural Phonology,* ed. A. Bruck, R. A. Fox, M. W. La Galy, 13–28. Chicago: Ling. Soc. 801 pp.
11. Bailey, C.-J. N. 1976. Phonology since generative phonology. *Pap. Z. Ling.* 11. In press
12. Bailey, C.-J. N. 1977. Isoglossic bundles or isolectal bundlings? In *Locational Analysis of Cultural Systems,* ed. C. L. Crumley, B. Bartel. In press
13. Bailey, C.-J. N. 1977. Old and new views of language history and language relationships. In a volume ed. H. Lüdtke. Berlin: de Gruyter. In press
14. Bailey, C.-J. N. 1977. Zum Problem der sprachlichen Variation. *Stud. Ling.* In press
15. Berdan, R. H. 1975. *On the nature of linguistic variation.* PhD thesis. Univ. Texas, Austin, Tex.
16. Bhat, D. N. S. 1970. A new hypothesis on language change. *Indian Ling.* 31:1–13
17. Bickerton, D. 1971. Inherent variability and variable rules. *Found. Lang.* 7:457–92
18. Bickerton, D. 1973. Quantitative vs. dynamic paradigms: the case of Montreal *que.* See Ref. 3, 23–43
19. Bickerton, D. 1973. The structure of polylectal grammars. In *Rep. 23rd Ann. Round Table Meet. Ling. Lang. Stud.,* ed. R. W. Shuy, 17–42. Washington DC: Georgetown Univ. Press. 351 pp.
20. Bickerton, D. 1975. *Dynamics of a Creole System.* London: Cambridge Univ. Press
21. Bickerton, D. 1975. Review of P. Trudgill's *The Social Differentiation of English in Norwich. J. Ling.* 11:299–308
22. Bickerton, D. 1976. Pidgin and creole studies. *Ann. Rev. Anthropol.* 5:169–93
23. Bloch, B. 1948. A set of postulates for phonemic analysis. *Language* 24:3–46
24. Carden, G. 1972. Multiple dialects in multiple negation. In *Pap. 8th Regional Meet. Chicago Ling. Soc.,* ed. P. M. Peranteau, J. N. Levi, G. C. Phares, 32–40. Chicago: Ling. Soc. 615 pp.
25. Carden, G. 1973. Dialect variation and abstract syntax. In *Some New Directions in Linguistics,* ed. R. W. Shuy, 1–34. Washington DC: Georgetown Univ. Press. 149 pp.
26. Cedergren, H. 1973. On the nature of variable constraints. See Ref. 3, 13–22
27. Cedergren, H. Sankoff, D. 1974. Variable rules: performance as a statistical reflection of competence. *Language* 50:333–55
28. Chomsky, N. 1965. *Aspects of the*

Theory of Syntax. Cambridge: M.I.T. Press. 251 pp.
29. Coleman, L. 1973. Why the only interesting syntactic dialects are the uninteresting ones. In *Pap. 9th Regional Meet. Chicago Ling. Soc.,* ed. C. Corum, T. C. Smith-Stark, A. Weiser, 78–88. Chicago: Ling. Soc. 709 pp.
30. DeCamp, D. 1958. The genesis of the Old English dialects: a new hypothesis. *Language* 34:232–44
31. DeCamp, D. 1971. Toward a generative analysis of a post-creole speech continuum. In *Pidginization and Creolization,* ed. D. Hymes, 349–70. Cambridge Univ. Press. 530 pp.
32. DeCamp, D. 1973. What do implicational scales imply? See Ref. 3, 141–48
33. Elliott, D., Legum, S. E., Thompson, S. A. 1969. Syntactic variation as linguistic data. In *Pap. 5th Regional Meet. Chicago Ling. Soc.,* ed. R. I. Binnick, A. Davison, G. M. Green, J. L. Morgan, 52–59. 462 pp.
34. Fasold, R. W. 1970. Two models of socially significant linguistic variation. *Language* 46:551–63
35. Fasold, R. W. 1972. *Tense Marking in Black English.* Washington DC: Cent. Appl. Ling. 254 pp.
36. Fasold, R. W. 1973. The concept of 'earlier-later': more or less correct. See Ref. 3, 183–97
36a. Fasold, R. W., Shuy, R. W., eds. 1975. *Analyzing Variation in Language: Papers from the Second Colloquium on New Ways of Analyzing Variation.* Washington DC: Georgetown Univ. Press. 327 pp.
37. Fischer, J. L. 1958. Social influences of the choice of a linguistic variant. *Word* 14:47–56
38. Greenbaum, S. 1973. Informant elicitation of data on syntactic variation. *Lingua* 31:201–12
39. Heringer, J. T. 1970. Research on quantifier-negative idiolects. In *Pap. 6th Regional Meet. Chicago Ling. Soc.,* 287–95. Chicago: Ling. Soc. 588 pp.
40. Katz, J. J. 1966. *The Philosophy of Language.* New York: Harper & Row. 326 pp.
41. Kiparsky, P. 1968. *How Abstract is Phonology?* Bloomington: Indiana Univ. Ling. Circle. 50 pp.
42. Kiparsky, P. 1971. Historical linguistics. In *A Survey of Linguistic Science,* ed. W. O. Dingwall, 576–642. College Park: Ling. Program, Univ. Maryland. 810 pp.
43. Kucera, H. 1973. Language variability, rule interdependency, and the grammar of Czech. *Ling. Inq.* 4:499–521
44. Labov, W. 1966. *The Social Stratification of English in New York City.* Washington: Cent. Appl. Ling. 655 pp.
45. Labov, W. 1972. Contraction, deletion, and inherent variability of the English copula. In *Language in the Inner City* by W. Labov, 65–129. Philadelphia: Univ. Pennsylvania Press. 412 pp.
46. Labov, W. 1973. The boundaries of words and their meanings. See Ref. 3, 340–73
47. Labov, W. 1973. The linguistic consequences of being a lame. *Lang. Soc.* 2:81–115
48. Labov, W. 1975. The quantitative study of linguistic structure. *Pennsylvania Work. Pap. Ling. Change Var.,* 1/3. Philadelphia: US Regional Survey. 66 pp.
49. Legum, S. E., Elliott, D., Thompson, S. A. 1973. *Considerations in the analysis of syntactic variation.* Presented at Ling. Soc. Am. meet., San Diego
50. Nessly, L. 1973. Nativization and variation in English phonology. See Ref. 3, 253–64
51. Parker, G. J. 1971. Comparative Quechua phonology and grammar V: the evolution of Quechua B. See Ref. 4, 3/3:45–109
52. Paul, H. Reprinted 1970. *Prinzipien der Sprachgeschichte.* Tübingen: Niemeyer Verlag. 428 pp. 8th ed.
53. Pfaff, C. W. 1973. *A sociolinguistic study of black children in Los Angeles.* PhD thesis, Univ. Calif., Los Angeles, Calif. High Wycomb, England: Univ. Microfilms
54. Quirk, R. 1965. Descriptive statement and serial relationship. *Language* 41:205–17
55. Ross, J. R. 1967. *Constraints on variables in syntax.* PhD thesis. Mass. Inst. Technol., Cambridge, Mass. Bloomington: Indiana Univ. Ling. Circle
56. Ross, J. R. 1973. A fake NP squish. See Ref. 3, 96–140
57. Sankoff, G. 1973. Above and beyond phonology in variable rules. See Ref. 3, 44–61
58. Trudgill, P. 1972. Sex, covert pres-

tige, and linguistic change in the urban British English of Norwich. *Lang. Soc.* 1:179–95

59. Weinreich, U., Labov, W., Herzog, M. I. 1968. Empirical foundations for a theory of language change. In *Directions for Historical Linguistics*, ed. W. P. Lehmann, Y. Malkiel, 95–195. Austin: Univ. Texas Press. 199 pp.

60. Wolfram, W. 1969. *A Sociolinguistic Description of Detroit Negro speech*. Washington DC: Cent. Appl. Ling. 237 pp.

61. Wolfram, W. 1973. On what basis variable rules? See Ref. 3, 1–12

62. Wolfram, W., Fasold, R. 1974. *The Study of Social Dialects in American English*. Englewood Cliffs: Prentice-Hall. 239 pp.

Ann. Rev. Anthropol. 1976. 5:107–31
Copyright © 1976 by Annual Reviews Inc. All rights reserved

KIN GROUPS: STRUCTURAL ANALYSIS AND THE STUDY OF BEHAVIOR

♦ 9572

Ladislav Holy

Department of Social Anthropology, Queen's University, Belfast, Northern Ireland

Surveying the progress of kinship studies in recent years, Goody made the following observation:

> . . . in recent years we have largely abandoned that whole middle ground that exists between the detailed analysis of single societies and the generalized discussion of concepts, such as filiation and descent, alliance and affinity. Both these other perspectives are necessary, but they do not exhaust the anthropological study of kinship; indeed they exclude what could be its most promising field, the theories of middle range. Some middle areas such as the study of lineage systems and prescriptive marriage have made progress, even though there has been a marked tendency for the writers in these fields to identify their interest with the study of kinship, even anthropology itself (34, p.ix).

The increasing tendency to ascribe important theoretical significance to the recent anthropological analyses to which Goody refers is a trend which is clearly observable not only in writings on kinship but in almost any other anthropological subject as well. It is a conscious or intuitive reflection on the present stage of the development of the anthropological discipline. This is a stage of perpetual and increasing questioning of the hitherto reigning paradigm, to use Kuhn's terminology, which manifests itself primarily in the fact that fewer and fewer anthropologists have been prepared to do what he calls "normal science" (47). It is difficult to establish when the present stage actually began. An increasing move in all fields of anthropological enquiry, from the homeostatic functional models constructed from social forms to dynamic models whose components are seen as social processes, has been noticeable over the last 20 years or so, and quite distinctly so in the past decade.

STRUCTURAL ANALYSIS

In considering how this move is reflected in the field of kin group studies, a brief outline of the basic methodological procedures of structural analysis is a fitting

107

point of departure, particularly because of the prominence of the concept of kin groups, or specifically descent groups, within its framework. In structural analysis, the social structure of a society was formulated by the investigator through various processes of abstraction from his observation of the behavior of actual individuals (cf 59, p. 192) and in explanation, the concrete behavior of individuals was seen as determined by demands of the social structure. In structural-functional anthropology, the analytical and explanatory model of descent groups as structures of jural obligations became a model of society par excellence. The reason for this lies in the second major methodological approach of structural anthropology: it is the endeavor to associate corporate groups with systems of activities. The result of this approach is a formulation of corporate groups normatively performing certain activities and a conception of certain activities as performed by members of a specific group. The overall structure of society is then formulated as the system of discrete groups, each of them performing a certain set of activities. In this model, the factors which determine the behavior of individuals are identical with the factors which form social structure (cf 83, pp. 2, 180). To be able to ascribe activities to groups, the groups which form the components of the structure have to be discrete, clearly bounded and not overlapping, and with unambiguous membership; they have to be segments [cf Middleton & Tait's (54) concept of "nuclear groups" and Sahlins' (68) concept of "residential proprietary segment"]. It was precisely these demands of the structural approach that led to the ascription of primary importance to the concept of descent and that determined the way in which descent was defined (cf 77, p. 75 on this point).

The definition of descent as employed by structural analysts goes back to the work of Rivers, who distinguished it analytically from inheritance and succession and defined it as the process regulating membership of a social group or class (64, p. 851; 65, p. 85 ff). Implied in his definition of descent is the notion that this term should be used only in reference to groups to which recruitment occurs automatically by virtue of birth, and which are exclusive in membership, clearly bounded, and do not overlap. In his usage then, descent was defined as a principle of recruitment into unilineal descent groups, as Leach (51, p. 130) has explicitly stated.

In the structural model, descent groups are conceptualized as corporate groups. The descent group has the identity of a single individual when viewed from outside or in relation to the jural-political sphere; it has an estate consisting of joint rights in material or immaterial property or differential privileges, and the relations within it are relations of incorporation and sharing. Not only is the recruitment of individuals into groups structurally determined by their descent, but also by their unquestionable and enduring loyalty to the group. Each individual derives his main social identity from his membership in the group. The concept of corporate unilineal descent group refers to formal jural criteria; in consequence, the rules governing each individual's behavior qua member of the group, as well as the intergroup relationships, are envisaged as having jural force (23, 24). As Buchler & Selby have observed (10, p. 92), this approach to the conceptualization of segments of the total social system arbitrarily seizes upon descent as one aspect of social life and gives it an inflated importance that may far outweigh its significance for ongoing social processes. LaFontaine, in her defense of the structural model, explicitly advocates this approach in the following way:

> It is clear that the principle of descent defined here is a means of allocating membership of segments of society. That is, an individual is placed within the society into which he is born by reference to his membership of a segment of it. It underlies the allocation of status, including political privileges and liabilities, and often legitimizes rights to various forms of property (48, p. 36).

The notion of descent as the main structural principle derives directly from African ethnography accumulated during fieldwork carried out in the 1940s and early 1950s. When new ethnography became extensively available from India, Burma, Ceylon, Indonesia, and South America, it became increasingly obvious that in explanation of the social structure of many societies in these areas, the main structuring importance could not be ascribed to the principle of descent. New structuring principles were sought and found in enduring alliances between groups. As a result of this development, the anthropological study of kin groups in the 1960s was dominated by the discussion between the proponents of the "alliance theory," developed mainly by Lévi-Strauss, Dumont, Leach, and Needham, and the proponents of "descent theory," developed mainly by Radcliffe-Brown, Evans-Pritchard, Fortes, Goody, Gough, Gluckman, and, to a certain extent, Firth (for a review of the discussion and bibliographical references, cf 10, 77).

On the ethnographical level, the discussion between "alliance" and "descent" theorists was basically the discussion between ethnographers working predominantly in Southeast Asia on the one hand and in Africa on the other. On the theoretical level it was a discussion between proponents of two kinds of structuralism: that of Lévi-Strauss, that depicts the structure as an entailment of perpetual alliance between segments, and the structural-functionalism of Radcliffe-Brown, that depicts the segmentary structure as a logical entailment of unilineal descent. Its central issue was the problem of how the social reality is structured or how the components of the structure are integrated into a system. Schneider pointed out clearly that

> (t)wo different kinds of system, each made up of identically structured segments, are really at issue. In one system, the segments are articulated into a logically interrelated system by the descent rule, the mode of classification of kinsmen, and the relationship of perpetual alliance between segments. In the other, the segments are defined by the descent rule, exogamy, and the variable bounding of the segments in terms of special functions (domestic, jural, political, residential, territorial, and so on) (77, p. 58).

The discussion and controversy between alliance and descent theorists was a discussion and controversy within one scientific paradigm. Underlying it was an agreement on societies existing as systems held in a state of equilibrium, and on actual physical segments being component parts of these systems.

Barth (6) recently distinguished another kind of system besides the alliance and descent systems. it is a system of some Middle Eastern societies where segments are defined by descent rule, but no rule of exogamy relates these segments in marriage exchanges with other segments of the same kind. Allowed or preferred marriages between patrilateral parallel cousins have important consequences for the internal structure of descent groups.

In this system, actors conceive of all kinship and affinal relations as basically "of the same kind." This limits considerably the range of descent group affairs. These focus primarily on property and the control of territory; they relate to a particular joint tangible estate. Political confrontations do not follow a segmentary pattern of fusion and fission; the opposed units are not unilineal descent segments but factions whose members are recruited on the basis of their friendship as well as on the basis of ties of cognatic, affinal, and some ties of agnatic kinship between them.

Although Barth's interest, like the interest of structural anthropologists, lies in formulating social structure, he departs from the structural analysis in that he treats as problematic the way in which structure is generated from the behavior of concrete individuals, and in that he specifically concentrates on the analysis of the processes through which structural premises and instances of individual behavior are connected (5, 6). The problems of anthropological enquiry he thus formulates were not—and could not have been—taken as problematic in the structural model. Most of the theoretical criticisms of the structural model have regarded it as deficient primarily for its inability to treat as problematic the relations between structural forms and actual behavior. Thus Schneider criticized it for its "failure clearly to distinguish the segment as a conceptual entity from its concrete counterpart as a group" (77, p. 75). Buchler & Selby pointed out that the model eliminates "the possibility of establishing correspondence rules that link theoretic constructs with behavioral systems. This is due to an exclusive concern with the system of jural constraints which structure the basic actual framework" (10, p. 102). Barth criticized the model "for seeking explanation too exclusively on the conceptual side of the dichotomy" between the segment as a conceptual entity and its counterpart as a group (5, p. 6). Smith, a long time before him, expressed a similar criticism when he argued that the "weakness of lineage theory and study . . . has been to mistake the ideology for actuality, and not to look behind it for the more general and abstract categories of action, in terms of which it is to be explained and its constitution determined" (78, p. 65).

All the criticisms raised against the model on the ethnographic plane address themselves equally to this problematic relation between the segment and its jural correlates as structural constructs and the observable behavior of living people. It has been noted many times that the behavior of the Nuer does not correspond in detail to Evans-Pritchard's description in ideal terms (28, 29, 35–37, 55, 68). Evans-Pritchard resolves the inconsistency between his model and the actual behavior which the model is purported to explain by declaring the principles on which the model is constructed as being unchallenged by the Nuer (16; 17, especially p. 28). This process of reasoning which Schneider has called "para-doxical obfuscation" (77, p. 74) amounts not so much to explaining the inconsistency as to dismissing it from consideration. Such dismissal was possible only because the whole analysis was geared to the description of the formal social structure of Nuer society, and the concrete instances of behavior were used merely as apt illustrations (cf 30) of the validity of the postulated structural principles.

NEW GUINEA AND MELANESIAN ETHNOGRAPHY

The problem of the relation between social structure and actual behavior could no longer be dismissed as nonexistent when new ethnographic data, mainly from societies in the New Guinea Highlands and in Melanesia, became increasingly available in the late 1950s and early 1960s. The fieldwork during which the data were collected was governed by the modern requirements of detailed ethnographic recording, supplemented by quantitative information obtained through census techniques. The quantitative data thus produced were not so easy to accommodate into the model of corporate, segmentary lineage systems as had been the basically qualitative descriptions on the basis of which the model had originally been built in the 1940s. The ethnographers working in the New Guinea Highlands pointed out that however much the ideology of patrilineal descent might have been normative there, the relation between the normative structure and the actually observable behavior was highly problematic. They were able to identify major territorially based political units within New Guinea societies, which they usually described as "clans." They reported that the clans were conceived by the natives as groups of agnatically related men and that they functioned as corporate groups with respect to land tenure, war, ceremonial exchange, and exogamy. The New Guinea ethnography demonstrated first of all that although the Highlanders might ideally recognize patrilineal descent as a principle of recruitment into corporate groups, in practice they disregard this principle to considerable extent and freely admit cognates and affines into the local descent group and, after a relatively short period of time, treat them as full members. On the other hand, nonresident agnates are very soon forgotten and become lost to the local descent group. Not only the ties of agnatic kinship, but cognatic and affinal ties as well, give people access to land. Agnates, cognates, and affines alike contribute to an individual's bridewealth, etc. All this led to the characterization of New Guinea societies as "loosely structured," as Held (38) and Pouwer (57) expressed it.

As the direct result of the theoretical development of social anthropology in the 1950s, the most obvious model to apply in the New Guinea Highlands was the model of corporate segmentary lineage system which envisaged the patrilineal lineage as the most important social group in the Highlands and as a segment of a more inclusive structure (cf 61, p. 11). Some anthropologists conceptualized the basic groups in New Guinea as descent groups, and considered patrilineal descent to be the most important structural principle (e.g. 7–9, 41, 66, 70, 71), though they expressed reservations about the direct applicability to the New Guinea scene of the model of corporate segmentary lineage systems described for uncentralized African societies. Other anthropologists, however, not only considered the basic groups in New Guinea to be lineage segments, but also maintained that the model of corporate segmentary lineage systems is applicable in New Guinea without modification (48).

In 1962, Barnes dismissed as a mirage the application of the model of African unilineal descent systems to New Guinea (2, p. 4). He argued that group ideology, processes of recruitment, and patterns of segmentation all make it doubtful whether New Guinea Highlands societies can be "characterized by patrilineal descent," and suggested that these societies might better be viewed as employing" cumulative patrifiliation . . . as a principle of group recruitment" (2, p. 6). Similarly, Scheffler has recently argued that native conceptualizations of the groups as composed of "brothers" or the "sons of one father" need not imply patrilineal constitution (76, p. 778). Although cognatic descent groups exist in some New Guinea societies (27), and patrilineal descent groups probably do exist in others (53; but cf also 3), according to Scheffler, the principal structural framework of many Highland societies is provided by the genealogical and social relations of paternal and fraternal kinship (76, p. 780). According to Scheffler, "such groups might therefore be described as patrifilial *kin* groups rather than patrilineal descent groups" (76, p. 780).

In response to Barnes's argument that in New Guinea systems cumulative patrifiliation rather than agnatic descent is the main principle of group affiliation, due probably to the special character of natural resources (2, p. 8), Meggitt suggested that "where the members of a homogeneous society of horticulturalists distinguish in any consistent fashion between agnates and other relatives, the degree to which social groups are structured in terms of agnatic descent and patrilocality varies with the pressure on available agrarian resources" (53, pp. 266, 280; cf also 63). Where land is scarce, the allocation of land to sisters' sons will be rare, movement of individuals between local groups will be restricted, and the composition of local groups will tend to be determined by agnatic descent. Barnes (3) and Strathern (80, p. 39 ff) rejected the scarcity of land as a possible factor shaping the de facto composition of local groups because of specific ethnographic cases which defy the hypothesis and because of the conceptual difficulty involved in the definition of "agnatic structure," which might refer to the conceptualization of group segments as well as to the processes of recruitment into them. In his criticism of the analysis correlating patrilineal group constitution with the scarcity of land, Scheffler points out that when land is scarce but rights in estates are divided rather than joint and brothers or classificatory brothers have reversionary interests in one another's parcels, "even though a mother's brother may wish to make a grant of land and may have the right to do so, he may effectively be prevented from making it by his brothers who have reversionary interests in his land and who may not wish to imperil their or their sons' interests in it" (76, p. 779). The resulting tendency of local groups to be composed of men related to one another through their fathers, their fathers'

fathers, etc need no more be a consequence of rigid adherence to a patrilineal group constitution than it is in the areas where land is not scarce and mothers' brothers freely allocate parcels of land to their sisters' sons (76, p. 780).

Allen (1), on the basis of his research among the Nduindui in the New Hebrides, argues that the tendency of a local group to be composed of men related to one another through patrifilial or patrilineal ties (the distinction is not critical to his argument) ceases to appear once a certain level of population density and land shortage is reached. Beyond this point the adaptation of groups to the fluctuation of resources, and to the population increase in some of these groups, cannot be resolved by warfare, and the only alternative is to employ mechanisms of adjustment based on the utilization of all available ties of kinship and affinity, leading to the crystallization of groups of co-residing cognates. In this way he reconciles Meggitt's hypothesis with that of Goodenough (32), who suggested that cognatic systems may be regarded as functionally advantageous in situations of high population density and heavy pressure on land resources (cf also 9, p. 75).

All participants in the ongoing discussion about the analysis and explanation of New Guinea ethnography have been addressing themselves to the problem of the formulation of an analytic and explanatory model applicable to these "loosely structured" societies. The discussion, however, differs in one significant respect from the discussion between alliance and descent theorists. Despite frequent disagreement whether and to what extent social structure and social segments are a formulation of empirical reality existing independently of the observer, or whether they are the anthropologist's construct (cf 77 for the survey of this discussion), there has been an agreement among the proponents of both alliance and descent theories that segments (whether as concrete or as conceptual entities) are the components of the structure. What has been disputed is how these components are integrated into a system. There is a much deeper disagreement among the participants in the current discussion. What is being disputed is not only how the components of the structure are integrated into a system in the New Guinea Highlands but also what these components actually are. What is at issue first of all is what the most important social groups or segments in the Highlands are and how they can properly be conceptualized. All ethnographers seem to be agreed that the most important social groups in New Guinea are the groups of co-residents in a given territory. As I have tried to show, where there has not been an agreement, what is the subject of ongoing controversy among anthropologists is in terms of which ties, other than the territorial ones, do the natives themselves conceptualize these groups, and in terms of which ties, other than the territorial ones, can the anthropologist best conceptualize them. Another issue is the definition of significant variables of the New Guinea systems and the relations between them.

Noting the widely reported lack of status discrimination against nonagnatic members of the New Guinea residential groups, de Lepervanche considers "locality as a primary structural principle" in the Highlands (13, p. 140). Although she herself does not intend to construct a model of Highland systems, it is obvious from her analysis that such a model would have to be one of a system of local groups in which warfare and the role of big men in political relations would be important structural principles. Her treatment of locality as a primary structural principle is very close to the position of other anthropologists (e.g. 14, 49, 50, 56, 58) who, like de Lepervanche herself, are aware of the inadequacy of African models in the Highlands and have likewise emphasized the structural importance of locality, warfare, and of big men in Highland social structure. Newman, for example, stresses that the sources of community integration lie in the power structure and not the kinship structure in that people think of themselves as a group because of their reciprocity and allegiance to a big man (56, pp. 59, 61).

In his attempt to construct an explanatory model of New Guinea Highland societies, Strathern (80) demonstrates, through a comparative study, that descent in these societies usually stresses the unity of the clan group, while recruitment to the group is through patrifiliation supplemented by using the ties of affinity and matrifiliation, the ties of common residence, participation in exchanges, joining the following of a big man, etc. He considers also the political and intermarriage alliances between groups, ties with affines and maternal kin, warfare, initiation rituals, and relations between the sexes as important structural principles. He concludes by saying that even when it can be suggested in the analysis of a single system how these principles are interrelated, it is much more difficult to incorporate them into a model applicable to all New Guinea societies.

Although the discussion about the interpretation and understanding of New Guinea ethnography has far from achieved its aim of formulating a model, alternative to the model of segmentary descent systems, which would be applicable to New Guinea societies, and although Barnes's observation that the task of understanding the significant variations in the New Guinea societies "is a long way from completion" (4, p. 4) is as true today as when it was made, the discussion has certainly had a positive result in formulating new problems for investigation. These issues could not have arisen in the framework of the structural analysis which treats all behavior as determined by the demands of social structure, as I have mentioned before. The very recognition of these problems clearly indicates the shift in emphasis in what is treated as problematic. The anthropologists working in New Guinea and Melanesia have been concerned not only with the formulation of the social structure and analysis of how this structure works, but also with the formulation of the structure in such a way that it would subsume not only the normative actions but all the variations in the actual behavior as well. In this way, what became one of their main concerns was the explanation of the actual behavior of living individuals. This considerable shift in emphasis was probably the result of the combination of two factors: (a) the confrontation with new data in need of explanation, and (b) new questions being asked about the data. Proponents of the model of the segmentary lineage system do not seem to have any difficulty in analyzing and interpreting these new data (cf 48), so asking new questions about the data obviously must have been a much more decisive factor. The whole shift in emphasis is thus due to changing "epistemological orientation rather than ethnographic fact" (10, p. 90), or as LaFontaine rightly observed, "what is involved here is a difference in emphasis which can be explained in terms of the history of anthropological theory rather than the geography of anthropological field-work" (48, p. 41).

LOCAL AND KIN GROUPS

One of the problems which discussion about the analysis and interpretation of New Guinea and Melanesian ethnography has brought into the forefront of methodological attention is the problem of relations between locality and descent or kin groups. Kroeber argued that traits connected with formal social organization, such as unilineal descent reckoning, are "in a sense epiphenomena to other underlying phenomena, such as place of residence" (46, p. 217). Evans-Pritchard similarly stressed the primacy of territory in his model of segmentary lineage structure (16, p. 265). On the other hand, Fortes holds lineage and locality to be independently variable, and he suggests that how they interact depends on other factors in the social structure. For him, local ties are of secondary significance, "for (they) do not appear to give rise to structural bonds in and of themselves" (23, p. 36; cf 78 for discussion of these two lineage models).

In ascribing structural importance to local ties, Langness (49) and de Lepervanche (13) seem to depart furthest from Fortes' position. But even if the "commitment to maintain the group strength can and does override descent as a recruitment principle (49, p. 169; similarly 13, p. 143), descent (Langness, de Lepervanche) or kinship (Scheffler) still seems to be an ideology in whose terms the solidarity of the local group is expressed. Immigrants seem to be quickly absorbed into the group and all male group members refer to one another as "brothers." They assert that they are descendants of a single ancestor and to that extent think of themselves as a group. Thus New Guinea data, including Langness's own, seem to give credence to Fortes's contention that locality does not give rise to structural bonds in itself unless the ties of co-residence are converted into the ties of kinship. It has often been pointed out that this process is facilitated by a lack of interest in genealogies or genealogical amnesia (e.g. 13, p. 134; 62, p. 35; 69, p. 106; 82, p. 28). Cook rightly rejects attributing a causal function to "genealogical amnesia" in the process of conversion of nonagnates into agnates among the Manga of New Guinea. He points out that "imputing an instrumental function to 'genealogical amnesia,' that is, as exterminating anomalies of 'agnatic derivation' . . . may be a case of giving post facto a cause to certain events; as such it does not constitute an explanation of those events" (12, p. 195). Recently specific attention has been paid to analyzing mechanisms which facilitate the conversion of resident nonmembers into members of the group with which they live. Strathern (82), following Salisbury's discussion of the Siane (72, 73) and his own ethnographic data on the Melpa, suggests that the process of conversion of co-resident cognates into full members of the agnatic group associated with a given locality is facilitated by the natives' parallel conceptualization of identity through locality and identity through descent. Clansmen share identity because they share substance through their descent from a common ancestor. Another way in which they share substance is through the consumption of food grown on clan land. Food creates substance just as procreation does, and thus it is a mediator between locality and kinship in the natives' conceptual world. Unlike Strathern, Cook (12) concentrates on the terminological system as a mechanism facilitating conversion. He demonstrates convincingly that among the Manga, who make a cross/parallel distinction of Seneca type which is ignored in the first descending generation, the terminology facilitates the nominal conversion of nonagnates into agnates. But in my opinion, he is not justified in deriving the conclusion from this process of terminological conversion that "genealogical amnesia" is an epiphenomenon of the kinship terminological system in the sense of being induced through terminological usage (12, p. 195).

First, if "genealogical amnesia" were induced solely through terminological usage, only those joined through one female link to the lineage with which they reside (i.e. those father's father's sister's son's children of the agnates with whom they reside) could count as its agnatic members; the genealogical links of other nonagnatic members of the lineage presumably would remain remembered. Second, if "genealogical amnesia" were induced solely by terminological usage, how could we account for it in societies with different terminological systems?

Although Cook is certainly right in stressing that genealogical amnesia does not cause anything (12, p. 195), it seems that rather than being an epiphenomenon of the kinship terminology, it may better be regarded as epiphenomenal to the behavioral patterns. Thus Scheffler (76) points out that co-residence of nonmembers with a group is a necessary but not a sufficient condition for their gradual conversion into group members. He argues that performance by nonmembers of duties normally deriving from membership in the group leads to the group granting them concomitant rights. By the same token, nonmembers holding rights in spatially fixed resources, which are allocated by descent but also acquirable by other means, will eventually come to be considered full members of the group (76, p. 777).

In the process of conversion of nonmembers into members, Scheffler thus ascribes equal significance to the performance of duties deriving from membership and to the holding of rights which normally derive from membership. This is probably not fully justified. It seems that the process of conversion outlined by Scheffler is rather strictly unidirectional in the sense that the performance of duties might lead to the granting of membership rights, but the holding of rights in spatially fixed resources does not necessarily have to lead to the performance of duties. It is precisely for this reason that nonmembers may only become identified as a separate lineage attached to the lineage associated with the given locality (cf 16, 21, 22). Moreover, in a situation where it is possible to obtain rights in local estate, not only on account of descent but on account of various ties of individual kinship as well, the holding of rights in spatially fixed resources is in no way indicative of the holder's group membership either to the outsiders or to the group members themselves.

In analyzing the process of conversion of nonmembers into members, it is useful to bear in mind Barth's reminder that "some empirical events are far more pregnant with consequences than others" (6, p. 4), and to realize that the performance of some activities is more indicative of group membership than the performance of others. In my analysis of the conversion of nonagnates into full members of agnatic lineages among the Berti (39, 40), I tried to show that participation in the interlineage compensation payments is indicative of group membership because it is an activity through whose performance the individual unequivocally proclaims his membership, and the group in which he claims membership, again unequivocally, either confirms it or rejects it. Although it is possible for an individual to contribute to compensation payments in two groups for some time and thus to claim membership in both, his membership in only one of them is clearly asserted through his own behavior and through the behavior of other group members when both groups are in conflict and the conflict is to be resolved by one group paying compensation to the other. I would hypothesize that not all rights and duties deriving from group membership will be equally strongly indicative of an individual's group affiliation; activities through whose performance he demonstrates his loyalty to one group and denies his loyalty to another, in situations when his simultaneous loyalties come into conflict, are "more pregnant with consequences" for the recognition of his group affiliation.

DESCENT IDEOLOGY AND BEHAVIOR

Another problem which the discussion concentrating on the interpretation of New Guinea data has clearly delineated, and made an object of theoretical interest reaching far beyond the limits of New Guinea ethnography, is the problem of the discrepancy between the ideology of descent and actual behavior or "statistical norms," as Langness put it (49, p. 182). The problem was implied for the first time by Read (60, p. 155) and Elkin (15, p. 169), who stated with reference to the Gahuku-Gama and the Wabag of the Central Highlands that patrilineality is the most important structural principle, although deviations with respect to group recruitment, political relations, and segmentation do exist. The problem has been explicitly formulated by Langness (49) and Watson (86) and recognized as such by Berndt (7).

De Lepervanche has noted that if the problem is formulated as "the discrepancy between ideology and statistical norms," "this sounds as if ideology descended from heaven upon a collection of Highlanders who did not conform to its demands" (13, p. 168). What kind of confusion is involved here? Fortes pointed out that what is "conducive to analytical confusion as well as to misinterpretation of the empirical data of kinship and social organization" is the "diffuse and discursive usage of such key concepts as 'descent' and 'descent group' " (25, p. 280). In my view, it is not so much the "diffuse and discursive usage" of key concepts which leads to confusion and disagreement about the interpretation of empirical data, but rather the continuing use of concepts developed within the framework of the structural theory for answering the questions asked outside this framework. The core of the confusion is not so much the interpretation of empirical data as such, or the disagreement about the definition of the concepts, as a failure to realize that a concept which had been defined in a specific way to cope with problems derived from a certain theoretical framework is not suitable for coping with problems formulated outside this framework. In other words, the core of the confusion is the failure to realize that a concept which might have its origin in a certain ethnography is not elevated to the status of an analytical concept because of its capacity to provide a kind of "metalanguage" by which a wide range of ethnographic data can be adequately described, but because it enables the analyst to organize his ethnographic data in such a way that he can accommodate them within his theoretical model. In the final analysis, a concept is not derived from ethnography but from theory. It is defined in such a way as to enable the analyst to explain his data within his theory.

The key concept in the formulation of the problem of discrepancy between ideology and actual behavior then, is the concept of descent; the problem of discrepancy arises because social groups are ideally but not actually patrilineal (cf 49). In Strathern's words, " 'the' ideology could thus be taken as read and sociological explanations advanced for the discrepancies between it and 'actual' behavior" (82, p. 25).

The problem could have been formulated in this way only because of the failure to realize that a concept of descent as a principle of recruitment into unilineal descent groups has not some universal heuristic value but is defined in this way "in the interest of protecting a typology of segmentary system" and of "the model of a segment as a physically distinct entity" (77, p. 75). If the Highlanders themselves use an agnatic idiom to express group solidarity, or if, as Watson puts it, patrilineal ideology provides "an idiom in terms of which local groups may speak of others and of themselves to others" (86, p. 14), the problem of discrepancy between ideology and actual behavior can arise only (a) when it is assumed that the concept the natives use is the concept of descent, and (b) when it is assumed at the same time that descent refers to principles of recruitment into groups (i.e. when the analyst fails to realize that the recruitment meaning attributed to the concept of descent is not a universally valid generalization of ethnographic fact but a meaning ascribed to the concept for the sake of maintaining consistency of a certain analytical and theoretical framework). The reasoning behind the formulation of the problem of discrepancy between ideology and actual behavior (or statistical norm) is thus the following: the natives conceptualize group solidarity in descent terms; they then ideally conceptualize their groups as descent groups in the sense that descent is a principle of recruitment into them; descent, however, does not govern actual behavior of living individuals which the anthropologist observed, hence the discrepancy between ideology of descent and actual behavior.

Such a discrepancy does not arise when the concept of descent ceases to be regarded "as both a translation term and an analytical concept relating to the definition of membership in bounded corporations" (81, p. 185) and is given a definition which would enable it to be employed as a translation term only. Scheffler has done precisely this. He has rejected the definition of descent as a "process whereby persons become members of corporate kin groups" (74, p. viii; cf also 75, p. 544; and for an analysis of a society with a descent rule but without descent groups, see 87). Following Fortes's definition of descent as a "relation mediated by a parent between himself and an ancestor, defined as any genealogical predecessor of the grandparental or earlier generation" (24, p. 207; 25, p. 281), he proposes to regard descent as "relationship by genealogical tie to an ancestor" (75, p. 542) and suggests that wherever such relationships are recognized in a particular society, we can speak of "descent constructs." He calls the norms which employ such constructs, "descent-phrased rules" (75, p. 543). Scheffler, criticizing Rivers' definition of descent, stresses that it is important

> "to distinguish between 1) cultural or ideological constructs and the social processes they may regulate or validate and 2) types of social processes and types of cultural forms, e.g. rules or their components. If we do this, we may distinguish group affiliation, succession and inheritance *processes* in terms of the kind of status involved in each, as Rivers had to do in any event; we may recognize as descent-constructs some of those genealogical forms which may occur in each of these three contexts of status transmission; and finally we may designate as descent-phrased rules those norms which incorporate, or in which are manifest, the various genealogical forms we call descent-constructs (75, p. 542–43).

What Scheffler advocates here is "the necessity to distinguish between ideational (cultural) forms and social transactional structures or processes" (75, p. 543). Such a distinction enables us to "look separately at what the structure of a people's constructs is and at the way in which these are utilized to determine a distinction of rights in their social life" (81, p. 185).

According to Scheffler, the confusion involved in the formulation of the discrepancy between ideology and actual behavior does not derive from the reification of the concept of descent in its limited meaning as the principle of recruitment (as I have tried to show), but from a more basic confusion of descent constructs with the simple recognition of several successive filial steps "which is a more general phenomenon constituting the basis of what we call kinship" (75, p. 543).

He argues that the New Guinea ethnographers wrongly assumed that the concept the natives themselves use to conceptualize solidarity of the local group is the concept of descent. He suggests that the position of fathers and sons and of brothers in a genealogical continuum is not at issue in New Guinea, and that although the natives describe their groups as composed of "brothers" or of "sons of one father," the relations between and within groups are conceptualized simply in terms of kinship and not descent (76, p. 778). Such generalization, however, is probably not fully justified. Strathern, who uses the concept of descent in its wider meaning of any genealogically reckoned relationship with an ancestor (81, p. 8), demonstrates convincingly that although the Melpa are recruited into their groups on the basis of filiation, the solidarity, continuity, and segmentation patterns of their social groups are referred to and symbolized at least partly in terms of descent-constructs (81, pp. 8, 24). The same seems to hold true for at least some other Highland societies [e.g. Daribi (85) or Siane (72, p. 170; 73)].

NATIVES' AND ANTHROPOLOGISTS' CATEGORIES AND CONCEPTS

The confusion which Scheffler points out in relation to the problem of discrepancy between ideology and actual behavior is basically a confusion between natives' and anthropologists' categories and concepts. In deciding on whether the natives conceptualize their groups in terms of relations of descent or kinship, the natives' own categories and the anthropologist's analytical categories might quite simply not have been clearly distinguished. Yet in deciding on what is the composition of the local groups in the New Guinea Highlands, and in attempts to find out how these groups might best be conceptualized by the anthropologist (in contradistinction to how they are conceptualized by the natives), a clear and conscious distinction between natives' categories and the anthropologist's own analytical categories is the important point of departure. Describing the composition of local groups in terms of his own analytical categories is thought to enable the anthropologist to establish what these groups represent in the world of the objective fact (again in contradistinction to whatever the natives might subjectively take them for). I would suggest that a confusion between natives' concepts and the anthropologist's analytical concepts is again involved in the anthropologist's procedure of establishing the "objective" fact, in the sense that ultimately it is not the anthropologist but the natives who define the members of the anthropologist's analytical categories.

Although Megitt defines "agnate" as a cognate related in male line only, in his distinction between "agnates" and "other cognates" among the Enga (53), McArthur (52) suggests that he does not follow this "strict anthropological usage" (52, p. 181) but rather the Enga's own classification, according to which his "quasi-agnates" (the children of co-resident sons of female agnates (53, pp. 31–32) and the offspring of quasi-agnates are categorized as "agnates." She points out that "in strict anthropological usage quasi-agnates and their offspring would be classed as cognates since they are descendants of a remembered female clan member" (52, p. 282). She concludes that comparing the composition of groups whose members have been classified according to different criteria can lead only to confusion, and that such confusion can hardly be avoided unless it is specified which procedures were followed in classifying quantitative data (52, p. 285). She indicates two possible comparisons: comparisons of figures based on people's own classifications, and comparisons of figures based on the anthropologist's classifications. Strathern seems to be in favor of comparisons in terms of the anthropologist's classifications, as the natives' classifications do not have to be isomorphic with one another (80, p. 40). In his study of the Melpa he follows his own and not the Melpa's definition of an agnate. Any such categorization involves well-known difficulties deriving from the fact that the anthropologist's classification of an individual as an agnate or otherwise is based on the anthropologist's reckoning upon that individual's genealogy as communicated to him by that individual himself and/or others. It has been shown many times that details of genealogies become altered in many ways. Cook, for example, states that 21.23% (76 out of 358) of the members of one Manga clan (wives excluded) who are or were theoretically co-resident, were or are genealogical nonagnates (12, p. 192). Obviously anybody is classified by Cook as a nonagnate whose genealogy in the span of five or six generations (the span of genealogical data available) is not fully agnatic. Yet it is quite clear that the genealogical knowledge serving as the basis for his classification is subject to alternation and manipulation. Of the 76 genealogical nonagnates, 62 are descendants of 9 female agnates, while there is a "sparsity of ascendant generation agnatic females in the genealogies" which he recorded (12, p. 192). Thus Cook classifies as agnates those who are either descended from an ancestor in an unbroken agnatic line or whose genealogy has been already altered to a purely and fully agnatic form. Even if he is following "strict anthropological usage" for classifying agnates, it is partly himself and partly his Manga informants who decide on the members of his category "agnate." As a result of this, his figure of 21.23% of nonagnatic members of one Manga clan is completely meaningless; it has no reference either in the Manga cognitive world or in the world of scientifically "objective" (biological?) fact. The figure refers solely to the category of people which Cook himself has defined.

To avoid this obvious difficulty, Strathern classifies as agnatic members of a Melpa clan those whose fathers' fathers were clan members themselves (or whose fathers' fathers joined the clan), and as nonagnates those whose fathers' fathers were not clan members (81, pp. 94–95). The reason for his not extending the definitional requirements beyond this level derives from his effort not to confuse the emic and etic stretches of genealogy (81, p. 94). Within the two generations above the level of currently married men, "it is possible to plausibly establish what at least some of the etic facts are" (81, p. 93). Apart from the fact that it is only possible to establish—as Strathern himself readily admits—what at least *some* of the etic facts are (which in itself does not make his classification any more etic than, for example, Cook's etic classification) Strathern's distinction between agnates and nonagnates raises a question about the reality to which his categories refer in yet another way. Strathern says that etic facts of actual genealogical relations within two generations above the level of contemporary adult men are recoverable, "although they are unlikely to be mentioned often by clansmen themselves, simply because they are largely irrelevant to contemporary affairs" (81, p. 94). Thus, using etic criteria, he distinguishes categories which have no reference to reality as known and lived by the Melpa. Consider a man whose father's mother returned to her natal group with her children after her divorce or widowhood. If he grew up as a member of his father's mother's group, he would be classified as a nonagnate by Strathern. On the other hand, a man whose father's father joined his wife's group (and whose father grew up as a member of this group) would be classified as an agnate by Strathern. The Melpa would not categorize these two men differently; both would be *wue-nt-mei,* a term which Strathern glosses as "man-bearing" member (81, pp. 18–19, 201–4). Strathern thus ultimately distinguishes categories which have ontological status only within the reality which he has himself defined.

There are at least two methodological confusions involved in Strathern's and similar approaches: (1) The criterion on the basis of which Strathern distinguishes his categories is that of agnatic descent. As his categorization is not paralleled by Melpa categorizations but rather cuts across the latter, he is in fact ascribing heuristic importance to the principle of agnatic descent which it need not necessarily have. Instead of making it possible to investigate what significance agnatic or cognatic descent might have in Melpa structure and action, he imposes the significance of agnatic descent on Melpa structure and action by analytical fiat. (b) Strathern distinguishes agnates and nonagnates to be able to analyze the processes of group affiliation and to investigate whether there is any discrimination against nonagnatic members of the group. He finds that there are only slight differences in status between agnates and nonagnates. At least some of these differences, as he himself points out, cannot be simply explained by the fact of agnation itself (81, p. 207).

The analysis of status differences among group members in terms of the anthropologist's instead of the natives' categories is misconceived on at least two counts. First, such an approach completely dismisses from consideration the natives' own categorizations and, in consequence, has to leave them unexplained. Strathern does this in spite of his earlier proclamation that these "classification should in fact *themselves* be made an object of study" (80, p. 40). One would assume that if the Melpa categorize the group members as the *wue-nt-mei* ("man-bearing" member), *amb-nt-mei* ("woman-bearing" member), and *tepa rǫndi wue* ["taken and (re-)planted man"] (81, pp. 18–19), they have some reason for doing it. One would further assume that if there are any differences in status among group members, these would probably concern the categories of group members as recognized by the Melpa. After all, it is only these categories which are meaningful to them and hardly the categories as distinguished by the anthropologist. Unfortunately, it is not possible to reorganize Strathern's figures concerning agnatic and nonagnatic clan members according to the Melpa's own categorizations of clan members. Strathern's figures, however, indicate that his category of nonagnates includes woman-bearing and man-bearing members as well as sons of "taken and (re-)planted men" (classified as man-bearing members or differently by the Melpa?). It would be interesting to see whether more meaningful correlations of status difference could be associated with these categories of group members than with the meaningless differentiation between agnates and nonagnates.

The second reason why the analysis of status differences among group members in terms of the anthropologist's categories is misconceived applies to Strathern's analysis only on a hypothetical level. Assuming that there were some differences among man-bearing members of the group that would correspond with the anthropologist's classifications of these members into agnates and nonagnates, how could these differences possibly be explained or interpreted? This question ceases to be hypothetical in the case of those anthropologists who analyze status differences among group members in terms of agnates and nonagnates, categorized as such by the analyst on the basis of actors' genealogies, and who find a positive correlation between these categories and status difference. For example, Ryan has found that nonagnates in Mendi subclans suffer certain handicaps in their marital lives (66, p. 269; 67, p. 170). His category of subclan nonagnates subsumes not only the three categories of nonagnates which the Mendi recognize (66, p. 265), but also some of those group members whom the Mendi categorize together with those whom Ryan calls "agnates." Should there not be any status discrimination against the latter category (Mendi agnates whom Ryan classifies as nonagnates), the obvious conclusion would be to say that the Mendi discriminate against those whom they classify as nonagnates, as indeed they seem to do according to Ryan's own data (cf 66, p. 265). As Ryan does not do this, it seems that there must be some Mendi agnates (Ryan's nonagnates) who suffer some disadvantages and some Mendi (and Ryan's) agnates who do not. Ryan explains the difference in status between the two by the difference in their group affiliation. However, as far as the affiliation of both members is concerned, no distinction is made by the Mendi (in the sense that both members are equally categorized); any observable differences in status between them obviously have their explanation in something other than their mode of affiliation. Ryan's approach, which dissects the Mendi category of agnatic members of subclans into agnates and nonagnates and then correlates the observable differences in status with his own categories, precludes even the formulation of what this "something other than the mode of affiliation" could be. In this way he cannot arrive at the explanation of any observable behavioral pattern through empirical research, but the explanation is already contained in his analytical model. It means that like the proponents of the model of corporate descent groups or of the alliance model, he does not need empirical data for constructing explanatory models but merely for substantiating the validity of the model.

DESCENT GROUPS AND DESCENT CATEGORIES

Another confusion which appears in the discussion about the interpretation of New Guinea and Melanesian ethnography is the failure to distinguish clearly between descent groups and descent categories. In his description of the general features of New Guinea ethnography, Barnes mentions that "in each generation a substantial majority of men affiliate themselves with their father's group and in this sense it acquires some agnatic continuity over the generations. It may be similar in demographic appearance and de facto ties to a patrilineal group" (2, p. 6). Objecting to this, LaFontaine points out that "group here means locality"; she argues that descent and residence are confused in conceptualizing locality as a group, and suggests that this confusion characterizes much of the New Guinea ethnography where " 'group' has an implicit spatial reference" (48, p. 38). In reference to Langness (49), who, according to her, is explicitly guilty of this confusion, she rejects the definition of group in terms of common residence or common action, since in such definition "the analytical concept is confused with ethnographic appearance and the actions of particular individuals" (48, p. 38). She declares her own position quite clearly: in New Guinea the "group" is a "descent group to which all men's sons are affiliated by virtue of their birth" (48, p. 38). Disregarding Scheffler's stricture that a communality of descent does not itself "make" a group (75, p. 544), she then goes on consistently treating as corporate groups those units of which men are members by virtue of their births. Since she explicitly rejected the definition of a group in terms of common action, one is left wondering what kind of definition of a group she is actually working with, and for what other possible reasons than the insistence on preserving the established structural approach she rejects offhand any distinction between categories and groups. I take it that Keesing had similar approaches in mind when he recently observed that "perhaps more theorists of kinship over the years have come to grief or caused confusion by losing track of the difference between social groups and cultural categories than by any other conceptual flaw" (44, p. 9) and that "the anthropological literature is full of confusions about 'clans' and 'lineages' and 'kindreds' where (the) distinction between groups and categories, corporations and action groups, have been blurred or overlooked" (44, p. 11; cf also 45).

If group is merely an analytical concept, as LaFontaine suggests, and when the object of the study is not the explanation of actual behavior but the explanation of the working of the social structure of a given society, the group can be ideologically defined, as Scheffler expresses it (75, p. 547), i.e. defined in terms of the ideology of group membership. A distinction between categories and groups is then not an issue, or at least not the major or main issue. For example, Goodenough, in his discussion of the taxonomy of kin groups (33), quite rightly points out that there is no need in such discussion to distinguish "groups" in a narrow sociological sense from other kinds of social division or category: "Their status as corporations, as solidary bodies, as entities whose members all assemble in connection with activities of some kind is, of course, germane for some discussion, but not for this one" (33, p. 42). In reference to the discussion about the structural differences between unilineal and nonunilineal (or cognatic) descent groups, de Lepervanche observed that "nowhere is the crucial distinction between categories and groups a basis for argument" (13, p. 170). It did not need to be, as descent ideology and the problem of whether descent alone closes the group, or whether additional criteria restrict membership, were the main theme of the discussion; nowhere was the substance, as opposed to the ideology, of group membership (cf 75, p. 546) the primary issue (for recent surveys of the discussion cf 33, 44).

When the object of study is human behavior in contradistinction to merely a study of social systems (cf 74, p. 291), or when, as Keesing expressed it, "we pay closer attention to who does what with whom" instead of trying "to explain the behavior of individuals as a product of (or deviation from) the system" (44, pp. 126, 122), the distinction between groups and categories becomes of crucial importance.

Scheffler has demonstrated the analytical importance of this distinction in his study of the Choiseul Island social structure (74). In his analysis of the *sinangge*, a kin unit consisting of all descendants, through both males and females, of an apical ancestor known to have founded the unit, he distinguishes cognatic descent categories (74, pp. 53–62) and descent groups which form the "primary residential proprietary segments" of Choiseulese society (74, p. 92 ff). This analytical distinction follows closely Choiseulese conceptualizations, according to which "the descent group is sometimes viewed as those of the *sinangge* who have, literally translating 'stayed put' as opposed to those who have 'gone out' " (74, p. 57).

The distinction between groups and categories is central also to Keesing's analysis of the Kwaio social structure (43). He points out that Kwaio social structure could be described as a set of primary segments (consisting of descent group members domiciled in their estate, plus their spouses) "forming discrete corporations and independent political units; but interlocked into a wider system by cross-cutting webs of cognatic kinship, by secondary interests of complementary filiation, and by affinal alliance" (43, p. 125). But such a model is deficient in that it confuses the realm of the actors' conceptual world with the realm of processual order (43, p. 126). Keesing argues that Kwaio individuals who live in the same settlement or territory cannot usefully be viewed as a "descent group." They rather "fall into a complex pattern of partially overlapping categories. Cultural principles governing interaction, rights, and transactions are structured in terms of these categories; and it is from these categories that different social groups are crystallized in defined contexts" (43, p. 126). Social groups crystallizing in various interactional situations are "descent groups" if they consist " of a cluster of persons acting in social identity relationships defined on the basis of descent . . . or assumed partly on grounds of descent entitlement or obligation" (43, p. 129).

Unlike Scheffler and Keesing, Tiffany denies the existence of descent categories in the Samoan social structure (84, p. 441), whose formal features resemble closely those of the Choiseul Island. A unit consisting of all descendants, through both males and females, of the reputed founding ancestor of the unit, is called '*āiga*. Tiffany classifies this unit as a corporate descent group. Each '*āiga* has its own named estate and those '*āiga* members who currently reside on that estate constitute the localized core of '*āiga* membership. Other '*āiga* members reside dispersed on estates attached to different '*āiga;* they count as members as long as they at least sporadically participate in the '*āiga's* affairs. This means that persons who have remained inactive for several generations may be permanently lost from the genealogical record of the '*āiga* in question. But there are inactive members whose cognatic links are still remembered and retained, and Tiffany's informants were adamant "that a mutually recognized consanguineal link is sufficient for an inactive member to gain re-entry, so to speak, into the affairs of an '*āiga*" (84, p. 432), i.e. to assume his descent group membership. Tiffany's analysis begs the following question: if the important factor influencing the genealogical recognition of a particular descendant of an '*āiga's* founding ancestor is that member's active participation in his or her '*āiga's* affairs, as she herself stresses, on what basis is a descendant whose genealogical links are still remembered and retained, but who has not shown any interest in the '*āiga's* affairs and even less actively participated in such affairs, considered to be a member of this '*āiga* conceptualized as a corporate descent group? Through disregarding the importance of the analytical distinction between categories and groups, Tiffany falls back on defining a corporate group on the basis of formal criteria of membership (cognatic descent from the apical ancestor) (cf also 11 for the same problem) and not on the basis of interaction in spite of her proclamation to the contrary.

In his discussion of "descent groups," Scheffler pointed out that "social units exhibit varying degrees of formal and informal organization and pertain to various activities and interests, and which one of these one wishes to dignify with the label 'group' . . . must depend upon the problem one has in mind" (78, p. 546). The groups crystallizing in different interactional situations which Keesing distinguishes as "descent groups" among the Kwaio, are what most sociologists and anthropologists would call action or task groups. Many sociologists and anthropologists would consider to be a group only such a unit that convenes and has a certain form and degree of continuity, corporateness, discreteness and organization, though these characteristics may be variously defined (cf, for example, 20, p. 36; 23, p. 36; 26, pp. 202–3; 31, pp. 9–14; 79, pp. 9–22). A "descent group" so conceived among the Kwaio has a continuing existence in one of its various manifestations only in the sense that the same cluster of actual persons recurrently assume the social identities defined on the basis of descent (43, p. 129).

Both Scheffler and Keesing define the group on the basis of interaction and not on the basis of some formal criteria of membership. Formal criteria define only membership in cultural or social categories. They stress the point that membership in a descent category does not assign members to a descent group or define its boundary (43, p. 128; 75, pp. 546–47); it only defines eligibility or entitlement to membership of the group. Goodenough implies a similar distinction when he talks about an individual activating his membership in a descent group to which he has a right by virtue of his ancestry (33, p. 58).

EPISTEMOLOGICAL REASSESSMENT

Concentration on the study of human behavior, rather than merely the study of social systems, and the redefinition of basic analytical concepts which this shift

in emphasis necessarily requires, are manifest in the work of those anthropologists who have studied societies with cognatic descent groups and
categories, or societies in which it was for various reasons difficult to classify the
main social groups as unilineal. But there have already appeared reanalyses of
societies with unilineal descent groups (or of societies which have been
classified as having such groups) which seriously question the explicative validity of structural models and concepts in whose terms these societies had been
studied.

In a comparative study of Kwaio and Tallensi ancestor worship, Keesing
makes the following observation:

> The gulf between the way Kwaio (and I as their ethnographer) conceptualize their
> system and the way Fortes and Goody conceptualize the African systems seems far
> wider than the gulf between what the Kwaio and Africans *do*. And if the gulf is
> generated more by the model than by the facts, we had better look very carefully at
> the models (42, p. 765).

He suggests that it is possible that Tallensi themselves recognize agnatic,
uterine, and cognatic descent constructs (42, p. 769) and that any Tale individual
belongs not only to an agnatic descent group but also to a multiplicity of cognatic
descent categories (42, p. 770). It is common descent, rather than cognatic
kinship, which is expressed in terms of his relationship to the ancestor in
contexts involving the corporation, territory, or shrine founded by that ancestor
(42, p. 772). In his reanalysis of Tallensi data, Keesing argues that it was the
analytical concept of complementary filiation (subsuming both a culturally secondary descent principle and relationships of cognatic kinship) which prevented
Fortes from recognizing the operation of the cognatic descent principle in the
Tallensi social structure (42, pp. 765, 767).

Faron (18, 19) has analyzed the Mapuche society in Chile in terms of the
structural model of segmentary descent groups. He considers the principle of
patrilineal descent to have long been an important integrative force in Mapuche
society. Its importance increased when Mapuche were confined to reservations
and there occurred a reintegration of social units around the principle of patrilineality (18, pp. xiii–xiv). He distinguishes five levels of segmentation of descent
groups (18, p. 76) which form the core of residential groups on reservations. The
everyday life, as well as land inheritance, distribution of authority, etc, are
organized in terms of lineage segments.

As a result of his recent fieldwork among the Mapuche which concentrated on
the analysis of the organizational principles of interpersonal relationships,
Stuchlik finds it impossible to accept Faron's classification of the co-residential
groups among the Mapuche as patrilineal lineages. He is aware that Mapuche
society could have changed since the time of Faron's fieldwork and, taking that
into account, he argues that to conceive of reservations simply as localized
patrilineages means to overestimate considerably the importance of patrilineality in Mapuche society (83, p. 58). The statistical predominance of viri-
patrilocal residence leads to the concentration of agnates on any given reserva-
tion. Stuchlik does not deny the possibility of distinguishing this group ana-

lytically as a patrilineal lineage; any such distinction would be, however, solely the anthropologist's construct. The Mapuche themselves do not conceive of people agnatically related to one another as a unit; the relations of agnatic descent (in contradistinction to patrifiliation) are not a principle of recruitment into any activity, and indeed there is no social context in which only agnates would appear as a corporate group to the exclusion of nonagnates (83, p. 64 ff). Even the inheritance of land, which for Faron is one of the main concerns of the patrilineage (18, p. 74), is organized in very different terms. Primary rights in land are vested in the elementary or joint-extended family, with the wider local group having only indirect control, and they are perpetuated through inheritance by children; sons have preference as heirs, but daughters are by no means excluded from inheritance, and children inherit land from both their parents (83, pp. 96–97). Analyzing the patterns of the choice of partners for interaction in a way similar to that of Keesing (43), Stuchlik concludes that the most important social groups among the Mapuche are egocentric groups of genealogically and/ or spatially near cognates and affines; however, neighborhood and friendship relations, only partially coterminous with kinship relations, are of considerable importance.

The reanalyses, together with work done in societies with cognatic descent groups or kin groups which cannot be unambiguously described as unilineal, indicate the growing dissatisfaction with existing anthropological classifications. This dissatisfaction so far has been mostly expressed in analyses of ethnographic data from societies only recently opened to intensive anthropological fieldwork. But it does not derive solely from this new data; more significantly, it is generated by asking new questions and by redefining what is treated as problematic. A distinct trend in a substantial corpus of contemporary anthropological writing on kin groups is a growing preoccupation with what people actually do and with whom they do it rather than with the formulation of jural norms and formal structures. This basic epistemological reassessment, or a critical reaction to it, are the main features which characterize the present stage of kin group studies.

Literature Cited

1. Allen, M. 1971. Descent groups and ecology amongst the Nduindui; New Hebrides. In *Anthropology in Oceania: essays presented to Ian Hogbin*, ed. L. R. Hiatt, C. Jaywardena, 1–25. Sydney: Angus & Robertson
2. Barnes, J. A. 1962. African models in the New Guinea Highlands. *Man* 62: 5–9
3. Barnes, J. A. 1967. Agnation among the Enga: a review article. *Oceania* 38: 33–43
4. Barnes, J. A. 1968. Foreword to R. M. Glasse. *Huli of Papua: A Cognatic Descent System*. Paris: Mouton
5. Barth, F. 1966. Models of social organization. *R. Anthropol Inst. Occas. Pap.* 23
6. Barth, F. 1973. Descent and marriage reconsidered. See Ref. 34, 3–19
7. Berndt, R. M. 1964. Warfare in New Guinea Highlands. In *New Guinea: the Central Highlands,* ed. J. B. Watson, 183–203. *Am. Anthropol.* 66, No. 4, part 2, special publication
8. Brookfield, H. C., Brown, P. 1963. *Struggle for land: agricultural and group territories among the Chimbu of the New Guinea Highlands.* Melbourne: Oxford Univ. Press in asso-

ciation with the Australian Natl. Univ.

9. Brown P., Brookfield, H. C. 1959–60. Chimbu land and society. *Oceania* 30: 1–75

10. Buchler, I. R., Selby, H. A. 1968. *Kinship and Social Organization: An Introduction to Theory and Method*. New York: Macmillan

11. Caplan, P. 1969. Cognatic descent groups on Mafia Island, Tanzania. *Man* (NS) 4:419–31

12. Cook, E. A. 1970. On the conversion of non-agnates into agnates among the Manga, Jimi River, Western Highlands District, New Guinea. *Southwest. J. Anthropol.* 26:190–196

13. de Lepervanche, M. 1967–68. Descent, residence and leadership in the New Guinea Highlands. *Oceania* 38:134–58, 163–89

14. du Toit, B. 1964–65. Filiation and affiliation among the Gadsup. *Oceania* 35:85–95

15. Elkin, A. P. 1952–53. Delayed exchange in Wabag Sub-District, Central Highlands of New Guinea. *Oceania* 23:161–201

16. Evans-Pritchard, E. E. 1940. *The Nuer: A Description of the Modes of Livelihood and Political Institutions of a Nilotic People*. London: Oxford Univ. Press

17. Evans-Pritchard, E. E. 1951. *Kinship and Marriage Among the Nuer*. London: Oxford Univ. Press

18. Faron, L. C. 1961. *Mapuche Social Structure: Institutional Reintegration in a Patrilineal Society of Central Chile*. Urbana: Univ. Illinois Press

19. Faron, L. C. 1964. *The Hawks of the Sun*. Univ. Pittsburgh Press

20. Firth, R. 1963. Bilateral descent groups: an operational perspective. In *Studies in Kinship and Marriage*, ed. I. Schapera, 22–37. *R. Anthropol. Inst. Occas. Pap.* 16

21. Fortes, M. 1945. *The Dynamics of Clanship Among the Tallensi*. London: Oxford Univ. Press

22. Fortes, M. 1949. *The Web of Kinship Among the Tallensi*. London: Oxford Univ. Press

23. Fortes, M. 1953. The structure of unilineal descent groups. *Am. Anthropol.* 55: 17–41

24. Fortes, M. 1959. Descent, filiation and affinity: a rejoinder to Dr. Leach. *Man* 59: 193–97, 206–12

25. Fortes, M. 1969. *Kinship and the Social Order: The Legacy of Lewis Henry Morgan*. Chicago: Aldine

26. Freeman, J. D. 1961. On the concept of kindred. *J. R. Anthropol. Inst.* 91:192–220

27. Glasse, R. M. 1968. See Ref. 4

28. Glickman, M. 1971. Kinship and credit among the Nuer. *Africa* 41: 306–19

29. Glickman, M. 1972. The Nuer and the Dinka: a further note. *Man* (NS) 7:586–94

30. Gluckman, M. 1961. Ethnographic data in British social anthropology. *Sociol. Rev.* 9:5–17

31. Goffman, E. 1961. *Encounters: Two Studies in the Sociology of Interaction*. Indianapolis: Bobbs-Merill

32. Goodenough, W. H. 1955. A problem in Malayo-Polynesian social organization. *Am. Anthropol.* 57:71–83

33. Goodenough, W. H. 1970. *Description and Comparison in Cultural Anthropology*. Chicago: Aldine

34. Goody, J., ed. 1973. *The Character of Kinship*. London: Cambridge Univ. Press

35. Gough, K. 1971. Nuer kinship: a reexamination. In *The Translation of Culture*, ed. T. Beidelman, 79–121. London: Tavistock

36. Greuel, P. J. 1971. The leopard-skin chief: an examination of political power among the Nuer. *Am. Anthropol.* 73:1115–20

37. Haight, B. 1972. A note on the leopard-skin chief. *Am. Anthropol.* 74:1313–18

38. Held, D. J. 1957. *The Papuas of Waropen*. The Hague: Nijhoff

39. Holy, L. 1967. Social consequences of *dia* among the Berti. *Africa* 37:466–79

40. Holy, L. 1974. *Neighbours and Kinsmen: A Study of the Berti People of Darfur*. London: Hurst

41. Kaberry, P. M. 1967. The plasticity of New Guinea kinship. In *Social Organization: Essays Presented to Raymond Firth*, ed. M. Freedman, 105–23. London: Cass

42. Keesing, R. M. 1970. Shrines, ancestors, and cognatic descent: the Kwaio and Tallensi. *Am. Anthropol.* 72:755–75

43. Keesing, R. M. 1971. Descent, residence, and cultural codes. See Ref. 1, 121–38

44. Keesing, R. M. 1975. *Kin Groups and Social Structure*. New York: Holt, Rinehart & Winston

45. Keesing, R. M., Keesing F. M. 1971. *New perspectives in Cultural Anthropology.* New York: Holt, Rinehart & Winston
46. Kroeber, A. L. 1952. Basic and secondary patterns of social structure. In *The Nature of Culture,* ed. A. L. Kroeber. Univ. Chicago Press
47. Kuhn, T. 1970. *The Structure of Scientific Revolutions.* Chicago: Univ. Chicago Press
48. LaFontaine, J. 1973. Descent in New Guinea: an Africanist view. See Ref. 34, 35–51
49. Langness, L. L. 1964. Some problems in the conceptualization of Highlands social structure. See Ref. 7, 162–82
50. Langness, L. L. 1966–67. Sexual antagonism in the New Guinea Highlands: A Bena Bena example. *Oceania* 37:161–77
51. Leach, E. R. 1962. On certain unconsidered aspects of double descent systems. *Man* 62:130–34
52. McArthur, M. 1966–67. Analysis of the genealogy of a Mae-Enga clan. *Oceania* 37:281–85
53. Meggitt, M. J. 1965. *The Lineage System of the Mae-Enga of New Guinea.* London: Oliver & Boyd
54. Middleton J., Tait, D., eds. 1958. *Tribes Without Rulers.* London: Routledge & Kegan Paul
55. Newcomer, P. J. 1972. Nuer are Dinka: an essay on origins and environmental determinism. *Man (NS)* 7:5–11
56. Newman, P. L. 1965. *Knowing the Gururumba.* New York: Holt, Rinehart & Winston
57. Pouwer, J. 1960. Loosely structured societies in Netherlands, New Guinea. *Bijdragen tot de Taal-, Land-, en Volkenkunde* 116:109–18
58. Pouwer, J. 1964. A social system in the Star Mountains: toward a reorientation of the study of social systems. See Ref. 7, 133–61
59. Radcliffe-Brown, A. R. 1952. *Structure and Function in Primitive Society.* London: Cohen & West
60. Read, K. E. 1951. The Gahuku-Gama of the Central Highlands. *South Pac.* 5:154–64
61. Read, K. E. 1954. Cultures of the Central Highlands of New Guinea. *Southwest. J. Anthropol.* 10:1–43
62. Reay, M. O. 1959. *The Kuma.* Melbourne Univ. Press
63. Reay, M. O. 1971. Structural co-variants of land shortage among patrilineal peoples. In *Politics in New Guinea,* ed. P. Lawrence, R. M. Berndt. Univ. West. Australia Press
64. Rivers, W. H. R. 1915. Mother right. In *Encyclopedia of Religion and Ethics,* ed. J. Hastings 8:851–59. Edinburgh
65. Rivers, W. H. R. 1924. *Social Organization.* London: Kegan Paul
66. Ryan, D. 1958–59. Clan foundation in the Mendi valley. *Oceania* 29:257–89
67. Ryan, D. 1969. Marriage in Mendi. In *Pigs, Pearlshells and Women,* ed. M. J. Meggitt, R. M. Glasse, 159–75. New Jersey: Prentice-Hall
68. Sahlins, M. D. 1961. The segmentary lineage: an organization of predatory expansion. *Am. Anthropol.* 63:322–45
69. Sahlins, M. D. 1965. On the ideology and composition of descent groups. *Man* 65:104–7
70. Salisbury, R. F. 1956. Unilineal descent groups in the New Guinea Highlands. *Man* 56:2–7
71. Salisbury, R. F. 1962. *From Stone to Steel.* Melbourne Univ. Press
72. Salisbury, R. F. 1964. New Guinea Highland models and descent theory. *Man* 64:168–71
73. Salisbury, R. F. 1965. The Siane of the Eastern Highlands. In *Gods, Ghosts and Men in Melanesia,* ed. P. Lawrence, M. J. Meggitt, 50–77. Melbourne Univ. Press
74. Scheffler, H. W. 1965. *Choiseul Island Social Structure.* Berkeley: Univ. California Press
75. Scheffler, H. W. 1966. Ancestor worship in anthropology: or, observation on descent and descent groups. *Curr. Anthropol.* 1966: 541–51
76. Scheffler, H. W. 1973. Kinship, descent and alliance. In *Handbook of Social and Cultural Anthropology,* ed. J. J. Honigman, 747–93. Chicago: Rand McNally
77. Schneider, D. M. 1965. Some muddles in models: or, how the system really works. In *The Relevance of Models for Social Anthropology,* 25–85. A.S.A. Monogr. 1. London: Tavistock
78. Smith, M. G. 1956. On segmentary lineage systems. *J. R. Anthropol. Inst.* 86:39–80
79. Sprott, W. J. H. 1958. *Human Groups.* Penguin Books

80. Strathern, A. 1969. Descent and alliance in the New Guinea Highlands: some problems of comparison. *Proc. R. Anthropol. Inst.* 1968:37–52
81. Strathern, A. 1972. One father, one blood: descent and group structure among the Melpa people. Canberra: Australian Natl. Univ. Press
82. Strathern, A. 1973. Kinship, descent and locality: some New Guinea examples. See Ref. 34, 21–33
83. Stuchlik, M. 1976. *Life on a Half-Share: Mechanisms of Social Re-*cruitment *Among the Mapuche of Southern Chile.* London: Hurst
84. Tiffany, S. W. 1975. The cognatic descent groups of contemporary Samoa. *Man* (NS) 10:430–47
85. Wagner, R. 1967. *The Curse of Souw: Principles of Daribi Clan Definition and Alliance in New Guinea.* Univ. Chicago Press
86. Watson, J. B. 1964. Anthropology in the New Guinea Highlands. See Ref. 7, 1–19
87. Wilson, P. J. 1967. Tsimihety kinship and descent. *Africa* 37:133–54

Ann. Rev. Anthropol. 1976. 5:133–48
Copyright © 1976 by Annual Reviews Inc. All rights reserved

UPPER PALAEOLITHIC ARCHAEOLOGY

Harvey M. Bricker[1]

Department of Anthropology, Tulane University, New Orleans, Louisiana 70118

INTRODUCTION

A review article on the Upper Palaeolithic could attempt to do various things, but I think it could not successfully attempt to cover all recent developments in our understanding of specific Upper Palaeolithic sequences unless it were very long and accompanied by profuse artifact illustration. Upper Palaeolithic specialists will have such information at their disposal, and anthropologists with other interests are unlikely to profit from a systematic textbook-like treatment. [For those who wish an encapsulated presentation of Upper Palaeolithic prehistory, the best source is still, in my opinion, the relevant portion of Bordes's (11) text.] I have assumed that the most useful approach would be topical and that the number of topics discussed should be sufficiently small so that something of consequence could be said about each one. Eschewing various topics of equal relevance and importance to those I have chosen (e.g. the geochronologic and chronometric framework of the Upper Palaeolithic; recent developments in typological analysis, paleoecology, etc; widespread changes at the end of the Upper Palaeolithic and their relevance to the establishment of food-producing economies), I have restricted my consideration to two topics. Because of my own research interests (centered for the moment on the Châtelperronian of southwestern Europe) and because of its implications for teachers and scholars in other fields of anthropology, the principal topic of this article is the origins of the Upper Palaeolithic and how ideas about this have been changed by recent developments. The second topic, to which I give much shorter treatment, concerns some recently acquired information about ritual, notation, and symbol in the Upper Palaeolithic. These aspects of the culture of early modern man have, I believe, an interest for a broad spectrum of anthropologists caring little or nothing for the arcane intricacies of local archaeological sequences. It is my intention in this article to speak to anthropologists whose interests are

[1] I am grateful to Mr. Antonio Rodriguez-Buckingham, Librarian of the Tozzer Library of Harvard University, for the cooperation extended to me during my stay in Cambridge, and to Mr. Marco J. Giardino, my colleague at Tulane University, for his help with the Italian literature.

133

sufficiently different from mine that we are unlikely to meet face-to-face; I beg the indulgence of my professional colleagues for repeating here what they already know perfectly well.

THE ORIGINS OF THE UPPER PALAEOLITHIC

The "Classic Model" of the Upper Palaeolithic

Any attempt to discuss some of the recent research on the archaeology of the Upper Palaeolithic raises immediately certain questions of concept and definition that are themselves crucial to the understanding of that research. The extensive modification of some aspects of the "classic" model of the Upper Palaeolithic, especially those relating to its origin, has been proposed and widely accepted during the past decade. Some historical comments are relevant to understanding how recent research has produced new and different results.

The concept of an Upper Palaeolithic, like that of man's "antediluvian" antiquity itself, was developed in Europe for application to European data. In the latter part of the nineteenth century, following the coining of the term "Palaeolithic" by Lubbock in 1865 (52) and the general acceptance of this term to apply to Quaternary prehistory, attempts to subdivide the Palaeolithic occasioned lengthy and sometimes bitter dispute over matters of evolutionary models, stratigraphic sequences, and preferred nomenclatures. The concept of an "Upper Palaeolithic," a period during which bone and antler were first extensively used for tools and weapons, appeared in the rapidly changing classificatory schemes of de Mortillet (75) as early as 1872 (25), but the basis of the subsequent understanding of the Upper Palaeolithic was Breuil's synthesis of 1912 (15). Although a few later authors (e.g. Garrod 35, Leakey 50) have attempted to define the Upper Palaeolithic as a purely temporal *period,* it has generally been understood and presented in summary works (e.g. Breuil & Lantier 16, Clark 23, Grahmann & Müller-Beck 41, Oakley 80) as a *stage,* having somewhat different temporal limits, especially for its end, in different areas.

In addition to establishing the so-called "classic" French sequence (Aurignacian, Solutrean, Magdalenian, and subdivisions thereof) that was later ill-advisedly extended to other parts of Europe, to Africa, and to Asia, Breuil (15) identified the dimensions of change—technological/typological, social, and anatomical—that he regarded as sufficiently important to merit recognition of the Upper Palaeolithic as a major cultural unit. What may be called the classic model of the Upper Palaeolithic, present in outline in Breuil's work and specified more fully by later workers, had several aspects of relevance here, as described below.

CHARACTERISTIC 1: DEFINITION AND DISTRIBUTION   A defining characteristic of the Upper Palaeolithic was its combination of technological and typological innovations—the first quantitatively important appearance in the archaeological record of end-scrapers, burins, etc made on blades produced from specially prepared blade cores and of various kinds of bone, antler, and ivory tools and weapons. Also included here (under a narrow "typological" or more broadly "cultural" rubric) was the first appearance of art, mobiliary and parietal, and of numerous objects of personal adornment.

Because assemblages with such technological/typological characteristics were limited in their geographical distribution (principally to Europe, North Africa, southwestern Asia, and Siberia), large areas of the Old World (much of sub-Saharan Africa, southern and southeastern Asia, and Australia) were considered not to have an Upper Palaeolithic. Contemporary assemblages in these areas were described in some other fashion, often stressing cultural conservatism or retardation.

CHARACTERISTIC 2: ANATOMICAL ASSOCIATIONS   The Upper Palaeolithic archaeological materials were the work of anatomically modern man (*Homo sapiens sapiens*), whereas the Mousterian or otherwise named Middle Palaeolithic materials were those of Neanderthal or other premodern man. This association of technology/typology with anatomy was taken to be a second defining characteristic of the Upper Palaeolithic.

It was assumed, at least for Europe (the original locus of the classic model), that the first appearance of the new technology/typology and the new anatomy were synchronous, occurring at the beginning of the second half of the last (Würm) glaciation——during what is now called the Würm II/III Interstadial in the French sequence, the Podhradem Interstadial in Central Europe, and the equivalent episode in other regional sequences.

CHARACTERISTIC 3: ORIGIN AND DIFFUSION   The Upper Palaeolithic was for Europe an allochthonous phenomenon that had been brought to that area in already developed form from elsewhere. The locus of origin was guessed at (maybe the Near East, maybe Africa, maybe Central Asia, etc) or left unspecified, but there was often an assumption of a *single* origin and subsequent diffusion from it.

The archaeological and anatomical innovations were not only synchronous, but also causally related. The Upper Palaeolithic originated outside Europe because modern man had done so, and its appearance in Europe was the archaeological manifestation of the replacement in Europe of Neanderthal man by *H. s. sapiens*. This reasoning, in good accord with reigning ideas in human paleontology, was sometimes applied to extra-European areas as well, where the appearance of "blade and burin" industries was allowed to stand for the "arrival" of modern man in the absence of skeletal material.

Modifications in the Model

DEFINITION AND DISTRIBUTION   The technological/typological definition of the Upper Palaeolithic in Europe is the element of the classic model that has undergone the least change. A paper by Mellars (69) on the differences between

Middle and Upper Palaeolithic industries in southwestern France deals with matters of more general application. The recognition of the importance of blade technology in the Upper Palaeolithic has been tempered by the knowledge that this was present (although not quantitatively dominant) at least as early as the Middle Palaeolithic, and Bordes (12, 13) emphasizes that even earlier technical roots occur in the Levallois blade technique. Conversely, tools made on flakes are quite common in some Upper Palaeolithic industries. Mellars (69) suggests that the real Upper Palaeolithic innovation was morphological—". . . the comparatively rapid development of entirely new forms . . ." of stone implements. The increased array of specialized tools and weapons in the Upper Palaeolithic is used by Binford (10) in a more general treatment of the effects of increasing technological efficiency upon the nature of the archaeological record. Brose & Wolpoff (17), in presenting an extreme view of the importance of a general transition to the Upper Palaeolithic, obscure the significance of their major thesis (see below) by their inappropriate handling of the data on stone tool assemblages. There is certainly continuity between *some* Middle Palaeolithic industries and *some* Upper Palaeolithic ones, but their comparative technique demonstrates nothing beyond the fact that scrapers, knives, etc were manufactured by artificers of both stages. Of all the things for which the de Sonneville-Bordes/Perrot type list may be useful, tracing continuity from the Middle to the Upper Palaeolithic on the basis of broad functional and even broader morphological presence or absence is not one of them.

Crude or technically simple osseous implements and articles of adornment certainly occur sporadically in earlier assemblages (13, 17), but Mellars (69) points out that the extensive, complex, and well-controlled modification of osseous materials remains an Upper Palaeolithic characteristic. Although the "embryo of art" (13)—evidence of pigment use and the presence of a few decorated objects—can be found in the Middle and Lower Palaeolithic [Marshack (67) discusses some of the more interesting European examples], no currently available data challenge the Upper Palaeolithic as the locus of the earliest coherent corpus of art.

The geographical range within which industries recognized as Upper Palaeolithic occur has been increased within the last several decades. The areas of particular relevance are India, Japan, and the Nile Valley.

Although a few "blade and burin" industries have been known in India for some decades, information about a true Indian Upper Palaeolithic has increased greatly recently. Ghosh (38, 39) discusses the occurrence in eastern India of punch-struck blades and characteristic Upper Palaeolithic tools in assemblages in which flakes are, however, quantitatively predominant; similar industries and ones in which blade technology dominates are reported for other parts of India by Murty (79), Misra (71), and Sankalia (83). A series of Upper Palaeolithic factory sites and their environmental context in the Pushkar Basin, northwestern India, have been studied by Allchin, Goudie, and Hegde (1–3). Although such Indian industries are not yet precisely dated, they seem to belong to the late Upper Pleistocene, prior to the Holocene microlithic industries. There is some evidence (39, 71) that the blade technology has its roots in the local,

Mousterian-like Middle Stone Age or Middle Palaeolithic, as is the case for some Upper Palaeolithic industries of Europe and elsewhere.

Knowledge of Upper Palaeolithic industries (or, indeed, Palaeolithic industries of any kind) in Japan is less than three decades old. Systematic synthesis of information from the hundreds of sites that have now been investigated is in an early stage, but recent summaries in English have been provided by Morlan (73, 74) and Chard (19). Chard points out that sites are often poorly dated and as yet poorly correlated from one region to another; furthermore, because of glacioeustatic fluctuations, most Pleistocene sites in the general region of the Japanese archipelago are probably now under water. The classic Upper Palaeolithic blade technology and characteristic tools (burins, etc) are particularly well represented in northern Japan, closest to the Siberian areas with which certain resemblances are seen; further south, diversified but possibly more indigenously developed industries are based more predominantly on flake technology (19). The several microblade technologies that appear in Japan at the end of the Upper Pleistocene are apparently closely related to similar ones appearing on the Asian mainland and later in the New World. In a recent summary, Smith (86) reviews the documentation for an apparent spread of what he calls "the northeast Asian-northwest American microblade tradition" from interior East Asia (present before 15,000 B.P.) to North America (present by 10,000–9,000 B.P.) and uses data recently presented by Okladnikov (81) and Mochanov (72) suggesting an origin for this technology in the area extending from northern China to southern Siberia.

Until the appearance of the results of the work done in the 1960s to salvage the antiquities of Nubia and Upper Egypt from the effects of the construction of the Aswan High Dam, it was generally thought that late Pleistocene Egypt was an area of cultural stagnation in which rather epigonal Levalloisian industries lasted on and from which Upper Palaeolithic "blade and burin" industries were absent (87). It is now known that several late Upper Pleistocene industries in this part of the Nile Valley had technological and typological characteristics that permit them to be considered as Upper Palaeolithic. Wendorf et al (95) report the existence of several such industries near Sohag in Upper Egypt. Further south in Upper Egypt, on the Kom Ombo plain, Smith (87) describes three different industries, which he has named Menchian, Silsilian, and Sebekian, and points out resemblances between them and various already known Upper Palaeolithic industries of southwestern Asia and northern Africa. South of Aswan, near Ballana in Egyptian Nubia, the Ballanan industry described by Wendorf (92, 93) appears to have close similarities to the Sebekian of Kom Ombo. Further south, in Sudanese Nubia, industries that could be called Upper Palaeolithic on technological criteria are not found, but several of them, notably the Khormusan, described by Marks (59), and the Gemaian, described by Shiner (84), ". . . underwent a fully equivalent development in stone tool typology, in such things as burins and scrapers, which parallel that of the Upper Palaeolithic in Europe" (94). Throughout Upper Egypt and northern Nubia, the simultaneous presence of these Upper Palaeolithic industries based on a blade technology and others based on the older flake technology makes this a zone of boundary and transition between the Mediterranean basin and sub-Saharan Africa in which great variety in technology, typology, and adaptation pattern existed at the end of the Pleistocene. Clark (21) explores the effects of this variation, which continued into the early Holocene, upon the development of new subsistence bases.

Some of the most exciting recent information about the distribution of Upper Pleistocene industries in which blade technology is well developed concerns some of the Middle Stone Age industries of southern Africa. It is probably not (yet?) justified to speak of these industries as Upper Palaeolithic in the classic sense; the evidence they provide of a very early development of blade technology is discussed below in a later section.

ANATOMICAL ASSOCIATIONS   The long held and often documented idea that Upper Palaeolithic industries are the work of anatomically modern man has not been seriously challenged, but its reciprocal—that modern man produced Upper Palaeolithic rather than Middle Palaeolithic tools—is apparently not without exception. Recent data from several sites indicate that some groups of anatomically modern man were making Mousterian tools.

One site that may very well fall into this category is the cave Darra-i-Kur, northeastern Afghanistan, excavated by Dupree (27, 28). A fragmentary human temporal bone was found in a level containing a Mousterian industry of Levallois facies; some of the Levallois points are made on Levallois blade blanks, but the industry is clearly Middle rather than Upper Palaeolithic (29). A radiocarbon date from the occupation level has a central value of ca 30,000 B.P., but both the nature of the sample and the lack of alkaline pretreatment indicate that the true age of the occupation is probably much older (28). According to Angel (5), the characteristics of the temporal bone contrast markedly with those of Neanderthal man, and the specimen can be considered at least transitional (in the sense of the Skhul population) and quite possibly modern. The difficulties of attempting a phyletic placement of such a fragmentary fossil are, of course, severe (58).

Much fuller and less ambiguous evidence is provided by Vandermeersch's (91) study of the skeletal material from Jebel Qafzeh, near Nazareth, Israel. A total of eight individuals, from the previous as well as the more recent excavations, were buried in a level containing a Mousterian industry of Levallois facies described as having ". . . absolutely no Upper Palaeolithic components . . ." (91) which underlay several meters of later Mousterian deposits. The preliminary report on the anatomy of the sample assigns the human remains to *Homo sapiens sapiens* rather than to *H. s. neanderthalensis*.

An eastern European fossil that has attracted attention for some time is a cranium from the Veternica cave, Jugoslavia. The specimen, described by Smith (85) as ". . . indistinguishable from modern hominid crania," was found in Level "h," which contains an undoubted Mousterian assemblage and which is dated geochronologically to the local equivalent of the Podhradem Interstadial (57). The excavator, Malez, has suggested that the fossil *may* be a burial intrusive from an overlying Aurignacian level, and this suggestion has been considered likely (85); however, the appearance of modern man at such a late date should occasion little surprise, even in association with Mousterian tools.

The situation in western Europe, the locus of the "Neanderthal problem" in at least some formulations, is complicated by our almost total ignorance of the anatomy of the makers of those industries which offer the strongest evidence of an archaeological transition from Middle to Upper Palaeolithic—the Mousterian of Acheulian Tradition. In commenting on this lacuna, Bordes (13) says that it would not be surprising if an association of modern man with that industry were eventually to be documented. Although such evidence is not yet at hand, one site in Spain appears to offer data similar to those from Jebel Qafzeh.

At La Cueva de la Carigüela, near Piñar in Granada, a series of sediments most probably of late Würm II age (54) contain Mousterian industries associated with human skeletal remains (4). Lumley's study (54) shows that there is great homogeneity and stability in the sequence of Mousterian assemblages (Levels 10 to 2), all of which can be described as Typical Mousterian of Levallois facies containing very few characteristically Upper Palaeolithic tools. Of great interest is the fact that the human remains from the lower levels, including a child's frontal from Level 9 subsequently studied by Lumley & García Sánchez (55, 56), are those of Neanderthal man, whereas a tibia from Level 3 and a mandible and parietal from Level 2 are said to be of anatomically modern man (34). If the anatomical assignment of the later remains is confirmed by corroborative studies and if the Würm II dating is correct, the importance of Carigüela for both the Palaeolithic archaeology and human paleontology of western Europe is obviously great.

In 1971, Brose & Wolpoff (17) suggested on theoretical grounds that the archaeological materials of the earliest anatomically modern man should be of the sort normally assigned to the Middle Palaeolithic. Although they did not then have specific data to document this expectation, it now appears that at least some representatives of modern man were indeed making Mousterian tools. What might be the "earliest" occurrence of anatomically modern man is a controversial problem in human paleontology, one which fortunately is not the topic of this review. The earliest appearance of an Upper Palaeolithic technology is another question fraught with ambiguity. As discussed below in a later section, the development and quantitatively significant use of blade technology appears in some areas well before the mid-Würm (II/III, Podhradem, etc) time horizon that is usually and correctly associated with the beginnings of the undoubted and continuing Upper Palaeolithic in many areas. Without providing clear processual and interpretative answers, some of the recent data appear to destroy the element of synchrony in the classic model, even for Europe; anatomy and technology must be considered separately.

ORIGIN AND DIFFUSION   A significant modification in the classic model of the Upper Palaeolithic is the present understanding that in Europe, as well as in other areas of the Old World, the technological/typological characteristics of the Upper Palaeolithic have local roots in specific local Middle Palaeolithic industries from which transitional change can be documented. Bordes's (13) recent summary of evidence for Upper Palaeolithic origins mentions five major areas of Eurasia where there is at least some documentation of a Middle-to-Upper Palaeolithic transition.

The initial Upper Palaeolithic industry whose origin is best documented is the Châtelperronian (or Lower Périgordian) of southwestern Europe, found in an area extending from central or perhaps northern France to northern Spain [see, for example, the syntheses of González Echegaray & Freeman (40), Moure Romanillo (76), and de Sonneville-Bordes (88)]. Summaries of the evidence—technological, typological, and distributional—for both the existence of the Châtelperronian and its transitional authocthonous development from the Mousterian of Acheulian Tradition have been presented recently by Delporte (26), Bordes (13), de Sonneville-Bordes (88), and Mellars (69). Its first appearance in the Würm II/III Interstadial is well documented geochronologically, especially by Laville (47–49) and others in southwestern France. Because of insoluble problems about the true provenience of the Combe-Capelle skeleton [e.g. Delporte (26); comments of Movius, Bordes, and Bosinski in de Sonneville-Bordes (88)], the anatomy of the Châtelperronian artificers must be considered as unknown (as essentially is that of their Mousterian *archaeological* predecessors).

The situation in Central Europe seems less clear (at least to the outside observer), if for no other reasons than the larger area involved and the greater diversity of both early Upper Palaeolithic industries and the research models and terminologies applied to them. The earliest relevant industry, occurring first in the *early* part of the Podhradem Interstadial, is the Szeletian, combining within single assemblages flake technology (for scrapers, points, etc), blade technology (for end-scrapers, burins, etc), and the occurrence of bifacial foliate points. Although some (e.g. Gavela 37) view the Szeletian as a Middle Palaeolithic phenomenon, most workers consider it the earliest Upper Palaeolithic representative in the area (e.g. Bordes 13, Kozłowski 46, Valoch 90). Its technological/typological roots are apparent in the foliate point (*Blattspitz*) Mousterian of Central Europe, and it is either an independent local transition from Middle to Upper Palaeolithic (like the Châtelperronian further west) or the result of technical acculturation to an already existing Aurignacian tool-making tradition. Although the later Szeletian and the Aurignacian were clearly contemporaneous (46), the independent origin of the Szeletian appears more likely because the earliest Aurignacian sites are placed by both geochronology and radiocarbon somewhat later than the early Podhradem Interstadial. The Jermanovician industry of Poland and nearby regions is sufficiently similar to the Szeletian to be grouped with it by some workers (e.g. Valoch 90). Chmielewski (20) and others (e.g. Fridrich 32) consider it, with its foliate points and Upper Palaeolithic technological and typological elements, to be another instance of an independent development from local Mousterian roots. The earliest Jermanovician sites are apparently of late Podhradem age.

Another early Upper Palaeolithic industry widespread in Central Europe is the Aurignacian. Although there have long been attempts to see this tool-making tradition as intrusive in Central Europe (as it certainly is in Western Europe), the earliest (late Podhradem) assemblages contain numerous Middle Palaeolithic types, and some local late Mousterian industries in which blade technology, burins, and carinate scrapers are prominent are considered to be directly transitional to the local Aurignacian (32, 90). Fridrich (32) argues that the so-called Kremsian industry, considered by others to be at most an Aurignacian variant, is another example of an independent development from local Mousterian roots.

In the European part of the Soviet Union, early Upper Palaeolithic industries, some of which may be as old as those of Central Europe despite problems with radiocarbon dating (43, 53), show great variation in both technology and typology. A group of similar assemblages from various sites, referred to collectively as the industry of a "Kostenki-Sungif culture," are considered by some workers (6, 13, 20) to have developed transitionally from local Mousterian industries of Levallois technology. However, Klein (43), who emphasizes the difficulties of understanding the typological variation in the relevant assemblages, strongly denies solid evidence of a Middle-to-Upper Palaeolithic transition anywhere in the European Soviet Union.

The possibility of local transitions from Mousterian to Upper Palaeolithic in the Near East has often been mentioned (13), and there are suggestions (39, 71) that the blade industries of India have specific roots in the local Middle Palaeolithic. Bordes's (13) discussion of the Far East concerns the possibly transitional assemblage from the site of Shuitungkou in the Ordos region of northern China. Chard (19; see also Okladnikov 81) summarizes information about the site of Moil'tyn-am in northern Mongolia, where a poorly dated sequence of assemblages suggests to Soviet archaeologists a transitional development from a pebble-tool and flake technology—invoking both Western (Mousterian) and East Asian connotations—to a true blade technology. The later assemblages at Moil'tyn-am may be relevant to the origins of the Siberian Upper Palaeolithic further north; Mongolia is considered a very probable source area for the first effective settlement of central and eastern Siberia by man, during the Sartan glacial stage beginning ca 30,000 B.P. Whereas similarities between the Siberian Upper Palaeolithic and that of Europe have long been recognized (42), recent work emphasizes relationships with other areas of East Asia.

Although information from some areas is clearer than that from others, there are now abundant data to support a view of Upper Palaeolithic origins as multiple and polycentric. The evidence would be much clearer were the chronology better controlled in some areas, thus denying more conclusively the kind of hyper-diffusionist arguments from principle abundant in the older literature and recast more recently by Klein (43). The crucial question is, of course, whether industries of *mixed* technological and typological characteristics (the existence of which is not in dispute) mean *transition* or a kind of technical acculturation to an already extant and diffusing tradition. The greater probability of the polycentric position seems indicated by the very specific nature of the typological continuities in certain local sequences, some with great time depth, and the general absence of such specific typological resemblances between and among earliest Upper Palaeolithic industries in different areas (the mischief done by the overextension of terminology—Aurignacian, Châtelperron point, *lamelle* Dufour, etc—can hardly be overestimated).

To accept the position that the Upper Palaeolithic originated several times, in different areas and perhaps at somewhat different dates, is *not* to suggest that all Middle Palaeolithic industries (or all Mousterian industries of Levallois technique) automatically and inexorably developed into Upper Palaeolithic ones—a point of view more than hinted at by Brose & Wolpoff (17). Detailed typological research in various areas—e.g. for southeastern France by Lumley & Lumley (55), for Middle Europe by Bosinski (14), for Central Europe by Valoch (90), for eastern Europe by Chmielewski (20), for North Africa by Tixier (89) and Camps (18)—gives abundant evidence of specific Middle Palaeolithic industries and complexes that did not "become" Upper Palaeolithic, even late ones contemporary with the Châtelperronian, Szeletian, etc. Furthermore, it is certainly the case that *some* early Upper Palaeolithic industries, and some later ones, have no satisfactory local roots in given areas and must be considered intrusive.

In addition to the Upper Palaeolithic industries discussed above (and, of course, many others) that date to the equivalent of the second half of the Würm, there is evidence from North Africa and the Near East and from southern Africa that industries produced principally or in large part by an "Upper Palaeolithic" blade technology and containing blade tool forms generally characteristic of the Upper Palaeolithic existed significantly earlier in the Upper Pleistocene. One such group of related industries—the Amudian or pre-Aurignacian—that is found in Libya and at the eastern end of the Mediterranean appears to date to the end of the Eem Interglacial or the beginning of the Würm (e.g. Garrod 36, McBurney 68). Technologically and typologically these fit quite well definitions of Upper Palaeolithic (although not particularly Aurignacian) industries, but the lack of continuity in their areas of occurrence prohibits regarding them as the origin of later developments.

Recent work on Middle Stone Age industries of southern Africa has emphasized the very early appearance there of the extensive (but not exclusive) use of Upper Palaeolithic-like blade technology and characteristic Upper Palaeolithic tool forms (end-scrapers, burins, backed tools) (33, 44, 45). The MSA industries apparently began no later than the beginning of the Eem Interglacial and ended no later than 40,000–30,000 B.P. Sampson's (82) summary of what he calls the "Pietersburg complex," beginning ca 60,000 B.P., is an example of a widespread group of industries in which characteristically Upper Palaeolithic technology and typology are prominent. The physical type associated with MSA industries in southern Africa is unknown, but there has been a suggestion that the Florisbad skull indicates a degree of anatomical modernity in the populations of that time (82). Clark (22) and others have pointed out that this very early development of blade technology is just one of several indications from recent data that sub-Saharan Africa can no longer be considered to have been culturally static, laggard, or peripheral.

The two "precocious" appearances of blade technology (North Africa/Near East and southern Africa) are, at least in part, contemporaneous. They are probably best regarded as independent of one another, separate examples of the polycentrism of origin of what are recognized as Upper Palaeolithic characteristics. Despite their early dating, it is not possible to seize on either of them as *the* origin of the later industries long considered Upper Palaeolithic.

That aspect of the classic model of the Upper Palaeolithic which saw these developments as coming into Europe from some external region of origin is no longer in accord with modern archaeological data, which demand a model of multiple, polycentric origins in various parts of the Old World, including Europe. These same archaeological data strongly suggest (but cannot, of course, directly demonstrate) that the appearance of Upper Palaeolithic technology/ typology in Europe, or in any other given area, cannot be viewed as the result of the intrusive entry of anatomically modern man. Other causal explanations for the temporally and spatially widely distributed technological changes must be sought. If these changes are systemically related to human anatomy (cf Brose & Wolpoff 17, Mann & Trinkaus 58), we can expect that the origins of modern man will be no less multiple and polycentric.

RITUAL, NOTATION, AND SYMBOL

Burials and Nonburials

Patterned ways of disposing of human dead, appearing first during the Middle Palaeolithic, become more numerous and complex during the Upper Palaeolithic. Of the various recent discoveries of human remains in Upper Palaeolithic sites, some are of particular interest.

Šandalja II is a cave site near the city of Pula in South Istria, Jugoslavia, excavated by Malez (57). Human remains have been found associated with a "Gravettian" industry in a level ("b") dated by radiocarbon to ca 12,000 B.P. A few fragments were found in 1963, but major discoveries in 1971 raise the total corpus to 29 separate skeletal fragments. How many individuals are represented is not clear, but there are apparently more than one. What is notable about the Šandalja II human remains is their condition and distribution. All bones, cranial and postcranial, were thoroughly smashed, and the fragments were widely strewn within the occupation level along with the nonhuman faunal refuse. The lack of burial and the other details suggest to Malez that cannibalism was being practiced, but he notes that there is no evidence of charring of the human bones. These circumstances are similar to those reported by Movius (77, 78; see also Billy 9 and Legoux 51) for the fragmentary remains of at least seven individuals found dispersed through Level 2 (Protomagdalenian) at the Abri Pataud (Dordogne), France. The bones of the Pataud individuals were not so severely smashed, but the scattering of dismembered chunks and the lack of stratigraphic evidence of burial remain puzzling.

Complex burial ritual associated with an Aurignacian occupation at Cueva Morín (Santander), Spain, is reported by Freeman & González Echegaray (30, 31). The four burials, of which two were only minimally disturbed, are highly unusual in that the human remains are not skeletons, but rather pseudomorphs or natural casts in fine clayey sediment that preserve the general shape and outline of the original organic material of the corpse. The best preserved, Morín I, was removed *en bloc* from the cave for later cleaning, study, and conservation in the laboratory. The burial ritual reconstructed for Morín I is as follows: (*a*) excavation of a grave trench with digging sticks into the underlying Middle Palaeolithic occupation levels; (*b*) "deepening" the grave by building low walls of clay clods around the circumference of the trench; (*c*) mutilation of the corpse of the very tall individual by decapitation and amputation of the feet (apparently in order to fit the dimensions of the grave) and placement of these body parts into the trench; (*d*) placement of grave goods—the body of a small ungulate, large butchered portions of game animals, and some flint implements—on top of the corpse and the placement of other grave goods (meat, ochre) into an offering pit beside the grave; (*e*) filling of the grave and construction of a low mound, incorporating red ochre, on top of it; and (*f*) lighting a fire on top of the mound.

A well preserved "Gravettian" burial was discovered in 1971 by Mezzena & Palma di Cesnola (70) in the Grotta Paglicci (Apulia), Italy. A tall young male was buried in extended position in a grave covered by a thin layer of red ochre. In addition to the flint and bone implements that were associated as grave goods, the excavators found evidence of some of the defunct's costume and articles of personal adornment; these include an ankle ring, a bracelet, and what was apparently a cap decorated with pierced deer teeth.

The richest evidence for the costume of Upper Palaeolithic man comes from the burials discovered by Bader (6–8) between 1964 and 1969 at Sungiŕ, near Vladimir in the northern part of the European USSR. Sungiŕ is an open-air, early Upper Palaeolithic site that contains, in addition to rich evidence of habitation, the complete or partial human skeletal remains of six individuals. The most important of these are found in two grave complexes, Sungiŕ I and II. Sungiŕ I consists of the primary interment of a 60-year-old male, the burial ritual for which has been reconstructed as follows: (*a*) excavation of the grave pit and the sprinkling into it of charcoal and red ochre; (*b*) placement of the corpse along with flint implements as grave goods; and (*c*) filling of the grave, including the emplacement of a thick layer of red ochre. A fragmentary female skull found in the top of this grave fill may represent part of the same ritual, but the upper zone was too seriously disturbed by solifluction to be certain of the association.

Sungiŕ II consists of the burial in a grave trench of two young boys, extended head-to-head, accompanied by rich and varied grave goods. The most spectacular of these are two long spears (lengths of 1.66 m and 2.42 m) made of split and artificially straightened mammoth tusk. A third skeleton and additional grave goods, found in the upper part of the grave fill and again badly disturbed and damaged by solifluction, may be part of the same burial complex.

By a very careful study of the distribution of beads in relation to the skeletal remains and of the patterns of soil discoloration, Bader and his co-workers have been able to suggest very detailed reconstructions of the articles of clothing worn by the Sungiŕ cadavers. These include: (*a*) a skin cap to which were sewn numerous bone beads; (*b*) a skin jacket or tunic, not open in front; (*c*) a short outer coat, open in front and held shut with ivory pins; (*d*) skin trousers, constricted and decorated at knee and ankle by bead-covered bands; and (*e*) soft, moccasin-like shoes, possibly sewn to the trousers.

Notation and Symbol

One aspect of the cultural remains of Upper Palaeolithic man that has long been recognized as extremely important is the frequent presence of art and decoration. Significant new discoveries are being made all the time, including important finds of hitherto unknown parietal art and associated material [e.g. the new chambers at Niaux reported by Clottes & Simonnet (24)], but an attempt to review these discoveries and the analytic and interpretative models applied to them would be the appropriate subject of a separate review article. One body of analysis has, however, been especially significant (in spite of or perhaps because of the controversy it has provided) because of the new dimensions of Upper Palaeolithic culture it appears to have made accessible to the anthropologist. The work of Marshack, in two recent monographs (62, 64) and a series of articles (e.g. 60, 61, 63, 65), suggests with great plausibility the use of similar conventions of notation by Upper Palaeolithic groups widely distributed in space and time. Marshack offers considerable documentation in support of his hypothesis that the notation was a system for recording time based on a lunar cycle. Other aspects of his work concern possible interpretations of Upper Palaeolithic iconography, and in a recent popularized paper (66) he reports preliminary results of his application of specialized photographic techniques to parietal art. If this research withstands the testing and challenges it has evinced, it could be an important contribution from the realm of Upper Palaeolithic archaeology to a more general anthropological study of man.

Literature Cited

1. Allchin, B., Goudie, A. 1971. Dunes, aridity and early man in Gujarat, western India. *Man* n.s.6:248–65
2. Allchin, B., Goudie, A. 1974. Pushkar: prehistory and climatic change in western India. *World Archaeol.* 5:358–68
3. Allchin, B., Hegde, K. Ṭ. M., Goudie, A. 1972. Prehistory and environmental change in western India: a note on the Budha Pushkar Basin, Rajasthan. *Man* n.s.7:541–64
4. Almagro, M., Fryxell, R., Irwin, H. T., Serna, M. 1970. Avance a la investigación arqueológica geo-
cronológica y ecológica de la cueva de La Carigüela (Piñar, Granada). *Trab. Prehist.* 27:45–60
5. Angel, J. L. 1972. A Middle Palaeolithic temporal bone from Darra-i-Kur, Afghanistan. See Ref. 27, 54–56
6. Bahder, O. N. 1971. Abitati dell' estremo Nord dell'Europa nel Paleolitico. *Riv. Sci. Preist.* 26:325–45
7. Bahder, O. N. 1967. Eine ungewöhnliche paläolithische Bestattung in Mittelrussland. *Quartär* 18:191–93 + Tafel XXVII
8. Bahder, O. N. 1970. Das zweite Grab in der paläolithischen Siedlung

Sungif im mittleren Russland. *Quartär* 21:103–4 + Tafel II

9. Billy, G. 1975. Etude anthropologique des restes humains de l'abri Pataud. See Ref. 78, 201–61

10. Binford, L. R. 1973. Interassemblage variability—the Mousterian and the 'functional' argument. In *The Explanation of Culture Change: Models in Prehistory*, ed. C. Renfrew, 227–54. Univ. Pittsburgh Press

11. Bordes, F. 1968. *The Old Stone Age*. New York: McGraw-Hill

12. Bordes, F., ed. 1972. *The Origin of Homo sapiens/Origine de l'homme moderne* (Ecologie et Conservation, 3). Paris: UNESCO

13. Bordes, F. 1972. Du Paléolithique moyen au Paléolithique supérieur: continuité ou discontinuité? See Ref. 12, 211–18

14. Bosinski, G. 1972. Late Middle Palaeolithic groups in northwestern Germany and their relations to early Upper Palaeolithic industries. See Ref. 12, 153–94

15. Breuil, H. 1912. Les subdivisions du paléolithique supérieur et leur signification. *C. R. 14e Congr. Int. Anthropol. Arch. Préhist.*, Genève:165–238

16. Breuil, H., Lantier, R. 1959. *Les hommes de la Pierre Ancienne (Paléolithique et Mésolithique)*. Paris:Payot. 2e ed.

17. Brose, D. S., Wolpoff, M. H. 1971. Early Upper Paleolithic man and late Middle Paleolithic tools. *Am. Anthropol.* 73:1156–94

18. Camps, G. 1974. *Les civilisations préhistoriques de l'Afrique du Nord et du Sahara*. Paris: Doin

19. Chard, C. S. 1974. *Northeast Asia in Prehistory*. Madison: Univ. Wisconsin

20. Chmielewski, W. 1972. The continuity and discontinuity of the evolution of archaeological cultures in central and eastern Europe between the 55th and the 25th millenaries B. C. See Ref. 12, 173–79

21. Clark, J. D. 1971. A re-examination of the evidence for agricultural origins in the Nile Valley. *Proc. Prehist. Soc.* 37(2):34–79

22. Clark, J. D. 1975. Africa in prehistory: peripheral or paramount? *Man* n.s.10:175–98

23. Clark, J. G. D. 1969. *World Prehistory: A New Outline*. Cambridge Univ. Press

24. Clottes, J., Simonnet, R. 1972. Le réseau René Clastres de la caverne de Niaux (Ariège). *Bull. Soc. Préhist. Fr.* 69:293–323

25. Daniel, G. E. 1950. *A Hundred Years of Archaeology*. London: Duckworth

26. Delporte, H. 1970. Le passage du Moustérien au Paléolithique supérieur. In *L'homme de Cro-Magnon*, ed. G. Camps, G. Olivier, 129–39. Paris: Arts et Métiers Graphiques

27. Dupree, L. 1972. Prehistoric research in Afghanistan (1959–1966). *Trans. Am. Philos. Soc.* n.s.62 (4):1–84

28. Dupree, L. 1972. Introduction: outline of work by season. See Ref. 27, 5–13

29. Dupree, L., Davis, R. S. 1972. The lithic and bone specimens from Aq Kupruk and Darra-i-Kur. See Ref. 27, 14–32

30. Freeman, L. G., González Echegaray, J. 1970. Aurignacian structural features and burials at Cueva Morín (Santander, Spain). *Nature* 226:722–26

31. Freeman, L. G., González Echegaray, J. 1973. *Los enterramientos paleolíticos de Cueva Morín (Santander)*. Santander: Patronato de las Cuevas Prehistóricas de Santander

32. Fridrich, J. 1973. Počátky mladopaleolitického osídlení Čech (Die Anfänge der jungpaläolithischen Besiedlung Böhmens). *Archeol. Rozhl.* 25:392–442

33. Gabel, C. 1975. Africa south: the last 30,000 centuries. *J. Field Archaeol.* 2:363–87

34. García Sánchez, M. 1960. Restos humanos del paleolítico medio y superior y del neo-eneolítico de Piñar (Granada). *Trabajos del Instituto "Bernardino de Sahagún" de Antropología y Etnología del Consejo Superior de Investigaciones Científicas* 15(2):17–72

35. Garrod, D. A. E. 1938. The Upper Palaeolithic in the light of recent discovery. *Proc. Prehist. Soc.* 4:1–26

36. Garrod, D. A. E. 1962. The Middle Palaeolithic of the Near East and the problem of Mount Carmel man. *J. R. Anthropol. Inst.* 92:232–59

37. Gavela, B. 1968. Szeletien-ski facies u paleolitu Srbije (Le faciès szélétien du Paléolithique en Serbie). *Starinar* 19:13–26

38. Ghosh, A. K. 1970. The Paleolithic cultures of Singhbhum. *Trans. Am. Philos. Soc.* n.s.60(1):1–68
39. Ghosh, A. K. 1972. Flake and flake-blade industries in India in the context of human evolution. See Ref. 12, 95–100
40. González Echegaray, J., Freeman, L. G. 1971. *Cueva Morín: excavaciones de 1966 a 1968.* Santander: Patronato de las Cuevas Prehistóricas de la Provincia de Santander
41. Grahmann, R. Müller-Beck, H. 1967. *Urgeschichte der Menschheit.* Stuttgart: Kohlhammer. 3. Aufl.
42. Klein, R. G. 1971. The Pleistocene prehistory of Siberia. *Quat. Res.* 1:133–61
43. Klein, R. G. 1973. *Ice-Age Hunters of the Ukraine.* Univ. Chicago Press
44. Klein, R. G. 1974. Environment and subsistence of prehistoric man in the Southern Cape Province, South Africa. *World Archaeol.* 5:249–84
45. Klein, R. G. 1975. Middle Stone Age man-animal relationships in southern Africa: evidence from Die Kelders and Klasies River Mouth. *Science* 190:265–67
46. Kozłowski, J. K. 1974. Quelques remarques sur la relation entre l'Aurignacien et le Szélétien. *Arheol. Rad. Raspr. (Acta Diss. Archaeol.)* 7:373–78
47. Laville, H. 1969. L'interstade Würm II-Würm III et la position chronologique du Paléolithique supérieur ancien en Périgord. *C. R. Acad. Sci. Paris Sér. D* 269:10–12
48. Laville, H. 1973. *Climatologie et chronologie du Paléolithique en Périgord: étude sédimentologique de dépôts en grottes et sous-abris.* Thèse de Doctorat d'Etat ès Sciences Naturelles. Université de Bordeaux I
49. Laville, H. 1975. Précisions sur la chronologie du quaternaire récent. *Bull. Soc. Préhist. Fr.* 72:15–17
50. Leakey, L. S. B. 1960. *Adam's Ancestors: The Evolution of Man and his Culture.* New York: Harper Torchbooks. 4th ed.
51. Legoux, P. 1975. Présentation des dents des restes humains de l'abri Pataud. See Ref. 78, 262–305
52. Lubbock, J. 1865. *Prehistoric Times.* London: Williams & Norgate

53. Lucius, E. 1969–1970. *Das Problem der Chronologie jungpaläolithischen Stationen im Bereiche der europäischen UdSSR* (Mitt. Prähist. Komm. Österr. Akad. Wissensch., 13/14). Wien: Kommissionsverlag der Österreichischen Akademie der Wissenschaften
54. Lumley, H. de 1969. Etude de l'outillage moustérien de la grotte de Carigüela (Piñar - Grenade). *Anthropologie* 53:165–206, 325–64
55. Lumley, H. de, Lumley, M.-A. de 1972. Les prédécesseurs de l'homme moderne dans le Midi méditerranéen. See Ref. 12, 37–48
56. Lumley, M.-A. de, García Sánchez, M. 1971. L'enfant néandertalien de Carigüela à Piñar (Andalousie). *Anthropologie* 75:29–56
57. Malez, M. 1974. Noviji rezultati istraživanja paleolitika u Velikoj pećini, Veternici i Šandalji (Neue Ergebnisse der Paläolithikum—Forschungen in Velika pećina, Veternica und Šandalja, Kroatien). *Arheol. Rad. Raspr. (Acta Diss. Archaeol.)* 7:7–44 + Tabla I–VIII
58. Mann, A., Trinkaus, E. 1973. Neandertal and Neandertal-like fossils from the Upper Pleistocene. *Yearb. Phys. Anthropol.* 17:169–93
59. Marks, A. E. 1968. The Khormusan: an Upper Pleistocene industry in Sudanese Nubia. See Ref. 92, 315–91
60. Marshack, A. 1969. Polesini: a reexamination of the engraved Upper Palaeolithic mobilary materials of Italy by a new methodology. *Riv. Sci. Preist.* 24:219–81
61. Marshack, A. 1970. Le bâton de commandement de Montgaudier (Charente): réexamen au microscope et interprétation nouvelle. *Anthropologie* 74:321–52
62. Marshack, A. 1970. *Notation dans les gravures du Paléolithique supérieur: nouvelles méthodes d'analyse.* Publs. Inst. Préhist. Univ. Bordeaux, Mémoire, 8. Bordeaux: Delmas
63. Marshack, A. 1972. Cognitive aspects of Upper Palaeolithic engraving. *Curr. Anthropol.* 13:445–77
64. Marshack, A. 1972. *The Roots of Civilization.* New York: McGraw-Hill
65. Marshack, A. 1972. Upper Paleolithic notation and symbol. *Science* 178:817–28
66. Marshack, A. 1975. Exploring the

mind of Ice Age man. *Natl. Geogr. Mag.* 147(1):64–89
67. Marshack, A. 1976. *Implications of the Paleolithic symbolic evidence for the origin of language. Am. Sci.* 64:136–45
68. McBurney, C. M. B. 1967. *The Haua Fteah (Cyrenaica) and the Stone Age of the South-East Mediterranean.* London: Cambridge Univ. Press
69. Mellars, P. A. 1973. The character of the middle-upper palaeolithic transition in southwest France. See Ref. 10, 255–76
70. Mezzena, F., Palma di Cesnola, A. 1972. Scoperta di una sepoltura gravettiana nella Grotta Paglicci (Rignano Garganico). *Riv. Sci. Preist.* 27:27–50
71. Misra, V. N. 1972. Evolution of Palaeolithic cultures in India. See Ref. 12, 115–20
72. Mochanov, Y. A. 1973. *Early migrations to America in the light of a study of the Dyuktai Paleolithic culture of north-east Asia.* Presented at 9th Int. Congr. Anthropol. Ethnol. Sci., Chicago
73. Morlan, V. J. 1967. The preceramic period of Hokkaido. *Arct. Anthropol.* 4(1):164–220
74. Morlan, V. J. 1971. The preceramic period of Japan: Honshu, Shikoko and Kyushu. *Arct. Anthropol.* 8(1):136–70
75. Mortillet, G. de 1872. Classification des diverses périodes de l'Age de la Pierre. *C. R. 6e Congr. Int. Anthropol. Arch. Préhist., Bruxelles:* 432–44
76. Moure Romanillo, J. A. 1972. Secuencia cultural del Paleolítico superior en la región cantábrica. *Trab. Prehist.* 29:9–16
77. Movius, H. L. Jr. 1961. The Proto-Magdalenian of the Abri Pataud, Les Eyzies (Dordogne). *Ber. 5. Int. Kongr. Vor- und Frühgesch., Hamburg, 1958:* 561–66 (Berlin: Gebr. Mann, 1961)
78. Movius, H. L. Jr., Ed. 1975. *Excavation of the Abri Pataud, Les Eyzies (Dordogne).* Harvard Univ., Peabody Mus., Am. Sch. Prehist. Res., Bull. 30. Cambridge: Peabody Mus.
79. Murty, M. L. K. 1968. Blade and burin industries near Renigunta on the south-east coast of India. *Proc. Prehist. Soc.* 34:83–101

80. Oakley, K. P. 1964. *Frameworks for Dating Fossil Man.* Chicago: Aldine
81. Okladnikov, A. P. 1973. *Mongolian Paleolithic (On the history of initial development by man of Central Asia).* Presented at 9th Int. Congr. Anthropol. Ethnol. Sci., Chicago
82. Sampson, C. G. 1974. *The Stone Age Archaeology of Southern Africa.* New York: Academic
83. Sankalia, H. D. 1972. The Middle Palaeolithic cultures of India, central and western Asia and Europe. See Ref. 12, 109–13
84. Shiner, J. L. 1968. The Cataract Tradition. See Ref. 92, 535–629
85. Smith, F. H. 1976. A fossil hominid frontal from Velika Pećina (Croatia) and a consideration of Upper Pleistocene hominids from Yugoslavia. *Am. J. Phys. Anthropol.* 44:127–34
86. Smith, J. W. 1974. The Northeast Asian—Northwest American microblade tradition (NANAMT). *J. Field Archaeol.* 1:347–69
87. Smith, P. E. L. 1966. The Late Paleolithic of northeast Africa in the light of recent research. *Am. Anthropol.* 68(2)(2):326–55
88. Sonneville-Bordes, D. de 1972. Environnement et culture de l'homme du Périgordien ancien dans le sud-ouest de la France: données récentes. See Ref. 12, 141–46
89. Tixier, J. 1972. Les apports de la stratigraphie et de la typologie au problème des origines de l'homme moderne dans le Maghreb. See Ref. 12, 121–27
90. Valoch, K. 1972. Rapports entre le Paléolithique moyen et le Paléolithique supérieur en Europe centrale. See Ref. 12, 161–71
91. Vandermeersch, B. 1972. Récentes découvertes de squelettes humains à Qafzeh (Israël): essai d'interprétation. See Ref. 12, 49–54
92. Wendorf, F. 1968. *The Prehistory of Nubia.* Dallas: Southern Methodist Univ.
93. Wendorf, F. 1968. Late Paleolithic sites in Egyptian Nubia. See Ref. 92, 791–953
94. Wendorf, F. 1968. Summary of Nubian prehistory. See Ref. 92, 1041–59
95. Wendorf, F. Said, R., Schild, R. 1970. Egyptian prehistory: some new concepts. *Science* 169:1161–71

Ann. Rev. Anthropol. 1976. 5:149–68
Copyright © 1976 by Annual Reviews Inc. All rights reserved

PHYSICAL ANTHROPOLOGY OF   ◆ 9574
THE LIVING POPULATIONS OF
SUB-SAHARAN AFRICA

Jean Hiernaux

Laboratory of Biological Anthropology, University of Paris 7, Paris, France

MATERIALS

This review is based on information made available after the compilation, published in 1968 (79), of all known anthropobiological means and frequencies that fulfill the following requirements: (*a*) the samples must concern well-defined African ethnic groups living south of 22° North, exclusive of those of European or Asiatic descent; (*b*) the samples must comprise at least 40 male subjects for adult anthropometry, 50 subjects for dermatoglyphics, and 100 subjects for blood traits; and (*c*) the techniques must be explicitly uniform. The same criteria have been used in compiling the data basic to this review.

Table 1 lists the populations and characteristics covered by new information in the areas of adult anthropometry, blood genetics, dermatoglyphics, and color blindness. Table 2 lists growth studies published after 1968. Other biological variables are dealt with in the text.

Compared with the past, the period covered here saw fewer studies undertaken for the sake of quantifying or classifying the differences between neighboring populations, but many more studies aimed at answering specific questions. In Africa as elsewhere, the Human Adaptability section of the International Biological Programme (IBP) has played a major role in promoting the careful planning of multidisciplinary studies aimed at solving problems of adaptation and response to the environment.

Without claiming to be comprehensive, the following analysis of the new studies addresses broad topics or questions.

FACTORS OF GROWTH AND MATURATION

The growing process is known to be controlled by heredity and a number of environmental factors. Some of the studies listed in Table 2 have been under-

149

taken not only for computing local norms (valid only for the studied gene pool in its momentary environmental conditions), but also for assessing environmental influences on growth. Rural Kongo children show a physical development inferior to that of the Kongo of Kinshasa, the capital city of Zaïre, but within this town physical development also varies between the districts according to the wealth of the inhabitants (65). At two years of age, Bantu children fed partly in a nursery school at Soweto near Johannesburg are taller and weigh more than urban Bantu children of Johannesburg, who in turn are taller and weigh more than rural Bantu children (141).

These results agree with what has been observed in the rest of the world. In Africa as elsewhere, the elucidation of environmental factors underlying the differences in growth according to social class, income, occupation, and urban vs rural residence remains incomplete. If nutrition and hygiene are generally accepted factors, Jürgens (104) is convinced that intellectual output is an incipient factor of differentiation in Tanzania.

A high proportion of the tabulated studies compare the growth of the Africans with that of Europeans (living in Europe or Africa) or of Euramericans. A generally slower growth of the Africans is shown as in previous studies. For the same height, weight attains the same value in Tanzania as in the United Kingdom (a situation rarely observed in Africa), but the Tanzanian children have thinner skin folds (42). Leiderman et al (113) retested the precocity in psychomotor development of the African infant during the first year in comparison to the European, a precocity already observed in several populations. On the basis of Bailey's tests in peri-urban Kikuyu infants of Kenya, Leiderman et al confirmed the African superiority in both the mental and the motor parts of the test, but contrary to previous observations they found that the test scores correlate positively with the father's income and education and with the modernity of the household. The causes of this African superiority are not yet clearly understood.

Nor are the causes of the generally late sexual maturation in Africa fully understood. The most frequently computed indicator of this phenomenon, the median age at menarche, is known in no more than ten African populations. Recent data concern the girls of Dakar in Senegal (117), 14.0 yr; the Nyakyusa of Tanzania (74), 14.9 yr; and the rural Somali of Somalia (69), 14.8 yr (the first two values are from status quo surveys analyzed by probits, the third one from recalled ages). These data confirm that socioeconomic status and rural vs urban residence influence the age at menarche as well as growth. For example, urban Somali girls of high status in Mogadishio have their menarche at 13.1 yr (69) (probit value). On the basis of seven values only (from probit series), Roberts (145) found a negative regression of the age at menarche in Africa on mean annual temperature; menarche is later in Africa than in Europe and Asia, in absolute terms and after the adjustment of continental means for effects of temperature. It is, possible however, that ambient temperature is not independent of nutrition and hygiene, two determining factors of the age at menarche.

Table 1   Sources of anthropobiological means and frequencies on populations of sub-Saharan Africa additional to those listed by Hiernaux (79, pp. 137–250)[a]

Popul.	Geogr. coord.	Anthro. attrib.	Refs.	Popul.	Geogr. coord.	Anthro. attrib.	Refs.
Amarar	21N 36E	ABO, Rh, MNS, KJs, Fy, Jk, Hb, Lu, P, G6PD, PGM, AK, 6PGD, AcP, Hb, Gm, Hp, Tf, Gc	49	Bedik	12N 13W	awl	67
				Bedik	12N 13W	20 metric	66
				Bedik	12N 13W	A_1A_2BO, Le, Rh, MNS, KJs; JK, I, P, G6PD, AcP, Hb, Gm, Hp, Tf, PChol, AlcP	18
Dongola	20N 30E	Hb	166				
Daza	18N 20E	Hb	19	Bedik	12N 13W	Hb	122
Shaikia	18N 32E	Hb	166	Bobo-Diula	12N $5W_1$	ABO, Rh	147
Gaaliin	17N 33E	Hb	166	Karaboro	11N 4W	5 metric, awl, trc	167
Wolof	16N 17W	G6PD	135	Gula	11N 18E	Hb	19
Baria	16N 37E	A_1A_2BO, Rh, MNS, KJs, Fy, P, G6PD, Hb	128	Nuba	11N 30E	Hb	166
				Dinka	11N 32E	Hb	166
				Dinka	11N 32E	Hb	53
Sarakole	15N 6W	Hb	57	Isa	11N 41E	A_1A_2BO, Rh, MN	52
Dogon	15N 4W	12 metric	95	Gadabursi	11N 41E	A_1A_2BO, Rh, MN	52
Dogon	15N 4W	awl, trc	64	Fali	10N 13E	awl, trc	62
Ful (Mali)	P15N 2W	awl, trc	64	Fali	10N 13E	20 metric	97
Fulse	15N 1W	4 metric	92	Fali	10N 13E	reflect	142
Fulse	15N 1W	awl, trc	61	Tupuri	10N 15E	ABO, Rh	15
Fulse	15N 1W	G6PD, Gm, Lnv	93	Sara-Majingay (rural)	10N 17E	22 metric	38
Fulse	15N 1W	awl, trc	64				
Kunama	15N 37E	A_1A_2BO, Rh, MNS, KJs, Di, P, G6PD, Hb	128	Sara-Majingay (rural)	10N 17E	A_1A_2BO, Le, Rh, MN, KJs, Fy, I, P, G6PD, PGM, AK, 6PGD, AcP, Hb, Gm, Inv, Hp, Tf, PChol	84
Fur	14N 25E	Hb	166				
Manding	13N 15W	Hb	122				
Ful (Bissau)	P13N 15W	awl, trc	118	Sara-Majingay (rural)	10N 17E	reflect	81
Koniagi	13N $14W_1$	ABO, Rh, MN, KJs, Fy, P, Hb	59	Salamat	10N 19E	Hb	19
Koniagi	13N $14W_1$	Gm, Hp, Tf	58	Shilluk	10N 31E	Hb	53
Bobo-Fing	13N 5W	ABO, Rh	147	Yoruba	9N 3E	PTC	105
Bobo-Ule	13N $4W_1$	ABO	147	Yoruba	9N 3E	G6PD	137
Ful (Haute Volta)	P13N 4W	ABO, Gm, Gc	170	Yoruba	9N 3E	ABO, Le, Se	6
Marka	13N $4W_3$	ABO, Gm, Hp, Gc, Lp	170	Yoruba	9N 3E	PGM	91
Mossi	13N 2W	ABO, Rh	147	Yoruba	9N 3E	ABO, Rh, MN, KJs, Hp, Tf, Gc, Rg	75
Mossi	13N 2W	A_1A_2BO, Rh, Hb, Gm, Hp	130				
Amhara	13N 37E	24 metric, A_1A_2BO, Le, Rh, MNS, KJs, Fy, Jk, Lu, P, G6PD, PGM, AK, 6PGD, AcP, Gm, Hp, Tf	73	Laka	9N 15E	Hb	19
				Sara-Majingay Vare	9N 17E	Hb	19
Danakil	13N 41E	A_1A_2BO, Rh, MN, Hb	51	Sara-Mbay (urban)	9N $17E_1$	17 metric	80

Table 1 (*Continued*)

Popul.	Geogr. coord.	Anthro. attrib.	Refs.	Popul.	Geogr. coord.	Anthro. attrib.	Refs.
Sara-Day				Binga	3N 17E	HLA	17
(urban)	9N 17E$_2$	17 metric	80	Karamojong	3N 34E	A$_1$A$_2$BO, Le, Se,	2
Sara-Kaba						Rh, MNS, Hb, Hp,	
(urban)	9N 18E$_1$	17 metric	80			Tf	
Sara-Kaba				Rendille	3N 37E	A$_1$A$_2$BO, Rh, MN	29
(rural)	9N 18E$_1$	19 metric	138	Mbuti	2N 28E	Gm	158
Sara-Ngama							54
(urban)	9N 18E	17 metric	80	Mbuti	2N 28E	ABO, Rh, MN,	60
Nuer	9N 31E	Hb	53			KJs, G6PD, Hb,	
Sidamo	9N 37E	Gm, Inv	159			Hp, Tf	
Baule	8N 5W	Gm, Inv	16				122
Yakuba	8N 8W	Gm, Inv	16	Mbuti	2N 28E	trc	63
Nago	BN 1E	14 metric	35	Sambur	2N 37E	A$_1$A$_2$BO, Rh, MN,	29
Fon	8N 2E	A$_1$A$_2$BO, Le, Rh,	35			Hp, Gc	
		MNS, KJs, P,		Kitosh	1N 34E	Hb	53
		G6PD, Hb, Hp,		Luyia	1N 34E$_4$	ABO	12
		Gc		Marama	1N 34E$_1$	Hb	53
Adja	8N 2E$_1$	14 metric	35	Nyore	1N 34E$_3$	Hb	53
Kotafon	8N 2E$_2$	14 metric	35	Luo	0S 34E$_1$	ABO	12
Hehe	8N 35E	awl, trc	146	Luo	0S 34E$_1$	Hb	53
Gagu	7N 6W	Gm, Inv	16	Luo	0S 34E$_1$	PGM, Hb, Gm,	77
Kru	7N 8W$_1$	Hb	21			Inv, Hp, Tf	
Wobe	7N 8W$_2$	Gm, Inv	16	Gusii	0S 34E$_2$	Hb	53
Ful Bororo				Maragoli	0S 34E$_4$	Hb	53
(RCA)	P7N 15E	11 metric	33	Nandi	0S 35E$_1$	ABO	12
Bamileke	6N 10E$_1$	awl	62	Kipsigis	0S 35E$_2$	Hb	53
Bamileke	6N 10E$_1$	ABO, Rh	15	Kikuyu	0S 36E	A$_1$A$_2$BO, Rh, MN,	28
Bamileke	6N 10E$_1$	A$_1$A$_2$BO, Rh, MN	76			Hb, Hp	
Bamileke	6N 10E$_1$	ABO, Rh, Hb	71				30
Baya	6N 14E	11 metric	32	Kikuyu	0S 36E	ABO	12
Nzakara	6N 22E	11 metric,	31	Kikuyu	0S 36E	G6PD	4
		A$_1$A$_2$BO, Rh, MN,		Konda			
		KJs, P, Hb, PTC		(Oto)	1S 19E$_1$	25 metric	89
Nzakara	6N 22E	Gc	155	Twa des			
Mundari	6N 31E	Hb	53	Konda	1S 19E$_2$	26 metric	89
Abua	5N 6E	dalton	144	Kamba	1S 38E	Hb	53
Ogoni	5N 7E$_4$	G6PD	72	Kamba	1S 38E	ABO	12
Ogoni	5N 7E$_4$	dalton	144	Pokomo	1S 39E	ABO, Hb	53
Banda	5N 16E	11 metric	32				54
Bari	5N 31E	Hb	53	Shi	2S 28E	ABO, Rh, MNS,	126
Fajelu	5N 31E$_2$	Hb	53			KJs, G6PD, Hp,	
Ewondo +						Tf	
Eton	4N 11E	Hb	56	Masai	2S 36E	Hb	53
Mbimu	4N 15E$_1$	10 metric	34	Tutsi	3S 30E$_1$	G6PD	126
Binga	3N 17E	awl	10	Teita	3S 38E$_1$	ABO, Hb	53
Binga	3N 17E	1 metric, A$_1$A$_2$BO,	23	Taveta	3S 38E$_2$	ABO, Hb	53
		Se, Rh, MNS, KJs,		Giriama	3S 39E$_2$	ABO	53
		Fy, He, PG6D,		Giriama	3S 39E$_2$	PTC	3
		AcP, Hb, Gm, Hp,		Giriama	3S 39E$_2$	G6PD	4
		Tf, Gc		Kabinda	4S 12E	6 metric	107
Binga	3N 17E	PGM	149	Hadza	4S 35E	awl, trc	8
Binga	3N 17E	Pep	148	Hadza	4S 35E	dalton, PTC	9

Table 1 *(Continued)*

Popul.	Geogr. coord.	Anthro. attrib.	Refs.	Popul.	Geogr. coord.	Anthro. attrib.	Refs.
Baka	5S 29E	Hb	53	Kuanyama	17S 16E	awl, trc	119
Sandawe	5S 35E	reflect, ABO, Rh	169	Kuanyama	17S 16E	Gm, Inv	103
Bondei	5S 38E	G6PD	4	Kuanyama	17S 16E	6PGD	101
			54	Ndonga	17S 17E	6PGD	101
Yaka	6S 17E₁	ABO, Rh, MNS,	126	Kwangar	17S 19E	1 metric (stature)	22
		KJs, Hp, Tf,		Kwangar	17S 19E	6PGD	101
		G6PD, Hb		Tonga	L7S 27E	Rh, He, Di	162
Wongo	7S 21E	G6PD	150	Tonga	L7S 27E	2 metric	163
Ngola	8S 15E	ABO, Le, Rh,	157	Shona	17S 31E₁	ABO	49
		MN, KJs, JK,		Zezuru	17S 31E₂	MN, KJs, Fy, P	116
		AcP, Hb, Gc		Sena	17S 35E₂	G6PD	139
Ngola	8S 15E	6 metric	166	Kwambi	18S 17E	6PGD	101
Shinji	8S 18E	G6PD	150	Kwambi	18S 17E	Gm, Inv	103
Lunda	8S 21E	G6PD	150	Hukwe			
Mbangala	9S 18E	G6PD	150	(Bushmen)	18S 22E	24 metric	70
Chokwe				Tewe	18S 33E	ABO	1
(north)	9S 20E	6 metric	107	Rue	18S 34E	ABO	1
Chokwe				Chuabo	18S 37E	awl, trc	120
(north)	9S 20E	ABO, Le, Rh,	157	Chuabo	18S 37E	ABO	139
		MN, KJs, JK,		Kung	19S 20E	AcP	100
		Acp, Gc		Kung	19S 20E	6PGD	101
Chokwe				Ndebele	19S 28E	Gm, Inv	103
(north)	9S 20E	G6PD	150	Dama	20S 15E	5 metric, ABO,	106
Songo	10S 17E	G6PD	150			Rh, MN, Gm, Inv,	
Minungu	10S 21E	G6PD	150			awl	
Luimbi	11S 17E	6 metric	166	Dama	20S 15E	6PGD	101
Tonga	11S 34E	Gm, Inv	103	Ndau	20S 33E	G6PD	139
Makonde	11S 39E	ABO	1	Mashangan	20S 34E₁	ABO	1
Makonde	11S 39E	A₁A₂B₀O, Rh, MN	174	Bangwe	20S 34E₂	ABO	1
Makonde	11S 39E	G6PD	139	Nyamban	20S 35E	Gm, Inv	103
Bieno	12S 17E	6 metric	166	Bushmen	21S 21E	Gm, Inv	103
Bieno	12S 17E	ABO, Le, Rh,	157	G/wi	21S 21E₂	6PGD	101
		MN, KJs, JK,		Venda			
		AcP, Gc		(rural)	22S 30E	11 metric	112
Nyanja	12S 34E	G6PD	139	Venda			
Makua	13S 37E	ABO	1	(rural)	22S 30E	28 metric	47
Makua	13S 37E	awl, trc	120	Venda			
Makua	13S 37E	A₁A₂BO, Rh,	175	(rural +			
		MN, Fy		urban)	22S 30E	PTC	46
Makua	13S 37E	G6PD	139	Magon	23S 35E	ABO, G6PD, Hb	99
Muila	15S 13E	6 metric	166	Magon	23S 35E	Gm, Inv, Hp, Tf	102
Ganguela	15S 18E₂	Hp	129	Shangan	23S 32E	G6PD	139
Lozi	15S 23E	Gm, Inv	103	Shangan	23S 32E	PGM, AK, 6PGD,	140
Lenje	15S 29E	Gm, Inv	103			AcP, Hp, Tf, Gc	
Nyungwe	15S 33E	awl, trc	120	Shangan	23S 32E	ABO, Rh, MNS,	121
Nyungwe	15S 33E	G6PD	139			KJs, Fy, JK, Lu,	
Humbe	16S 14E	7 metric	171			P, Gm, Inv, Hp,	
Humbe	16S 14E	awl, trc	119			Gc	
Mbukuso	16S 20E₁	1 metric (stature)	22	Shangan	23S 32E	Gm, Inv	103
Mbukuso	16S 20E₁	Gm, Inv	103	Thonga	23S 35E	ABO	1
Mbukuso	16S 20E₁	6PGD	101	Thonga·	23S 35E	ABO, Rh, MNS,	121
Kuanyama	17S 16E	7 metric	171			KJs, Fy, JK, Lu,	

Table 1 *(Continued)*

Popul.	Geogr. coord.	Anthro. attrib.	Refs.	Popul.	Geogr. coord.	Anthro. attrib.	Refs.
		P, Gm, Inv, Hp, Gc		Tswana	27S 21E	6PGD	101
				Tswana	27S 21E	AcP	100
Thonga	23S 35E	G6PD	139	Zulu	28S 31E	6PGD	101
Chopi	24S 35E	G6PD	139	Zulu	28S 31E	awl, trc	68
Pedi	25S 29E	28 metric, awl, trc, dalton, PTC, MPP	48	Zulu	28S 31E	Gm, Inv	103
				Sotho	29S 28E	ABO, Rh, MNS, Hp, Tf	127
Pedi	25S 29E	AcP	100				
Pedi	25S 29E	Gm, Inv	103	Sotho	29S 28E	ABO	136
Pedi	25S 29E	6PGD	101	Sotho	29S 28E	awl	134
Swazi	25S 31E	Gm, Inv	103	Sotho	29S 28E	Gm, Inv	103
Ronga	25S 32E	G6PD	139	Sotho	29S 28E	6PGD	101
Ronga	25S 32E	awl, trc	120	Sotho	29S 28E	AcP	100
Ronga	25S 32E	ABO	1	Pondo	30S 29E	Gm, Inv	103
Khoikhoi				Baca	31S 28E	Gm, Inv	103
(Nama)	26S 16E	AcP	100	Xhosa	33S 27E	Gm, Inv	103
Khoikhoi				Xhosa	33S 27E	AcP	100
(Nama)	26S 16E	6PGD	101	Xhosa	33S 27E	6PGD	101
Tswana	27S 21E	Gm, Inv	103	Hlubi	33S 28E	Gm, Inv	103

[a] awl = fingerprint patterns; trc = total ridge count; dalton = color-blindness; MPP = middle phalanx pilosity.

Frisch & McArthur (55) suggested that a critical fatness (in terms of fat deposits in percentage of body weight) is the major determinant of the onset of menstrual cycles. This could explain the earlier menarche in the cities and in the upper classes, in which a richer diet, a lower incidence or severity of debilitating diseases, and a less physically active way of life determine thicker fat deposits. However, fatness, or at least mean weight for height, does not vary in Africa in response to environmental factors only; it also exhibits genetic variation (78). If Frisch's hypothesis is correct, the late menarche (16.5 yr) of the genetically tall, elongated, and relatively lightweight Tutsi girls of Rwanda may have a genetic determinant in common with their slender physique: one that controls a relatively low fat deposition.

Skeletal maturation is also generally delayed in Africans in comparison to Europeans, at least at some ages (114, 125), a difference for which a genetic component has been suggested (114).

FACTORS OF THE ADULT PHYSIQUE AND PHYSIOLOGY

In the field of human biology, IBP recommended studying how populations respond to a changed environment, especially their response to heat, cold, and altitude. Since the biological response may comprise reversible short-term changes, irreversible modifications in the expression of the genome (through an

Table 2 Growth studies in sub-Saharan Africa published since 1968[a]

Population or place	Country	Sex	Ages (yr)	No. of metric variables	Refs.
El Kalakla	Sudan	♂♀	0.25–14	7	161
Gondar	Ethiopia	♂♀	6–20	5	44
Addis Ababa	Ethiopia	♂♀	5–16	5	50
Wolof of Dakar	Senegal	♂♀	0–7	11	117
Dakar	Senegal	♂♀	2–15	4	117
Sara of Sahr	Chad	♂♀	3–10	34	86
Kinshasa	Zaïre	♂	6–12	5	65
Bantu of Dar es Salam	Tanzania	♂♀	7–15	2	42
Bantu (rural, urban)	Tanzania	♂♀	7–16	7	42
Bantu	Tanzania	♂♀	7–24	3	104
Masai	Tanzania	♂	11–17	3	104
Nyakyusa	Tanzania	♀	9–17	14	74
Kisi	Tanzania	♀	9–14	14	74
Chokwe and Lunda	Angola	♂♀	0–20	1	151
Lourenço Marques	Mozambique	♂♀	6–18	3	40
Lower Shire	Malawi	♂♀	<5	3	20
Bantu (rural, urban)	S. Africa	♂♀	2–6	2	141
Bantu of Pretora	S. Africa	♂♀	6–15	11	154
Bushmen	Botswana	♂♀	b	2	11

[a] Longitudinal studies.
[b] Unknown.

alteration of the growth processes), and genetic adaptation, such studies require a comparison of populations of similar origin who dispersed into different habitats. The potential output of the study is enriched if a variation in the number of generations spent in a new habitat can be taken into account.

Although Africa does not offer human habitats at an altitude as high as in the Andes or the Himalayas, a team under Harrison performed a study of altitude adaptation in Ethiopia (73). Three groups of Amhara, living at 1500, 3000, and 3700 m above sea level, were compared. The first two groups were adequately sampled. No difference in allele frequency at 14 loci was found between them, which confirms their common origin. The third group is significantly greater in weight, lateral dimensions, thorax size, and vital capacity. The causal factors are not evident: if altitude itself is the most probable factor in the larger thorax and increased vital capacity, its action on the other variables is more probably indirect, through differences in food intake and occurrence of diseases such as malaria. People living at lower altitudes who migrated to higher altitudes in adulthood do not differ from the highland natives in vital capacity. Whether this is due to adult plasticity or to selective migration, the data do not tell.

Once the effect of altitude is removed, there is not much variation in mean annual temperature in tropical Africa. However, annual rainfall and seasonal variation in temperature and air moisture largely differ between the equatorial forest and the open biomes. In the forest, climate is relatively uniform during the year; the air is still and the sun's rays are filtered by clouds and tree-cover. The savanna is more sunny and windy, with alternating dry and wet seasons and higher peaks of heat. When men, who evolved in the tropical savanna, migrated into the equatorial forest (a process that started about 20,000 years ago), they became subject to different climatic pressures.

This particular case of human adaptation has been studied by Hiernaux and his collaborators (38, 80, 81, 84, 85, 89). They compared three populations: The Sara in the savanna of southern Chad, and the two castes (vassal and suzerain) of the Konda ethnic group who live side by side in the equatorial forest of Zaïre—the Twa and the Oto. The Pygmoid Twa, settled in the forest for a long time, live predominantly by hunting and gathering, whereas the Oto, an offshoot of a relatively recent wave of Bantu-speaking invaders, live mainly by agriculture and fishing. This team synthesized its results with those obtained on the Binga Pygmoids of the Central African Republic by Cavalli-Sforza and his collaborators (23), who concluded that the Binga, the Mbuti Pygmies, and the Central African agriculturalists have a common origin, that there is no clear-cut evidence for a mixed origin of the Binga, and that the Mbuti and Binga ancestral lines either diverged independently from the Central African line (the Mbuti line before the Binga), or diverged from a common line early after the latter's branching from the Central African one.

The anthropometric comparison of the Twa-Oto (Konda) pair of populations with three other pairs of Pygmy or pygmoid hunters vs forest agriculturalists also suggests that several independent lines of "pygmyization" have evolved from a common Central African stock in different areas of the rain forest, and probably during different times, to give birth to the present Pygmy and Pygmoid populations—a case of parallel evolution.

Multivariate analysis of the data also suggests that gene migration, everywhere unidirectional, between the members of the same pair of populations, flows in the suzerain-to-vassal direction in the Konda, but in the reverse direction in the other pairs, in keeping with the ethnological data on the caste identification of the crossbreeds.

Size reduction in the forest owes nothing to malnutrition: the Pygmies have a relatively high weight for their height. Its biological advantage seems to lie in an increase in the body surface/body volume ratio, which apparently is achieved through a lower speed of growth (88). A possible mechanism by which the genome could determine small body size—a tissue subresponsiveness to human growth hormone—is suggested by endocrinological studies on the Binga (123, 124, 143).

Diet is an unquestionable factor influencing human physique. The array of diet-sensitive measurements now includes the skin folds, which permit, in combination with other measurements, estimates of body composition. They are frequently included in anthropometric studies (31–35, 38, 73, 80, 89, 112, 163).

As already stated in the growth section, fatness may vary, at both the individual and the population levels, with the genome as well as with the environment. This may be true for other diet-sensitive variables like biochemical levels. Despite a diet rich in cholesterol, the Masai herders of East Africa present low levels of blood cholesterol and β-lipoproteins; compared to Europeans, they compensate for a higher capacity to absorb the dietary cholesterol by a higher capacity to block the synthesis of endogenous cholesterol (90). The data do not allow a distinction to be made between genetic and nongenetic determinants of these characteristics.

Like the Masai, the Hadza of Tanzania, who until recently were hunter-gatherers, have a low cholesterol level, low blood pressure, and no (or only a slight) increase of these two variables with age (7). A low, age-stable blood pressure has also been observed in the Mbuti Pygmies, the Bushmen of the Kalahari, the Fali of North Cameroon, and the Kurumba of Upper Volta (94). All these are populations leading a very active life, but this seems to be but one of the factors involved. In the level and age dependence of their blood pressure, they contrast with urban populations like the Venda of Johannesburg (112) and the Yoruba of Ibadan (5), but also with some rural populations like the rural Ganda (152), Venda, and Yoruba, although the last two groups have a lower mean blood pressure than their urban conterparts.

Such cases bear witness to the many instances of changing ways of life in Africa that put a stress on human adaptability, cultural and biological: from nomadic to settled, as in the Hadzas studied by the late N. Barnicot and his co-workers (7, 8, 9, 13, 14); from rural to urban; or as part of relocation schemes. They all imply deep demographic, socioeconomic, dietary, and sanitary changes. Several IBP projects have been concerned with adaptation of Africans to urban life: in the Venda (47, 112), Malawi (131), and the Sara (37).

In Africa as elsewhere, the measurement of work capacity is frequently included in recent adaptation studies, such as in the study of Ethiopians at two altitude levels (111) and in the comparison of Twa and Oto in Zaïre (65) and of rural and urban Venda (165). However, the measurement of maximum O_2 intake requires elaborate laboratory equipment, much time, and the cooperation of the subjects; samples are therefore usually low and there is a risk that they suffer from biases. Moreover, the conclusions may differ according to whether the populations are compared for absolute O_2 intake, O_2 intake per unit of body weight, or O_2 intake per unit of another biometric function such as lean body weight. Simpler methods, like the step test used in the Fali of Cameroon (96), do not give easily comparable results. A study of young adult Africans in Dar es Salaam and their comparison with English samples showed that the maximum O_2 intake measured on an ergometric bicycle is a linear function of the lean leg volume as computed from external measurements of the lower limb; the function is the same for both sexes and both ethnic groups (41). The environmental factors of variation of work capacity seem therefore to be those that control muscle mass: diet, hygiene, and exercise.

Heat tolerance has been studied recently in only a few places in Africa. Nigerian villagers, and, in Lagos, students and workers in both the light and heavy industries have been compared for heat tolerance, as well as work capacity (133); the heavy industrial workers show evidence of physical adaptation to both heat and exercise. In Southern Africa, Bushmen, ten groups of Bantu, and subjects of European origin have been compared for adaptation to heat and cold. In their natural states, the heat reactions of the Bushmen are better than those of Bantu, which in turn are better than those of Europeans. This agrees with the prediction based on the average body surface/height ratio, but the data do not permit us to say how much of the difference in heat tolerance is due to differences in morphology and how much to differences in physical activities and environmental heat stress in their everyday lives. The Europeans stand the severe cold better, perhaps resulting more from their thicker subcutaneous fat than from their lower surface/weight ratio (173).

The study of some classical anthropobiological characteristics has been revived recently thanks to technological advances. This is the case for skin color, which can now be measured objectively by reflectometry. Since 1968, skin reflectance data have been published on the Amhara of Ethiopia (73), the Xhosa of South Africa (168), the Chopi of Mozambique (172), the Sandawe and Nyaturu of Tanzania (169), the Fali of Cameroon (142), the Yoruba of Nigeria (132), the Sara of Chad (81), and the Twa and Oto castes of the Konda in Zaïre. A Sara-Oto-Twa sequence of increasing reflectance of the inner arm at 685 nm is observed, in agreement with the hypothesis that melanin concentration in the skin is adaptive to the dose of ultraviolet radiation (85).

So far, this analysis of the factors of variation in anthropobiological characteristics has considered only a fraction of the metric data referred to in Table 1: those collected for answering specific questions in human ecology. Another ecological approach has used most of the above data plus those published in 1968: J. Hiernaux and A. Froment (unpublished) have computed the correlations between the means of frequencies of 31 anthropobiological variables and 5 climatic variables, thus revising the first author's 1968 estimates.

NUMERICAL TAXONOMY

Another use of the current set of means and frequencies has been to extract from it, or from a section of it, a subset of values for computing multidimensional distances between a number of populations. From the matrix of distances may then be derived a two- or three-dimensional map, a dendrogram, or a cluster analysis. Most often the scholar has to compromise between two needs: of comparing many populations, and of basing the comparison on many attributes.

All works published since 1968 along these lines have used either biometrical means or the frequencies of blood genetic polymorphisms. Anthropometric maps have been published (on the basis of nine, ten, and ten variables respectively) for 15 populations of the Kivu-Rwanda-Burundi area (82), 32 populations of sub-Saharan Africa (83), and four pairs of suzerain vs vassal castes in Zaïre and the Republic of Central Africa (89), and dendrograms of 16 populations of Southwest Africa on the basis of 10 variables (107). The Mbuti, Binga, and Central African agriculturalists have been mapped for six polymorphisms (23), and nine populations (including the Sara Majingay) for nine polyporphisms (84). At the Congress of Anthropological and Ethnological Sciences in Chicago in 1973, Jenkins, Harpending, and Nurse presented a paper on the genetic distances between 18 populations of Southern Africa for 14 polymorphisms.

Most authors of these studies were aware that a given set of human populations does not necessarily lend itself to a meaningful classification, and felt more concerned with interpreting the matrices and maps in terms of selection, gene migration, mutation, and genetic drift than with defining taxa. The application to Africa of a recent development of the distance studies has started with the comparison of maps locating the same populations for different variables or sets of variables, which has elsewhere proved to be helpful for understanding human differentiation. The discrepancies between the metrical and blood polymorphism distances in the equatorial forest have been interpreted in terms of a different sensitivity of the two categories of variables to the climate (89). A close correlation between metrical and geographical distances in a set of eight Sara villages (138) calls for a simple model of differentiation. Within the Bantu-speaking area, linguistic and biometrical distances between 11 populations are fairly well correlated, but a twelfth population, the Mbundu of Angola, is strongly discordant, which allows for several possible explanations (87).

THE STUDY OF THE DISTRIBUTION OF SINGLE ATTRIBUTES

The distribution of some of the attributes listed in Table 1 has been studied (or restudied) recently. A simple case is that of a qualitative attribute, a variant of which is present in some populations only. This seems to be the case for the $Gm^{1, 13}$ haplotype, which has not been found in Africa north of Southern Africa, where it is the commonest haplotype in the San (or Bushmen) and the second commonest in the Khoikhoi (or Hottentots) (160). Hence the hypothesis that this haplotype arose by mutation in an ancestral Khoisan population, and its utilization for quantifying Khoisan admixture in the Bantu-speaking populations of southern Africa (103).

The P^r allele of the red cell acid phosphatase system has also been used for quantifying this admixture (103). However, its presence in populations living far away from Southern Africa, like the Bedik of Senegal and the Sara of Chad, in whom no Khoisan admixture is suspected, suggests that it could be widely distributed in Africa. Its high frequencies in Southern Africa, with the highest ones in the Khoisan, could therefore result either from genetic drift in the ancestral Khoisan, or from genetic adaptation to a factor peculiar to the Southern African environment. In the latter case, convergent selection would add its pressure to that of Khoisan admixture for determining the P^r frequencies in those populations brought to Southern Africa by the Bantu expansion since the first centuries AD.

A somewhat similar but better understood case is that of the hemoglobin polymorphism: both S and C alleles are absent from a number of populations, many more for C than for S. On a world basis, Livingstone (115) listed all data on the frequency of hemoglobin variants, thalassemia, and glucose 6-phosphate dehydrogenase deficiency published between 1967 and 1973, and discussed them by continents. He concludes that, in presence of holoendemic malaria, S tends to replace any other abnormal hemoglobin. If so, now that S is present in the West African bastion of C, C is on the way to elimination. However, within the range of possible selective fitness of the hemoglobin genotypes in a malarial environment, some sets of fitness induce the replacement of S by C, and still other ones maintain an A-S-C polymorphism (24, 39). More precise estimates of the fitness of the various hemoglobin genotypes in different habitats are needed for further elucidation of the natural history of the abnormal hemoglobin alleles.

Indeed, the understanding of the distribution of any biological attribute requires knowing the selective fitness of its genotypes or, at least, of its phenotypes. The search for significant associations between anthropobiological frequencies or means and environmental variables (e.g. in the fields of climate, nutrition, disease, and culture) has helped in building specific hypotheses about selective factors for a number of attributes, mono- or polygenic. Such associations at least call for an explanation, like the significant differences found between leprous and nonleprous Makwa of Mozambique for five blood polymorphisms (156). However, in Africa, differences in survival and fertility have been demonstrated only in some of the blood polymorphisms involving anomalies or deficiencies, and only one recent work has sought and found direct evidence of both stabilizing and directional selection in the domain of anthropometry (38).

In some cases, the adaptive value of a trait looks evident e.g. that of adult lactose tolerance in the pastoral societies of East Africa, where the evidence is in favor of a genetic component (27, 36).

The nature of some morphological attributes has been disputed: are they genetic or acquired? This is the case for the tablier, or elongation of the *labia minora,* which attains a frequency near to 100% in the Bushmen, in whom it seems to be genetic (45, 164). Possibly sexual selection has been at work on this trait.

STUDIES ON MICRODIFFERENTIATION

A developing strategy in anthropobiology consists of the thorough demographic, genealogical, historical, and biological study of populations small enough to make the examination of all their members practicable. In sub-Saharan Africa, one such population has been studied in this way: the Bedik of eastern Senegal, by Gomila and his co-workers (18, 66, 108–110). This population of nearly 1500 individuals inhabits six villages within a small area that displays no marked environmental heterogeneity. It exchanges very few mates with the surrounding populations. It is divided into two social fractions; the rate of endogamy varies between villages. Intervillage biological differentiation depends little on geographic distance; in the field of anthropometry, it seems to depend partly on the rate of endogamy, although the two sexes show conflicting pictures in this respect. Intervillage distances based on blood polymorphisms are independent from anthropometric distances, which indicates different factors or mechanisms of differentiation.

Also thoroughly studied from the viewpoint of demography and genealogies have been the Kel Kummer, a group of nomadic Twareg who live near the Mali-Niger boundary. Their genealogies have been traced back to 1610, and biologically validated by the study of blood polymorphisms; no case of paternity exclusion was discovered. Special attention was paid to the *HL-A* haplotypes, which proved their usefulness for reconstructing the history of the parting of three related Twareg groups, including the Kel Kummer. A complete or nearly complete absence of *HL-A* homozygotes was another major finding of this research (25, 26, 43, 98).

CONCLUSION

Anthropobiological research has been very active in sub-Saharan Africa during the last seven years. By the variety of its human habitats and ways of life, by the rapid changes of its human ecosystems, and by the persistence of a number of communities leading relatively undisturbed ancestral ways of life, this area needs and hopefully will attract still more research in the near future. The growing participation of Africans in the current anthropobiological effort is encouraging.

Literature Cited

1. Alberto, M. S. 1962. Elementos de estudo para la organizaçao da carta sero-antropologica da populaçao negra de Mocambique (com base no sistema ABO). *Mem. Inst. Cient. Moc.* 4:1–192
2. Allbrook, D., Barnicot, N. A., Dance, N., Lawler, S. D., Marshal, R., Mungai, J. 1965. Blood groups, haemoglobin and serum factors of the Karamojo. *Hum. Biol.* 37:217–37
3. Allison, A. C. 1951. A note on taste-blindness in Kenya Africans and Arabs. *Man* 51:119–20
4. Allison, A. C. 1960. G6PD deficiency in red blood cells of East Africans. *Nature* 186:531
5. Akinkugbe, O. O., Ojo, O. A. 1969. Arterial pressure in rural and urban populations in Nigeria. *Br. Med. J.* 2:222–24
6. Ball, P. A. J. 1962. Influence of the Secretor and Lewis genes on susceptibility to duodenal ulcer. *Br. Med. J.* 11:948:50
7. Barnicot, N. A., Bennett, F. J., Woodburn, J. C., Pilkington, T. R. E., Antonis, A. 1972. Blood pressure and cholesterol in the Hadza of Tanzania. *Hum. Biol.* 44: 621–48
8. Barnicot, N. A., Mukherjee, D. P., Woodburn, J. C., Bennett, F. J. 1972. Dermatoglyphics of the Hadza of Tanzania. *Hum. Biol.* 44: 621–48
9. Barnicot, N. A., Woodburn, J. C. 1975. Colour blindness and sensi-

tivity to PTC in Hadza. *Ann. Hum. Biol.* 2:61–68
10. Barrai, I. 1968. Dermatoglyphics in Babinga Pygmies. *Atti Assoc. Genet. Ital.* 12:92–94
11. Beaton, G. R. 1969. A growth study of Bushman and Bantu children. *S. Afr. J. Sci.* 65:17–27
12. Beecher, J. L. 1967. ABO blood group distribution in some Kenya tribes. *East Afr. Med. J.* 44:134–41
13. Bennett, F. J., Barnicot, N. A., Woodburn, J. C., Pereira, M. S., Henderson, B. E. 1973. Studies on viral, bacterial, rickettsial and treponemal disease in the Hadza and a note on injuries. *Hum. Biol.* 45:243–72
14. Bennett, F. J., Kagan, I. G., Barnicot, N. A., Woodburn, J. C. 1970. Helminth and protozoal parasites of the Hadza of Tanzania. *Trans. R. Soc. Trop. Med. Hyg.* 64:857–80
15. Bernard-Schwebel, A., Nicoli, R. M., Ranque, J., Battaglini, P. F. 1965. Etudes séro-anthropologiques. Recherches sur la population du Cameroun. *Afr. Med.* 28:165–66
16. Blanc, M. 1970. "Applications du système sérique Gm et Inv à l'étude des populations humaines." Toulouse: Centre d'hémotypologie du CNRS
17. Bodmer, J. G., Bodmer, W. F. 1970. Studies on African Pygmies. IV. A comparative study of the HL-A polymorphism in the Babinga Pygmies and other African and Caucasian populations. *Am. J. Hum. Genet.* 22:396–411
18. Bouloux, C., Gomila, J., Langaney, A. 1972. Hemotypology of the Bedik. *Hum. Biol.* 44:289–302
19. Boyer, S. H., Crosby, E. F., Fuller, G. F., Ulenurm, L., Buck, A. A. 1968. A survey of haemoglobins in the Republic of Chad and characterization of haemoglobin. *Am. J. Hum. Genet.* 20:570–78
20. Burgess, H. J. L., Wheeler, E. 1971. *Lower Shire Nutrition Survey.* Blantyre, Malawi: Ministry of Health
21. Cabannes, R., Sy-Baba, Schmitt-Beurrier, A. 1968. Etude des hémoglobines en Côte d'Ivoire. *Ann. Univ. Abidjan Méd.* 2:108–15
22. Castro, M. E., De e Almeida. 1968. Alguns caracteres antropologicos de Mucussos e Cuangares (Angola). *Mem. Junta Invest. Ultramar Port.* II 55:109–36

23. Cavalli-Sforza, L. L., Zonta, L. A., Nuzzo, F., Bernini, L., De Jong, W. W., Meeka Khan, P., Ray, A. K., Went, L. N., Siniscal, M., Nijenhuis, L. E., van Loghem, E., Modiani, G. 1969. Studies on African Pygmies. I. A pilot investigation of Babinga Pygmies in the Central African Republic (with an analysis of genetic distances). *Am. J. Hum. Genet.* 21:252–74
24. Cavalli-Sforza, L. L., Bodmer, W. F. 1971. *The Genetics of Human Populations.* San Francisco: Freeman
25. Chaventré, A. 1973. *Etude généalogique d'une tribu saharo-sahélienne: les kel Kummer et apparentés.* Thèse Doct. Etat ès Lett. et Sci. Hum. Univ. Sorbonne, Paris
26. Chaventré, A., Degos, L. 1975. Rôle et importance du système HL-A en anthropologie. Applications aux Kel Kummer. *Bull. Mém. Soc. Anthropol. Paris* 2:99–116
27. Cook, G. C. 1969. Lactate deficiency: a probable ethnological marker in East Africa. *Man* (NS) 4:265–67
28. Corrain, C. 1972–1973. Distribuzione dei caratteri emotipologici tra le populazione Kykuyu del Kenya. *Riv. Antropol.* 43:265–80
29. Corrain, C., Capitanio, M. 1973. Alcune ricerche antropologiche tra le populazione del Kenya. *Atti Mem. Accad. Pata. Sci. Lett. Arti* 85(2):49–62
30. Corrain, C., Capitanio, M., Erspamer, G. 1974. Emoglobine normale in populazione del Kenya. *Atti Mem. Accad. Patav. Sci. Lett. Arti* 86(2):5–13
31. Cresta, M. 1965. Antropologia morfologica e sierologica dei N'zakara della Republica Centrafricana. *Quad. Ric. Sci.* 28:9–20
32. Cresta, M. 1965. Note antropologiche sui Baya ed i Banda della Republica Centrafricana. *Quad. Ric. Sci.* 28:59–68
33. Cresta, M. 1965. Contributo alla conoscenza antropologica dei Fulbe Bororo. *Quad. Ric. Sci.* 28:69–80
34. Cresta, M. 1965. Contributo alla conoscenza antropologica dei Babinga. *Quad. Ric. Sci.* 28:81–102
35. Cresta, M., Spedini, G. 1968. Antropologia morfologica ed ematologica del basso Dahomey: I. Caratteri morfologici. *Riv. Antropol.*

55:163–78; II. Caratteri emotipologici. Ibid, pp. 179–88; III. Cresta, M., Spedini, G., Olivieri, V. Caratteri chimici. Ibid, pp. 189–202

36. Cox, J. A., Elliott, F. G. 1974. Primary adult lactose intolerance in the Kivu area: Rwanda and the Bushi. *Am. J. Dig. Dis.* 19:714–24

37. Crognier, E. 1967. Données biométriques sur l'état de nutrition d'une population africaine tropicale: les Sara du Tchad. *Biom. Hum.* 4:37–54

38. Crognier, E. 1973. Adaptation morphologique d'une population africaine au biotope tropical: les Sara du Tchad. *Bull. Mém. Soc. Anthropol. Paris* 10:3–151

39. Crozier, R. H., Briese, L. A., Guerin, M. A., Harris, T. R., McMichael, J. L. Moore, C. H., Ramsey, F. R., Wheeler, S. R. 1972. Population genetics of hemoglobins S, C and A in Africa: equilibrium or replacement? *Am. J. Hum. Genet.* 24:156–67

40. Da Costa Martins, D. 1971. Height, weight and chest circumference of children of different ethnic groups in Lourenço Marques, Moçambique, in 1965 with a note on the secular trend. *Hum. Biol.* 43:253–64

41. Davies, C. T. M., Mbelwa, D., Crockford, G., Weiner, J. S. 1973. Exercise tolerance and body composition of male and female Africans aged 18–30 years. *Hum. Biol.* 45:31–40

42. Davies, C. T. M., Mbelwa, D., Doré, C. 1974. Physical growth and development of urban and rural East African children, aged 7–16 years. *Ann. Hum. Biol.* 1:257–68

43. Degos, L., Chaventré, A., Jacquard, A. 1973. Le polymorphisme du système HL-A est-il maintenu par un désavantage des homozygotes? *C. R. Acad. Sci. Paris* 277:1553–56

44. Dellaportas, G. J. 1969. Growth of school children in Gondar area, Ethiopia. *Hum. Biol.* 41:218–22

45. De Villiers, H. 1969. The morphology and incidence of the tablier in Bushman, Griqua and Negro females. *Proc. 8th Int. Congr. Anthropol. Ethnol. Sci.* 1:48–51

46. De Villiers, H. 1970. A note on taste blindness in Venda males. *S. Afr. J. Sci.* 66:26–28

47. De Villiers, H. 1972. A study of morphological variables in urban and rural Venda male populations. *Human Biology of Environmental Change,* ed. D. J. M. Vorster, 110–13. London: IBP

48. De Villiers, H. n.d. Morphological variables and genetic markers in urban and rural Pedi male populations. Polycop. Dep. Anat., Univ. Witwatersrand, Johannesburg

49. El Hassan, A. M., Godber, M. J., Kopec, A. C., Mourant, A. E., Tills, D., Lehmann, H. 1968. The hereditary blood factors of the Beja of the Sudan. *Man* 3:272–83

50. Eksmyr, R. 1971. Anthropometry in Ethiopian school children. CNU Rep. No. 40. *Nutr. Metabol.* 13: 7–20

51. Fourquet, R. 1969. Etude hémotypologique ABO, MN et Rh de l'èthnie Afar. *Med. Trop. Marseille* 29:669–79

52. Fourquet, R. 1970. Etude hémotypologique des Somali Issa et Gadaboursi. *Med. Trop. Marseille* 30:352–62

53. Foy, H., Kondi, A., Timms, G. L., Brass, W., Bushra, F. 1954. The variability of sickle-cell rates in the tribes of Kenya and the Southern Sudan. *Br. Med. J.* I:294–97

54. Fraser, G. R., Giblett, E. R., Motulsky, A. G. 1966. Population genetic studies in the Congo. III: Blood groups (ABO, MNSs, Rh, JS$^\alpha$). *Am. J. Hum. Genet.* 18:546–52

55. Frisch, R. E., McArthur, J. W. 1974. Menstrual cycles: fatness as a determinant of minimum weight for height necessary for their maintenance or onset. *Science* 185: 949–51

56. Gamet, A., Labes, A. 1964. Première étude sur les hémoglobinoses au Centre-Cameroun. *Bull. Soc. Pathol. Exot.* 57:1125–33

57. Gentilini, M., Pannetier, J. 1969. Résultats de l'étude de l'électrophorèse systématique de l'hémoglobine de quinze cents travailleurs migrants de l'Ouest africain. *Ann. Soc. Belge Med. Trop.* 49:193–98

58. Gessain, R., Moullec, J., Gomila, J. 1965. Groupes d'haptoglobine et de transferrine et groupes Gm des Coniagui et des Bassari. *Bull. Mém. Soc. Anthropol. Paris* 8:19–22

59. Gessain, R., Ruffié, J., Kane, Y., Kane, O., Cabannes, R., Gomila, J. 1965. Note sur la séro-anthropologie de trois populations de Guinée et du Sénégal: Conaigui, Bassari et Bedik.

Bull. Mém. Soc. Anthropol. Paris 8:5–18

60. Giblett, E. R., Motulsky, A. G., Fraser, G. R. 1966. Population genetic studies in the Congo. IV: Haptoglobin and transferrin serum groups in the Congo and in other African populations. *Am. J. Hum. Genet.* 18:553–58

61. Glanville, E. V. 1967. Dermatoglyphics of the fingers and palms of the Kurumba from Upper Volta. *Proc. K. Ned. Akad. Wet. Ser. C* 70:535–42

62. Glanville, E. V. 1968. Digital and palmar dermatoglyphics of the Fali and Bamileke of Cameroons. *Proc. K. Ned. Akad. Wet. Ser. C* 71:529–36

63. Glanville, E. V. 1969. Digital ridge-counts of Efe Pygmies. *Am. J. Phys. Anthropol.* 31:427–28

64. Glanville, E. V., Huizinga, J. 1966. Digital dermatoglyphs of the Dogon, Peul and Kurumba of Mali and Upper Volta. *Proc. K. Ned. Akad. Wet. Ser. C* 69:664–74

65. Ghesquière, J. L. 1972. Physical development and working capacity of Congolese. See Ref. 47, pp. 117–20

66. Gomila, J. 1971. *Les Bedik (Sénégal oriental). Barrières culturelles et hétéogénéité biologique.* Univ. Montréal Press. 273 pp.

67. Gomila, J., Pée-Laborde, L., Lestrange, Th. 1967. Dermatoglyphes digito-palmaires et plis de flexion dans l'isolat Bedik, Sénégal oriental (résultats préliminaires). *Anthropos* 19:103–18

68. Grace, H. J., Ally, F. E. 1973. Dermatoglyphs of the South African Negro. *Hum. Hered.* 23:53–58

69. Grassivaro Gallo, P. 1975. The age at menarche in Somalia. *Ann. Hum. Biol.* 2:197–200

70. Gusinde, M. 1966. Von gelben und schwarzen Buschmännern. Graz, Austria: Akad. Druck–V. Verlagsanstalt

71. Happi, C. 1959. *Recherches Hématologiques chez les Bamiléké au Cameroun: groupes sanguins, drépanocytose.* Thèse Doct. Méd. Univ. Paris, Paris, France

72. Harris, R., Gilles, H. M. 1961. G6PD deficiency in the peoples of the Niger Delta. *Ann. Hum. Genet.* 25:199–205

73. Harrison, G. A., Küchemann, C. F., Moore, M. A. S., Boyce, A. J., Baju, T., Mourant, A. E.,

Godber, M. J., Glasgow, B. G., Kopeć, A. C., Tills, D., Clegg, E. J. 1969. The effects of altitudinal variation in Ethiopian populations. *Philos. Trans. R. Soc. London Ser. B* 256(805):147–82

74. Hautvast, J. 1973. Sexual development in relation to ecological, socio-economical and somatometrical factors. A comparative study of two groups of schoolgirls in Tanzania. *Anthropol. Anz.* 34:23–31

75. Heiken, A., Balogun, R. A., Swan, T., Rasmuson, M. 1974. Population genetic studies in Nigeria. *Hereditas* 76:117–36

76. Henninot, E., Polaert, J., Happi, C. 1958. Recherches sur les groupes sanguins de populations Bamiléké (Bafang, Cameroun). *Bull. Mém. Soc. Anthropol. Paris* 9:340–51

77. Herzog, P., Bohatova, J., Ortova, A. 1970. Genetic polymorphism in Kenya. *Am. J. Hum. Genet.* 22:287–91

78. Hiernaux, J. 1964. Weight/height relationship during growth in Africans and Europeans. *Hum. Biol.* 36:273–93

79. Hiernaux, J. 1968. *La Diversité Humaine en Afrique Subsaharienne,* ed. Inst. Soc. Univ. Lib. Bruxelles, Bruxelles. 261 pp.

80. Hiernaux, J. 1969. Investigations anthropobiologiques au Moyen-Chari (République du Tchad) préliminaires à des recherches multidisciplinaires. *Homo* 20:1–11

81. Hiernaux, J. 1972. La réflectance de la peau dans une communauté de Sara Majingay (République du Tchad). *Anthropologie Paris* 76:279–99

82. Hiernaux, J. 1972. The analysis of multivariate biological distances between human populations: principles, and applications to sub-Saharan Africa. *The Assessment of Population Affinities in Man,* ed. J. S. Weiner, J. Huizinga, pp. 96–114. Oxford: Clarendon

83. Hiernaux, J. 1973. Numerical taxonomy of man: an application to a set of thirty-two African populations. *Physical anthropology and its extending horizons,* ed. A. Basu, A. K. Ghosh, S. K. Biswas, R. Ghosh, pp. 151–61. Calcutta: Orient Longman

84. Hiernaux, J. 1976. Blood polymorphisms in the Sara Majingay of Chad. *Ann. Hum. Biol.* 3:127–40

85. Hiernaux, J. 1976. Skin color and

climate in Central Africa: a comparison of three populations. *Hum. Ecol.* 4:69–73

86. Hiernaux, J., Asnes, D. 1974. La croissance des enfants Sara de 3 à 10 ans à Fort-Archambault (République du Tchad). *Bull. Mém. Soc. Anthropol. Paris* 1:427–53

87. Hiernaux, J., Gauthier, A. M. 1976. Comparaison des affinités linguistiques et biologiques de douze populations de langue bantoue. *Cah. Etud. Afr.* In press

88. Hiernaux, J., Rudan, P., Brambati, A. 1975. Climate and the weight/height relationship in sub-Saharan Africa. *Ann. Hum. Biol.* 2:3–12

89. Hiernaux, J., Vincke, E., Commelin, D. 1976. Les Oto et les Twa des Konda (zone de l'Equateur, Zaïre). *Anthropologie Paris,* Vol. 80

90. Ho, K. J., Biss, K., Mikkelson, B., Lewis, L. A., Taylor, C. B. 1971. The Masai of East Africa: some unique biological characteristics. *Arch. Pathol.* 91:387–410

91. Hopkinson, D. A., Harris, H. 1966. Rare phosphoglucomutase phenotypes. *Ann. Hum. Genet.* 30:167–81

92. Huizinga, J. 1968. New physical anthropological evidence bearing on the relationships between Dogon, Kurumba and the extinct West African Tellem populations. *Proc. K. Ned. Akad. Wet. Ser. C* 71:16–30

93. Huizinga, J. 1968. Human biological observations on some African populations of the thorn savanna belt. I + II. *Proc. K. Ned. Akad. Wet. Ser. C* 71:356–90

94. Huizinga, J. 1972. Casual blood pressure in populations. See Ref. 47, pp. 164–69

95. Huizinga, J., Birnie-Tellier, N. F. 1966. Some anthropometric data on male and female Dogons. *Proc. K. Ned. Akad. Wet. Ser. C* 69:675–88, 689–95

96. Huizinga, J., Reijnders, B. 1974. Heart rate changes during exercise (step test) among the Fali of North Cameroon. *Proc. K. Ned. Akad. Wet. Ser. C* 77:283–94

97. Huizinga, J., Reijnders, B. 1974. Skinfold thickness and body fat in adult male and female Fali of North Cameroon. *Proc. K. Ned. Akad. Wet. Ser. C* 77:496–503

98. Jacquard, A. 1972. Evolution du patrimoine génétique des Kel Kummer. *Population* 27:784–800

99. Jenkins, T., Blecher, S. R., Smith,

A. N., Anderson, G. G. 1968. Some hereditary red-cell traits in Kalahari Bushmen and Bantu: hemoglobins, G6PD deficiency and blood groups. *Am. J. Hum. Genet.* 20:299–309

100. Jenkins, T., Corfield, V. 1972. The red cell acid phosphatase polymorphism in Southern Africa: population data and studies on the R, RA and RB phenotypes. *Ann. Hum. Genet.* 35:379–91

101. Jenkins, T., Nurse, G. T. 1974. The red-cell 6PGD polymorphism in certain Southern African populations; with the first report of a new phenotype. *Ann. Hum. Genet.* 38:19–29

102. Jenkins, T., Steinberg, A. G. 1966. Some serum protein polymorphs in Kalahari Bushmen and Bantu: gamma-globulins, haptoglobins and transferrins. *Am. J. Hum. Genet.* 18:399–407

103. Jenkins, T., Zontendyk, A., Steinberg, A. G. 1970. Gammaglobulin groups (Gm and Inv) of various Southern African populations. *Am. J. Phys. Anthropol.* 32:197–218

104. Jürgens, H. W. undated. *Examination of the physical development of Tanzanian youth.* München: Inst. Wirtschaftsforschung

105. Kalmus, H. 1967. The frequency of PTC non-tasters in schoolchildren at Ibadan, Western Nigeria. *Hum. Biol.* 39:32–34

106. Knussmann, R., Knussmann, R. 1969. Die Dama. Eine Altschicht in Südwestafrika? *J. Südwestafrika Wiss. Ges.* 24:9–32

107. Knussmann, R., Rösing, F. W. 1974. Die ähnlichkeitsverhältnisse im südwestlichen Afrika nach anthropometrischen merkmalen. *Bevölkerungsbiologie,* ed. W. Bernhard, A. Kandler, pp. 125–53. Stuttgart: Fischer

108. Langaney, A. 1974. Structures génétiques des Bedik du Sénégal oriental. *Cah. Anthropol. Ecol. Hum.* 2:11–124

109. Langaney, A., Gomila, J., Bouloux, C. 1972. Bedik: bioassay of kinship. *Hum. Biol.* 44:475–88

110. Langaney, A., Gomila, J. 1973. Bedik and Niokholonko intra- and inter-ethnic migration. *Hum. Biol.* 45:137–50

111. Lange-Andersen, K 1972. The effect of altitude variation on the

166   HIERNAUX

physical performance capacity of Ethiopian men. See Ref. 47, pp. 154–63

112. Laubscher, N. F. 1972. The South African multidisciplinary Venda study: a multivariate statistical analysis. See Ref. 47, pp. 199–204

113. Leiderman, P. H., Babu, B., Kagia, J., Kraemer, H. C., Leiderman, G. F. 1973. African infant precocity and some social influences during the first year. Nature 242:247–49

114. Levine, E. 1972. The skeletal development of children of four South African populations. Hum. Biol. 44:399–412

115. Livingstone, F. B. 1973. Data on the abnormal hemoglobins and glucose-6-phosphate dehydrogenase deficiency in human populations 1967–1973. Ann Arbor, Mich.: Mus. Anthropol., Univ. Mich. 287 pp.

116. Lowe, R. F., Gadd, K. G., Chitiyo, M. E. 1971. The MN, P, Kell and Duffy blood group systems of the Zezuru tribe of Rhodesia. Cent. Afr. J. Med. 17:207–9

117. Massé, G. 1969. Croissance et maturation de l'enfant à Dakar. Rev. Soc. Biom. Hum. Biotypol. 4:13–23

118. Matznetter, Th. 1964. Hautleistenuntersuchung an sechs afrikanischen Negerstämmen. Z. Morphol. Anthropol. 55:315–34

119. Matznetter, Th. 1967. Untersuchungen über das Papillarsystem südwestangolanischer Negerstämme. Mitt. Anthropol. Ges. Wien 96/97:21–56

120. Matznetter, T. 1973. Enweiterte studien über hautleisten von Bantu-Negern nördlich und südlich des Sambesi von Moçambique. Mitt. Anthropol. Ges. Wien 102:64–83

121. Matznetter, T., Spielmann, W. 1969. Blutgruppen moçambiquanischen Bantustämme. Z. Morphol. Anthropol. 61:57–71

122. Mauran-Sendrail, A., Bouloux, C., Gomila, J., Langaney, A. 1975. Comparative study of haemoglobin types of two populations of eastern Senegal. Bedik and Niokholonko. Ann. Hum. Biol. 2:129–36

123. Merimee, T. J., Rimoin, D. L., Cavalli-Sforza, L. L. 1972. Metabolic studies in the African Pygmy. J. Clin. Invest. 51:395–401

124. Merimee, T. J., Rimoin, D. L., Cavalli-Sforza, L. L., McKusick,

V. A. 1968. Metabolic effets of human growth hormone in the African Pygmy. Lancet 2:194–95

125. Michaut, E., Niang, I., Dan, V. 1972. La maturation osseuse pendant la période pubertaire. A propos de l'étude de 227 adolescents dakarois. Ann. Radiol. 15:767–79

126. Motulsky, A. G., Vandepitte, J., Fraser, G. R. 1966. Population genetic studies in the Congo. I: G6PD deficiency, hemoglobin S and malaria. Am. J. Hum. Genet. 18:514–37

127. Moullec, J., Mendrez, C., Nguyen Van Cong 1966. Les groupes sanguins au Lessouto. Bull. Mém. Soc. Anthropol. Paris 9:363–66

128. Mourant, A. E., Kopeć, A. C., Ikin, E. W., Lehmann, H., Bowen-Simpkins, P., Fergusson, I. L. C., Hellier, M. D., Jones, R. D., Roberts, I. A. M. 1974. The blood groups and haemoglobins of the Kunama and Baria of Eritrea, Ethiopia. Ann. Hum. Biol. 1:383–92

129. Moura-Pires, F., Silveira-Nunes, M. A., Barros, F. 1964. Fréquence des haptoglobines dans quatre groupes éthniques du Sud de l'Angola. Sangre 9:53–56

130. N'gatchou Hagoua, J. 1965. Contribution à l'étude séro-anthropologique des Mossi (Haute-Volta). Thèse Doct. d'Et. en Pharm. Univ. Lille, Lille, France. No. 311

131. Nurse, G. T. 1972. The body size of rural and peri-urban adult males from Lilongwe District. See Ref. 47, pp. 105–9

132. Ojikutu, O. 1974. Skin pigmentation and pigmentary changes in man. See Ref. 107, pp. 104–17

133. Ojikutu, R. U., Fox, R. H. Davies, C. T. M., Davies, T. W. 1972. Heat and exercise tolerance of rural and urban groups in Nigeria. See Ref. 47, pp. 132–44

134. Olivier, G., Mendrez, C. 1966. Les dermatoglyphes digitopalmaires au Basutoland (Lessouto). Bull. Mém. Soc. Anthropol. Paris 9:355–61

135. Pene, L., Sankale, M., Linhard, J., Bernou, J. C., Diebolt, G., Gueye, I. 1967. Etude de l'évolution du paludisme rural africain en fonction des glucose-6-phosphate-deshydrogénases. Med. Afr. Noire 14:257–59

136. Pijper, J. 1930. The blood groups of the Bantu. Trans. R. Soc. S. Afr. 18:311–15

137. Porter, I. H., Boyer, S. H., Watson-Williams, E. J., Adam, A., Szeinberg, A., Siniscalco, M. 1964. Variation of glucose-6-phosphate-deshydrogenase in different populations. *Lancet* I:895–99
138. Ramirez Solano, M. E. 1975. *Différenciation morphologique parmi huit villages Sara.* Thèse Doct. 3e Cycle, Univ. Paris VII. 113 pp.
139. Reys, L., Manso, C., Stamatoyannopoulos, G. 1970. Genetic studies on Southeastern Bantu of Mozambique. I. Variants of G6PD. *Am. J. Hum. Genet.* 22:203–15
140. Reys, L., Manso, C., Stamatoyannopoulos, ·G., Giblett, E. 1972. Genetic studies on Southeastern Bantu of Mozambique II. Serum groups, hemoglobins, and red cell isozyme phenotypes. *Humangenetik* 16:227–33
141. Richardson, B. D. 1973. Growth standards. An appraisal with special reference to growth in South African Bantu and white pre-school children. *S. Afr. Med. J.* 47:699–702
142. Ritgers-Aris, C. A. E. 1973. Réflectométrie cutanée des Fali (Cameroun). *Proc. K. Ned. Akad. Wet. Ser. C* 76:500–11
143. Rimoin, D. L., Merimee, T. J., Rabinowitz, D., McKusick, V. A., Cavalli-Sforza, L. L. 1967. Growth hormones in African Pygmies. *Lancet* 2:523–26
144. Roberts, D. F. 1967. Red/green colour blindness in the Niger Delta. *Eugen. Q.* 14:7–13
145. Roberts, D. F. 1969. Race, genetics and growth. *J. Biosoc. Sci. Suppl.* 1:43–67
146. Roberts, D. F., Chavez, J., Redmayne, A. 1974. Dermatoglyphics of the Hehe (Tanzania). *Man* (NS) 9:31–43
147. Sanguiolo-Brabançon, Chr., Nicoli, R. M., Ranque, J., Battaglini, P. F. 1965. Recherches sur les populations de la Haute Volta dans le cercle de Bobo-Dioulasso. *Afr. Med.* 28:169–73
148. Santachiara-Benerecetti, S. A. 1970. Studies on African Pygmies. III. Peptidase c polymorphism in Babinga Pygmies: a frequent erythrocytic enzyme deficiency. *Am. J. Hum. Genet.* 22:228–31
149. Santachiara-Benerecetti, S. A., Modiano, G. 1969. Studies on african Pygmies. II. Red cell PGM studies in Babinga Pygmies. *Am. J. Hum. Genet.* 21:315–21
150. Santos-David, J. H. 1965. A deficiencia da deidrogenase da G6PD nos eritrocitos dos nativos da Lunda e Songo (Angola). *Arq. Anat. Antropol.* 33:141–52
151. Santos-David, J. H. 1972. Height growth of melanodermic natives of northeastern Lunda (Angola). *S. Afr. J. Med. Sci.* 37:49–60
152. Shaper, A. G., Saxton, G. A. 1969. Blood pressure and body build in a rural community in Uganda. *E. Afr. Med. J.* 46:228–45
153. Simbeye, A. G. A. 1972. A study of some haemoglobin variants, haptoglobin types, ABO and Rh blood groups in a sample of Liberians. *Hum. Hered.* 22:286–89
154. Smit, P. J. 1974. Variability in the anthropometric status of four South african populations. *S. Afr. Med. J.* 48:643–57
155. Spedini, G. 1964. Il sistema sieroproteico Gc nei Negri N'Zakara (R. C. A.). *Ric. Sci. Parte 2, Sez. A* 34:229–36
156. Spielmann, W., Teixidor, D., Renninger, W., Matznetter, T. 1970, Blutgruppen und lepra bei Moçambiquanischen Völkerschaften. *Humangenetik* 10:304–17
157. Spielmann, W., Teixidor, D., Matznetter, T. 1973. Blutgruppen bei Bantu populationen aus Angola, zugleich ein Beitrag zur Berechnung der Vaterschaftswarschenlichkeit bei Gutachten mit Negern als eventualvatern. *Blut* 27:322–35
158. Steinberg, A. G. 1966. Correction of previously published Gm(c) phenotypes of Africans and Micronesians. *Am. J. Hum. Genet.* 18:109
159. Steinberg, A. G. 1973. Gm and Inv allotypes of some Sidamo Ethiopians. *Am. J. Phys. Anthropol.* 39:403–8
160. Steinberg, A. G., Jenkins, T., Nurse, G. T., Harpending, H. C. 1975. Gammaglobulin groups of the Khoisan peoples of Southern Africa: evidence for polymorphism for a $Gm^{1,5,13,14,21}$ haplotype among the San. *Am. J. Hum. Genet.* 27:528–42
161. Sukkar, M. Y., Johnson, D., Abdel Gadir, A. M., Yousif, M. K. 1971. The nutritional status of children in rural Khartoum. *Sudan Med. J.* 9:23–38

168 HIERNAUX

162. Tobias, P. V. 1966. The peoples of Africa South of the Sahara. In *The biology of human adaptability*, ed. P. T. Baker, J. S. Weiner, pp. 111–200. Oxford: Clarendon

163. Tobias, P. V. 1972. Physique and body composition in Southern Africa. *J. Hum. Evol.* 1:339–43

164. Tobias, P. V. 1972. Recent human biological studies in Southern Africa, with special reference to Negroes and Khoisans. *Trans. R. Soc. S. Afr.* 40:109–33

165. Van Graan, C. H., Strydom, N. B., Greyson, J. S. 1972. Determination of the physical work capacities of urban and rural Venda males. See Ref. 47, pp. 129–31

166. Vella, F. 1966. Haemoglobin S and sickling in Khartoum Province. *Trans. R. Soc. Trop. Med. Hyg.* 60:48–52

167. Wangermez, I., Lamontellerie, M. 1974. Les dermatoglyphes des Karaboro (Haute Volta). Fréquence comparée des tourbillons en Afrique tropicale. *Bull. Mém. Soc. Anthropol. Paris* 1:357–71

168. Wassermann, H. P., Heyl, T. 1968. Quantitative data on skin pigmentation in South African races. *S. Afr. Med. J.* 42:98–101

169. Weiner, J. S. 1971. A preliminary report on the Sandawe of Tanzania. *Proc. Anthropol. Congr. dedicated to A. Hrdlicka, Prague and Humpolec, 1969*, ed. V. V. Novotny, pp. 481–84. Prague: Academia

170. Wendt, G. G., Ermert, A., Kirchberg, G., Kindermann, I. 1967. ABO Blutgruppen und Serumgruppen bei den Negerstämmen Peulh und Marka. *Humangenetik* 4:74–80

171. Weninger, M. 1967. Anthropologische Beobachtungen an Bantu-Negern Angolas (1964). *Homo 9. Tag. Dtsch. Ges. Anthropol.*:216–25

172. Weninger, M. 1969. Spektrophotometrische untersuchungen der Haut an einem BantuStamm (Chope) aus Moçambique. *Anthropologie Brno* 7:53–58

173. Wyndham, C. H. 1972. Man's adaptation to heat and cold in Southern Africa. See Ref. 47, pp. 145–53

174. Xavier Da Cunha, A., Font Xavier Dacunha, F. A. 1969. Os groupos sanguineos dos Macondes de Moçambique. *Rev. Cienc. Biol. Ser. A* 2:103–13

175. Xavier Da Cunha, A., Font Xavier Dacunha, F. A. 1970. Grupos sanguineos da populacaõ Macua da ilha de Moçambique. *Rev. Cienc. Biol. Ser. A* 3:97–107

Ann. Rev. Anthropol. 1976. 5:169–93
Copyright © 1976 by Annual Reviews Inc. All rights reserved

PIDGIN AND CREOLE STUDIES ◆ 9575

Derek Bickerton

Department of Linguistics, University of Hawaii, Honolulu, Hawaii 96822

INTRODUCTION

Since pidgin and creole languages have not previously been surveyed in this review series (nor, save as a sub-subdepartment of linguistics, in its biennial predecessor), it may be appropriate to begin by very briefly summarizing the history and development of the field before proceeding to discuss the work that is currently taking place therein.

Until relatively recently, pidgin and creole languages were regarded, even by most linguists, as constituting objects hardly worthy of attention from serious students of language. Despite the fact that attempts to describe such languages date back at least to the second half of the eighteenth century (90), and that a few nineteenth-century linguists, in particular Schuchardt (115), had observed their possible relevance to any general theory of linguistic change, the popular view that they constituted merely "corrupted" versions of European languages was widely accepted. As a result, development of the field was delayed, and when it came was very uneven. According to a survey by Hancock in the Hymes collection (72), there exist at present over 200 pidgin and creole languages (59), but of these, only about six could be said to have acquired an extensive literature (Haitian Creole, Sranan, Papiamentu, Jamaican Creole, Hawaiian Pidgin-Creole, and Neo-Melanesian or Tokpisin), while many are known only through anecdotal reference and have never been described at all. Similarly, there has never been complete agreement even on the precise boundaries of the field. Although the definitions of Hall (57)—that a pidgin is a language with "sharply reduced" grammatical structure and vocabulary, native to none of its users, while a creole is a pidgin that has acquired native speakers—would probably still be accepted by a majority of linguists, we will find that more recently some linguists have tried to narrow the first definition and others to broaden the second, while still others, adopting what has been called the "domestic" theory of creole origins, have attempted to short-circuit Hall's cycle.

As mentioned in the previous paragraph, early interest in pidgins and creoles centered around their origins and the extent to which—at a time when the *Stammbaum* theory of genetic relationships was ascendant—they might prove counterexamples to such a theory. Adherents of the theory claimed, for in-

169

stance, that there could be no such thing as a "mixed language," and yet pidgins and creoles seemed to show signs of precisely such a mixture; although, in the case of at least the best-known examples, vocabulary was preponderantly (+90%) drawn from the Indo-European parent, the syntax seemed to contain a number of non-IE features. Was it the case that [as Sylvain (127) argued for Haitian Creole] a creole language was simply the grafting of a European lexicon on an African grammar? Or did the European component outweigh all others on every linguistic level? While a number of writers (66, 128–130, 140) argued for at least a modified version of the former position, the majority (41, 55–57, 75, 149) continued to maintain the latter view. This was hardly surprising, since both the tradition of Indo-European philology and the currently (i.e. prior to 1960) dominant school of structural linguistics both regarded phonology and morphology as central to the study of language and syntax as relatively peripheral.

However, the nature of the genetic debate was radically changed by the introduction in the 1960s of a *tertium quid* in the form of the monogenetic hypothesis (122, 132, 150). According to this hypothesis, the similarities found worldwide among pidgins and creoles were the result of their having had a common ancestor, perhaps dating back as far as the medieval Lingua Franca (150), but certainly to an Afro-Portuguese pidgin that is assumed to have developed in fifteenth-century Guinea. Monogenesis, which for all its apparent heterodoxy represents a means of saving many of the assumptions of traditional historical linguistics, entails a belief in relexification (122), the replacement of a vocabulary originally Portuguese by English, French, Spanish, or Dutch words, without any effect on other areas of the grammar.

For reasons which remain mysterious to this reviewer, this volume's predecessor, *The Biennial Review of Anthropology* (1959–1971) consistently listed works dealing with pidgins and creoles in the section on "Sociolinguistics," despite the fact that very little work in the field could properly be called sociolinguistic; an article by Alleyne on language and Jamaican politics (4), a curious essay by Fanon that surprisingly endorses educated French attitudes to pidgins and creoles (42), and an entertaining if rather impressionistic dissertation by Reisman on the ethnography of speaking in Antigua (107) are three of the very few pre-1970 examples that spring to mind. For the most part, when it did not seek to delve into origins, work on pidgins and creoles was purely descriptive, and in general, prestructuralist (e.g. 41, 89), early structuralist (25, 37, 54), or tagmemic (95) in orientation; only one study, B. Bailey's (6) analysis of the syntax of Jamaican creole, was within the framework of generative grammar. However, during the last few years, several aspects of this picture have changed, and there has been a considerable rebirth of interest in pidgins and creoles as possible testing grounds for issues in contemporary theory. Three developments in general linguistics have helped to foster this interest. First, the revival of historical linguistics, under generative auspices, created a climate favorable to the study of the processes of linguistic change. Second, the study of linguistic variation, long considered minor or irrelevant by most linguists, became a legitimate and even respectable field. Third, and perhaps most important for future studies, the view that languages are illimitably different was largely replaced by the view that all languages are fundamentally similar, and this in turn stimulated the search for universals of language.

In consequence, the last 5 years have seen a sharp increase both in the number of writings on pidgins and creoles and the range of topics that such writings have covered. Although many of these topics overlap, the lack of any single clear direction in the field makes it necessary, for purposes of review, to subdivide the material according to the major centers of interest.

DEFINITIONS

A recurring problem in the field has been the precise definition of its boundaries. As numerous writers have pointed out, pidgins and creoles have traditionally been defined in extralinguistic terms, so that (in contrast with the areal fields) it is not possible to establish the allegiance of any given language simply by looking at its sound system, grammatical structure, and lexicon, and then comparing these with those of putatively related languages. At the International Conference on Pidginization and Creolization (Jamaica, 1968) a rather fruitless morning was spent discussing "simplification" as a possible formal criterion for pidginization, but "simplification" itself proved quite impossible to define. In practice, extralinguistic definitions have been altered and refined. For example, Hall's acceptance, as a pidgin, of any improvised contact language between persons not sharing a common tongue has been challenged by Whinnom (151); according to the latter's view, contact languages produced by a meeting of only two language communities (like the *hapa-haole* of nineteenth century Hawaii, or the Italo-Spanish *cocoliche* of Buenos Aires) represent phenomena too transitory and unstable to be classed as distinct languages. The term "pidgin" would be reserved by Whinnom for situations where a reduced or simplified form of L_1 was used mainly by native speakers of L_2, L_3, L_4, etc to communicate with one another, rather than with speakers of L_1, thus freeing their speech from being corrected in the direction of L_1 and enabling it to develop as an independent entity. This view, which would sharply reduce the importance in pidginization of any deliberate simplification by L_1 speakers (contrary to the views expressed in 19, 44, 96, etc), would probably now be shared by a majority of pidginists.

Another distinction which is sometimes attempted is that between "trade jargons" and pidgins proper (9, 134). It is not clear that such a distinction is meaningful or can be consistently maintained. It appears to be motivated at least in part by a recognition that some pidgins are relatively rudimentary and highly unstable, whereas others are more developed and have relatively homogeneous grammars. But it is not clear that there is any necessary correlation between the pidgin's function and its linguistic status. Hawaiian pidgin, which was certainly not a "trade jargon," and indeed gave birth to a creole, never achieved grammatical complexity or stability. It would rather seem that all contact languages, whatever their primary function, develop through a series of stages; trade jargons may be likelier to be trapped in the more primitive stages than other types of pidgin, but there is no other obvious typological difference.

If the trend in pidgin studies has been to limit the area of application of the term "pidgin," creole studies have shown precisely the reverse tendency. Studies by Goodman (51) and Southworth (119) served to raise the possibility that pidginization or creolization might have intervened at some stage in the historical development of a given language, even where no historical evidence for such processes has survived. While the cases they present—those of Mbugu and Marathi respectively—seem fairly plausible, there is obviously a danger that any unusual historical change may be "explained" in these terms. Indeed, C. J. Bailey (7, p. 134) has come perilously close to equating creolization with linguistic change in general:

> I am taking it for granted that mixtures of systems spoken by native speakers—i.e. creoles—may occur in different proportions and degrees. . . . Let scientists borrow *pairwise* from German . . . and let *wise* become a productive formative in ordinary speech for deriving adverbs from nouns, and this is creolization!

Admittedly, he goes on to state that "one would not wish to speak of creolization where only a few lexical items were borrowed," but the supposition that creoles are simply any "mixed languages" leads logically to such a position, which in effect makes "creolization" a redundant term.

A Baileyan view of creolization would, of course, remove creoles from any necessary connection with antecedent pidgins; and, indeed, from three other sources have come suggestions that creoles, properly so described, may exist without any prior process of pidginization. The first was a paper by Gumperz & Wilson (53), which showed how Marathi, Kannada, and Urdu, as spoken in the Indian village of Kupwar, had undergone so much convergence as to virtually share a common surface syntax, even though the standard forms of these languages show many syntactic differences. It was claimed that such convergence, based on close contact over an extended period, yielded phenomena closely similar to those which characterized creolization, and should therefore be regarded as special cases of the latter. The second was the suggestion, implicit in Valkoff's work on Portuguese creoles (144), but made more explicit by Tonkin (135) and Hancock (61), that pidgins themselves may have had a creole origin. According to this theory, the most likely locus for the origin of any contact language on the West Coast of Africa lay not in the necessarily fleeting contacts of traders (in which, as some historical evidence attests, interpreters and even phrase-books were often used) but in the families of *lançados,* those Europeans (Portuguese in the first instance, later of other nationalities) who settled in Guinea and married into various tribal societies. Languages thus developed, it is argued, subsequently became contact languages throughout West Africa, and were the ancestors of Caribbean and other creoles. The third source is a note by Voorhoeve (145) which pointed out a consequence of the monogenetic theory that apparently had not been realized before: that "if the theory of relexification holds true, a historical Portuguese pidgin has been relexified in contact with French masters, without passing through an intermediate French pidgin stage." Thus acceptance of monogenesis virtually abolishes pidginization as a productive process; one is forced to assume a single invariant pidgin being transmitted from speaker to speaker just like any other language.

With respect to all of these definitional proposals, the most one can say is that they show how much we still have to learn about linguistic change processes, language transmission, and the various kinds of language-contact situations. Unfortunately, the questions they raise, though of considerable importance, are far from easy to answer. Many of the types of situation which gave rise to creole or creole-like phenomena in the past may not be replicated in the twentieth century; those that produced the European-based creoles—episodes of Western imperialist expansion—are unlikely ever to be repeated, at least in a similar form. Thus these questions are unlikely to be resolved by empirical study, while the only other possible source of solutions, historical reconstruction, is made extremely difficult by the virtual absence of recorded texts.

At the same time, there is a clear danger that a broadened definition of creoles may simply serve to distract attention from what have been traditionally known as creoles, i.e. the offspring of pidgin languages. As I shall show in a later section, there may be reason to believe that these represent differences in kind, rather than in degree, from other kinds of language change, whether contact-generated or internal. If creolization is redefined as no more than massive linguistic change due to interlingual contact, then these differences may be glossed over, and a potential source of valuable insights into the basic structure of language may be lost.

ORIGINS

As mentioned earlier in this review, the debate about origins has occupied much of the history of pidgin and creole studies. Though the monogenetic case was widely accepted in the late 1960s (cf DeCamp 29), this was due more to a prolonged stalemate between previous competing views than to any massive display of supporting evidence. Alleyne (5) pointed out in 1971 that no one had so far attempted to reconstruct the hypothesized Proto-Pidgin, and this lack still has not been remedied. A paper by Voorhoeve (146) which seeks to prove relexification in the case of two of the three Surinam creoles—Sranan and Saramaccan—represents almost the only recent substantive argument in favor of the monogeneticist position, and even this is not a new argument, but rather a gathering of fresh evidence in support of an old one. Indeed, the view that pidgins and creoles are predominantly simplifications of their respective super-strates has enjoyed a mild revival (21, 68, 96, 97, 143). Work along these lines has produced some new evidence, mainly historical, which serves directly or indirectly to suggest that deliberate simplification by superstrate speakers may indeed have existed during early pidginization. However, such work continues to ignore, downplay, or distort both the number of creole rules which are demonstrably nonsuperstratal in origin, and the widespread typological similarities between creoles of different genetic affiliation which formed the lynch-pin of the monogeneticist case. Thus it is typical of the "simplificationist" school of thought that it concentrates on superficial morphology rather than underlying semantics. Such writers on French creoles as Valdman (143) and Chaudenson (21), for instance, are quite content to repeat the traditional derivations of creole tense-aspect markers from French periphrastic constructions, without taking into account that the *meanings* of the creole forms by no means always match those of the periphrastic forms, though the semantic structure of French creole tense-aspect systems does match those of at least some non-French creoles, and these systemic similarities owe nothing to French or any other European language.

What has vitiated the origins debate has been an insistence on premature position-taking. For every ten studies that have determined, on the basis of often superficial, partial, and unsystematic evidence, that a given creole unquestionably belonged to one family or another, we have been lucky to get one which eschewed partisan stances and got down to the business of comparison in workmanlike fashion. One of the few pre-1970 examples of the latter genre is Goodman's comparative study of French creoles (50). Subsequently there have been studies by Hancock (60) and Alleyne (still unpublished) of the relationships between the English-based Atlantic pidgins and creoles, but no comparable work on Portuguese creoles apart from a somewhat sketchy and anecdotal treatment by Valkoff (144) and a brief article by Ferraz on the Bight of Benin creoles (45); a comparative study of these four creoles (São Thomé, Angolar, Príncipe, and Annobón) with the Crioulo of Guinea, Cape Verde creole, Papiamento, and Papia Kristang would seem to be essential, not merely in its own right, but for the light it might shed on the contention that a Portuguese-based pidgin was the progenitor of all the European-based creoles.

Another largely unfilled need is that for comparisons between pidgin or creole languages and related non-European languages. Most studies in this area concentrate on some fairly isolated segment of the grammar such as serial verbs (e.g. 11, 71, 147, 152), while studies which attempt to embrace a wide variety of grammatical phenomena, such as Camden's comparison of South Santo with New Hebrides Bislama (20), are all too rare. However, two novel forms of comparative analysis deserve mention. The first, by Huttar (70), involves taking a list of polysemic root morphemes in a given creole (in this case, Djuka) and determining the extent to which their range of meanings is shared by both putatively related and unrelated languages; for instance, whether, as in Djuka, the morpheme that means "mouth" is also used to refer to arrowheads and other pointed objects. The results (which Huttar admits are tentative and need confirmation from other sources) seem clearly to disconfirm the predictions of monogenesis—creoles with no African substratum scored lower on similarity than many unrelated indigenous languages—and were hardly more favorable to those of any "universals" theory. Pidgins and creoles, as a class, scored only marginally higher than a wide sample of indigenous and in the main unrelated languages. Huttar found that the major semantic influence, at least at this lexical level, came from the substratum: creole languages with an African substratum and some (by no means all) West African languages showed the highest level of similarity. The second, by Lee & Vaughn-Cooke (83), compared Nigerian pidgin to English and a group of substratal languages on the basis of Chomsky-Hallean feature marking. If a pidgin were really "simpler" than its related languages, their argument ran, its phonology ought to be less marked; in fact, that of Nigerian pidgin turned out to be more marked, at least with respect to its phonetic inventory, than some of its contributing languages. Such innovative approaches as these will, one hopes, help to break some of the ideological deadlocks which have hampered pidgin-creole studies in the past.

At the same time, one must not neglect the information that can be derived from more traditional studies. Though historical data on the development of pidgins and creoles is notoriously sparse, there can be no doubt that patient gleaning can still yield many more useful facts. Hancock (63) in particular has stressed the importance of such evidence, although an attempt to provide a genealogy for the Lingua Franca reaching back to Egyptian times contains too much speculation and partisan interpretation to serve as a model of its kind. Rather more solid work has been done by Mühlhäusler (94) on the early stages of Pacific pidgins; in particular, he has shown the previously unsuspected existence of a pidgin closely related to Tokpisin on German plantations in nineteenth-century Samoa, and has argued plausibly, if not quite convincingly, for the role of these plantations in the formation and stabilization of Pacific pidgins generally. Evidence has been discovered by Bill Wilson, a graduate student at the University of Hawaii (reported in 18), that a pidginized Hawaiian antedated, and may well have been the ancestor, of an English pidgin in Hawaii. If, as seems likely, this language, rather than English pidgin, was the plantation language for the first 70 years of sugar cultivation in Hawaii, a number of cherished sociolinguistic axioms about plantations may have to be rethought. Chaudenson (21), as a by-product of his monumental work on the Réunion lexicon, has shown that one widespread assumption among creolists—that the similarities between Mascarene and Caribbean French creoles could be explained in terms of a common West African pidgin ancestor—cannot be maintained: too few Africans came to the Indian Ocean, and far too late, for their speech to have had more than marginal influence on the creoles of Réunion, Mauritius, and the Seychelles. Such enquiries, though they cannot themselves yield an adequate theory of origins, should furnish at least some of the facts on which such a theory may eventually be based.

However, the debate about origins has definitely ceased to hold the center of the stage, not because it has come anywhere nearer being settled, but because interest has largely shifted to a different, if related, area—the extent to which language universals, rather than existing individual languages, contribute to the structure of pidgins and creoles.

UNIVERSALS

The possibility that there might be some connection between pidgins and creoles on the one hand and universals of language on the other was voiced as early as 1939 by Hjelmslev (67). However, the intellectual climate of the time did not encourage work on universals. It was not until the present decade that serious attention was given to the idea.

What was possibly the main impulse came from linguists whose major interests lay outside pidgins and creoles. Labov, in a widely circulated but never-published paper (81), began to ask questions which related specifically to the functional effectiveness of pidgins. If they were reduced or simplified forms of language, how was communication adequately maintained? If pidgins were adequate for communication, why did creoles complicate them? These were questions that had long gone unasked and had badly needed asking; unfortunately, the data on which Labov based his tentative answers was of a quality far inferior to that of his other studies, and led him to a number of incorrect conclusions. More explicitly concerned with universals was a paper by Kay & Sankoff (76), which circulated in manuscript for 2 years before its appearance in DeCamp & Hancock's book (31), and which advanced the hypothesis that in a pidgin situation speakers discard constructions from their own languages which are syntactically marked and are left with a small set of unmarked structures which show little or no difference between their deep and surface forms; in other words, they are able to employ their *faculté de language* to select a kind of lowest common denominator of simplest forms. Such a lowest common denominator would, it was suggested, approximate to the structure of a universal base. At about the same time, and apparently independently, similar suggestions were made by a number of younger scholars in the field—Agheyisi (3), Mühlhäusler (93), Givón (48)—while Traugott, who had entered the field from historical linguistics, motivated by an interest in change processes, began to develop a theory of "natural syntax" which was strongly influenced by the work of Labov and Kay & Sankoff (136).

This group of scholars labored under the disadvantage that several of them had little or no first-hand experience of pidgins, while those who did (Agheyisi, Sankoff) were most familiar with pidgin languages (Nigerian Pidgin, Tokpisin) which had been in existence for a considerable period of time. Yet obviously, if pidgin speakers did have the power to reduce their language to some kind of universal base, this power would have to be exercised at the beginning, rather than the middle or end, of the pidginization process. In fact, such evidence as is obtainable about more primitive pidgins hardly supports the Kay-Sankoff hypothesis. In a long and thoughtful article on Chinook jargon, Silverstein (117) showed that its speakers, far from working from any common base structure, rather derived similar surface structures from the distinctive deep structures of their own native languages. Nagara (95), analyzing the pidgin English of Japanese plantation workers in Hawaii, found that much of their phonology and syntax could be explained in terms of a direct transference of Japanese language patterns. Subsequent investigation by Bickerton (18) has confirmed that Hawaiian pidgin, virtually the only true plantation pidgin which is recoverable today, showed internal differences so gross that it is possible to determine the ethnicity of the speaker from written texts and on grounds of syntax alone. The theory that pidgin speakers have access to universals cannot, therefore, derive any support from empirical studies.

Traugott's picture of a natural syntactic base, derived partly by analogy from Stampian natural phonology (121), is a persuasive one:

> If we can accept an unordered semantic base, one which is essentially cognitive, and which reflects a kind of semantic weighting . . . then we can argue that a natural syntactic process is one which gives spatio-temporally ordered expression to this unordered cognitive base, in certain restricted ways. I hypothesize, for example, that there are natural tendencies to give analytic expression to such grammatical elements as negation, tense, aspect, mood, logical connectives and so forth (136, p. 315).

However, she errs in attributing to pidgin speakers the capacity to recover such a level of structure. (I will point out again, at the risk of boring the reader, that according to the arguments of both sides, "pidgin speaker" *must* here be read as "speaker of a pidgin in the early stages of its formation"; to claim it can also have, in this context, its normal meaning of "anyone who speaks a pidgin language," and thus include "a speaker of a pidgin language that has been established for several generations," is simply a fudge. That Traugott shares my definition is quite clear from her remarks on pp. 318–19 about the capacity to simplify language.) Linguists often write about pidgins as if people in the original contact situation had sat down and said, "We cannot understand one another, therefore let us see if we can devise a pidgin." In fact, pidgin speakers are generally under the impression that they are speaking some existing language, albeit in broken form. Typical is an anecdote by Reinecke (104, p. 102) about a Chinese laborer in Hawaii, unable to understand the instructions of his new white supervisor, who exclaimed "Wasamalla this Haole? He no can speak haole!" Indeed, such an attitude may persist long after the pidgin has stabilized and become a creole; a native speaker of Saramaccan, describing to me some of the differences between Saramaccan and its more Europeanized neighbor Sranan, repeatedly referred to the former as "the African language."

If this is the case, then what the pidgin speaker thinks he is doing is trying to learn an existing language, and the result of his efforts may most profitably be compared with attempts at second language learning under extremely adverse conditions (16, 17). Now, while the thought-experiment pidgin speaker flies unerringly to universals, the more earthbound foreign language learner hugs his syntactic home ground closely, and behaves very much as early-stage pidgin speakers do. Indeed, there is something highly counter-intuitive about what is unwittingly implied by Traugott and other members of the "pidgin-universal" school—that the adult speaker's *faculté de langage* is shackled, qua foreign language learner, but completely unbound, qua pidgin speaker. Whether one agrees or disagrees with the Halle-Lenneberg thesis (58, 88) that language acquisition is severely inhibited after puberty, there can be no doubt that the language-learning abilities of children are considerably greater than those of adults. For this reason, it would seem more natural to find access to universals among the children of early pidgin speakers, rather than among those speakers themselves.

The theory that creoles, rather than pidgins, come closest to language universals has been most explicitly stated by Bickerton (15). This paper suggested that the similarity of creole tense-aspect systems the world over could be explained only by hypothesizing the existence of an innate tense-aspect system, based on human cognitive capacities, which surfaced intact, instead of being partially suppressed in Stampian, language-particular ways, whenever the input to the child's language acquisition device failed to find adequate data. Such a situation would certainly obtain in an early-pidgin plantation community, where that data would consist partly of the itself unstable and communicationally inadequate pidgin, partly of a largely unlearnable mix of the previous generation's native tongues. This theory is still too new and controversial to be satisfactorily evaluated. So far it has been welcomed by Givón (49), whose earlier work (48) had pointed in a similar direction, and Slobin (118), who found support for the underlying semantic categories proposed in the paper in his own and others' work on child language acquisition; however, it has been criticized by Neff (98), who questions the interpretation of some of the Hawaiian data, and Traugott (137), who finds the universals proposed to be "overly explicit." Obviously its predictions must be tested empirically and over as wide a range of languages as possible. Its most obvious advantage qua theory of creole development (for its implications extend to areas outside this field) is that it accounts for and explains precisely those facts which have been put forward to justify the monogenetic hypothesis.

The debate on universals, though the newest in the field, seems likely to be the most crucial and far-reaching in years to come. It has already attracted to pidgins and creoles the attention of a number of specialists from other fields, and provides an issue that is of potential interest to everyone seriously interested in the inner mechanics of human language. However, only the next few years will determine whether it will uncover data rich enough to make its contentions credible, or, like the "origins" debate before it, degenerate into a theoretical stalemate, with partisans selecting, out of a broad array of facts, those and only those that buttress their own particular case.

VARIABILITY

If the study of universals includes more theory than fact, the same cannot be said for another recent development—the study of variation in pidgins and creoles, particularly in the decreolization process. As noted by Valdman (141), pre-1970 orthodoxy had ignored or at least downgraded the amount of variability to be found in these languages. To a large extent this was a political decision, rendered inevitable by popular accusations that they "had no grammar"; thus Hall (57, p. 107) felt constrained to argue that ". . . investigations by unprejudiced investigators, using modern techniques of linguistic observation and analysis, have demonstrated conclusively that all pidgins and creoles, even the simplest, are as amenable to description and formulation as are any other languages." Since those "other languages" were supposed to have regular, invariant grammars, pidgins and creoles must be equally regular if they were to be deemed equally worthy of study.

However, the facts of variation had been noticed at least as early as Reinecke's work in the 1930s (104, 105), and were observed in the Caribbean somewhat later by DeCamp (28). In a penetrating and ahead-of-its-time article by Stewart (126) that appeared in 1969, the connection between synchronic variation and diachronic change was made explicit for the first time. Almost simultaneously, DeCamp was working out the formalism for implicational scaling, which was to become the major operational tool for the variation studies of the 1970s (30). His research in Jamaica had indicated that variation was far from the chaos which B. Bailey had implied when she wrote that "a given speaker is likely to shift back and forth from Creole to English . . . within a single utterance," and that "the lines of demarcation are very hard to draw" (6, p. 1). DeCamp cut this Gordian knot by refusing to draw lines; to him, the "dialect mixture" of somewhere like Jamaica was a "post-creole continuum" with no "structural break" between the furthest creole extreme [which came to be known as the "basilect," a term first used by Stewart (123)] and the form nearest to that of the standard language [described as the "acrolect" in a paper by Tsuzaki (138)]. DeCamp claimed that for any linguistic feature found in the continuum, its presence in the output of a given speaker would predict the presence of one set of features, while its absence would predict the absence of another set (although presence would make no predictions about absence, and vice versa). The type of table thus produced is illustrated in Table 1:

Table 1 Form of implicational scales

Lects	Features						
	F_1	F_2	F_3	F_4	F_5	F_6	F_7
1	−	−	−	−	−	−	−
2	−	−	−	−	−	−	×
3	−	−	−	−	−	×	+
4	−	−	−	−	×	+	+
5	−	−	−	×	+	+	+
6	−	−	×	+	+	+	+
7	−	×	+	+	+	+	+
8	×	+	+	+	+	+	+
9	+	+	+	+	+	+	+

Table 1 illustrates an exceptionless implicational scale. Minuses indicate the absence of a given feature; pluses represent its presence. Crosses indicate a state that was not taken into account in DeCamp's original formulation, but which subsequent work showed to be necessary, i.e. that in which a speaker sometimes uses a given feature and sometimes, even where the opportunity exists, does not. Scales such as this should best be viewed, not as descriptions of data, but as abstract measures against which the degree of deviation in actual outputs can be measured. They make certain predictions about these outputs: for instance, Table 1 predicts that a speaker who lacks feature 5 will also lack features 1 through 4, and that a speaker who possesses feature 3 will also possess features 4 through 7. However, we can make no predictions about what will occur to the right of a minus—a speaker lacking feature 5 may categorically lack, or variably or categorically possess, feature 7, for example—and similarly no predictions can be made to the left of a plus. However, we can say that if a speaker whose output would otherwise concur with Lect 2 should possess feature 3, or one who would otherwise occupy Lect 7 should lack feature 6, he violates the predictions of the scale, and demands either a revision of that scale such as will serve to accomodate him, or at the very least some attempt to explain why he deviates from the majority pattern.

The ontological status and statistical validity of implicational scales have been the subject of debate, but there can be no question that they have served to bring to light many linguistic phenomena which were unobserved or inexplicable before. In particular, they have shed extensive light on the hitherto puzzling process of "decreolization"—that by which a creole in contact with its superstrate may progressively lose creole characteristics and eventually come to appear as no more than a rather deviant dialect of that superstrate. In turn, an understanding of decreolization has helped to change radically the prevailing opinion about the origins of Black English (see below). It has also been possible to replicate studies and achieve closely similar results. For instance, Day (26) found a hierarchy of environments for copula deletion in Hawaii identical to that which Labov (79), using a variable-rule format, had found in Black English. Similarly, Washabaugh (148) found that the environments for the replacement of the complementizer *fi* or *fu* by *tu* in Providencia were identical with those specified by Bickerton (13) in Guyana. However, his explanation of the phenomenon differed in a way that illustrates the limitations, as well as the capabilities, of implicational analysis.

Bickerton had argued that *fi/fu* replacement was determined by three semantic categories of preceding verb: (*a*) modals and inceptives, (*b*) "psychological" verbs, and (*c*) all other classes. Washabaugh, however, argued that these categories were poorly motivated—there was no obvious reason why *fi/fu* replacement should be determined by them—and that both his and Bickerton's results could be explained more parsimoniously in terms of lexical diffusion. It is probable that in this instance, Washabaugh's analysis is the correct one. However, the general conclusion which he draws from this case—that decreolization is above all a matter of surface forms, and that it is nowhere conditioned by the semantic level—is hardly tenable in the light of subsequent work by Bickerton (14, 16). The first of these studies shows that the Guyanese mesolectal pronoun system comes into being by the establishment of an across-the-board gender distinction which obliterates a preexisting case distinction in the basilect; restructuring and regularization in the light of semantactic categories, rather than any mere filtering down of superstrate models, must be the mechanisms operating here. In the second, extensive evidence is given to show that the underlying Guyanese tense-aspect system goes through several quite complex mutations before it arrives at an approximation to the English system, each mutation representing a slightly different semantic analysis of the nature of states, actions, and events; incidentally, it illustrates one case—the acquisition of "strong" past forms—where lexical diffusion might have been expected to operate but where it fails to do so.

The moral of all this is that implicational scales can never determine the form of the grammar. Though they can be used effectively to display the data that needs to be accounted for—as has been done by Day (26), Odo (100), Peet (102), and Perlman (103) for parts of the Hawaiian continuum, for instance—and may serve to suggest grammatical explanations, these suggestions may be misleading (as the case discussed indicates) and in any case need to be supplemented by traditional methods of linguistic analysis. Awareness of this need to provide adequately motivated explanations is clearly present in the work of younger Caribbean scholars such as Cooper (22), Roberts (111), and especially Rickford (109, 110), who has demonstrated the interaction of phonological and semantactic considerations in the workings of the decreolization process, in particular tracing the disappearance of the *doz* habitual aspect marker in mesolectal creoles, which he argues, very convincingly, helped to produce the "distributive *be*" of Black English.

Although most studies of creole variation have used a continuum-type model based on DeCamp's original, mention should be made of an alternative explanation, suggested by Tsuzaki for Hawaii (139) and at least partially endorsed by Labov (80), i.e. that of "co-existent systems." In fact, no study has yet succeeded in drawing any kind of satisfactory boundary line between a creole and its related standard (an apparent exception will be examined in the next paragraph), or in dividing a creole into any of the subsystems which from time to time have been hypothesized. We must therefore conclude that "co-existent systems" are lacking in reality. All that can positively be argued in their favor is that speakers of creoles may regard them as "real," i.e. any creole speaker will tell you unhesitatingly whether a given sentence is creole or not (trouble only starts when you get two creole speakers to do this). But one should beware of confusing "psychological reality"—a popular rallying cry—with "what the man in the street thinks is going on." If what people do in their daily life contradicts what they say they do, one should regard as "psychologically real" that which underlies their consistent actions, rather than the way those actions may be rationalized. In fact, when one asks creole speakers about their language, one is likely to tap, not some level of intuitive folk wisdom, but residues of the untruths about language taught them in the schools.

It will have been noted that virtually all the evidence for decreolization has been drawn from English-related creoles. No work of a similar nature has been done on Portuguese-based creoles, although the dialect continuum of the Cape Verde islands cries out for such treatment, and of the only two approaches to French creoles from this viewpoint (84, 142) the former concluded that there was no such thing as a continuum between French and Creole. However, Lefebvre's conclusions still leave doubts. In the first place, they accord rather too neatly with longstanding establishment beliefs about French-Creole relationships—a fact that would not matter so much if, prior to the studies described above, similar beliefs had not been held about English-Creole relationships. Secondly, there is some factual evidence (e.g. Valdman 141) that in Haiti, if not in the Lesser Antilles, the French-Creole distinction is by no means so sharp. Thirdly, there is the fact that Lefebvre's analysis is based, not on natural speech, but on retellings of a specified folk-tale, in which speakers were directly requested to provide two versions, one "Creole" and one "French"! One can hardly conceive of a methodological framework more loaded in favor of its conclusion, and it seems likely that any study which (like all the other studies mentioned in this section) based itself on spontaneous speech in relatively natural settings would yield quite different results. In regions where historically related languages are in contact over extended periods, it is hardly plausible to suggest that no results should follow from this fact.

Perhaps the most significant insight so far derived from the study of creole variation is that its synchronic variability may simply represent what might under other circumstances have been diachronic change (16, 126). A similar conclusion by Labov with respect to English sound changes (78 and numerous subsequent works) has helped modify and expand our understanding of historical change in phonology; it seems reasonable to suppose that present and future studies of synchronic variation in creole syntax may help to improve our knowledge of a still-less-understood area, that of syntactic change.

THE BLACK ENGLISH CONTROVERSY

One specific result of decreolization studies has been a clarification of the debate over the origins of Black English. The traditional position (77, 91, etc) was that Black English derived from general English—perhaps with some aberrations due to purely "social" causes—and that it showed no influence whatsoever from African or other sources. This position began to be attacked in the early 1960s by a school of which the most vehement spokesmen were Dillard (32–34) and Stewart (124, 125). Their criticisms were twofold: that the "Anglicist" case could only be supported by positing a wholly random and unprincipled selection of features from the whole gamut of English dialects (Dillard's "cafeteria principle"), and that it ignored or misanalyzed a number of features which by no stretch of the imagination could be derived from English. The latter features were claimed to be clearly of creole origin. However, in the form in which it was first stated, their case won only a limited degree of acceptance. Black English was, in the main, mutually intelligible with White dialects, whereas the Caribbean creoles were not; indeed, if one made a three-cornered comparison between White English, Black English, and the kind of Jamaican Creole described by B. Bailey (6), there could be little doubt that synchronic Black English stood closer, on virtually any measure of evaluation, to the former than to the latter. But at a time when (as mentioned earlier) creoles were supposed to prove their linguistic respectability by showing that they possessed rules as regular as those of other languages, Bailey and almost all other descriptivists in the field felt obliged to treat them as unitary systems; moreover, to avoid the slur that creoles were merely corrupted versions of standard languages, those systems had to be shown to differ maximally from their superstrates. It followed inevitably that descriptions of creoles, even creoles that were really continuums, turned out to be descriptions of absolute basilects. There was thus (as far as "Anglicists" were concerned) nothing to bridge the structural gulf between creoles and English except for literary and historical evidence. This the "Creolists" had in abundance, but most of it was ruled inadmissible by the "Anglicists"; ironically, the more liberal attitudes towards race that were then becoming prevalent made it easy to dismiss the kind of dialogues found in eighteenth and nineteenth century memoirs, histories, plays, novels etc as attempts to disparage blacks and render them ridiculous, rather than honest efforts to reproduce their speech. A recent example of the power to distract that this red herring still retains is given in Fasold's review of Dillard (43). Fasold, who still apparently labors under the misapprehension that any kind of "simple and ungrammatical" language is "creole-like," is so worried about "racism" that he manages to miss the whole thrust of Dillard's argument—that these allegedly "invented" literary forms happen to coincide with actually existing forms in contemporary Caribbean creoles, about which eighteenth and nineteenth-century authors, were they never so prejudiced, can hardly have known. However, as "Creolists" have developed their claims by drawing attention to the role of decreolization—Stewart's already-cited paper (126) is perhaps the most lucid example of this—and as the works listed in the previous section made clear the workings of the decreolization process, hostility to the "Creolist" case weakened and in some quarters disappeared. When a semipopular work by Dillard appeared and was widely reviewed in 1972 (35), it met with a measure of acceptance that would have been unthinkable a decade earlier.

The position of Gullah is also critical in this debate. Since Turner's classic study (140), no one had seriously disputed that Gullah was a creole. However, Rickford has pointed out (109) that even recent descriptions of Gullah (e.g. 24) treated it on the pattern of other creoles—i.e. as if only the basilect existed—and that it was therefore possible to go on regarding it as something quite distinct from Black English. However, as has been shown by Rickford's own work, and as will be shown more comprehensively by Stewart's ongoing, but still unpublished, work in the Sea Islands, there exists a complete linguistic continuum linking Gullah with Black English, which closely resembles similar continuums in the Caribbean and Hawaii.

However, it is likely that a full and satisfactory understanding of the origin and development of Black English must await a full and satisfactory explanation of pidgins and creoles. In an interesting paper by Berdan, favorably disposed to the "Creolist" case (12), the author begins by taking for granted the majority opinion in the field, that pidgins represent "simplifications" of the superstrate language and creoles represent "complications" of the pidgin. If (as some of the evidence in this review suggests) this view is too simplistic, and should be dropped in favor of the theory that pidgins constitute a grossly handicapped case of second language learning while creoles show a partial recourse to the *faculté de langage* (which does not, of course, exclude retention of rules and features from any of the contributing languages) which later may be subject both to natural changes and changes due to superstrate pressure, then Berdan's argument, that some Black English constructions such as "relative clause reduction" can be "viewed as simplifications of Standard English grammar," will prove not so much incorrect as irrelevant.

SOCIOLINGUISTICS

Although pidgins and creoles have traditionally been regarded as somehow "sociolinguistic" in themselves, there was not, prior to the present decade, very much work on them that could properly be so termed. In recent years, this lack has to some extent been remedied. Sociolinguistic studies of Caribbean creoles —pidgins and creoles of other areas have hardly even been considered in this light—fall roughly into two general classes.

The first class is modeled on the Labovian, survey-oriented approach. Work along these lines has been carried out by Winford in Trinidad (153, 154); a much more ambitious study has been carried out by Le Page in Belize (85–87). While Winford has concentrated mainly on establishing the speech varieties that correlate with class and ethnic divisions, Le Page and his associates have been more concerned with the language of the individual as an expression of his general social allegiance. In the immense linguistic complexity of Belize (where the presence of Spanish, Indian languages, and Black Carib alongside the usual Caribbean-English continuum provides an unusually wide set of options for the speaker), each speaker, according to Le Page, "creates the systems for his verbal behavior so that they shall resemble those of the group or groups, with which from time to time he may wish to be identified" (87, p. 2). While this statement in essence is correct, the word *creates* seems hardly apt here; it suggests that the speaker can actually "make things up," or at least select quite freely from the whole range of features that the continuum contains. In fact, the studies described in Section 4 indicate that this is far from being the case. The creole menu is not á la carte, it rather consists of a series of "chef's specials," congeries of features in which if you select one, you must select all. Moreover, it is surely premature to speak of selection until you know what is on the menu; the rather inadequate descriptions of past tense and pluralization in Belize creole contained in (85) leave it quite unclear what is being meant, sociolinguistically or in any other way, when a Belizean selects *mi kom* over *kom,* or *di taiga-dem* over *taiga.* A similar connection between group allegiance and linguistic level within the continuum is shown in Edwards' work on Providencia/San Andres creole (38–40). Here, while again the grammatical analysis may not be above reproach, Edwards was one of the first writers on creoles to appreciate the implicational nature of their structure: the fact that any choice of features is constrained by, and in its turn serves to constrain, other choices.

The second class of sociolinguistic studies concerns itself with what Hymes has called "the ethnography of speaking": roughly, who says what to whom, under what circumstances, and for what purpose. Studies along these lines have been produced by Abrahams (1), Abrahams & Bauman (2) and Reisman (108). Such studies are valuable in that they concentrate on something which in strictly linguistic studies is seldom mentioned, and indeed usually ignored altogether—what speaking in particular ways *means* to the participants themselves. Good studies of this kind can add flesh to the bare bones of formal descriptions, but they run certain risks, from which the examples mentioned are not exempt. Two sources of danger are the amorphous nature of the material, with its concomitant problem of what, out of an infinite array of facts, may be relevant and what may not, and the continuing lack—perhaps inevitable in view of the newness of the field—of any substantial body of theory. These factors make for mainly anecdotal treatments; moreover, and perhaps in an attempt to compensate for this, there has been an unfortunate tendency in some studies to return to a dichotomistic approach, with creole, African-derived and "anti-establishment" expressions, attitudes, etc on one side of the fence, and English, white-oriented, "pro-establishment" expressions, attitudes etc on the other. Granted these two strands are seen as being interwoven, often in subtle ways, but one feels there is more to it than that: that the mesolect is no mere artefact of linguistic description, but represents a middle ground in its own right, which (for better or for worse) serves as the home base of many people, perhaps even a majority, in the Caribbean. There are any number of ways, linguistic and nonlinguistic, in which such people can define themselves as distinct and separate both from the White culture which they increasingly see as exploitative, and the deep creole culture which they still, unfortunately, perceive as "low" and "vulgar." Any simple dichotomy means that the life-styles and speech patterns of this important group are placed outside the scope of analysis.

DESCRIPTIVE STUDIES

The present survey has concentrated on those areas of the field which seemed of general theoretical interest, and has in consequence mentioned only such descriptive works as might have some bearing on current theoretical issues within the field. There is no intent to disparage other studies; on the contrary, the field suffers from a lack of straightforward, observationally adequate grammars such as are taken for granted in many other fields of linguistics. To some extent, this lack is due to the nature of the field; there are (or were until recently) fewer pidginists and creolists than there were pidgins and creoles to be described, and, to make matters worse, many languages which have been included under the pidgin-creole rubric have only the sketchiest of typological resemblances. If one's field is Romance or Polynesian languages, one may reasonably be expected to know something substantive about all the languages within it; to do the same in pidgin/creole studies demands the competence of a polyglot and the memory of an elephant! I will therefore merely list, far from exhaustively, what seem to me to be some of the more interesting descriptive studies that have appeared over the last few years, several of which are included in the proceedings of the 1975 Honolulu conference (27).

It was mentioned earlier that one of the problems in the field was the unavailability, synchronically, of certain stages in the pidgin-creole cycle. While its social circumstances do not exactly reproduce those of the classic pidgin situations, the migrations of foreign workers to Germany and Australia have produced linguistic phenomena which resemble pidginization. A number of papers, mainly unpublished, have attempted to describe the background situation and the types of speech produced (23, 36, 47, 92). The main problem in dealing with such phenomena is that we still do not know for certain whether the line between a "true pidgin" and "foreigner's English" is an unbroken one, or whether there is a sharp distinction in kind, rather than one of degree (and if so, which side of the line *gastarbeiter* speech falls); hopefully, more and fuller descriptions of both *gastarbeitersprachen* and true pidgins will make detailed comparisons possible.

Growing interest in pidgins and creoles leads to a seemingly never-ending succession of new examples coming to light. Among more recent discoveries are pidgins, possibly creolizing or already creolized, in Nagaland, the Sudan, and the Northern Territory of Australia. The Australian aboriginal example—Roper River Creole, described by Sharpe (116)—is clearly a close relative of Tokpisin, although its phonology shows a different substratal influence (for instance, it has no voiceless consonants, so that *talk,* which serves as the phonetic model for the verb meaning "speak, say" in virtually all Anglo pidgins and creoles becomes *dog* rather than the usual *tok* or *taak*). The description of Naga pidgin—which seems to be a blend of a Naga koine with Assamese—by Sreedhar (120) is unfortunately too brief and compressed to give much idea of the language to anyone unfamiliar with its related languages. The same is true of the descriptions of Juba Arabic, an Arabic-related pidgin spoken in the Southern Sudan, and Ki-Nubi, reportedly a creole offspring of Juba Arabic, by Bell (10) and Nhial (99). According to Bell (personal communication), however, there are possible similarities between the tense-aspect system of Ki-Nubi and that of the European-language-related creoles. Obviously, pidgins and creoles which claim no European ancestors present much more of a problem for the Western linguist, especially when, as in both the Naga and Ki-Nubi cases, contributions to the contact language must have come from at least two distinct language families. However, their importance would be hard to overstress. Any theory about pidginization and creolization that is based exclusively on European-influenced models cannot but be suspect, especially if it claims universal significance; unfortunately, clear and unambiguous cases of non-European pidgins creolizing have not so far been proven to exist. It is therefore vital in the future to collect as much data as possible on any situation where it is believed that, prior to European contact, pidginization or creolization may have taken place; so far only Sango (113) and Chinook Jargon (74, 117) have received more than cursory attention, apart from work by Heine (64, 65) on pidginized versions of African languages.

With regard to better-known pidgins and creoles, some of the more interesting papers have been concerned with the lexicon. In addition to the paper by Huttar already cited, one may mention a paper by Frake (46)—unfortunately not followed up by subsequent publications—on the remarkable principles according to which the lexicon of Zamboangueno is divided between words of Philippine and Spanish origin; a comparative word-list for Djuka, Sranan, and Saramaccan by Huttar (69) which indicates some fascinatingly divergent routes followed by phonological change in the three languages; and a paper by Hancock (62) on "incoining"—his own coinage for the processes by which a creole can expand its vocabulary without increasing its stock of loan words.

In phonology, Tinelli (133) has analyzed nasalization in Haitian creole, Papen (101) has examined the rules affecting verb suffixes in Mascarene creoles, and Johnson (73) has described morpheme-structure rules in the Atlantic Anglo-creoles. All these papers show a familiarity with modern methods of grammatical analysis which is less often shared by the writers on syntax. In that field, one of the most interesting contributions is Sankoff's study (112) of the marking of relative clauses in Tokpisin, which illustrates the development of quasi-obligatory grammatical markers out of what were originally purely functional discourse devices (and which even now cannot be satisfactorily described without taking discourse factors such as speaker presupposition into account). Also discourse-oriented was a study of narrative patterns in Saramaccan by Grimes & Glock (52). Since functional discourse characteristics would seem a priori likely to have universal status, studies such as these should help to open up an important new approach to future comparative studies in the field.

One thing which that field conspicuously lacks for any of its languages is the type of compendious reference grammar represented by e.g. Schachter & Otanes' work on Tagalog (114). A work of this type on any pidgin or creole would serve as an invaluable base for the exhaustive cataloguing of similarities and dissimilarities which needs to be carried out during the next decade. Most attempts to produce grammatical overviews of individual pidgins and creoles deserve, and many modestly claim, only the title of "sketch," but Tokpisin has been better served than many by two accounts from Laycock (82) and Wurm (155). These grammars, though pedagogically oriented, give good general outlines of the language and have the added advantage that they contain a number of interesting texts; similar remarks would also apply to Baker's (8) study of Mauritian creole.

The field still lacks a good general introduction. Hall's introductory volume (57), which was not above criticism when it appeared nearly 10 years ago [see Taylor's (131) penetrating review], has now been outdated in very many respects by the research of the last decade. However, the only general work to have appeared since (Todd 134), while it updates many of Hall's conclusions, is unduly brief and selective in its coverage. Fortunately, by the time this review appears, the compendious bibliography of the field by Reinecke et al (106) should at last be available. This work, with its several thousand annotated references, covers all generally recognized pidgins and creoles, is virtually exhaustive up to 1970, and contains many of the more important titles published subsequently; it should prove an indispensable aid to every scholar in the field. Also of service to present and future scholars should be the *Journal of Creole Studies*, under the editorship of Edgar Polomé and Ian Hancock, which is also scheduled to appear in 1976. This journal, which will contain articles on literary and social matters relating to creole studies as well as purely linguistic treatments, will supplement but not supplant what has hitherto been the only organ devoted solely to pidgins and creoles—the *Carrier Pidgin*, a quarterly newsletter formerly edited by Barbara Robson, in the future to be edited by Stanley Tsuzaki and John Reinecke.

SUMMARY AND FORECAST

As the foregoing account should have indicated, the study of pidgins and creoles has been passing through a period of rapid growth and diversification. Ten years ago it was regarded as little more than a quaint backwater of linguistics; now it tends to be treated with interest and some respect, mixed perhaps with a measure of mild scepticism as to whether it can really deliver all that its more vocal adherents have promised. Only time will tell whether it can maintain its growth rate and achieve its potential, but there can be little doubt that that potential is a considerable one. The pidgin/creole field is unique among fields of linguistic study in that it unites the concern for specific languages of the various areal fields with an obligation to deal in processes which, if not necessarily universal, are at least more than family-specific. The difficulties which this involves have already been mentioned; one should not underestimate the compensating advantages.

However, the field still has a long way to go. This review, as well as chronicling its achievements, has tried also to indicate some of the limitations which it must overcome. It should not be forgotten that its resources, in terms of scholars and sheer finance, are far less than those of many areal fields, and yet need to be spread over a vaster area of ground. The spread so far has been remarkably uneven. It is hardly surprising perhaps that of the only three studies of pidgins or creoles that have obtained financial support on a really generous scale, two have been in the United States (in what are almost the only two pidgin-creole areas America has, Hawaii and the Sea Islands) while the third has been in a politically sensitive dependency of Great Britain (British Honduras). There is nowhere any institute or university department devoted to the study of pidgins or creoles; there is no chair of pidgin and creole languages in any European university. Considering the potential that the field has for adding to our knowledge of the human language faculty, and through that faculty to our knowledge of the human mind itself, one can but hope that these deficiencies will be speedily remedied. But the remedying of them will in turn depend on the capacity of the field, within the next decade, to maintain its present rate of development and prove beyond doubt the indispensability of its contribution to a complete science of man.

Literature Cited

1. Abrahams, R. D. 1972. The training of the man of words in talking sweet. *LinS* 1:15–29
2. Abrahams, R. D., Bauman, R. 1971. Sense and nonsense in St. Vincent; speech behavior and decorum in a Caribbean community. *Am. Anthropol.* 73:762–72
3. Agheyisi, R. N. 1971. *West African Pidgin English: simplification and simplicity.* PhD thesis. Stanford Univ., Calif.
4. Alleyne, M. C. 1963. Communication and politics in Jamaica. *Caribb. Stud.* 3:22–61
5. Alleyne, M. C. 1971. Acculturation and the cultural matrix of creolization. See Ref. 72, 169–86
6. Bailey, B. 1966. *Jamaican Creole Syntax.* Cambridge: C. U. P. 164 pp.
7. Bailey, C. J. N. 1973. *Variation and Linguistic Theory.* Washington DC: Cent. Appl. Ling. 162 pp.
8. Baker, P. 1972. *Kreol, a Description of Mauritian Creole.* London: Hurst. 221 pp.
9. Baron, N. S. 1977. Trade jargons and pidgins: a functionalist approach. See Ref. 27
10. Bell, H. 1977. Pidgin Arabic and the language survey of the Sudan. See Ref. 27
11. Bendix, E. H. 1970. Serial verbs in Creole and West African. Presented at 69th Ann. Meet. Am. Anthropol. Assoc., San Diego
12. Berdan, R. 1977. Sufficiency conditions for a prior creolization of Black English. See Ref. 27
13. Bickerton, D. 1971. Inherent variability and variable rules. *Found. Lang.* 7:457–92
14. Bickerton, D. 1973. The nature of a creole continuum. *Language* 49:640–69
15. Bickerton, D. 1974. Creolization, linguistic universals, natural semantax and the brain. *Work. Pap. Ling.* 6.3:125–41. Univ. Hawaii Dep. Ling.
16. Bickerton, D. 1975. *Dynamics of a Creole System.* Cambridge: C. U. P. 224 pp.
17. Bickerton, D. 1976. Pidginization and creolization: language acquisition and language universals. In *Pidgin and Creole Linguistics,* ed. A. Valdman. Bloomington: Indiana Univ. Press
18. Bickerton, D., Odo, C. 1976. Report on NSF Grant No. GS-39748, Part 1: general phonology and pidgin syntax. Univ. Hawaii (mimeo)
19. Bloomfield, L. 1933. *Language.* New York: Holt. 566 pp.
20. Camden, W. G. 1977. Parallels in structure of lexicon and syntax between New Hebrides Bislama and the South Santo language spoken at Tangoa. See Ref. 27
21. Chaudenson, R. 1974. *Le Lexique du Parler Créole de la Réunion.* Paris: Librairie Honore Champion. 1249 pp.
22. Cooper, V. O. 1977. On the notion of decreolization and St. Kitts Creole personal pronouns. See Ref. 27
23. Clyne, M. G. 1977. German and English working pidgins. See Ref. 27
24. Cunningham, I. A. E. 1970. *A syntactic analysis of Sea Island Creole (Gullah).* PhD thesis. Univ. Michigan, Ann Arbor
25. D'Ans, A. M. 1968. *Le Créole Français d'Haiti.* The Hague: Mouton. 181 pp.
26. Day, R. R. 1972. *Patterns of variation in copula and tense in the Hawaiian post-creole continuum.* PhD thesis. Univ. Hawaii, Honolulu. 169 pp.
27. Day, R. R., Bickerton, D. 1977. *Papers from the International Conference on Pidgins and Creoles, Honolulu, 1975.* Honolulu: Univ. Hawaii Press. In press
28. DeCamp, D. 1961. Social and geographic factors in Jamaican dialects. In *Creole Language Studies,* ed. R. B. Le Page, 61–84. London: Macmillan
29. DeCamp, D. 1971. The study of pidgin and creole languages. See Ref. 72, 13–39
30. DeCamp, D. 1971. Towards a generative analysis of a post-creole speech community. See Ref. 72, 349–70
31. DeCamp, D., Hancock, I. A., eds. 1974. *Pidgins and Creoles: Current Trends and Prospects.* Washington DC: Georgetown Univ. Press. 137 pp.
32. Dillard, J. L. 1967. Negro children's dialect in the inner city. *Fla. FL Rep.* 5.3:7–10
33. Ibid 1968. Non-standard Negro dialects—convergence or divergence? 6.2:9–12
34. Ibid 1970. Principles in the history

of American English—paradox, virginity and cafeteria. 8.1/2:32–34

35. Dillard, J. L. 1972. *Black English: its History and Usage in the United States.* New York: Random House. 361 pp.

36. Dittmar, N., Klein, W. 1974. Untersuchungen zum Pidgin-Deutsch spanischer and italienischer arbeiter in der BRD. Deutsches Seminar der Universität Heidelberg (mimeo)

37. Dwyer, D., 1969. *Introduction to West African Pidgin English.* East Lansing: Afr. Stud. Cent., Michigan State Univ. 572 pp.

38. Edwards, J. D. 1968. Social linguistics on San Andres and Providencia Islands. Louisiana State Univ. (mimeo)

39. Edwards, J. D. 1970. Aspects of bilingual behavior on San Andres Island, Colombia. Louisiana State Univ. (mimeo)

40. Edwards, J. D. 1974. African influences on the English of San Andres Island, Colombia. See Ref. 31, 1–26

41. Faine, J. 1937. *Philologie Créole.* Port-au-Prince: Imprimerie de l'Etat. 303 pp.

42. Fanon, F. 1952. Le noir et le langage. In *Peau Noire, Masques Blancs,* F. Fanon, 33–52. Paris: Editions du Seine. 237 pp.

43. Fasold, R. 1975. Review of Ref. 35, *Language in Society* 4:198–221

44. Ferguson, C. A. 1971. Absence of copula and the notion of simplicity: a study of normal speech, baby talk, foreigner talk and pidgin. See Ref. 72, 141–50.

45. Ferraz, L. 1977. The origin and development of four creoles in the Gulf of Guinea. See Ref. 27

46. Frake, C. O. 1971. Lexical origins and semantic structure in Philippine Creole Spanish. See Ref. 72, 223–42

47. Gilbert, G. G., Orlovic, M. 1977. Pidgin German spoken by foreign workers in West Germany: the definite article. See Ref. 27

48. Givón, T. 1973. Prolegomena to any creology. Univ. California, Los Angeles (mimeo)

49. Givón, T. 1975. Postscript to Ref. 48. Univ. California, Los Angeles (mimeo)

50. Goodman, M. F. 1964. *A Comparative Study of French Creole Dialects.* The Hague:Mouton. 143 pp.

51. Goodman, M. F. 1971. The strange case of Mbugu (Tanzania). See Ref. 72, 243–54

52. Grimes, J. E., Glock, N. 1970. A Saramaccan narrative pattern. *Language* 46:408–25

53. Gumperz, J. J., Wilson, R. 1971. Convergence and creolization: a case from the Indo-Aryan/Dravidian border. See Ref. 72, 151–68

54. Hall, R. A. Jr. 1948. The linguistic structure of Taki-taki. *Language* 24:92–116

55. Hall, R. A. Jr. 1952. Pidgin English and linguistic change. *Lingua* 3:138–46

56. Hall, R. A. Jr. 1958. Creole languages and genetic relationships. *Word* 14:367–73

57. Hall, R. A. Jr. 1966. *Pidgin and Creole Languages.* Ithaca: Cornell Univ. Press. 188 pp.

58. Halle, M. 1964. Phonology in generative grammar. In *The Structure of Language,* ed. J. A. Fodor, J. J. Katz, 334–52. Englewood Cliffs, NJ: Prentice-Hall. 612 pp.

59. Hancock, I. A. 1969. A map and list of pidgin and creole languages. See Ref. 72, 509–23

60. Hancock, I. A. 1969. A provisional comparison of the English-derived Atlantic Creoles. *Afr. Lang. Rev.* 8:7–72

61. Hancock, I. A. 1972. A domestic origin for the English-derived Atlantic Creoles. *Fla. FL Rep.* 10.1/2:7–8, 52

62. Hancock, I. A. 1975. The use of historical evidence in the reconstruction of the genesis and development of pidgins and creoles. Univ. Texas, Austin (mimeo)

63. Hancock, I. A. 1977. Lexical expansion within a closed system. See Ref. 27

64. Heine, B. 1970. *Status and Use of African Lingua Francas.* New York: Humanities Press. 206 pp.

65. Heine, B. 1977. Some generalizations on African-based pidgins. See Ref. 27

66. Herskovits, M. J. 1941. *The Myth of the Negro Past.* New York: Harper. 374 pp.

67. Hjelmslev, L. 1939. *Caractères grammaticaux des langues créoles.* Presented at Congr. Int. Sci. Anthropol. Ethnol., Copenhagen

68. Hull, A. 1977. On the origin and chronology of the French-based Creoles. See Ref. 27

69. Huttar, G. L. 1972. A comparative word list for Djuka. In *Languages of the Guianas,* ed. J. E. Grimes, 12–21. Summer Inst. Ling. 91 pp.

70. Huttar, G. L. 1975. Sources of creole semantic structures. *Language* 51:684–95
71. Huttar, G. L. 1977. Some Kwa-like features of Djuka syntax. See Ref. 27
72. Hymes, D., ed. 1971. *The Pidginization and Creolization of Languages.* Cambridge: C. U. P. 530 pp.
73. Johnson, M. C. 1974. Two morpheme-structure rules in an English proto-creole. See Ref. 31, 118–29
74. Johnson, S. V. 1977. Chinook Jargon variations: towards the Compleat Chinooker. See Ref. 27
75. Jourdain, E. 1956. *Du Français aux Parlers Créoles.* Paris: Klincksieck. 334 pp.
76. Kay, P., Sankoff, G. 1974. A language-universals approach to pidgins and creoles. See Ref. 31, 61–72
77. Krapp, G. P. 1925. *The English Language in America.* New York: Century. 2 vols. 594 pp.
78. Labov, W. 1966. *The Social Stratification of English in New York City.* Washington DC: Cent. Appl. Ling. 655 pp.
79. Labov, W. 1969. Contraction, deletion and inherent variability of the English copula. *Language* 45:715–62
80. Labov, W. 1971. The notion of 'system' in creole languages. See Ref. 72, 447–72
81. Labov, W. 1971. On the adequacy of natural languages: I. The development of tense. Univ. Pennsylvania (mimeo)
82. Laycock, D. 1970. *Materials in New guinea Pidgin (Coastal and Lowlands).* Canberra: Aust. Natl. Univ. 99 pp.
83. Lee, M. H., Vaughn-Cook, A. F. 1977. On inventories and syllable-structures. See Ref. 27
84. Lefebvre, C. 1974. Discreteness and the linguistic continuum in Martinique. *Anthropol. Ling.* 16.2:47–78
85. Le Page, R. B. 1972. Preliminary report on the sociolinguistic survey of Cayo District, British Honduras. *Lang. Soc.* 1:155–72
86. Le Page, R. B. 1973. The concept of competence in a creole/contact situation. *York Pap. Ling.* 3:31–50
87. Le Page, R. B., Christie, P., Jurdant, B., Weekes, A. J., Tabouret-Keller, A. 1974. Further report on the sociolinguistic survey of multilingual communities: survey of Cayo District, British Honduras. *Lang. Soc.* 3:1–32
88. Lenneberg, E. H. 1967. *Biological Foundations of Language.* New York: Wiley. 489 pp.
89. Lenz, R. 1928. *El Papiamento, la Lengua Criolla de Curazao.* Santiago de Chile: Balcells. 341 pp.
90. Magens, J. M. 1770. *Grammatica over det Creolske Sprog.* Copenhagen: Gerhard Giese Salikath
91. McDavid, R. I. Jr., McDavid, V. G. 1951. The relationship of the speech of American Negroes to the speech of Whites. *Am. Speech* 26:3–17
92. Meisel, J. M. 1975 *The language of foreign workers in Germany.* Presented at 4th Int. Congr. Appl. Ling., Stuttgart
93. Mühlhäusler, P. 1972. *Pidginization and simplification of language.* MPhil thesis. Univ. Reading, England. 179 pp.
94. Mühlhäusler, P. 1975. *Samoan Plantation Pidgin English and the origin of New Guinea Pidgin.* Presented at 1975 Ann. Conf. Ling. Soc. Australia, Canberra
95. Nagara, S. 1972. *Japanese Pidgin English in Hawaii: a Bilingual Description.* Honolulu: Univ. Hawaii Press. 322 pp.
96. Naro, A. 1973. *The origin of West African Pidgin.* Presented at 9th Reg. Meet. Chicago Ling. Soc., Chicago
97. Naro, A. 1977. *The origin of Pidgin Portuguese.* See Ref. 27
98. Neff, K. J. 1977. *Go* in Hawaiian Creole. See Ref. 27
99. Nhial, A. A. J. 1977. Ki-Nubi and Juba Arabic: the relationship between a creole and a pidgin of the Arabic language. See Ref. 27
100. Odo, C. 1970. English patterns in Hawaii. *Am. Speech* 45:234–39
101. Papen, R. A. 1977. *Nana k nana, nana k napa* or the strange case of 'e-deletion' verbs in Indian Ocean Creole. See Ref. 27
102. Peet, W. Jr. 1973. Omission of subject relative pronouns in Hawaiian English restrictive relative clauses. In *Towards Tomorrow's Linguistics,* ed. R. W. Shuy, C.-J. N. Bailey, 253–66. Washington DC: Georgetown Univ. Press
103. Perlman, A. M. 1973. *Grammatical structure and style-shift in Hawaiian Pidgin and Creole.* PhD thesis. Univ. Chicago, Ill. 284 pp.
104. Reinecke, J. 1969. *Language and Dialect in Hawaii.* Honolulu: Univ. Hawaii Press. 254 pp.

105. Reinecke, J., Tokimasa, A. 1934. The English dialect of Hawaii. *Am. Speech* 9:48–58, 122–31

106. Reinecke, J., DeCamp, D., Hancock, I. A., Tsuzaki, S., Wood, R. 1975. *A Bibliography of Pidgins and Creoles*. Honolulu: Univ. Hawaii Press

107. Reisman, K. M. L. 1965. *The isle is full of noises: a study of Creole in the speech patterns of Antigua, West Indies*. PhD thesis. Harvard Univ., Cambridge, Mass.

108. Reisman, K. M. L. 1977. Remarks on conflict and meaning in 'continuous' systems. See Ref. 27

109. Rickford, J. R. 1974. The insights of the mesolect. See Ref. 31, 92–117

110. Rickford, J. R. 1977. How does *doz* disappear? See Ref. 27

111. Roberts, P. A. 1977. The importance of certain linguistic theories for showing important relationships in a creole language. See Ref. 27

112. Sankoff, G., Brown, P. 1975. *On the origins of syntax in discourse: a case study of Tok Pisin relatives*. Univ. Montreal. 86 pp. (mimeo)

113. Samarin, W. J. 1967. *A Grammar of Sango*. The Hague: Mouton. 284 pp.

114. Schachter, P., Otanes, Fe. T. 1972. *Tagalog Reference Grammar*. Berkeley: Univ. California Press. 566 pp.

115. Schuchardt, H. E. M. 1909. Die lingua franca. *Z. Rom. Philol.* 33: 441–61

116. Sharpe, M. C. 1974. Notes on the 'Pidgin English' Creole of Roper River. *Aust. Inst. Aboriginal Stud. Newsl.* (new ser.) 2:2–12

117. Silverstein, M. 1972. Chinook jargon: language contact and the problem of multilevel generative systems. *Language* 48: 378–406, 596–625

118. Slobin, D. I. 1975. *The more it changes. . . . On understanding language by watching it move through time*. Presented at Stanford Child Language Forum, Stanford, Calif.

119. Southworth, F. C. 1971. Detecting prior creolization: an analysis of the historical origins of Marathi. See Ref. 72, 255–74

120. Sreedhar, M. V. 1977. Standardization of Naga Pidgin. See Ref. 27

121. Stampe, D. 1972. *A dissertation on natural phonology*. PhD thesis. Univ. Chicago, Ill. 79 pp.

122. Stewart, W. A. 1962. Creole languages in the Caribbean. In *Study of the Role of Second Languages in Asia, Africa and Latin America*, ed. F. A. Rice, 34–53. Washington DC: Cent. Appl. Ling. 128 pp.

123. Stewart, W. A. 1965. Urban negro speech: sociolinguistic features affecting English teaching. In *Social Dialects and Language Learning*, ed. R. W. Shuy, 10–18. Champaign, Ill.: Natl Counc. Teach. Engl. 157 pp.

124. Stewart, W. A. 1967. Sociolinguistic factors in the history of American Negro dialects. *Fla FL Rep.* 5.2:11–30

125. Ibid 1968. Continuity and change in American Negro dialects. 6.1:3–18

126. Stewart, W. A. 1969. Historical and structural bases for recognition of Negro dialect. *Proc. 20th Ann. Round Table, Georgetown Univ.*, 239–47

127. Sylvain, S. C. 1936. *Le Créole Haitien: Morphologie et Syntaxe*. Port-au-Prince: Puillet. 180 pp.

128. Taylor, D. 1959. On function versus form in 'non-traditional' languages. *Word* 15:485–89

129. Taylor, D. 1960. Language shift or changing relationship? *Int. J. Am. Ling.* 26:144–61

130. Taylor, D. 1963. The origin of West Indian Creole languages: evidence from grammatical categories. *Am. Anthropol.* 65:800–14

131. Taylor, D. 1967. Review of Ref. 57. *Language* 43:817–24

132. Thompson, W. A. 1961. A note on some possible affinities between the creole dialects of the old world and those of the new. In *Creole Language Studies*, ed. R. B. Le Page, 107–13. London: Macmillan. 130 pp.

133. Tinelli, H. 1974. Generative and creolization processes: nasality in Haitian Creole. *Lingua* 33:344–66

134. Todd, L. 1974. *Pidgins and Creoles*. London: Routledge & Kegan Paul. 106 pp.

135. Tonkin, E. 1971. Some coastal pidgins in West Africa. In *Social Anthropology and Linguistics*, ed. E. Ardener, 129–55. London: Tavistock. 318 pp.

136. Traugott, E. C. 1973. Some thoughts on natural syntactic processes. In *New Ways of Analyzing Variation in English*, ed. C.-J. N. Bailey, R. W. Shuy, 313–22. Washington DC: Georgetown Univ. Press. 373 pp.

137. Traugott, E. C. 1976. Pidginization, creolization and language change. In *Pidgin and Creole Linguistics*, ed. A. Valdman. Bloomington: Indiana Univ. Press

138. Tsuzaki, S. M. 1966. Hawaiian English: pidgin, creole or dialect? *Pac. Speech* 1.2:25–28

139. Tsuzaki, S. M. 1971. Co-existent systems in language variation: the case of Hawaiian English. See Ref. 72, 327–39

140. Turner, L. D. 1949. *Africanisms in the Gullah Dialect*. Chicago: Univ. Chicago Press. 317 pp.

141. Valdman, A. 1969. The language situation in Haiti. In *Research Resources of Haiti*, ed. R. Schaedel, 155–203. New York: Res. Inst. Study of Man. 624 pp.

142. Valdman, A. 1973. Some aspects of decreolization in Creole French. *Current Trends in Linguistics*, 11; 507–36. The Hague: Mouton. 604 pp.

143. Valdman, A. 1977. A pidgin origin for Creole French? See Ref. 27

144. Valkoff, M. F. 1966. *Studies in Portuguese and Creole*. Johannesburg: Witwatersrand Univ. Press. 282 pp.

145. Voorhoeve, J. 1971. A note on reduction and expansion in grammar. See Ref. 72, 189 .

146. Voorhoeve, J. 1973. Historical and linguistic evidence in favor of the relexification theory in the formation of Creoles. *Lang. Soc.* 2:133–46

147. Voorhoeve, J. 1977. Serial verbs in creole. See Ref. 27

148. Washabaugh, W. 1974. *Variability in decreolization on Providence Island, Colombia*. PhD thesis. Wayne State Univ., Detroit, Mich.

149. Weinreich, U. 1958. On the compatibility of genetic relationship and convergent development. *Word* 14:374–79

150. Whinnom, K. 1965. The origin of the European-based pidgins and creoles. *Orbis* 14:509–27

151. Whinnom, K. 1971. Linguistic hybridization and the 'special case' of pidgins and creoles. See Ref. 72, 91–115

152. Williams, W. R. 1971. Serial verb constructions in Krio. *Stud. Afr. Ling.*, Suppl. 2:47–65

153. Winford, D. 1972. *A sociolinguistic description of two communities in Trinidad*. PhD thesis. York Univ., England

154. Winford, D. 1977. The creole situation in the context of sociolinguistic studies. See Ref. 27

155. Wurm, S. A. 1971. *New Guinea Highlands Pidgin: Course Materials*. Canberra: Aust. Natl Univ. 175 pp.

Ann. Rev. Anthropol. 1976. 5:195–208
Copyright © 1976 by Annual Reviews Inc. All rights reserved

THEORY IN THE STUDY OF CULTURAL TRANSMISSION

◆ 9576

B. Allan Tindall
Department of Physical Education, University of California,
Berkeley, California 94720

The amount of research work being conducted on the process of cultural transmission has led to an active interest in theories of the process by which individuals learn to be members of their culture. Most research work conducted today is generated by some theoretical concern, and should ultimately be useful for clarifying those concerns. My task was to take stock of the theories of cultural transmission, but that stock taking indicates that there are no theories of the process of cultural transmission, and that there are only two theories concerned with that portion of the total process that occurs in social interaction.

My feeling is that we need theories, true theories, in order to understand that which draws our curiosity, in order to be in a position to take action in the process of cultural transmission, and, until we do understand, we need theories to communicate our thoughts, our research findings, and our conclusions.

Since we need theory but do not have one, I will present a review of where we are. In this review I shall define a theory and distinguish it from theory work. I shall present theory work which conceptualizes the process of cultural transmission as involving two component processes, and present theory work on those two component processes. The theory work will be used as the best advice available for conceptualizing the process of cultural transmission. I shall then compare two theories of the interactive aspect of cultural transmission to a synthetic conceptual framework.

In this review I confine myself to work which is addressed to the process of cultural transmission. I will not consider reports of empirical research which may contain theoretical propositions, either explicitly or implicitly. I will not consider theories of schooling, nor shall I attempt to make explicit propositions which are implied in many review articles.

THEORY AND THEORY WORK

Theories are descriptions of empirical phenomena (1, p. 294; 12, p. 107; 13, pp. 951–52) intended to communicate that which has been learned by the scientist.

But descriptions, even in the form of precisely defined concepts, are not theories.

> Concepts and their definitions are certainly part of a theory, but they are not sufficient by themselves to constitute a theory. Concepts are names for properties of nature, and a theory does not even begin to exist until propositions are stated about contingent relationships of the general form x varies as y between the properties. The reason is obvious: A theory is a deductive system, and no deductions can be made from concepts alone; propositions are absolutely necessary (13, p. 957).

Theory then is more than simple description: it is a description of relationships between conceptually distinct elements. A propositional description explains some property of the social process by specifying the exact nature of a relationship. The specification of the relationship of x to y is also implicitly a prediction that within certain boundaries wherever you observe x and y you will observe the relationship specified in the proposition (13, pp. 951–52).

Theory then can be defined as a set of propositions which describe the relationship between conceptually distinguished elements of the social process. Theories are heuristic descriptions insofar as the stated propositions facilitate the deduction of new propositions. As a theory describes, explains, and predicts elements of social process, it functions to communicate knowledge and to prod us to make further inquiries into poorly explained elements of that process.

Theories function to communicate what a scientist has learned, but just as theory must be distinguished from theoretical work on the basis of the presence of propositions, different orders or levels of theory must be distinguished on the basis of the complexity of the phenomena described and on the basis of the audience for which the description is intended.

Homans is quite correct that theories can be distinguished on the basis of ". . . what one wants to explain or predict" (13, p. 953). But his discussion of the distinction between "high-order" propositions and "low-order" propositions based on the extent to which they are more or less "general" explanations of various elements of the social process (pp. 952–53) fails to be clear about how a scientist moves to the more inclusive and general level and why such movement is necessary.

Clarification can be obtained from a discussion of two salient points: (a) that elements in the social process and in the process of social science cannot be described in terms of themselves (2, pp. 293, 298; 12, p. 107); and (b) that it is the observer who constructs the concepts used in description (2, p. 294; 12, pp. 109–10).

> Bateson, arguing from a logic developed by Bertrand Russell states: Russell's central notion is the truism that a class cannot be a member of itself. The class of elephants has not got a trunk and is not an elephant. . . . A class of commands is not itself a command and cannot tell you what to do (2, p. 293).

Goodenough agrees:

> . . . we cannot describe the primitive elements in terms of themselves. To describe these, we need some independent perceptual and conceptual frame, one that a linguist

brings with him into the descriptive task and that is part of a culture and is represented symbolically in a language he already knows and shares with the audience to whom he presents his description (12, p. 107).

The second point brings into sharp focus the logic of description as there must be a logic which distinguishes how informants describe the culture, how an anthropologist describes his informants' culture, and how anthropologists describe schemes for representing their representations of their informants' culture.

> It is the observer who creates messages (i.e. science) about the system which he is studying, and it is these messages that are of necessity in some language or other and must therefore have *order;* they must be of some or other Logical Type or of some combination of types (2, p. 294).
>
> . . . there is also a hierarchy of propositions and messages, and within this latter hierarchy [the hierarchy of propositions which correspond to a hierarchy of names, classes, and classes of classes] the Russellian discontinuity between types must also obtain. We speak of messages, of meta-messages, and meta-meta-messages; . . . (2, p. 293).

Goodenough has argued essentially the same point in his discussion of the terms emic and etic; the particular and the general (12, pp. 108–9). He points out that it is the observer who formulates the concepts which provide a description of the elementary (emic) features of a culture: a description which is based upon another logic, an etic logic. Finally, in order to compare cultures, artifacts of cultures, or extracultural phenomena, another order or system of description is required: a typology developed from etic concepts; a conceptual system, a meta-conceptual system, and a meta-meta-conceptual system.

Naroll and his colleagues (17, 18) have suggested the substitution of the term *theoric* (17, p. 2) for the term typology. Their logic is exactly the logic used by Bateson and Goodenough: as you intend to explain different orders of phenomena you must use propositions composed of a different order of concepts.

> . . . emic concepts are those used in a specific culture by the natives thereof to classify a given semantic domain. Etic concepts are those used by social scientists to analyze the conceptual distinctions made by emic systems. . . . Theoric concepts are those used by social scientists to explain variations in human cultures (18, p. 134).

The interdependent points made by Bateson and Goodenough clarify for anthropologists the necessity behind the distinction between "high order" and "low order" theories, and how a scientist moves to the most general level of theory. Homans has not clearly argued that the social scientist needs, in order to describe a conceptual order in such a way that comparisons can be made between different orders of complexity to the ultimate goal of explaining humanity, to select his concepts from a conceptual system one degree more abstract than the system he wants to describe (2, pp. 297–99). A social scientist moves toward inclusiveness and greater generality by moving from one conceptual scheme (language) to another.

A theory is distinct from theoretical work in that it is composed of propositions which allow deductions to be made. Theories can be distinguished insofar
as they seek to explain (describe, predict) different phenomena, and they can be
distinguished insofar as they seek to explain different orders or levels of complexity of a phenomenon. I shall use Narroll's labeling system (emic, etic,
theoric) because it is more manageable than message, meta-message, and meta-
meta-message.

THEORY WORK: THE PROCESS OF CULTURAL TRANSMISSION

A review of theoretical work makes it clear that there are *no* theories of the
process of cultural transmission. No scholar or group of scholars has created a
deductive system of theoric propositions which describe, explain, and predict
the process by which individuals come to full membership in their cultural
system. Two groupings of work have made major contributions to the development of a conceptual framework which *defines* the total process of cultural
transmission; both of them are nearly identical in their approach.

Kimball (16) stresses that the process of cultural transmission is the variable
relationship between the

> . . . social and cultural environment, which prescribes the method and content of
> education, and the individual in whom experience is organized and internalized (16, p.
> 160).

Gearing & Tindall (9) define the process of cultural transmission as:

> . . . constituted in regularly occurring patterns of encounter, wherein are transacted
> various *equivalences of meaning,* which equivalences together form a network and
> are the cultural system of the community in question. A network of equivalent
> meanings is constituted by similarities of shared perception . . . (9, p. 96).

Both of these works define cultural transmission as involving two conceptually
distinct processes: (*a*) the *inter*-psychic interactive social and cultural process,
and (*b*) the *intra*-psychic process of learning which takes place within the
individual.

According to Kimball, the details of the interactive aspect of cultural transmission lie in the specification of:

> . . . who teaches what to whom, how, where, and under what circumstances. One
> must also observe the situations in which, although there is no apparent effort to
> teach, the youthful observers successfully imitate the behavior they have witnessed
> (16, p. 99)

The work of Gearing and his associates identified the central concerns of the
inter-psychic study of cultural transmission as "What is transmitted?"; "Who
transacts with whom?"; and "How do transactions proceed?" (9, pp. 96–102)

Kimball is more explicit than Gearing about the cognitive process which must
take place within each individual (16, p. 155 ff), but Gearing also clearly recog-

nizes that the processing of stimuli which leads to "equivalencies" and "shared perceptions" must take place within the individual according to an intra-psychic process.

Finally, as a component of both what must be learned and what must be enacted in the interactive process, both authors clearly make a qualitative distinction between rather superficial knowledge and cultural premises. Kimball distinguishes between two orders of content: (a) world view, ". . . which contains the unstated premises that order thought and feeling" (16, p. 147); and (b) the "specific content" of culture, which I take to mean among other things ". . . bodily functions, kinship behavior, and household skills" (16, p. 160). Gearing makes the same distinction:

> . . . clusters of information would seem to vary as to complexity of the sets of interconnected categories, as to whether the categories are digital or typological in form, and as to the presence or absence of verbal labels for the categories and connections (10, pp. 7–8).

Complex typologic information is ". . . what we have called cultural premises . . ." (10, p. 8), while more simple digital information is what Kimball has called the "specific content" of culture.

These two groupings of work provide a strikingly similar definition for the process of cultural transmissions. To summarize, cultural transmission is constituted in two interrelated processes; the *inter*-psychic process which is concerned with who (actors) does what (interactive form or mode including setting or circumstance) about what topics (content of communication and complexity of information), and the *intra*-psychic process of cognition wherein people organize the stimuli which are made available to them in their social and cultural environment. A complete theory of the process of cultural transmission would then be a system of propositions composed of theoric concepts from which deductions could be made to define, explain, and predict the process in any community.

Below I shall discuss selected examples of theory work which contribute to an elaboration of the conceptual specifications for the intra and inter psychic processes involved in cultural transmission. The work reviewed is presented as being sound advice by scholars in the field as to what must be included in a theory of the intra and inter psychic processes involved in cultural transmission.

THEORY WORK: THE INTRA-PSYCHIC PROCESS

Only a few of the works that I have reviewed deal with the cognitive process which take place within each individual learner of a culture. Cole & Scribner (2–5) address themselves to a conceptualization of the variation in the *intellectual tasks* required in various cultures or within cultures, while Spindler (19) and Kimball (16) are concerned with conceptualizing the nature of the cognitive activity which must take place during cultural transmission.

In a series of recent writings, Cole & Scribner attend to the differences between what can be observed with respect to cognitive content, and what must be inferred with respect to cognitive processes (2, p. 72). In this concern they conceptualize the cross-cultural differences in remembering tasks. Given that there are "remembering tasks" (i.e. cognitive activity), the problem is to discover the ". . . kinds of 'memory skills' that members of different cultural groups, or specialists within each group, could be expected to develop" (5, p. 226) by isolating indigenous examples of peoples remembering in a variety of situations, and experimentally manipulating variables to determine: (a) the cultural variations in remembering tasks, and (b) the intellectual activity required to enact those remembering tasks.

Cole & Scribner are concerned with describing culturally specific intellectual requirements in order to know what intellectual abilities must be developed. Following such description, presumably attention can be paid to the process by which individuals in each culture come to acquire the required capacities.

Spindler (19) argues that learning to be a culture member is a matter of choosing among alternative "instrumental linkages." A cultural system is a system of behaviors which produces predictable results in terms of the achievement of goals. Such a system of behaviors has at its core, in the minds of the culture members, a system of perceived instrumental linkages between behaviors and goals. Belief systems of the culture support the linkages, and the educational institutions and processes (schools, churches, initiation ceremonies, families) teach children ". . . what the linkages are, how they work, and why some are better than others . . ." (19, p. 4)

It is when a child chooses between alternative sets of linkages that he acquires a cultural "identity;" ". . . a cathexis with certain instrumental linkages that are central to one's presentation of self in the context of one's life style." A knowledge of the available linkages and a cathected identity establish a sense of "cognitive control;" ". . . the ability of the individual to maintain a working model in his mind of potentially productive instrumental linkages and their organization."

If we are to study the intra-psychic dimension of cultural transmission we must focus on the process by which the individual selects instrumental linkages, derives an identity from those linkages, and establishes a sense of cognitive control over his world.

Kimball (16) argues that the process of cultural transmission is a variable relationship between the social and cultural environment on the one hand and the individual, who organizes and internalizes experience, on the other. His argument stresses the need to inquire into both variables. However, for my purposes I shall abstract his comments about what it is the individual must do intra-psychically in order to become a member of his culture.

Kimball argues that the individual must learn knowledge in three areas: (a) affect, which he calls the ethos or world view of the culture; (b) skills, such as language, kinship, household skills; and (c.) cognitive behavior, affect and cognitive behavior being more complex than skills. In both the family (including peer associations) and in institutional organizations ". . . the child learns body skills and affective and cognitive behavior, although the emphasis will vary from one to another" (16, p. 160)

It is the learning of "cognitive behavior" or "cognitive learning" that makes an individual a member of his culture. Cognitive learning involves learning: (a) ". . . a set of categories that permit him to distinguish and classify individuals, things, qualities, events, and processes" (16, p. 157); and (b) "cannons of discrimination:"

> The individual must also learn the criteria that make identification possible and permit classification of the items of experience in the larger whole. Not only must each individual learn the basis upon which items are classified, but he must also learn the criteria that permit him to evaluate and hence respond (16, p. 158).

The cognitive process is the process by which things are classified by a set of criteria. The focus of intra-psychic inquiry into cultural transmission (and any theoretical work done) must then be on the individual's organization and internalization of the category system and the system of criteria.

Three sets of work propose conceptual boundaries which define what must be included in any research or theoretical work on the intra-psychic process. Kimball and Spindler differ in one dimension while they are in agreement on another. They differ in that Spindler believes that the basis for the intra-psychic process is the learning of a finite set of instrumental linkages, while Kimball believes that what is pivotal is the learning of a process which enables each individual to make sense out of the world around him. The difference here is with respect to dynamics. Spindler argues that change can only take place with the introduction of new linkages, the locus for the production of which is not at all clear (19, p. 4), while Kimball argues that change is built into the criteria for categorization (16, pp. 158–61)

Kimball and Spindler are in agreement that the boundaries of the intra-psychic process are known, and all that remains is to do research and to construct theories about the details of that process. In this agreement they differ with the team of Cole and Scribner, in that the latter are more cautious in outlining what must be researched. Cole & Scribner have argued for a clear understanding of the elements involved in the process of cognition, and are implicitly suggesting that more detailed theoretical work must await a firm knowledge of just what intellectual activities are required to be developed in various cultures, or within specialized groups with specific cultures.

Finally, Cole & Scribner and Kimball demand that research and theoretical work attend to both the individual cognitive process and the cultural environment in which the individual acts. There is little detailed theory work in educational anthropology which defines the boundaries of the intra-psychic study of cultural transmission. Perhaps this is due to a wealth of theoretical work in psychology, social psychology, and psychological anthropology on the cognitive processes. That work may be complete enough to eliminate the need for a unique set of concepts for the study of the cognitive process in cultural transmission.

The implied difference between Cole & Scribner on the one hand and Kimball and Spindler on the other is not of any significance. Whether or not we are ready to theorize is an empirical question answerable only when a theory is generated and put to a test. But the answer is progress, for it will further clarify the intricacies of the process of cognition in cultural transmission.

Spindler's argument that the learning to be a culture member is constituted in learning a finite range of instrumental linkages seems to ignore the dynamics of human behavior. Kimball's argument is far more appealing because it outlines a process which in the form of a theory could potentially account for change among the members of a cultural system (as in status changes, maturation, etc) as well as changes in the entire system.

I conclude from this that we need to move toward the specification of a system of propositions at the etic level at least, from which researchers can deduce new propositions which will move us toward a complete description, explanation, and prediction of the intra-psychic processes of cultural transmission. Only when such a theory appears can we move toward a complete theory of the process of cultural transmission.

THEORY WORK: THE INTER-PSYCHIC PROCESS

The previously cited work of Kimball and Gearing defined the concepts salient to the study of the inter-psychic process of cultural transmission: (a) the mode of interaction; (b) the participants in the interactive environment; and (c) the content of the interaction. Simply put: who does what to whom about what topics?

In this section I shall discuss these conceptual areas as they are dealt with by various scholars. I shall not make this discussion elaborate since that would be somewhat redundant with the first review of the field (9), and since it would prematurely necessitate a discussion of the theory developed by Gearing and associates.

The Interactive Mode of Cultural Transmission

Kimball and Gearing note that a crucial concern is the conceptualization of how cultural transmission proceeds. The work of Hymes (14) is concurrent and provides details for a conceptual elaboration. Hymes expounds upon the need to understand communication in context. He points out that the concept of "language" is simultaneously too general and too specific to be sufficient for understanding people's communications. A new concept is needed and

> . . . must be more specific than "language," because often a person is not adequately described as "speaking English," but as speaking in some variety of English, . . .; as speaking in some recognizable manner, according to a general type of situation, . . .; or according to some specific type of scene or genre, . . .; according to some particular role or relationship,. . . . At the same time the concept that we need must be more general than that of "language," because in many communities the available means of speech extend beyond any one language, or linguistic norm, to comprise a variety of levels. . . . Finally, the concept must be more general than "language" because in all communities language is but one means of communication among others (14, pp. xxii–xxiii).

According to Hymes, we must attend to the "difference that makes a difference," and we can do that by conceptualizing the mode of cultural transmission as "communicative repertoire," the aspects of which ". . . can be taken as defining general questions to be asked, whether with reference to persons, groups, or communities:

(1) What is the set of means available. . . .? What are the meanings associated with these means?
(2) What are the contexts of situations for communication, including speaking, as defined by the person, group or community? What meanings are associated with these contexts?
(3) What relations of appropriateness (and inappropriateness) obtain between means of communication and situations . . .? . . . In particular, what is the meaning of the use of one means as against another?

The mode or form of cultural transmission must be seen as including means which include but are not restricted to verbal language: nonverbal behavior must be considered. Context must also be considered, because meaning (that is ultimately the content of what is transmitted) is determined by the relationship between the means used for communication and the context in which communication takes place. This perspective links the form of communication with the second conceptual concern, the participants in social interaction, and implies the link to the third, the content of cultural transmission.

The Participants in Cultural Transmission

Kimball and Gearing define as relevant who interacts with whom. That is: who are the people present in any interactional encounter, or what is the social context of interaction? There seems to be some agreement that each cultural system maintains a category system for classifying people (9, 15, 16). The social nature of a context is defined by the people present, and as noted, the mode of communication used in cultural transmission is intimately related to the social context.

Kimball has made the distinction between family and institutional contexts in order to discuss the degree to which the holders of information are "strangers" to those who do not have, and seek, or are sent to obtain that information (16, pp. 150–52)

Gearing has been more precise in pointing out that the life careers of people can be described in terms of a wider range of interactive "encounters." The full array of emic social identities, in all possible combinations, describes the potential range of encounters that any person or category of people might engage in. An encounter profile for a person or category of people would be a discription of the actual encounters they participated in, from that full range (7, 9).

How cultural transmission takes place is seen to be related to the communicative form (language plus other means, presumably kinesic) and to social context. Social context describes the nature of interactive encounters as the presence or absence of types of people, but the presence or absence of types of people is also related to the content of the communications in context.

The Content of Cultural Transmission

Ultimately cultural transmission involves the presentation or display of information which can be learned (the process of how or if it is learned is an *intra*-psychic concern): the content of communications. The concern is with conceptualizing what information must be made available to learners, and that concern is ultimately tied to the interactants because they either do or do not possess certain types of information. It is obvious that if none of the parties in an encounter possess certain information, then those parties cannot communicate about that information, and no transmission can occur in that encounter about that information.

Gearing and Kimball distinguish between simple, specific information and complex, typologic premises, although the exact procedures for the specification of the degree of simplicity or complexity is not clear. Kimball (16) identifies three types of information which must be learned: (*a*) world view, perspective, or ethos (which is complex); (*b*) body skills, kinship, etc (which is specific); and (*c*) the system for categorizing people and events, and the criteria by which categorizations are made (which is neither simple nor complex). Gearing (10) makes a distinction along two axis: simple to complex on the vertical axis, and digital or typologic on the horizontal axis.

Certainly some information is discrete and simple: names of people, events; some information is complex: how to learn (deutero-learning) (2), the premise of man's relationship to man (10), the criteria for determining "work" or "play" (10); some information clearly neither simple nor complex: whole category systems without the associated criteria. Much of what has been reviewed here identifies information which must be the content of communication: categories of social identity (9, 10, 15, 16); knowledge of the means of communication, of social contexts, and the criteria for appropriate communicational behavior (14); the components parts of and the structure of instrumental linkages (19); and much more.

Finally, we must be concerned with the degree to which the content of cultural transmission is explicit. If cultural premises are unstatable (10, 16), they must constitute implicit communicational content. At the other extreme is explicit content which deals with discrete, easily named items of information. Other information may be communicated by partially implicit and partially explicit means.

Cultural transmissive content must then be conceptualized as involving implicit and explicit messages about simple and complex information, which is in the possession of certain people who enact those messages.

To summarize: the inter-psychic process of cultural transmission must be conceptualized as involving modes of communications among particular people in social contexts which contain implicit and explicit messages about simple and complex information.

Any theory of the inter-psychic dimensions of cultural transmission must be composed of deductive propositions which stipulate the relationships between these conceptual elements. Such a theory must define the specific modes of communication which are used, the categories of people who group themselves (or are grouped) into social contexts for interaction, and must define the explicit and implicit messages about simple and complex information. The theory must then stipulate the relationship between people's communications about information in a manner which explains and predicts how it is that the information which enables cultural membership gets from those who have it to those who do not have it. Preferably such a theory would be theoric in that the concepts used were meta-meta-messages about cultural transmission as a human process, rather than an etic formulation which was a message about some emic system for the transmission of a culture.

THEORIES OF THE INTER-PSYCHIC PROCESS

There are only two works which can properly be called theories of the inter-psychic process of cultural transmission. There are many descriptive ethnographies in which implicit deductive propositions can be found. There are additionally deductive propositions about selected aspects of the total inter-psychic process of cultural transmission. Spindler has formulated a deductive proposition concerning culture change as a function of the presence or absence of new instrumental linkages (19). Kimball has specified the relationship between the type of role relationship between teachers and students in a manner which predicts the extent of student involvement in the "learning process," and ultimately the continuance of the society now constituted in the United States (16). Wilson has constructed a framework for conceptualizing the relationship between the evolution of culture and the evolution of education in a manner which lends itself to the deduction of specific propositions (20). These deductive systems are here excluded because they do not deal with the entire inter-psychic process on a theoric level.

Marion Dobbert (6) has presented a deductive system which defines the process of cultural transmission to be the variable relationships between: 1. Relevant aspects of persons, as (a) "learners" and (b) "other persons"; 2. "Cultural settings and locals"; and 3. "Cultural Information Stored in Social Patterns," as between "Organized Group Patterns, " and "Possible Individual Act [action?] Patterns."

Dobbert has not specified any propositions, although her work contains several. An example would be: The "culture" that a person can learn at any given time varies with that person's "age stage and sex." This is explicated by the following series of propositions:
1. Age stage and sex limit one's access to cultural settings.
2. Limited access to cultural settings limits the range of activities available for observation and/or participation.
3. Limits to the available activities limits the specific cultural content which can be learned to:
   (a) The objects, group size, relational content, and emotional content of those activities.

(b) The values and ideals of the people present.

(c) Specific instrumental acts.

This is a theoric level theory because it utilizes the etic concepts (although they are not thoroughly defined) of "age stage and sex," cultural settings, etc to specify, and thus define and explain in a manner which is deductive, their relationship to the inter-psychic process of cultural transmission (a theoric concept).

However, this formulation fails to consider two points stressed in the discussion above. Nowhere in her brief discussion does Dobbert mention the *mode* of cultural transmission. She does mention "observation and participation" by the learner, but that is not a statement of communication in context. She also fails to be explicit about the relative simplicity or complexity of the *content* of what is transmitted. This theory then falls short of containing all the concepts that are perceived by scholars in the field to be salient to the inter-psychic process of cultural transmission.

The only other theory which attempts to explain and predict the inter-psychic process of cultural transmission has been written by Fred Gearing and his associates (8, 10, 11). This theory is quite elaborate and complex, and I can only outline its major variables, the essence of its five propositions, and its sufficiency as a true theory of the inter-psychic process of cultural transmission.

The theory seeks to explain and predict the interactional circumstances in which culture gets transmitted. We have concluded that culture is transmitted through the carefully controlled exchange of information in (at least) dyadic encounters. In those encounters, information of the simple digital, simple typologic, complex digital, and complex typologic type is exchanged or not exchanged, through complex series of linguistic and kinesic messages, as a function of the *social identity* of the parties to an encounter and as a function of the nature of information as *property*.

"Exchange" means passed back and forth between the parties; not exchanged means it is displayed as a message and is not returned, or is not displayed.

The types of information, as between simple and complex, is the same as that which was discussed above.

Social identity means the perceived category into which a person is classified.

Property gives wealth, power, or status. Information of certain types can be instrumental to wealth, power, and status, and as such information is property.

There is one qualification in pragmatic effect though not in principle: if there be, within the bounded community under analysis, items of information displayed by each with all, those items are not property-like within that community (but would be found to be property-like in some more inclusive community) (10, p. 3).

There are five propositions stipulated in "A Cultural Theory of Education," which are paraphrased here:

Proposition 1a and 1b jointly predict the patterns of (simple) information exchange (one of three types) which will occur as a function of the social identities of the parties to the encounter (and the probability of mobility from one identity to another where the parties are not in the same category) and as a function of the property-like nature of the information exchanged (8, p. 14 ff).

Proposition 2 predicts the pattern of relationship between the "leader" of the exchange and the "follower" as a function of the type of encounter (as in proposition 1). Simply that "old hands" (those who possess simple information) lead and "newcomers" (those who seek information, regardless of age) follow (8, p. 23 ff).

Proposition 3 predicts a cybernetic control over exchanges of simple information in multipartied encounters, wherein the parties are not of the same social identity, such that the least common denominator is used to determine what items of information will be exchanged. (8, p. 26 ff).

Proposition 4 predicts the establishment of leading and following in encounters involving complex information, according to tacit patterns of leading and following established in exchanges of simple information (8, p. 27 ff).

Proposition 5 predicts the establishment of tacit leading and following as a function of the familiarity of the parties with the topic in question (8, p.29).

This theory deals explicitly with the various forms of verbal and nonverbal communication (i.e. the mode) as individuals of various social identities are parties to an encounter (the participants) in which certain types of (simple and complex) information exchanges take place (the content) as a function of the social identity of the parties and the property-like nature of the information. The processual relationship between modes of communication, participants, and cultural content are defined, explained, and thus predict, for any given community, the inter-psychic constraints to the nonrandom distribution of information. This is a theoric level formulation, which in its full form deals with all of the conceptual elements discussed above in a series of deductive propositions.

WHERE WE ARE AND WHERE WE MUST GO

When I began this review I was convinced that I would find many theories, because in every discussion of research the touchstone is theoretical development, and because each researcher is striving to clarify some theory. Now I am puzzled. Can it be that educational anthropologists do not know the difference between a theory and theory work? Do we need a George Casper Homans (13) to instruct us? Should we reexamine our graduate level training? Or is it that the field is so new that the construction of theories of cultural transmission are only now possible? I hope the latter is true.

We are not too far, as we have a long way to go. I am of course partial to what is called the "Gearing theory," but my partiality extends beyond my own ego investment. The work of Kimball, Hymes, and many others indicates that our work is moving in the right direction. But that is only half of a full theory of cultural transmission.

The other half must be brought forward: we need to know what is cognitively involved in learning culture; we need to know if there is something unique about cognition in cultural transmission; and we need to know how conceptual descriptions of the cognitive process can be linked relationally in deductive propositions; we need a theory of the intra-psychic processes in cultural transmission.

But that will not take us to where we want to go. At such time that a full theoric level intra-psychic theory is available, additional work will be necessary to define the exact nature of the interrelatedness between the intra- and inter-psychic aspects of cultural transmission. We have a long way to go but unless we are constantly traveling, constantly reexamining, constantly reformulating, we will not be able to communicate. Theory, after all, is the meta-meta-language which is our emic system for conceptualizing the world, for taking action in the world, and for guiding our search for understanding.

Literature Cited

1. Bateson, G. 1958. *Naven.* Stanford Univ. Press. 312 pp. 2nd ed.
2. Cole, M. 1973. Toward an experimental anthropology of thinking. In *Learning and Culture,* ed. S. T. Kimball, J. H. Burnett, 59–74. Seattle: Univ. Washington Press. 264 pp.
3. Cole, M. 1974. Toward an experimental anthropology of education. *CAE Q.* 5:7–11
4. Cole, M., Scribner, S. 1974. *Culture and Thought: A Psychological Introduction.* New York: Wiley. 277 pp.
5. Cole, M., Scribner, S. 1975. Theorizing about socialization of cognition. *Ethos* Summer:249–68
6. Dobbert, M. L. 1975. Another route to a general theory of cultural transmission: a systems model. *CAE Q.* 6:22–26
7. Gearing, F. O. 1973. Where we are and where we might go: steps toward a general theory of cultural transmission. *CAE Newsl.* 4:1–10
8. Gearing, F. O. A cultural theory of education. In *Toward a General Cultural Theory of Education,* ed. F. O. Gearing, L. Sangree. The Hague: Mouton. In press
9. Gearing, F. O., Tindall, B. A. 1973. Anthropological studies of the educational process. *Ann. Rev. Anthropol.* 2:95–105
10. Gearing, F. O., Tindall, B. A., Smith, A., Carroll, T. 1975. Structures of censorship, usually inadvertent: studies in a cultural theory of education. *CAE Q.* 6:1–22
11. Gearing, F. O., Carroll, T., Hughes, W., Precourt, W., Smith, A., Tindall, B. A., Topfer, S. A general theory of education. Work. pap. #6. See Ref. 8
12. Goodenough, W. H. 1970. *Description and Comparison in Cultural Anthropology.* Chicago: Aldine. 173 pp.
13. Homans, G. C. 1964. Contemporary theory in sociology. In *Handbook of Modern Sociology,* ed. R. E. L. Faris, 951–77. Chicago: Rand McNally. 1088 pp.
14. Hymes, D. 1972. Introduction. In *Functions of Language in the Classroom,* ed. C. B. Cazden, V. P. John, D. Hymes, xi–lvii. New York: Teachers Coll. Press. 394 pps.
15. Ianni, F. A. J. 1974. Social organization study program: an interim report. *CAE Q.* 5:1–8
16. Kimball, S. T. 1974. *Culture and the Educative Process.* New York: Teachers Coll. Press. 285 pp.
17. Naroll, R., Naroll, F. 1973. *Main Currents in Cultural Anthropology.* Englewood Cliffs, NJ: Prentice-Hall. 410 pp.
18. Naroll, R., Michik, G. L., Naroll, F. 1974. Hologeistic theory testing. In *Comparative Studies by Harold E. Driver and Essays in His Honor,* ed. J. G. Jorgensen, 121–48. New Haven: HRAF Press. 245 pp.
19. Spindler, G. D. 1974. From Omnibus to Linkages: cultural transmission models. *CAE Q.* 5:1–6
20. Wilson, H. C. 1973. On the evolution of education. See Ref. 2, 211–41

Ann. Rev. Anthropol. 1976. 5:209–25
Copyright © 1976 by Annual Reviews Inc. All rights reserved

STATUS OF SOCIAL-CULTURAL ANTHROPOLOGY IN INDIA

♦ 9577

Gopāla Śarana
Department of Anthropology, Karnatak University,
Dharwar 580003 (Karnataka), India

Dharni P. Sinha[1]
Center for Educational Policy and Management, Administrative
Staff College of India, Hyderabad 500475 (AP), India

INDIAN ANTHROPOLOGY IN FOCUS

Although we have been invited to write on the status of social-cultural anthropology in South Asia, we prefer to confine our remarks to India for various reasons. To the best of our knowledge, anthropology has not been accorded independent academic recognition in Afghanistan, Pakistan, Nepal, and Bangladesh, although there are some anthropologists working in basically non-anthropological institutions. Sri Lanka has produced some well-known anthropologists, but their talent is being utilized by other countries.

In India, on the other hand, anthropology has been recognized by academic and nonacademic bodies and institutions for many decades. Before detailing the background of contemporary anthropology in India, we should like to say a few words about the discipline in general. We have been invited to write on social-cultural anthropology, the study of man. But it is appropriate to state at the outset that social-cultural anthropology in India is a subdivision of anthropology in the sense that the term is understood in the English-speaking countries. The other two major subdivisions of anthropology are physical (biological) anthropology and prehistory or archaeological anthropology. In recent years, some institutions of higher learning and research have begun to teach linguistic anthropology as well. As this account makes clear, we realize that there are areas of interest which the Indian social-cultural anthropologists share with Indian so-

---

[1]We acknowledge with sincere thanks the considerable assistance received from J. L. Plakkoottam of the Administrative Staff College of India.

209

ciologists. But in the procedures, the manner of conceiving research problems, areas of research, theoretical orientations, and involvement with problem-solving there is a large difference between Indian sociologists as a whole, on the one hand, and Indian anthropologists as a whole, on the other. We firmly believe that social-cultural anthropology is neither a branch of sociology in India nor coterminus with it. This account, however, is not to be taken to mean that we are against meaningful cooperation or even collaboration with sociologists in India.

Among the colonialized nations, which became free after the Second World War, India has had a unique position. After the British entrenched themselves in this country, a group of English scholars began deriding the earlier rash accounts of "primitiveness" and "barbarism" of the native Indians as painted by some particularly egoistic and ill-intentioned British administrators. It did not take long for the West to realize that India had one of the oldest uninterrupted cultural traditions among all countries of the world. Sir William Jones's statement in 1776 about a more than accidental affinity between Sanskrit, Greek, and Latin and the consequent growth in comparative philology, with Sanskrit occupying the focal point of interest, contributed much toward changing the Western scholars' opinion of India. However, we do not agree with some of our fellow anthropologists in this country who believe that anthropology in India began with the establishment in 1774 of the Asiatic Society of Bengal. It is true that the Asiatic Society was responsible for the publication of materials concerned with antiquarian and anthropological interests.

In our view, the origin of anthropology in India goes back to the days of British colonial administration in the latter half of the nineteenth century. The British administrators gradually realized that a good acquaintance with the natives and their culture was a basic prerequisite for governing them properly without falling foul of their customs and thus causing avoidable irritations. Therefore, the administrative needs of the British rulers forced them to use official machinery to gather information about the social institutions, economic conditions, and religious beliefs and practices of the native Indians, who could be grouped easily into tribes and castes. H. H. Risley first published his accounts of tribes and castes of Bengal in 1891. He later became famous as head of census operations in India, which resulted in his most celebrated book, *The People of India*. He was able to establish an ethnographic survey as a wing of the census operations in 1905. This may be taken as a landmark in the development of anthropology in India. Crooke, Thurston, Grierson, Blunt, Mills, Dalton, O'Malley, Russel, Hutton, and others of the Indian Civil Service also contributed toward the founding and establishment of anthropology in India. The efforts of these British administrators gave us compendia of tribes and castes for different parts of India, district gazetteers covering almost every district of British India, the Imperial Gazetteer of India, and census reports. The report of the 1931 census conducted under the direction of J. H. Hutton is particularly notable for its ethnographic notes and comments on different communities of India. After India became independent in 1947, a social studies division was added to the office of the Registrar General of India, who is in charge of census operations in this country.

The preceding account highlights the fact that anthropological studies in India were the offshoot of colonial rule. They were undertaken by British administrators (39) to enable "the rulers to take stock of their position and to see how it has fared with the people committed to their charge" (39, p. 2). In some cases anthropological studies were motivated by genuine curiosity about the variety of different peoples of India and their exotic customs. A few notable consequences of these studies are worth mentioning. The early anthropological studies were not academic but utilitarian in their nature. The contributors were all foreigners who were studying the cultures of the natives. They were all based in India and did not have direct contact with the academic anthropologists like Tylor, Frazer, and others who were conducting researches at Cambridge, Oxford, and London universities. Thus their work did not become a part of British anthropology, which would have been the case had they been inspired by the British academic anthropologists or the colonial office in London. But in one sense their contributions were in tune with the main theme and ethos of the late nineteenth and early twentieth century anthropology. Their contributions were anthropological, in spite of the utilitarian bias, because they were often studying curious customs of people belonging to other cultures.

This early affiliation of anthropology with government agencies continued even after independence. There are certain research institutions that are doing anthropological studies. They are autonomous or semi-autonomous establishments and are financed by federal or state governments. The most notable research institution, probably the largest of its kind in the world, is the Anthropological Survey of India with its headquarters at Calcutta. It has seven regional stations and employs over a hundred professional anthropologists. It has been carrying on research in both social-cultural and physical anthropology. It has the best library of anthropology in India.

Several state governments have established tribal research institutes or bureaus in their states to collect information and plan the development of the tribal people residing in their states. In some states, anthropologists, besides working in the tribal institutes, are also associated with the *Harijan* and social welfare departments. Some other national institutes where anthropologists have been working are the National Institute of Community Development, National Institute of Family Planning, International Centre for Population Studies, and Indian Agricultural Research Institute. Anthropology in India is trying to carve out a unique place for itself in the holistic anthropological study under the Satellite Instructional Television Experiment (SITE) at the Space Applications Centre, Ahmedabad.

Anthropologists not only find places in governmental research institutions, but in some governmental investigating agencies as well. Some of these are the Office of the Commissioner for Scheduled Castes and Scheduled Tribes, social welfare departments of the Government of India and the state governments, the Office of Registrar General of India, and the Gazetteer Division of the state information departments. Anthropology's association with museums in this country is also quite old. Indian Museum at Calcutta and National Museum at New Delhi have separate anthropology divisions. Among the state museums, the Government Museum at Madras has a very good section on anthropological exhibits and its curators are professional anthropologists. The Prince of Wales Museum at Bombay has an anthropology section, and Gujarat Vidyapith in Ahmedabad has a good collection of material culture items from the different tribes of Gujarat.

Until now we have talked about the recognition accorded to anthropology by nonacademic agencies. It is notable that even though anthropology had not been introduced as a regular subject of study in an Indian university, it was accorded recognition by the Indian Science Congress Association in its first session held at Calcutta. The Indian Science Congress began with a section on anthropology, which has remained a part of the Congress. Until recently it was the only social science discipline represented in the Indian Science Congress. This situation is parallel to that of the British and American Associations for the Advancement of Science. It may not be out of place to mention here that anthropology has been associated with the National Institute of Sciences of India (now called Indian National Science Academy) from its very inception. Anthropology also has a place in the Council of Scientific and Industrial Research, Indian Council of Medical Research, and Indian Council of Social Science Research. Anthropologists are associated with the Planning Commission of India as well.

A discipline cannot be said to have made its mark until it is accorded recognition as a subject of teaching and research at the university level. Contrary to the popular idea that anthropology is a new subject, it entered the field of university education in 1920 at Calcutta University. Curiously, although the first inspiration for both academic and nonacademic anthropology in India came from Great Britain, Indian anthropological teaching has not followed the British pattern. At present, full-fledged departments of anthropology, covering all branches of the discipline, are conspicuous by their absence in British universities. Most of the famous British universities have departments of social anthropology, not anthropology. But in India, beginning with Calcutta University, practically all the universities teach anthropology as an integrated discipline although there has been more emphasis on the development of social-cultural anthropology. Out of over 100 universities in this country, provision for teaching anthropology at masters' level has been made in about 20. At the bachelors' level one paper in anthropology is usually given as a part of the sociology course in most universities.

Unfortunately, the growth of anthropology as a subject of higher study and research has not been rapid, at least not as rapid as that of sociology. Besides the regular universities, anthropology has carved out a small niche in technical and professional institutions as well. The Indian Institute of Management at Calcutta and the Administrative Staff College of India at Hyderabad have anthropologists on their faculty who are trying to extend the traditional boundaries of anthropology. Some anthropologists have also been recruited as members of the faculty of the social science and humanities division of the Indian Institutes of Technology, to train engineers. In our view in the last half-century the growth of Indian anthropology in general and of social-cultural anthropology in particular has been notable, though not spectacular. Despite its under developed economic conditions and the lack of employment opportunities for many of its graduates, India probably is second only to the United States in the number of professionally trained anthropologists working in different institutions.

SPHERES OF INFLUENCE AND CHANGING PERSPECTIVES

In the previous section, we referred to the colonial background of Indian anthropology. It may be worthwhile to repeat that the British administrator began anthropological studies in this country with a purely utilitarian purpose. He was an alien and looked at all kinds of native Indians with "non-involvement." Like his fellow countrymen studying peoples of Africa, Oceania, or the West Indies, his studies of Indian people were also "other-culture" studies. His contributions normally would have formed the Indian studies wing of British anthropology, but the British administrators conducted their studies of Indian institutions and customs as servants of the government of India while they were stationed in this country. Not the academic interests of British anthropology but administrative requirements motivated these early studies. Most of the writings were either official or semiofficial documents of the government of India.

At the turn of the century, L. K. Ananthakrishna Iyer and S. C. Roy entered the field of anthropological studies. Iyer, like the British administrators, worked on a serial publication. (24 a, b) on the tribes and castes. Roy's work had a different flavor. Although not an academic anthropologist himself, he was in close touch with the leading Western anthropologists like Frazer, Rivers, Marett, and Dixon. He wrote detailed ethnographic accounts of several tribes of Chotanagpur, beginning with his first publication in 1912 entitled *Mundas and Their Country* (39a). Roy has himself called his procedure "the orthodox method of ethnographical monographs," which consisted of concise classified presentation of the different aspects of a culture as a whole. Roy considered his procedure to be different from the functional method of Malinowski. He was convinced, at the end of his career, that he would adopt the functional method if he were to do his anthropological studies over again.

It is strange that even these very able pioneering anthropologists of Indian origin did not think that their work should be different from that of the British administrator-anthropologists who were studying an alien culture. Roy was not a foreigner, but he quickly adopted the prevailing fashion of the day of studying tribals who were called animists by Tylor. Both Iyer and Roy thought that a study of tribal people through first-hand field work was central to anthropology. Other anthropologists of Indian origin followed the lead of these pioneers by choosing to work among the tribal people. Thus for a fairly long time (until the end of the 1940s) Indian anthropology was *primarily* a study of tribal people of India who were considered to be separate from the rest of the Indian population

214   SARANA & SINHA

and thus could be studied with the same kind of detachment that Western anthropologists had adopted in studying cultures of simple people, usually outside their own national boundaries.

In those days anthropology's exclusive concern was with exotic and non-literate peoples. The American anthropologists were primarily engaged in synchronic and historical studies of the American Indian. The "other-culture" perspective of American anthropology would not have developed in sharp focus if they had continued to study the American Indian alone. However, it was soon realized that a mere historical approach was inadequate for understanding the American Indian culture. After World War II, the American anthropologists started taking an interest in global ethnography and developed area specializations. They thus reinforced the anthropological practice of studying cultures other than their own and contributed to the further development of the other-culture perspective and methodology. Even though American anthropology had begun with the study of the natives at home, the situation of the British and continental anthropologists was quite different because nonliterate peoples were not living within their national boundaries. They therefore had to go to Africa, Asia, or Australia and the Pacific regions for their anthropological studies of nonliterate (other) cultures. As pointed out above, the Indian anthropologist considered it quite legitimate to concentrate on the Indian tribal population. Our pioneers thought that they could study the Oraon, the Munda, the Birhor, and other Indian tribes as though they were studying other cultures like the English administrator—anthropologists or other academic anthropologists from the West who had started taking an interest in India in the late 1940s. After World War II, the foreign anthropologists who worked in India were academicians and not administrators. Some of them studied tribes. In due course, interest shifted from the study of tribes to that of castes. The transition was natural and smooth for both the foreign anthropologists and the Indian academic anthropologists who succeeded such pioneers as Iyer and Roy.

In changing the focus from tribe to caste, there was some difference in the nature of anthropological enquiry (3, 34, 36, 52). The tribes usually were compact, manageable, and more or less homogeneous communities with relatively little contact with the outside world. The anthropologists could not study castes under the same conditions. Therefore, many studies in the early 1950s of castes were attempted within the territorially defined limits of a village. Village studies were very popular at least for a decade and some are still being conducted. We are not sure of the ultimate value of village studies conducted by different anthropologists without any similarity in framework or plan of study. Such studies do not seem to be motivated by a desire to cover systematically the different subregions and regions of India to provide knowledge about the way people live in village India. We hope that those involved in village studies are fully aware that the results of their investigations, either individually or collectively, will not by themselves give us a proper understanding of the complexities of Indian civilization. However, this is not to deny that they will bring forth valuable concrete details of the ordinary aspects of life. But they are unlikely to tell us much about what Kroeber has called "the larger heightened elements" of the total culture, such as "the national power, leadership, guidance, genius, resources and achievements" (29).

What has been said above should not be taken to mean that we are against community studies in general and studies of village communities in particular. However, interest in the study of castes did not allow the anthropologist— foreign or Indian—to confine himself to one particular village. The study of caste was bound to spill over from the village to a group of villages, to a region, and to figure in the national context as well. Here the traditional pull of the holistic approach was compelling the anthropologist to confine himself in his field research to only a village. That is why caste studies and village studies, for at least a while, seemed to be one and the same, but not for long. Both Western and Indian anthropologists have been primarily concerned with the study of caste (1, 37). This is borne out by the papers published in *Structure and Change in Indian Society* by the Indianists of the United States of America (50, 51). Four of the six sections of the book deal with caste under the following headings: "Caste and Social Structure," "The Structure of Inter-Caste Relations," "Is the Caste System Changing?," and "Caste in Politics, Economics and Law."

Let us pause here to examine the genesis and implications of the convergence of interest of the foreign and Indian anthropologists in Indian studies. A foreign anthropologist comes to India to study a culture other than his own. India is too complex and too vast a country to be covered fully by one or more empirical anthropological enquiry. The foreign anthropologist knows this full well. Therefore he has to strike a balance between knowing a small part of India very intensively and having a fairly good knowledge of the country as a whole. This is a basic prerequisite for recognition as an area specialist of South Asia in the country of his origin. He also fulfills the basic professional requirements of studying another culture by grappling with the entirely different, exotic, extremely complex, and exciting Indian culture. When he comes to India he brings with him concepts and theoretical frameworks, as well as research procedures, developed by Western anthropologists in their studies of simple, nonliterate, and relatively homogeneous and isolated communities that are quite unlike those in complex India. True to the anthropological tradition of his country, he has to conduct an empirical enquiry. He therefore chooses a village, a few contiguous villages, or a small region for his detailed empirical study. Sometimes his analysis is very penetrating because he goes into the minutest detail. There is no doubt that many of these studies prove to be quite illuminating even to the intelligent native laymen as well as scholars in understanding certain aspects of their own culture. We are fully aware that a well-trained native anthropologist who does a "self-study" on similar lines may miss some facets of the social dimensions because he takes many things in his own culture for granted, whereas they are brought to the surface by a foreign investigator due to cultural shock. The latter has to be especially alert to unravel the finer details to understand and account for the alien cultural system that he studies.

We are fully convinced of the desirability and importance of the anthropological study of other cultures and greatly regret that the Indian anthropologists are deficient in this area. But the requirements of anthropological self-study must be different. For instance, as initial training in the specifics of anthropological field work, the native anthropologist may investigate problems similar to those studied by anthropologists working in an alien culture. For an Indian anthropologist born in India an account of how a joint family breaks up into two or more family units by having separate *chulhas* (hearths), how a caste Panchayat decides on violation of caste norms, or how a caste is ranked in a particular village should not be considered a significant contribution to knowledge, although they may be so for a British or an American anthropologist specializing in Indian studies. In India *anthropology as self-study* should throw light on those aspects of Indian culture that we are more competent to deal with than any foreigner because we have learned the goals, values, and ideals of our culture through enculturation. This means that we have to undertake to study those aspects of our culture that are of vital importance but that have not been investigated hitherto. This may sometimes result in dealing with the very basic and elementary aspects of life, not excluding those concerned with material culture. We must also devise special schemes for holistic description of different levels of organization, such as cities, regions, and the entire nation.

Let us return to the discussion begun earlier about the problems of a foreign anthropologist studying the complex Indian culture. As Kroeber aptly remarked, anthropologists have always desired to apperceive and conceive the subject matter of their study both empirically and holistically. The holistic urge has been most distinctive of anthropologists as a group, possibly because their investigations began with small-scale or simple "authentic" societies that can be viewed as discrete wholes. But when the anthropologist studies a complex society the scene changes drastically. How is he going to perceive and conceive the phenomena both empirically and holistically? To earn the right to be called a specialist on India in his country, a foreign anthropologist spends a year or more in an Indian village. Through time-honored first-hand field work he can study empirically only a small segment of the complex Indian society. But a community, a village, or even a group of villages is not an autonomous society. Therefore, the anthropologist for the first time realizes that he is empirical but not holistic in his approach. He has no better tool at his disposal than that of enthnographic investigation in a face-to-face situation. We are not denying the important contributions that can be made even by ethnographic procedure by concentrating on the study of linguistically or geographically defined communities within complex civilizations like India. But it should be made abundantly clear that the ethnographic procedure may always remain subsidiary in dealing with the existing documents in a complex civilization. A composite picture of Indian culture cannot easily be painted by combining only the results of several ethnographic accounts of different village communities. The problem of combining empiricism and holism in the study of the complex Indian society is difficult, though not impossible, to solve. The Western anthropologists working in India tried to solve this dilemma by positing concepts of "economic frontier," "text and context," "great tradition and little tradition," etc (32). It is a pity that we in India adopted these concepts and could not evolve anything better of our own than "Sanskritization" (57). There is a lot of truth in what N. K. Bose wrote in 1952 about Indian anthropologists (7). Indian anthropologists have not made any problem peculiarly their own. They have failed to let their problems of research grow out of the life of their own people. Most of them have followed the paths beaten by anthropologists in the powerful Western countries.

R. Nicholas (35) says that "the position of South Asian specialists in anthropology—whether British, American, Indian or Ceylonese—appears to me to be less favorable than that of specialists in several other world areas" (35, p. 12). In our view this is so for two reasons. First, the South Asian specialist has treated his complex society data with the concepts and frames of reference developed elsewhere in the study of simple societies lacking written history. Second, a unique opportunity existed in India for a dialog between the foreign anthropologists who studied this culture from the "other-culture" perspective and the anthropologists born in India who did self-study of parts of their own culture, but this dialog has failed to materialize. Unfortunately, the India-born anthropologists are more to blame because instead of breaking new grounds, they became mere camp followers. We should have left it to the foreign anthropologists to be concerned with the infinite and minute details of behavior. They could perceive the bits and pieces of information that may have proved crucial in anthropological interpretations and analyses, although they might escape the attention of, or seem to be superfluous to, the native anthropologist. We wish we could have taken up the study of patron-client relationships, the position and role of women in different spheres of life, the dynamics of the joint family system, and the study of reciprocity and redistribution in economic as well as noneconomic transactions in different spheres of life.

We should also mention here some of the positive consequences of the involvement of Indian anthropologists in the study of segments of their own society and culture. We have imbibed the holistic spirit of anthropology and have demonstrated the utility of detailed and long-term face-to-face field work in the study of one's own culture or a part thereof. Almost all the major tribes of India have been covered through ethnographic studies. We are no longer obsessed with the exploration of merely the unusual and the exotic. One of our greatest drawbacks is the lack of other-culture studies by Indian anthropologists. It is high time that we did develop expertise in this field because research among other cultures has been the forte of anthropology. Such research will broaden the vision of Indian anthropologists and will help them understand their own culture better. However, what has until now been our weakness will prove to be a source of strength in the very near future. We do not think there is any other country in the world where anthropological self-study has been conducted by native-born anthropologists for almost seven decades. Before long, anthropologists of all countries, particularly the developing countries, will have to start studying their own culture. We cannot anticipate the kinds of problems these native anthropologists will face. This new aspect of anthropology in almost every country will encounter growing pains. The only exception then will be anthropology in India, which has long passed that stage. This does not mean that we will have no problems, but they certainly will be different from those of anthropologists elsewhere. Moreover, our experiences during the early periods of growth of anthropology in India will prove useful to others. In yet another way Indian anthropology is unique. In most countries of the world, local problems and issues are dealt with by sociologists, economists, psychologists, and political scientists, but not by anthropologists. By concentrating on tribal studies for almost half a century, the Indian anthropologists carved out a permanent place for their discipline in this country. Therefore when they moved from the study of tribes to the study of communities, castes, and other more complex segments of the Indian population, they did so without losing their identity as anthropologists. As we show in the next section, in grappling with more complex issues of development, welfare, and nation-building, anthropologists have been trying to make their own contributions, although sometimes working in collaboration with other social scientists. Whatever may be the nature of anthropological investigation in the future, it is unlikely that Indian anthropology will wither away by merging its identity with one or more disciplines.

CONTINUING INTERESTS AND EMERGING TRENDS

In the days of colonial anthropology the Indian anthropologists were unconcerned with national issues, which in those days were centered around the struggle for liberation from foreign rule. Elwin's "national park" thesis recommended that the tribal people be left alone to develop along their own lines, free from exploitation of the neighboring caste Hindus (17, 18). This position created bad publicity for anthropology. Anthropology became suspect in the eyes of the nationalist forces, as it was taken to stand for separation between the tribals and nontribals by advocating that the former be kept in "reservations" and "scheduled areas." Thus it was supposed that anthropology was a handmaiden of colonialism and stood against the integration of different sections of Indian population into one nation. Ghurye (21) tried to repudiate the national park thesis, but he was not willing to go far enough to face the realities squarely. He viewed the tribal people as "aborigines so-called." It was left to the British administrator—turned—academic anthropologist, J. H. Hutton (24), to unhesitatingly declare that the tribals were nothing but backward Hindus and that their gradual assimilation into the Hindu fold had been going on for a very long time.

Later the Indian anthropologists became involved with the nontribal people in their academic pursuits like the foreign anthropologists who served as their mentors and trailblazers. The Indian anthropologist considered it necessary to be detached and uninvolved. But such a state of affairs could not continue for long. The first few years of India's independence were full of turmoil and upheaval. The country was rocked with massive transfers of populations across the national borders, creating the problem of refugee rehabilitation. The communal riots and Pakistani conflict with India over Kashmir kept the new nation on its toes. The situation drastically changed once the dust settled and the country decided to embark upon planning economic development and social reconstruction. A great challenge was thrown before all the social sciences in this country. The Indian social scientist could no longer remain in his ivory tower. He had to face the challenge. For anthropology the task has been far from easy. An agonizing process of reappraisal has set in. The goals and ideals of the discipline are not yet clearly defined, but we know that we can no longer escape our responsibility in the name of pursuing detached scientific enquiry. Most of our recent research is not related to the major issues of the day and is not concerned with the national goals and aspirations. Many of us still publish to gain approval from our peers and mentors in the West. S. C. Sinha (55) has rightly asked us to enquire as "to what extent academic patronage and linkages with Western *Gurus* and *Guru-Bhais* continue to be a decisive factor in shaping the contour of a scholarly enterprise in anthropology in India today" (55, p. 5).

In India today a debate has been going on as to what role the social sciences, including anthropology, must play. Almost everyone has pointed out the fact of borrowed techniques, concepts, and frames of reference. Time and again we are told of the triviality or the theoretical and methodological barrenness of the social science enterprises in this country. Among anthropologists also there is a strong feeling that we have to get away from Western models, which are unsuited for our purposes in this country because they are either created from data from simpler peoples or result from Westerners' responses to their own cultural requirements. Efforts are being made to identify the native institutions and areas for growth, development, and socioeconomic progress. But on the whole Indian anthropology's response to the Indian challenge has been ad hoc, diffused, and without focus or direction. We discuss these matters below, but note here that Indian anthropology has not altogether failed in its attempt to meet the new challenge. After all, the challenge is quite new and anthropologists elsewhere have not much that can be used as an example to be emulated. Moreover, the process of meeting the challenge is still going on and its success or failure can be assessed only after some time. Before discussing the new ground being broken, we would like to mention a few things that have been done on the usual topics and familiar areas of anthropological research.

Tribal ethnography has been the most researched area in Indian anthropology. In the past it was common to write an ethnographic account of a tribe, covering most of the important facets of its life. After a lapse of two decades in the 1970s the anthropologists have once more started taking interest in the study of tribes (12, 41). Most of the tribal ethnography is being done by government research institutions. Many of the tribes in Arunachal Pradesh about whom no literature existed were studied by the former North East Frontier Agency (NEFA) administration. Tribal research institutes in the states are also paying attention to tribal ethnography. Indian anthropologists feel that many monographs on the well-known tribes of India have become out of date. Therefore, the Indian Council of Social Science Research (ICSSR) has planned a restudy of tribes covering most regions of the country. The study will at first be confined to a few selected tribes like the Chenchu, the Khasi, the Munda, the Kadar, the Naga, the Bondo, the Baiga, etc. Unfortunately, no outstanding functional study along the lines of Malinowski and his students exists for an Indian tribe. Verrier-Elwin's *The Muria and their Ghotul* is the most celebrated and well-documented study of one tribal institution, although it still cannot be called a functional study. Some scholars in the universities have attempted to study one facet of tribal life, and this trend is likely to be more popular with academically minded anthropologists interested in tribal studies. Study of health, sanitation, education, land alienation, and impact of industrialization and urbanization on the tribal people is likely to be more popular with future researchers. One reason for this trend may be the availability of more funds from governmental agencies for research on such topics rather than for investigating conventional tribal ethnography. The important difference in the attitude of the contemporary Indian anthropologists towards the tribal people is in marked contrast to what was true of our early forebears. Nobody now talks of tribes as if they were not a part of the total Indian population. The increase of consciousness among the tribal people and the knowledge of special privileges available to them under the constitution of India has changed the situation in the former tribal areas drastically. States of Nagaland and Meghalaya are populated almost exclusively by those whom we have known as tribal people.

The concept of caste is so uniquely Indian that some students of Indian social systems will always be interested in it. As pointed out in the previous section, soon after independence, both foreign and Indian anthropologists tried to synchronize the study of castes and villages. But since then the study of caste in wider horizons, beyond the village, has been more common (4, 13, 23, 27, 28). The role of caste in politics has attracted the attention of not only anthropologists but other social scientists as well (2, 5, 19, 22, 33, 38). Some political scientists, who are influenced by the concept of political culture, have paid particular attention to caste and its role in elections, factions and the functioning of political parties at regional as well as national levels. The attention paid to the scheduled castes and the funds available for conducting research to find out the kinds of discrimination they are subjected to and ways to ameliorate their condition have been the topic of research by some foreign as well as Indian anthropologists. In short, much of the empirical research on caste deals with the relationship between castes, status, power, stratification, and economic consequences flowing from them (6).

One of the most outstanding studies on caste to appear in the last 30 years is L. Dumont's *Homo Hierarchicus* (16). It is a work in which a perceptive anthropologist makes good use of the empirical field material that he and others have collected in the past few decades. But he wisely does not confine his attention to the minutest details of stratification in a particular village. He rises above the empirical data to present a most illuminating account of the ideology of a caste society and distinguishes it from that of an egalitarian society. Unlike Indian as well as Western critics, Dumont does not condemn a caste society and refuses to consider it inferior to the so-called democratic Western society.

Recent research on kinship, marriage, and family has been conducted as in the past (31, 58). Some anthropologists have covered areas such as the Lakshadweep islands, which were not studied by others. But nothing strikingly new from a theoritical point of view has yet emerged. The position of family studies is somewhat different. Some anthropologists and nonanthropologists have studied the dimensions of the Indian family in nonrural settings.

Partly due to behavioral orientation in American political science during last decade or so and partly due to anthropological studies of political behavior and institutions in the newly independent Asian and African countries, there have been some studies in political anthropology also. We have already mentioned the study of impact of caste on politics. There have also been studies of voting behavior and political movements (30), and of rural leadership (20). Unfortunately, the Indian anthropologists have not tried to bridge the gap between the micro-level political behavior studies and the study of the forces and processes involved in nation-building. We feel that study of the cultural background of the Indian nation-building during the freedom movement and after independence requires the particular attention of anthropologists. Lloyd Fallie's study of nationalism in Uganda and similar studies may provide particularly valuable leads to Indian anthropologists.

The shift from tribal studies to urban studies is a big jump. The field of urban anthropology is quite new; therefore it is not surprising that anthropologists in India have not made much headway. The association of anthropologists with the Calcutta Metropolitan Planning Organization has been long-standing. The late Nirmal Kumar Bose brought his knowledge of geography and anthropology to bear upon the study of Calcutta (9, 61). Vidyarthi (59) had posited the idea of the sacred complex in the study of a priestly community in a city in Bihar. Several American and Indian anthropologists have been involved in the study of the sacred complex of Bhubaneshwar and Puri under the leadership of Cora Du Bois. B. N. Saraswati (46) has been engaged in a long-term and multidirectional study of the holy city of Varanasi. These studies are going to break new ground. At Calcutta, S. C. Sinha (56) made a notable attempt to bring together experts from different fields of academics and the performing arts to present what he called the profiles of a city. Work in these areas may produce notable contributions by India to the science of anthropology.

India is in ferment after living through four Five-Year Plans and two decades of democratic rule. A great change has occurred in the thinking processes of people in many sections of India. Tremendous progress and remarkable achievements in agricultural production, industrial growth, irrigation facilities, and power supply have raised the level of aspiration, of the common man. It has also resulted in an increasing gap between the rich and the poor. The unfortunate stigma that has been attached to the untouchable castes for centuries has created much resentment among these people. They have not been able to rise above their traditional status despite massive governmental assistance. Poverty has become a major issue economically as well as socially. Those who are socially downtrodden are also among the economically most impoverished. People are no longer willing to accept poverty as the dictate of fate that cannot be changed. Studies of the poor with a view to reduce the economic disparity, eradicate social discrimination, and ensure justice for every citizen has acquired a very prominent place in the present scheme of things in this country.

Anthropologists and other social scientists are charged with the responsibility of providing information so that the standard of living may be raised for the teeming millions who are steeped in poverty and underprivileged. In this context the concepts of relevance and of priorities of sociocultural research has acquired much importance (14, 15, 40, 47, 48, 60). The funding agencies do not say that fundamental research cannot be conducted. Yet it is expected that social scientists who are being funded from the limited resources available to the country will realize their responsibility toward the nation. They are required to help in the task of nation-building and national reconstruction. For this reason, more and more stress is being laid upon problem-oriented and theme-oriented research that may have a bearing on some issues the nation is trying to resolve. The Anthropological Survey of India has launched a study of the weaker sections of the population in different parts of the country. Some tribal research institutes have been charged with the responsibility of preparing regional plans for the development of tribal people and tribal areas. Anthropologists, therefore, will have to strike a balance between conducting research for their academic or aesthetic satisfaction as well as for planning for development of certain sections of our country. It is too early to determine the outcome of the present ventures. We hope that too narrow a view of relevance will not be taken. Otherwise anthropology will be converted into a mere problem-solving discipline, which in our view will be contrary to the spirit of the discipline.

Two of our deceased elder anthropologists are to be credited with some research trends that need to be pursued with zeal and devotion. As a result of her kinship studies, I. Karve (25, 26) was trying to formulate ideal types of North Indian and South Indian subcultural zones. Her study of Mahabharata from an anthropological point of view we hope will be a pacesetter for historical-culture studies. N. K. Bose (8) was a man of diverse interests. His studies of temple architecture and the culture of the Puri temple are examples of an early interest in topics not commonly pursued by Indian anthropologists. His attempt to identify similarities and differences among selected items of material culture covering different regions of India needs to be explored further. This should produce a notable contribution to Indian anthropological studies.

In the past decade anthropologists, especially those working in the field of management, have turned their attention to the study of complex organizations —those built around tasks, industry, government, hospitals, etc. N. R. Sheth's work on *Social Framework of Indian Industry* (49) and D. P. Sinha's *Culture Change in an Inter-tribal Market* (53) are examples of this trend. To these anthropologists a territorial frame of reference is of limited consequence. More important are issues and problems, as well as institutions for social action. The study of small groups in organizations by Sinha (54) is an attempt to identify indigenous institutions for action systems. Ethnographic description and social analysis is not enough. Study of alternative choices and their consequences and implications are of great significance in contemporary anthropology. We may mention here G. Chattopadhyay & Sinha's work on the sociocultural relevance of new educational technology and the study of authority and dependency in Indian culture (10, 11).

Although methodology has recently been discussed in several forums, interest in problems of general theory and methodology is not reflected in the writings of Indian anthropologists. In 1959 critical appraisals of Radcliffe-Brown's concepts, except those on kinship by Murdock, were rare, but in an article in 1959 G. Sarana showed how Radcliffe-Brown confused the distinction between social structure and social organization (42). He further wrote on this theme in 1969 showing that Malinowskian functionalism was not "formless." He clarified the distinction between "functioning" and "having a function," pointing out its significance in understanding Malinowski's and Radcliffe-Brown's contributions to anthropology. In a paper presented at the American Anthropological Association meeting in 1965 in Denver, Colorado, Śarana made a critical appraisal of Lévi-Strauss's concept of model and his procedure for the analysis of myth (43). He anticipated Leach's assessment of Lévi-Strauss, which appeared several years later.

Śarana's interest in anthropological methodology is also longstanding. He has made a critical appraisal of the methodological premises of the German-Austrian historical school of ethnology. He has demonstrated the importance of reinterpretation through the analysis of the Swazi data in his recent essay on the anthropological procedures (44). But it is Śarana's contribution to the analysis of methods of comparison in social-cultural anthropology that is most notable. In his 1975 book, *The Methodology of Anthropological Comparisons,* he makes a systematic analysis of the comparative methods from the point of view of the units, purposes, and techniques and methods of comparison (45). The three methods of comparison are: (*a*) illustrative comparison (*b*) complete universe comparison, and (*c*) hologeistic sampled comparison. Śarana goes on to examine the relationship between ethnographic procedure, comparative methods, and explanation in social-cultural anthropology.

A most notable advance in anthropological studies is associated with space research. India has been experimenting for the last 6 months with the Satellite Instructional Television programs (SITE), which are screened in selected rural centers in a few chosen states of the country. Long before the SITE program was inaugurated on 15 August 1975 a team of anthropologists were preparing to make holistic studies on the impact of these programs on people for the duration of the experiment. The results of these investigations are anxiously awaited by the other anthropologists in this country. These will be another first to the credit of Indian anthropology.

224   SARANA & SINHA

Literature Cited

1. Ahmed, I., ed. 1973. *Caste and Social Stratification among the Muslims.* Delhi: Manohar
2. Atal, Y. 1971. *Local Communities and National Politics (A Study in Communication Links and Political Involvement).* Delhi: Natl. Publ.
3. Aurora, G. S. 1972. *Tribe-Caste-Class Encounters: Aspects of Folk-Urban Relations in Alirajpur Tehsil.* Hyderabad: Admin. Staff Coll. India
4. Bailey, F. G. 1957. *Caste and the Economic Frontier.* Bombay: Oxford Univ. Press
5. Beteille, A. 1971. *Caste, Class and Power: Changing Patterns of Stratification in a Tanjore Village.* Berkeley: Univ. Calif. Press
6. Beteille, A. 1974. *Studies in Agrarian Social Structure.* Delhi: Oxford Univ. Press
7. Bose, N. K. 1952. Current research projects in Indian anthropology. *Man in India* 32:121-33
8. Bose, N. K. 1967. *Culture and Society in India.* Bombay: Asia Publ.
9. Bose, N. K. 1968. *Calcutta-A Social Survey.* Bombay: Lalvani
10. Chattopadhyay, G. 1975. Dependency in Indian culture: from mud-huts to company board rooms. *Econ. Polit. Weekly* 10 (22): M-30-39
11. Chattopadhyay, G., Sinha, D. P. 1970. Social organization and interpersonal relevance of sensitivity training. *Ind. Relat.* 22:213-29
12. Chauhan, B. R. 1970. *Towns in the Tribal Setting.* Delhi: Natl. Publ.
13. D'Souza, B. G. 1975. *Goan Society in Transition-A Study of Social Change.* Bombay: Popular Prakashan
14. Dube, S. C. 1971. *Explanation and Management of Change.* New Delhi: Tata McGraw Hill
15. Dube, S. C. 1974. *Contemporary India and its Modernization.* Delhi: Vikas
16. Dumont, L. 1970. *Homo Hierarchicus.* Delhi: Vikas
17. Elwin, V. 1947. *The Muria and their Ghotul.* London: Oxford Univ. Press
18. Elwin, V. 1960. *A Philosophy of NEFA.* Shillong: NEFA Admin.
19. Fox, R. G. 1969. *From Zamindar to Ballot Box: Community Change in a North Indian Market.* Ithaca, NY: Cornell Univ. Press
20. Gaekwad, V. R., Tripathi, B. L., Bhatnagar, G. S. 1972. *Opinion Leaders and Communication in Indian Villages.* Ahmedabad: Indian Inst. Manage.
21. Ghurye, G. S. 1943. *The Aborigines So-Called and Their Future.* Poona: Gokhale Inst. Polit. Econ.
22. Gould, H. A. 1967. Towards a Jati model of Indian politics. *Econ. Polit. Weekly* 4 (5): 291-97
23. Hiebert, P. G. 1971. *Konduru: Structure and Integration in a South Indian Village.* Minneapolis: Univ. Minn. Press
24. Hutton, J. H. 1961. *Caste in India: Its Nature, Function and Origin.* Bombay: Oxford Univ. Press
24a. Iyer, L. K. A. 1908, 1912. *Cochin Tribes and Castes,* Vols. 1, 2. London: Higginbotham
24b. Iyer, L. K. A. 1928, 1930, 1935. *The Mysore Tribes and Castes,* Vols. 1-3. Mysore Univ. Press
25. Karve, I. 1961. *Hindu Society-An Interpretation.* Poona: Deccan College
26. Karve, I. 1969. *Yuganta-The End of an Epoch.* Poona: Deshmukh Prakashan
27. Kessinger, T. G. 1974. *Vilayatpur 1848-1968: Social and Economic Change in a North Indian Village.* Berkeley/Los Angeles/London: Univ. Calif. Press
28. Khare, R. S. 1970. *The Changing Brahmans.* Chicago Univ. Press
29. Kroeber, A. L. 1963. *An Anthropologist Looks at History.* Berkeley/Los Angeles: Univ. Calif. Press
30. Leaf, M. J. 1972. *Information and Behavior in a Sikh Village-Social Organization Reconsidered.* Delhi: Oxford Univ. Press
31. Madan, T. N. 1965. *Family and Kinship: A Study of the Pundits of Rural Kashmir.* Bombay: Asia Publ.
32. Marriott, M., ed. 1955. *Village India.* Univ. Chicago Press
33. Mehta, S. 1971. *Social Conflicts in a Village Community.* Delhi: Chand
34. Nakane, C. 1968. *Garo and Khasi: A Comparative Study in Matrilineal Systems.* Paris: Mouton
35. Nicholas, R. W. 1969. Suggestions for future anthropological research. In *Urgent Research in Social Anthropology,* ed. B. L. Abbi, S. Saberwal. Simla: Indian Inst. Adv. Study

36. Orans, M. 1965. *The Santhal: A Tribe in Search of a Great Tradition.* Detroit: Wayne State Univ. Press
37. Paranjpe, A. C. 1970. *Caste, Prejudice and the Individual.* Bombay: Lalvani
38. Parvatamma, C. 1971. *Politics and Religion: A Study of Historical Interaction between Socio-Political Relationship in a Mysore Village.* New Delhi: Sterling
39. Risley, H. H., Gait, E. A. 1903. *Census of India 1901,* Vol. 1. Calcutta: Gov. India
39a. Roy, S. C. 1912. *Mundas and Their Country.* Calcutta: City Bar Libr.
40. Sahay, B. N. 1969. Socio-cultural development. In *Pragmatism in Development.* Delhi: Bookhouse
41. Sahay, K. N. 1968. Impact of Christianity on the Chainpur belt in Chotanagpur: an analysis of its cultural process. *Am. Anthropol.* 70 (5): 923–42
42. Sarana, G. 1959. A few comments on some of Radcliffe-Brown's basic concepts. *East. Anthropol.* 12:202–9
43. Sarana, G. 1967. Model and myth in Lévi-Strauss' anthropology. *J. Indian Anthropol. Soc.* 2: 159–68
44. Sarana, G. 1970. Rituals and rebellion: The Swazi case re-examined. *East. Anthropol.* 23: 141–62
45. Sarana, G. 1975. *The Methodology of Anthropological Comparisons: An Analysis of Comparative Methods in Social and Cultural Anthropology.* New York: Wenner Gren Found. Anthropol. Res.
46. Saraswati, B. N. 1970. *Contributions towards Understanding Indian Civilization.* Dharwar: Karnatak Univ.
47. Sen, L. K., Roy, P. 1966. *Awareness of Community Development in Village India.* Hyderabad: Natl. Inst. Commun. Dev.

48. Sen, L., et al 1971. *Planning Rural Growth Centres for Integrated Area Development: A Study in Miryalguda.* Hyderabad: Natl. Inst. Commun. Dev.
49. Sheth, N. R. 1968. *The Social Framework of an Indian Factory.* Bombay: Oxford Univ. Press
50. Singer, M. 1959. *Traditional India: Structure and Change.* Philadelphia: Am. Folklore Soc.
51. Singer, M., Cohn, B. S., eds. 1968. *Structure and Change in Indian Society.* New York: Wenner-Gren Found. Anthropol. Res.
52. Singh, S. K., ed. 1972. *Tribal Situation in India.* Simla: Indian Inst. Adv. Study
53. Sinha, D. P. 1968. *Culture Change in an Inter-tribal Market.* Bombay: Asia Publ.
54. Sinha, D. P. 1973. Small groups in anthropological inquiry. *East. Anthropol.* 26:118–32
55. Sinha, S. C. 1971. Is there an Indian trend in social-cultural anthropology? *J. Indian Anthropol. Soc.* 6:1–14
56. Sinha, S. C. 1974. *Profile of a City– Calcutta.* Calcutta: Indian Anthropol. Soc.
57. Srinivas, M. N. 1966. *Social Change in Modern India.* Bombay: Allied
58. Vatuk, S. 1972. *Kinship and Urbanization: White Collar Migrants in North India.* Berkeley: Univ. Calif. Press
59. Vidyarthi, L. P. 1961. *The Sacred Complex in Hindu Gaya.* Bombay: Asia
60. Vidyarthi, L. P., ed. 1968. *Applied Anthropology in India.* Allahabad: Kitab Mahal
61. Vidyarthi, L. P. 1969. *Cultural Configuration of Ranchi.* Calcutta: Basu

Ann. Rev. Anthropol. 1976. 5:227–48
Copyright © 1976 by Annual Reviews Inc. All rights reserved

SOCIAL STRATIFICATION ◆ 9578

Frank Cancian

School of Social Sciences, University of California, Irvine, California 92717

Social stratification is a basic element of social organization in all human and some animal societies. Interpersonal and intergroup relations of dominance and submission, rank or hierarchy appear wherever people live together; and most studies of social relations say something relevant to the topic of stratification. Thus, I have found no useful way to draw a line, even a hazy line, around the relevant literature.

Given the extensiveness and diffuseness of the literature on social stratification, I have chosen to focus the review on the three issues that seem to me most important in terms of past or potential contributions by anthropologists: 1. the relation of material surplus, population size, and population density to stratification; 2. the comparability of patterns of stratification and mobility in industrial and "anthropological" (non-Western, preindustrial) societies; and 3. the relation of ideology and behavior in the working of stratification systems. Under each topic the discussion is pushed toward general issues in social theory. This seems appropriate because there is now no generally accepted paradigm in which an anthropologist studying stratification may work.

SURPLUS AND STRATIFICATION

A great transformation has taken place in thinking about the relation of productivity to the evolution of systems of social stratification. The received wisdom of two decades ago saw surplus beyond subsistence needs as the key to stratification: the greater the surplus, the greater the stratification. In this view, there could be stratification only when one individual could produce enough to sustain more than one individual. Those who somehow managed to live off the work of others constituted the higher ranks. This idea, as a basic explanatory element in the evolution of stratification systems, needs a postulated stage in which early people struggled mightily for physical survival. In that stage everybody had to work and everybody was thereby more or less equal. With improved food production techniques, the emergence of surplus over subsistence needs permitted the emergence of rulers, and the existence of rulers

227

signaled the existence of surplus. This simple materialistic interpretation of the emergence of stratification was found in important works until a decade ago (32, 33, 44).

In the early stages of the surplus debate a crack appeared in the old facade. Pearson (39) found absolute surplus over subsistence needs difficult to define in simple materialistic terms. He argued that subsistence level is always socially, not biologically, defined; thus the illusion of an objectively measurable causative variable burst. Pearson's surplus was essentially an arbitrary quantity relative to the society that, by social convention, created it.

In his response to Pearson, Harris (21) found the courage to carry materialism out to its logical extreme, thus resolving an inconsistency in previous thinking. Previous thinking had seen the problem of physical survival as environmentally imposed in early human existence, but as socially manipulated and controlled in modern societies after the creation of a physical surplus. Harris's Neo-malthusian invocation of unrelenting population pressure, as exotic and patently false as it might seem to the affluent academic contemplating him or herself as part of the supported classes, undercut this dichotomous characterization of history. Harris argued that population pressure eliminates any superfluous surplus in the long run, and that seemingly unproductive social institutions (many of which involve stratification) are socially necessary for material survival. While an outpouring of adaptivist reinterpretations of "superfluous" ritual and rank institutions followed Harris's paper (22, 31, 41), neither his full-fledged materialism nor Pearson's extreme "societal voluntarism" have come to dominate.

The facade was cracked further and irreparably by the new view of hunting and gathering societies (29). The idea that early people had to continually struggle for physical survival tumbled in the face of studies of actual work patterns in contemporary technologically simple societies and the simultaneous realization that many genuinely impoverished contemporary technologically simple societies are poor because they have been driven to marginal habitats by technologically more complex societies. It is now clear that simple societies cannot win a competition with larger more complex societies that desire their territory. It is still not clear that all simple societies lived securely when they had their pick of habitats, but many certainly did. Most important, it is clear that many simple societies, that lived in the most egalitarian of observed social arranagements, could have survived from the physical point of view on the work of a proportion of their membership. The potential for one person living off the work of another was there.

Two points have emerged in this transformation of thinking about the relation of productivity, surplus, and stratification. First, if there is a struggle for physical survival at the bottom of modern systems of stratification, it is as likely to be a recent creation as it is to be a vestige of earlier forms of human adaptation. Environmental control and material want for "them" (early people) and human and social control of physical and material needs for us is no longer a tenable basic orientation. The course of history can no longer be seen as a gradual ascent to postindustrial society. Second, and more important for the theory of the evolution of stratification: the emergence of social stratification in technologically simple societies was not restrained by the inability of a worker to produce a surplus that could be used to support a ruler. Thus the emergence of stratification cannot be explained by the technological possibility of producing a surplus.

There is no new conventional wisdom as far as I can see, but two major trends have emerged from the basic reorientation described above. One is the replacement of the physical surplus idea with the more sophisticated social surplus idea that has taken place among some Marxist anthropologists. The other is the shift of attention from physical production as the causative variable to a view of stratification mediated through the consequences of population aggregation. I will review each briefly. Neither trend, it should be pointed out, has produced an idea to replace the simple evolutionary causal dynamic that was contained in the physical surplus idea.

Sahlins's work published in *Stone Age Economics* (45) is crucial to the popularization of the Marxist side of things, broadly defined. His statement of the observation that hunters and gatherers must move around, and that, lacking efficient transportation, they necessarily limited their possessions, neatly explains the lack of stratification based on the ownership of the means of production—though it does not explain the failure of some hunters and gatherers to appropriate the labor of others. And his observation that domestic units, if left alone, will not produce more than they desire for themselves, sets the stage for his discussion of the political aspects of appropriation of household production for extra-household consumption. He sees the political life as a stimulus to production. Deftly including himself in the old guard, he creates the new interpretation as follows:

> . . . the chief creates a collective good beyond the conception and capacity of the society's domestic groups taken separately. He institutes a public economy greater than the sum of its household parts.
>
> This collective good is also won at the expense of the household parts. Too frequently and mechanically anthropologists attribute the appearance of chieftainship to the production of surplus (for example, Sahlins, 1958). In the historic process, however, the relation has been at least mutual, and in the functioning of primitive society it is rather the other way around. Leadership continually generates domestic surplus. The development of rank and chieftainship becomes, *pari passu,* development of the productive forces (45, p. 140).

While the argument just quoted appears to be a suitable interpretation, for prestate societies, of the essence of a socially created and controlled surplus, O'Laughlin (35), in her review of Marxist anthropology, criticizes Sahlins for displaying vestiges of his former self:

> In analysing the development of political chiefdoms, Sahlins argues that such political structures evolve from a contradiction between forces and relations of production. This sounds like a Marxist argument, but Sahlins' contradiction is immanent rather

than material; there is a difference between what people could produce and what they actually produce. Political structures therefore evolve as a means of realizing the surplus that is implicit but unactualized in the system. In fact, the contradiction that Sahlins finds lies within the forces of production, that is, within the technological system itself. Unless one ahistorically assumes the teleological rationalization of economic efficiency as the essence of human evolution, there is no way of moving from this supposed contradiction to the emergence of political hierarchies. In other words, there is a distinct continuity between Sahlins' early evolutionary work and that of his recent Marxian stage (35, p. 355).

Though she explicitly eschews any attempt at general explanation of the evolution of stratification in favor of a more orthodox insistence on historical specificity, O'Laughlin emphasizes the social nature of surplus in her own exposition of the Marxian perspective. The various Marxian arguments about the social nature of surplus developed by Sahlins, O'Laughlin, and others (see especially the journal *Economy and Society*) all contrast with the simple materialist position taken by Marxists (33) and non-Marxists before the recent revolutionary reconceptualization of technologically simple societies.

Orans's seminal paper on "Surplus" (36) represents the alternative explanation of stratification in terms of population size and density. He argues that the differences in social stratification in the societies Sahlins studied in *Social Stratification in Polynesia* (44) may be the result of population size, not increased physical surplus available for appropriation by and support of people of high rank. He shows that Sahlins has not demonstrated greater productivity on the part of individual workers in the more stratified societies, and argues that it is the greater number involved in a single exchange network that leads to the greater stratification. Always careful to acknowledge alternative arguments, including clear historical instances of stratification resulting from political conquest, Orans does nonetheless speculate about cause:

> Even if it is true that population and degree of stratification are closely correlated, one might well argue that they are not causally related; apart from the correlation I can think of two reasons why they might be causally related, i.e., why an increase in population might contribute to increased stratification: 1) to administer a more populous society, *ceteris paribus,* may require more layers of administrative control endowed with more real power; 2) it may be easier to establish and maintain wide differences in prestige and privilege in a large society than in a small one where all relationships tend to be based on kinship and/or face-to-face (36, p. 30).

A more openly Hobbesian version of Orans's second argument is presented by Foster (18). It is simply that as a group gets beyond the size where individuals can know everyone else, responsibility for social control must be delegated, for unknown people cannot be trusted. This leads to ever increasing stratification as group size grows.

A third element in this population package is provided by Harris's interesting juxtaposition of data on the technoenvironmental efficiency of various systems of production (24). While the data are scanty, it is apparent that the shift from hunting and gathering to slash and burn to hoe agriculture for the cases Harris reviews does not increase the productivity of work substantially. Rather the technological change brings more people together on ever decreasing amounts of land. Thus, the result of technological change at these levels may be, not increased production which is appropriated in a system of stratification, but increased aggregation of population which leads to similar results. Where he does see an increase of productivity, Harris also sees a distinct decrease of leisure and deterioration of working conditions. Boserup (5) pictures a related trend in her contra-Malthusian argument for population increase as the cause of technological innovation which permits intensification of agriculture on ever more densely populated land.

The population density arguments include an interesting series of explanations based on materials from relatively sparsely populated Africa (20, 53, 55). Stauder (53) in particular exposes the obverse of the Hobbesian argument from density by arguing that institutions of social control are less important if offending individuals can simply move away until time dulls the conflict.

All these arguments, both Marxist and non-Marxist, emphasize the social creation of stratification in situations where sufficient numbers of people accumulate and must share space. While they are just as consistent with their times (the late 1960s and early 1970s) as the emphasis on physical surplus was a decade or two earlier, they are better, it seems to me, because they abolish the separation of primitive and modern people on the basis of relation to the environment. We now see ourselves as continuing the struggle attributed to our most distant ancestors. The old hope that in postindustrial society we could free ourselves from stratification through producing abundance passed with the illusion of material control. And so did the idea that stratification resulted from the creation of a material surplus.

STRATIFICATION AND MOBILITY IN ANTHROPOLOGICAL SOCIETIES

Anthropologists pay little attention to a number of questions about stratification systems that have been the central concern of sociologists. In large part this difference seems to stem from the fact that sociologists focus on the Western industrial societies where they live while anthropologists focus on other societies. And sociologists considering stratification systems think in terms of national systems while anthropologists work at the local level. Anthropologists concentrate on societies which they view as undifferentiated except in terms of kinship and personal characteristics. And anthropologists concentrate on cultural-ideal descriptions of institutions in more complex non-Western societies. In addition, anthropologists have traditionally avoided the quantitative analysis of anonymous individuals employed by sociologists in the study of Western industrial society and its historical antecedents. While the division of labor and diversity of approach has been productive in many ways, I believe it has led to oversimplified views of the "other" kind of society in each discipline, and that this oversimplification has in turn blocked realistic comparison across societies.

Moreover, sociologists are routinely viewed as apologists for or critics of the establishment, while anthropologists are viewed as more benign. In fact, the interpretation of social stratification in anthropological societies is important to the maintenance of the sociocultural systems in which we live. As is often observed: in interpreting "them" we are defining ourselves.

What follows is divided into three parts. I will review first the arguments for and against the idea that anthropological and industrial societies are different from each other, second the recent trends in attention to stratification by anthropologists, and third recent work on comparative social mobility. What follows includes frequent interpretation of the general theoretical and political implications of the material, because I believe these considerations are part of full understanding of the issues. This effort requires more speculation than I am comfortable with, but since every reader is a native, he or she may judge the analysis for him or her self and reject what is not useful.

The Shape and Character of Stratification Systems

Many anthropologists see a distinction between social stratification and other forms of social inequality along the lines developed by Fried (19). They seem to favor separate analysis of phenomena in the two or more categories the distinction creates. Others see a similarity among diverse forms of structured social inequality. They emphasize the similarities first and the subtypes and complexities second.

At the surface of the difference between the positions is a simple semantic confusion that must be clarified. "Social stratification" may be used in the general (broad) sense intended in the title of this paper to include all forms of social inequality from caste and rigid occupation classes to age and sex stratification. In this sense it is essentially equivalent to "social inequality" as it is currently used. "Social stratification" may also be used in a specialized (narrow) sense to include only certain kinds of inequality in which society-wide strata are clearly recognized.

The problem goes much deeper than the labels employed, for the use of the term "social stratification" exclusively at the lower (specialized) level of contrast embodies a commitment to a substantive difference between stratified systems of social inequality and others. Thus the distinction carries heavy theoretical weight, and the two approaches tend to be associated with political or value positions on the nature of human society. In the long run, I believe, the association need hold only in simplistic conceptualizations of the issues. Nonetheless, it is crucial in any current statement on the anthropological study of social stratification.

Here I want to characterize the extreme positions as displayed in recent books by Fallers (17) and Plotnicov & Tuden (42, 58). Plotnicov & Tuden represent the position that distinguishes "social stratification" from other forms of social inequality:

Social stratification . . . is a fundamental feature in the organization, maintenance, and changes of a complex society. Stratified societies display a distinctive structural anatomy. Characteristically, each has *social groups* that (1) are ranked hierarchically, (2) maintain relatively permanent positions in the hierarchy, (3) have differential control of the sources of power, primarily economic and political, relative to their rankings, (4) are separated by cultural and invidious distinctions that also serve to maintain the social distance between the groups, and (5) are articulated by an overarching ideology which provides a rationale for the established hierarchical arrangements. Since these features vary in different societies, it is difficult to construct an ideal model of a stratified society which can incorporate all varieties.

Not all societies, however, are stratified. In unstratified societies individuals are ranked merely on the bases of sex, age, and kinship statuses (42, pp. 4–5).

Though they state that "All societies have a division of labor, evaluation of statuses, and unequal distribution of rewards and valuables, with the result that some form of social inequality is universal" (58, p. 4), Tuden & Plotnicov explicitly counter the idea that all societies are stratified.

> ... the belief that stratification is universal indicates a confusion among stratification, ranking, and individual differences within societies. Ranking—the evaluation of individuals and roles—is universal. But societies composed of ranked social groups that are organized on bases other than kinship statuses or biological factors, like age and sex, are not everywhere the rule (58, p. 4).

The contrasting position stresses the appropriateness of looking at the ranking of persons and "localized" groups in an unbroken status continuum. In his critique of the stratigraphic or "layer cake" image of society, Fallers takes this position:

> The stratigraphic image of society, then, seems to have crystallized in the late eighteenth-century ideological clashes over hereditary power and status and to have been taken over by Marx as a means of conceptualizing the new inequalities of industrial capitalism. Weber's view was a more differentiated one which societies as arenas in which groups of various kinds—especially occupational ones—struggle for cultural and political dominance, in the process reducing old inequalities and producing new ones (sic). This view, it seems to me, captures the modern situation more adequately than does Marx's stratigraphic scheme. Nevertheless, the idea of society-wide strata has remained prominent in Western social science, including that part of it which has been concerned with American society (17, p. 16).

Fallers concludes his essay on the "uses and abuses of the stratigraphic image of society" as follows:

> The term "social stratification," then, has a certain historical appropriateness in contemporary Western societies. I suggest, nevertheless, that it is a poor term for which social scientists might well substitute "inequality." Not only is it quite misleading when applied to the many non-Western societies in which thought and action about inequality center much more upon interpersonal relations of superiority and inferiority; it also oversimplifies by attempting to capture with a single graphic image the multiple bases of differentiation and inequality which exist within Western societies. Race, ethnicity, occupation, and regionalism are not reducible to "class" or "stratum," and all these terms, to the extent to which they have meaning in non-Western societies, very often have different meanings there. . . . (17, p. 29).

The positions represented by Plotnicov & Tuden on the one hand and Fallers on the other may be identified with classic positions in the history of the study of social stratification. In very broad terms, the former fits with the radical tradition and the latter with the conservative tradition. Lenski, who characterizes each tradition in detail (32), is criticized by Dahrendorf (11) for oversimplifying the issues. Yet there seems little doubt that Plotnicov & Tuden are conscious of their affinity with the Marxist end of the political-theoretical spectrum, and that Fallers is appropriately placed at the Parsonian functionalist end. The radical position, simply conceived, must stress the possibility of real, society-wide groups or classes, while the functionalist perspective, simply conceived, must stress the complexity, interconnectedness and cross-cutting individual member-ships in all kinds of social groups.

Since I find the reality of class or group interests obvious and compelling as an explanation of human behavior, and the importance of contradictory cross-cutting ties just as obvious and compelling, I am at a loss to choose between the orientations. I do think both positions have been used to underemphasize the importance of stratification in anthropological societies while they have differ-ent positions (stressing and underplaying stratification, respectively) with re-gard to modern industrial society. For this reason I believe they must be understood and eventually rejected as guides to the interpretation of stra-tification in anthropological societies.

The basic issue remains the degree to which anthropological societies will be considered comparable to Western industrial societies. There is little doubt that larger, more complex societies are different from decapitated peasant commu-nities and small preindustrial societies in many ways. Yet if we attend to Fallers, they are not—except in certain unique historical periods—characterized by the kind of clear, distinct social groups described by Tuden & Plotnicov. While Tuden & Plotnicov make the standard disclaimer that all the elements of their ideal type are seldom found in any single empirical society, the contrast they set between stratified and other societies represents an idea that has long been popular among anthropologists.

My experience is almost totally consistent with Fallers's contention that anthropologists' thinking is dominated by the stratigraphic, "layer-cake" image of stratification. This image does not cause them to find classes in an-thropological societies. It has rather the opposite effect. Since anthropologists seldom find the kind of clear strata and unambiguous groups described in ideal types, they usually conclude that they are working in an unstratified society, and emphasize the homogeneity of the population or the personal characteristics of economically and politically dominant individuals. This implicit comparison with an ideal type obscures patterns of stratification in anthropological societies. These patterns are often similar to patterns in industrial societies that also fail to conform to the ideal type.

When viewed in terms of their political implications the two positions are more complicated for anthropologists than they are for sociologists and other students of industrial societies. For some, anthropological societies represent the alternative forms of humanly possible institutional structure that could exist in a reformed state of industrial societies. Thus the anthropologist who sees no clear patterns of stratification in nonindustrial societies offers an alternative societal type to the reformer who sees class in our society and hopes to change it. And the anthropologist who sees stratification in nonindustrial societies that is comparable to stratification in industrial societies cuts off that simple alternative. These issues make the choices involved in the analysis of stratification in anthropological societies particularly loaded ones.

Stratification Involving Anthropological Societies

Any student of rural people in other countries knows that a large proportion of the world's population, as it is studied by anthropologists, falls between Plotnicov & Tuden's (42) stratified type and kinship rank type. This amorphous majority of non-Western people, usually labeled peasants, is commonly treated as an undifferentiated mass residing in homogeneous communities that occupy the bottom rung of the national stratification system. In recent years two different steps away from the homogeneous conceptualizations that impede study of stratification have been taken. Anthropologists have begun to study both the regional, national, and international systems in which peasant communities are embedded on the one hand, and the internal differentiation of peasant communities on the other. Both these very different trends involve greater anthropological attention to social stratification.

The first trend focuses on the *larger system* and includes the rapidly expanding literature on internal colonialism, dependency theory, and core-periphery relations to which anthropologists are minority contributors. Broadly conceived, the literature includes the culturally oriented development from the dual society conception to cultural pluralism at one extreme and the world system ideas of the sociologists like Wallerstein (61) at the other. The former has tenuous credentials for the study of social stratification, for, as Benedict points out, the cultural pluralism concept "may be more useful for work on cultural differences within a society than for examining the political and economic structure of that society" (2, p. 29). And the latter, as O'Laughlin (35) points out, demands almost complete abandonment of anthropology's disciplinary boundaries. The middle range of this literature includes the work of many anthropologists who have actively studied the context of local communities and the larger systems themselves. Some of these are: R. N. Adams (1), G. A. Collier (10), A. Leeds (30), S. F. Silverman (46), G. W. Skinner (48), C. A. Smith (49), R. Stavenhagen (54), and E. R. Wolf (62–64).

While in some senses this literature may be seen as the belated, self-conscious extention of Kroeber's classic definition of peasant societies as part-societies and part-cultures that cannot exist without the city, it represents a very important reorientation of anthropological effort away from the local level and toward regional, national, and international systems that include the peasant community as a dynamic element. Peasants are tied to the larger system, albeit in an asymmetrical way. They become full-fledged, if severely disadvantaged, actors in the larger society. In this analysis peasant communities often remain internally undifferentiated, but they are no longer the pristine cultural isolates so common a decade or two ago.

The second trend focuses on *internal differentiation* in peasant communities, and emphasizes the wealth and prestige differences within the societies that anthropologists have commonly treated as homogeneous. While the focus on the larger system discussed above abandons the local emphasis of anthropology and retains the view of the peasant communities as homogeneous, this approach abandons the homogeneity and retains the local emphasis. It adopts some of the anonymous, quantitative, sociological classification of people which conflicts with traditional anthropological explanations in terms of kinship and individual characteristics. The work of F. Cancian (6, 8), B. DeWalt (13), S. F. Silverman (47), and R. A. Thompson (56), among others, shows that the division of small, poor communities into rich and poor, high and low prestige people reveals internal behavior patterns very similar to those found in Western industrial societies. This attempt to generalize across diverse societies, and the related relegation of cultural differences to secondary status in the analysis, threatens to raise many of the issues of comparability that dominated the abortive debate between the substantivist and formalists in economic anthropology (7). Pelto & Pelto (40) have pointed out how this type of analysis of intra-cultural, intra-societal diversity relieves people in anthropological societies of the indignity of culturally dominated lives that they suffer when viewed as homogeneous and different from people in Western industrial societies.

Both the trends discussed here run counter to the tendency to separate anthropological societies from industrial societies in the study of social stratification. While typological differences between societies will remain an important area of anthropological concern, it is clear that the characteristic isolation and homogenization of anthropological societies that impeded the study of social stratification is lessening. Anthropologists are becoming active students of stratification, rather than simple reporters of contrastive systems.

Mobility and Openness of Stratification Systems

In most conceptions of stratification, individuals or groups have both a position in the hierarchy and a potential for changing that position. Systems where change is seen as relatively frequent are labeled open or flexible; those where change is seen as relatively rare are labeled closed or rigid. The latter are often identified with traditional agrarian societies where position is in large part ascribed, the former with modern industrial societies where position is in large part achieved. Since anthropologists tend to work with traditional societies, mobility has not been a subject of great concern. This is especially true, of course, because they have not concentrated on the internal differentiation that logically must precede mobility. With the advent of "modernization," however, anthropologists have been drawn to comparison of traditional and "modern" periods in anthropological societies, and to comparison of mobility rates.

The accumulated evidence is far from adequate to support firm conclusions, but two very important generalizations are emerging. First, insofar as it is possible to compare traditional and modern societies, modern societies may be less open. Kelley & Perlman (26), who set their study of mobility among the Toro of Western Uganda in the context of the relevant sociological literature, conclude, as does Fallers (17), that the modern educational system leads to greater rigidification rather than greater openness. While both these cases are from East Africa, where relatively abundant land may create a special situation, the generalization is nonetheless fascinating. More findings along these lines would upset the received wisdom about traditional and modern societies, and force reevaluation of the conclusion about relative mobility rates that has been uncritically drawn from the conceptual distinction between ascribed and achieved status systems.

Second, comparative studies by sociologists suggest that it is difficult to establish differences in mobility rates among industrial societies given current approaches to the problem. The best available studies do not show substantial differences in the commonly expected directions, e.g. between the United States and Europe (27, 57). Kelley (personal communication) has found few existing anthropological studies with data adequate for comparison with industrial societies.

This theoretical disarray and need for data and new generalizations creates an opportunity for substantial contributions by anthropologists focusing on traditional societies. The process would involve two steps, neither of which is common in current anthropological work. First, patterns of stratification must be identified in communities where they have traditionally been ignored or treated as culturally specific, rigid, ascribed role allocations; and second, intergenerational mobility must be studied.

Since the few actual comparisons do not support the received wisdom distinguishing traditional and modern societies, it is hard to avoid the speculation that the received wisdom stems from blinders created by our position in society. It may be that the characterization of traditional societies as less mobile than modern societies serves to relieve the contradiction between egalitarian ideology and actual stratification in the Western industrial democracies where most scholars who make these characterizations work.

EXPERIENCE AND IDEOLOGY IN STRATIFICATION

The importance of ideology and subjective experience, of meaning and mental culture, is the subject of great debate in the study of social stratification. The explicitly stated positions extend across the entire current range of ideas on the status of mental and cultural phenomena, and display the chasm that separates symbolic and behavioral anthropology. I will first review recent positions on the relation of ideology and behavior—the question that dominates the debate viewed over a long time span; then concentrate on the study of ambiguity in ideological systems that has become a major focus for many anthropologists in recent years.

Ideology and Behavior

It is useful to begin with three concepts: ideology, behavior, and action. The distinction between ideology and behavior is related to the old theory-practice, thinking-doing distinction, which itself parallels the older mind-body distinction; but, once again, antiquity and ubiquity are guarantees that the problem will persist, not promises of a solution. At the outset I want to assign cultural assumptions, cognitive apparatus, conceptions of the desirable, values and norms to ideology. Behavior is what happens outside the mind—observable behavior conceptualized and reported by the investigator. At this point, a commitment on the role of the investigator in the construction of observations seems unnecessary. Action is a term commonly used for behavior complete with the ideology that gives it meaning, or, if you take the other point of view, of ideology complete with the behavior that gives it mundane expression.

There often appears in the discussion of the relation of behavior and ideology the idea that ideology is, by its nature, shared among individuals and therefore connected with social theories that begin with the group—with society as a precondition for the existence of the individual; and the corresponding idea that behavior is connected with an individualistic bias under which the existence of the individual is a precondition for the existence of society. While largely correct as a generalization about the history of theories of society, this distinction has no clear and forceful logical standing. Its application in the study of social stratification is beautifully illustrated by Dumont's *Homo Hierarchicus* (15), a polemical work on the Hindu caste system. In what follows I will review Dumont's position, the work of Berreman and others who do not support Dumont's view of the caste system, and the work of Ossowski and Dahrendorf relevant to the general problem of ideology and experience in social stratification.

DUMONT   Dumont presents a clear set of assertions favoring the predominance of ideology in social reality. Beginning his study with a wholesale commitment to a Durkheimian position on the importance of mind and its social character, he uses the language of action:

> . . . the social is often considered exclusively as a matter of the behavior of individuals, individuals who are assumed to be fully formed in advance. In this regard, it is enough to observe that actual men do not *behave:* they *act* with an idea in their heads, perhaps that of conforming to custom. . . .
>
> It is the prime merit of French sociology to have insisted, in virtue of its intellectualism, on the presence of society in the mind of each man (15, pp. 5–6).

This starting point leads Dumont to the formula which characterizes the non-ideological component of action as a residual:

Once what happens on the plane of observation O is related to a first plane of reference, the plane of ideology I, it brings to light another component situated in the residual plane R (o=i+r). From observation and ideology we deduce by "subtraction" the residual empirical component of each observed phenomenon (15, p. 38).

The strength of Dumont's commitment to the predominant importance of ideology is perhaps best communicated by his scholarly qualification, in a footnote, that ideology ". . . is not the *whole* of social reality" (15, p. 264).

Dumont's goal is to understand the ideology of the caste system. For the Westerner to do this, he insists, he must first break the Western preconception that people are first individuals, then members of society. Dumont's thumbnail sketch of Western thought leads him to the conclusion that "After a long period dominated by a tendency which led to atomization, the essential problem for contemporary thought is to rediscover the meaning of wholes and systems" (15, p. 41). It is in this spirit that he offers the caste system as an example of a system that begins with the principle of hierarchy, a principle stated at the system level and including the individual only as part of the system. Dumont's book is dedicated to the task of loosening the Western mind sufficiently to allow it to comprehend such a starting point.

The principle of equality and the principle of hierarchy are facts, indeed they are among the most constraining facts, of political and social life. There is no space here to dwell upon the question of the place of ideology in social life; as far as methodology is concerned, all that follows, both in outline and in detail, aims to answer this question (15, p. 3).

More concretely, Dumont is concerned to show that, by virtue of its ideology, the caste system is more than simply a super rigid and explicit class system. For from his point of view, which starts with ideology, the caste system is clearly distinct from a class system which combines rigid and clear behavioral class with egalitarian ideology. And, of course, insofar as action is the focus of attention, hierarchical ideology plus rigid groups in which membership is determined by birth, are clearly different from egalitarian ideology plus rigid groups in which membership is determined by birth. Dumont is particularly concerned to draw out the implications of the difference for egalitarians who engage in self-flagellation over the antirational character of stratification and Hindus who presumably accept the naturalness of hierarchy (14).

BERREMAN AND OTHERS ON CASTE   Berreman's views on "Caste in India and the United States" (3) provide a clear contrast though they were published before Dumont's work in response to earlier proponents of the position Dumont exemplifies. Berreman defines a caste system without regard to ideology: "a *hierarchy of endogamous divisions in which membership is hereditary and permanent*" (3, p. 120), but his attention to the role of ideology is nevertheless direct. Responding to views like Dumont's which distinguish nonconflictual and acceptant attitudes toward caste in India from less acceptance of race relations in the United States, he says:

Central to these distinctions is that caste in India is passively accepted and indorsed by all on the basis of the religio-philosophical explanations which are universally subscribed to, while Negro-white relations in America are characterized by dissent, resentment, guilt and conflict. But this contrast is invalid, resulting, as it does, from an idealized and unrealistic view of Indian caste, contrasted with a more realistic, pragmatic view of American race relations; Indian caste is viewed as it is supposed to work rather than as it does work; American race relations are seen as they do work rather than as they are supposed, by the privileged, to work. The traditional white southerner, asked to describe relations between the races, will describe the Negro as happy in his place, which he may quote science and Scripture to justify. This is similar to the explanations offered for the Indian system by the advantaged (3, p. 121).

Thus, Berreman challenges Dumont's implicit assumption that Hindu caste ideology is monolithic; and his challenge is consistent with the accumulating evidence that the rhetoric of caste ideology is no more a reliable guide to Hindu behavior than the rhetoric of egalitarian ideology is a guide to American behavior. It may still be that Hindu caste ideology is a better approximation to Hindu behavior than American ideology is to American behavior, but this is a subtle comparative question, a question of degree, that has not yet been successfully conceptualized, let alone researched.

The relevant facts in this behavioral attack on the uniqueness of the caste system may be divided into three types. First, there is the actual mobility of entire castes within local hierarchies and the accomodation of the ideology to this relaxation of preordained rigidity. This phenomenon is reported by many and elucidated by Srinivas under the master concept Sanskritization (50, 51). As Srinivas has pointed out, the strength of the caste system as a system of stratification is that it co-opts the dissident group into using the rhetoric of the system in its demands for mobility, thereby yielding rank to those who forcefully support the intricacies of the rank system (50). This highly intellectual exercise in social redefinition does not obviate the fact of mobility and its inconsistency with the basic tenets of caste ideology.

Second, there are many reports of success in avoiding the rigid prescriptions of occupational specialization, especially those involved in the jajmani system under which service castes in rural areas perform services in return for annual payment from farmers' crops. Orans (37), in a study of 40 villages, tries to show that the ideology of caste seldom holds individuals to traditional jajmani relations if there are viable economic alternatives within reach. Epstein's (16) blacksmith who finds a relative to take his traditional obligations and traditional compensation so that he can be freed to pursue commercial dealings on the open market is another example of the "flexibility" of the system. It is important to note that Epstein's blacksmith, like many lower caste individuals whose occupation is set by their birth into a caste, is a part-time farmer. In fact, empirical studies show that many service caste members own land. Thus, while caste membership is a virtually absolute and enduring ascribed characteristic of individuals seen in terms of the belief system, it is not an adequate index of socioeconomic rank in general. In this situation it is hard to believe that Indian villagers are oblivious to other systems of rank, especially economic rank.

Finally, close study of behavior under caste ideology reveals practical transformations of the overarching ideology of purity and pollution in contexts where
human interaction takes place across caste lines. Food exchange and pipe
smoking practices described by Dumont (15, pp. 86–87, based on A. C. Mayer's
data) indicate that Indian villagers behave in only very approximate accordance
with the concept of society provided by caste ideology.

In sum, while caste is clearly the dominant rhetoric for conceptualizing social
relations for some Indians, the evidence suggests that it is neither a universally
accepted ideological charter for actual relationships, nor a reliable guide to
behavioral practice. It can hardly be denied that it is different in content from
other ideologies, but how that difference affects experience and practice in India
is an unresolved question. Differences in experience and behavior are clearly
not as extreme as differences in ideologies.

OSSOWSKI   In his seminal work, *Class Structure in the Social Consciousness*
(38), Ossowski, a Polish sociologist writing in the 1950s, provides a useful
counterpoint to the positions reviewed above. His work covers a broad range of
Western thinkers on stratification, but his pivotal empirical observation is that
ideologists in both the United States and the Soviet Union see their own society
as one characterized by "non-egalitarian classlessness." Each sees substantial
differences between people in the social and economic rewards they receive,
and each concludes that these differences do not constitute classes in his/her
society. Thus, allowing for differences in political expression between the
societies, Ossowski finds the arguments of Soviet and American ideologists and
sociologists about their own societies to be very similar. At the same time,
Soviet emigres and American observers see classes in Soviet society, while
Soviet observers see classes in American society.

These observations of the way people think and talk about stratification lead
Ossowski to the conclusion that:

> Interpretations of class structure are social facts, which constitute a response to
> emergence or persistence of certain types of human relationships. Thus, the typology
> of the modes of interpreting such structures may be correlated with the typology of
> the actual structures (38, p. 172).

In establishing his types of correlation between interpretations and actual structures Ossowski separates: A. the beliefs and milieux of the analyst, B. the
interpretation of the society, and C. the actual structure of the society. B is the
ideology. A is used to explain which particular B is used to view C.

The common sense appeal of this scheme and Ossowski's convincing discussion of historical cases notwithstanding, the problems of infinite regress
inherent in any scheme which can be applied to itself become apparent. Is C
knowable without B? In fact, is even A knowable without B? But, of course, B is
a function of A and C.

Ossowski solves this problem with the implicit assertion that it is nonetheless
possible to make meaningful statements about the relation of interpretations to

actual structures. This position is consistent with his treading the thin line between Marxist emphasis on historical specificity and commitment to the importance of generalizing across social systems. From the outset he asserts that ideology is important because: "A view of the social structure which is widely held is an element in the social situation, and thus exerts an influence on the nature of human relations" (38, p. 6).

DAHRENDORF   Dahrendorf's display of synthethizing virtuosity in his paper "On the Origins of Inequality among Men" (12) offers the best theoretical orientation which encompasses the various positions reviewed above. He views a normative order as essential to the functioning of a community, but sees it as imposed by those in power (those in power being those who are able to impose a normative order) and inevitably subject to dispute by those who the prevailing order relegates to low positions in the stratification system. From Dahrendorf's point of view, both a prevailing normative order (ideology) and change in the prevailing normative order are basic parts of social reality. The normative order guides the application of sanctions to deviants, and deviants are inevitably produced by the system of stratification headed by those who define the normative order to their own advantage.

CONCLUSIONS   Two general conclusions follow from the material reviewed above. First, it is not appropriate to treat ideology as a set of rules from which behavior can be predicted. The relation of norms to behavior is not a simple isomorphic one, even with an ample allowance for "deviant" behavior which does not conform to norms and is sanctioned according to a subsidiary set of rules. Second, it is not appropriate, in the absence of extensive empirical research yielding positive results, to assume that ideology is part of mental culture or cognitive orientation shared by all or most members of a society. In fact, at a more specific level, there is reason to believe that people in advantaged positions in a society will articulate an ideology which implies shared norms supporting the extant social relationships, while people in disadvantaged positions in a society will hold contrary views about the nature of society.

What remains of the action framework after the observation that ideology varies with social position and social purposes? Certainly the commonplace fact that people "feel" constrained by rules and state rules in justification of behavior is not obviated by this observation. What is lost is the principle that generally shared meaning precedes specific meaning. In terms of the contrasts between group-oriented and individual-oriented theories of society stated at the beginning of this section of the paper, this means a rejection of the group-oriented theories insofar as they assume simple ideological homogeneity. It does not imply support for the individual-oriented theories. For investigators of social stratification, at least, the implication seems to be simply that ideology and meaning are relative to position in the stratification system. This is neither a group nor an individual characteristic, and the analysis of action, ideology, and behavior that follows from this fact supercedes the simplistic notions with which I began.

These conclusions to which the study of social stratification have led are not new in this generation of anthropological thought. They are consistent with: 1. the doubts about intracultural cognitive uniformity expressed by Wallace (60); 2. the proposal for study of intracultural diversity by Pelto & Pelto (40); and 3. the war on mentalism led by Harris (23). Moreover, they fit with the new directions advocated by sociologists working on ethnomethodology, labeling theory, and social construction of reality (9, 43); and finally, they are consistent with the increasingly popular conflict views of society and history taken by Marxist and non-Marxist anthropologists. While it is not clear if and when we will reach another dominant consensus of the order of the Parsonian view in sociology and the cultural uniformity-cultural determinist view in anthropology, it is clear that these paradigms can no longer guide study of the role of experience and ideology in social stratification.

The Uses of Ambiguity: Experience and Ideology Continued.

The lively discussion in symbolic anthropology of the ambiguity, multivocality, and manipulability of symbols has as its counterpart in the study of social stratification the attention to the existence and functions of ambiguity. Moore (34) and Turner (59), who bridge symbolic and political anthropology, note how these characteristics of symbols are useful in political action. They are likewise an important characteristic of social stratification systems, for the ability to redefine and manipulate relative rank can transform the experience of social stratification. Whatever the ultimate practical significance of such transformations, they are clearly a frequent feature of behavior in stratification systems. Here I will first review some interpretations of stratification systems which emphasize ambiguity, then discuss the relationship of the scientific mode of inquiry to the study of these phenomena. While the issues discussed below are closely related to those discussed immediately above, I have chosen to separate them because I do not want to confuse the debate about the direct relation of ideology and behavior with the more recently popular discussion of the existence and functions of ambiguity.

For the purposes of discussion it is useful to distinguish three components of the role of ambiguity in the system of stratification. First, ambiguity in cultural conventions, in the roles and the symbols associated with rank, exists in many if not all societies. Where populations of individuals or groups interact as relevant alters there seem to be many rules for specifying rank and many interpretations of the symbols of rank. More are available than are used. The way in which any concrete situation will be defined in terms of the available array of rules and symbols is difficult to know. Second, people or groups vying for rank in any concrete situation will attempt to apply the conventions that enhance their rank. Third, any "resultant" situation may include several different definitions of social reality and remain viable. Normative or cultural consensus need not be characteristic of the situation. In the three examples cited below, the contrast between Leach's early recognition of these characteristics of conventions surrounding stratification and Srinivas's later statement illustrates the way in which the overall orientation has shifted away from the framework presuming normative (cultural) consensus.

Leach's classic statement in *Political Systems of Highland Burma* (28) 20 years ago comes out of an earlier conception of the relation of ideology and behavior, but includes a clear statement of the functions of ambiguity. He begins:

> To be frank, Kachin *gumsa* theory about class differences is almost totally inconsistent with Kachin practice. I want then to explain not only what the Kachin theory is but also how the inconsistencies in actual behavior affect the total social structure.
>
> In theory rank depends strictly upon birth status; all legal rules are framed as if the hierarchy of aristocrats, commoners and slaves had a caste-like rigidity and exclusiveness. In Kachin theory rank is an attribute of lineage and every individual acquires his rank once and for all through the lineage into which he happens to be born. It is easy to see that this theory is a fiction, but less easy to understand just what kind of fiction is involved (28, pp. 159–60).

Leach goes on to show how individuals strive for higher rank by garbling evidence and otherwise manipulating the complicated Kachin rules of succession to optimize the position of their lineage and thereby their own position. "These elaborate rules not only allow for much controversy, they also make it relatively easy for any influential aristocrat to reconstruct remote sections of his geneology in his own favor" (28, p. 166). Leach clearly identifies the functions of ambiguity but, in keeping with the dominant orientation of normative (cultural) consensus when he wrote, takes "Kachin theory" seriously, and thus sees the functions of ambiguity as extraordinary.

Srinivas, writing more recently, has shown how Hindu caste, the most elaborated, hierarchical, and rigid of ideologies, is subject to the same type of manipulation in practice.

> Thus the Harijan Holeyas are able to point to the Smiths as their inferiors, and as "evidence" of their superiority, to the fact that they do not accept food and drinking water from Smiths. . . . On their side, the Smiths would dismiss the Harijan claim as absurd, and point to their Sanskritized style of life, and to their not accepting food cooked by any except Brahmins and Lingayats as evidence of their high status. This kind of ambiguity regarding the position of several castes was not only a function of the flexibility of the system but also facilitated its acceptance (52, p. 73).

Hodge, an American sociologist working with traditional quantitative data on education, occupation, and income of individuals, finds the correlation between the types of rank low enough to conclude that the system is not "crystallized" and makes a parallel interpretation for the American system which has one of the most elaborately antihierarchical of modern ideologies.

> The absence of a crystallized status system in which education, occupational prestige, and income are so closely interwoven that any one of them may be utilized as a surrogate for the others implies that the vast majority of individuals will have some legitimate claim upon the various rewards of the society (25, p. 183).

All these statements affirm the importance of ambiguity as a part of social reality, and none ultimately confuses it with (a) a deficiency in understanding of the system, or (b) an imperfection in the fit between ideology and behavior. They are consistent with the emphasis on the ambiguity of the symbolic-ideological aspect of social reality that is characteristic of recent and current symbolic anthropology, and inconsistent with earlier views that emphasized the logical coherence and primacy of ideology in meaningful human behavior.

This earlier view in the Durkheimian-Parsonian tradition, it seems to me, came out of a pressure for isomorphism between the clarity, coherence, and order of scientific study and the character of the social reality studied. More recently a similar kind of pressure has led to an implicit isomorphism between complicated social reality and the complicated humanistic approaches to its study. Both are based on the incorrect premise that fuller knowledge is attainable when the form of knowing approximates the form of the known. The premise itself perhaps stems from the hope that fairly complete and objective knowledge is possible.

The genuine ambiguity which exists in social reality, like the disparity which exists between the ideology of high and low ranking people and groups in stratification systems, seems to contribute to the ability of many to live in systems that would seem tolerable to only a few.

CONCLUSIONS

Important insights derived from the study of other societies have accumulated over the years, yet anthropological study of social stratification remains in its infancy. This is particularly true of our understanding of agrarian (peasant) societies, but it is also reflected in the recent revolution in thinking about hunting and gathering societies. While exceptions abound and present trends may be cyclical variation rather than unidirectional progress, growth in the anthropological study of social stratification seems to be part of a movement away from emphasis on the isolation, homogeneity, and uniqueness of other societies and towards their comparability with industrial societies.

The older antiquarian emphasis of anthropology encouraged conceptualization in terms of implicit differences between our sociocultural system and that of anthropological societies. And the older conception of culture emphasized descriptions of autonomous cultural systems in terms of paradigms dominated by a value on coherence and completeness.

This is changing as the ambiguity of symbols and rules is increasingly recognized, and as "norms" become "ideology" and "ideology" becomes "rhetoric" in the standard conceptual tool kit. It changes further as conflict, disarray, incompleteness, and revolution become aspects of social reality rather than signs of scientific inadequacy, and as the recognition of differentiation and change in other societies makes them similar to our vision of ourselves.

The study of social stratification, by its very nature, involves the conceptualization of differences among individuals and groups within a single system of analysis. And the substance of social stratification, freed of the assumptions of cultural homogeneity and ideological dominance, involves conflict and continuing change in social reality.

DISCLAIMERS

The disclaimers and accompanying rationalizations in a paper of this sort could themselves fill a substantial part of the space available. I want to make them brief and to distinguish motivated exclusions from exclusions resultant from lack of space, time, or competence. I am sorry about the latter category, and hope that others will fill out the picture.

The context of this paper includes theories of society that anthropologists share with sociologists, but I have not attempted to review recent American sociology because the literature is enormous and because I believe Beteille is fundamentally correct when he says, "The poverty of their approach derives from an obsessive concern for 'methodology' and scientific precision at the expense of sociologically significant problems" (4, p. 10).

I have tried to avoid "political anthropology" as such because it is too large a field to handle, and because it has an orientation that concentrates on the upper ranks and getting things done at the societal level. I am concerned with issues better viewed without emphasis on the top.

I have not tried to systematically review Marxist approaches, quasi-Marxist approaches, and non-Marxist approaches that emphasize relations of local systems with the larger system, especially the nation-state and the international politico-economic system, both because the literature has become too large and because I believe they draw needed attention away from internal differentiation in small communities.

I have excluded contributions by prehistorians and primatologists because I am not competent to review them, and studies of sex and ethnic stratification because they are special cases of general principles and because they are currently popular and warrant separate reviews.

Finally, with great regret, I have excluded reviews clustered around a limited number of institutional complexes which I had hoped to include. Caste, the potlatch, the big man system, intentional communities, etc, viewed as stratification systems would produce very useful theoretical insights, I think, as well as valuable intellectual histories of anthropological contributions to social theory.

ACKNOWLEDGMENTS

I am indebted to Francesa Cancian for very useful comments on various drafts of this paper, and to George Collier, Jane Collier, Bridget O'Laughlin, G. William Skinner, and Katherine Verdery for helpful suggestions.

Literature Cited

1. Adams, R. N. 1970. Brokers and career mobility systems in the structure of complex societies. *Southwest. J. Anthropol.* 26:315–27
2. Benedict, B. 1970. Pluralism and stratification. In *Essays in Comparative Social Stratification,* ed. L. Plotnicov, A. Tuden, 29–41. Univ. Pittsburgh Press. 349 pp.
3. Berreman, G. D. 1960. Caste in India and the United States. *Am. J. Sociol.* 66:120–27
4. Beteille, A. 1969. Introduction. In *Social Inequality: Selected Readings,* ed. A. Beteille, 9–14. Baltimore: Penguin. 397 pp.
5. Boserup, E. 1965. *The Conditions of Agricultural Growth.* Chicago: Aldine. 124 pp.
6. Cancian, F. 1965. *Economics and Prestige in a Maya Community.* Stanford Univ. Press. 238 pp.
7, Cancian, F. 1966. Maximization as norm, strategy, and theory. *Am. Anthropol.* 68:465–70
8. Cancian, F. 1972. *Change and Uncertainty in a Peasant Economy.* Stanford Univ. Press. 208 pp.
9. Cancian, F. M. 1975. *What Are Norms?* New York: Cambridge Univ. Press. 212 pp.
10. Collier, G. A. 1975. *Fields of the Tzotzil.* Austin: Univ. Texas Press. 255 pp.
11. Dahrendorf, R. 1966. Review symposium on Lenski's power and privilege. *Am. Sociol. Rev.* 31:714–18
12. Dahrendorf, R. 1968. On the origin of inequality among men. In *Essays in the Theory of Society,* 151–78. Stanford Univ. Press. 300 pp.
13. DeWalt, B. 1975. Inequalities in wealth, adoption of technology, and production in a Mexican ejido. *Am. Ethnol.* 2:149–68
14. Dumont, L. 1960. Caste, racism and "stratification." In *Social Inequality,* ed. A. Beteille, 337–61. Baltimore: Penguin. 397 pp.
15. Dumont, L. 1970. *Homo Hierarchicus.* Univ. Chicago Press. 386 pp.
16. Epstein, S. 1967. Productive efficiency and customary systems of rewards in rural South India. In *Themes in Economic Anthropology,* ed. R. Firth, 229–52. London: Tavistock. 292 pp.
17. Fallers, L. A. 1973. *Inequality: Social Stratification Reconsidered.* Univ. Chicago Press. 330 pp.
18. Foster, G. M. 1960–61. Interpersonal relations in peasant society. *Hum. Organ.* 19:174–84
19. Fried, M. H. 1967. *The Evolution of Political Society.* New York: Random House. 270 pp.
20. Goody, J. 1971. Class and marriage in Africa and Eurasia. *Am. J. Sociol.* 76:585–603
21. Harris, M. 1959. The economy has no surplus? *Am. Anthropol.* 61: 185–99
22. Harris, M. 1966. The cultural ecology of India's sacred cattle. *Curr. Anthropol.* 7:51–66
23. Harris, M. 1974. Why a perfect knowledge of all the rules one must know to act like a native cannot lead to knowledge of how natives act. *J. Anthropol. Res.* 30:242–51
24. Harris, M. 1975. *Culture, People, Nature.* New York: Crowell. 694 pp.
25. Hodge, R. W. 1970. Social integration, psychological well-being, and their socioeconomic correlates. In *Social Stratification: Research and Theory for the 1970s,* ed. E. O. Laumann, 182–206. Indianapolis: Bobbs-Merrill. 280 pp.
26. Kelley, J., Perlman, M. L. 1971. Social mobility in Toro. *Econ. Dev. Cult. Change* 19:204–21
27. Kerckhoff, A. C. 1974. Stratification processes and outcomes in England and the U.S. *Am. Sociol. Rev.* 39:789–801
28. Leach, E. 1954. *Political Systems of Highland Burma.* Cambridge: Harvard Univ. Press. 324 pp.
29. Lee, R. B., DeVore, I., eds. 1968. *Man the Hunter.* Chicago: Aldine. 415 pp.
30. Leeds, A. 1973. Locality power in relation to supralocal power institutions. In *Urban Anthropology,* ed. A. Southall, 15–41. New York: Oxford Univ. Press. 489 pp.
31. Leeds, A., Vayda, A. P., eds. 1965. *Man, Culture, and Animals.* Washington DC: Am. Assoc. Advan. Sci., Vol. 78. 304 pp.
32. Lenski, G. 1966. *Power and Privilege.* New York: McGraw-Hill. 495 pp.
33. Mandel, E. 1968. *Marxist Economic Theory,* Vol. 1. New York: Monthly Review Press. 379 pp.
34. Moore, S. F. 1975. Epilogue: Uncertainties in situations, indeterminacies in culture. In *Symbols*

248   CANCIAN

and Politics in Communal Ideology,
ed. S. F. Moore, B. G. Myerhoff.
Ithaca: Cornell Univ. Press. 245 pp.
35. O'Laughlin, B. 1975. Marxist approaches in anthropology. *Ann.
Rev. Anthropol.* 4:341–70
36. Orans, M. 1966. Surplus. *Hum. Organ.* 25:24–32
37. Orans, M. 1968. Maximizing in
jajmaniland. *Am. Anthropol.* 70:
875–97
38. Ossowski, S. 1963. *Class Structure
in the Social Consciousness.* New
York: Free Press. 202 pp.
39. Pearson, H. J. 1957. The economy
has no surplus. In *Trade and Markets in the Early Empires,* ed. K.
Polanyi, C. M. Arensberg, H. W.
Pearson, 320–41. Glencoe: Free
Press. 382 pp.
40. Pelto, P. J., Pelto, G. H. 1975. Intracultural diversity. *Am. Ethnol.*
2:1–18
41. Piddocke, S. 1965. The potlatch
system of the Southern Kwakiutl.
Southwest J. Anthropol. 21:244–64
42. Plotnicov, L., Tuden, A. 1970. Introduction. In *Essays in Comparative Social Stratification,* ed. L.
Plotnicov, A. Tuden, 3–25. Univ.
Pittsburgh Press. 349 pp.
43. Rubington, E., Weinberg, M. S.
1968. *Deviance: The Interactionist
Perspective.* New York: Macmillan.
422 pp.
44. Sahlins, M. D. 1958. *Social
Stratification in Polynesia.* Seattle:
Univ. Washington Press. 306 pp.
45. Sahlins, M. 1972. *Stone Age Economics.* Chicago: Aldine. 348 pp.
46. Silverman, S. F. 1965. Patronage
and community-nation relationships
in central Italy. *Ethnology* 4:172–89
47. Silverman, S. F. 1966. An ethnographic approach to social
stratification. *Am. Anthropol.* 68:
899–921
48. Skinner, G. W. 1964–65. Marketing
and social structure in rural China,
Parts, I, II, and III. *J. Asian Stud.*
24:3–43, 195–228, 363–99
49. Smith, C. A. 1975. Examining
stratification systems through peasant marketing arrangements. *Man*
n.s. 10:95–122

50. Srinivas, M. N. 1952. *Religion and
Society among the Coorgs of South
India.* Oxford: Clarendon. 267 pp.
51. Srinivas, M. N. 1956. A note on
Sanskritization and Westernization.
Far Eastern Q. 15:481–96
52. Srinivas, M. N. 1975. The Indian
village, myth and reality. In *Studies
in Social Anthropology,* ed. H. H.
Beattie, R. G. Lienhardt, 41–85.
Oxford Univ. Press
53. Stauder, J. 1972. Anarchy and ecology: Political society among the
Majangir. *Southwest. J. Anthropol.*
28:153–68
54. Stavenhagen, R. 1975. *Social
Classes in Agrarian Societies.* Garden City: Anchor. 266 pp.
55. Stevenson, R. F. 1968. *Population
and Political Systems in Tropical
Africa.* New York: Columbia Univ.
Press. 306 pp.
56. Thompson, R. A. 1974. *The Winds
of Tomorrow: Social Change in a
Maya Town.* Univ. Chicago Press.
182 pp.
57. Treiman, D. J. 1975. Problems of
concept measurement in the comparative study of occupational mobility. *Soc. Sci. Res.* 4:183–230
58. Tuden, A., Plotnicov, L. 1970. Introduction. In *Social Stratification
in Africa,* ed. A. Tuden, L. Plotnicov, 1–29. New York: Free Press.
392 pp.
59. Turner, V. 1975. Symbolic studies.
See Ref. 35, 145–61
60. Wallace, A. F. C. 1961. *Culture
and Personality.* New York: Random House. 213 pp.
61. Wallerstein, I. 1974. *The Modern
World System.* New York: Academic. 410 pp.
62. Wolf, E. R. 1955. Types of Latin
American peasantry. *Am. Anthropol.* 57:452–71
63. Wolf, E. R. 1956. Aspects of group
relations in a complex society. *Am.
Anthropol.* 58:1065–78
64. Wolf, E. R. 1967. Levels of communal relations. In *Handbook of Middle American Indians,* gen. ed., R.
Wauchope, vol. ed., M. Nash,
6:299–316. Austin: Univ. Texas
Press

Ann. Rev. Anthropol. 1976. 5:249–64
Copyright © 1976 by Annual Reviews Inc. All rights reserved

ANTHROPOLOGICAL STUDIES OF CITIES

◆ 9579

Richard E. Blanton
Department of Sociology and Anthropology, Purdue University,
West Lafayette, Indiana 47907

INTRODUCTION

In this paper I will review and expand upon a theoretical and methodological approach to the study of cities that, in my view, has been unduly neglected by anthropologists interested in cities. This approach, usually referred to as regional analysis, is based on the central place theory of geography. I believe that we need to expand our theoretical horizons because traditional theories of cities utilized by anthropologists are both misleading and limited in scope. In order to demonstrate the value of a regional approach to studies of cities, I will first critically (and very briefly) review traditional theories of cities, then offer a regionally based definition of cities and explore some of the implications of the regional approach for explaining the cross-cultural variability and dynamic features of cities and systems of cities.

Perhaps the most prominent feature of traditional theories is that they regard cities as the sources of social change—they are a kind of special environment, almost with a life of their own. These "city-centric" theories have been based on Durkheim's *The Division of Labor in Society* (who, in turn, was influenced by Spencer's *Principles of Sociology*), on the sociology of George Simmel, and the philosophy of Oswald Spengler. Martindale (32) has written a convenient review of the development of these theories, which he refers to as "socio-psychological" theories of cities. Hauser (19), for example, following Durkheim and Spencer, writes that ". . . aggregative living has produced in the social realm a major transformation the equivalent of genetic mutation in the biological realm." Park, in the classic statement of the "Chicago School" of urban sociology (38), described the city as a "psychophysical mechanism"; Wirth (59), in the same volume, writes of the city that its ". . . growth is so rapid and its energy so great that it changes its complexion almost daily, and, with it, the character of mankind itself" (see also 60). As proposed by Redfield & Singer (42), the city, whether the center of "orthogenetic change" (". . . carrying forward into systematic and reflective dimensions an old culture") or "heterogenetic change" (". . . creating of original modes of thought that have authority beyond or in conflict with old cultures and civilizations"), is ". . . a place in which culture change takes place" (42, p. 58).

Robert Redfield's famous "Folk-Urban Continuum" (41) was developed under the influence of the "Chicago School." This proved to be the focus of anthropological theorizing about cities for years, until gradually the work of a number of people (too numerous to review completely here) demonstrated that not only could the "Folk-Urban Continuum" not be attributed the status of theory, but that it could not even stand as an adequate empirical generalization (cf Hauser 20; Lewis 28, 29).

In spite of the serious criticisms which have been leveled at the Simmel-Wirth-Redfield trio, there is no shortage of "socio-psychological" theories of cities in the more recent literature in anthropology and its sister disciplines. Friedmann (15) writes that cities are ". . . an active force in the ongoing processes of social transformation," and, according to Epstein (13), most urban anthropologists in Africa assume that ". . . towns inevitably act as instruments of social transformation" (see also Jacobs 22 and Moore 37). Although many criticisms could be made of these traditional ways of looking at cities, the major objections, as I see them, are: (*a*) If urbanism is regarded as a way of life, how can one account for the cross-cultural and diachronic variability in cities and in the ways of life within cities? The attempt by Redfield & Singer (42) to differentiate between cities which are the centers of "orthogenetic" or "heterogenetic" change by no means does justice to the wide variety in kinds and functions of cities. (*b*) As stated by Lewis (28, p. 432), the ". . . folk-urban conceptualization of social change focuses attention primarily on the city as the source of change, to the exclusion or neglect of other factors of an internal or external nature." The folk-urban continuum fails to aid our understanding of the rates of social change, or when and where change is likely or not likely to occur.

In the remainder of this paper I will attempt to demonstrate that a regional theory of cities, in contrast with "socio-psychological" theories, is explicitly oriented to provide explanations for the cross-cultural differences in cities, while avoiding the fallacy of overemphasizing the role of cities in social change.

CITIES DEFINED

I will assiduously avoid the use of the terms urban and urbanism, for although both these terms have something to do with cities, no two researchers agree on what the association is. Similarly, much ink has been spilled by scholars over what cities are and what they are not, without, to date, a satisfactory resolution of the definitional problem. Instead of reviewing this bulky and frustrating literature here, I refer the reader to two useful summaries by Paul Wheatley (57, pp. 371–99; 58).

Perhaps the greatest obstacle in the definition of cities as a special type of human community has been the establishment of a set of indispensable criteria which can be applied cross-culturally. In the most widely read work on pre-industrial cities (Sjoberg 47), for example, it is argued that the presence of a literate elite is the single best criterion to distinguish cities from other types of early settlements, clearly a cross-cultural error of no small magnitude. Wheatley (56) suggests that these definitional problems could be resolved by the use of his concept of "ethnocity." Here attention is paid to ". . . nodes of concentration of people and shelters in the continuum of population distribution over the face of the earth. Such of these as attain a certain size and perform appropriate functions are designated by the terms appositely translated in English as 'city' or 'town'. . . . These nodes are induced by forces operating within, and sometimes peculiar to, the specific culture" (56, pp. 166–67). This approach is desirable because it avoids the necessity for discovering indispensable criteria, and instead focuses on the hierarchy of central places in a society.

Such a functional definition of cities emphasizes the disposition in space of what might be called central institutions—institutions that mediate between specialized subsystems within a society. In order to optimally service a population, these central institutions are not likely to be randomly dispersed over the landscape. Instead, they will tend to occur clustered in places that become the central places of the society, or, in other words, the cities and towns. Cities (and towns) then are a product of the process called *segregation,* one of the two basic cultural evolutionary processes described by Flannery (14). Segregation, according to Flannery, has to do with ". . . the amount of internal differentiation and specialization of subsystems . . ." (The other basic evolutionary process described by Flannery, *centralization,* refers to the ". . . degree of linkage between the various sub-systems and the highest-order controls in the society . . .", and is less relevant to the discussion at hand). In the present context, segregation refers to the extent to which households or groups of households are independent—in more evolved systems they are less independent, necessitating various kinds of linkages in the society between specialized subsystems. Linkages between specialized subsystems may take the form of transactions in the context of central institutions. Chieftainships, governments, and markets are examples of such central institutions. The general description of central institutions is that they link specialized subsystems by the conversion of inputs to outputs via a set of transactions (cf Meier 34). The kinds of inputs and outputs vary—markets involve mostly material inputs and outputs, while governments more often convert information inputs to outputs in the form of directives.

For our purposes here, the most salient characteristics of central institutions are that they require energy to function, and that the transactions take time. Energy is supplied by subsystems of producers, who must work more than would be necessary in the absence of such institutions. The fact that there is always a finite amount of energy in the environment of any society, and that producers can be pushed or otherwise encouraged to produce only so much surplus, means that central institutions always have a maximum size and are always limited to a finite number of transactions per unit of time. These energy-related limitations can be circumvented by technological or organizational changes that bring energy savings or increase the society's ability to capture energy from its environment, but new limits will be reached if central institutions continue to grow.

Time is as important a constraint on central institutions as energy. Participants may attempt to minimize the amount of time spent in transactions in order to have time available for other activities, and slowly operating central institutions may fail to meet deadlines. We might expect, therefore, given time and energy constraints, that in all societies we will find the presence of strategies that minimize both the time and energy costs of central institutions. Although there undoubtedly will be considerable cross-cultural variability in the form of these strategies and the extent to which minimization is actually achieved, there is probably no society in which there is complete disregard for the energy and time costs of these mediating central institutions. Such energy and time optimization strategies would become more and more important in evolving systems, since the costs of subsystem intermediation increase rapidly as societies become more complicated (Flannery 14, pp. 411–12).

One of the most obvious energy and time optimization strategies has to do with the disposition of central institutions over the landscape—specifically, we might expect central institution transactions to occur centrally, in localities that allow minimization of the time and energy costs of travel. According to Friedmann, ". . . distance is a physical obstacle that can be overcome most rationally by centralizing certain functions within geographic space" (15, p. 86). This is perhaps most obvious in connection with central institutions that involve exchanges of goods, since these might be heavy to carry and may spoil, but the same will be true for information processing central institutions. For this latter type of institution, there is the additional problem that excessive travel time may increase the probability of "noise" entering the flow of information—that is, information may be lost or confused in transport, or directives may not be fully and accurately transmitted.

The process of time and energy optimization will have as a product the growth of a place or places which become the foci of central institution transactions (called central places). It is at this point that we begin to borrow from the central place theory of geography, a theory that is largely the work of Christaller (10), with some recent modifications (Berry & Garrison 6, Berry & Pred 7). Following this theoretical approach, we may refer to the range of central place functions, or the area beyond which a given function at a given place will not operate because of the friction of distance and/or competition from other central places offering the same function. Low-order central place functions have small ranges, and therefore will tend to be widely and frequently distributed over the landscape in order to maximally service the population. High-order functions have large ranges, so that only a few places in a region will offer these. In a simple society such as a chiefdom with few central institutions, usually one community serves as the focus of central transactions. In more evolved systems, there may be both more kinds of central institutions and a hierarchical division of labor within central institutions. These will produce a hierarchy of central places in a region, ranging from communities which have a wide range of central place functions, including high-order functions, to a series of small, scattered places with fewer functions, and functions of smaller range. The population size of central places, as geographers have shown (e.g. Gun-awardena 16, Stafford 53) will tend to vary depending on the number of central place functions present. In a society with a hierarchy of central places, cities are those communities in the highest range of the hierarchy, while towns are those communities occupying the middle and lower ranges of the hierarchy. Where the researcher draws the boundary between what are called cities and what are called towns is always arbitrary and will vary from society to society.

The regional approach to the definition of cities is not peculiar to Wheatley, myself, or others who have borrowed from central place studies in geography. Wolf (61), for example, has written that the city is ". . . a settlement in which a combination of functions are exercized, and which becomes useful because in time greater efficiency is obtained by having these functions concentrated in one site." And, according to Arensberg (3), the city ". . . is a permanently massed, large concentration of people in a community having nodal function or functions, somehow providing for the lacing together (not necessarily the subordination) of some hinterland of the other, perhaps lesser communities of a society." My only complaint with Arensberg's definition is that it includes the caveat that a city must have a "large" and "massed" concentration of people. This begs the question of how large is large enough, and how massed is massed enough for a community to be called a city. The advantage of the functional definition of cities I presented above is that any community that is a central place is a city or town (depending on its place in the central place hierarchy of the society), irrespective of its form or population size. Central places in societies smaller and less segregated than our own may lack large or massed central places, but they still have what Arensberg refers to as "nodal functions," and so should be referred to as cities and towns.

I should point out in concluding this section that while I have borrowed from central place studies in geography in developing this definition of cities, I have tried to word it to avoid the overemphasis on the movement of goods through systems, or, in other words, the economic functions of central places that, in my opinion, characterize this field (cf Haggett 17). Part of Christaller's original work on the geometry of central place systems had to do with what he called the "administrative" or "$K=7$" principle (10), which I will discuss in more detail below. Unfortunately, more recent work by geographers has dealt almost exclusively with the "marketing" and "transport" principles, both concerned with tertiary economic functions. The kinds of transactions I am referring to in the context of central institutions involve the movement of goods and/or information. The overemphasis on economic functions of central places has led, in my view, to some confusion in the literature. Coe (11), for example, wrote that interior Cambodian and lowland Classic Maya civilizations had no "true" cities. His argument is that since both geographic areas lacked environmental diversity it is not likely that there was regional economic specialization and trade, and therefore both areas lacked cities. This is not only overly environmentally deterministic (since he has almost no direct archaeological evidence for the lack of specialization and trade), but it also overlooks the fact that there were obviously central places, manifested as large groupings of civic-ceremonial buildings and palaces. Even if it were true that these were not economic centers, they were clearly centers of information processing and so should be referred to as cities as defined above. Donna Taylor (54) has demonstrated for a group of East African middle range hierarchical societies a ". . . close positive relationship between settlement hierarchy and political-jurisdictional hierarchy . . .," and that ". . . in hierarchical societies the relative size of the centers of higher rank is closely related to the extent of centralization in decision-processing" (54, p. 13). Interestingly, this set of East African chiefdoms and simple states, unlike those portrayed in the generalized descriptions of societies of this type by Service (46) and Sahlins (44), ". . . were not typically redistributive societies. . . . Local groups tended to be largely self-sufficient in material . . . needs, and the organized collection and redistribution of regional production specialties is described for only one of the most centrally organized societies examined" (54, p. 81). From the same perspective I must add a criticism to Wheatley's contention that the early "cult centers" (as he calls them) that evolved in regions of primary state formation were centers of redistribution (57, p. 389). The presence or absence of redistribution in ancient central places must always remain hypothetical until demonstrated by direct archaeological evidence.

In the next section I will explore some of the interrelationships between information processing central place hierarchies and economic central place hierarchies. This point of view, I argue, will contribute to an understanding of the nature and dynamic properties of systems of cities and towns.

THE LOCATIONAL PATTERNS

Anthropologists interested in the application of central place theory to problems in peasant marketing systems have found Christaller's (10) original formulation most applicable (cf Crissman 12, Hodder & Hassall 21, Johnson 24, Skinner 48, and Smith 52). According to some geographers (cf 5), the transformations of the Christallerian model proposed by Lösch (30) may prove to be a more accurate representation of reality for modern industrialized societies, but there is no consensus on this point. For these reasons, and because Lösch was relatively less interested in administrative location, I will also depend here primarily on Christaller's formulation. Rather than repeat the assumptions and geometric properties of the Christallerian model, I refer the reader to a recent synthesis by Smith (51).

The major difference between Christaller's two economically relevant locational principles (the K=3 "marketing" principle, and the K=4 "transport" principle) on the one hand, and the K=7 "administrative" principle on the other hand, has to do with the extent to which competition can occur between centers of the same level in the hierarchy. (The K numbers refer to the ratio of low-order places to high-order places, a matter not relevant to this discussion. I use the K designations only as a convenient means of referring to the different locational patterns.) In the case of the two economic principles, centers of a lower level in the settlement hierarchy are "nested" midway in space between centers of the next highest rank. In the K=3 case, such centers are located between three higher-level centers, while in the case of the K=4 pattern, such centers are located midway between two higher level centers, on the road between them. Centers of the same level in hierarchy, therefore, compete to service lower-level centers, particularly near the edges of their maximum spheres of influence. As a consequence, all consumers tend to be served equally, without monopolistic pricing. As Christaller correctly perceived, the locations of administrative centers should differ from the K=3 or K=4 patterns, since they do not compete for "customers"; instead, they should have discrete, tightly bounded ranges, with the center conveniently situated near the center of the servicing region. As Smith (52, p. 98) notes, the K=7 principle ". . . is admirably suited to carving up administrative districts, since each higher-order center controls its dependent centers and hinterland exclusively." Although I will not deal explicitly here with religious-administrative hierarchies (which are usually inextricably woven with political administration), in those cases where they are discrete, autonomous institutions (such as in Medieval Europe), they should exhibit the K=7 pattern, since each "parish" is a discrete unit, and competition is not likely to occur.

IMPLICATIONS OF THE LOCATIONAL PATTERNS FOR UNDERSTANDING VARIABILITY IN CENTRAL PLACE HIERARCHIES

In the following sections, I will outline the basic patterns of articulation between economic central institutions and decision-making central institutions, and explore the implications of these patterns for understanding some of the cross-cultural variability in sizes and functions of central places, and certain of their dynamic features. I do this in three sections. The first two sections, which deal with "primate" centers and "disembedded capitals," pertain to the interaction of economic and decision-making central institutions at the upper levels of central place hierarchies, while the last section deals with the patterns of articulation of these central institutions on the lower levels.

Primate Centers

Purely from theoretical considerations, one should not expect locational isomorphism between administrative and economic central place hierarchies, since the two locational patterns are incompatible (cf Skinner 48, p. 31). There are two major exceptions to this general rule.

REDISTRIBUTIVE SYSTEMS   In redistributive economic systems, in which exchange is entirely administered, the centers of redistribution are also centers of decision-making.

PRIMATE SYSTEMS   In a marketing central place hierarchy in which the range of the highest order functions is equivalent to the maximum extent of the society as a whole, only one highest ranking center will exist, since only that center will be able to offer the entire range of products in the system. This center can also be the highest ranking administrative center, since the maximum range of these functions is also equivalent to the maximum extent of the whole society. The combination of the widest possible range of economic and administrative functions in one place can produce a "primate" distribution in the settlement hierarchy, i.e. a situation in which the major central place is exceptionally large relative to other centers (Berry 4). A large center of this type can actually retard the growth of lower-ranking centers, thereby intensifying its regional dominance, for the following reasons:

(*a*) One of the assumptions of Christaller's classical formulation of central place theory is that consumers will always go to the closest market, in order to minimize the energy and time costs of transportation. Crissman (12) has argued that this will not always be true because ". . . motivations for marketing at one place rather than another are exceedingly complex and vary from one context to another." Specifically, Crissman suggests that ". . . marketing areas for particular goods associated with given levels in the central place hierarchy, vary significantly in size depending on the level in the hierarchy of the center supplying them" (12, pp. 347, 393). Trips to higher-order centers may be more frequent than theoretically predicted, he argues, because of the possibility of multipurpose trips, ". . . price differentials between low and high-level centers owing to fewer middlemen at the former . . .", and lower prices in larger centers due to ". . . competition between multiple firms offering the same goods . . ." Added to these economic considerations, he argues, are a variety of social, political, religious, and recreational reasons for going to one town rather than another. We might expect that the beauty and impressiveness of the massive civic, ceremonial, and palace constructions, manifesting the power of the highest administrative level, would be an added incentive to visit the major political center in spite of the tribulations of travel. For a variety of reasons then, the presence of a primate center could retard the growth of other centers because people will tend to go out of their way to complete transactions in the large center, bypassing better-located places.

(*b*) Carol Smith (52) has described a situation in highland Guatemala which may add to our understanding of the nature of "primate" settlement distributions. There the massed purchasing power of the Ladino elites, who control the government from a few centers, has resulted in a situation in which rural production is oriented to these large centers alone. Thus all economic networks in the region ". . . converge on a single center rather than on different nodes of a multi-centered, unbounded system. Because of this convergence, there is no competition among equivalent centers for the commerce of smaller centers" (52 p. 100). The outcome of these processes, she argues, will be the growth of "solar" or "dendritic" market systems in which secondary centers in the region are poorly developed, and most production is geared for the primate center. Such situations lend themselves to poor economic development of the hinterland, since populations far away from the main center cannot participate in the society's economic system as effectively as those closer in (52; see also Johnson 23).

(*c*) According to central place theory, secondary centers should arise far away from the major center, where the "pull" of the major center is weakest due to the friction of distance. This is not realizable in some cases, however, because secondary centers far enough away from the major center to effectively compete with it may be near the borders of the society. Because their market ranges are therefore distorted and smaller than necessary to support higher level functions, they will tend to remain poorly developed, the demand being met for higher-order goods only at the main center. According to Johnson (23, p. 131), border ". . . cities are inherently fragile economically since national borders artificially cut up geographically complementary regions" (see also 51, p. 179).

(*d*) Because long-distance exchange is often directly administered or is at least under some degree of political control, high-ranking administrative centers are often also the foci of interregional exchange activities, and this, too, could add to the already overbearing domination of a region by a primate center (cf Vapnarsky 55).

Disembedded Capitals

In cases where the highest-order goods in a society have a range which is less than the extent of the society as a whole, there should be multiple highest ranking economic centers instead of the primate pattern. In this case, I suggest, it is less likely that the highest-order place in the administrative hierarchy will be located in one of the commercial central places, for at least two reasons:

(*a*) The location of any one of the multiple commercial central places, which might be optimal for servicing its region but not the whole society, might not be suitable for the location of central administrative transactions pertaining to the whole society. Suboptimal locations of highest ranking central places in the administrative system, as I mentioned above, increase the likelihood that "noise" could enter into communications with poorly serviced zones, decreasing the effectiveness of the administration.

(*b*) Merchants in existing high-order commercial central places might resist placement of high-order administrative functions in any existing center (except their own), because of the commercial advantages that would accrue to that center, especially insofar as such placement would increase the prestige of the one center and mass the purchasing power of high ranking elites there.

I predict that in systems with multiple high-order commercial central places of nearly equivalent rank, the political capital will be located in a neutral position, away from existing commercial central places. This situation would also obtain in a region inhabited by a group of autonomous political units joined in a league or confederacy, perhaps for the purpose of taking advantage of their mutual military capabilities in interregional warfare or control of interregional long distance exchange, but where all of the co-joining units are of nearly equivalent power. There are, in other words, situations in which one would expect the highest-order decision-making institution to be spatially "disembedded" from the remainder of the central-place hierarchy. There appear to be several different kinds of "disembedded capitals."

CAPITAL CENTERS   The capital is a permanent but neutrally located special function community involved primarily in decision making at the regional level. Examples of this pattern include Washington DC (which was located away from the existing centers of Boston, New York, and Philadelphia, midway between the southern and northern states, at the insistence of the southerner, Thomas Jefferson), pre-Periclean Athens, Brazilia, Ottawa, New Delhi, and Canberra. I have argued that early Monte Albán, the ancient Zapotec capital in Oaxaca, Mexico, was a center of this type (Blanton 9).

ROVING PALACES   Highest-ranking elites move around periodically or at random from center to center, never staying long enough in one place to augment permanently the influence of any given center. Examples of this pattern include the roving palaces of ancient Egypt and certain periods and regions in premodern Europe. According to Russell (43), the failure to establish permanent places for ruler and court in Medieval Germany and Iberia precluded the rise of single, dominant central places.

TEMPORARY CAPITALS   Rulers build entirely new capitals when they come into office. Part of Coe's (11) argument that the ancient inland Cambodian capitals were not "true" cities was that each new ruler built a new facility, an impossible situation, Coe thought, for a commercial center. It is likely that he was dealing instead with a situation in which the capitals were disembedded from the remainder of the central place hierarchy. Unfortunately, the paucity of archaeological evidence makes it difficult to test this hypothesis.

I feel it would be worthwhile to investigate certain of the dynamic properties of the two kinds of central place hierarchies just described. Specifically, it occurs to me that the first pattern, the primate pattern with a weakly developed hierarchy of commercial central places, might exhibit less long-term stability than the second pattern, in which the whole population is serviced by a more completely developed series of marketing central places. The class-like differences that are likely to develop, given the primate pattern, between the well-serviced, relatively affluent groups in and near the main center versus those in poorly serviced, distant areas, could produce internal tensions that could erupt as warfare or revolution. Too, the primate pattern might be a more brittle one because populations distant from the main center might tend to break away politically and economically from the society as a whole, especially if allegiance to an adjacent system with a well-developed commercial central place hierarchy becomes a possibility.

Political Control of Marketing Hierarchies

Although classical central place theory predicts a lack of spatial isomorphism between administrative and commercial central place hierarchies (with the exception of the primate pattern described above), in reality there is often considerable spatial intertwining of the two types of central institutions. One reason for this undoubtedly has to do with the energy and time savings derived from the "agglomeration of functions." Skinner writes concerning rural China:

That the market town is a natural site for administration of its dependent area is obvious: Marketing periodically brings to town representatives of households throughout the administrative unit and village leaders can, on market days, readily consult their administrative superiors (50, p. 382).

Another factor to consider in explaining the overlap of political and commercial hierarchies is the extent to which the decision making central institution eyes the exchange system as a source of revenue and power. In this case, locating administrative and marketing activities together facilitates control and taxation. In spite of the obvious advantages of conformity between economic and decision hierarchies, however, there still exists the built-in incompatability between the two. This is probably why Skinner found little overlap between administration and market places in rural China on the whole, especially in the lower levels of the central place hierarchy (48, p. 9).

I suggest that the most fruitful method for explaining the cross-cultural and diachronic variability in relations between administrative and marketing hierarchies will be to investigate the following three variables:

(a) *The power of the state:* This refers specifically to the extent to which the administrative institution is able to distort the economically desirable $K=3$ and $K=4$ patterns into the administratively more efficient $K=7$ pattern. According to Smith (52, p. 99) the $K=7$ pattern usually resembles the "solar" marketing pattern. Here, ". . . poor market articulation occurs because the requirement of force overrides market efficiency. . . . A $K=7$ system almost always suggests imposition of the economic system by rulers . . ." I predict that such administratively imposed patterns would always be temporary, because the more an administration meddles in markets, the less efficient marketing becomes. For example, the $K=7$ pattern could easily lend itself to monopolistic pricing, since equivalent centers no longer compete. Producers, under these conditions, might choose to participate less in the market institution, lowering over-all productivity, and thereby lowering state revenues from the market. This would coincide with the added costs incurred by the administration in its attempts to gain control over markets. These two factors operating together should force lessened administrative control of markets, probably first in lower ranking markets, which are the most numerous and therefore require the most personnel to administer. This process is nowhere better illustrated than in Skinner's description of the attempts of the communist regime in China to administer peasant marketing (50). The first such attempts resulted in considerable dislocations in the market and in reduced productivity. The response by the regime to the lowered productivity was to attempt to obviate rural marketing by absorbing it ". . . entirely into an expanded official structure, thereby shifting onto hundreds of thousands of local cooperative branches the functions of the standard market" (50, p. 365). This tactic only exacerbated the problem, until finally the regime reversed its position: "The rightist solution [to the marketing problem], which by August, 1956, had carried the day, was to overcome the malfunctions in the existing system by relaxing controls and giving freer rein to the marketing mechanism."

(b) *The relative power of the state and participants in the market institutions:* A politically powerful marketing institution might force the diminution of administrative distortions of the marketing hierarchy. This process is well illustrated in the history of Medieval Europe, where the emerging commercial middle class gradually swamped the power of the nobility. To quote Pirenne (40, p. 203), the legal codes of the commercially oriented cities ". . . not only did away with personal servitude and restrictions on land, but also caused the disappearance of the seignioral rights and fiscal claims which interferred with the activity of commerce and industry." This resulted in the elimination of, among other things, market tolls, seigniorial monopolies on ovens and mills, and the right of shelter for the nobility.

The possibility exists that there could develop in such cases a kind of market-state dynamic, such that, if for some reason the state begins to lose control over the market institution, an increase in market productivity would result, increasing in turn the power of the marketing institution, which could further exacerbate the power and revenue losses of the administrative institution—a deviation-amplifying, mutual-causal process, in the phraseology of Maruyama (33). Administrative expansion in control of markets, however, will normally be dampened as a result of revenue losses incurred in distortion of the marketing hierarchy, in combination with increased costs of administration.

(c) *The information processing capacity of administrative institutions:* This refers to the extent to which a decision making institution can absorb an increase in the amount of information in the environment, for example, in the context of an expanding, evolving system. Any institution has a finite transactional capacity, limited by energy, personnel, and time, allowing it to respond only to a finite "communications load." According to Meier:

> Communications load is best measured as the rate of requests for service or other forms of satisfying response, such as cogent explanations as to why the service cannot be provided. It represents the initiation rate for social transactions effected by the institution. The output, or transaction completion, rate is what generates rewards for the institution over the long run. When the output rate fails to keep up with the initiation rate, some queues and backlogs develop. If all other factors remain equal, the resultant performance of the institution begins to deviate more and more from the ideal as load increases, until a peak in output rate is reached. As certain resources and internal stocks-on-hand are expended, the output becomes less with increasing load. The output rate may drop precipitately [resulting in breakdown] or it may seek a level which is 'good enough to get by.' The *capacity* of the organization for completing transactions will lie somewhere between the peak performance that could not be maintained and the level chosen for 'satisficing'. . . . In this framework the capacity of an institution for completing a flow of transactions is equivalent to the *channel capacity* of a communications system for coding and decoding messages (34, pp. 79–80).

(See also J. G. Miller 35 and Wright 63.)

Several different kinds of institutional responses to communications overload are possible, as Meier points out (including expansion in size if the institution can capture more energy to fund growth), but the kind of response most relevant to this discussion is for the institution to redefine its limits inward. An administrative institution, in the context of stress due to communications overload (for example in an evolving system), might respond by allowing certain previously administered transactions to operate autonomously. I suggest that in such cases one of the first areas in which control hierarchies would relinquish control would be in the context of exchange-related institutions. This is because economic institutions will tend, in the absence of administration, to exhibit self-regulation, or at least will tend to operate with a minimum of administrative regulation. This response would free energy and personnel for more urgent problems in the areas of offense and defense, long-distance trade, and adjudication. The arguments presented above, based especially on Skinner's analyses, strongly suggest that economic institutions actually do better with minimal administration because of the built-in incompatabilities of the marketing and administrative central place hierarchies. This kind of response to information overload could explain the transition from redistributive economies (the most highly administered exchange systems) to markets, as well as being a possible explanation for why an administration might relinquish control of existing markets.

CONCLUSIONS

I have argued that traditional theories of cities utilized by anthropologists fail because they cannot adequately account for the cross-cultural variability in the nature of cities, and because they are inadequate for dealing with the dynamic properties of cities and the societies of which they are a part. I have suggested that one avenue anthropologists could take to resolve the shortage of adequate theory is to adopt a regional approach to studies of cities, based on the powerful central place theory of geography. This theory focuses attention on the disposition of central institutions over the landscape. Those places that are the foci of central institution transactions are a society's system of cities and towns—its central-place hierarchy. This theory not only provides the means for explaining some of the cross-cultural variability in systems of cities and towns, but also provides a means for dealing with certain of the dynamic properties of societies. To accomplish this, I argued, the regionally oriented researcher should investigate the spatial relationships of the two basic kinds of central institutions, those that are economic and those that pertain to information processing and decision making. I outlined the basic kinds of articulation between these two genre of central institutions, described the patterns in the central place hierarchy which result from these relationships, and explored some of the implications of these varying patterns for understanding social change. The three patterns explored are the following:

(a) The primate pattern obtains in a region in which the major commercial central place is also the political capital. This center will tend to dominate the region in such a way that the development of secondary centers, as predicted by Christaller's economic location principles, is retarded. This can result in a "dendritic" market pattern on the peripheries, such that regions distant from the main center are poorly serviced economically. This pattern is typically associated with the "dual economies" described by Johnson (23), in which great wealth differentials develop between those populations close to or in the center, and those populations in distant, poorly serviced areas. Such societies, I argued, might exhibit relatively little long-term stability because these wealth differentials could lead to internal conflict, and because poorly serviced peripheral regions might tend to break away politically and economically from the society as a whole.

(b) The second pattern I described is one in which there is more complete development of the commercial central place hierarchy, as predicted by Christaller. The primate pattern is absent, in part, because the political capital is typically "disembedded" from the marketing hierarchy, and so does not artificially distort that hierarchy away from what would be expected on theoretical grounds alone (i.e. following Christaller's K=3 and K=4 locational principles).

(c) Lastly, I discussed the nature of the lower ends of central place hierarchies. The nature and spatial distribution of low-order central places in a society, I argued, depends largely on the extent to which a decision making institution is able to "distort" the economically desirable K=3 and K=4 patterns into the administratively desirable K=7 pattern, in order to more closely regulate and tax rural production. Following the work of Skinner (50) as an example, it is clear that marketing efficiency depends on maintenance of the K=3 or K=4 patterns. Administrative meddling in the marketing hierarchy brings a reduction in marketing efficiency, and therefore, overall declines in productivity of participants in the marketing institution. As a result, I suggest, administrative distortions of commercial central place hierarchies should tend to be short-term, since an administration loses revenues at the same time that it is incurring the added costs of market administration.

I hope this brief, and not nearly complete, exercise in central place theorizing will be an inducement to other anthropologists interested in cities to adopt a regional approach as one method for explaining the variability and dynamic features of systems of cities and towns. Relatively few anthropologists have employed such an approach. The prominent works are those I have already described at length, those of Skinner (48–50), Smith (52), and Crissman (12). To this list I can add the publications of Johnson (24–26), Wright (63), Adams (1), and Adams & Nissen (2), for ancient Greater Mesopotamia; Marcus (31), and Hammond (18) for the ancient lowland Maya area; the publications of participants in the "Valley of Mexico Project" (Blanton 8, Millon 36, Parsons 39, Sanders 45, Wolf 62); as well as Blanton (9) and Kowalewski (27), writing about the ancient Valley of Oaxaca. This small but growing movement, I feel, will prove to be a significant new addition to anthropological studies of cities.

ACKNOWLEDGMENTS

I am grateful for helpful comments received on an earlier version of this paper from Gary Feinman, Greg Johnson, Steve Kowalewski, Susan Lees, John Pfeiffer, John Speth, Donna Taylor, and Paul Wheatley. Responsibility for any errors is my own.

Literature Cited

1. Adams, R. McC. 1965. *Land Behind Baghdad: A History of Settlement on the Diyala Plains.* Univ. Chicago Press
2. Adams, R. McC., Nissen, H. J. 1972. *The Uruk Countryside.* Univ. Chicago Press
3. Arensberg, C. M. 1968. The urban in crosscultural perspective. In *Urban Anthropology: Research Perspectives and Strategies,* ed. E. Eddy, 2:3–15. Proc. South. Anthropol. Soc. Athens: Univ. Georgia Press
4. Berry, B. J. L. 1961. City size distribution and economic development. *Econ. Dev. Cult. Change* 9:573–88
5. Berry, B. J. L. 1967. *Geography of Market Centers and Retail Distribution.* Englewood Cliffs: Prentice-Hall
6. Berry, B. J. L., Garrison, W. L. 1958. Recent developments in central-place theory. *Proc. Reg. Sci. Assoc.* 9:107–20
7. Berry, B. J. L., Pred, A. 1961. *Central Place Studies: A Bibliography of Theory and Applications.* Philadelphia: Reg. Sci. Res. Inst.
8. Blanton, R. E. 1972. *Prehispanic Settlement Patterns of the Ixtapalapa Peninsula Region, Mexico.* University Park: Penn. State Univ. Dep. Anthropol.
9. Blanton, R. E. 1976. The origins of Monte Albán. In *Cultural Change and Continuity,* ed. C. Cleland. New York: Academic
10. Christaller, W. 1933. *Die Zentralen Orte in Suddeutschland.* Transl. C. W. Baskin, 1966. *Central Places in Southern Germany.* Englewood Cliffs: Prentice-Hall
11. Coe, M. D. 1961. Social typology and tropical forest civilizations. *Comp. Stud. Soc. Hist.* 4:65–85
12. Crissman, L. W. 1973. *Town and country: Central place theory and Chinese marketing, with particular reference to southwestern Changhua Hsien, Taiwan.* PhD thesis. Cornell Univ., Ithaca, NY
13. Epstein, A. L. 1967. Urbanization and social change in Africa. *Curr. Anthropol.* 48:275–95
14. Flannery, K. V. 1972. The cultural evolution of civilizations. *Ann. Rev. Ecol. Syst.* 3:399–426
15. Friedmann, J. 1961. Cities in social transformation. *Comp. Stud. Soc. Hist.* 4:86–103
16. Gunawardena, K. 1964. *Service centers in southern Ceylon.* PhD thesis. Univ. Cambridge, England
17. Haggett, P. 1965. *Locational Analysis in Human Geography.* New York: St. Martin's Press
18. Hammond, N. 1972. Locational models and the site of Lubaantún: A classic Maya centre. In *Models in Archaeology,* ed. D. Clarke, 757–800. London: Methuen
19. Hauser, P. M. 1965. Urbanization, an overview. In *The Study of Urbanization,* ed. P. M. Hauser, L. Schnore, p. 12. New York: Wiley
20. Hauser, P. M. 1965. The folk-urban ideal types: Observations on the urban-folk and urban-rural dichotomies as forms of Western ethnocentrism. See Ref. 19, 503–17
21. Hodder, I., Hassall M. 1971. The non-random spacing of Romano-British walled towns. *Man* 6:391–407
22. Jacobs, J. 1969. *The Economy of Cities.* New York: Random House
23. Johnson, E. A. J. 1970. *The Organization of Space in Developing Countries.* Cambridge: Harvard Univ. Press
24. Johnson, G. A. 1972. A test of the utility of central place theory in archaeology. In *Man, Settlement, and Urbanism,* ed. P. J. Ucko, R. Tringham, G. W. Dimbleby, 769–85. London: Duckworth
25. Johnson, G. A. 1973. *Local Exchange and Early State Development in Southwestern Iran.* Anthropol. Pap. 51. Ann Arbor: Univ. Michigan Mus. Anthropol.
26. Johnson, G. A. 1975. Locational analysis and Uruk local exchange systems. In *Ancient Civilization and Trade,* ed. J. A. Sabloff, C. C. Lamberg-Karlovsky, 285–339. Albuquerque: Univ. New Mexico Press
27. Kowalewski, S. 1976. *Prehistoric settlement patterns of the central part of the valley of Oaxaca, Mexico.* PhD. thesis. Univ. Arizona, Tucson, Ariz.
28. Lewis, O. 1951. *Life In a Mexican Village. Tepoztlán Restudied.* Urbana: Univ. Illinois Press
29. Lewis, O. 1965. The folk-urban ideal types: Further observations on the folk-urban continuum and urbanization with special reference to Mexico City. See Ref. 19, 491–503
30. Lösch, A. 1940. *Die räumliche Ordnung der Wirtschaft.* Transl. H.

Woglom, W. F. Stolper, 1954. *The Economics of Location.* New Haven: Yale Univ. Press

31. Marcus, J. 1973. Territorial organization of the Lowland Classic Maya. *Science* 180:911–16
32. Martindale, D. 1958. Prefatory remarks: The theory of the city. In *The City,* M. Weber, 9–62. Transl. D. Martindale, G. Neuwirth, New York: Free Press
33. Maruyama, M. 1963. The second cybernetics: Deviation-amplifying mutual-causal processes. *Am. Sci.* 51:164–79
34. Meier, R. 1962. *A Communications Theory of Urban Growth.* Cambridge: M. I. T. Press
35. Miller, J. G. 1965. Living systems: Basic concepts. *Behav. Sci.* 10:193–257
36. Millon, R. 1973. *Urbanization at Teotihuacán, Vol. I. The Map.* Austin: Univ. Texas Press
37. Moore, K. 1975. The city as context: Context as process. *Urban Anthropol.* 4:17–25
38. Park, R. 1925. The city: Suggestions for the investigation of human behavior in the urban environment. In *The City,* ed. R. Park, E. Burgess, R. McKenzie, pp. 1–46. Univ. Chicago Press
39. Parsons, J. R. 1972. *Prehistoric Settlement Patterns in the Texcoco Region, Mexico.* Mem. 3, Mus. Anthropol., Univ. Michigan. 447 pp.
40. Pirenne, H. 1925. *Medieval Cities: Their Origins and the Revival of Trade,* p. 203. Princeton Univ. Press
41. Redfield, R. 1941. *The Folk Cultures of Yucatan.* Univ. Chicago Press
42. Redfield, R., Singer, M. 1954. The cultural role of cities. *Econ. Dev. Cult. Change* 3:53–73
43. Russell, J. C. 1972. *Medieval Regions and Their Cities,* p. 36. Bloomington: Indiana Univ. Press
44. Sahlins, M. D. 1968. *Tribesmen.* Englewood Cliffs: Prentice-Hall
45. Sanders, W. T. 1965. *Cultural Ecology of the Teotihuacán Valley, Mexico.* University Park: Penn. State Univ. Dep. Anthropol.
46. Service, E. R. 1971. *Primitive Social Organization.* New York: Random House. 2nd ed.
47. Sjoberg, G. 1960. *The Preindustrial City, Past and Present.* Glencoe: Free Press
48. Skinner, G. W. 1964. Marketing and social structure in rural China: Part I. *J. Asian Stud.* 24:3–43
49. Ibid 1965. Marketing and social structure in rural China: Part II, 195–228
50. Ibid. Marketing and social structure in rural China: Part III, 363–99
51. Smith, C. A. 1974. Economics of marketing systems: Models from economic geography. *Ann. Rev. Anthropol.* 3:167–201
52. Smith, C. A. 1975. Examining stratification systems through peasant marketing arrangements: An application of some models from economic geography. *Man* 10:95–122
53. Stafford, H. A. Jr. 1963. The functional bases of small towns. *Econ. Geogr.* 39:165–75
54. Taylor, D. 1975. *Some locational aspects of middle-range hierarchical societies.* PhD. thesis. City Univ. New York, NY
55. Vapnarsky, C. 1969. On rank-size distributions of cities: an ecological approach. *Econ. Dev. Cult. Change,* 17:584–95
56. Wheatley, P. 1963. What the greatness of a city is said to be: Reflections on Sjoberg's "Preindustrial City." *Pac. Viewpoint* 4:163–88
57. Wheatley, P. 1971. *Pivot of the Four Quarters, A Preliminary Inquiry into the Origins and Character of the Ancient Chinese City,* Chicago: Aldine
58. Wheatley, P. 1972. The concept of urbanism. See Ref. 24, 601–37
59. Wirth, L. 1925. A bibliography of the urban community. See Ref. 38, p. 172
60. Wirth, L. 1938. Urbanism as a way of life. *Am. J. Sociol.* 44:1–24
61. Wolf, E. R. 1966. *Peasants,* p. 11. Englewood Cliffs: Prentice-Hall. 116 pp.
62. Wolf, E. R., ed. 1976. *The Valley of Mexico: Studies in Ecology and Society.* Albuquerque: Univ. New Mexico Press
63. Wright, H. T. 1969. *The Administration of Rural Production in an Early Mesopotamian Town.* Anthropol. Pap. 38. Ann Arbor: Univ. Michigan Mus. Anthropol.

Ann. Rev. Anthropol. 1976. 5:265–88
Copyright © 1976 by Annual Reviews Inc. All rights reserved

HUMAN ETHOLOGY

◆ 9580

Robin Fox
Department of Anthropology, Livingston College, Rutgers University,
New Brunswick, New Jersey 08903

Usher Fleising
Department of Anthropology, University of Calgary, Calgary 44, AB, Canada

INTRODUCTION

A variety of developments in the biological and social sciences over the last decade have led to an upsurge of interest in the origins and evolution of human behavior. Since the paradigm for much of this enquiry has been that of classical European ethology, the designation "human ethology" has gained some currency; but other claimants are "biosociology" and "biosocial anthropology" (63). "Social biology" has already been appropriated by eugenics and demography, while "sociobiology" has come to be associated with a particular school of evolutionary genetics (171).

The labels are immaterial. What matters is that across a wide area of the social and natural sciences there has been a revival of interest in the phylogenetic approach to behavior under the aegis of the neo-Darwinian synthesis. The spectacular success of ethology proper under Lorenz and Tinbergen has obviously been influential, but equally influential have been the renaissance of primatology under Washburn, the growing importance of ecology, the advances in molecular biology, endocrinology, and the neurosciences, the new wealth of data on fossil man, and the growing sophistication of models for the evolution of complex genetic systems governing behavior. This has corresponded to a growing interest in the analysis of innate mental properties in the work of transformational grammarians like Chomsky and structuralists like Lévi-Strauss and Piaget.

The essence of the ethological approach is the acceptance of the synthetic theory of evolution as the master paradigm for the analysis of all life processes, including such uniquely human processes as language and culture. Human behavior then, like the behavior of any life form, must be analyzed in terms of its evolution and *patterns of adaptation*. This is of great importance to anthropology as a science, since such a holistic approach can serve to reintegrate physical and cultural anthropology, which have drifted even farther apart as a result of too naive an emphasis on culture as "superorganic" (62).

265

We should stress that the germs of such an approach were always present in anthropology, but a lack of both data and theory on the one hand, and a hostile superorganic environment on the other, left them undeveloped. The early 1960s, however, saw a surge of interest largely initiated by Count's (37) extraordinary paper and by physical anthropologists such as Spuhler (147), Washburn (164), Howell & Bourlière (92), and DeVore (42). Tiger & Fox (152) and Freeman (67), in successive issues of *Man,* called the attention of social anthropologists to the possibilities of the ethological approach. Alland (5) had made an ambitious attempt to reintroduce a Darwinian perspective, and many papers in the volumes edited by Tax (148) testified to the same interest, as did the volume by Roe & Simpson (135). Not all of this was specifically "ethological" in orientation by any means, and many students of the evolution of behavior would undoubtedly reject much of ethology considered as a school of comparative zoology. What there was in common during this period was the intense interest in the possibilities of linking Darwinian theory to the material of physical and cultural anthropology to produce an evolutionary account of human social behavior and culture. By 1970 Callan (29) felt ready to produce an extended criticism of the ethology-anthropology possibilities, and by 1971 Tiger & Fox (153) felt prepared to attempt an ambitious synthesis aimed at the reconversion of the social sciences to the Darwinian mandate.

Anthropology is the most obvious science to serve as the nerve center of this convergent evolution of interest in behavioral phylogeny. While the influence of this approach is being felt in fields such as ecology, sociology, psychiatry, political science ("biopolitics" is now a recognized subdiscipline), medicine, and urban planning, we concentrate here on four areas of development that we judge to be of most immediate interest to anthropologists. Space does not allow us to discuss the important developments in the neurosciences, which deserve a paper of their own.

COMPARATIVE ETHOLOGY

Following our identification of human ethology with evolutionary theory, we can expect a substantial body of material on comparative behavior at the level of the individual, the population, or the species. This expectation derives from Darwin's own contribution to the comparative method (70), and the belief that this is a crucial technique for deriving and testing evolutionary hypotheses.

A survey of the literature reveals, however, a considerable hiatus in studies of comparative behavioral systems. The number of such systematic studies within the mammalian order is particularly disappointing (cf 20). Whether one is interested in convergent or homologous behavior (168), human ethology will remain incomplete unless it directs more of its attention to the study of adaptive significance or *teleonomy* (44, 128, 170) which, as we have argued, is its distinctive characteristic.

Teleonomic studies are two-pronged: they deal with the long-term survival of a pattern, and with the more immediate function of the behavior or behavioral syndrome being analyzed.

Dewsbury (44) outlines three methods in the study of teleonomy: experimental, behavior genetic, and adaptive correlation.

We shall focus on adaptive correlation, because it has been little used and holds much promise, and is the most appropriate for the ethological anthropologist who is interested in analysis at the species level.

Briefly, the method of adaptive correlation involves the comparison of several species on a number of dimensions, e.g. ecological, behavioral, morphological. The idea is ". . . to infer the function of a character from the nature of other characters with which it appears to be consistently associated," (44, p. 150).

Thus Dewsbury (43) classified male mammalian copulatory behavior according to 16 possible patterns in order to determine their functional significance. This work is an excellent example of the use of adaptive correlation in the pursuit of teleonomic problems. His statement about adaptive correlation and copulatory patterns is worth quoting:

> Adaptive correlation entails relative variations in copulatory pattern to other characteristics in reproductive physiology, morphology, social behavior, and ecology. The adaptive significance of the total pattern or reproduction can then be studied. Copulatory patterns cannot profitably be studied in isolation from these other characteristics (pp. 23, 24).

The correlates of copulatory patterns examined thus far have been morphological (for 24 species of the family *Cricetidae*). This is now being extended to ecological and behavioral variables. The correlations of primate (including *Homo sapiens*) copulatory patterns have still to be investigated. From this perspective, Hafez (77) has already collated some of the primary data.

Glickman & Sroges (71) studied curiosity in over 100 species represented in 200–300 animal subjects and showed that variation was related not only to taxonomic position, but to other variables as well, e.g. the type of food eaten and the method of feeding.

Parker (125, 126) studied the manipulative propensity and diversity of ten species of primates and found that the great apes demonstrated a higher degree of behavioral diversity on the indexes used. Parker concludes that "creativity rather than trainability may be the apes' forte."

Alcock (2) reviewed the available information on tool use in animals, detailing the possible origins, transmission, and evolution of this behavior. He argued for the origin of tool use as a modification of a preexisting behavior pattern (some of which may have been performed accidentally) and demonstrated how the pattern once established came under selective pressures.

Dewsbury (44) describes research in comparative psychology which is addressed to the adaptive function of behavior, particularly research relating to learning mechanisms. Bolles (23) related species-specific defense reactions to avoidance learning. Garcia et al (68) relate survival in the rat's habitat to learning with exceptionally long conditioned stimulus-unconditioned stimulus intervals. Glickman & Schiff (72) see reinforcement as related to species-typical responses in adaptation, while Rozin & Kalat (136) and Warren (162) repeat what Lorenz (110) claimed in his book, *Evolution and Modification of Behavior,* i.e. that learning capacities are subjected to selection the same as any other trait. Thus behaviors crucial to the survival of the organism are "easy" to learn. Sex differences in aggression have been related to the ease with which it can be learned by males (79, 90, 151). The learning of aggressive behavior in males, particularly at adolescence, is probably related to their higher levels of testosterone. (An interesting area of cross-specific research would be a study of the onset of adolescence, correlating physiological, anatomical, and behavioral variables.)

Attachment behavior describes the complex of behaviors involved in maintaining the mother's (or caregiver's) proximity to the infant (25). Bowlby described the patterns of attachment for several nonhuman primates, and showed that as one ascends the phylogenetic scale from monkey to ape, the infant displays increased dependence upon the caretaking adult for the maintenance of proximity. He then interpreted infant-typical behaviors—smiling, babbling, crying, grasping, reaching, and orientation movements—as having adaptive significance. Those forces which resulted in longer periods of childhood dependence were balanced by mechanisms which insured the infants' survival.

It has been suggested (100) that the strength of the attachment between mother and offspring is related to the degree of arboreality. A preliminary survey by one of the authors indicates some concurrence. The problem, however, is that although data on primate arboreality are readily available, assessments of the strength of attachment between mother and infant are difficult to operationalize.

Thompson (150), in a very elegant piece, combines adaptive correlation with hypothesis testing to examine his thesis on the convergence of hominid and carnivore behavior. Using taxonomic inclusion as the independent variable, Thompson selected variables dealing with naturalistic behavior of carnivores (3 families, 11 species) and primates (6 families, 15 species including *H. sapiens*) which could be dichotomized on a 2 × 2 table. For example, he looked at food sharing, food storing, cannibalism and surplus killing (whether present or absent), also group defense (male or both sexes) and number of adults feeding one young (mother versus more than one). He concluded that much human behavior does indeed converge with that of the carnivores (cf 98, 142).

The comparative physiology, ecology, and behavior associated with primate feeding and digestion is being investigated by Philip Spaulding at the University of Calgary (personal communication). He is concerned that there is very little information on primate digestive physiology, particular on how this relates to ecology and evolutionary development. In particular he wonders why the human digestive system is so efficiently constructed to handle carbohydrates. What were the selective pressures that produced such a system? Spaulding believes that physical anthropologists have spent too much time on teeth and bones, to the neglect of human physiology, and believes "that there is an evolutionary tale to be told between the teeth and the bowels."

Blurton Jones (20, pp. 85–90) suggests several lines of inquiry that would fuse behavioral, anatomical, and physiological variables using the method of adaptive correlation. There is much information, for example, on mammalian infant and child-care patterns, and outside of Bowlby's work these data have not been collated. Blurton Jones (20, p. 86), citing Orians (123) and Trivers (155) states ". . . that infant care and characteristics of population replacement and reproduction are major influences on the nature of societies." However, Elliott (55), in criticizing Orians who maintained that polygamy was an advantage for males, argued that individual female fitness is critical in explaining the evolution of polygamy and should not be treated as an outcome of different strategies of males and females. One would therefore like to see a compilation of infant care data and the variables with which they are associated.

Barash (12) discusses the importance of the evolutionary development of interspecies recognition as a precurser of social behavior. His research on two "solitary" carnivores, the racoon and the red fox, indicates that neighbors recognize each other (measured under laboratory conditions). Thus Barash suggests that a rudimentary form of social structure is present in these "solitary" species. It would be interesting to extend his study of recognition to a wider range of mammalian species, incorporating the work of Lewis (108) and Eckerman (46) on human infants and the primate material of, for example, Mason (111). Since interspecific patterns tend to resemble intraspecific ones (119), a phylogenetic comparison could indicate more clearly the situations under which social cohesion will tend to evolve from solitariness.

There are other interspecific studies dealing with behavioral and ecological variables which are germane to an understanding of intraspecific behavior patterns (76, 120, 143). For example, interspecific dominance-mediated niche-partitioning is necessarily related to intraspecific aggression, and the former may be related to body size as well (120, 143).

On the theme of body size, Blurton Jones (20, p. 86) would like to see a comparison of the composition of adult breeding groups with sex differences in adult size. He argues ". . . that marked size difference in mammals goes with a high proportion of breeding females to breeding males." This should be tested against Washburn's & McCown's (165) statements about the basic primate anatomy being female with an added male apparatus for aggressive behavior. Geist's (69) research on ungulates may help in sorting some of the variables since he does consider the relationship between body size, ecology, and social evolution. Concerning combat adaptations he concludes that these ". . . are an important non-ecological variable in the social behavior and social organization of ungulates." (p. 217).

Play behavior has been examined cross-specifically (14, 109), and Fagen (59), in reviewing this literature, classifies these studies into functionalist and structuralist approaches to play, and also focuses on the psychological and evolutionary mechanisms associated with play behavior. What is still lacking is a systematic treatment of play along the same lines employed by Dewsbury in his study of mammalian copulatory patterns.

Bischof (16) asks if indeed it is true, as is often expressed in anthropology, that the incest taboo differentiates man from his animal brethren? His comparative study of incest avoidance in mammals is a clear demonstration of a pattern of social behavior that must have been under some kind of selective pressure.

Bischof argues that consistent outbreeding in mammalian reproductive strategies is a logical extension of the selective advantages of biparental reproduction.
Shepher (143a) considers the remarkable data on "spontaneous" incest avoidance and exogamy among kibbutz children to be a case of "negative imprinting"
at a critical period.

In the same volume in which Bischof's material appears, Fox (64), in an
extensive survey of primate social behavior, contends that primate social patterns conform to two basic models: one appears to be based on a principle of
"alliance," and the other conforms to a model based on "descent." The human
innovation, according to Fox, was the fusion of these two systems to produce
"elementary" human kinship system. [This argument is aided by King's (99)
speculations on the origins of band organization.] Fox's paper is part of a larger
argument (61) which attempts to integrate data from primatology and human
evolution in an investigation of the origin of kinship systems.

A critical variable in Bischof's and Fox's argument is the dispersion of males.
Differences in the strength of attachment between mother and male and mother
and female infants could be hypothesized to coincide with different patterns of
male dispersion. Timing of separation is probably also important. There exists
data on ungulates (100) and other animals which could be used to good effect
(28).

Mazur (116) tackled the very difficult task of comparing dominance hierarchies cross-specifically (see also 160), and Edelman & Omark (47) and
Omark, Omark & Edelman (122) conducted cross-cultural studies of dominance
hierarchies in young children.

The concept of dominance, however, has an ambivalent status in ethology.
Measures of dominance are not uniform and although dominance may be viewed
as a relational concept (60, 133), it is probably correct to assign it the status of an
intervening variable which has some effect on group social organization. Recent
studies of dominance hierarchies with nursery school children (59a, 147a) have
also stressed dominance as an intervening variable.

The most promising new departure in the study of rank-ordering has been
Chance's thesis of "attention structure" (32, 33). The basic premise is simple:
that "dominance" can be measured by the relative attention paid by one animal
to another. The evidence, from human and nonhuman sources, has been gathered together in *The Social Structure of Attention* by Chance & Larsen (33a).
Chance has distinguished two modes of attention: hedonic-based on display,
and agonistic-based on threat, and related these to, among other things, the
development of creative intelligence. [For an interesting discussion of the relation between dominance and "prestige," see (13).]

Dealing with a very different set of mechanisms, Snyder (146) developed an
evolutionary theory of dreaming based on a phylogenetic study of REM state
data. Snyder proposed that ". . . the REM state serves a sentinal function,
bringing about brief but periodic awakenings after preparing the organism for
immediate fight or flight" (p. 121).

Allison & Van Twyver (6) studied mammalian sleep patterns and correlated
these with both type of sleeping place and predation. They distinguish "good

sleepers" and "poor sleepers." Good sleepers—e.g. ground squirrel, cat, ma-
caque, man—have secure sleeping places or are predatory. Poor sleepers—e.g.
rabbit, goat, donkey, baboon—are subject to predation at all hours.

Winson (172) has discovered that the theta rythms associated with waking
behavior and REM sleep are species-specific. In other words, animals dream
about "species-typical" behaviors.

Continuing on the theme of comparative mental functions, Medin (118) investigated procedures involved in a comparative study of memory. Warren (161)
advocates increased use of comparative studies to understand the prefrontal
cortex, and we have still to make full advantage of the studies of Lettvin et al
(105), Maturana & Frank (112), and Hubel & Wiesel (93).

Lettvin et al related units of neural firing to specific natural stimuli in the life of
frogs; Maturana & Frank discuss selective responsiveness in pigeons; and
Hubel & Wiesel did the same for amphibians and the cat. Considering our
increased knowledge of primate cognitive functions, both human and nonhuman
(94–96), there is considerable opportunity for relating cognitive studies to natural behavior, especially as this relates to learning. There exist studies of pattern
preference in birds and fish (131) and human infants (138, 166), and there is data
on habitat selection in birds (40, 101, 104). Klopfer & Hailman's study (101), for
instance, showed that the North American finch (*Spizella pesserina*) displays a
preference for features relating to shape of foliage rather than density.

An attempt has also been made to deal with emotions on a comparative basis
(34, 129), and several ideas have been advanced concerning the evolution of the
expression of emotions (51, 78). These studies, of course, derive their inspiration from Darwin's (39) book on the same theme.

The primate literature correlating social behavior with ecology (35, 41, 49) has
not been mentioned because this has been reviewed by Jolly (94a) and Crook
(37a). Also, the field of physical anthropology has fixated on these studies to the
neglect of the kinds of material reviewed above. We feel it is important to
emphasize that physical anthropology has yet to take full advantage of the fact
that ". . . anatomy and physiology are fossilized behavior" (20, p. 85).

Comparative ethology can provide an arena for the interpretation of just such
material, for it has the firm advantage that it is of necessity wedded to a
phylogenetic approach, and can take advantage of the wealth of data existing in
comparative psychology, medicine, zoology, and even physics and biochemistry. It is here that we can expect the strongest thrust in conjunction with
sociobiology (see below) in the direction of a phylogenetic interpretation of
human behavior.

CHILD ETHOLOGY

The transmission of culture has been of central importance to anthropology
since the pioneering work of the culture and personality school in the 1930s. A
good deal of the more sophisticated observation and recording, such as that
developed by the Whitings (167), has much in common with the classical methods of ethological observation (20). What the anthropological approach has

lacked, however, has been ethology's fine-tuned analysis and the cross-specific perspective. Also, the anthropological paradigm sees the child largely as a receiver of culture, while the ethological sees the existence of a dynamic program of interaction between parent and child in which the child is as much an initiator as the parent. The child, as it were, "demands culture," but demands it with a repertoire of behaviors shaped by evolution which, in interaction with the parental responses similarly shaped, provides a framework for cultural acquisition.

We should note that many developmental psychologists who have embraced the techniques of ethology have not maintained a consistent evolutionary perspective, despite persistent reminders that "ethology" without this perspective is not really ethology (*Human Ethology Newsletter,* 1975, Nos. 6 and 9).

Ethological research on children employs a normative-descriptive approach using a natural-history model (18, pp. 10–14; 31) to generate testable hypotheses from the data collected. Smith & Connolly (145, p. 73) summarize the motivations which led them and other psychologists to turn to ethology.

> In summary some characteristics of the early literature on social behavior which limit its value in present-day terms are:
> (1) a prevalent bias in the categories used and situations examined towards behaviors considered desirable or undesirable by teachers and parents;
> (2) uncritical use of categories of a high level of complexity, often defined in motivational terms, with resultant emphasis on high interobserver agreement after considerable training;
> (3) reliance on methods of time sampling, or incident sampling, with a lack of sequential analysis of behavior sequences, or temporal association of behavior clusters in specific situations;
> (4) little interest in looking for explanations of behavior in terms of underlying motivations and immediate environmental influences;
> (5) lack of interspecies perspective.

The picture is not quite this gloomy, and a good deal of child-oriented research from the 1930s that has largely been ignored should, in the estimation of the above authors, be reexamined. However, the biased nature of eliciting techniques, rating scales, and interview data is recognized by ethologists (17, p. 22) who prefer to use a large variety of simple observable features of behavior as raw data.

Following the lead of the animal ethologists, the procedure for child ethologists is to create a list of objectively definable behavioral units and to describe, on the basis of this list, the organization and development of behavior. Ideally this list is an "ethogram," i.e. ". . . the precise catalogue of all behavior patterns of an animal" (48, p. 11). Differences do, however, occur in the number of items included in the lists. Thus Grant (73–75) published a list of 118 items he used in his various studies; Blurton Jones (18) defines 31 behavioral units; McGrew (117) defines 42; and Brannigan & Humphries (26) catalogue 136 units of behavior. Young & Decarie (176) define 52 facial and vocal behaviors for infants; and Young & Wolf (unpublished manuscript) catalogue 40 behavior responses of infants to objects.

The quantitative differences are not discrepancies but result from a different research focus. Brannigan & Humphries list 40 units in the mouth region and specify 7 smiles, while Blurton Jones uses two types (three if one includes "laugh"). The former authors are more concerned with the structure and information function of nonverbal behavior, whereas Blurton Jones's research focuses on the organization of behavioral units within a social setting.

Although it is recognized that the criteria for defining behavioral units are not uniform and can lead to problems of interpretation (10, 17), as long as each element can be objectively defined by motor and structural components, then replication and finer-tuned analysis are more plausible. In fact, ethology has for a long time relied on replication as a test of validity (17; 19, p. 293).

The natural history approach of the ethologist is useful in that it provides a data base from which hypotheses can be generated. The raw data of the ethologist and its generation in the behavioral stream challenges the unitary concepts of developmental and social psychology, e.g. "agression," "attachment," or "anxiety." What kinds of behaviors are we talking about when we use these terms? Why is a given action "aggression" rather than something else?

Sequential and factor analytic techniques (144, 169) are used extensively in animal ethology and these have been applied to human ethology as well. The goal is to identify a group of behaviors for which one can show there are shared causal factors.

For example, Blurton Jones (18) labeled as social the items "point," "give," "receive," "talk," and "smile," which all occurred together. An interesting developmental difference occurred when Blurton Jones looked at the grouping "fixate," "frown," "hit," "push," "take-tug-grab," which he labeled "aggression." These occur together for older children but "take-tug-grab" separates from the others in 2-year-olds. This raises the possibility that taking an object has little to do with aggression (confirmed by 59a). This factor analysis produced for Blurton Jones three principal factors which he labeled:

1. rough and tumble versus work (highest loading for "work")—positive—and "laugh," "run," "jump," "hit at," "wrestle"—negative;

2. aggression (highest loadings for "fixate," "frown," "hit," "push," "take-tug-grab");

3. social (highest loadings for "point," "give," "receive," "talk," "smile").

McGrew (117) investigated several dimensions of early child behavior including agonistic behavior, group formation, dominance, density and social behavior, and periodicity. Concerning the latter, for example, he found when comparing children in the first and fifth day at nursery school that there were significant differences in "immobility," "automanipulation," "glancing," and (total) "looking," but no significant differences for "run," "walk," and "verbalization." There were significant long-term decreases in "immobility," "automanipulation," and (total) "looking."

Connolly & Elliott (36) observed spontaneous tool use in 3 and 5-year-olds, reviewing first the comparative material available on nonhuman primate hand structure and function. They describe in detail the variation in grasps and movements and also their frequency of occurrence. An increase in the tendency to use the right hand is reported, and it is concluded that for this age group the hand is not fully developed in several important respects.

Similarly Young & Wolf (unpublished manuscript) are investigating laterality of behavior and its relation to hemispheric specialization in infancy. Young & Wolf observed infants' (3 and 8 months old) responses to objects and identified 40 "unit behavior responses." These elements are presently being used by these investigators ". . . to determine the evolving relationship of manual specialization, hemispheric specialization, and cognitive (Piagetian) skill." (See also 126.)

Infant-oriented research has blossomed with the shift in perspective to the infant as an active rather than a passive integer in initiating and maintaining social contact (132, 134, 177). Ainsworth (1), Lewis & Rosenblum (107), Anderson (8), Blurton Jones & Leach (21) are among those responsible for detailing the stages of the mother-infant relationship showing how variables such as proximity, smiling, crying, and touching have specific temporal configurations. Kagen (96), Wolf (173, 174), Ambrose (7), and Young & Dècarie (176) have detailed the behavioral inventory available to the infant. Lewis et al (108) and Eckerman, Whatley & Kutz (46) are just beginning to trace the process of peer recognition in one-year-olds, and have already demonstrated that these infants can and do discriminate "friends" from "strangers."

The bulk of the above research, however, concentrates on the developmental side of infant and child behavior. It does not address evolutionary questions, despite the impetus given by John Bowlby (25). Bowlby used the ethological method, but always he maintained a consistent phylogenetic perspective in his explanation of the infant's behavior in terms of its adaptive significance (see above). Freedman's (65, 66) work is also consistent in its evolutionary perspective. Freedman's concern is with *variation* in infant behavior, and his cross-cultural studies demonstrate the lability of behavior at birth and its possible adaptive significance.

Blurton Jones & Konner (20a), and Konner (102, 103) have looked at Zhun/Twa(! Kung) Bushman infants. This work is important because the kind of data gathered are readily accessible for cross-specific comparisons. Konner presents data on the temporal (years) sequence of body contact between mother and child, and gives curves for maternal responsiveness. These are readily comparable with measures collected for nonhuman primates (91).

The specification of variables at the level of analysis used by human ethologists has the advantage of identifying hitherto hidden relationships; in his study of mother-infant behavior, Anderson (8) showed that waving by toddlers signals the onset of interaction rather than farewell. This could certainly not have been predicted by traditional psychological methods. Another example is found in the work of Krebs (cited in 19, p. 282) ". . . who found that children low in the peck-order smiled more when initiating an interaction with high-ranking children than high-rankers when initiating interactions with low. However, smiling in response to smiles is commoner in those high in the peck-order." It is possible that some homologous relationship might exist between situations which elicit the fear grin and similar displays in nonhuman primates, and those situations which evoke human smiling (18, p. 282, for further discussion; also 178).

The use of these sophisticated observational methods not only introduces a new dimension into the study of enculturation, but because of its potential cross-specific reference it establishes a basis for evolutionary analysis. In this perspective we can examine the program of infant-parent interaction, within which cultural transmission takes place, as a dynamic interplay between genetic potentialities and cultural specifics.

FUNCTIONAL ANATOMY

An area of traditional concern for physical anthropologists is the investigation of the functional side of the anatomy and physical structure of primates (cf 121, 157), but the relationship between form and function, previously viewed in static terms, has recently acquired a dynamic aspect in which behavior is a significant variable. It is now apparent that while much bone form is genetically determined, it can be altered during the lifetime of the individual by stressing it during its growth period (15, p. 227). There is evidence that external bone form is influenced by the activities and life-style of an individual; variations in skeletal features between, for example, zoo and natural living animals can be explained as resulting from differential bone response to the exigencies of these environments. Birdsell (15, p. 228) indicates that dental stress (in addition to the angle of the forehead) contributes to the form of brow ridges. Different life histories can apparently shape bone structure.

> Thus squatting facets, or flattened places on the long bones constituting the knee joint, were thought to be characteristic of primitive living men. In fact, they turned out to be the result of hunting men squatting around campfires all of their life and producing the flattened planes through continuous pressure (15, p. 228).

The consequence of this is that we must temper our genetic interpretations of variations in bone structure with considerations of the actual behavior of the individuals being studied. Washburn (163) long ago stressed the importance of adding behavioral considerations to our structural investigations.

In a series of papers, Sarles, (139–141) takes the dynamics of bone plasticity a step farther and suggests, on the basis of work by Enlow (56) and his own unpublished work with Ordean Oyen, that one must consider the dynamics of bone shaping in terms of social interaction; in particular they are interested in "how the face comes to look as it does."

As stated above, functional anatomists now believe that hard tissue does not develop and grow unless it is kept under reasonably constant dynamic tension (a muscular process). Sarles and Oyen therefore believe that speaking (a muscular activity) affects facial and skull formation, which can therefore be seen as results of action as much as physical maturation. This G. H. Mead approach, as Sarles calls it, to the human body (especially the face) leads him to speculations about the development of facial features and expressions. For example, children come to resemble their parents because, in effect, their facial muscular movements mimic those of their caretakers, and "It appears that one tends to 'use' his face much like the people in his family, community, etc." (141). Much of what we do with our faces and bodies is influenced by what others do with their faces and bodies. Franz Boas (22), Sarles notes, found that the skulls and faces of second and third generation immigrants to America were literally changing shape. These observations were left essentially unexplained as physical anthropology went in other directions. The search for fossil bones became intensified; but interpretation of them was as rigid as the bones themselves. If bone is fluid, however, then some of our reconstructed prehistory is open to serious reinterpretation (15; Sarles, in preparation), and comparison of the dynamic interaction of bone, soft tissue, and environment (physical and social) is imperative.

Ekman & Friesen (54) have recently made a breakthrough in the understanding of the relationship between the surface skin and the deeper muscular structures that could contribute significantly to an understanding of the interplay between facial form, structure, and the environmental influences on these. In their search for meaningful units of facial behavior, they have succeeded in developing a facial atlas defined in terms of functional anatomy. Their atlas divides muscular units in terms of their effects on the appearance-change of the face.

This produces a facial ethogram, and one can, on the basis of the precise measurements the atlas allows, ask questions about combinations of muscle units into larger "meaningful units." The lists prepared by human ethologists of "meaningful" facial units are now subject to more intense empirical verification, and one can pursue with renewed vigor the cross-specific work initiated by Darwin (39) and carried on in more detail by Andrew (9), van Hoof (158, 159) and Chevalier-Skolnikoff (34).

The search for homologies in facial expressions (48, p. 480) and ritualization of behaviors occurring on the face are now also subject to more detailed empirical investigation.

Variation in use and nonuse of certain muscle-unit combinations occurs both intra and interculturally (50, 52). Individual variation also occurs in relation to the points of attachment of muscle fibers to underlying facial tissue (53). Given this variation, we have a system that has obviously been under sexual selection pressure if nothing else, and probably still continues to be so.

It should be possible to get a similar atlas for various other primates. Sarles (141) reports that one of his students is working on baboon facial studies, and has developed a technique for dissecting from the inside out, a procedure which preserves the relationship of skin to the underlying structures.

In a piece of work more closely related to traditional physical anthropology, Cartmill (30) claims that the primate structures traditionally associated with adaptation to arboreal locomotion, i.e. grasping extremities and closely apposed eyes, are better explained as structures specialized for the capture of prey on slender supports. Comparing the functional anatomy of sciurids, primates, and the Felidae, Cartmill presents a visual predation hypothesis which challenges the conventional explanations for the development of grasping extremities and stereoscopic vision.

Such an interpretation has obvious bearings on interpreting hominid evolutionary trends. Considering the now abundant data for primate predation (89, 149) and the field observations on the use of the forelimbs in the capture, killing, and dismembering of prey, Cartmill's hypothesis is extremely attractive. Recalling also Errington's (57) statement that predation is a phylogenetically very old behavior, perhaps Ardrey (11) is correct in emphasizing this trait as significant in human social evolution. It is unfortunate that Cartmill chooses not to include the behavioral data on observed primate predation in support of his argument.

It would be possible in this context to review extensively much of the data on human evolution. We have been careful, however, to point out only some possibilities of integrating *behavioral* analysis with the analysis of anatomical and physiological function. (For a survey of some physiological correlates of behavior, see 151.) It is only through such an integration that true ethological interpretation of anatomical data—fossil and contemporary—can be achieved.

SOCIOBIOLOGY

The newly christened discipline of sociobiology attempts to apply principles of evolutionary biology to the problem of the emergence and maintenance of social behavior. It therefore attempts a general theory of social behavior embracing all forms from social amoebas to human communities. If it succeeds as a paradigm, it should provide the explanatory framework within which the data we have discussed can be analyzed.

The recent synthesis by Wilson (171) brings together the work on evolutionary genetics and animal behavior that has gathered force over the last 10 years. It represents an important amalgamation of two trends with long histories that only burgeoned in the 1930s, and which even then did not come together—evolutionary biology in the tradition of Fisher, Wright, and Haldane, and ethology of the classical European school. Wilson's title inevitably recalls Julian Huxley's *Evolution: The Modern Synthesis* (93a), which, while doing much to further a neo-Darwinian approach, did not have enough of the animal-behavior material that would have put flesh on the mathematical bones. Wilson also has the advantage of the work of comparative zoologists and primatologists who are not specifically of the ethological school, plus his own incomparable knowledge of insect societies. He has been able, therefore, to take the concept of behavioral evolution and suggest the actual evolutionary mechanisms by which certain behavioral patterns are selected. He draws on the work of several theorists in particular who have been concerned to reject the notion of *group selection* and return to a modified Darwinian model of *individual selection*.

The problems with group selection—as classically recorded in the works of Keith (97) and Wynne-Edwards (175)—are well known. It is difficult to envisage how traits in individual animals that are held to have evolved for the benefit of the group, population, or species *in the long run,* can have evolved in the first place. It would require both extraordinary genetic prescience and an indifference to Darwinian fitness measured in terms of the number of offspring an individual leaves. The actual mechanisms by which it might work have never been demonstrated (114, 170).

On the other hand, proponents of the classical Darwinian model have been faced with the paradox of seemingly "altruistic" behavior which clearly benefits the group, but which apparently reduces the fitness of the individual animal. Thus the self-sacrificing behavior of bees, the existence of sterile castes in insects, a host of warning behaviors in birds and animals, and the willingness of mammalian parents to sacrifice themselves for their young have been hard to explain fully in terms of individual fitness.

It was Hamilton (80) who first proposed a solution to the problem, although Maynard Smith (113) actually coined the term *kin selection* (see also Hamilton, 81–88). The point was really quite simple: if one took the individual's *genes* rather than the individual *organism* as the unit of selection—which is perfectly correct in measuring its fitness—then there were clearly cases where the individual would increase its fitness more by protecting other individuals that carried replicas of its genes than by protecting itself and possibly losing the relatives. The obvious case is that of a parent with several viable offspring, all themselves likely to have offspring, all of which would carry replicas of the parental genes. Kin selection is then an extension of this principle to an understanding of altruistic acts among related organisms. Hamilton expressed this in the now famous formula $k = 1/r$, where k is the ratio of gain to loss in fitness resulting from the altruism, and r is the relatedness of the two individuals measured by the fraction of genes they share. The degree of relatedness of A to B, the benefit B would derive, and the relative magnitude of the cost to A would together determine the likelihood of A acting altruistically toward B.

This led Hamilton to introduce a modification of the concept of reproductive fitness which he has termed *inclusive fitness:* the individual's "personal fitness" (the number of offspring he leaves), and also his effects on the fitness of his neighbors (the number of offspring they leave) multiplied by the fraction of his relatedness to them. Thus it measures fitness in terms of an individual's *total effect on the gene pool,* both directly and indirectly. In short, an individual can, by acting to his own detriment, actually increase his inclusive fitness by helping to preserve the genes of others who share genetic relatedness with him.

The factors favoring kin selection mechanisms in a population appear to be: long lifetime, low dispersal rate, and high mutual dependence. Since what ultimately counts in measuring fitness is the totality of the individual's genes in the pool, this model makes perfect sense of "altruism" without recourse to group selection arguments.

It leaves unexplained, however, the paradox of altruistic acts directed towards nonrelatives and even towards members of other species. Trivers (154) expanded the idea to apply beyond kin in what he called *reciprocal altruism.* In kin selection, the altruist does not act with any expectation of return: the "return" is the preservation of its gene replicas. If the individuals are only slightly related, however, or even totally unrelated, altruism will most likely occur when the individual can expect, at some time in the future, an altruistic act in return. If the cost to the altruist is relatively low, if the individual in distress is well known, if interactions are frequent, and if the population at large is exposed to the risk, then the probability of an altruistic act is increased. Again, it is the altruistic individual's fitness that is increased by the act, but there is more of a real gamble involved than in kin selection. The difference is one of degree, however, with the cost-benefit ratio looming larger in the case of reciprocal altruism.

Triver's main problem was with the possibility of cheating in systems where "altruistic" genes were inclined to spread. Without some checks, it would seem, nonaltruists ("cheaters") could be expected to increase at the expense of altruists. Clearly there would be disaster if they succeeded altogether, since the population would consist entirely of takers and no givers. But nevertheless the cheaters are at a certain parasitical advantage unless controlled. Human populations, as they grew larger in the course of evolution, were particularly open to cheating. This is a concomitant of humans being the most highly developed species as regards reciprocal altruism.

It is Trivers' analysis of the psychological mechanisms which evolved to support reciprocal altruism and control cheating that takes us from the theoretical base for altruism and the animal examples into the realms of human behavior. In Trivers' own words: ". . . friendship, dislike, moralistic aggression, gratitude, sympathy, trust, suspicion, trustworthiness, aspects of guilt, and some forms of dishonesty and hypocrisy, can be explained as important adaptations to regulate the altruistic system." For example, "moralistic aggression" against a cheater can be seen as having a double tendency; on the one hand it prevents the altruist from continuing altruism in the absence of reciprocity simply for his own emotional reward, and on the other it intimidates the cheater. The other emotions on the list, many of which when expressed seem out of all proportion to the acts provoking them, are viewed as part of a biological repertoire evolved to handle an altruistic species given to reciprocity. They can, of course, be much modified by local circumstances. Indeed, *behavioral plasticity* is an important outcome of just such an evolutionary system.

One of Trivers' more far-reaching conclusions is of great importance for the reintegration of physical and cultural anthropology: "Given the psychological and cognitive complexity the system rapidly acquires, one may wonder to what extent the importance of altriusm in human evolution set up a selection pressure for psychological and cognitive powers which partly contributed to the large increase in hominid brain size during the pleistocene." Many writers have held that increasing sociocultural complexity exerted such a selection pressure, but few have been very specific about the content. Trivers opens up an important new dimension in this respect. Also his stress on *reciprocity* should interest those social anthropologists who find inspiration in the work of Marcel Mauss and the extension of his theories by Lévi-Strauss (106), Tiger and Fox (153, chap. 5), and others. Mauss would have acknowledged readily that he was dealing with deep-rooted human tendencies, and we should be grateful to the sociobiologists for showing how these might have evolved.

Further extensions of the Hamilton-Trivers arguments, both by the principals and others, have taken two forms: theoretical modifications of the model, and applications both to species not considered in the original formulations and to man.

For example, Darlington (38) proposed a nonmathematical model for the evolution of altruism that reintroduced the principle of group selection. But by "group selection" in this context he in effect means *differential extinction* of populations already formed by individual selection. This could lead to rapid shifts in gene frequencies, and, assuming that relatively nonaltruistic populations suffer extinction (because of their failure to cooperate internally), can aid in the spread of altruistic genes. A similar point is made by Wilson (171), reviving the Darwin-Keith hypothesis of genocide and genetic absorption as agents of rapid evolution. This would be a more intensive version of the "Sewall Wright effect," in which relatively inbred populations occasionally exchange genes, causing rapid change in frequencies. The difference is that with genocide and the absorption of perhaps some of the females of the destroyed group, the incidents need only be infrequent to have the same dynamic effect. (For an example of an ongoing process of this kind see 30a.)

Since altruism will evolve more rapidly the greater the relatedness of individuals in a group, this model would suggest that self-sacrifice and xenophobic aggression are two sides of the same evolutionary coin, certainly a familiar enough picture in human history. Hamilton (88) extends this argument, in particular dealing with problems of migration and their effects. Eshel (58) has also stressed low demographic mobility, but as promoting the *neighbor effect:* the reduction of the frequency of *nonaltruists*. This is interesting since most explanations have dealt with factors increasing the number of altruists. Boorman & Levitt (24) have taken the argument beyond altruism to "sociality" in general, although this social cooperation is in essence dependent on altruism itself. They postulate a "threshold effect": once the threshold is reached, cooperative genes "explode" and fixate rapidly. They feel this is especially applicable to groups of cooperatively hunting carnivores, and hence relevant to the evolution of human behavior. (It also ties in with Trivers' point quoted earlier.) Orlove (124) proposed a model of kin selection not requiring coefficients of relationship, and Brown (27) put forward a three-stage development of altruism in jays which may well be a general model. It involved an initial (or "K") stage of high competitiveness, moved to increasing kin selection with the development of high relatedness, and ended with "kin-group" selection, in which the successful altruistic populations succeeded better than the others. Again, high extragroup aggression in this model is a correlate of high intragroup unselfishness.

Eberhard (45) has worked out a model that takes care of the seemingly awkward case of altruism by descendants and even very distantly related individuals. She introduces the idea of "subordinate" behavior—so spectacular in the primates—as a form of altruism in which the subordinate is a reproductively inferior but related individual to the dominant. There is always a precarious balance, it seems, between selection for selfishness on the one hand and altruism on the other, the arbiter being inclusive fitness.

For example, Trivers, in a series of papers, has developed his own ideas further with particular reference to *parental investment* and *parent-offspring conflict* (155, 156). The interests of parents and children do not necessarily totally harmonize, and conflict can develop over the investment of time and effort by the parent. Parents wish to spread the effort among all offspring as a rule, while each offspring wishes to monopolize the parental effort. The result is both inter-generational strife and sibling rivalry. (This represents a framework in which the child ethologists might examine their data.) Trivers also explores differential *reproductive strategies*. Males and females in sexually reproducing species must of necessity develop different strategies, especially where births are limited and maturation delayed. A female can improve her inclusive fitness best by careful nurture of her own young and those of related females; a male does this by spreading his genes as widely as possible, while preventing the females he controls from accepting the genes of other males (see the argument in 55).

The "cost-benefit" analysis mentioned earlier has been developed into a theory of aggressive conflict by such analysts as Parker (127), Maynard Smith & Price (115), and Popp & DeVore (130). Here again the cost or gain in inclusive fitness becomes the measure of the payoff to the combatants in escalating or de-escalating a conflict.

Generous attempts to weld this kind of material into a general theory of the evolution of aggression and reciprocity in humans have been made by Alexander (3, 4). He ingeniously correlates Sahlins' (137) theories of human reciprocity with those of the sociobiologists, and shows how aspects of human kinship systems such as polyandry and the role of the mother's brother can be understood from the viewpoint of kin selection. Where "confidence of paternity" is low, it pays a brother, in terms of Trivers' reproductive strategies, to invest in the children of his sister whose relatedness is high and 100% certain. "Nepotism" in this context comes to have far-reaching significance.

Thus Fox (60) and Tiger & Fox (153, chap. 3) have pointed out that crucial to an understanding of human kinship systems is the separation of the conjugal (husband-wife) bond and the consanguineous (brother-sister) bond, and the employment of *either* for "parental" purposes. Sociobiology may well go a long way towards telling us why *this* potentiality (as opposed to the oversimplified "pair bond," for example) has evolved. Fox has contrasted the patrilineal and matrilineal "strategies" in human kinship systems as "gaining control over a wife" as opposed to "hanging onto the sister"—and ultimately controlling the offspring of one or the other (60). It is easy to see how kin selection, with its peculiarly human components, can account for the evolution of these tendencies.

Even from this incomplete survey we can see that numerous issues in the study of human systems of kinship and exchange can be looked at afresh from the synthesizing perspective of sociobiology, to say nothing of aggression, cooperation, xenophobia, migration, justice, cheating, morality, genocide, and sibling rivalry. This is going to take better communication between anthropologists and biologists, but the signs are promising. Ultimately, anthropologists must work out a way to integrate their data from cultural and physical anthropology with that from animal behavior, neuroscience and comparative psychology, within the broadly "ethological" framework we have described. This would not be to constitute yet another unnecessary subdiscipline, but to reconstitute anthropology itself, and return to it its distinctiveness and force among the sciences.

ACKNOWLEDGMENTS

This cooperative effort was made possible by a grant from the Harry Frank Guggenheim Foundation. We should like also to acknowledge the research assistance of Jay Callen.

Literature Cited

1. Ainsworth, M. D. S. 1973. The development of infant-mother attachment. In *Review of Child Development Research*, ed. B. M. Caldwell, H. N. Ricciuti, 3:1–94. Univ. Chicago Press
2. Alcock, J. 1972. The evolution of the use of tools by feeding animals. *Evolution* 26:464–73
3. Alexander, R. D. 1974. The evolution of social behavior. *Ann. Rev. Ecol. Syst.* 5:325–83
4. Alexander, R. D. 1975. The search for a general theory of behavior. *Behav. Sci.* 20:77–100
5. Alland, A. 1967. *Evolution and Human Behavior*. New York: Nat. Hist. Press
6. Allison, T., Van Twyver, H. B. 1970. The evolution of sleep. *Nat. Hist.* 79 (2):56–65
7. Ambrose, J. A. 1961. The development of smiling response in early infancy. In *Determinants of Infant Behavior*, Vol. I, ed. B. M. Foss. New York: Methuen
8. Anderson, J. W. 1972. Attachment behavior out of doors. In *Ethological Studies of Child Behavior*, ed. N. G. Blurton Jones, 199–216. Cambridge Univ. Press
9. Andrew, R. J. 1963. Evolution of facial expression. *Science* 142:1034–41
10. Andrew, R. J. 1972. The information potentially available in mammal displays. In *Nonverbal Communication*, ed. R. A. Hinde, 179–205. Cambridge Univ. Press
11. Ardrey, R. 1966. *The Territorial Imperative*. New York: Dell
12. Barash, D. P. 1974. Neighbor recognition in two "solitary" carnivores: the racoon (*Procyon lotor*) and the red fox (*Vulpes fulva*). *Science* 185:794–96
13. Barkow, J. H. 1975. Prestige and culture: a biosocial interpretation. *Curr. Anthropol.* 16:553–72
14. Bekoff, M. 1972. The development of social interaction, play and metacommunication in mammals: an ethological perspective. *Q. Rev. Biol.* 47:412–34
15. Birdsell, J. B. 1975. *Human Evolution: An Introduction to the New Physical Anthropology*. Chicago: Rand McNally. 2nd ed.
16. Bischof, N. 1975. Comparative ethology of incest avoidance. See Ref. 63, 37–68
17. Blurton Jones, N. G. 1972. Characteristics of ethological studies of human behavior. See Ref. 8, 3–36
18. Ibid. Categories of child-child interaction, 97–128
19. Blurton Jones, N. G. 1972. Nonverbal communication in children. See Ref. 10, 271–96
20. Blurton Jones, N. G. 1975. Ethology, anthropology and childhood. See Ref. 63, 69–92

20a. Blurton Jones, N. G., Konner, M. J. 1973. Sex differences in behavior of London and Bushman children. In *Comparative Ecology and Behavior of Primates*, ed. R. P. Michael, J. H. Crook, 689–750. New York: Academic

21. Blurton Jones, N. G., Leach, G. M. 1972. Behaviour of children and their mothers at separation and greeting. See Ref. 8, 217–48

22. Boas, F. 1931. Changes in bodily form of descendants of immigrants. In *Source Book in Anthropology*, ed. A. L. Kroeber, T. T. Waterman. New York: Harcourt, Brace

23. Bolles, R. C. 1970. Species-specific defense reaction and avoidance learning. *Psychol. Rev.* 77:32–48

24. Boorman, S. A., Levitt, P. R. 1973. A frequency-dependent natural selection model for the evolution of social cooperation networks. *Proc. Natl. Acad. Sci. USA* 70:187–89

25. Bowlby, J. 1969. *Attachment and Loss: Attachment*, Vol. I. New York: Basic Books

26. Brannigan, C. R., Humphries, D. A. 1972. Human non-verbal behaviour, a means of communication. See Ref. 8, 37–64

27. Brown, J. L. 1974. Alternate routes to sociality in jays—with a theory for the evolution of altruism and communal breeding. *Am. Zool.* 14:63–80

28. Brown, J. L., Orians, G. H. 1970. Spacing patterns in mobile animals. *Ann. Rev. Ecol. Syst.* 1:239–62

29. Callan, H. 1970. *Ethology and Society: Towards an Anthropological View*. Oxford: Clarendon

30. Cartmill, M. 1974. Rethinking primate origins. *Science* 184:436–43

30a. Chagnon, N. A., Neel, J. V., Weitkamp, L., Gershowitz, H., Ayres, M. 1975. The influence of cultural factors on the demography and pattern of gene flow from the Makiritare to the Yanomama Indians. In *Man and Nature*, ed. F. S. Hulse, 287–301. New York: Random House

31. Chance, M. R. A. 1969. The study of social behavior in subhuman primates. In *Psychiatry in a Changing Society*, ed. S. H. Foulkes, G. S. Prince. London: Tavistock

32. Chance, M. R. A. 1975. Social cohesion and the structure of attention. See Ref. 63, 93–114

33. Chance, M. R. A., Jolly, C. J. 1970. *Social Groups of Monkeys, Apes and Men*. New York: Dutton

33a. Chance, M. R. A., Larsen, R. 1976. *The Social Structure of Attention*. New York: Wiley

34. Chevalier-Skolnikoff, S. 1973. Facial expression of emotion in nonhuman primates. See Ref. 51, 11–90

35. Clutton-Brock, T. H. 1974. Primate social organization and ecology. *Nature* 150:539

36. Connolly, K., Elliott, J. 1972. The evolution and ontogeny of hand function. See Ref. 8, 329–84

37. Count, E. W. 1958. The biological basis of human sociality. *Am. Anthropol.* 60:1049–85

37a. Crook, J. H. 1975. *Social Systems and Evolutionary Ecology*. New York: Macmillan

38. Darlington, P. J. Jr. 1972. Nonmathematical models for evolution of altruism, and for group selection. *Proc. Natl. Acad. Sci. USA* 69:293–97

39. Darwin, C. 1872. *The Expression of Emotions in Man and in Animals*. New York: Appleton. Reprinted Univ. Chicago Press, 1965

40. Davis, D. E., Ed. 1974. *Behavior as an Ecological Factor*. Stroudsburg, Pa: Dowden, Hutchinson & Ross

41. Denham, W. W. 1971. Energy relations and some basic properties of primate social organization. *Am. Anthropol.* 73:77–95

42. DeVore, I., Ed. 1965. *Primate Behavior. Field Studies of Monkeys and Apes*. New York: Holt, Rinehart & Winston

43. Dewsbury, D. A. 1972. Patterns of copulatory behavior in male mammals. *Q. Rev. Biol.* 47:1–33

44. Dewsbury, D. A. 1973. Comparative psychologists and their quest for uniformity. *Ann. NY Acad. Sci.* 223:147–67

45. Eberhard, M. J. W. 1975. The evolution of social behavior by kin selection. *Q. Rev. Biol.* 50:1–33

46. Eckerman, C., Whatley, J., Kutz, S. 1975. Growth of social play with peers during the second year of life. *Dev. Psychol.* 11:42–49

47. Edelman, M. S., Omark, D. R. 1973. Dominance hierarchies in young children. *Soc. Sci. Inform.* 12:103–10

48. Eibl-Eibesfeldt, I. 1975. *Ethology: The Biology of Behavior*. New

York: Holt, Rinehart & Winston. 2nd ed.

49. Eisenberg, J. F., Muckenhirn, N. A., Rudran, R. 1972. The relation between ecology and social structure in primates. *Science* 176:863–74

50. Ekman, P. 1971. Universals and cultural differences in facial expressions of emotion. *Nebr. Symp. Motiv.* 1970:107–284

51. Ekman, P., Ed. 1973. *Darwin and Facial Expression.* New York: Academic

52. Ibid. Cross-cultural studies of facial expression, 169–222

53. Ekman, P. 1975. *Facial Atlas: Measuring Facial Muscular Expression.* Presented at 3rd Int. Human Ethol. Workshop, Sheffield, England

54. Ekman, P., Friesen, W. V. 1975. *Unmasking the Face.* Englewood Cliffs, NJ: Prentice-Hall

55. Elliott, P. F. 1975. Longevity and the evolution of polygamy. *Am. Nat.* 100:281–87

56. Enlow, D. H. 1968. *The Human Face.* New York: Harper & Row

57. Errington, P. 1967. *Of Predation and Life.* Ames: Iowa State Univ. Press

58. Eshel, I. 1972. On the neighbor effect and the evolution of altruistic traits. *Theor. Popul. Biol.* 3:258–77

59. Fagen, R. 1974. Selective and evolutionary aspects of animal play. *Am. Nat.* 108:850–58

59a. Fleising, U. 1976. *Sequential analysis of interpersonal behavior and the determination of dominance hierarchies: the organization of social interaction in preschool children.* PhD thesis. Rutgers Univ., New Brunswick, NJ

60. Fox, R. 1967. *Kinship and Marriage: An Anthropological Perspective.* London and Baltimore: Penguin Books

61. Fox, R. 1972. Alliance and constraint: sexual selection in the evolution of human kinship systems. In *Sexual Selection and the Descent of Man, 1871–1971,* ed. B. Campbell, 282–331. Chicago: Aldine

62. Fox, R. 1974. *Encounter with Anthropology.* New York: Harcourt, Brace & Jovanovich

63. Fox, R., Ed. 1975. *Biosocial Anthropology.* London: Malaby Press; New York: Halsted Press

64. Ibid. Primate kin and human kinship, 9–36

65. Freedman, D. G. 1971. An evolutionary approach to research on the life cycle. *Hum. Dev.* 14:87

66. Freedman, D. G. 1974. *Human Infancy: An Evolutionary Perspective.* Hillsdale, NJ: Erlbaum

67. Freeman, D. 1966. Social anthropology and the scientific study of human behaviour. *Man: J. R. Anthropol. Inst.* 1:330–42

68. Garcia, J., Ervin, F. R., Koelling, R. A. 1966. Learning with prolonged delay of reinforcement. *Psychon. Sci.* 5:121–22

69. Geist, V. 1974. On the relationship of social evolution and ecology in ungulates. *Am. Zool.* 14:205–20

70. Ghiselin, M. T. 1969. *The Triumph of the Darwinian Method.* Berkeley: Univ. Calif. Press

71. Glickman, S. E., Sroges, R. W. 1966. Curiosity in zoo animals. *Behaviour* 26:151–88

72. Glickman, S. E., Schiff, B. B. 1967. A biological theory of reinforcement. *Psychol. Rev.* 74:81–109

73. Grant, E. C. 1965. *An Ethological Description of Some Schizophrenic Patterns of Behavior.* Leeds Symp. Behav. Disorders

74. Grant, E. C. 1968. An ethological description of non-verbal behavior during interviews. *Br. J. Med. Psychol.* 41:177–84

75. Grant, E. C. 1969. Human facial expression. *Man* 4:525–36

76. Grant, P. R. 1972. Interspecific competition among rodents. *Ann. Rev. Ecol. Syst.* 3:79–106

77. Hafez, E. S. E. 1971. *Comparative Reproduction of Nonhuman Primates.* Springfield, Ill: Thomas

78. Hamburg, D. A. 1963. Emotions in the perspective of human evolution. In *Expression of the Emotions in Man,* ed. D. Knapp, 300–17. New York: Int. Univ. Press

79. Hamburg, D. A. 1974. Ethological perspectives on human aggressive behaviour. In *Ethology and Psychiatry,* ed. N. F. White, 209–19. Univ. Toronto Press

80. Hamilton, W. D. 1963. The evolution of altruistic behavior. *Am. Nat.* 97:354–56

81. Hamilton, W. D. 1964. The genetical evolution of social behavior. *J. Theor. Biol.* 7:1–52

82. Ibid 1966. The moulding of senescence by natural selection. 12:12–45

83. Hamilton, W. D. 1967. Extraordinary sex ratios. *Science* 156:477–89
84. Hamilton, W. D. 1970. Selfish and spiteful behaviour in an evolutionary model. *Nature* 228: 1218–20
85. Hamilton, W. D. 1971. Geometry for the selfish herd. *J. Theor. Biol.* 31:295–311
86. Hamilton, W. D. 1971. Selection of selfish and altruistic behavior in some extreme models. In *Man and Beast: Comparative Social Behavior,* ed. J. F. Eisenberg, W. S. Dillon, 57–91. Washington DC: Smithsonian Press
87. Hamilton, W. D. 1972. Altruism and related phenomena, mainly in social insects. *Ann. Rev. Ecol. Syst.* 3:193–232
88. Hamilton, W. D. 1975. Innate social aptitudes of man: an approach from evolutionary genetics. See Ref. 63, 131–55
89. Harding, R. S. O. 1973. Predation by a troop of olive baboons (*Papio anubis*). *Am. J. Phys. Anthropol.* 38:587–92
90. Hinde, R. A. 1974. *Biological Bases of Human Social Behaviour.* New York: McGraw Hill
91. Hinde, R. A., Spencer-Booth, Y. 1968. The study of mother-infant interaction in captive group-living rhesus monkeys. *Proc. R. Soc. B.* 169:177–201
92. Howell, F. C., Bourlière, F., Eds. 1964. *African Ecology and Human Evolution.* Chicago: Aldine
93. Hubel, D. H., Wiesel, T. N. 1965. Receptive fields and functional architecture in two non-striate visual areas of the cat. *J. Neurophysiol.* 28:229–89
93a. Huxley, J. 1942. *Evolution: The Modern Synthesis.* New York: Harper
94. Jarrard, L. E., Ed. 1971. *Cognitive Processes of Nonhuman Primates.* New York: Academic
94a. Jolly, A. 1972. *The Evolution of Primate Behavior.* New York: Macmillan
95. Kagen, J. 1970. The determinants of attention in the infant. *Am. Sci.* 58:199–306
96. Kagen, J. 1971. *Change and Continuity in Infancy.* New York: Wiley
97. Keith, A. 1948. *A New Theory of Human Evolution.* London: Watts
98. King, G. E. 1976. Society and territory in human evolution. *J. Hum. Evol.*
99. King, G. E. 1975. Socioterritorial units among carnivores and early hominids. *J. Anthropol. Res.* 31:69–87
100. Klopfer, P. H. 1962. *Behavioral Aspects of Ecology.* Englewood Cliffs, NJ: Prentice Hall
101. Klopfer, P. H., Hailman, J. P. 1965. Habitat selection in birds. In *Advances in the Study of Behavior,* ed. D. S. Lehrman, R. A. Hinde, E. Shaw, 279–303. New York: Academic
102. Konner, M. J. 1972. Aspects of the developmental ethology of a foraging people. See Ref. 8, 285–304
103. Konner, M. J. 1976. Maternal care, infant behavior and development among the Zhun/twa (!Kung) Bushmen. In *Studies of Bushman Hunter-Gatherers,* ed. R. Lee. Cambridge, Mass.: Harvard Univ. Press
104. Lack, D. 1937. The psychological factor in bird distribution. *Br. Birds* 31:130–36
105. Lettvin, J. Y., Maturana, H. R., McCulloch, W. S., Pitts, W. H. 1959. What the frog's eye tells the frog's brain. *Proc. Inst. Radio Eng.* 47:19–40
106. Lévi-Strauss, C. 1949. *Les structures élémentaires de la parenté.* Paris: P.U.P.
107. Lewis, M., Rosenblum, L., Eds. 1974. *The Effect of the Infant on its Caregiver.* New York: Wiley
108. Lewis, M., Young, G., Brooks, J., Michelson, L. 1976. The beginning of friendship. In *Friendship and Peer Relations: The Origins of Behavior,* Vol. 3, ed. M. Lewis, L. Rosenblum. New York: Wiley
109. Loizos, C. 1966. Play behaviour in higher primates: a review. In *Primate Ethology,* ed. D. Morris, 176–218. New York: Doubleday
110. Lorenz, K. 1965. *Evolution and Modification of Behavior.* Univ. Chicago Press
111. Mason, W. A. 1975. Comparative studies of social behavior in *Callicebus* and *Saimiri:* behavior of male-female pairs. *Folia Primatol.* 22:113–23
112. Maturana, H. R., Frank, S. 1963. Directional movement and edge detectors in the pigeon retina. *Science* 142:977–79
113. Maynard Smith, J. 1964. Kin selec-

tion and group selection. *Nature* 201:1145–47

114. Maynard Smith, J. 1966. *The Theory of Evolution*. London: Penguin Books

115. Maynard Smith, J., Price, G. R. 1973. The logic of animal conflict. *Nature* 246:15–18

116. Mazur, A. 1973. A cross-species comparison of status in small established groups. *Am. Sociol. Rev.* 38:513–30

117. McGrew, W. 1972. *An Ethological Study of Children's Behavior*. New York: Academic

118. Medin, D. L. 1974. The comparative study of memory. *J. Hum. Evol.* 3:455–63

119. Miller, R. S. 1967. Pattern and process in competition. *Adv. Ecol. Res.* 4:1–74

120. Morse, D. H. 1974. Niche breadth as a function of social dominance. *Am. Nat.* 108:818–30

121. Napier, J. R. 1966. Functional aspects of the anatomy of the hand. In *The Hand: Clinical Surgery 7*, ed. R. G. Pulvertaft. London: Butterworths

122. Omark, D. R., Omark, M., Edelman, M. S. 1976. Formation of dominance hierarchies in young children: action and perception. In *Psychological Anthropology*, ed. T. Williams. The Hague: Mouton

123. Orians, G. 1969. On the evolution of mating systems in birds and mammals. *Am. Nat.* 103:589–603

124. Orlove, M. J. 1975. A model of kin selection not invoking coefficients of relationship. *J. Theor. Biol.* 49; 289–310

125. Parker, C. E. 1974. Behavioral diversity in ten species of nonhuman primates. *J. Comp. Physiol. Psychol.* 87:930–37

126. Parker, C. E. 1974. The antecedents of man the manipulator. *J. Hum. Evol.* 3:493–500

127. Parker, G. A. 1974. Assessment strategy and the evolution of fighting behavior. *J. Theor. Biol.* 47:223–43

128. Pittendrigh, C. S. 1958. Adaptation, natural selection, and behavior. In *Behavior and Evolution*, ed. A. Roe, G. G. Simpson, 390–416. New Haven: Yale Univ. Press

129. Plutchik, R. 1970. Emotions, evolution and adaptive process. In *Feelings and Emotions: Loyola*

Symposium. Personality and Psychopathology Ser., ed. M. B. Arnold, 7:3–24. New York: Academic

130. Popp, J. L., DeVore, I. n.d. *Aggressive competition and social dominance theory*. Presented at 62nd Burg-Wartenstein Symp., Wenner-Gren Found.

131. Rensch, B. 1958. Die Wirksamkeitt ästhetischer Faktoren bei Wirbeltieren. In *Z. Tierpsychol.* 15:447–61

132. Rheingold, H. L. 1969. The social and socializing infant. In *Handbook of Socialization Theory and Research*, ed. D. A. Goslin. New York: Rand McNally

133. Richards, M. P. M. 1971. Social interaction in the first weeks of human life. *Psychiatr. Neurol. Neurochir.* 74:35–42

134. Richards, M. P. M., Bernal, J. F. 1972. An observational study of mother-infant interaction. See Ref. 8, 179–99

135. Roe, A., Simpson, G. G., Eds. 1958. *Behavior and Evolution*. New Haven: Yale Univ. Press

136. Rozin, P., Kalat, J. W. 1971. Specific hungers and poison avoidance as adaptive specializations of learning. *Psychol. Rev.* 78:459–86

137. Sahlins, M. D. 1965. On the sociology of primitive exchange. In *The Relevance of Models for Social Anthropology*, ed. M. Banton. London: Tavistock

138. Salapatek, P. 1968. Visual scanning by the human newborn. *J. Comp. Physiol. Psychol.* 66:247–58

139. Sarles, H. 1972. *The dynamics of facial expression*. Presented at ann. meet. Int. Assoc. Dental Res., Las Vegas, Nev.

140. Sarles, H. 1973. *A human ethological approach to communication*. Presented at 9th Int. Congr. Anthropol. Ethnol. Sci.

141. Sarles, H. 1974. Facial expression and body movement. In *Current Trends in Linguistics*, ed. T. Sebeok, 12:297–310. The Hague: Mouton

142. Schaller, G. B., Lowther, G. R. 1969. The relevance of carnivore behavior to the study of early hominids. *Southwest. J. Anthropol.* 25:307–41

143. Schoener, T. W. 1974. Resource partitioning in ecological communities. *Science* 185:27–39

143a. Shepher, J. 1971. *Voluntary im-*

position of incest and exogamic restrictions in second generation kibbutz adults. PhD thesis. Rutgers Univ., New Brunswick, NJ

144. Slater, P. J. B. 1973. Describing sequences of behavior. In *Perspectives in Ethology*, ed. P. Klopfer, P. P. G. Bateson. New York: Plenum

145. Smith, P. K., Connolly, K. 1972. Patterns of play and social interaction in pre-school children. See Ref. 8, 65–96

146. Snyder, F. 1966. Toward an evolutionary theory of dreaming. *Am. J. Psychiatry* 123:121–42

147. Spuhler, J. N., Ed. 1959. *The Evolution of Man's Capacity for Culture*. Detroit: Wayne State Univ. Press

147a. Strayer, F. F., Strayer, J. 1975. *An ethological analysis of dominance relations among young children*. Presented at biennial meet. SRCD, Denver

148. Tax, S. 1960. *Evolution after Darwin*. Univ. Chicago Press

149. Teleki, G. 1973. The omnivorous chimpanzee. *Sci. Am.* 228:32–42

150. Thompson, R. 1975. A cross-species analysis of carnivore, primate and hominid behavior. *J. Hum. Evol.* 4:113–24

151. Tiger, L. 1975. Somatic factors and social behavior. See Ref. 63, 115–32

152. Tiger, L., Fox, R. 1966. The zoological perspective in social science. *Man: J. R. Anthropol. Inst.* 1:75–81

153. Tiger, L., Fox, R. 1971. *The Imperial Animal*. New York: Holt, Rinehart & Winston

154. Trivers, R. L. 1971. The evolution of reciprocal altruism. *Q. Rev. Biol.* 46:35–57

155. Trivers, R. L. 1972. Parental investment and sexual selection. See Ref. 61, 136–79

156. Trivers, R. L. 1974. Parent-offspring conflict. *Am. Zool.* 14:249–64

157. Tuttle, R., Ed. 1972. *The Functional and Evolutionary Biology of Primates*. Chicago: Aldine

158. Van Hoof, J. A. R. A. M. 1962. Facial expressions in higher primates. *Symp. Zool. Soc. London* 8:97–125

159. Van Hoof, J. A. R. A. M. 1972. A comparative approach to the phylogeny of laughter and smiling. See Ref. 10, 209–38

160. Van Krevald, D. 1970. A selective review of dominance-subordination relations in animals. *Genet. Psychol. Monogr.* 81:141–73

161. Warren, J. M. 1972. Evolution, behavior and the prefrontal cortex. *Acta Neurobiol. Exp.* 32 (2):581–93

162. Warren, J. M. 1973. Learning in vertebrates. In *Comparative Psychology: A Modern Survey*, ed. D. A. Dewsbury, D. A. Rethlingshafer. New York: McGraw Hill

163. Washburn, S. L. 1953. The strategy of physical anthropology. In *Anthropology Today*, ed. A. L. Kroeber. Univ. Chicago Press

164. Washburn, S. L., Ed. 1961. *The Social Life of Early Man*. New York: Wenner-Gren Found. Anthropol. Res.

165. Washburn, S. L., McCown, E. R. 1973. *Aggression and the evolution of the skull*. Presented at Am. Anthropol. Assoc. 72nd Ann. Meet., New Orleans

166. Watson, J. S. 1966. Perception of object orientation in infants. *Merrill-Palmer Q.* 12:73–94

167. Whiting, B., Whiting J. 1973. Methods for observing and recording behavior. In *Handbook of Method in Cultural Anthropology*, ed. R. Naroll, R. Cohen, 282–315. New York: Columbia Univ. Press

168. Wickler, W. 1973. Ethological analysis of convergent adaptation. *Ann. NY Acad. Sci.* 223:65–69

169. Wiepkema, P. R. 1961. An ethological analysis of the reproductive behavior of the bitterling. *Arch. Neerl. Zool.* 14:103–99

170. Williams, G. C. 1966. *Adaptation and natural selection: a critique of some current evolutionary thought*. Princeton Univ. Press

171. Wilson, E. O. 1975. *Sociobiology: The New Synthesis*. Cambridge and London: Belknap Press of Harvard Univ. Press

172. Winson, J. 1972. Interspecies differences in the occurrence of Theta. *Behav. Biol.* 7:479–87

173. Wolf, P. 1966. The causes, controls and organization of behavior in the neonate. *Psychol. Issues 5* (17, Ser. No. 1)

174. Wolf, P. 1969. The natural history of crying and other vocalizations in early infancy. In *Determinants of Infant Behavior*, Vol. 4. New York: Methuen

175. Wynne-Edwards, V. C. 1962. *Ani-*

mal Dispersion in Relation to Social Behavior. New York: Hafner

176. Young, B., Decarie, T. G. 1974. An ethology-based catalogue of facial/vocal behaviors in infancy. *Educ. Test. Serv.* RB 74–51. Princeton, NJ: ETS

177. Zigler, E., Child, I. L. 1969. Socialization. In *The Handbook of Social Psychology,* Vol. 3, ed. G. Lindzey, A. Aronson. Reading, Mass: Addison-Wesley

178. Zivin, G. 1975. *Facial gestures as status signals in preschool boys.* Presented at Ann. Meet. Eastern Psychol. Assoc., New York

Ann. Rev. Anthropol. 1976. 5:289–328
Copyright © 1976 by Annual Reviews Inc. All rights reserved

THE ANTHROPOLOGICAL ◆ 9581
STUDY OF CHILDREN'S PLAY

Helen B. Schwartzman[1]
Institute for Juvenile Research, 1735 West Taylor Street, Chicago, Illinois 60612

INTRODUCTION

The study of play was a topic of serious concern to a number of anthropologists and folklorists at the turn of this century. Inspired by the arguments of Tylor (e.g. 280) about the diffusion of games such as *pachisi* to the Americas, a number of authors (68, 71, 140, 249) contributed articles to the early issues of the *American Anthropologist* discussing the games of many North American Indian groups. It was also at this time that the extensive game collections of Newell (195), Gomme (112, 113) and Culin (64, 66) were published. However, with the exception of Best's *Games and Pastimes of the Maori* (30) and Lesser's *The Pawnee Ghost Dance Hand Game* (170), the study of play did not advance much beyond the early investigations of Culin until the late 1950s. In 1959, Roberts, Arth & Bush (inspired again by Tylor) published an article (216) attempting to develop a theoretical framework for the study of games, explaining both their geographical distribution and sociocultural significance. This article served effectively to reopen the field of play research for anthropologists, and in 1974 The Association for the Anthropological Study of Play (TAASP) was organized.[2]

In contrast, the study of child socialization has been a recognized subject for anthropological inquiry for some time. Early in this century investigators such as Chamberlain (57) began to pursue the study of "primitive" children, and since that time a number of significant studies of child socialization have appeared (e.g. 69, 168, 183, 184, 292–294). More recently, in a series on education and culture edited by George and Louise Spindler, a variety of ethnographies of childhood have been published (e.g. 142, 154, 169, 295).

Unfortunately for the study of children's play, ethnographers interested in this topic at the turn of the century often reported information only on the games and leisure time activities of adults, considering children's play to be much too

[1]I would like to thank John Schwartzman, John M. Roberts, and Brian Sutton-Smith for valuable comments and criticism; Linda Barbera for bibliographic assistance; and Mary Dell Onley and Drue Cass for typing assistance.
[2]Information in regard to TAASP membership, publications, etc may be obtained by writing to Elinor Nickerson, Box 297, Alamo, California 94507.

frivolous and ephemeral to merit serious examination. Socialization researchers, on the other hand, have concentrated on the study of how children learn to become culturally appropriate adults. Children's play has not always been seen to contribute significantly to this process, and so it has seldom been extensively investigated. Nevertheless, over the years many important reports on the play activities of children have accumulated in the anthropological literature. However, because there has never been an organized body of literature available for researchers' contributions, the literature appears in scattered and sometimes obscure places, and the research itself often looks scattered and unfocused. As this is the first review of children's play to appear in the *Annual Review of Anthropology,* I have organized this chapter in an attempt to provide a general overview, systematization, and assessment of this rapidly growing area of research in anthropology. Although there are many studies of adult play and games and nonhuman primate play available in the anthropological literature, these investigations are considered here only insofar as they have influenced studies of children's play.

Research on children's play appears in two forms in the anthropological literature. The fact that young humans play in one way or another in all societies in the world is illustrated by the numerous descriptions of this activity appearing in ethnographies. In Table I, which appears at the conclusion of this chapter, a listing by author and geographic area of many of these reports is presented. A brief overview of these accounts is included in this review, and certain selected reports are discussed.

The second type of literature available on this subject consists of attempts on the part of investigators to formulate specific definitions and/or theoretical statements about the play behavior of children. Because anthropologists have often used the studies of sociologists, psychologists, and psychiatrists to inform their research in this regard, relevant literature from these disciplines is also reviewed here. In evaluating this research I do not want to perpetuate the notion that studies of play must always be justified in terms of what they tell us about other more "serious," and presumably more important, activities. Research on children's play can and should be evaluated on the basis of what is learned about children's play (not cognition, or social structure, or culture contact). To facilitate this assessment I use Sutton-Smith's (269) recent contrast between the *texts* (i.e. descriptions of the play or game event itself) and *contexts* (i.e. the social, psychological, or environmental correlates of the event) of play, assuming that those studies which provide information on both texts and contexts are most complete and most useful for future investigations.

In the conclusion of this chapter a discussion of future prospects for research on children's play in anthropology is offered. Here a number of research needs in this field are described as they were suggested to me in the preparation of this review.

Play: Definitions, Classifications, and Reductions

In this chapter a variety of definitions, classifications, and reductions utilized by anthropologists and others in their studies of children's play are considered. A word, however, must be said briefly about what I consider to be this "triple threat" to play. I say this not because I devalue attempts to define, classify, or reduce (by metaphorical transformation) phenomena in the research process, but because I am critical of the way definitions, classifications, and reductions of children's play have been formulated and used in the past. Definitions, for example, are often speculative attempts by investigators to arbitrarily define the nature of play, with little attempt made to actually collect information or data on the subject. Classifications, on the other hand, have frequently been formulated by researchers desperate to "make sense" out of the range of materials which they may actually have collected. Often such classifications are a useful first step, but all too frequently a classification scheme is formulated and that is all. Finally, in theorizing about play, a metaphorical transformation is often made (e.g. play is likened to a psychological projection, or play is viewed as a cognitive process). Unfortunately, this transformation is often disregarded and soon play *is* a psychological projection, or play *is* a function of cognitive processes, as the metaphor is now taken literally (cf 278). When this happens, a reduction of play to some other phenomenon occurs. I would suggest that by forgetting the intrinsically playful, "as if" quality of theorizing, an injustice is done to all phenomena, but an injustice is done particularly to play.

As there is clearly no single agreed-upon definition, classification, or metaphor/reduction of play available in the literature, I have chosen to offer a brief description of one form of this activity collected by William Bascom (19) for a group of Yoruba children. I do this because I think it captures and illustrates the complexities of translation and transformation so characteristic of play, and as will be seen, anthropology as well.

> During my work with their father these three children invented a new game, playing anthropologist. One sat in my chair on my cushion, with paper and pencil in hand. The second sat in their father's chair, acting as "interpreter," while the third sat on a bench as the informant customarily did. The second child turned to the first and said, "You are my master," and then to the third child, saying in Yoruba, "The white man wants you to tell about Odua." The third child replied in Yoruba and the second turned to the first and "interpreted," making a series of meaningless sounds which were supposed to sound like English. The first child scribbled on the paper, and replied with more nonsense syllables and the second child turned to the third with a new question in Yoruba (19, p. 58).

Ethnographic Descriptions of Children's Play

A review of the ethnographic literature of Africa and South America by Schwartzman & Barbera (231) suggests that there are four implicit metaphors utilized by anthropologists in presenting and interpreting information on children's play behavior. This view was confirmed in the analysis of reports for the remaining geographic areas of the world undertaken in the preparation of this chapter. The most common approach taken by ethnographers is to view play as imitation of and/or preparation for adult life, and therefore functional for the enculturation and socialization of children. This approach is discussed and critiqued here in the ROLE STUDIES section. A second perspective is found in frequent descriptions of children's play as game activity. This view is expressed in many early monographs where a special section of the report is specifically devoted to descriptions of games and toys. In most cases, however, while the material implements involved in a game are meticulously described, little information is provided on the social process of the activity. In adopting this view the anthropologist rarely reports information on children's unstructured play activity. This approach is illustrated most clearly in the DIFFUSIONISM AND ANTIQ-UARIANISM and the CROSS-CULTURAL, INTRA-CULTURAL COMPARATIVE STUDIES sections. A third metaphor, employed by fewer anthropologists, treats children's play as if it is a projective test that reveals a child's anxieties and hostilities which are assumed to be engendered by the child-rearing patterns of a culture. This view is discussed in the CROSS-CULTURAL, INTRA-CULTURAL COMPARATIVE STUDIES and the *Psychological Orientation* sections.

Finally, a fourth perspective characterizes children's play as an essentially trivial pastime. This view, of course, reflects Western societies' general disregard for play phenomena (see Norbeck 196), and it leads anthropologists to report little if any information on this topic. Often the ethnographer has collected material on the subject, but as there has been no organized body of literature available for such contributions, the material is excluded from the monograph. For example, in Paul and Laura Bohannan's descriptions of the Tiv, the ethnographic reports (e.g. 33, 34) do not discuss children's play; however, their published field notes do contain descriptions of this activity (35, pp. 374–79).

Ethnographic descriptions of children's play are generally thought to be illustrative of a particular society's patterning and influence on this behavior. However, as I suggest here, these accounts may also be related to the culture of the anthropologist as well as to the particular theoretical approach which he/she chooses to adopt. It is at the point of interaction between an ethnographer and a particular view of, or theory about, culture and cultural behavior that implicit metaphors for play are made explicit. These theoretical schools are discussed below.

The Anthropological/Sociological Orientation[3]

DIFFUSIONISM AND ANTIQUARIANISM Studies of play by anthropologists and folklorists began in the late nineteenth century at a time when it was

---

[3]In this review, two types of studies are presented. Those which attempt to look at children's play in its various sociocultural contexts are reported in the *Anthropological/ Sociological Orientation* section. Studies attempting to account for and/or explain play in terms of psychological processes are reviewed in the *Psychological Orientation* section. Obviously these divisions are arbitrary and inconsistencies develop whereby psychologists' works are reviewed in the anthropological category and vice versa. I can only say that I have attempted to review the study in relation to the general *orientation* adopted by the investigator for the study or explanation of play, and not in relation to his/her particular disciplinary identity (e.g. anthropologist, psychologist, psychiatrist, etc).

fashionable to collect and compile examples of the customs of various "primitive" peoples. As Western children at this time were often equated with "primitives" (e.g. 8), their customs, in the form of their games and rhymes, were likewise considered appropriate for collection and preservation. The chapters on children's play in Gomme's two-volume work on *The Traditional Games of England, Scotland, and Ireland,* published in 1894 and 1898 (112, 113), were intended to serve these archival purposes. This is also true for the earlier well-known collection of American children's games by Newell (195). Here game texts are catalogued according to specific play themes: love games, histories, playing at work, humor and satire, guessing games, games of chase, and so forth. Newell utilized a diffusionist approach in interpreting the significance of these games by asserting that it could be illustrated that they were "almost all entirely of old English origin" (195, pp. 1–2). Newell and Gomme also believed that children's games were survivals, in childish form, of earlier societies' more serious adult activities. For example, the English child's game of "Nuts in May" was thought by Gomme to be derived from the early custom of marriage by capture. This view, of course, relates to G. Stanley Hall's recapitulation theory of play which is discussed here in the *Psychological Orientation* section. Both of these writers likewise shared the view that children's play activities, just like "primitive" people's customs, were destined for extinction.[4]

Tylor's (280–282) interest in the study of the geographic distribution of games (for use in support of his specific theories of culture contact) encouraged a number of early ethnographers to report information on children's (e.g. 15, 71) and adults' (e.g. 140, 249) games. It was left to Culin, however, to produce what are still today the most comprehensive anthropological collections of games available (e.g. 63–66). In these reports, Culin proposed his own views on game diffusion, which often conflicted with Tylor's interpretations, and he also suggested that games were universal features of all cultures. Generally information is only reported on adult games, particularly those involving material implements. There is often, however, incidental mention of children's play, and at least one of Culin's articles (63) is devoted specifically to a discussion of Brooklyn children's games.

The study of children's play as a game activity was further fostered by the tendency at this time for anthropologists to concentrate on discriptions of spectacular, conspicuous, and ritualized events. Games were seen as the most obvious form of play and so anthropologists began to search for ways to learn about the "pure" (i.e. nonacculturated) games of a society's past. This approach affected the study of children's play by encouraging ethnographers to use adults, as opposed to children, as informants, urging them to reminisce about the games of the past (e.g. 71, 209, 248). Unfortunately, in utilizing this technique

[4]Of course as we now know children's "customs" have survived, and probably will continue to do so in the future, although recently some (e.g. 242) have suggested that television and other devices emphasizing sedantism and passive involvement for children may actually extinguish their more active and imaginative play activities. This, however, remains to be seen.

anthropologists often ignored the present-day activities of children which were likely to include variations on traditional, or possibly innovative, games created in response to new physical and/or social environments.

More recent collections of play texts have been made by a number of investigators. One of the most productive in this regard is Brewster, a folklorist, who has compiled an impressive amount of material on the games of children and adults in various societies of the world (see various works listed by geographic area in Table I). Brewster suggests that there are a number of important reasons for anthropologists to study games, most specifically because of the evidence they offer of specific culture contact between peoples (46). His most detailed study of children's play is his 1953 report on American (North Carolina) children's games, *Children's Games and Rhymes* (41). His study of *American Nonsinging Games* (42) also includes detailed descriptions of children's games. Brewster's method of collecting games is typical of nineteenth century armchair anthropology in that he relies on reports of others to provide him with information for his studies. However, in spite of this somewhat dubious methodology, his works are very important for he maintained an interest in play during a time when anthropologists and many folklorists would have none of it.

Dorothy Howard, an American folklorist who has studied both Australian and American children's games, and Iona and Peter Opie, English folklorists writing on the language, jokes, pranks, and games of English school children, both employ a more ethnographic and observational approach in their research studies. Howard's works include several articles describing, for example, the hopscotch games (143), ball bouncing "customs" and rhymes (144), gambling implements (145), and marble games (146) of Australian children. The Opies have published two major works on child lore: *The Lore and Language of Children* (198) and *Children's Games in Street and Playground* (199). In this latter report, 11 types of games which children play "of their own accord" are described. Games emphasizing chasing, catching, seeking, hunting, racing, dueling, exerting, daring, guessing, acting, and pretending are all discussed. Although both Howard and the Opies employ techniques (e.g. observation and interviews) and informants (i.e. generally children and not adults) which mark them off in contrast to the approach of the past, the motivation for their studies still appears to be the collection and preservation of play texts with little attention given to play contexts (cf 269, p. 9).

Brian Sutton-Smith, a developmental psychologist, exhibits a variety of orientations in his research studies on children's play (e.g. archival, anthropological, psychological and sociological). As an archivist he has produced an important collection, classification, and historical analysis of the games of New Zealand Pakeha children (256), matching here the earlier work by Best (29, 30) on Maori children's games. The effect of European culture on Maori children's unorganized games has also been considered (267). In a more recent study with Rosenberg (276), Sutton-Smith presents an analysis of patterns of change in the game preferences of American children. Here it is reported that these children evidence an increasing preference (over a 60-year time period) for informal, spontaneous games as opposed to more formalized play activities (e.g. parlor or team guessing games).

A specific collection of jump rope rhymes is available by Abrahams (1). The history of this game is discussed (e.g. in the recent past it was a boys' activity whereas now it is clearly a girls' game) and a brief review of relevant literature on this subject is offered. Examples of other games to have received special attention from collectors are singing games (61, 195), counting out rhymes for games (111, 195), and string figure games (39, 84). (String games, it should be noted, were particularly important to the early diffusionists for use as evidence in support of particular culture contact theories.) Finally, a useful list of early collections of children's games is available by Newell (195).

CROSS-CULTURAL AND INTRA-CULTURAL COMPARATIVE STUDIES. In 1959 Roberts, Arth & Bush published an article (216) entitled "Games in Culture." Here an important distinction is drawn between amusements and games. A game is said to be characterized by organization, competition, two or more sides, criteria for determining a winner, and agreed-upon rules, whereas noncompetitive activities (e.g. string figure making) are described as "amusements" (p. 597). A çlassification of games constructed on the basis of how game outcome is determined is presented. Three types of games are enumerated: games of physical skill (e.g. marathon races, hockey); games of strategy (e.g. chess); and games of chance (e.g. dice, high card wins).

On the basis of their analysis of ethnographic and Cross-Cultural Survey File material, the authors suggest that games are expressive cultural activities similar to music and folktales. Games are also said to be models of various cultural activities and therefore exercises in cultural mastery (e.g. games of skill are related to mastery of specific environmental conditions; games of strategy are related to mastery of the social system; and games of chance are related to mastery of the supernatural).[5] Associations between complexity of cultures and complexity of games (e.g. "simple" societies do not generate a "need" for games of strategy, whereas in complex societies all types of games are present) are also noted and commented on in the study. This finding is often used to contradict earlier statements by diffusionists about the universal existence of games in all cultures (e.g. 268).

Even though this article relates most specifically to the study of adult games, it is crucial for understanding the direction taken in the 1960s for the cross-cultural study of children's games. In 1962, building on the work of Roberts, Arth & Bush (216) and Whiting & Child (294), Roberts & Sutton-Smith (217) developed a *conflict-enculturation hypothesis*, intended to explain relationships existing between types of games, child-training variables, and cultural variables. Briefly stated, the hypothesis holds that conflict engendered by the specific child-training procedures of a culture leads to an interest and involvement in specific

---

[5]This view of play as mastery is most directly related to Freudian and psychoanalytic theories which are reviewed here in the *Psychological Orientation* section.

types of game activities which pattern this conflict in the role-reversals sanctioned by the game-rules. It is argued further that involvement over time in these activities leads to mastery of appropriate behaviors which have functional and culturally useful value (269, p. 10). The hypothesis was tested in a manner similar to the Roberts, Arth & Bush (216) study and found to hold cross-culturally. This approach has generated further studies attempting to show that the same relationships hold in American culture (e.g. 218, 272). The notion that games serve as models of cultural power relationships and in this capacity serve as "buffered learning situations" is also described by Sutton-Smith & Rosenberg (275). A number of more complete summaries of the Roberts and Sutton-Smith studies on children's play are available (268, 269, 273).

Eifermann (80, 81), in her recent study of children's games in Israel, tested this hypothesis by predicting that rural children, with more opportunity to engage in the adult world than urban children, would develop less intense conflicts and therefore less interest in competitive games which model these conflicts. However, in analyzing her data, the opposite was found to occur. Millar (185) has also criticized this hypothesis in a fashion similar to Eifermann. Sutton-Smith (136) argues, however, that Eifermann's findings do not contradict the hypothesis, basically because she groups all competitive games into one category (pp. 268–69).

It was also during the late 1950s and early 1960s that the child socialization study known as the *Six Cultures* project (292) was initiated. Games were described in this study, following the work of Roberts, Arth & Bush (216), as expressive mastery activities for children, and investigators were encouraged to view and report this behavior in this fashion. Unfortunately, as I have argued elsewhere (230), because games are defined as useful only insofar as they might contain information about the more important "behavioral systems" of succorance, nurturance, self-reliance, achievement, responsibility, obedience, dominance, sociability, and aggression (292, p. 7), detailed information on the unorganized play, as well as games, of children in these cultures is not available. There are, however, interesting differences in amount of play activity reported in the various societies studied (e.g. Gusii children are said to engage in almost no fantasy play, whereas descriptions of this activity for New England and Okinawan children are quite prevalent). Sutton-Smith (269) has recently suggested possible reasons for these differences.

Quantitative studies of cross-cultural and intra-cultural variation in children's play in England, Norway, Spain, Greece, Egypt, and the United States (233) and in three American subcultures (e.g. White, Mexican-American, and Black) (234), have recently been made by Seagoe. She has also studied, with Murakami (235), differences in Japanese and American children's play. In all of these investigations, variation in children's "play socialization" is determined by children's answers to a series of questions derived from a "play report" (e.g. what do you spend most of your time playing at school? and what do you like to play most?) (see 232). Differences in play noted here are associated with age, sex, type of schooling, cultural and ethnic factors.

Georges (103) has recently criticized the Roberts and Sutton-Smith studies by suggesting that relationships are made by these researchers solely on the basis of information derived from observation and testing of American children and from data obtained from the Cross-Cultural Survey Files (HRAF). Georges states that "there are no indications in their publications that Roberts and Sutton-Smith have actually attempted to test these generalizations cross-culturally" (p. 9). Eifermann (81) essentially makes the same statements in her study. Sutton-Smith (269), however, appears to indicate that such studies are underway (p. 10).

Sutton-Smith (269) has recently offered his own criticism of this research. For example, he suggests that even though these investigations reopened the issue of play and games in anthropology, ultimately they represent more of an empirical than theoretical breakthrough. And he states that perhaps the emphasis on the sociocultural functions of games ultimately served to reduce play phenomena to these more serious activities (p. 9). Finally, he argues that these studies are in the end investigations of play *contexts* (i.e. asserted relationships about the psychogenic and sociogenic correlates of games) without much reference to play *texts* (p. 11). This criticism is certainly applicable to all cross-cultural quantitative research, as well as to many early diffusionist studies. However, an alternate view can also be proposed. That is, that these studies tend to ignore not only text but also context. A "search and seize" methodology is characteristic of both these research schools. In both instances games are pulled from their original sociocultural systems and placed in artifically constructed contexts for analysis (those set up by either statistical or diffusionist design). In these instances I would suggest that both text and context are ignored.

ROLE STUDIES: THE ROLE PLAY OF CHILDREN AND THE ROLE OF PLAY IN SOCIETY   According to Loizos, the most commonly accepted theory of play is to view it as practice for adult activity (175, p. 236). The pre-exercise theory of Groos (120, 121) is an early example of this approach. Children's role play has frequently been interpreted from this perspective and in this way the seemingly non-purposeful actions of play are transformed into activities functional for the perpetuation of the social order.

George H. Mead reflects this view in his classic study of the conditions which give rise to the objectification of the self (182). In this work, Mead pays particular attention to the development of language, play, and games in children. Play and game activity are clearly differentiated here as they are thought to have distinct functions in relation to the development of the child's sense of self. For Mead, "ordinary" play (e.g. playing Indians) allows the child to imagine himself in various social roles and by so doing to "build up" his own character. In order to play games, however, the child must be able "to take the attitude of everyone else involved," and to see that "these different roles must have a definite relationship to each other" (p. 151). For example, in the game of baseball the child must know his own role in the game (e.g. as a catcher) and also be able to take the role of others (e.g. the pitcher) by being willing to risk his own identity for the sake of the "generalized other" (e.g. the team). In Mead's view, once the child is able to take the attitude of the other he/she is on the way to "becoming an organic member of society" (p. 159).

The most common expression of this approach, as adopted by anthropologists, is to describe children's play as imitative or mimetic activity and therefore functional as an enculturative mechanism. Malinowski illustrates this perspective by contending that play should be studied for its educational value and in relation to its "function as preparation for economic skills" (180, p. 107). The use of this imitation/preparation metaphor is widespread in ethnographies. Turnbull's description of the play of Mbuti Pygmy children is quite typical.

> Like children everywhere, Pygmy children love to imitate their adult idols. . . . at an early age boys and girls are "playing house" or "playing hunting". . . . And one day they find that the games they have been playing are not games any longer, but the real thing for they have become adults. . . .(279, p. 129).

I suggest that implicit in these interpretations is the child-centered view of many Western, and also many non-Western, *adults*. That is, if adults as parents are thought to direct a large portion of their time and energy toward children (e.g. to raise or rear them), then it becomes expected that children will reciprocate by directing the major portion of their time in play toward adults (i.e. by imitating them). Perhaps the view of play as imitation is just a sophisticated version of, and rationalization for, this common-sense (i.e. adult) interpretation (cf 179). However, these types of assumptions need to be questioned, evaluated, and researched before becoming incorporated into anthropological works.

Fortes's (93) study of the "Social and Psychological Aspects of Education in Taleland" includes one of the most significant and insightful investigations of children's play available in the ethnographic literature. Play, according to Fortes, "is the paramount educational exercise of Tale children" (p. 44). It is never, however, simple and mechanical reproduction of adult activities. In this article Fortes recognizes the need for anthropologists and others to rethink their view of imitation.

> Writers on primitive education have often attributed an almost mystical significance to "imitation" as the principal method by which a child learns. The Tallensi themselves declare that children learn by "looking and doing," but neither "imitation" nor the formula used by the Tallensi help us to understand the actually observable process. Tale children do not automatically copy the actions of older children or adults with whom they happen to be without rhyme or reason and merely for the sake of "imitation" (p. 54).

If anyone doubts (and apparently many still do, judging by recent ethnographies) that so-called "primitive children" actually do engage in imaginative, and not "mere imitative," play behavior, I refer them to Fortes' description of a typical play situation in Taleland (p. 59–61) as well as to Raum's extensive discussion of the play of Chaga children (211).

Lancy (161) has recently noted that the idea that play functions to enculturate children is very common, but it has rarely been tested. In order to explore its validity Lancy has used a variety of techniques (e.g. participant observation, interviews, and experiments) in studies of African (Kpelle) and, more recently, American children (160–162; unpublished observations). His studies suggest that "The evidence for the learning of adult roles, patterns of thought and values in play, while not impressive, is at least encouraging to a theory of play in enculturation" (161, p. 31).

A variation on the play as imitation/enculturation view is evidenced in Smilansky's study of Israeli children's sociodramatic play (242). In this work Smilansky indicates that children's make-believe play aids imitation and is, in fact, a technique by which the child's limitations can be overcome and "by which a richer reproduction of adult life is made possible" (243, p. 7). Smilansky's studies have also led her to suggest that certain groups of children have less facility for imaginative role play than others. In her study, children of North African and Middle Eastern parents are said to engage in this play with much less frequency and with less ability than children of European parents.

Sutton-Smith (268) uses these results as well as the earlier study of Roberts, Arth & Bush (216) to suggest that there may be "two cultures of games." Children in "ascriptive game cultures" are said to engage in imitative and nonimaginative play activities. Play is hierarchical, where one child bosses all the others and is quite often aggressive. Central person games, and later games of physical skill, are most common. The types of societies associated with these games are not clearly described by Sutton-Smith except insofar as they are said to be characterized by: (a) extended and not nuclear families; (b) leading individuals dominate by arbitrary power; and (c) children and adults are not separated from one another (268, p. 299). Children in "achievement game cultures" are said to play imaginatively and in a more egalitarian style. Likewise there is less physical aggression and less emphasis on ritualized and formalistic games (e.g. singing games). Western (i.e. Western middle-class) societies are typical of "achievement game cultures." Here children are segregated from the rest of society and nuclear families predominate (pp. 303–9).

As Sutton-Smith particularly uses the work of Smilansky to support his "two cultures" view, it is important to again consider Eifermann's recent studies of children's play in Israel (81). In this study she challenges Smilansky's findings by suggesting that the form of play (i.e. sociodramatic/imaginative) behavior which Smilansky reports to be lacking in her sample of "disadvantaged" children appears at a later age (i.e. at age 6–8 rather than 3–6) for a comparable group of children in her own study. And she states that her analysis indicates that at this later age, "culturally deprived" children not only develop the ability to engage in symbolic play but "they also engage in such play at a significantly higher rate than do their 'advantaged' peers" (81, p. 290). I would also suggest here that facilities for "imaginative play activity" may be displayed in various ways by children. Individual, subcultural, and cultural play styles all affect the way that a child will play and so, for example, a child may not engage in imaginative sociodramatic play activity in the way that American middle-class children do and yet he/she may display imaginative abilities in other ways. Another particularly difficult problem here is the fact that there are many, sometimes conflicting, views of what constitutes "imaginative play" behavior.

All in all, I think a clarification is in order, by Sutton-Smith, of his "two cultures of games."

A number of studies have been made investigating types of roles and status positions in specific games and relationships between these roles and the larger social context. In a study by Gump & Sutton-Smith (124), an attempt is made to classify rule games on the basis of the kinds of status positions they contain (e.g. leader, follower, attacker, defender, taunter, taunted), and the controls over the allocation of such positions (e.g. leader chosen by popularity, leader chosen by chance, leader chosen by defeat or triumph). After classifying a variety of games in this way the authors proceed to analyze the status positions and allocation of power in "It" games (e.g. tag, King of the Mountain, etc), with the idea that such roles offer players the opportunity to gain experience and/or practice in handling such positions. Examples of other similar studies conducted by Sutton-Smith are those investigating relationships between sex roles and play choices (277), and sibling relationships and role involvement in play (265, 274). In one study (265), a role reversal phenomenon is noted in which it is found that first-born children who occupy a dominant/leader role in sibling relations within the family often act in nondominant/follower roles in peer play situations.

In relation to this earlier work, Sutton-Smith has recently undertaken a study of role reversals and inversions apparent within the structure of certain children's games (263,269). He calls these the "games of order and disorder" and relates them to the various forms of symbolic inversion (e.g. rites of reversal) which anthropologists have frequently described (see Norbeck 196). Examples of such games are: Ring-Around-the-Rosy, Poor Pussy, Queen of Sheba. Sutton-Smith states that these games are significant particularly because they suggest that play and games are not always socializing and social ordering activities, as they may in fact seek to challenge and reverse the social order. This is so because these games often model the social system "only to destroy it" (e.g. everyone acts in concert and then collapses) (269, p. 12). These games also often mock conventional power roles and frequently provide unconventional access to such roles (e.g. everyone gets a turn). In these games Sutton-Smith suggests that one may find "seeds of potential novelty for the larger society."

A current interest of anthropologists, sociologists, and psychologists is the study of sex roles in various societies. Children's play has been investigated as a vehicle for the learning and practicing of culturally appropriate sex roles by a number of researchers (e.g. 110, 177). Lever's recent studies of sex differences in children's play and game behavior are useful to consider here (171, 172). In this research a group of American white, middle-class fifth grade children is investigated to determine: (a) if there are any sex differences in their play patterns; and (b) if involvement in particular games affects the performance of adult roles. Most specifically, an attempt is made to test whether boys' games are more "complex" (in the way that complexity is defined in formal organizations) than girls' games. It is argued that if this is so, then it can be proposed that boys' games better prepare them "for successful performance in a wide range of work settings in modern complex societies" (172, p. 3). The dimensions of game complexity outlined and analyzed here are: role differentiation; interdependence between players; size of play group; degree of competition and explicitness of goals; number and specificity of rules; and degree of team formation. On the basis of her analysis, Lever reports that "with respect to each of these six dimensions, boys' activities were more often complex" (172, p. 12).

In searching for ways to understand the learning of sex roles, it may be useful to consider the role inversions and role mocking behavior said to be characteristic of the "games of order and disorder." Perhaps in these games children have been questioning and/or mocking culturally stereotyped sex roles all along (and as adults, or course, we thought they were just being socialized).[6] I suggest that these types of play activities have only recently been recognized because role studies have tended to concentrate on the contexts (i.e. social function) of play. In order to correct this emphasis, I offer a brief play text from Goodman (114) of two 4-year-old boys caricaturing the behavior of an adult woman, simultaneously "convulsed by their own wit":

Jack: It's *lovely* to see you!
Danny: I'm *so* happy to see you!
Jack: How *are* you? How have you been?
Danny: Sorry I have to go so quick (114,p. 138).

The role of play in society has been considered by a number of investigators, but the studies of Huizinga (147) and Caillois (54) stand out in this regard. Huizinga has frequently been said to have inaugurated an anthropology of play in his famous work *Homo Ludens* (147). Here he suggests that play must be studied "in itself" because "it is a significant function" and there "is some sense to it" (pp. 1–2). Huizinga attempts to capture the "sense" of play by defining it as: (*a*) a voluntary activity existing outside "ordinary" life; (*b*) totally absorbing; (*c*) unproductive; (*d*) occurring within a circumscribed time and space: (*e*) ordered by rules; and (*f*) characterized by group relationships which surround themselves by secrecy and disguise (p. 13). He utilizes this definition to delineate the "play element" in such activities as law, war, philosophy, and art.

Caillois, in *Man, Play, and Games* (54), criticizes and elaborates on Huizinga's definition. Most specifically he suggests that it is too narrow for it stresses only the competitive character of play. In order to add to this definition Caillois develops a classification scheme in which four types of play are identified: *agôn* (competition); *alea* (chance); *mimicry* (simulation); and *ilinx* (vertigo). Superimposed on this scheme is a continuum of ways of playing running from *ludus* (controlled and regulated play) to *paidia* (spontaneous play) (78, p. 31). Neither of these investigators concentrates on the specific study of children's play; however, their works are frequently cited and have often provided guidance for students of this topic. An excellent description and critique of Huizinga's and Caillois' writings is offered by Ehrmann (78).

---

[6]Another explanation for these types of games is that they provide opportunities for practice of what Goffman (108) has termed *role distance*.

COMMUNICATION STUDIES   In the 1950s Bateson (20, 21) initiated the development of a comprehensive theory of communication (and epistemology) using play as a prototype. This approach has since conceptually linked the study of such seemingly diverse phenomena as psychotherapy (e.g. 128), schizophrenia (e.g. 23), and humor (e.g. 98). According to Bateson, play can only occur among organisms able to meta-communicate and therefore able to distinguish messages of differing logical types. These messages act as "frames" or contexts providing information about how another message should be interpreted. Therefore, in order to understand an action as play it must be framed by the message "this is play." Bateson suggests that this message generates a paradox of the Russellian or Epimenides' type wherein a negative statement contains an implicit negative meta-statement (21, p. 180). Therefore the message "this is play" states: "These actions in which we now engage do not denote what these actions *for which they stand* would denote." In a play fight, for example, the message would be "this bite is not a bite." In these terms the texts and contexts of play are intimately and systemically related and cannot be considered in isolation from one another. This relationship is most clearly expressed in Bateson's metalogues (22) in which the structure and content of an interaction are comments on one another.

Bateson also makes an important distinction between play and game communication. In games the paradoxical reference system of play is embodied in a codified system of rules which organize the use of objects, space, time, as well as player activities. Here it is not necessary for play communication to occur continually to define players etc, as this is achieved by the game's explicit rule structure. In games then the ambiguity and paradox inherent in play, which necessitates constant and consistent communication and interpretation for maintenance of the event, has been "ruled" out. Bateson suggests this view in his description of similarities between play and psychotherapy and his contrast between these two activities and games (21, p. 192).

Miller (186) incorporates Bateson's notion of meta-communication in his attempt to arrive at a definition of play capable of encompassing all the various activities (e.g. playing puppies, playing house, playing games, etc) referred to by this label. He reviews a variety of material on the subject of both human and nonhuman primate play, specifically considering reports on the various forms, as well as presumed functional attributes, of this behavior, and he suggests that there are a number of patterns, or "motifs," to be found in all these diverse activities. In describing these motifs, Miller uses Bateson's notion of frames to suggest that play is a context or mode of organization in which "ends are not obliterated" but do not, as is true for other behaviors, "determine the means" (186, p. 92). Play is also distinguished by a psychological process which Miller refers to as "galumphing," that is, "the voluntary placing of obstacles in one's path." In this article Miller attempts to deal with one of the main "obstacles" presented to the student of play (i.e. how can we talk about play as a unitary category of behavior when its manifestations appear to be so diverse?).

Geertz has also suggested an approach to the study of play utilizing the notions of text and context. In his study of the Balinese cockfight as "deep play," he presents an analysis of this play form as a social text which comments on "the whole matter of assorting human beings into fixed hierarchical ranks and then organizing the major part of collective existence around that assortment" (102, p. 26). In short, it is a text which can only be understood in its larger sociocultural context and which itself is "interpretive" of that context. In this sense, "it is a Balinese reading of Balinese experience; a story they tell themselves about themselves."

Sutton-Smith (269) has also recently proposed an approach for the study of both the texts and contexts of play. Here he discusses the importance of considering the "antecedent" (e.g. previous exploratory activity, power relationships, signal activity), and "postcedent" (e.g. the outcomes of novelty, flexibility, and revival) contexts of play and their relationship to cultural ideologies. Sutton-Smith suggests that the textual structures of play may be described from several perspectives. Cognitively, they may be viewed as a form of abstraction whereby "the child creates meaning and organization out of his prior experience," whereas conatively, they may be seen as a form of power reversal and affectively as a type of vivification experience (p. 14).

In another work entitled "Boundaries," Sutton-Smith suggests the importance of studying "the codes that govern entries and exits" in play and differential "ludic techniques" used by children "to cross such boundaries" (258, pp. 103–4). He relates this discussion to Goffman's (109) description of types of integrations in play encounters and, of course, both of these studies can be related to Bateson's earlier investigation of play frames. This association is most clearly illustrated in Goffman's recent work, *Frame Analysis* (109).

In a recent study (229, 230) of the symbolic play communication of a group of American preschool children, the author has also suggested the importance of interpreting play texts in specific social contexts. Following Bateson (20, 21), Geertz (102), and Ehrmann (78), it is suggested that symbolic or pretend play can be analyzed as a text in which players act as both the subjects and the objects of their jointly created event. In this sense, as Ehrmann (78) suggests, the players become the "stakes" of their "game." Therefore in play *texts*, the players as *subjects* of these events are able to interpret and comment on their relationships to each other (as these are developed in specific social *contexts* like a day care center) as the *object* of their play. This approach also adopts a view of play as communication characterized (after Bateson 21) by its production of paradoxical statements about persons, objects, activities, and situations. Individuals' play styles are described in reference to the way they communicate their intention to act as both the subject and the object of their play. In these terms, in order to be a successful player, one must be able to communicate information that simultaneously defines one as a play-*subject* (e.g. adopting the play role of witch, mother, etc) and as an actual person in the defining social context and therefore a play-*object*. In short, an attempt is made here to describe the *texts in context* and the *context in texts*.

STRUCTURAL STUDIES   The idea that play can be studied by an analysis of its intrinsic elements has been suggested by a number of investigators (e.g. 12, 75,

147, 214, 262). Dundes, for example, suggests that certain ordered units of action, or *motifemes*, may be isolated as the "minimum structural units" of both games and folktales (75, pp. 276–77). In this study he follows the work of the Russian folklorist Propp (208) on the morphology of folktales; however, he states that games are structurally different in one important way from folktales. In games one finds that two sequences of actions occur simultaneously, whereas in folktales only one action sequence is described at a time. Dundes proposes that Propp's notion of the distribution of functions among the *dramatis personae* of folktales (e.g. villany, struggle, and pursuit, relate to the villain's action sphere) may be used to describe the motifemic elements in games. In order to illustrate this approach Dundes analyzes a number of children's games, such as Hare and Hounds, Hide and Seek, The Witch, and Steps (Mother May I?), in terms of this schema. Georges has criticized Dundes's use of this approach because it was formulated originally for the analysis of folktales and not games, and it is questionable whether the two activities can be considered to be equivalent (103, pp. 5–6).

Other attempts to describe and define specific structural features or dimensions of game activities appear in Redl (214), Redl, Gump & Sutton-Smith (215), and Avedon (12). In their article entitled "The Dimensions of Games," Redl, Gump & Sutton-Smith outline 30 significant features of games "which are thought relevant to the behavior that games may provoke" (215, p. 408). Examples of these dimensions are: type of body contact required, type of bodily activity required, skill requirements, competition factors, use of space, time considerations, prop usage, role-taking factors, rule complexity, interdependence of players. Avedon (12) also presents an analysis of games isolating ten significant features of this activity.

Based on his study of New Zealand children's games, Sutton-Smith (262) presents what is described as a formal analysis of the meaning of the game "Bar the Door" ("Red Rover," "Anty Over"). This analysis is presented in terms of a description of five basic features of the game: (*a*) the game challenge; (*b*) player participation; (*c*) performance; (*d*) spatial scene; and (*e*) temporal structure. Sutton-Smith (271) has more recently attempted to compare Piagetian developmental structures with specific structural elements apparent in fantasy narratives (i.e. free form stories) of American children.

Examples of studies attempting to categorize and describe significant features of play or games from the perspective of the players themselves have been made by Parrott (201) and von Glascoe (286). Parrott, in "Games Children Play: Ethnography of a Second Grade Recess," describes three significant categories of game and play behavior used by a group of American second-grade boys to classify their own play activities. The three categories are: "games" (e.g. Kick the Can), "goofing around" (e.g. sucking icicles), and "tricks" (e.g. tripping someone). This information was elicited in several interview sessions with the children. The distinguishing features of "games," from the players' perspective, are said to be: (*a*) types of boundaries; (*b*) existence or absence of penalties; (*c*) types of roles; (*d*) outcome of the activity; (*e*) presence or absence of teams; and (*f*) rule structure. The basic features of "tricks" were more difficult to establish, but Parrott reports that they may be characterized, from the players' perspective, by unexpectedness, physical activity, opposing force, and (Parrott's own interpretation) players' intentions. "Goofing around" is characterized, in comparison with games, by its lack of teams, roles, competition, or goals, and also by the fact that "you can do it alone" as opposed to "games" which "you cannot do alone." It is interesting to note here that Parrott's "emically" derived categories appear to correspond quite readily with the "etic" categories utilized by Redl, Avedon, and Sutton-Smith for analyses of game structure and meaning. Von Glascoe (286) also uses the approach of ethnoscience to describe the system of game classification and the patterning of game preferences for Yucatan children, adolescents, and adults.

Studies of verbal play have been infrequently made by anthropologists because to comprehend this form of play, it is necessary to have an intimate knowledge of a society's language (196). Consequently there are few ethnographic studies of children's linguistic play available; however, there are some useful descriptions of Chaga children's verbal play available in Raum (211), as well as Haas's (125) analysis of two language games of Thai children, and Dundes, Leach & Ozkök's (76) description of Turkish boys' verbal dueling rhymes. The Opies' (198) collection and classification of English school children's language games and Chukovsky's (59) study of Russian children's word play are also significant in this regard. Two interesting attempts to classify the verbal play form of jump rope rhymes by the nonverbal motor patterns involved in jumping are also available (48, 51). A number of other studies (10, 29, 41, 256) include significant descriptions of children's verbal play.

Structural and linguistic investigations of children's play may be characterized by their tendency to focus on textual, as opposed to contextual, analysis, and in this way these studies may be related to the archival approach. However, here the texts are not analyzed according to diffusionist or survivalist theories, but rather structural-linguistic models are utilized.

ETHOLOGICAL AND ECOLOGICAL STUDIES Ethological studies of nonhuman primate play have been made by a number of investigators (see 175 or 185 for reviews of these studies). This approach has also been utilized for the study of children's behavior (e.g. 31, 32) and the specific study of children's play (e.g. 244). The ethologist's emphasis on the observation and description of anatomically defined items of behavior has led to an interest in the development of a behavioral definition of play, one capable of use for making interspecies comparisons.

Loizos presents one of the most useful discussions of this sort by suggesting a number of ways in which motor patterns may become transformed in play actions: (*a*) a behavioral sequence may be reordered; (*b*) movements may be exaggerated; (*c*) movements may be repeated; (*d*) movements may be repeated and exaggerated; (*e*) a sequence may be broken off or fragmented, irrelevant activities will be introduced, and later the sequence will be resumed; and (*f*) a sequence is not completed and the incomplete element is repeated (175, p. 229)

In attempting to develop such definitions of play, ethologists have, however, often encountered great difficulties in trying to distinguish play from other forms of behavior. Some investigators, exasperated by this problem, have suggested that play itself should be eliminated as a special behavioral category (e.g. 228); while other researchers have attempted to explore relationships between play and the behaviors with which it is so frequently confused.

Exploration is one such behavior. And Hutt's (149) study of the exploratory activities of a group of English children 3–5 years old presents important information on this problem. On the basis of this research, Hutt states that exploration may actually be seen to consist of two different classes of behavior (i.e. specific and diversive exploration). She suggests that specific exploration "seeks to reduce uncertainty and hence arousal or activation produced by . . . novel or complex stimulation"; whereas diversive exploration is an attempt "to vary stimulation in order to sustain a certain level of activation" (149, p. 248). Hutt suggests that play exhibits more similarity to this latter form of exploration; however, due to the failure of investigators to distinguish between these two forms of exploration, the behaviors of exploration and play have often been confused.

An ethological study reporting information on the play behavior of a group of 40 English nursery school children is reported by Smith & Connolly (244). Here a number of behaviors (e.g. talking, smiling, standing, crying, laughing, fighting) are defined according to facial expressions, vocalization, body posture, and motor patterns, and recorded in relation to their occurrence during the children's free play activity (p. 76). Recognizing the difficulty of rigidly defining play behavior, the investigators choose instead to describe it as presumably occurring when the child is in contact with play objects (e.g. toys, apparatus such as slides, books, etc) or is engaging in fantasy activity (e.g. pretending to be dead) (p. 80). Different types of play are also defined by the researchers (e.g. self, parallel, and group play). The behaviors defined and recorded in the above fashion are examined in relation to data collected on age, sex, family structure, environmental setting, and other variables. On the basis of their analysis, the investigators report, for example, that: (a) social play and talking occurred more frequently in the older group; (b) talking and sucking behaviors were more frequent among girls, whereas play horses and rough and tumble play were more frequent among boys; (c) outdoors there was more running, laughing, rough and tumble play, and less aggressive behavior (pp. 81–82). An ethological description of the specific, and in the past often ignored, rough and tumble play category for children is available in Blurton-Jones (31, pp. 450–54).

In the 1930s a number of observational studies emphasizing the importance of investigating ecological, or play context variables, were conducted. For example, Van Alstyne (284) noted that play materials such as dishes, dolls, wagons, and telephones encouraged conversation between children, whereas materials such as clay, scissors, puzzles, and books related to a more passive type of cooperation. Johnson (155) found that playgrounds with less equipment encouraged both social contact and social conflict among children whereas playgrounds with more equipment encouraged the opposite. Other studies of this type were also conducted at this time by Parten (203) and Updegraff & Herbst (283).

More recent studies of relationships existing between play setting and play activity have been reported by Gump & Sutton-Smith (123) and Gump, Schoggen & Redl (122). In this latter study, an interesting analysis comparing the play of one boy in his home environment and in a camp environment is available. Examples of other recent studies utilizing this ecological perspective and providing information on children's play behavior are available in works by Barker (17), Shure (239), and Doyle (73). Doyle makes a useful distinction between single-niche play settings (i.e. those that encourage solitariness or competitiveness, like puzzles or riding a bicycle) and multiple-niche play settings (i.e. those that encourage sociality and cooperativeness like teeter-totters). A lengthier review of these ecological studies may be found in a book edited by Herron & Sutton-Smith (136, pp. 77–82); and a discussion and methodological critique of the early ecologists in comparison with more recent ethological studies is available in an article by Smith & Connolly (244).

In these studies useful descriptions of play contexts (particularly environmental contexts) are quite common, and discussions of associations between contextual factors and types of play are also frequently offered. Unfortunately, however, there is often a lack of detailed information on specific play texts. The ethologists' interest in formulating behavioral definitions of play on the basis of careful observations of this behavior are also significant, although here I note a tendency on the part of researchers to seek to remove themselves from the actual context of activity by acting as passive or "unresponsive" observers (e.g. 31, p. 440), or by using one-way mirrors or videotape techniques. In regard to this approach, it is my suggestion that researchers who attempt to study children's play in "naturally occurring contexts" must recognize the part they have "to play" in such contexts; and if they do not, then the investigation will be neither ethologically or ecologically sound.

Psychological Orientation

EARLY EVOLUTIONARY STUDIES   Evolutionary theories of children's play have had more impact in psychology than anthropology. Hall's (129) *recapitulation theory* is probably the best known in this regard. Hall believed that "The best index and guide to the stated activities of adults in past ages is found in the instinctive, untaught, and nonimitative plays of children . . ." (129, p. 202). He assumed that the play "stages" of children recapitulated the entire biocultural history of mankind.[7] Following the work of Hall, Reany (213) proposed a scheme of children's "play periods" thought to be comparable to man's various evolutionary stages. For example, the *animal stage* or period (birth to age 7) was reflected in swinging and climbing games; the *savage stage* (7 to 9)

---

[7]Gilmore (106, p. 312) notes that Hall was the first theorist to suggest the idea of play "stages."

exhibited hunting and throwing games; the *nomad stage* (9 to 12) was reflected in simple skill and adventure games, as well as "interest in keeping pets"; the *pastoral stage* and the *tribal stage* (12 to 17) were characterized by doll play, gardening, and finally team games (p. 12). Interpretations of play as a cultural survival, as found in Gomme (112, 113) and Newell (195), are earlier examples of this recapitulation theory. This view of play has been widely criticized and is no longer taken seriously by most investigators.[8]

PSYCHOANALYTIC STUDIES   Psychoanalytic theories of play, as developed initially by Freud (95–97), are a special case of more general cathartic theories of this phenomenon (106, p. 320). Freud's explanations of this behavior are varied, but the idea that children act out and repeat problematic situations in play in order to *master* them predominates in his writings. This view has been repeated, revised, and/or expanded by many, including Alexander (4), Bühler (52), Peller (204), Waelder (288), and Winnicott (296).

Two brief examples of Freud's interpretation of play are presented here. The first, commonly cited, incident is found in *Beyond the Pleasure Principle* (96), where Freud discusses the behavior of an 18-month-old boy who had developed the habit of throwing all available objects into a corner of his room or under his bed at those times (which were apparently quite frequent) when his mother left him. Freud noticed, however, that the boy took special care to fling over the edge of his bed a small reel with a string attached to it, which, after throwing away, he would pull back and then repeat the action over and over. Freud suggested that this activity represented the child's "great cultural achievement," in which he was able to allow his mother to go away by compensating himself for this by "staging the disappearing and return of objects within his reach" (p. 33). Freud's indirect, but by now very famous, treatment of "Little Hans" (95) also includes information on his diagnostic use of play. Here the boy's development of a sudden fear of horses, presumably acted out by his pretending to be a horse, is interpreted as symptomatic "of those fears and adjustments with which the boy was trying to cope at the time," specifically, anxieties about himself and his feelings toward his father, mother, and a new baby in the home (185, p. 225).

Both of these incidents illustrate the major themes in psychoanalytic interpretations of children's play behavior: most specifically the view that in play the child is able to deal with anxiety provoking situations by making himself/herself the active master, as opposed to passive victim, of the situation. In so doing the child is often thought to project his own anxious or hostile feelings on to others or objects (e.g. the witch roasts the mother doll in the stove) (185, p. 27). Freud also suggested that the wishes and conflicts of each of his psychosexual stages would be expressed in play (e.g. blowing bubbles might reflect oral frustration; sand

[8]However, Langness has recently noted that the influential child development studies of Piaget are closely related to the early evolutionary ideas of psychologists such as Hall (164, pp. 33–38).

and water play would substitute for "soiling and wetting" and so forth). Finally, as expressed most clearly in *Jokes and their Relation to the Unconscious* (97), Freud believed that all children wish to "grow up," and therefore by imitating adults in their play, children are able to make possible what is at present impossible and thereby once again master a frustrating (although in this case not necessarily psychically painful) situation.

The most obvious use, as well as expansion, of Freud's theory of children's play is apparent in the widespread utilization of play for diagnostic and therapeutic purposes. Anna Freud, however, is significant for her suggestion that play may serve defensive purposes by promoting denial by the child of anxious feelings (106, p. 321). Generally she does not stress the importance of play in children's analysis, however, suggesting that "instead of being invested with symbolic meaning it may sometimes admit of a harmless explanation" (94, p. 35).

Klein (157) chose to focus specifically on the use of the symbolic play of children in analysis, suggesting that this behavior was in fact an appropriate substitute for the verbal free associations traditionally used in adult analysis. To encourage and facilitate projective play of this type, Klein developed the use of miniature toys (generally dolls representing family figures) in her analytic sessions with children. This doll play approach, adopting, as it does, a view of play as a projective eliciting device similar to a TAT or Rorschach, has now become widely used for clinical (e.g. 14) as well as research (e.g. 173) purposes. In these instances, play *texts* are used as a *context* for the diagnosis and treatment or research investigation of children's nonplay behavior.

Erikson's (85, 86, 88, 89) numerous studies of children's play stress the importance of viewing this activity in terms of its growth enhancing, as opposed to anxiety reducing, qualities. In *Childhood and Society* (89), for example, he suggests that "the child's play is the infantile form of the human ability to deal with experience by creating model situations and to master reality by experiment and planning" (p. 322). Erikson has also studied the phenomenon of "play disruption" (85) and sex differences as these are reflected in play configurations and constructions (86, 88).

A recent psychoanalytically oriented study by Gould (115) is available in which an attempt is made to present an analysis of children's spontaneous play fantasy productions. This work is unusual in its presentation of a number of specific play texts collected for Gould by teachers in an American middle-class nursery school. In her interpretation of these texts, she draws on the studies of Piaget, Freud, and many others to relate these events to the cognitive and affective developmental level of individual children. In this way she expands on the early synthetic work of Issacs (151, 152).

Examples of attempts to interpret non-Western children's play from a psychoanalytic perspective are available in Erikson's studies (87, 89) of Ogalala Sioux and Yurok children and Roheim's reports (219) on Duau (Normanby Island) children. The clearest example of anthropologists' employment of this perspective is found in Jules & Zunia Henry's *Doll Play of Pilagá Indian*

Children (134). Likewise the Roberts & Sutton-Smith studies (266), as well as the *Six Cultures* project (292), exhibit this approach in their descriptions of play and games as expressive activities and exercises in cultural mastery. Finally, Maccoby, Modiano & Lander's (178) social psychological analysis of "Games and Social Character in a Mexican Village" utilizes this perspective, and Landy (163) also adopts this approach in his use of doll play for the study of Vallecañese children.

DEVELOPMENTAL STUDIES   The tendency to associate types of play activities with specific stages or sequences of child development has already been noted in the works of Hall, Reany, Freud, and others. But the preeminent developmental theorist for children's play is Piaget. Piaget is well known for his extensive studies on the intellectual development of children. He has, however, also been a student of children's play. In his study of moral development in children (205), Piaget investigates how children learn the rules for playing the game of marbles. The various stages of rule conceptualization are discussed (e.g. younger children believe that the rules are absolute and immutable whereas older children view them as derived from social consensus), and a lengthy description of the game and its variations in Geneva and Neuchâtel are offered.

Piaget's most significant study of children's play appears in *Play, Dreams, and Imitation in Childhood* (206). This work is based on observations of his own three children's play activities. In analyzing this material, relationships between play and intellectual functioning are clearly drawn. According to Piaget there are two major aspects of cognition: accommodation and assimilation. Accommodation is that process whereby the child (or any organism) modifies his/her own mental set in response to external demands. In contrast, assimilation is that process whereby the child incorporates elements of the external world into his/her own schemata. Both processes are thought to be a part of all actions; however, at times one may predominate over the other, while at other times they may be in balance or "equilibrium." Acts characterized by the "primacy of assimilation over accommodation" are described as play, whereas imitation occurs when accommodation predominates over assimilation (p. 87). Intelligent adaptation is said to occur when there is a stable equilibrium achieved between these two processes. The assumptions implicit in this theory, as they influence Piaget's specific theory of play, are discussed here in the COGNITIVE STUDIES section.

For Piaget the ontogeny of play must be viewed in relation to the development of intelligence in the child and therefore each cognitive stage, which Piaget has outlined, exhibits a characteristic type of play activity. Play in the *sensory-motor* period is characterized by repeated performance of newly mastered motor abilities and evidence of pleasure in engaging in such activity. Symbolic play, "where actions appropriate to one object are used on a substitute," corresponds with the *representational* or *pre-operational* phase of development in Piaget's schema (185, pp. 54–55). Make-believe or sociodramatic play is said to be characterized by this symbolic pretense whereby a child acts "as if" he/she were a father, witch, etc. This form of play is "pure assimilation" reflecting, according to Piaget, the child's repetition and distortion of expressions or activities of adults. Corresponding with the *concrete operational* phase is the appearance of *games-with-rules*. Through the use and development of collective, as opposed to individualized, symbols (as this is promoted in games and other activities engaged in at this time) the child's reasoning becomes more logical and objective, and therefore presumably closer to reality, preparing him/ her finally for the *formal operational* period.

There are many questions to be asked of this developmental approach. For example, does assimilative play become less frequent as one grows up? Is this schema applicable only for the Swiss upper-middle-class children of Piaget's studies? Does one note the same sequence of play for other Western children, and what about the ontogeny of play in non-Western children?

In relation to the first question, Piaget recognizes that games with rules, characterized by assimilation, do occur among adults and so in this sense play does not cease to exist in the formal operational period. However, he also argues that over time play becomes "more and more adequately adapted to reality," characterized less by "the deformation and subordination of reality to the desires of the self," and so in this sense play does decrease with age (207, p. 339). In contrast, Sutton-Smith suggests that play is "not displaced by reality or by greater rationality, nor does it cease to be a vital function with age" (259, p. 339). The recent studies of Singer (240) on daydreams and Klinger (158) on fantasy would seem to indicate that, contrary to Piaget, adults do engage in a variety of assimilative play activities.

A number of investigators have also recently commented on the fact that Piaget's play sequences do not appear in the same fashion in their own studies. For example, Singer (241, p. 3) notes his personal participation in make-believe football games in early adolescence. The Opies' (199) work tends to confirm this observation, at least for British children, in that they report a great deal of group fantasy behavior between the ages of 5 and 12. As reported by Singer, Smilansky suggests that play does not necessarily become more realistic during later childhood, but rather with a greater range of experience it becomes possible "for children at older ages to engage in bizarre and strange stories, albeit more organized from an adult standpoint" (241, p. 15). She also proposes that the symbolic, imaginative play said to be characteristic of early childhood by Piaget may be related more to cultural and socioeconomic factors than to developmental ones, although of course Eifermann has challenged these particular findings on the basis of her own studies. Research reports by El'Konin (83) on the play of Russian nursery school children indicates that play for these children consists of redundant and realistic, as opposed to imaginative, replications of the activities of adults.

Eifermann's (80, 81) research also reports contradictory findings for certain of Piaget's statements. Most specifically, she states that her findings (p. 295) generally disconfirm Piaget's claim that "games with rules increase in number, both relatively and absolutely, with age" as they replace sensory-motor and symbolic play activities. Instead she found that an absolute decline in participation in games with rules appears around 11 years but a relative decline in participation appears at a somewhat later age. In relation to this decline she reports a corresponding rise in participation in unstructured play activities, particularly types of practice play (e.g. jump rope, running, etc). Eifermann's information does support Piaget's claim (although he did not specify this in terms of socioeconomic level) that symbolic play for "high" schools (upper-middle-class children) is already rare at ages 6 to 8, while in the "low" schools children are found to actively engage in symbolic play in the first two grades (pp. 295–96).

Anthropological studies of the play of non-Western children have tended not to focus on developmental considerations. In many instances the three types of play discussed by Piaget are noted by those ethnographers who choose to describe this activity; however, the age of children engaged in such activities is often not reported, although this is less true in more recent studies. Clearly, more detailed studies of the *sociocultural contexts* of play must be conducted in order to answer many of the questions posed by Piaget's theory as well as the recent studies of Eifermann, El'Konin, and Smilansky.

Erickson (89) has also proposed a series of play stages in conjunction with his more general theory of psychosexual development. Play in this schema develops first as *autocosmic* play consisting of "exploration by repetition of sensual perceptions, of kinesthetic sensations, of vocalizations, etc" (p. 220). Play in the *microsphere* is often solitary play, and it relates to play with "manageable toys," and is engaged in when the child "needs to overhaul his ego" (p. 221). This play has its dangers, however, as it can promote the expression of anxious themes and lead therefore to play disruption. Generally, Erickson states, play in the microsphere will lead to pleasure in mastery of toys and mastery of traumas projected on them. At nursery school age play occurs in the *macrosphere*. This is "the world shared with others," and often others "are treated as things, are inspected, run into, or forced to 'be horsie.' " Bateson & Mead, in *Balinese Character* (24), include a lengthy discussion and photographic illustration of autocosmic play and symbols (pp. 131–43), and here there is also an excellent description and sequence of photographs of the play activities of a group of girls (pp. 207–11).

Examples of other discussions of developmental sequences for play are given by Gesell (105), Hurlock (148), and Lowenfeld (176).

COGNITIVE STUDIES   Piaget is the main proponent of theories on play as cognition. His specific approach to the interpretation of play has already been described briefly. A variety of critiques of this approach are available (106, 185, 241). However, by far the most sustained analysis of Piaget's view has been formulated by Sutton-Smith (259).

Sutton-Smith (259) suggests that due to Piaget's "copyist epistemology" and concern with directed thought (e.g. understanding the operations of the physical world) as opposed to undirected thought (e.g. understanding imaginative thought), he has been unable to account for play and has therefore reduced it to a function of cognition. Sutton-Smith argues that for Piaget, concepts are ultimately copies derived from "an external reality," and since play is said to distort this reality it can have no constitutive role within thought (pp. 329, 335). In short, "Intelligence cannot proceed without imitation. It can proceed without play" (p. 329). Because Piaget cannot explain play in terms of his own system, Sutton-Smith asserts that he resorts to a series of affective explanations for this behavior (e.g. play functions to serve "ego continuity").

Piaget responds to this critique by stating that he does not exhibit a copyist epistemology, because it is his belief that "concepts are the expression of an assimilation by schemes of transformation" (207, p. 337). He reiterates his view that in play one sees "the primacy of assimilation over accommodation" whereby reality may be transformed without the necessity of submitting this transformation "to the criterion of objective fact" (p. 338). However, Piaget stresses that play in his system is never subordinated to "accommodative imitation" and cannot be reduced to such imitation because it is always "assimilation of reality to the self."

Sutton-Smith (257) replies to these comments by suggesting that Piaget still does not indicate what the vital cognitive *function* of play is in early childhood. Secondly, he states that Piaget continues to focus on the way play corresponds with adaptive cognitive structures at various age levels rather than the structural uniqueness of particular play *transformations*. The result, according to Sutton-Smith, is that imagination is subordinated to reason (pp. 341–42).

In other statements Sutton-Smith (260, 261, 269) has suggested his own view as to play's relation to cognitive functioning. For example, he proposes that the child's adoption of an "as if" attitude in play illustrates his/her ability to *conserve* imaginative identities even in the presence of contrary stimuli (261). However, it is not until the ages of 5 to 7 years that children "can conserve class identities of phenomena such as number, quantity, space," etc (p. 256). If the "as if" attitude of play is viewed as a representational set, Sutton-Smith suggests that the ability to use such sets in play perhaps facilitates the adoption of representational categories on a cognitive level.

Bateson's (20, 21) theory of play communication also suggests that play is itself an important learning arena. Here Bateson proposes that in play the important thing that is learned is not the specific role or activity that is being played, but rather "that behavior can be set to a logical type or to a style . . . and the fact that the choice of style or role is related to the frame and context of behavior . . ." (20, p. 265).

The study of children's play "symbolics" has recently been undertaken by a number of Russian researchers. Most of these studies have not been translated into English, but a useful review is available in El'Konin (83). The most interesting thing to be noted in these studies is the importance of adults for inspiring, by example or suggestion, the symbolic play of children. For example, by noting the history of the use of certain objects like sticks, and following the play of children on a daily basis, it is found that a stick may be called a "thermometer" because the teacher who gave it to the child called it by that name (p. 225). These studies also suggest that play may be crucial for understanding the development of abstract thought in children because in play symbolization there occurs the "emancipation of the word from the thing" (p. 230). However, as Vygotsky has stated, it is also possible to "over-intellectualize" play and transform the child into "an unsuccessful algebraist who cannot yet write the symbols on paper, but depicts them in action" (287, p. 8).

A useful reader edited by Almy (5) is available containing various articles related to cognitive and motivational studies of early childhood play. Bruner's (49, 50) more recent studies of relationships between play and learning are also important to consider, particularly his most recent suggestion that play makes possible the "practice of subroutines of behavior that later come together in useful problem solving" (50, p. 81). And finally, a number of articles discussing the pros and cons of formulating learning games (e.g. math, spelling, history games) for use in the classroom situation are presented in Avedon & Sutton-Smith's *The Study of Games* (13).

One of the problems in all these studies is their tendency (as noted by Sutton-Smith for Piaget) to reduce play to cognitive functioning, and in the process to transform play into the "serious business" of children. However, I suggest that if researchers are to learn anything significant about play from these investigations, they will have to focus on what children *learn in play,* and not what children *distort* by playing, and not what children can be taught by *using* play.

EXPERIMENTAL STUDIES Experimentalists have frequently used play as a context (i.e. a testing ground) for the study of other aspects of children's behavior. Recently, however, a number of studies have appeared which use play as a testing ground but also make it the subject of the test. Examples of both types of investigations are described briefly here.

A useful review of experimental research conducted between 1920–1932 is available by Hurlock (148). She pays specific attention to studies related to developmental aspects of children's play. Britt & Janus (47) consider a number of experimental studies up to 1941, and Jerome & Dorothy Singer (242) have prepared a review of more recent experimental studies of children's imaginative play.

In the 1940s, the use of the doll play technique (originally developed by Klein) in personality research studies became quite common. Levin & Wardwell's (173) review of these studies includes a wide range of material from approximately 1940–1960. The value of this approach, as stated by the authors, is that "it is possible to study a great variety of human problems 'in miniature' " (p. 156). Examples of the various types of problems investigated are: (a) aggression and its relation to age, sex, and child-rearing factors (e.g. 237); (b) stereotypy (e.g. 16); (c) parental identification (e.g. 7); (d) effect of child's separation from parents (e.g. 16, 237); and (e) racial and religious identifications and biases (e.g. 6).

The best example of this approach in anthropology is Jules & Zunia Henry's *Doll Play of Pilagá Indian Children* (134), in which the doll play technique is used for the investigation of sibling rivalry among Pilagá children. Following the work of Levy (174) on sibling rivalry of American children, the Henrys adopted this approach for use in a field work context to study the patterning of this behavior in a non-Western culture. Although this study provides important information on the phenomenon of sibling rivalry in Pilagá culture, due to its use of a play as projection metaphor, it does not provide detailed material on children's play.

Gewirtz (104) has also used the doll play technique to investigate cultural differences in the expression of aggression by Sac and Fox and midwestern white children. Here it is found that Fox boys exhibit more doll play aggression than girls; however, both Fox boys and girls exhibit less aggression than the midwestern white children. Again, because play is used as a context for the investigation of aggression in this study, we learn nothing significant about the children's play behavior.

More promising research in this regard is currently being conducted by a number of psychologists (e.g. 90, 101, 106, 241, 242). In *The Child's World of Make-Believe: Experimental Studies of Imaginative Play* (241), Singer presents a useful summary of theories of children's play, particularly imaginative play, as well as discussions of methodological problems in, and solutions for, the recording, noting, and categorizing of this behavior. Discussion of the measurement of imaginative predispositions in children is also offered and chapters reporting experimental play interventions are included. For example, Freyberg (Chapter 6) discusses changes in the imaginative behavior of urban "disadvantaged" kindergarten children exposed to a specific "training" program in make-believe (pp. 129–54).

A major interest of these studies is the development of techniques like the above training program for facilitating pretend play for children. Investigations such as Freyberg's, as well as studies of television programs, are being conducted to determine what affects children's spontaneous play behavior. There are, however, many questions to be raised about these efforts (e.g. is it possible to "measure" imagination and spontaneity; and likewise is it possible to train someone to "be spontaneous"?). Specifically, "training" the "poor," "urban disadvantaged," etc in make-believe or sociodramatic play is questionable although many investigators (e.g. Smilansky, Sutton-Smith, Singer) would seem to argue to the contrary. I have suggested elsewhere that expressions of imagination may appear in various forms, and it is also clear to me that the research so far is not at all conclusive on the fact that children, other than middle-class children, are "imaginatively disadvantaged."

One of the most recent and interesting experimental studies available is reported by Garvey & Berndt (101). By observing a number of previously acquainted 3 to 5-year-old American children engaged in play, in a laboratory context, the investigators collected information on how children communicate pretending, how they organize these play episodes in terms of plans, and the types of play roles and activities they most frequently adopt. Pretend play is defined here as an action involving "some transformation of the Here and Now in which the child is actually situated" (p. 1). The authors report that there are at least five types of communication involved in pretending: The first type is called *negation of pretend* whereby an ongoing pretend state is transformed back to the "Here and Now" (e.g. "I'm not the dragon anymore") (p. 4). The second type of communication is labeled *enactment* and relates to actions, gestures, attitudes, tone of voice, etc, engaged in by the player to signify his/her pretend identity. *Play signals* are the third variety discussed, said to be markers of a play orientation such as giggling, grinning, winking, etc. *Procedural* or *preparatory behaviors* are also necessary so that objects may be apportioned correctly (e.g. "This is my telephone") and that rights may be clarified (e.g. "I didn't get a turn"), as well as general references to interaction (e.g. "Do you want to play with me?") (p. 5). Finally *explicit verbal mention of pretend transformations* is said to occur in a number of ways (e.g. the child may mention a partner's role, "Are you going to be a bride?"; or his/her own role, "I'm a work lady at work," and so forth) (p. 7). The authors discuss the importance of these verbal transformations by suggesting that to some extent, for children of this age, "the saying is the playing" (p. 9). The importance of this observation is the authors' recognition of the intimate relation existing between play texts and play contexts, and it is this view which makes this study significant.

Reference Material

The nineteenth century studies of Schiller (227), Spencer (246), and Groos (120, 121) are still worthy of consideration by students of children's play who are interested in understanding the historical context out of which most twentieth century theories of play developed. Ariès (9) and Stone (250) enlarge this perspective in their discussions of the emergence of children and child's play in Western societies. The interpretive works of Huizinga (147) and Caillois (54) are also important reading for play researchers.

A number of survey books, articles, readers, and bibliographies have recently appeared on the specific topic of children's play. One of the best in this regard is Herron & Sutton-Smith's *Child's Play* (136). This book contains a useful collection of many of the most important articles written over the years on this subject. The experimental, ecological, psychoanalytic, cognitive, and developmental perspective are all included in this work, as is the Sutton-Smith/Piaget debate, but many of the more recent studies available are not reported here. However, reviews by Sutton-Smith (270) and J. & D. Singer (242) cover this more recent literature. Sutton-Smith's *The Folk-Games of Children* (266) provides a useful and needed compilation of many of his most significant publications on this topic. Included here in its entirety is his 1959 study of *The Games of New Zealand Children*, as well as examples of many of the Roberts & Sutton-Smith studies. In Goodman's *The Culture of Childhood* (114), a brief survey of anthropological studies of children's play, games, and humor is available. A discussion of anthropological studies of play is also provided by Norbeck (196) in a *Natural History* special supplement devoted to the topic of play. Articles by other play researchers (e.g. Sutton-Smith, Leacock) are also included here. Millar's *The Psychology of Play* (185) is also an important resource, because until recently many of the most significant studies of children's play have been made by psychologists.

The most extensive bibliography on children's play, to my knowledge, has been compiled by Herron et al (135). This work contains psychological, psychiatric, anthropological, and sociological references. In Avedon & Sutton-Smith's *The Study of Games* (13) selected bibliographies on general studies of children's games, children's games in specific cultures, singing games, string figure games, as well as a reference list of studies of children's games published in languages other than English between 1955 and 1965 are offered. Finally, less extensive bibliographies on children's games in folklore and anthropological sources are available by Daiken (67) and Hymes (150). A recent bibliographic compilation of studies of traditional games, including children's play, in Mexico has been prepared by Scheffler (226).

CONCLUSTION: FUTURE DEVELOPMENTS

Children's play has been studied from a number of perspectives. Researchers adopting an anthropological or sociological orientation tend to examine either its textual or contextual manifestations, even though Bateson (21) demonstrated in 1955 that this was quite impractical. Psychologists and psychological anthropologists, on the other hand, generally use play as a context for the examination of children's nonplay behavior. Recent studies (101, 160, 230, 269) indicate, however, that researchers are beginning to develop more systemic as well as systematic approaches for the investigation of this phenomenon.

Anthropologists should contribute to these studies by producing "ethnographies of children's play" which are both textual and contextual in orientation. Currently there are few such ethnographies available, and because of this almost all theorizing about play has been done on the basis of studies of Western children. Due to this lack of information differences between Western and non-Western children's play are often interpreted as evidence of deficiency in play styles rather than as evidence of variation in play styles. As anthropologists know from their studies of other topics, such views generally last only as long as there is a deficiency of rich ethnographic material.

There are a number of more specific topics which need to be examined cross-culturally. These are briefly listed here. (*a*) Studies of the varying, and widening, contexts of children's play (e.g. play in the immediate family, in the compound, village, neighborhood, school, etc) should be made in order to explore not only how contexts may affect texts, but also how texts may transform contexts. (*b*) Adopting this latter focus, the "games of order and disorder" which symbolically invert the social order, as Sutton-Smith has suggested, should be investigated to determine the nature and degree of their existence in other cultures. (*c*) Studies of relationships between play and sex roles, occupational roles, and cognitive skills are all important to pursue in attempting to determine what children actually learn in play. Do they, in fact, learn specific social roles and skills, or are they more generally "learning to learn" (Bateson,

20, 22)? (*d*) Cross-cultural studies focusing on developmental issues should be formulated specically to put Piaget's and others' theories of play "stages" to the ethnographic test. In regard to such studies I note a particular lack of information in the ethnographic literature on early infant play. (*e*) Studies of the various forms of children's verbal play (e.g. puns, riddles, etc) should also be much more thoroughly investigated by anthropologists.

I have one final suggestion to offer prospective researchers and that is that they should expect to find that, whatever else it may be, child's play is *not* easy.

Table 1   Children's play: Selected references organized by geographical area[a]

AFRICA
General
Leacock (166)
Schwartzman & Barbera (231)
West Africa
Bascom (19)
Beárt (25)
P. & L. Bohannan (35)
Fortes (93)
Grindal (118)
Lancy (160–162)
Leis (169)
Central and South Africa
Brewster (37)
Centner (56)
Gowlett (116)
Kidd (156)
Leacock (166)
Read (212)
Sanderson (225)
Turnbull (279)
Van Zyl (285)
East Africa
Castle (55)
Harrison (132)
Lambert (159)
Leakey (167)
Raum (211)

CENTRAL AND SOUTH AMERICA
Central America
Edmonson (77)
Garcia (99, 100)
Maccoby, Modiano & Lander (178)
Modiano (192)
Nerlove et al (194a)

K. & R. Romney (220)
Scheffler (226)
von Glascoe (286)
Caribbean
Beckwith (25a)
Elder (82)
Landy (163)
Parsons (202)
South America
Cooper (60)
J. & Z. Henry (134)
Hilger (138)
Jackson (153)
Schwartzman & Barbera (231)
Shoemaker (238)

NORTH AMERICA
General
Abrahams (1)
Babcock (15)
Barker & Wright (17)
Brewster (38, 41, 42)
Browne (48)
Buckley (51)
Chase (58)
Cox (61)
Culin (63)
J. & A. Fischer (92)
Goldstein (111)
Hall (130)
Hostetler & Huntington (142)
Monroe (193)
Newell (195)
Parrott (201)
Schwartzman (229, 230)
Stearns (248)

Table 1 (*Continued*)

Sutton-Smith & Rosenberg (276)
Wolford (298)
North American Indians
General
Culin (66)
Southeast
Hassrick & Carpenter (133)
Rowell (223)
Speck (245)
Northcentral and Plains
Daniel (68)
Dorsey (71)
Erikson (89)
Gilmore (107)
Grinnell (119)
Hilger (137)
Lesser (170)
Searcy (236)
Walker (289)
Southwest
Dennis (69)
Hodge (140)
Leighton & Kluckhohn (168)
Mook (194)
Opler (200)
Stevenson (249)
California
Erikson (87)
Stearns (248)
Northwest Coast
Wolcott (297)
Alaska
Ager (2, 3)
Lantis (165)
Ramson (210)

ASIA
Brewster (43)
Culin (64)
Haas (125)
Minturn & Hitchcock (188)
Mistry (189–191)

EUROPE
Ariès (9)
Brewster (39, 44)
Chukovsky (59)

Crombie (62)
Douglas (72)
Gomme (112, 113)
Milojkovic-Djuric (187)
I. & P. Opie (198, 199)
Watson (290)

NEAR EAST
Brewster (45)
Dennis (70)
Dundes et al (76)
Eifermann (79–81)
Granqvist (117)
Smilansky (243)
Spiro (247)

OCEANIA
Melanesia
Aufenanger (10, 11)
Barton (18)
Burridge (53)
Haddon (127)
Hogbin (141)
Mead (184)
Roheim (219)
Rosenstiel (221)
Watt (291)
Micronesia
T. & H. Maretzki (181)
Polynesia
Best (29, 30)
Bolton (36)
Culin (65)
Emerson (84)
Firth (91)
Hocart (139)
Mead (183)
Pukui (209)
Stumpf & Cozens (252, 253)
Sutton-Smith (254–256, 264, 267)
Australia
Berndt (28)
Haddon (126)
Harney (131)
Howard (143–146)
Leakey (167)
Roth (222)
Salter (224)

Table 1 (*Continued*)

Indonesia	Jocano (154)
Bateson & Mead (24)	W. & C. Nydegger (197)
Beran (26, 27)	Storey (251)
DuBois (74)	Williams (295)

[a]In this table selected references of descriptive accounts of children's play drawn from the anthropological and folklore literature are grouped according to geographical area. In certain instances reports or studies from other disciplines (e.g. psychology, education) are included. The publications are listed by the author(s) name and the number of the reference as it appears in the bibliography.

Literature Cited

1. Abrahams, R. D., ed. 1969. *Jump-Rope Rhymes: A Dictionary*. Austin: Univ. Texas Press (publ. for Am. Folklore Soc.)
2. Ager, L. P. 1974. Storyknifing: an Alaskan girls' game. *J. Folklore Inst.* Indiana Univ. Publ. 11
3. Ager, L. P. 1976. Cultural values in Eskimo children's games. *Problems and Prospects in the Study of Play*, ed. D. Lancy, B. A. Tindall. Proc. 1st Ann. Meet. Assoc. Anthropol. Study of Play. New York: Leisure Press. In press
4. Alexander, F. 1958. A contribution to the theory of play. *Psychoanal. Q.* 27:175–93
5. Almy, M., ed. 1968. *Early Childhood Play: Selected Readings Related to Cognition and Motivation*. New York: Simon & Schuster
6. Ammons, R. B. 1950. Reactions in a projective doll-play interview of white males two to six years of age to differences in skin color and facial features. *J. Genet. Psychol.* 76:323–41
7. Ammons, R. B., Ammons, H. S. 1949. Parent preferences in young children's doll-play interviews. *J. Abnorm. Soc. Psychol.* 44:490–505
8. Appleton, L. E. 1910. *A Comparative Study of the Play Activities of Adult Savages and Civilized Children*. Univ. Chicago Press
9. Ariès, P. 1962. A modest contribution to the history of games and pastimes. *Centuries of Childhood*, 62–99. New York: Vintage
10. Aufenanger, H. 1958. Children's games and entertainments among the Kumngo tribe in Central New Guinea. *Anthropos* 53:575–84
11. Ibid 1961. A children's arrow-thrower in the Central Highlands of New Guinea. 56:633
12. Avedon, E. M. 1971. The structural elements of games. See Ref. 13, 419–26
13. Avedon, E. M., Sutton-Smith, B. 1971. *The Study of Games*. New York: Wiley
14. Axline, V. M. 1969. *Play Therapy*. New York: Ballantine
15. Babcock, W. H. 1888. Games of Washington children. *Am. Anthropol.* 1:243–84
16. Bach, G. R. 1946. Father fantasies and father typing in father-separated children. *Child Dev.* 17:63–80
17. Barker, R., Wright, H. F. 1966. *One Boy's Day*. Hamden, Conn: Archon
18. Barton, F. R. 1908. Children's games in British New Guinea. *J. R. Anthropol. Inst.* 38:259–79
19. Bascom, W. 1969. *The Yoruba of Southwest Nigeria*. New York: Holt, Rinehart & Winston
20. Bateson, G. 1971. The message 'this is play.' See Ref. 136, 261–66
21. Bateson, G. 1972. A theory of play and fantasy. See Ref. 22, 177–93
22. Bateson, G. 1972. *Steps To An Ecology of Mind*. New York: Ballantine
23. Bateson, G., Jackson , D., Haley, J., Weakland, J. 1972. Toward a theory of schizophrenia. See Ref. 22, 201–27
24. Bateson, G., Mead, M. 1942. *Balinese Character: A Photographic Analysis*. New York Acad. Sci.
25. Beárt, C. 1955. *Jeux et jouets de l'ouest africain, II*. Dakar: IFAN
25a. Beckwith, M. W. 1922. Folk-games of Jamaica. *Publ. Folklore Found.*, Vassar College, No. 1
26. Beran, J. A. 1973. Characteristics

of children's play and games in the Southern Philippines. *Silliman J.* 20:100–13

27. Ibid. Some elements of power in Filipino children's play, 194–207

28. Berndt, R. M. 1940. Some Aboriginal children's games. *Mankind* 2:289–93

29. Best, E. 1922. Pastimes of Maori Children. *NZ J. Sci. Technol.* 5:254

30. Best, E. 1925. Games and pastimes of the Maori. *Dom. Mus. Bull.* Wellington, No. 8

31. Blurton-Jones, N. 1969. An ethological study of some aspects of social behavior of children in nursery school. In *Primate Ethology*, ed. D. Morris, 437–63. New York: Doubleday

32. Blurton-Jones, N., ed. 1972. *Ethological Studies of Child Behavior.* Cambridge Univ. Press

33. Bohannan, L., Bohannan, P. 1953. *The Tiv of Central Nigeria.* London: Int. Inst. (West. Afr., Part 8, in Ethnogr. Survey of Afr.)

34. Bohannan, P. 1965. The Tiv of Nigeria, *Peoples of Africa*, ed. J. Gibbs, 513–46. New York: Holt, Rinehart & Winston

35. Bohannan, P., Bohannan, L. 1958. A source notebook on the Tiv life cycle. *Three Source Notebooks in Tiv Ethnography.* New Haven: HRAF

36. Bolton, H. C. 1891. Some Hawaiian pastimes. *J. Am. Folklore* 4:21–26

37. Brewster, P. G. 1944. Two games from Africa. *Am. Anthropol.* 46:268–69

38. Brewster, P. G. 1945. Johnny on the pony, a New York State game. *NY Folklore Q.* 1:239–40

39. Brewster, P. G. 1951. A string figure series from Greece. *Laographia* 101–25

40. Brewster, P. G. 1951. Four games of tag from India. *Midwest Folklore* 1:239–41

41. Brewster, P. G. 1952. Children's games and rhymes. *The Frank C. Brown Collection of North Carolina Folklore*, 1:32–219. Durham, NC: Univ. Press

42. Brewster, P. G. 1953. *American Nonsinging Games.* Norman: Univ. Oklahoma Press

43. Brewster, P. G. 1955. A collection of games from India, with some notes on similar games in other parts of the world. *Z. Ethnol.* 80:88–102

44. Brewster, P. G. 1957. Some games from Czechoslovakia. *South. Folklore.* 21:165–74

45. Brewster, P. G. 1960. A sampling of games from Turkey. *East and West* (Rome) 11:15–20

46. Brewster, P. G. 1971. The importance of collecting and study of games. See Ref. 13, 9–17

47. Britt, S. H., Janus, S. Q. 1941. Toward a social psychology of human play. *J. Soc. Psychol.* 13:351–84

48. Browne, R. B. 1955. Southern California jump-rope rhymes: a study in variants. *West. Folklore* 14:3–22

49. Bruner, J. S. 1972. Nature and uses of immaturity. *Am. Psychol.* 27: 687–708

50. Bruner, J. S. 1975. Play is serious business. *Psychol. Today*, 81–83

51. Buckley, B. 1966. Jump-rope rhymes—suggestions for classification and study. *Keystone Folklore Q.* 11:99–111

52. Bühler, K. 1930. *The Mental Development of Children.* New York: Harcourt

53. Burridge, K. O. L. 1957. A Tangu game. *Man* 57:88–89

54. Caillois, R. 1961. *Man, Play, and Games.* New York: The Free Press

55. Castle, E. B. 1966. *Growing Up in East Africa.* London: Oxford Univ. Press

56. Centner, T. 1962. *L'enfant africain et ses jeux.* Elisabethville: CEPSI

57. Chamberlain, A. F. 1901. *The child: A Study in the Evolution of Man.* London: Scribner

58. Chase, H. 1905. Street games of New York City. See Ref. 136, 71–72

59. Chukovsky, K. 1968. *From Two to Five.* Berkeley: Univ. California Press

60. Cooper, J. M. 1949. A cross-cultural survey of South American Indian tribes: games and gambling. *Bur. Am. Ethnol. Bull.* 143:503–24

61. Cox, J. H. 1942. Singing games. *South. Folklore.* 6:183–681

62. Crombie, J. W. 1886. History of the game of hop-scotch. *J. R. Anthropol. Inst.* 15:403–8

63. Culin, S. 1891. Street games of boys in Brooklyn. *J. Am. Folklore* 4:221–37

64. Culin, S. 1895. *Korean Games, with Notes on the Corresponding Games of China and Japan.* Philadelphia: Univ. Pennsylvania Press

65. Culin, S. 1899. Hawaiian games. *Am. Anthropol.* 1:201–47

66. Culin, S. 1907. *Games of North American Indians*. 24th Ann. Rep. Bur. Am. Ethnol.

67. Daiken, L. H. 1950. Children's games: a bibliography. *Folklore* 61:218–22

68. Daniel, Z. T. 1892. Kansu: a Sioux game. *Am. Anthropol.* 5:215–16

69. Dennis, W. 1940. *The Hopi Child*. New York: Appleton-Century

70. Dennis, W. 1957. Uses of common objects as indicators of cultural orientation. *J. Abnorm. Soc. Psychol.* 55:21–28

71. Dorsey, J. O. 1891. Games of Teton Dakota children. *Am. Anthropol.* 4:329–46

72. Douglas, N. 1931. *London Street Games*. London: Chatto & Windus

73. Doyle, P. H. 1975. The differential effects of multiple and single niche play activities on interpersonal relations among preschoolers. See Ref. 3

74. DuBois, C. 1944. *Peoples of Alor*. Minneapolis: Univ. Minnesota Press

75. Dundes, A. 1964. On game morphology: a study of the structure of non-verbal folklore. *NY Folklore Q.* 20:276–88

76. Dundes, A., Leach, J., Ozkök, B. 1972. Strategy of Turkish boys' verbal dueling rhymes. *J. Am. Folklore* 83:325–49

77. Edmonson, M. S. 1967. Play: games, gossip and humor. *Handbook of Middle American Indians*, ed. R. Wauchope, 191–206. Austin: Univ. Texas Press

78. Ehrmann, J. 1968. Homo Ludens revisited. *Yale Fr. Stud.* 41:31–57

79. Eifermann, R. R. 1970. Cooperation and egalitarianism in Kibbutz children's games. *Hum. Relat.* 23:579–87

80. Eifermann, R. R. 1971. *Determinants of children's game styles*. Jerusalem: Isr. Acad. Sci. Hum.

81. Eifermann, R. R. 1971. Social play in childhood. See Ref. 136, 270–97

82. Elder, J. D. 1965. Song games from Trinidad and Tobago. *Publ. Am. Folklore Soc. 16*

83. El'Konin, D. 1966. Symbolics and its functions in the play of children. See Ref. 136, 221–30

84. Emerson, J. S. 1924. Hawaiian string games. *Publ. Folklore Found.*, Vassar College, No. 5

85. Erikson, E. H. 1940. Studies in the interpretation of play: part I: clinical observations of play disruption in young children. *Genet. Psychol. Monogr.* 22:557–671

86. Erikson, E. H. 1941. Further exploration in play construction: three spatial variables and their relation to sex and anxiety. *Psychol. Bull.* 38:748

87. Erikson, E. H. 1943. Observations on the Yurok: childhood and world image. *Univ. Calif. Publ. Am. Archeol. Ethnol.* 35, No. 10

88. Erikson, E. H. 1951. Sex differences in the play configurations of American pre-adolescents. *Am. J. Orthopsychiatry* 21:667–92

89. Erikson, E. H. 1963. *Childhood and Society*. New York: Norton

90. Fein, G., Apfel, N. 1975. *Elaboration of Pretend Play During the Second Year of Life*. Presented at Ann. Meet. Am. Psychol. Assoc., Chicago

91. Firth, R. 1930. A dart match in Tikopia: a study in the sociology of primitive sport. *Oceania* 1:64–96

92. Fischer, J., Fischer, A. 1963. The New Englanders of Orchard Town, U.S.A. See Ref. 292, 869–1010

93. Fortes, M. 1970. Social and psychological aspects of education in Taleland. *From Child to Adult*, ed. J. Middleton, 14–74. New York: Natural History Press

94. Freud, A. 1964. *The Psychoanalytical Treatment of Children*. New York: Schocken

95. Freud, S. 1955. *The Cases of 'Little Hans' and the 'Rat Man,'* complete works, Vol. 12. London: Hogarth

96. Freud, S. 1959. *Beyond the Pleasure Principle*. New York: Bantam

97. Freud, S. 1963. *Jokes and Their Relation to the Unconscious*. New York: Norton

98. Fry, W. F. Jr. 1963. *Sweet Madness: A Study of Humor*. Palo Alto, Calif: Pacific Books

99. Garcia, L. I. 1929. Children's games. *Mex. Folkways* 5:79–85

100. Ibid 1932. Children's games. 7:63–74

101. Garvey, C., Berndt, R. 1975. *The organization of pretend play*. Presented at Ann. Meet. Am. Psychol. Assoc., Chicago

102. Geertz, G. 1972. Deep play: notes on the Balinese cockfight. *Daedalus* 1–37

103. Georges, R. A. 1969. The relevance of models for analyses of traditional play activities. *South. Folklore Q.* 33:1–23

104. Gewirtz, J. L. 1950. An investigation of aggressive behavior in the doll play of young Sac and Fox Indian children, and a comparison to the aggression of midwestern white preschool children. *Am. Psychol.* 5:294–95

105. Gesell, A. 1946. *The Child from Five to Ten.* New York: Harper

106. Gilmore, J. 1971. Play: a special behavior. See Ref. 136, 311–25

107. Gilmore, M. R. 1926. Some games of Arikara children. *Indian Notes* 3:9–12

108. Goffman, E. 1961. *Encounters.* Indianapolis: Bobbs-Merrill

109. Goffman, E. 1974. *Frame Analysis.* New York: Harper & Row

110. Goldberg, S., Lewis, M. 1969. Play behavior in the year-old infant: early sex differences. *Child Dev.* 40:21–31

111. Goldstein, K. S. 1971. Strategy in counting out: an ethnographic folklore field study. See Ref. 13, 167–78

112. Gomme, A. B. 1894. *The Traditional Games of England, Scotland and Ireland,* Vol. 1. London: Nutt

113. Ibid 1898, Vol. 2.

114. Goodman, M. E. 1971. Play, games and humor. *The Culture of Childhood,* 131–42. New York: Teachers Coll. Press

115. Gould, R. 1972. *Child Studies Through Fantasy.* New York: Quadrangle

116. Gowlett, D. F. 1968. Some secret languages of children in South Africa. *Afr. Stud.* 27:135–39

117. Granqvist, H. 1975. *Birth and Childhood Among the Arabs.* New York: AMS Press

118. Grindal, B. 1972. *Growing Up in Two Worlds.* New York: Holt, Rinehart & Winston

119. Grinnell, G. B. 1923. *The Cheyenne Indians.* New Haven, Conn: Yale Univ. Press

120. Groos, K. 1898. *The Play of Animals.* London: Chapman & Hall

121. Groos, K. 1901. *The Play of Man.* New York: Appleton

122. Gump, P. V., Schoggen, P., Redl, F. 1963. The behavior of the same child in different milieus. *The Stream of Behavior,* ed. R. Barker, 169–202. New York: Appleton-Century-Crofts

123. Gump, P. V., Sutton-Smith, B. 1971. Activity-setting and social interaction. See Ref. 136, 96–102

124. Gump. P. V., Sutton-Smith, B. 1972. The 'It' role in children's games. See Ref. 266, 433–41

125. Haas, M. 1964. Thai word games. See Ref. 150, 301–3

126. Haddon, A. C. 1902. Australian children's games. *Nature* 66:380–81

127. Haddon, A. C. 1908. Notes on children's games in British New Guinea. *J. R. Anthropol. Inst.* 38:289–97

128. Haley, J. 1963. *Strategies of Psychotherapy.* New York: Grune & Stratton

129. Hall, G. S. 1904. *Adolescence,* Vol. I. New York: Appleton

130. Hall, J. 1941. Some party games of the Great Smokey Mountains. *J. Am. Folklore* 54:68–71

131. Harney, W. 1952. Sport and play amidst the Aborigines of the Northern Territory. *Mankind* 4:377–79

132. Harrison, H. S. 1947. A bolas-and-hoop game in East Africa. *Man* 47:153–55

133. Hassrick, R., Carpenter, E. 1944. Rappahannock games and amusements. *Primitive Man* 17:29–39

134. Henry, J., Henry, Z. 1974. *Doll Play of Pilagá Indian Children.* New York: Vintage

135. Herron, R. E., Haines, S., Olsen, G., Hughes, J. 1967. *Children's Play: A Research Bibliography.* Champaign: Univ. Illnois Motor Performance Lab., Children's Res. Cent.

136. Herron, R. E., Sutton-Smith, B., eds. 1971. *Child's Play.* New York: Wiley

137. Hilger, I. M. 1951. Chippewa child life and its cultural background. *Bur. Am. Ethnol. Bull.* 146

138. Hilger, I. M. 1957. *Araucanian Child Life and Its Cultural Background.* Washington DC: Smithsonian Misc. Collect. 133

139. Hocart, A. M. 1909. Two Fijian games. *Man* 9:184–85

140. Hodge, F. W. 1890. A Zuni footrace. *Am. Anthropol.* 3:227–31

141. Hogbin, H. I. 1946. A New Guinea childhood: from weaning till the eighth year in Wogeo. *Oceania* 16:275–96

142. Hostetler, J., Huntington, G. 1971. *Children in Amish Society: Socialization and Community Education.* New York: Holt, Rinehart & Winston

143. Howard, D. 1958. Australian

'hoppy' hopscotch. *West. Folklore* 17:163–75

144. Howard, D. 1959. Ball bouncing customs and rhymes in Australia. *Midwest Folklore* 9:77–87

145. Howard, D. 1960. The 'toodlem-buck'—Australian children's gambling device and game. *J. Am. Folklore* 73:53–54

146. Howard, D. 1971. Marble games of Australian children. See Ref. 13, 179–93

147. Huizinga, J. 1955. *Homo Ludens: A Study of the Play Element in Culture.* Boston: Beacon

148. Hurlock, E. 1971. Experimental investigations of childhood play. See Ref. 136, 51–70

149. Hutt, C. 1971. Exploration and play in children. See Ref. 136, 231–51

150. Hymes, D. 1964. Children's games and speech play: a topical bibliography. *Language in Culture and Society: A Reader in Linguistics and Anthropology,* ed. D. Hymes, 303–4. New York: Harper & Row

151. Issacs, S. 1930. *Intellectual Growth in Young Children.* London: Routledge & Kegan Paul

152. Issacs, S. 1933. *Social Development in Young Children.* London: Routledge & Kegan Paul

153. Jackson, E. 1964. Native toys of the Guarayu Indians. *Am. Anthropol.* 66:1153–55

154. Jocano, F. L. 1969. *Growing Up in a Philippine Barrio.* New York: Holt, Rinehart & Winston

155. Johnson, M. W. 1935. The effect on behavior of variations in the amount of play equipment. *Child Dev.,* 6:56–68

156. Kidd, D. 1906. *Savage Childhood: A Study of Kafir Children.* London: Black

157. Klein, M. 1955. The psychoanalytic play technique. *Am. J. Orthopsychiatry* 25:223–37

158. Klinger, E. 1971. *Structure and Functions of Fantasy.* New York: Wiley

159. Lambert, H. E. 1959. A note on children's pastimes. *Swahili* 30: 74–78

160. Lancy, D. F. 1974. *Work, play, and learning in a Kpelle town.* PhD thesis. Univ. Pittsburgh, Pa.

161. Lancy, D. F. 1975. *The Role of Games in the Enculturation of Children.* Presented at 74th Ann. Meet. Am. Anthropol. Assoc., San Francisco

162. Lancy, D. F. 1976. The play behavior of Kpelle children during rapid cultural change. See Ref. 3

163. Landy, D. 1965. *Tropical Childhood: Cultural Transmission and Learning in a Rural Puerto Rican Village.* New York: Harper & Row

164. Langness, L. L. 1974. *The Study of Culture.* San Francisco: Chandler & Sharp

165. Lantis, M. 1960. *Eskimo Childhood and Interpersonal Relationships.* Seattle: Univ. Washington Press

166. Leacock, E. 1971. At play in African villages. *Natural History,* December, spec. suppl. on play: 60–65

167. Leakey, L. S. B. 1938. A children's game: West Australia and Kenya. *Man* 38:176

168. Leighton, D., Kluckhohn, C. 1974. *Children of the People.* New York: Farrar, Straus & Giroux

169. Leis, P. *Enculturation and Socialization in an Ijaw Village.* New York: Holt, Rinehart & Winston

170. Lesser, A. 1933. *The Pawnee Ghost Dance Hand Game: A Study of Cultural Change.* Columbia Univ. Contrib. to Anthropol. 16

171. Lever, J. 1974. *Games children play: sex differences and the development of role skills.* PhD thesis. Yale Univ., New Haven, Conn.

172. Lever, J. 1975. *Sex-Role Socialization and Social Structure: The Place of Complexity in Children's Games.* Presented at Ann. Meet. Pac. Sociol. Assoc., Victoria, BC

173. Levin, H., Wardwell, E. 1971. The research uses of doll play. See Ref. 136, 145–84

174. Levy, D. M. 1936. Hostility patterns in sibling rivalry experiments. *Am. J. Orthopsychiatry* 6:183–257

175. Loizos, C. 1969. Play behavior in higher primates: a review. *Primate Ethology,* ed. D. Morris, 226–85. Garden City, NY: Doubleday

176. Lowenfeld, M. 1967. *Play in Childhood.* New York: Wiley

177. Maccoby, E. E. 1959. Role-taking in childhood and its consequences for social learning. *Child Dev.* 30:239–52

178. Maccoby, M., Modiano, N., Lander, P. 1964. Games and social character in a Mexican village. *Psychiatry* 27:150–62

179. Mackay, R. 1974. Conceptions of children and models of socialization. *Ethnomethodology,* ed. R. Turner, 180–93. Harmondsworth: Penguin

180. Malinowski, B. 1960. *A Scientific Theory of Culture*. New York: Oxford Univ. Press

181. Maretzki, T., Maretzki, H. 1963. Taira: an Okinawan village. See Ref. 292, 363–539

182. Mead, G. H. 1934. *Mind, Self, and Society*. Univ. Chicago Press

183. Mead, M. 1928. *Coming of Age in Samoa*. New York: Morrow

184. Mead, M. 1930. *Growing Up in New Guinea*. New York: Morrow

185. Millar, S. 1968. *The Psychology of Play*. Harmondsworth: Penguin

186. Miller, S. 1973. Ends, means, and galumphing: some leitmotifs of play. *Am. Anthropol.* 75:87–98

187. Milojkovic-Djuric, J. 1960. The Jugoslav children's game 'Most' and some Scandinavian parallels. *South. Folklore Q.* 24:226–34

188. Minturn, L., Hitchcock, J. 1963. The Rājpūts of Khalapur, India. See Ref. 292, 203–361

189. Mistry, D. K. 1958. The Indian child and his play. *Sociol. Bull.* (Bombay) 7:137–47

190. Ibid 1959. The Indian child and his play. 8:86–96

191. Ibid 1960. The Indian child and his play. 9:48–55

192. Modiano, N. 1973. *Indian Education in the Chiapos Highlands*. New York: Holt, Rinehart & Winston

193. Monroe, W. S. 1904. Counting out rhymes of children. *Am. Anthropol.* 6:46–50

194. Mook, M. A. 1935. Walapai ethnography: games. *Mem. Am. Anthropol. Assoc.* 42:167–73

194a. Nerlove, S. B., Roberts, J. M., Klein, R. E., Yarbrough, C., Habicht, J-P. 1974. Natural indicators of cognitive development: an observational study of rural Guatemalen children. *Ethos* 2:265–95

195. Newell, W. W. 1883. *Games and Songs of American Children*. New York: Harper

196. Norbeck, E. 1971. Man at play. *Natural History*, December, spec. suppl. on play: 48–53

197. Nydegger, W., Nydegger, C. 1963. Tarong: an Ilocos barrio in the Philippines. See Ref. 292, 693–867

198. Opie, I., Opie, P. 1959. *The Lore and Language of School Children*. New York: Oxford Univ. Press

199. Opie, I., Opie, P. 1969. *Children's Games in Street and Playground*. Oxford: Clarendon

200. Opler, M. 1946. *Childhood and Youth in Jicarilla Apache Society*. Los Angeles: Southwest Mus.

201. Parrott, S. 1972. Games children play: ethnography of a second grade recess. *The Cultural Experience*, ed. J. Spradley, D. McCurdy, 207–19. Chicago: Sci. Res. Assoc.

202. Parsons, E. C. 1930. Ring games and jingles in Barbados. *J. Am. Folklore* 43:326–29

203. Parten, M. 1971. Social play among preschool children. See Ref.136, 83–95

204. Peller, L. E. 1971. Models of children's play. See Ref. 136, 110–25

205. Piaget, J. 1948. *The Moral Judgment of the Child*. New York: Free Press

206. Piaget, J. 1962. *Play, Dreams and Imitation in Childhood*. New York: Norton

207. Piaget, J. 1971. Response to Brian Sutton-Smith. See Ref. 136, 337–39

208. Propp, V. 1958. *Morphology of the folktale*. *Int. J. Am. Ling.* Part III, Vol. 24

209. Pukui, M. K. 1943. Games of my Hawaiian childhood. *Calif. Folklore Q.* 2:205–20

210. Ramson, J. E. 1946. Children's games among the Aluet. *J. Am. Folklore* 59:196–98

211. Raum, O. 1940. *Chaga Childhood*. London: Oxford Univ. Press

212. Read, M. 1968. *Children of Their Fathers: Growing Up Among the Ngoni of Malawi*. New York: Holt, Rinehart & Winston

213. Reany, M. J. 1916. *The Psychology of the Organized Group Game*. Cambridge Univ. Press

214. Redl, F. 1959. The impact of game ingredients on children's play behavior. *Transactions of the Fourth Conference on Group Processes*, 31–81. New York: Macy Found.

215. Redl, F., Gump, P., Sutton-Smith, B. 1971. The dimensions of games. See Ref. 13, 408–18

216. Roberts, J. M., Arth, M. J., Bush, R. R. 1959. Games in Culture. *Am. Anthropol.* 61:597–605

217. Roberts, J. M., Sutton-Smith, B. 1962. Child training and game involvement. *Ethnology* 2:166–85

218. Roberts, J. M., Sutton-Smith, B., Kendon, A. 1963. Strategy in games and folk tales. *J. Soc. Psychol.* 61:185–99

219. Roheim, G. 1943. Children's games and rhymes in Duau (Normanby Island). *Am. Anthropol.* 45:99–119

220. Romney, K., Romney, R. 1963. The Mixtecans of Juxtlahuaca, Mexico. See Ref. 292, 541–691
221. Rosenstiel, A. 1976. The role of traditional games in the process of socialization among the Motu of Papua, New Guinea. See Ref. 3
222. Roth, W. E. 1902. Games, Sports, and amusements. *North Queensland Ethnogr. Bull. No. 4:7–24* (Brisbane)
223. Rowell, M. K. 1943. Pamunky Indian games and amusements. *J. Am. Folklore* 56:203–7
224. Salter, M. A. 1967. *Games and Pastimes of the Australian Aboriginal.* Edmonton: Univ. Alberta Print. Dep.
225. Sanderson, M. G. 1913. Native games of Central Africa. *J. R. Anthropol. Inst.* 43:726–36
226. Scheffler, L. 1976. The study of traditional games in Mexico: bibliographical analysis and current research. See Ref. 3
227. Schiller, F. 1875. *Essays, Aesthetical and Philosophical.* London: Bell
228. Schlosberg, H. 1971. The concept of play. See Ref. 136, 212–15
229. Schwartzman, H. B. 1973. 'Real pretending': an ethnography of symbolic play communication. PhD thesis, Northwestern Univ., Evanston, Ill.
230. Schwartzman, H. B. 1976. Children's play: a sideways glance at make-believe. See Ref. 3
231. Schwartzman, H. B., Barbera, L. 1976. Children's play in Africa and South America: a review of the ethnographic literature. See Ref. 3
232. Seagoe, M. V. 1970. An instrument for the analysis of children's play as an index of degree of socialization. *J. Sch. Psychol.* 8:139–44
233. Ibid 1971. A comparison of children's play in six modern cultures. 9:61–72
234. Ibid. Children's play in three American subcultures, 167–72
235. Seagoe, M. V., Murakami, K. A. 1961. A comparative study of children's play in America and Japan. *Calif. J. Educ. Res.* 11:124–30
236. Searcy, A. 1965. *Contemporary and Traditional Prairie Potawatomi Child Life.* Lawrence: Univ. Kansas Press
237. Sears, R. R. Pintler, M., Sears, P. S. 1946. Effect of father separation on pre-school children's doll

play aggression. *Child Dev.* 17:119–243
238. Shoemaker, N. 1964. Toys of Chama (Eseejja) Indian children. *Am. Anthropol.* 66:1151–53
239. Shure, M. 1963. Psychological ecology of a nursery school. *Child Dev.* 34:979–92
240. Singer, J. L. 1966. *Daydreaming: An Introduction to the Experimental Study of Inner Experience.* New York: Random House
241. Singer, J. L. 1973. *The Child's World of Make-Believe: Experimental Studies of Imaginative Play.* New York: Academic
242. Singer, J. L., Singer, D. G. 1976. Imaginative play and pretending in early childhood: some experimental approaches. *Child Personality & Psychopathology,* ed. A. David, Vol. 3. New York: Wiley. In press
243. Smilansky, S. 1968. *The Effects of Sociodramatic Play on Disadvantaged Preschool Children.* New York: Wiley
244. Smith, P. K., Connolly, K. 1972. Patterns of play and social interaction in pre-school children. See Ref. 31, 65–95
245. Speck, F. W. 1944. Catawba games and amusements. *Primitive Man* 17:19–28
246. Spencer, H. 1873. *The Principles of Psychology.* New York: Appleton
247. Spiro, M. E. 1965. *Children of the Kibbutz.* New York: Schocken
248. Stearns, R. E. C. 1890. On the Nishinam game of 'Ha' and the Boston game of 'Props.' *Am. Anthropol.* 3:353–58
249. Stevenson, M. C. 1903. Zuni games. *Am. Anthropol.* 5:468–97
250. Stone, G. P. 1971. The play of little children. See Ref. 136, 4–14
251. Storey, K. S. 1976. Field study: children's play in Bali. See Ref. 3
252. Stumpf, F., Cozens, F. W. 1947. Some aspects of the role of games, sports, and recreation activities in the culture of modern primitive peoples: the New Zealand Maoris. *Res. Q.* 18:198–218
253. Ibid 1949. Some aspects of the role of games, sports, and recreation activities in the culture of modern primitive peoples: the Fijians. 20:2–20
254. Sutton-Smith, B. 1951. New Zealand variants of the game Buck-Buck. *Folklore* 63:329–33
255. Sutton-Smith, B. 1952. The fate of

English traditional games in New Zealand. *West. Folklore Q.* 11:250–53

256. Sutton-Smith, B. 1959. *The Games of New Zealand Children.* Berkeley: Univ. California Press

257. Sutton-Smith, B. 1971. A reply to Piaget: a play theory of copy. See Ref. 136, 340–42

258. Ibid. Boundaries, 103–6

259. Ibid. Piaget on play: a critique, 326–36

260. Sutton-Smith, B. 1971. The playful modes of knowing. *Play: The Child Strives Toward Self Realization,* 13–25. Washington DC: Natl. Assoc. Educ. Young Children

261. Sutton-Smith, B. 1971. The role of play in cognitive development. See Ref. 136, 252–60

262. Sutton-Smith, B. 1972. A formal analysis of game meaning. See Ref. 266, 491–505

263. Sutton-Smith, B. 1972. *Games of order and disorder.* Presented at Am. Anthropol. Assoc., Toronto

264. Sutton-Smith, B. 1972. Marbles are in. See Ref. 266, 455–64

265. Ibid. Role replication and reversal in play, 416–32

266. Sutton-Smith, B. 1972. *The Folkgames of Children.* Austin: Univ. Texas Press

267. Sutton-Smith, B. 1972. The meeting of Maori and European cultures and its effect upon the unorganized games of Maori children. See Ref. 266, 317–30

268. Ibid. The two cultures of games, 295–311

269. Sutton-Smith, B. 1974. Toward an anthropology of play. *Assoc. Anthropol. Study of Play Newsl.* 1:8–15

270. Sutton-Smith, B. 1975. *Current Research and Theory on Play, Games and Sports.* Presented to 1st Natl. Conf. Ment. Health Aspects of Sports, Exercise and Recreation (Am. Med. Assoc.), Atlantic City

271. Sutton-Smith, B. 1975. *Developmental structures in fantasy narrative.* Presented at Ann. Meet. Am. Psychol. Assoc., Chicago

272. Sutton-Smith, B., Roberts, J. M. 1972. Studies in an elementary game of strategy. See Ref. 266, 359–400

273. Ibid. The cross-cultural and psychological study of games, 331–40

274. Sutton-Smith, B., Roberts, J. M., Rosenberg, B. G. 1964. Sibling associations and role involvement. *Merrill-Palmer Q.* 10:25–38

275. Sutton-Smith, B., Rosenberg, B. G. 1970. *The Sibling.* New York: Holt, Rinehart & Winston

276. Sutton-Smith, B., Rosenberg, B. G. 1972. Sixty years of historical change in the game preferences of American children. See Ref. 266, 258–94

277. Sutton-Smith, B., Rosenberg, B. G., Morgan, E. F. Jr. 1972. Development of sex differences in play choices during preadolescence. See Ref. 266, 405–15

278. Turbayne, C. 1971. *The Myth of Metaphor.* Columbia, SC: Univ. South Carolina Press

279. Turnbull, C. 1961. *The Forest People.* New York: Simon & Schuster

280. Tylor, E. B. 1879. On the game of Patolli in ancient Mexico, and its probable Asiatic origin. *J.R. Anthropol. Inst. G.B. Irel.* 8:116–31

281. Ibid 1880. Remarks on the geographical distribution of games. 9:23–30

282. Tylor, E. B. 1971. On American lot-games as evidence of Asiatic intercourse before the time of Columbus. See Ref. 13, 77–93

283. Updegraff, R., Herbst, E. K. 1933. An experimental study of the social behavior stimulated in young children by certain play materials. *J. Genet. Psychol.* 42:372–91

284. Van Alstyne, D. 1932. *Play Behavior and Choice of Play Materials of Pre-School Children.* Univ. Chicago Press

285. Van Zyl, H. J. 1939. Some of the commonest games played by the Sotho people of Northern Transvaal. *Bantu Stud.* 13:293–305

286. von Glascoe, C. 1976. The patterning of game preferences in the Yucatan. See Ref. 3

287. Vygotsky, L. S. 1967. Play and its role in the mental development of the child. *Sov. Psychol.* 5:6–18

288. Waelder, R. 1933. The psychoanalytic theory of play. *Psychoanal. Q.* 2:208–24

289. Walker, J. R. 1906. Sioux games, II. *J. Am. Folklore* 19:29–36

290. Watson, W. 1953. Play among children in an East Coast mining community. *Folklore* 64:397–410

291. Watt, W. 1946. Some children's games from Tanna, New Hebrides. *Mankind* 3:261–64

292. Whiting, B. B., ed. 1963. *Six Cul-*

tures: Studies of Child Rearing. New York: Wiley

293. Whiting, J. M. 1941. *Becoming a Kwoma.* New Haven: Yale Univ. Press

294. Whiting, J. M., Child, I. L. 1953. *Child Training and Personality: A Cross-Cultural Study.* New Haven: Yale Univ. Press

295. Williams, T. R. 1969. *A Borneo Childhood: Enculturation in Dusun*

Society. New York: Holt, Rinehart & Winston

296. Winnicott, D. W. 1971. *Playing and Reality.* New York: Basic Books

297. Wolcott, H. F. 1967. *A Kwakiutl Village and School.* New York: Holt, Rinehart & Winston

298. Wolford, W. J. 1916. *The Play Party in Indiana.* Indianapolis: Indiana Hist. Comm.

Ann. Rev. Anthropol. 1976. 5:329–50
Copyright © 1976 by Annual Reviews Inc. All rights reserved

HISTORY AND SIGNIFICANCE OF THE EMIC/ETIC DISTINCTION

◆ 9582

Marvin Harris
Department of Anthropology, Columbia University, New York, NY 10027

Cultural materialism shares with other scientific strategies an epistemology which seeks to restrict fields of inquiry to events, entities, and relationships that are knowable by means of explicit, logico-empirical, inductive-deductive, quantifiable public procedures or "operations" subject to replication by independent observers. This restriction necessarily remains an ideal aim rather than a rigidly perfected condition, for it is recognized that total operationalization would cripple the ability to state principles, relate theories, organize empirical tests. It is a far cry, however, from the recognition that unoperationalized, vernacular, and metaphysical terms are necessary for the conduct of scientific inquiry to Feyerabend-like invitations (13,14) to throw off all operational restraints. The plain fact of the matter is that many social scientists literally do not know what they are talking about and cannot communicate with each other because they cannot ground any significant portion of their discourse in a coherent set of describable observational practices. Under such circumstances, it is sheer obscurantism to promote the further expansion of unoperationalized terms.

Mind Versus Behavior Stream

Cultural materialism rests on a second epistemological postulate which is uniquely relevant to the operationalization of the broad class of phenomena—the field of inquiry—with which it is concerned. This postulate holds that there are two fundamentally distinct kinds of sociocultural entities, events, and relationships.

On the one hand there are the phenomena which comprise the human behavior stream (1)—all the body motions and environmental effects produced by such motions, large and small, of all the human beings who have ever lived. On the other hand there are all the thoughts and feelings which we human beings experienced within our minds. The existence of this duality is guaranteed by the distinctive operations that groups of observers must employ to make statements about each realm. To describe the universe of human mental experiences, one must employ operations that are capable of penetrating inside of other people's heads (16). But to describe body motions and the external effects produced by

329

body motions, it is not necessary to find out what is going on inside of other people's heads—at least it is not necessary if one adopts the epistemological stance of cultural materialism. For reasons to be made clear in a moment, the operations suitable for discovering patterns with respect to what goes on inside of people's heads have come to be known as "emic" operations, while those which are suitable for discovering patterns in the behavior stream have come to be known as "etic" operations.

The Central Question of Materialist Epistemology

To speak of a choice between materialist and idealist strategies presupposes that we are capable of identifying "material" sociocultural entities independently of the ideational constructions that reside in or emanate from the minds of the people being studied. How is this independence to be achieved?

In *The German Ideology*, Marx & Engels (37) proposed to upend the study of sociocultural phenomena by focusing on the material conditions that constrain human life. Integral to this materialist upending was knowledge of "real" people situated as they "really are":

> The Social structure and the state are continually evolving out of the life process of definite individuals, but of individuals not as they may appear in their own or other people's imagination, but as they really are. . . .
>
> In direct contrast to German philosophy which descends from heaven to earth, here we ascend from earth to heaven. That is to say, we do not set out from what men say, imagine, conceive, nor from men as narrated, thought of, imagined, conceived in order to arrive at men in the flesh. We set out from real active men. . . .
>
> In the first method of approach, the starting point is consciousness (mistaken) for the real living individual; in the second, it is the real, living individuals themselves, as they are in actual life. . . .(37, pp. 13–15).

What did Marx & Engels mean by "individuals as they really are," "real active men," and "real living individuals"? What did they mean by "actual life"? We are only told that real men and women are those who "are effective, produce materially and are active under definite limits . . . and conditions independent of their will."

It is clear that the main concern here is to draw a distinction between the entities and processes of social life that are real and important to the participants versus entities and processes which by virtue of their scientific status are capable of efficaciously explaining (and changing) social thoughts and activities, regardless of whether they are real or important from the participant's point of view. However, the terminology in which Marx & Engels propounded this distinction is inadequate, especially in its conjunction of the ideal with the imaginary or unreal, and of the real with materiality. Cultural materialism, like all empirical sciences, seeks to separate thoughts about wholly imaginary entities, such as Carlos Castaneda's 100 foot gnats and flying shamans, from thoughts about empirically known gnats and the effects of gravity on people who jump out of windows. But cultural materialism rejects an implication that the thoughts themselves are "unreal" or that matter (whatever that might be) is more real than ideas. Recognition is also accorded the fact that purely imaginary, unreal entities can be cognized by ethnographers as well as by native participants. The statement of the basic materialist principles of sociocultural determinism rests instead upon the separation of conscious or unconscious autocognitions of actors from the conscious cogitations of the scientifically informed observer. In Lenin's words: "In all social formations . . . people are not conscious of what kind of social relations are being formed. . . . Social consciousness *reflects* social being—that is Marx's teaching" (34, p. 335). What is the nature of this social consciousness (or unconsciousness) as opposed to the nature of "social being"? I believe that the discussion of etic and emic options can make a decisive contribution to the clarification of this central epistemological problem (which Lenin, by attacking positivism, failed to solve).

Operationally, emic refers to the presence of an actual or potential interactive context in which ethnographer and informant meet and carry on a discussion about a particular domain. This discussion is deemed productive to the extent that the ethnographer discovers principles that represent and account for the way in which that domain is organized or structured in the mental life of that informant. As Ward Goodenough has written, emics is "The method of finding where something makes a difference for one's informants" (21, p. 144; see also 20). Emic operations necessarily result in the identification of phenomena and structures that correspond to what Marx & Engels were writing about when they rejected that form of philosophy that sets out from and effectively confines itself to what men imagine, conceive, and think. (What they "say" and "narrate" requires separate consideration, see below).

The operational meaning of etics, in contrast, is defined by the logically nonessential status of actor-observer elicitation. Interaction between anthropologist and actors is deemed productive only to the extent that principles of organization or structure that exist outside of the minds of the actors have been discovered. These principles may in fact be contrary to the principles elicitable from the actors themselves with respect to the manner in which they organize their imaginations, concepts, and thoughts in the identified domain. It is clear that the analytic results of an etic strategy correspond to what Marx & Engels intended by "real living individuals" as they are in "actual life." Once again, however, let me categorically reject any notion of superior and inferior realities associated with emic and etic epistemological options. Everything that we human beings experience or do is real. But everything we experience or do is not equally effective for explaining why we experience what we experience and do what we do.

Origin of the Terms "Etic" and "Emic"

"Etics" and "emics" are neologisms coined by the linguist Kenneth Pike from the suffixes of the words phon*etic* and phon*emic* in his book, *Language in Relation to a Unified Theory of the Structure of Human Behavior* (42). Phonetic accounts of the sounds of a language are based upon a taxonomy of the body parts active in the production of speech utterances and their characteristic environmental effects in the form of acoustic waves. Thus the linguist discriminates between voiced and unvoiced sounds, depending on the activity of the vocal cords; between aspirated and nonaspirated sounds, depending on the activity of the glottis; between labials and dentals depending on the activity of the tongue and teeth. On the other hand, phonemic accounts of the sounds of a language are based on the implicit or unconscious system of sound contrasts which native speakers have inside of their heads and which they employ to identify meaningful utterances in their language.

Pike's stated intention in coining these terms was to apply a single comprehensive research strategy to language and behavior based on analogies with the concepts and principles of structural linguistics, the school of language study responsible for the development of the concept of the phoneme. In structural linguistics, phonemes—the minimal units of contrastive sounds found in a particular language—are distinguished from nonsignificant or nondiscriminatory sounds and from each other by means of a simple operational test. If one sound substituted for another in the same sound context results in a change of meaning from that of one word to another, the two sounds exemplify (belong to the class of) two different phonemes. Sounds enjoy the status of phonemes, not because they are inherently (whatever that may mean) different, but because native speakers perceive them to be in "contrast" when one is substituted for the other.

Pike's Behavioremes

What Pike tried to do was to apply the principles by which linguists discover phonemes, morphemes, and other emic units of language behavior to the discovery of emic units—which he called "behavioremes"—in the behavior stream. To do this Pike recast the specific bimodal principles of *complementary* and *contrastive* distribution into a trimodal form of analysis involving what he called (*a*) *feature,* (*b*) *manifestation,* and (*c*) *distribution* modes. (*a*) An emic unit or "eme" in language or more general behavior has certain features which stand in contrast with other features. In language, the fundamental criterion of contrast is a difference of *form-meaning* attached to an utterance. For nonverbal behavior-stream events, it is a difference in form-purpose associated with an activity. Emes viewed in their feature mode are thus form-meaning or form-purpose composites. (*b*) The manifestation mode covers the fact that emes comprise classes whose members or variants—like the allophones of phonemes—manifest themselves in different forms in different contexts. (*c*) Finally, the distribution mode refers to the fact that emes occur in particular "slots." Thus, analogous to the restrictions on the occurrence of morphemes, there are behavioral distributions such that, to use Pike's examples, orange juice normally precedes cereal at breakfast, or the collection plate follows the sermon at a church service.

By identifying behavioremes, Pike hoped to extend the research strategy which had proved effective in the analysis of languages to the study of the behavior stream. Pike never considered the possibility of studying the behavior stream in its own right, apart from what it meant to the people whose behavior it exhibited. The paradigmatic unity which he sought was a unity of reduction, not of synthesis. Pike rejected virtually without discussion the possibility that an etic approach to the behavior stream might yield more interesting generalizations than an etic approach to language, and conversely that an emic approach to the behavior stream might yield far less interesting results than an emic approach to language.

To the extent that one could even talk about the existence of etic behavior stream units, they were for Pike necessary evils, mere stepping stones to higher emic realms. Observers necessarily begin their analysis of behavior stream events with etic categories, but the whole thrust of their analytical task is the replacement of such categories with the emic units that constitute structured systems within the minds of the social actors. In Pike's words (42, p. 38): "etic data provide access into the system—the starting point of analysis" . . . "the initial etic description gradually is refined, and is ultimately—in principle, but probably never in practice—replaced by one which is totally emic" (p. 39).

This position clashes with the epistemological assumptions of cultural materialism. In the cultural materialist research strategy, etic analysis is not a stepping stone to the discovery of emic structures, but to the discovery of etic structures. The intent is neither to convert etics to emics nor emics to etics, but rather to account for the divergence and convergence of both etic and emic structures.

Emics, Meaning and Purpose

Pike's scheme in its totality amounts to nothing less than the analogizing of every level of sociocultural phenomena to the levels of linguistic analysis. Society as a whole is viewed as the analogue of a language. In its feature mode, language has the purpose: "fruitful communication between its members," whereas in its feature mode society's purpose is "maintaining orderliness of personal interaction" (42, p. 644). Kinship groups are compared with phenomes and voluntary associations are like morphemes:

> As phonemic units can arbitrarily be joined to form morpheme units such as *cat* and *dog,* so individuals who in their selection cross over kin group lines may be joined into various units for particular purposes. . . . The purpose of such a group (e.g. a football team), when it is specifically goal-oriented, has this lexical-like flavor, as over against the much more diffuse purpose of a kinship group (42, p. 647).

Grammatical rules are paralleled by social rules defining slots or statuses. The meaning of the rule is the role defined in terms of expected behavior. Sentences have their analogues in the total activity of such groups as college football teams which are organized for the purpose of "playing the game according to the written rules" (p. 649).

This brief recapitulation of Pike's grand design should suffice to dispose of the opinion expressed by linguists that my use of the term emic and etic is deviant. Mridula Durbin (11), for example, claims that emic ought to be restricted to units identified strictly on the basis of the criteria of contrastive and complementary distributions. Taking a kind of "strict constructionist" view of things, Durbin argues that the "significant feature of the phonemic model"—the major achievement of structural linguistics—"is that the functional criterion of classification is operationally shifted to distributional criteria" (11, p. 384). What this shift comprised historically was that structural linguistics sought to minimize the importance of knowing the meaning of an utterance as a step in its phonemic analysis. Not so for Pike, however. Pike explicitly rejects the "extreme of the 'fundamental purely formal definition (associated with the work of Bloomfield and Zelig Harris) in which a morpheme is an arrangement of phonemes' . . . without the meaning as part of the basic definition itself" (42, p. 185). In other words, he explicitly rejected Durbin's "significant feature of the phonemic model."

Pike repeatedly insists that in their feature mode, emes involve composite form-meaning contrasts and that neither form nor meaning alone suffices for the identification of language or behavior stream units. Thus for Pike, emic analysis is certainly not tied to the strict distributional criteria characteristics of the phonemic level. If it had been so severely restricted, he could never have proposed the grandiose scheme of analogies a small part of which I have set forth above.

While I do not reject Pike's emphasis on the importance of the form-meaning, form-purpose composite, I insist that the essential operational ingredient in the emic approach remains the matter of "contrast," as exemplified in phonemic analysis. On this level—the level of phonemes—there is no question of the specific meaning of an eme. The phoneme (p) doesn't mean anything; hence, the form-meaning composite (p) consists merely of a particular sound and its contrast to other sounds in the minds of native speakers of English. The crucial criterion is not whether the contrast is a contrast of specific meanings, but whether with or without specific meanings, the contrast is significant because it is loaded with significance (carries meaning) inside the heads of the actors. Any language unit that observers deem to be contrastive because native actors carry out discrimination of similarity and difference *inside their heads* on the basis of its presence or absence is an emic unit.

Burling's Critique

Following Pike's usage, therefore, I previously defined emics and etics as follows:

> Emic statements refer to logico-empirical systems whose phenomenal distinctions or "things" are built up out of contrasts and discriminations significant, meaningful, real, accurate, or in some other fashion regarded as appropriate by the actors themselves (23, p. 571).
>
> Etic statements depend upon phenomenal distinctions judged appropriate by the community of scientific observers (p. 575).

Like Durbin, Robbins Burling condemns this usage as non-Bloomfieldian:

By these definitions, the Bloomfieldian phoneme is not an "emic" unit, since the Bloomfieldians were firmly, even obstinately opposed to any sort of mentalistic interpretation of language (9, p. 826).

All this proves, however, is that neither Pike nor I are followers of Bloomfield.

Moreover, despite Bloomfield's desire to exclude specific meanings from the definition of phoneme, the fact remains that (*a*) the operation of minimal pairs requires elicitation of judgments of same or different from native speakers; and (*b*) that even Bloomfieldian phonemes had to be capable of being combined into utterances that were meaningful, real, appropriate, etc to the native speakers (regardless of whether or not the linguist knew what the utterances meant)! It seems to me difficult to deny the mentalistic character of phonemic distinctions even if Bloomfield did wish to reduce the mental component to a minimum. As Emmon Bach has put it:

> The data of linguistics are not mere physical events, but physical events together with judgments of native speakers about these events . . . language as a cultural product cannot be adequately studied apart from the native speaker's judgments.
> The native speaker judges some utterances as being repetitions of the same sentence, phrase or word. And it is only the native speaker's judgment that can tell us about this fact (2, p. 34).

It is true that at one point Pike emphasizes the importance of distributional data in identifying the purpose of a nonverbal activity: "We assume that the basic purpose or meaning of a nonverbal activity, like that of a verbal one, is to be detected by the objective evaluation of objective distributional data of elicited responses" (42, p. 157). What this means is that the purpose of an activity may not be directly elicitable from the actors.

The analogous situation in language analysis is the establishment of the meaning of *ly* in lovingly. The actors may not consciously detect the meaning, but the linguist can infer it on the basis of the recurrence of *ly* at the end of verbs. Similarly, actors may not consciously detect the purpose of some activities, but by noting their distribution and by *eliciting* responses concerning their appropriateness in various contexts, observers may endow them with a specific purpose. At no point, however, does Pike state that direct elicitations of purposes are operationally forbidden. Ultimately, to paraphrase Bach, it is only the native actor's judgment that can tell us that some acts are repetitions of the same behavioreme.

How To Get Inside of People's Heads

The question of whether a construct is emic or etic depends on whether it describes events, entities, or relationships whose physical locus is in the heads of the social actors or in the stream of behavior. In turn, the question of whether or not an entity is inside or outside some social actor's head depends on the operations employed to get at it. Pike formulated an operational definition of emic and etic. "Two units," he wrote, "are different etically when instrumental measurements can show them to be so. Units are different emically only when they elicit different responses from people acting within the system" (42, p. 38). But Pike's phrase, "elicit different responses from people acting within the system," must be clarified in order to render the crucial operation explicit. As it stands, Pike's eliciting operation might be taken to mean that when an event E_1 occurs in the behavior stream and people react to it differently from event E_2, then E_1 and E_2 are emically different. But what has to be made clear is that you cannot get inside of people's heads by observing what they do during the natural course of behavior stream events. Observing what people do during the natural course of behavior stream events leads to etic not emic distinctions. Of course it is always possible to make inferences concerning what is going on inside of people's heads from purely etic data. But as Pike and so many others have insisted, strangers who do so will be led astray by their own projections. For example, during the course of fieldwork in a small Brazilian town, I noticed that a number of children came to school or went to the weekly market wearing only one shoe or sandal. A reasonable inference about what was going on inside their heads was that being children they preferred to go barefoot, and that wearing one shoe was therefore better than wearing two. The emic purpose of the activity, as determined by questioning children and their parents, was something else. Informants argued that it was better to wear two shoes; the purpose of wearing only one was to have siblings share the same pair of shoes, an important economy for poor households.

The way to get inside of people's heads is to talk with them, to ask questions about what they think and feel. When such questions are presented in formal, organized fashion aimed at mapping how participants view the world, we may speak of *eliciting operations*. As Frake (16, p. 76) has indicated, the basic methodological concept advocated by cognitive anthropologists is "the determination of the set of contrasting responses appropriate to a given, culturally valid eliciting context." The paradigmatic model for eliciting operations is the identification of phonemic contrasts by means of minimum pairs. In Pike's scheme, the equivalent test with respect to wearing shoes should involve eliciting a native's judgment if the wearing of one and two shoes are manifestations of the same or different form-purpose unit (the feature and manifestation modes) and if they are "appropriate" performances in the slot constituted by children walking to school (the distribution mode).

Eliciting operations are based on the assumption that social actors have learned to regard certain kinds of differences in thought and behavior as contrastive and others as noncontrastive and to regard the occurrence of certain kinds of thoughts and behaviors as appropriate or nonappropriate with respect to different contexts. The aim of emic analysis is to describe the structure of the "program" which generates these native judgments of contrast and appropriateness.

The Locus and Reality of Cognitive Rules

According to Burling (10), residence rules, grammatical rules, and kinship terminology rules, as well as Bloomfieldian phonemes, "stand or fall on their ability to account for observable phenomena," and "whether or not they are in any sense cognitively or psychologically real is an entirely separate question" (10, p. 826). I submit, on the contrary, that these are entirely separate questions only if one has no interest in providing a scientific explanation for speech acts, residence patterns, and domestic organization. If by "account for" one means the ability of a rule inside of the observer's head, or as expressed in writing, to summarize or predict the probable state of such noncognitive etic phenomena as residential alignments and domestic organization, the question of whether the rule is in some sense also inside the heads of the actors is indeed moot (17, 28). But if one intends to "account for" emic cognitive phenomena—grammatical competence, kinship taxonomy, residential·preference—it would be senseless to view the appropriate rules as existing exclusively inside the heads of the observers and outside the heads of the actors. How can such rules account for what goes on inside of actors' heads, if they are not inside them? Shall we posit that they account for the actor's cognitions by virtue of their location within the head of the family cat?

Burling has confused two facts here: (*a*) that observers frequently make rival inferences concerning what kinds of rules exist inside of other people's heads with (*b*) the fact that there are also etic *rules*, which make no claims at all about what goes on inside of people's heads. It is perfectly true, of course, that rival hypothetical emic structures, none of which accurately portray what goes on inside of people's heads, can be erected on the basis of erroneous inferences from inadequate data. The way such inadequacies are normally detected is by predictive failures concerning informant's elicited judgments of appropriateness or acceptability. For example, from a knowledge of a rule prohibiting sexual relations between close genealogical relatives one might erroneously predict that informants will accept the statement "mother brother's daughter and father sister's son must not marry each other." The psychological "reality" of a rule can only be measured by its predictive success. If two competitive emic rules are equally successful, they must be accorded equal psychological "reality" (9).

This problem—the problem of alternative emic algorithms and alternative logical models—is to be distinguished from that of consciousness. "Real" rules need not be conscious rules, as we have seen.

Transformation algorithms and other rules acquire an ambiguous epistemological status to the extent that they are not systematically tested through eliciting techniques aimed at exposing their predictive inadequacies—an unavoidable lapse when one lives in New Haven and relies on published reports of kinship terminologies attributed to anonymous or deceased informants in the Trobriand Islands (5, 25, 26, 29, 30, 32, 36).

Accounting for Behavior Stream Events

The most important source of Burling's epistemological quandary is the conflation of attempts to "account for" residence rules, taxonomies, symbol systems, moral codes, etc, with the attempt to "account for" the flow of speech acts, scenes, and other components of the behavior stream. The notion that mental rules (even the most "accurate" and "real" ones) can account for behavior stream events is the dominant principle of idealist as opposed to materialist research strategies. "Accounting for" in this context must mean "prediction," and materialists deny that a knowledge of emic rules can provide the basis for accurate predictions about behavior stream events. It is not surprising therefore that Burling accuses me of a "simplistic" dichotomy: "Harris' simplistic bifurcation into idealist 'emics' and materialist 'etics' is in danger of squeezing out the middle ground between them" (10, p. 821).

I do intend to squeeze out this middle ground because I believe that the inability to decide whether a datum is an idea in an actor's head or an event in the behavior stream is epistemologically intolerable. This does not mean that systemic relationships between ideas and behavior stream events cannot be found, but rather that it is unlikely that they will be found if they (emic and etic events) are not first distinguished.

Idealists may not like to see the concept of emics harnessed to the task of defining a strategy which challenges their own. But my authorization for defining emics as an aspect of the mental life of informants is thoroughly consistent not only with Pike's original definition but with the definitions of most anthropologists and linguists. The linguist William Bright, for example, writes: "First, a division must be made between the observational, or etic, universe, to which 'word' and 'object' belong, and the structural or 'emic' universe, within the human mind" (8, p. 20). Pelto in tracing the history of the emic approach, quotes Boas (7) to the effect: "If it is our serious purpose to understand the thoughts of a people the whole analysis of experience must be based on their concepts, not ours" (40, p. 69). He quotes Sapir (46) to the effect that an outsider cannot produce description that "would be intelligible and acceptable to the natives themselves."

Emics and Consciousness

Pike and others who have used linguistics as the model for emic analysis stress the fact that the immediate products of elicitation do not necessarily furnish the structured program that is the desired end product of emic analysis. For example, in determining whether the two /p/'s in *paper* (the first is aspirated) are phonemically same or different, we cannot rely on the native's conscious powers of autoanalysis. Nonetheless, Pike did provide for what he called *hypostasis*, namely the elicitation of conscious structural rules, such as "don't use double negatives." When one turns to elicitations that are concerned with the structure of thought and behavior as distinct from the structure of language, hypostasis is far more common. The answer to questions like: "Why do you do this?" or "What is this for?" "Is this the same as that?" and "When or where do you do this?" "What ought you to do in these circumstances?" are essential for specifying the trimodalities of Pike's emes. There is nothing antithetical therefore in attributing to emic structures both conscious and unconscious dimensions. Working with elicited responses, the observer is free to abstract and construct all manner of emic structures, conscious or unconscious, such as plans, cognitive maps, rules, themes, values, symbols, moral codes, and so forth.

Mary Black (6, p. 524) has taken Pelto (39, p. 83) to task for claiming that "the ethnographer termed by some 'emicist' goes about collecting 'verbal statements *about* human action' while an eticist is out there observing human action first hand." Black insists that it is the structure of the system of beliefs, including beliefs about action, that is studied in emic research, not the statements about the beliefs themselves. Joining the chorus of anthropologists who find contrary views "simplistic," Black writes:

> . . . the idea that ethnoscience is interested in language and linguistics for the purpose of having informants *make statements about their patterns of behavior* is rather simplistic and can be held only by those who have not done ethnosemantic work (6, p. 526).

It is not simplistic, it seems to me, to acknowledge that emics is concerned both with the content of elicited responses and with the structure that may be found to underlie that content at several different levels. Structural rules can be elicited directly in certain domains (for example, how to play football or poker, or how to make a shrunken head). Goodenough's (21) concept of "duty scale" involves directly elicited rules. Also, comparison of rules elicited from officials in bureaucratized organizations with those elicited from the organization's workers (47), or rules elicited from males and females, landowners, and peasants may achieve structural significance at the level of manifest content. Furthermore Black's notion of what constitutes authentic "ethnosemantic work" would seem to exclude sociological surveys and opinion polls which acquire structural significance as soon as their results are tabulated. The fact that ethnosemantic studies have not concerned themselves with manifest ideological structures is merely a reflection of their predilection for dealing with static, esoteric, and politically trivial taxonomies. Fortunately, emic studies are not restricted to the analysis of terminological distinctions. If Black wants to plant the flag of "ethnosemantic work" in the most static, esoteric, and politically trivial emic domains, she is welcome to exclusive full proprietary rights.

Etics as Observable

I should also comment at this point on Burling's and Bright's understanding of the term "etic" as data that are "directly observable." Having proposed a series of "rules" which hypothetically govern the formation of households in India, Burling notes:

> I think it not unreasonable, and in accordance with general usage, to call all ordinary grammatical rules and my rules of household composition "emic," because they represent theoretical statements, separated in certain respects from (and not algorithmically derivable from) the more directly observable "etic" data, such as households on the ground or sequences of noise, but at the same time the rules provide a means of interpreting and understanding the observable (and "etic") data of real households or real sentences. Of course it is silly to argue about the meaning of a word, but even if we decide that "emic" is not appropriate for such descriptions, it is still important to keep them distinct from the more directly observable "etic" phenomena (10, p. 827).

This definition of etic is inadmissable because there is no such thing as "direct observation." The "on-the-ground" composition of household cannot be directly observed, any more than a neutrino, a gene, or any other event, thing, or relationship can be directly observed. Moreover, Burling's example is especially infelicitous in view of the controversy surrounding the emic definition of residence among anthropologists (4, 15, 18, 40) and the excruciating consequences of different definitions of residence in political-economic contexts such as taxation, labor conscription, and welfare (4, 43, 50).

Behavioral and Mental vs Etic and Emic

If the locus of emic events lies in the actor's mind, while the locus of etic events lies in the behavior stream, are not Pike's neologisms redundant and scientifically dispensable? Why not simply contrast "mental events" with "behavioral events"? The answer is that both actors and observers are capable of describing the events in the behavior stream. Pike's unique contribution among idealists was precisely his attempt to emicize the description of the behavior stream (as distinct from more fashionable attempts to elicit grammars, folk taxonomies, symbol systems, values, and moral codes). That is, for Pike, descriptions of behavior which do not involve phenomenal distinctions—contrasts and distributions—that are significant and meaningful to the actors are unacceptable. In other words, Pike sought to situate the structural aspects of the behavior stream within the minds of the actors. But behavior stream events seen through actor's categories remain, in one sense at least, behavioral events, just as behavior stream events seen through observer's categories might in another sense be called mental events, because they are what the observers think them to be. Emic and etic are therefore not redundant with respect to mental and behavioral events because these neologisms invoke a separation of observers and actors and their respective phenomenologies of behavior stream events in ways not foreseen in the controversies between psychologists following mentalist and behaviorist strategies.

If behavioral events are described in terms of categories and relationships that arise from the observer's strategic criteria of similarity, difference, and significance, they are etic; if they are described in terms of criteria elicited from an informant, they are emic. A clear and historically crucial case is the much celebrated choice made by Goodenough in his description of Truk locality patterns. In a number of Truk households, John Fischer (1950) had described as patrilocal the residence pattern in which married male ego lived with father who was living with father's mother-in-law. Goodenough classified this same situation as avunculocal, even though mother's brother resided elsewhere, on the grounds that the people of Truk were traditionally matrilineal and that they therefore could not be practicing patrilocality: "Patrilocal residence . . . can occur in Truk only following upon a fundamental change in . . . cultural principles" (18, pp. 35–36). As Goodenough (21, p. 104) now explains, the source of the difference between himself and Fischer was "our different conception of the objects of residential choice as the Trukese perceive them." In fact, the difference was that Fischer had followed an implicitly etic strategy while Goodenough had followed an explicitly emic one. As Glenn Petersen (41) has pointed out, Fischer's view was at least as viable as Goodenough's, since the Truk pattern of residence was in fact shifting to ambilocality or even partilocality.

Etic and Emic Use of Informants

The distinction between mental and behavioral descriptions of behavioral events is more complex for anthropologists than for behaviorist psychologists who work with infra-human organisms. As a matter of practical necessity, anthropologists must frequently rely on native informants to obtain their basic information about who has done what. Recourse to informants for such purposes does not automatically settle the epistemological status of the resultant descriptions.

Depending on whose categories establish the framework of discourse, informants may provide either etic or emic descriptions of the events they have observed or participated in. When the description is responsive to the observer's categories of time, place, weights and measure, actor types, numbers of people present, body motion, and environmental effects, it is etic. Roger Sanjek (45), for example, has shown that network analyses can be carried out in two quite distinct ways, although in both instances actual, on-the-ground, behavioral phenomena are being reported. In the emic version informants provide information only about "significant others," filtering out individuals judged not to be essential to their social world; in the etic version, informants are encouraged to recall all interactive alters, regardless of their lack of emic significance.

Obviously, reliance upon informants for etic descriptions represents a methodological compromise. But as I stated at the beginning of this article, no one expects to achieve absolute operational purity.

Emics, Etics, and Cross-Cultural Comparisons

Among the criteria listed by Pike (42) as characteristic of emics and etics are the following:
Etic units: cross-culturally valid
Emic units: culturally specific, applied to one language or culture at a time

Much to my astonishment, prominent theoreticians apparently believe that this aspect of the emic/etic contrast lies at the very heart of the definition intended by Pike. Raoul Naroll (38), for example, actually defines emics and etics exclusively by reference to the distinction between concepts of particular cultures and pancultural concepts: "Emics are the study of concepts peculiar to particular cultures. Etics on the other hand, are the study of concepts for the study of culture in general—panculture" (38, p. 2).

My astonishment derives from the fact that this approach to the definition of emics and etics evades the epistemological issues with which Pike was concerned as reflected in elaborate discussion of the form-purpose, manifestation and distribution modes. It is this discussion alone which demands that the emic/

etic distinction be assigned a role in the historic development of competitive philosophical and scientific paradigms and strategies. To assert that certain statements about a field of inquiry are restricted to the particularities of one portion of that field, while other statements apply more generally, yields no clarification whatever concerning the epistemological status of either type of statement. The question of the degree to which emic events and relationships are replicated cross-culturally obviously cannot be settled without empirical tests. It is of course theoretically possible to so refine the particularities of a phonemic system, kinship terminology, moral code, or football team, that no comparable phenomena can be found anywhere in the world (one might, for example, insist that all relevant concepts be rendered exclusively in the native language). But this option is not closed to etic descriptions; no two etic events repeat themselves if they are looked at closely enough. In any field of inquiry, the claim "everything is different" is as true as the claim "everything is the same"; both lead equally to a total collapse of empirical testing. The normal resolution of this conundrum is to extract some similarities and ignore some differences; to specify ranges and limits; to construct logical and empirical classes and categories. Thus there is nothing that prevents us from finding less-than-perfectly described emic events, categories, and relationships approximately replicated in more than one culture. And this is exactly what anthropologists have devoted most of their efforts to. As Naroll (38), following "a brilliant chapter by Ward Goodenough" (21), illustrates with the example of kinship studies: "the pan-cultural analysis of kinship terms has proceeded from a crude description of particular kinship practices (read *ideas*) to an inventory of key distinctions which may or may not be important in particular kinship systems, and from these distinctions has come the componential analysis of particular kinship terminologies." He then lists the eight key concepts: 1. Consanguinity/affinity; 2. Generation;   3. Sex;   4. Collaterality;   5. Bifurcation;   6. Relative Age; 7. Decadence; and 8. Genealogical Distance; and he correctly identifies the work of Alfred Kroeber (31) as the most important source of these "components." The only trouble is that following Goodenough and William Sturtevant (1964), Naroll identifies the concepts of consanguinity, generation, sex, etc., as etic concepts. "These are the eight key etic concepts. . . . The inventory . . . is validated by the fact that every known emic kin-term system can be most parsimoniously defined by using the eight etic concepts" (38, p. 3).

As I have previously maintained (23, p. 557), Kroeber's kin terminology components are emic not etic. They are emic because (*a*) they refer to a phenomenological reality whose locus is inside of the heads of the actors; and (*b*) they are built up out of forms and meanings that are intended to reflect significant and appropriate distinctions within the heads of the actors in each of the cultures in which they occur. To repeat, the whole point of Kroeber's famous article was to replace L. H. Morgan's sociological treatment of kinship with a linguistic treatment, i.e. to make the meanings of kin-terms dependent on how they reflected cognized properties rather than on how they reflected the functioning of domestic groups.

Goodenough admits that Kroeber was indeed saying that "kinship termi-nology must be understood from the point of view of . . . what we would now call cognition . . ." but nonetheless my (Harris's) characterization of componential categories as emic is incorrect. They are etic, Goodenough insists.

What Harris seems to mean by etics is evidently not what Pike (1967), who coined the term, I, or others he criticizes mean by it. Harris has failed to learn the "culture" of those he criticizes.

What I allegedly fail to understand is that improved emics lead to improved etics, which in turn lead to improved emics.

As I have said, emic description requires etics, and by trying to do emic descriptions we add to our etic conceptual resources for subsequent description. It is through etic concepts that we do comparison. And by systematizing our etic concepts we con-tribute to the development of a general science of culture. Therefore, I agree heartily with Harris about the fundamental importance of etics. But unlike him I see etics as bogging down in useless hairsplitting and over-preoccupation with recording hard-ware, unless it is accompanied by a concern for emics. For Harris, concern with emic description competes with the development of etics; for me, it contributes most directly to it (21, p. 113).

Thus, for Goodenough, Kroeber's identification of the basic semantic di-mensions of kinship terminology "increased our potential for systematic com-parison" and "componential analysis is requiring us to make further refinements in our etic kit and in laying the basis for an even more systematic account of how the properties of genealogical space can be employed in their various combi-nations to describe the emic categories of kinship relationships" (21, p. 114).

In rebuttal, I can only repeat my earlier comment (23, p. 577): emic entities cannot be transmuted into etic entities. If *emes* recur cross-culturally, they remain *emes*. Once an eme, always an eme.

How is it possible for such divergent interpretations to persist? I think there is considerable merit to Goodenough's charge that I have failed to understand the "culture" of those I have criticized. More charitably put, "culture" here means paradigm or research strategy. I see emics and etics from the perspective of a research strategy that is radically different from Goodenough's. I see Pike's emic/etic distinction as providing the key epistemological opening for a materi-alist approach to the behavior stream. Goodenough "sees" emics and etics from an idealist perspective in which the entire field of study—culture—is off limits to materialist strategies. That is, for Goodenough and other cultural idealists, culture designates an orderly realm of pure idea while the behavior stream is a structureless emanation of that realm. In Goodenough's words:

The great problem for a science of man is how to get from the objective world of materiality, with its infinite variability, to the subjective world of form as it exists in what, for lack of a better term, we must call the minds of our fellow man . . . (19, p. 39).

In the strategy of Cultural Materialism, on the other hand, culture is not a realm of pure idea; rather, culture designates both patterns of thought and patterns of behavior. Furthermore, in the strategy of cultural materialism behavior is not regarded as an emanation of thought; rather, thought is regarded as an emanation of behavior (24). It is clear that Goodenough has failed to learn the "culture" of cultural materialism.

Emics, Etics, and Speech Acts

Considerable misunderstanding has arisen concerning the relationship between etic behavior stream analysis and communication events. Does the emic/etic option apply to such events? Since language is the primary mode of human communication, and since it is the function of language to convey meanings, one might readily conclude that the emic mode is the only feasible approach to language as the conveyor of meaning. In the strategy of cultural materialism, however, there are both emic and etic approaches to communication behavior.

Those who would describe the behavior stream of any higher organism must confront the task of identifying activities that are primarily communicative or that achieve (their environmental effects primarily through the intermediation of communicative acts (3). Dell Hymes (27, p. 13) defines communicative acts in terms of the concept "message." He lists seven criteria of messages: 1. code or codes in terms of which the message is intelligible; 2. participants, minimally an addressor and addressee; 3. a transmission event; 4. a channel; 5. a setting or context; 6. a definite form or shape to the message; 7. a topic—saying something about something. But for Hymes, messages must also possess an emic status which he defines as the "intersubjective objectivity . . . of the participants in the culture" (27, p. 11). Hence the above criteria cannot alone identify messages, just as "what counts as phonemic feature or religious act cannot be identified in advance."

The apodictic restriction of the ethnography of speech to emic meanings is a form of dogmatism not uncommon among idealists like Hymes, for whom "culture" is a term that cannot be applied to the behavior stream (48).

It is obvious however that an ethnography of messages can be based on etic as well as emic operations. It is obvious because psychologists, ethologists, and primatologists routinely study the messages exchanged between infra-human organisms independently of any eliciting conversations. Chimpanzees cannot be asked if a whisper or a whine changes the meaning of an utterance. Note that asking such a question is not to be confused with experimental manipulation of signals in order to test the etically derived meaning—as in observing the response of a duck to a duck call, or of a gorilla to prolonged eye contact. Only humans can carry on discussions involving requests for information, with the exception of a computer and a few chimpanzees who at great cost have been programmed to participate in rudimentary discourse.

With respect to the natural communicative acts that occur among infra-human species, it is possible to identify all seven of Hymes's basic criteria for messages.

Why therefore is it forbidden to identify etic messages and their meaning among humans? I think the objections of Hymes and other idealists boils down to this: they fear that if human messages are not approached from an emic point of view, the messages will be "misunderstood." But this objection applies with equal force to the interpretation of messages exchanged between ducks or between gorillas. As Franz Kafka long ago pointed out, if an ape could address a learned society, we would be astonished by all the things it had on its mind. Lacking such an ape, we do not know if messages which chimpanzees exchange have the same meaning for them as they do for Jane Van Lawick-Goodall (33). In the human case, however, we are more fortunate. We have the opportunity of finding out what messages mean according to two different meanings of meaning: first what messages mean independent of emic eliciting operations, and second what messages mean in response to elicitations concerning their meaning.

In my original approach to this problem (22), I was content to identify a "talking actone" and to propose that identification of the meaning of specific speech messages was accessible only through emic operations. In 1968 (23, p. 579) I stated: "From an etic point of view, the universe of meaning, purposes, goals, motivations, etc is . . . unapproachable." What I should have said was that from an etic point of view the universe of meaning, purposes, goals, motivations, etc is in the messages and not in the heads of the actors. That is, from an etic point of view nothing is asserted about what is going on inside of the heads of the actors when they exchange messages which have a determinate etic meaning. From an etic point of view, to counter Wittgenstein, as quoted by Searle (49, p. 145), people can say "it's cold here" and mean "it's warm here."

Etic Meanings of Speech Acts

The difference between etic meanings and emic meanings is the difference between the first level surface meaning of a human utterance and its total psychological significance for speaker and hearer respectively. I can explain this distinction by reference to videotape studies of behavior stream scenes in New York households (12, 44, 51). These studies have attempted to describe patterns of superordination and subordination in terms of the responses which members of households make to an *etic* category of speech acts which we (the observers) call "requests." This class of speech acts includes "requests for attention," "requests for action," and "requests for information" (Mom!; "Take the garbage out"; What time is it?). In English, observers can operationally define requests as speech acts involving certain grammatical and tonal features (such as omission of pronouns and emphatic or rising tones). It is presumed that while "requests" would have to be identified by different specific criteria in different languages, all human languages (and many infra-human communication systems) have provisions for sending messages which the sender would use if the sender seriously intended to alter the behavior of the hearer in a specific fashion. The need for discriminating between the surface meaning or the etic content of a message and its psychological or emic meaning is dramatically evident when one is confronted with the fact that in the households studied to date, hearers on the average do not comply with requests about one and one-half times more frequently than they comply with them. Several emic interpretations which do not involve the assumption that the speaker seriously intended to communicate the surface meaning of the message are compatible with this situation. For example, consider the speech acts in the following behavior stream events involving a mother and her 8-year-old son as recorded on videotape. Starting at 10:50 A.M., the mother repeats a series of requests to her son in which she asks him to stop playing with the dog.

Time	Request
10:50	R., leave him (the dog) alone.
11:01	Leave him alone.
11:09	Leave him alone.
11:10	Hey don't do that.
11:10	Please leave him alone.
11:15	Leave him alone.
11:15	Leave him alone.
11:15	Why don't you stop teasing him?
11:16	Leave Rex alone, huh?
11:17	Leave him alone.
11:17	Leave him alone.
11:24	Keep away from him.

During the same scene the mother also requests the same child to turn down the volume on the radio in the living room, as follows:

10:40	Keep your hands off that (radio).
10:41	I don't want to hear that.
11:19	Lower that thing (the radio).
11:20	Come on, knock it off.
11:20	Lower that.
11:20	Get your own (radio in another room).
11:20	Keep your hands off this thing (the radio).
11:26	Alright, come on. I've got to have that lowered.
11:27	Leave it alone.
11:27	Leave it alone.
11:29	Turn it off right now.
11:29	You're not to touch that radio.
11:29	Keep your hands off that radio.

It is clear that one cannot simply assume that a component in the meanings of the above requests is the intention of the speaker to be taken seriously about turning the radio off or leaving the dog alone. If the mother intends to be taken seriously, why does she repeat the same requests 12 or 13 times in less than an hour? One cannot argue that repetition is a token of her seriousness (like a prisoner who repeatedly tries to escape from jail) because she has numerous alternatives—she herself can turn the radio off, for example, or she can segregate the child and the dog in different rooms. Her failure to take decisive action may very well indicate that there are other semantic components involved. Perhaps she really intends merely to show disapproval. Or perhaps her main intention is to punish herself by making requests with which she knows her son will not comply. The emic ambiguities are even more marked when we examine the hearer's role. One possibility is that the child rejects the surface meaning of the request, knowing that his mother isn't really serious. Another possibility is that the child thinks that the mother is serious but rejects her authority. Or does the child interpret the repetitions to mean that his mother would rather punish herself than punish him? To disambiguate these meanings one must employ eliciting operations, and these alone are the hallmark of emic events. The etic meanings however, remain the same, regardless of the ultimate result of the elicitation process (which incidentally need not result in speaker or hearer meaning the same emic things). Emic meanings are inside of the heads of the actors. But etic meanings are inside the message in the speech act viewed as a behavior stream event.

To all of the above, I expect the rejoinder: You have now admitted that to identify and understand requests and other speech acts it is necessary to know the language in which the speech acts are made. Since the surface meaning of a speech act ultimately derives from semantic distinctions that are meaningful and appropriate to the native speakers, the surface meanings really are located inside of the native speakers' heads, are knowable through elicitations, and are therefore emic. And once an eme always an eme. Thus any codings of speech acts must necessarily be emic.

The rebuttal is as follows: To be a human observer capable of carrying out scientific operations presumes that one is competent in at least one natural language. Thus, in identifying speech acts in their own native language, observers are not dependent on eliciting operations and can readily agree that a particular utterance has a specific surface meaning whose locus is in the behavior stream.

That such surface meanings are also probably shared by the actors is not a decisive operational criterion, although it is a reasonable assumption.

This line of reasoning can easily be extended to include foreign speech acts, if we grant the proposition that all human languages are mutually translatable. This means that for every utterance in a foreign language, there is an analogue in one's own. While it is true that successful translation of a foreign speech act is facilitated by the collaboration of a native informant, the locus of the cognitive reality of the translation remains inside the observers' heads. That is, what the observers intend to find out is which linguistic structures inside their own heads have more or less the same meaning as the utterances in the behavior stream of the foreign actors. Thus the translation amounts to the imposition of the observers' semantic categories on the foreign speech acts, and as previously explained, the use of native informants is perfectly compatible with etic descriptions. Of course, in any competent translation we again assume that there is a close correspondence between the observers' surface meaning and the native speakers' surface meaning. But once this correspondence has been established, the observers have in effect enlarged their competence to include both languages, and hence they can proceed to identify the surface meanings of foreign speech acts as freely as native speakers of English are able to identify the speech acts listed above. Indeed, in the actual identification of requests in the videotape study from which the above examples are drawn (12), there were several coders who were not native speakers of English.

It should not come as any surprise that a *comprehensive* etic approach to the behavior stream presumes a knowledge of the language of the participants. In studying the behavior stream of infra-human species, we expect to include communication acts. Exactly the same assumptions about surface meanings are made in the infra-human case, except that the assimilation of these meanings to our shared language competence cannot be facilitated by native informants acting as translators. I italicize *comprehensive* because the argument I have just presented does not lead to the conclusion that the etic approach like an emic approach *necessarily* demands a knowledge of the social actors' language; on the contrary, many etic operations, including the study of some aspects of communication phenomena, can proceed entirely without foreign language competence.

The Emics of the Observer

A theme in the critique of the emic/etic distinction which is especially valued by partisans of obscurantist strategies is that etics, after all, are "nothing but the emics of the observers" (35). This statement has a grain of truth in it because one cannot deny that the locus of the reality of the behavior stream lies in part inside the heads of the observers. But it amounts to nothing more than a rerun of Bishop Berkeley's argument on behalf of an idealist ontology. Those who maintain that the behavior stream *only* exists inside of the minds of the observers, to be consistent must also believe that the observers themselves have no existence except as a sophistic figment. Why therefore don't they lapse into silent contemplation of their brain waves and let those of us who are so benighted as to believe that there are pluralities of minds and bodies out there go about our business?

Literature Cited

1. Barker, R., ed. 1963. *The Stream of Behavior*. New York: Appleton, Century, Crofts
2. Bach, E. 1964. *An Introduction to Transformational Grammar*. New York: Holt, Rinehart & Winston
3. Bauman, R., Sherzer, J. 1975. The ethnography of speaking. *Ann. Rev. Anthropol.* 4:95–120
4. Bender, D. 1967. A refinement of the concept of household: Families, co-residence and domestic functions. *Am. Anthropol.* 69:493–503
5. Berreman, G. 1966. Anemic and emetic analysis in social anthropology. *Am. Anthropol.* 68:346–54
6. Black, M. 1973. Belief systems. In *Handbook of Social and Cultural Anthropology*, ed. J. Honigman, 509–77. Chicago: Rand McNally
7. Boas, F. 1943. Recent anthropology. *Science* 98:311–14, 334–37
8. Bright, W. 1968. Languages and culture. *Encycl. Soc. Sci.* 9:18–22
9. Burling, R. 1964. Cognition and componential analysis: God's truth or hocus-pocus? *Am. Anthropol.* 66:20–28

10. Burling, R. 1969. Linguistics and ethnographic description. *Am. Anthropol.* 77:817–27

11. Durbin, M. A. 1972. Linguistic models in anthropology. *Ann. Rev. Anthropol.* 1:383–410

12. Dehavenon, A. L., Dehavenon, H. M. n.d. *Hierarchical Behavior in Domestic Groups: A Videotape Analysis.* (Mimeo)

13. Feyerabend, P. 1963. Explanations, predictions, theories. In *Philosophy of Science: The Delaware Seminar,* ed. B. Baumrin, 2:3–39. New York: Interscience

14. Feyerabend, P. 1970. Problems of empiricism, Part II. In *Nature and Function of Scientific Theories,* ed. R. Colodny, 275–353. Univ. Pittsburgh Press

15. Fisher, J. 1958. The classification of residence in censuses. *Am. Anthropol.* 60:508–17

16. Frake, C. 1962. The ethnographic study of cognitive systems. In *Anthropology as Human Behavior,* ed. T. Gladwin, W. Sturtevant, 72–85. Washington DC: Anthropol. Soc. Washington

17. Geoghegan, W. 1969. *Decision Making and Residence on Tagtabon Island.* Work. Pap. 17, Lang. Behav. Res. Lab., Univ. California, Berkeley

18. Goodenough, W. 1956. Residence rules. *Southwest, J. Anthropol.* 12:22–37

19. Goodenough, W., ed. 1964. Introduction. In *Exploration in Cultural Anthropology,* 1–24. New York: McGraw Hill

20. Goodenough, W. 1969. Frontiers of cultural anthropology, social organization. *Proc. Am. Philos. Soc.* 113:329–35

21. Goodenough, W. 1970. *Description and Comparison in Cultural Anthropology.* Chicago: Aldine

22. Harris, M. 1964. *The Nature of Cultural Things.* New York: Random House

23. Harris, M. 1968. *The Rise of Anthropological Theory.* New York: Crowell

24. Harris, M. 1975. Why a perfect knowledge of all the rules that one must know to act like a native cannot lead to the knowledge of how natives act. *J. Anthropol. Res.* 30:242–51

25. Hymes, D. 1968. Linguistics: The field. *Encycl. Soc. Sci.* 9:351–71

26. Hymes, D. 1970. Linguistic method in ethnography: Its development in the United States. In *Method and Theory in Linguistics,* ed. P. Garvin. The Hague: Mouton

27. Hymes, D. 1974. *Foundations in Sociolinguistics: An Ethnographic Approach.* Philadelphia: Univ. Pennsylvania Press

28. Kay, P. 1970. Some theoretical implications of ethnographic semantics. *Bull. Am. Anthropol. Assoc.* 3(3), pt. 2

29. Keesing, R. M. 1972. Paradigm lost: the new ethnography and the new linguistics. *Southwest. J. Anthropol.* 28:299–332

30. Keesing, R. M. 1974. Theories of culture. *Ann. Rev. Anthropol.* 3:73–79

31. Kroeber, A. 1909. Classificatory systems of relationship. *J. R. Anthropol. Inst.* 39:77–85

32. Kronenfeld, D. 1973. Fanti kinship: The structure and terminology of behavior. *Am. Anthropol.* 75:1577–95

33. Lawick-Goodall, J. van 1972. A preliminary report on expressive movements as communication in the Gombe Stream chimpanzees. In *Primate Patterns,* ed. P. Dolhinow, 25–84. New York: Holt, Rinehart & Winston

34. Lenin, V. I. 1927. *Materialism and Empirio-Criticism: Critical Comments on a Reactionary Philosophy.* New York: International Publ.

35. Lévi-Strauss, C. 1974. Structuralism and ecology. In *Readings in Anthropology, 1975–76,* ed. A. Weiss, 226–33. Guilford, Conn: Dushkin

36. Lounsbury, F. 1965. Another view of Trobriand kinship categories. *Am. Anthropol.* 67(2):142–285

37. Marx, K., Engels, F. 1942. *The German Ideology.* New York: International Publ.

38. Naroll, R. 1973. Introduction. In *Main Currents in Anthropology,* ed. R. Naroll, F. Naroll, 1–23. New York: Appleton, Century, Crofts

39. Pelto, P. 1970. *Anthropological Research: The Structure of Inquiry.* New York: Harper & Row

40. Pelto, P., Pelto, G. 1975. Intra-cultural diversity: Some theoretical issues. *Am. Ethnol.* 2:1–18

41. Petersen, G. n.d. *American Anthropology and the Colonial Experience in Micronesia.* (Mimeo)

42. Pike, K. L. 1967. *Language in Re-*

lation to a Unified Theory of the Structures of Human Behavior. The Hague: Mouton. 2nd ed.

43. Pivin, F., Cloward, R. W. 1971. *Regulating the Poor: The Function of Public Welfare.* New York: Random House

44. Reiss, N. 1975. *The Ethnography of Speaking and the Ethnography of Doing.* Unpublished paper presented at 74th Ann. Meet. Am. Anthropol. Assoc., San Francisco

45. Sanjek, R. 1974. What is network analysis and what is it good for? *Rev. Anthropol.* 1:588–97

46. Sapir, E. 1949. Selected writings of Edward Sapir. In *Language, Culture, and Personality,* ed. D. Mandelbaum. Berkeley: Univ. California Press

47. Schein, M. D., Diamond, S. G. 1966. *The Waste Collectors.* Unpublished Masters essay. Columbia, Univ., New York, NY

48. Schneider, D. 1968. *American Kinship: A Cultural Account.* Englewood Cliffs, NJ: Prentice Hall

49. Searle, J. 1972. What is a speech act? In *Language and Social Context,* ed. P. Giglioli, 136–54. Baltimore: Penguin Books

50. Stack, C. 1974. *All Our Kin: Strategies for Survival in a Black Community.* New York: Harper & Row

51. Sharff, J. 1975. *The Advocate.* Unpublished paper presented at 74th Ann. Meet. Am. Anthropol. Assoc., San Francisco

Ann. Rev. Anthropol. 1976. 5:351–81
Copyright © 1976 by Annual Reviews Inc. All rights reserved

DEMOGRAPHIC THEORY AND ANTHROPOLOGICAL INFERENCE

♦ 9583

Kenneth M. Weiss

Center for Demographic and Population Genetics, University of Texas
Graduate School of Biomedical Sciences, Houston, Texas 77030

INTRODUCTION: REGULARITY AND IRREGULARITY

Anthropology is basically an evolutionary science in which we attempt to understand the processes by which change is imposed on regularity in the joint evolution of human biology and culture. Like other evolutionary sciences, we often are unable to observe those processes directly, since they occur slowly relative to our brief observations. We also must deal with the problems of the instability of small populations. It is for these reasons that anthropology is in need of a solid theoretical foundation, expressed in terms of variables which can be observed, and from which to make meaningful indirect inference.

In recent times, theoretical constructs from various aspects of demography have been shown to be immensely useful in developing this theoretical foundation, and it has become clear that demographic variables can form a unifying metric for anthropology. The study of birth, death, and growth rates, of population size and dispersion, and of mating and migration, all have advanced with the use of demographic theory. Yet demography was developed by national political statisticians accustomed to massive bodies of data, where great precision was both expected and attainable. Demographers have seemed quite disinterested in the dynamic problems of biocultural evolution in small societies, where irregularities in vital processes are more apparent (though no more real) than they are when millions of records are aggregated. Perhaps this is why one demographer (190) has criticized anthropology harshly for what seemed our naive use of a science which is foreign to us. Yet work by anthropologists, including reviews of demographic anthropology (11, 62, 236) as well as new research collections (31, 65, 99, 193b, 234, 252, 277) has clearly shown that when used by us for our own goals, demographic theory has led to new insights, and that we can adapt and make of it a vital tool in an important natural science.

In this review I wish to show selected ways in which this adaptation has been made. Stress will be placed not so much on technical details as on the philosophy and logic of inference of anthropological demography. Our problem is to explain the biocultural dynamics within, and variation among, the generally small popu-

351

lations in which humans have lived, when we know that there is great variability and internal adjustment in these processes, and that this is compounded by the many occasional events which can severely affect small populations.

If the triumph of nineteenth century science was to show that nature is better viewed in terms of processes than of types, then that of the twentieth century has been to show repeatedly that the laws of nature are inextricably the laws of chance. The boundary between "signal" and "noise" has been forced to recede to such a degree that there is now only a very tenuous, and philosophically vulnerable, justification for separating observation into those categories. Thus, while we would like to explain human biocultural evolution with theories of adaptive processes, we must know not to expect perfect adaptation from a being whose perceptions are fallible and whose responses must therefore be inexact. While we may view human populations as "striving" toward biological and social equilibria, we must not introduce an artifice of stasis in our theoretical models for mathematical convenience, when we know fully that equilibrium can at best only approximately and temporarily be attained. In fact, one must seriously wonder whether we are justified in treating sporadic deviation from theory as unimportant "experimental" error, rather than as the very driving engine of human evolution itself.

This is the "stochastic problem" which I believe will become central to serious anthropological theory, and it will be demographic data which are used to solve it. To understand the biological forces controlling our lives and the social forces controlling our associations, the soundest formal approach seems to me to be first to determine the underlying average processes which appear to operate, even if they are hypothetical and never exactly attained, and then to analyze the way in which sporadic or stochastic factors modify those processes to produce actual observations. I hope in what follows to show ways in which progress has been made, or problems clarified, in this quest.

THE AGE PATTERNS OF BIRTH AND DEATH

Demographic theory begins with the fundamental statement that population change is the sum of births and immigration less deaths and emigration ($\Delta N = B + I - D - E$). These terms are then partitioned or expanded in ways depending on the problems to be studied. It is commonly assumed that statistical fluctuations in these terms are insignificant and that migration is zero. For anthropologists, the second assumption aids some aspects of our analysis and is probably reasonable if either migration consists mainly of spouse exchange, in which case both migrants are of about the same age and sex (hence net migration is zero), or if villages are being aggregated, in which case migration between villages is not counted. The statistical assumption will be discussed later in this review.

A. J. Lotka, the father of modern demographic theory, provided a detailed theoretical treatment of the demography of a large closed population with fixed age-specific rates of fertility and mortality. This is called a *stable population* under his assumptions, and it has been elaborated in many works (28, 57, 126, 154, 156, 219). The stable population has the property that the set of age-specific fertility and mortality rates ("vital rates") produces an annual number of births which approaches exponential growth at a rate "intrinsic" to the vital rates. No matter what the initial *age distribution* (proportion in each age class) of a population, the entire population will eventually grow at this rate. The age distribution of the population will become closer and closer to a fixed one, which is also determined by the vital rates. Disturbance of the population temporarily will only cause transitory deviations from the stable age distribution and growth rate, which will return. Even if birth and death rates change, the population will "track" on a determined path, so that any two populations subject to the same pattern of changing rates will become inexorably closer in age distribution.

Real populations do not fit these assumptions exactly, of course, but the stable population model has proved itself to be an extremely useful approximation. In those anthropological contexts where a population has not been severely disturbed recently, the model is very valuable and forms the foundation of theoretical demographic anthropology. This is due to the fact that our observations are nearly always restricted to a single census from a small group briefly visited, along with some other assorted and fragmentary data.

Stable population theory relates the birth, death, and growth rates to the age distribution they produce. Thus, from values of some of these parameters, values of others may be inferred; this *relationship between variables* is the critical advantage of stable population theory for anthropologists dealing with very incomplete data. In particular, if we can estimate the growth rate, the (growth-corrected) age distribution will be proportional to the age-specific mortality rates. Since we can seldom observe the age pattern of death directly, our knowledge of it usually must be derived from this property of stable populations. Only under special circumstances, such as the existence of extended missionary birth and death records, could we observe age patterns closely; we should, of course, make every effort to locate and use such data where they are available. Many other parameters can be estimated by similar kinds of inference; for example, the survival of family lines or clans (156, 197, 273), the rate at which orphans are produced (155), the number of social dependents, potential spouses, or children born to women of given ages, the future effects of present social practices as periodic functions of the age structure (127), or the degree of internal differentiation ("entropy") within the population (69). Many relationships between variables, under the assumptions of stable population theory, have been computed in detail (28, 57, 126, 199, 221). The anthropologist who attempts demographic studies without first obtaining a firm understanding of stable population theory is crippled to a degree which is no longer justifiable.

Population theory can be used to model the dynamics of populations with certain characteristics. For example, Goodman (89) and Coale (57) show how certain changes in birth and death schedules affect the age distribution. Such models usually deal with growing or diminishing populations. Yet it is clear that most human populations until recent centuries have had virtually zero average

354   WEISS

growth, since even small positive growth rates would otherwise have over-populated the earth many times over. Demographic theory which adequately deals with the dynamics of populations fluctuating about zero growth is as yet poorly developed, and presents an important area for future research. This is especially true since the assumption of zero growth, when growth has really been nonzero, can also lead to substantial error in life tables so derived (6a, 15, 44, 175). We can expect that small local populations always manifest irregular patterns of growth and decline, and must not overemploy the concept of an equilibrium with regard to individual local groups in the short run.

Coale (57) has given a demonstration that any characteristic of a population which has an age-specific distribution of incidence rate has an extremum of per capita frequency when the mean age of that distribution is the same as the mean age of the population; he also shows the way that the incidence of the trait changes as the two mean ages differ. Since many cultural and social aspects of a population, as well as diseases, have characteristic age patterns, this theorem will find important application in anthropology. In particular, we may expect to find that adjustments in social mechanisms optimize the biological and eco-logical strength of a tribe or set of villages with regard to the incidence of such things as disease. Surely one reason for human culture is to act in some senses as a servomechanism protecting by small adjustment against the everpresent forces of disruption.

Most theoretical developments in population have been made with a *continu-ous-time* mathematical approach, but since actual data are grouped by one or more whole years, a *discrete-time* approach is needed if the theory is to be applied. A matrix approach to population dynamics was developed by Lewis (146) and Leslie (144, 145), and its properties have been analyzed in several recent works (88, 126, 188, 192, 238). This has become the standard method of population dynamic analysis. Its results are, of course, consistent with the analogous continuous-time model.

The basic product of demographic study is usually the *life table*, which is built on a discrete-time approach. Because we must rely on theory and not on actual observation of the age-specific demographic processes, we generally employ "synthetic cohort" life tables, which in essence represent the mortality to be experienced by typical newborns assuming that age-specific rates do not change and are represented by a current census. The construction of life tables is discussed in several works for general readers (12, 126, 128, 221) and for anthropologists in at least two (1, 255). Many recent studies have used life tables or their equivalent (10, 15, 34, 41, 95, 109–111, 130, 163, 168, 172, 184, 210, 211, 235, 241, 256, and many others). The three greatest dangers in this kind of work are: (*a*) poorly met assumptions of stability, (*b*) statistically insufficient single population samples, and (*c*) the temptation to explain differences between life tables from several populations when they are too small to be significant (statis-tically or otherwise).

A point of interest is that it seems from preliminary investigations that if data were standardized on maximum life span, many of the characteristics of prim-itive human populations would also typify certain other primate groups, such as chimpanzees. This is an important question, although sufficient field data do not exist to answer it in detail (but see 114, 125a, 163); if our own demographic experience and that of related animals differ only in their time calibration, then fundamental biological inferences might be made concerning the evolution of longevity (note also 68a).

Sample Size Considerations

One of the most troublesome assumptions that we generally must make is that our censuses are statistically stable and representative of the demographic phenomena *generally* occurring (of course, they are always exactly representative of the events which *did* occur, since complete censuses are not samples). The theoretical approach to this issue rests on the observations that: (*a*) all well-studied human populations show the same basic age pattern of mortality, and (*b*) these regularities may be approximated by certain mathematical functions which have biological rationale. Thus, while statistical factors undoubtedly operate to produce variability in vital rate patterns, these factors seem in general to be laid onto fairly stable underlying average birth and death rates which can be important to estimate.

These facts justify smoothing the age distribution of a small population by some mathematical, empirical, or graphical means to remove assumed statistical irregularity (14, 46, 107, 126, 128, 173). However, this can be done only if we can safely assume that major demographic disturbance has not occurred recently or regularly; otherwise the population is not stable and we would err in using a theory which assumed it were.

A somewhat different approach from ad hoc smoothing is to assume that the population behaves similarly to other like-cultured groups. If so, then the age patterns of vital rates should be similar. There are many sets of *model life tables* constructed just for this purpose, and based on the aggregated experience of many populations. These each consist of a graded series of life tables following the empiric mortality of their base populations and conveniently parameterized for access; their construction has variously been based on: the observed correlation between successive age-specific mortality rates (245), correlation of mortality rates with life expectancy values (58), a two-parameter slope-and-rotation approach to the mortality curve (32, 46), and a mathematical smoothing of anthropological data (255).

Model life tables not based on anthropological data must often be extrapolated beyond their data base to be used for primitive populations; however, some of these approaches are among the most sophisticated, especially those of Brass (32, and see 46). Different sets of model life tables have been exceptionally useful (e.g. 33, 45, 109, 184, 234), although the most often-used set, by Coale & Demeny (58), may have difficulty in anthropological application due to the high juvenile mortality our populations often experience (2, 33). Bourgeois-Pichat (28) gives lengthy and detailed discussion of means to fit sets of model tables to empirical data, and his is the best treatment of that problem available. The techniques of Carrier and Hobcraft and the methods of Bourgeois-Pichat would, if combined with anthropologically based model life tables, probably produce an optimum life table approach among present alternatives.

The opinion is widespread that our populations are too small to be studied by stable population theory for which population size is not a consideration. It is thus of interest to know what the statistical variability in vital rates, and its consequents, are, so that we can quantify our risks. This has been dealt with only sketchily (e.g. 126, 174, 196, 237), and although these studies were dealing with sampling variability they apply to our total censuses of small groups. They compute the variances in such measures as life expectancy, which result from sampling variation in vital rates; however, the distributions themselves are not known so that probability statements still cannot be placed on the estimates. Here is a fertile area for future work.

Angel (8) has argued against life tables for paleoanthropology because of the assumption of unchanging rates, and Moore et al (175) show that the life table can be subject to such statistical variability in the underlying average vital rates as to produce a wide array of census results in different populations with those same average rates; thus estimates of these rates from the single censuses with which we typically must work would be of very limited use. Similar thoughts have been expressed with regard to population size (e.g. 6a, 6b; see 161, 222, 269). Indeed, this follows from branching process theory, which shows that most populations of small size, subject to constant birth and death probabilities, will eventually become extinct merely due to the statistical nature of these processes. This issue has in fact stimulated a wealth of simulation work in anthropological genetic demographic theory, about which there is more below.

The reason for some of this statistical instability of small groups is not, however, intrinsic to the groups *but to the theory used to model them.* Stable population theory assumes fixed vital rates, yet we know from overwhelming evidence that man is like all mammals in being active in regulating his own population growth and size (72). In medium or long-term studies, we are simply wrong to use a fixed vital rate model for human populations, and instead we must use a model in which birth and death rates at every age are negative-feedback functions of present conditions relative to some equilibrium. Three papers have examined the effects of demographic feedback of this kind on the stability of a population (225, 257, 260). When a population of 100 was projected with this kind of model by simulation, it was found to be very stable, and even after centuries the death rates derivable from the census and stable population theory, that is, the underlying average rates toward which the population tended, were accurate to within about 10 percent. Analysis of the variance of the results showed that the degree of error does not vary much from population to population. Thus an improved biological model shows that small size alone will "usually", in the statistical sense, not disrupt estimates of mortality rates beyond the accuracy needed by anthropologists (see also 222, 269).

Paleodemography

Studies of prehistoric populations, although based on actual data from the period, are one step deeper into all of the problems confronting the ethnological situation. Not only do we have all the statistical uncertainties, but (*a*) there are difficult problems of ascertainment of age and sex of specimens; (*b*) juveniles are almost always under-represented; (*c*) skeletal deposition may vary with respect to age groups; and (*d*) population size must be inferred from various totally indirect evidence (6a, 62, 113, 226, 276b).

The problems of aging of skeletons have been dealt with in several ways. Lovejoy (157) has provided some simple statistics with which two burial sets may be compared to see if their age distributions differ significantly. Weiss (254) has noted a systematic sexing bias in favor of males which must be taken into account, and Acsádi & Nemeskéri (1) deal at length with the theory of aging and sexing of skeletons, providing the best algorithm yet devised for reliable study of large data sets. There are several recent discussions of theoretical problems involved with paleodemography (36, 81, 82, 110, 218, 235, 236, 241, 253–257).

The most critical treatment of these problems has come from Masset (165 a–c), which must be read by all archeologists comtemplating demographic work. He shows that systematic errors in aging and sexing occur, which may all tend to make populations seem to have low life expectancy and excess female adult mortality. These are due, he argues, to manifestations of sex and age in bone and the inherent misidentification they produce, which are confounded so that we cannot be sure of our age-at-death distributions. Means to solve these problems must be found before our confidence in skeletal demography can be increased; however, archeological data from different sites or different times at the same site produce similar demographic results, so we can have confidence that whatever we are doing, we are doing consistently.

Perhaps a more critical assumption we tacitly make in paleodemography is that the population processes and basic population structure of past populations are closely approximated by the ethnographic present. We have been criticized for our use of this kind of analogy (190), though Swedlund & Armelagos (236) think it is largely unnecessary for the productive use of present-day primitive societies to understand the past. Indeed, there is reason to believe that some basic sociopolitical processes of present populations are not ethnographic survivals from previous times. These must be taken into account. For example, the mating network and relations between local paleolithic populations may differ fundamentally from present populations (271); also, the means of birth spacing, and hence fertility patterns, may have differed in hunting-gathering cultures from all subsequent groups (112, 141). Howell (112) notes, however, that this *uniformitarian* assumption that the processes in paleodemographic populations were similar to those observable in present, can find much empirical support, particularly in the age patterns of fertility and mortality. She provides a cogent discussion of this problem, showing that uniformitarianism, carefully applied, is a useful and probably needed assumption in paleodemography. It is also a central western metaphysic about nature's processes which must not lightly be discarded.

Mortality

Although the life table gives us the age pattern of net mortality, it is important that we be able to augment this by an understanding of the way in which the actual forces of mortality bring it about. Unfortunately, the causes of mortality in anthropological societies are largely unknown, nor do we have a firm understanding of the details of changes in them which cultural evolution has brought about (although see 9). Standard epidemiological theory would predict little epidemic infection, since sparsely dispersed populations cannot provide a sufficient number of susceptibles (e.g. 24, 40); of course, we know relatively little of the evolution of the ecology of present human epidemic and endemic diseases. Several studies have shown that primitives' exposure to a wide variety of antigens is common (e.g. 24, 35, 47, 170, 179–181) as reflected in gamma-globulin levels, and Dunn (73) finds common evidence for various types of parasitic disease. Armelagos (9, 236) gives a good summary of the kinds of evidence available to skeletal paleopathologists, such as evidence of rates and types of trauma or growth modification, or disease.

I have shown (255) that previous estimates of average life expectancy of stages in human demographic history have probably been about 10 years too high, but this does not help answer the question of the causes responsible. The central question to which attention must be directed is: What kills in primitive populations? It is important to remember that even with a high death rate, an observer for a short time in a small group will observe only a very small number of deaths. This puts a theoretical and practical limit on our ability to observe the cause of death structure of such groups, for death "rates" are experienced only in the statistical sense here: they are not the death ratios (number dead against number susceptible) generally observed in large nations. The development of a basic theory of mortality and the human life span is critical to an understanding of the diseases of old age which strike modern societies.

There has been some work done on the analysis of competing causes of mortality, using data from national censuses, by Preston and colleagues (198, 200, 201), giving a complete analysis of the correlation structure among causes of death, allowing us to relate recent cultural change to mortality changes, and providing a regression analysis by which we can take an observed age pattern of mortality and estimate, in theory, how the various known causes combined to produce it. The cause of death structure is intricate, since various causes interact, yet it involves all of the ecological relationships of the population. It is one of the most refractory, yet most important, of problems for anthropological demographers.

Fertility

The study of fertility is perhaps the most vigorous area of contemporary population science; most of this work, however, has to do with conception, birth, and birth control, and simulation thereof, or with studies of population regulation in general (e.g. 76, 92, 193, 193a, 193b, 220). The structure of marriage models has also been studied, by mathematical methods (170, 171, 189, 197). The parameters in such studies are usually far too complex and detailed to be estimable in anthropological circumstances; however, the details of fertility patterns must be better incorporated in models of human biology and genetics (181, 230).

One area of active research in anthropology has been to understand the factors which may cause birth spacing in largely contraception-free (in the Western sense) populations to be two to three years greater than expected (72, 227). This is the case for most anthropological populations [and for chimpanzees (114)]. One factor held by many to be of prime importance has been the effects, indirect and direct, of the extended lactation in anthropological societies relative to industrial ones. In the absence of stored, soft foods, hunter-gatherers have had to nurse their children far longer than is the case for agricultural peoples. Their life styles require such large distances to be traveled in the gathering of food, at least in desert or savannah environments, that only a single child can be carried at any time (39, 43a, 72, 84, 132, 141, 228, but 134a). Howell (112) argues that the anovulatory effect of lactation is related to the amount of body fat, and that women in hunter-gatherer societies are at reduced risk of pregnancy as long as they must nurse their infants; this is an effect observed in other animals as well (e.g. 80a). After agriculture, this effect is of limited importance, since sufficient foods may be available for women's critical body fat level to be restored sooner. Mathematical models of the lactation effect are available (e.g. 85, 86, 220), but the parameters require more data than we generally have in order to be estimated. Even without this direct physiological effect, the effects of *cultural* practices often associated with lactation, such as intercourse taboos, may be sufficient to explain much of the fertility-regulating role extended lactation plays in primitive societies (222).

The characterization of age patterns of fertility has seen some progress in anthropological demography; since we can only rarely observe actual age-specific fertility "rates" in small villages, use of stable population theory would be seriously hampered if we could not estimate these rates with reasonable accuracy in some indirect way. Use of a "typical" schedule of relative age-specific fertility has been made in this context. Several authors have shown that similar cultures have similar patterns of fertility at each age between menarche and menopause, relative to other ages in that range (33, 46, 104, 239, 246, 255). The general similarity of the results supports their use (see 252), and the error so introduced is probably not prohibitively great for many purposes.

The average fertility of women by age is important for many demographic studies, but it is far more biologically (and socially) important to know how this average number is distributed among those women. If all women had exactly the same chance of giving birth (e.g. no mortality, no unmarried women, no change with age), then the family size distribution would theoretically be Poisson, with the variance equal to the mean (30, 118, 119). However, the different experiences of each woman introduce increased variability among them, and a negative binomial distribution is more often observed (30, 48, 131, 167, 204). Some empirical studies show evidence for a Poisson (115, 167, 184, 185), probably due to relative cultural homogeneity and to birth control practices, which reduce the variance in fertility. This reduction has been magnified by modern culture and is of significant genetic importance, although the heritability of fertility differentials in man may be small (115, 119, 121, 167, 182, 243). Since we know virtually nothing about male fertility rates, a satisfactory understanding of the genetic, biological, and cultural ramifications of human reproductive behavior eludes us.

Indices of Demographic Status and Evolution

Often the details of the life table are too numerous for one to comprehend, and there is some purpose in devising simple measures which aggregate the information in a theoretically meaningful way. Life expectancy at birth summarizes all of the mortality table, for example, and Lotka's stable population growth rate (r) derives from both mortality and fertility schedules (126). A measure of genetic relevance is R. A. Fisher's Reproductive Value: the amount of reproduction remaining, on average, to an individual, relative to that of a newborn (67). A modification of his Fundamental Theorem of Natural Selection has been given by Crow (66); now called the Index of the Opportunity for Selection, it has been used frequently by anthropologists. The total variability in completed reproduction by individuals in a population is the most evolutionary differentiation which can exist among them, and hence the most which could be due to genetic selection; this can be partitioned into an index of components due to differential mortality and to differential fertility. It represents only the *potential* amount of natural selection, but can be used to compare the demographic features of populations without reference to genetics. This must be done cautiously, however, since cultural changes can cause compensating effects on the index (119, 121). The index reflects many important phenomena, such as cultural effects of population planning and the relative importance of fertility differentials versus mortality differentials during the eons of primitive cultural existence (226a).

A more purely demographic index is presented by Goodman (90), who gives the relative rate by which a change in mortality would affect r in relation to that which would result from equally changed fertility. Two similarly motivated measures have been produced by anthropologists. First, Henneberg's (104) Biological State Index relates death rates in skeletal series to the amount of reproduction possible if there were no pre-menopausal mortality, given a model of fertility; this has some difficulties in application (252). Secondly, an Index of Growth Regulation (254, 255) compares the relative degree to which fertility limitation, and mortality, reduce population growth from its potential maximum to its observed value. Although fertility damping has always been present, it has been the prominent factor in reducing human growth only since industrialization, in terms of this index.

Changes in mortality, fertility, and age distribution, as well as in the ages of childbearing, will directly affect the rates at which genetic or genetically related diseases are expressed (79, 108, 166, 186). In turn, the genetic fitness of those with such disorders can only be measured with a knowledge of the details of the fertility, as well as mortality, rates (26, 48, 224), another clear relationship between culture and human biology which is seen only when the metric of demography is used. The recent social concentration of childbearing into a short period of years will also have important genetic and epidemiological effects (79,

121, 167, 202). Thus genes cannot be thought to have any inherent "value" in the majority of cases, for fitness is inherently related to a cultural context.

DEMOGRAPHIC THEORY AND ANTHROPOLOGICAL GENETICS

Since human populations are not composed of equal-age individuals mating completely at random, several aspects of population genetics theory are basically demographic in nature; general discussions of these, with bibliography, are available in many recent works (42, 48, 65, 96, 176, 177, 181, 215–217, 229, 258, 277); a few points can be mentioned here.

Standard population genetics models are based on the assumption of discrete generations with no age structure and with synchronized reproduction (67, 119). When generations overlap and intermarry, theoretical problems arise in the estimation of gene frequency change, fitness, etc. This problem has been dealt with in several papers recently (7, 51–56, 82a, 119, 129, 194, 195), perhaps most significantly by Brian Charlesworth. Though not yet applied to anthropological problems, this work shows that gene frequencies, their rates of change, and hence their distribution among small demes, may depend on demographic patterns which are nonspecific with regard to genotypes. Density-dependent reaction in birth and death rates for various genotypes also may produce different gene frequency distributions in different ecological environments; again, a better model of biological feedback in vital rates is called for, as we have stressed earlier. This is highly relevant for those using genetic variation to reconstruct population histories and phylogenies for human microevolution, for under some circumstances the short-term demographic effects can be significant.

Overlapping generations affect the so-called "effective population size" which is a measure of the size an ideal population with discrete generations would have in order to be as genetically variable as the observed population. Many formulae have been advanced to compute this value given schedules of age-specific vital rates (48, 68, 78, 106, 166). Throughout most of human evolution, it can be shown that the effective population size, for females, was about 40 percent of the total census size; on varying computational grounds, estimates of the ratio of N_e to N have been found to be 20 to 30 percent (139, 210) or 40 to 60 percent (148). However, in the absence of good two-sex models of demography, which require knowledge of male fertility and its variance, we cannot deal adequately with effective size.

An important genetic question for small populations has to do with relatedness between individuals (more specifically, between genes) within the population, usually loosely referred to as "inbreeding," "genetic drift," or "consanguinity." Few anthropologists are aware of the great variety of meanings attached to various coefficients of inbreeding or their proper use, and hence a lot of attention has been paid in almost ritual fashion to a poorly understood concept for which formulae can be computed. Excellent reviews of this are available (119, 120, 203), demonstrating how equivalent mathematical expressions for genotype frequency distributions may refer to fundamentally different processes: (a) individuals marrying relatives more often than would occur by chance alone; (b) a loss of variability through the random elimination of genes in small populations; (c) marriage preference for individuals genetically alike, or unlike, oneself; and (d) subdivision of the population into small independent subunits. All of these factors affect genetic homozygosity, but their long-term evolutionary importance and interpretation have been greatly overemphasized. This is because other processes, such as mutation, natural selection, migration, and especially sociocultural factors interfere with the processes generating this homogeneity (e.g. 123, 140, 151, 183, 232, 248, 249).

The factor most affecting gene frequency distributions, insofar as we are generally concerned, is probably migration. Anthropological populations, through their regular mate exchange, have large migration distances and high migration rates. For recent historical populations, as well as those of other species, the distribution of migration distance has been shown repeatedly to be leptokurtic, that is, skewed toward shorter distances on average than primitives (98, 236). Clans, which may provide social division, probably provide little in the way of genetic barriers (149, 178), and several studies have shown that the effect of migration like that in primitive societies shortens "genetic distances" between widely separated demes and allows a dispersed species to evolve while simultaneously generating local ("racial") differences (22, 37, 38, 159, 259). Many papers have examined the effects of migration among anthropological peoples of various types, or of isolation of such populations (29, 80, 87, 93, 100, 136–138, 147, 183, 205–207, 229, 231, 233, 244, 248–250). In the long term, even an occasional long-range migrant can be an effective homogenizing force regardless of the short-term, short-range, culture-specific migration patterns. Yet the analysis of local genetic heterogeneity may show, as is the case with the Yanomama, that recent patterns of migration/expansion are primarily responsible for gene frequency differences (251).

Computer Simulation

Many questions are too complex to be formulated with demographic mathematics, but are still amenable to quantitative analysis through the semitheoretical means of Monte Carlo computer simulation. Reviews of anthropological work done in this area are available (76, 122a, 158). If there is an adequate foundation in the demographic processes expected to be operating, then one should find observable demographic parameters to show a distribution of values, centered at their expected underlying (average) values and scattered about those values by the chance aspects of life and death. Variations in age distribution, birth and death rates, inbreeding statistics, and so on are of this type, and we can simulate these on a computer to determine if chance alone, and the theory used, are sufficient to produce the observed values, or whether other factors or new theories are called for, or to see which changes are most important to the overall population structure. Many anthropological demographic studies do not take sufficient heed of this; hence, for example, interpopulation variability is explained with complex ratiocination when it is more reasonably explained simply as the expected chance variability of natural processes.

There are several anthropological demographic applications readily amenable to computer simulation: 1. One can determine the effect of small population size on the survival ability of the population, the ability to realize a particular mating pattern, or the effect on the population of enforcing prescriptive mating rules (43, 76, 160, 161, 223). 2. Age-specific vital rates may be estimated by simulation approximations to observed data (13, 75, 76, 117). 3. Mating patterns, population structure, and the frequency of consanguineous marriages can be simulated. Such "inbreeding" studies have used many approaches, often taking frequencies of inbred marriages to estimate the effective size of local groups within larger populations, and relations between deterministic theory and real populations have been examined by simulation (50, 82a, 94, 161, 162, 249). Notable among the conclusions is the fact that single gene loci, whose genotype frequencies are often used to test "inbreeding," can vary so much that reliable interpretations of the population structure and recent history must be made with many loci and all alleles at each locus (251); random factors and migration, not genetic selection, may often be sufficient to explain patterns of genetic diversity (204): simulation serves to keep us from invoking too much theory to explain our data, as important a function as the theory itself. 4. The development of genetic clines under selection may best be demonstrated with simulation models since there are many demographic factors to be considered simultaneously (22, 37, 159, 259, 263). 5. The basic demographic nature of band society is directly amenable to simulation (see below).

THE ECOLOGICAL DEMOGRAPHY OF ANTHROPOLOGICAL POPULATIONS

The Structure of Hunter-Gatherer Populations and its Relation to Mating Patterns

Several authors have tried to develop a basic model for the structure of the hunter-gatherer populations which seem to have characterized most of hominid existence. These efforts have examined environmental as well as social aspects of the problem, calling mainly on data from the ethnographic present (19, 93, 98, 140, 242). There has come to be general agreement that hunter-gatherers typically have lived in local bands of about 25 people, and that these bands have been organized into larger tribal units of about 500 (often called dialectic or linguistic tribes, z-tribes, mating networks, or connubia). These units are packed approximately in the most efficient regular way in which territories can be arrayed on a plane surface, namely, in hexagonal territories. This basic demographic model has been derived in several different ways (18–21, 23, 23a, 143, 263, 269–271). Williams (263) supports it with data from ethnological, ethological, and primatological sources and provides a formal theoretical development of the local patrilineal band as the fundamental hunter-gatherer polity. The model has been used to study the biological and social dynamics of hunter-gatherers. Williams showed that in addition to social stability, such groups are genetically somewhat more stable than had been thought. This finding is consonant with other studies showing ecological stability in such groups (191, 267), and with the principles of demographic feedback relations which we have stressed in this review.

Wobst has worked extensively with the social and economic aspects of early settlement patterns under this model of band society as it may be studied by the paleolithic archeologist (269–271). He first examines the nature of incest and exogamy, finding that they require fertility levels too high for a very small band to sustain. Thus, he argues that such mating rules did not come about until larger mating networks of several bands had developed for other reasons (see also 95b, 151). In another study (271), he argues that a "tribe" of local bands hexagonally dispersed around a central band may have demanded that peripheral band members travel excessively long distances with no rewards for doing so. Instead, he argues that until cultural or extractive conditions rewarded such clustering, *each* band would establish a mating network in which it was the center. Thus, the standard tribe model generally accepted, and based on the ethnographic present, may not apply for much of early cultural evolution, and hunter-gatherers may not represent the dominant first stage of culturel evolution after all. Wobst suggests some archeological patterns which would support this view, such as clinal artifact style distributions as compared with discretely distributed local styles. His model would result in even greater migration, and hence gene flow, than already is attributed to hunters, adding to the factors homogenizing the human species. Harpending & Yellen (98) also relate the degree of social nucleation to resource distributions, which in turn relate to linguistic, artifactual, and genetic patterns. Zubrow (276b, 277a) has given means, based on theories of locational geography, to assay population changes from archeological site-size distributions for early agricultural populations. We must note here that archeological remains probably will be equivocal on these points, and more importantly that the constant changing conflicts and alliances within and between human bands, along with stochastic elements in birth and death, lead to a fission-fusion process among local villages (181), so that the standard "hexagonal" village dispersion can only be thought of as the statistical average pattern in a field of Brownian motion. General long tenure for local primitive populations is far from well documented.

One of the factors which has been important in these studies of the demographic structuring of band societies is the availability of appropriate mates. If one models this problem with a theory that considers only two sexes, monogamy, and exogamy, statistical forces will generally lead one to predict large excesses of one sex with many people unable to marry (105, 170). At a higher level of model complexity, age-specific vital rates can be used to compute the expected number of a person's living kin of any given relationship, as a function of age (91). Such an exercise is important in determining the expected probability that one would find a potential mate—that is, opposite sex, proper age, and permissible kinship relation—in a group of given size. Detailed treatment of the relationship between age structure, population size and dispersion, and consanguinity (marriage rates between kin) have been given recently (49, 94, 119). Hajnal (94) has found that (*a*) a culturally realistic definition of "random mating" (as opposed, for example, to inbreeding) is that the chance of mating between any two individuals depends solely on the age difference between them; (*b*) cultural practices regarding marriage ages will limit potential mates available; and (*c*) under given demographic conditions, the number of consanguineous matings of a specific type is independent of population size. However, agreement between this theory and data is only fair, so that actual behavior has meaningful complexities not yet taken into account.

Several simulation and mathematical studies have examined the problem of available mates (e.g. 74, 83, 135, 152, 153, 160). Williams (264) and Yengoyan (274, 275) have produced models of Australian aboriginal social structures to show that they correspond to an optimization of mating possibilities for given demographic and ecological conditions. Recently the effects of the more common regular clan systems on consanguinity levels have been studied (43, 223). Although results are as yet not definitive, they suggest that the accumulation of genetic identity-by-descent does not necessarily vary as a function of the clan structure.

Ecological Balance: The Determinants of Population Growth and Size

Recently there have been several works attempting to analyze human population growth in a quantitative manner, and some of these have relevance to the work of anthropologists and primatologists. Coale (57) and Pollard (197) give detailed treatment of the mathematical relationships between age-specific parameters and growth rates. These follow from the assumption of a great deal of smooth and systematic demographic behavior in the population, even when stochastic elements are included (e.g. fixed average vital-rate schedules). However, there is evidence that population size in primitive societies is as much the result of sporadic (e.g. fission/fusion) processes among villages as it is the result of smooth and predictable vital rates (50a, 69a, 134a, 181). Such sporadic effects may have great importance in the biological properties of these societies, and we must be careful not to assume too much regularity merely because it is mathematically neater (6a).

In some contexts, associations between humans or other primates may be "casual," and group size at any time may be described by relatively simple stochastic models of birth, death, immigration, and emigration. Cohen has given several models for such group size distributions, applying it to temporary social subgroups of humans and monkeys, to monkey troop sizes, or to sleeping-group size in baboons (59–61). Such models predict group size based on a few parameter values related to fixed probabilities of entry to or exit from the group. They may have wider application than merely to casual groups, for although the comings and goings of individuals in primitive bands are usually rationalized in some purposeful cultural terms (such as kinship obligations), many of these constant changes in band composition might be predictable solely as the result of chance phenomena with estimable parameters. Even when simple stochastic models are sufficient to describe population size changes, it is important to attempt to understand what factors control the parameter values for the observed probability distributions.

Harpending and colleagues have recently employed mathematical models to examine the effect of periodicity or stochasticity in environmental factors on the size of human populations (97, 125; see also 6a, 142). They show that populations react to various frequencies of environmental oscillation in different ways; for example, agricultural populations can store food and are able to survive short-term fluctuations in weather, but they may be more vulnerable than hunter-gatherers to longer term cycles. The closer the reaction ties of a population to the input variables, the more vulnerable it is to short-term variation, and in fact perturbations of resources may even be magnified by the population. Of course, one would expect ad hoc adjustments to take place before such positive feedback became too severe, and the use of this approach to study long-term behavior, or to specify the consequent archeological manifestations of such behavior, may be quite tentative. However, this work does specify the kinds of archeological data one might expect to find and how to interpret it in light of the models proposed, and thus may lead to testable hypotheses.

Harpending (96) suggests that populations should usually be found to exist at levels well below "carrying capacity." The entire question of resource base, carrying capacity, cultural evolution, and population growth has been given extensive airing recently (6a, 6b, 17, 63, 64, 71, 72, 134a, 187, 226, 227, 234, 236, 276, 276a, 277; see also *World Archeology,* Vol. 4). Models to analyze overall population growth with very simple mathematics have been proposed by Sanders (212), although I personally find these to be too oversimplified and somewhat uncritical about ecological balance. Hayden (102, 103) argues that the concept of the carrying capacity is too difficult to define for humans, and suggests instead a measure of mortality and morbidity related to resource overexploitation, an approach difficult to test with present data. Boserup (27) and much of the book edited by Spooner (226) argue that pressure for population growth inheres to human populations, and that this pressure has forced agricultural and technological innovation leading to increased carrying capacity and larger populations. This argument seems to me to be contrary to much of what is known in biology, and Cowgill (63, 64) has argued against it on cultural grounds. The extensive chicken-or-egg debate over whether population growth or increased carrying capacity is the prime mover in the dynamics of human populations has been based on such fragile data that reliable conclusions cannot be drawn (e.g. 169). Several other papers have dealt with this issue, usually siding on the population-pressure view (e.g. 164, 213), although some papers have seen this question as one of adapting systems (e.g. 25, 63). Zubrow (276a, 276b, 277) has developed sets of formal propositions with which one may begin to test available archeological and ethnological evidence regarding the determinants of population size and growth. Ammerman (6a) has argued that we may typically have thought of carrying capacity and population size in too rigid a manner, giving insufficient attention to stochastic factors and to feedback relationships.

A similar kind of approach to population growth is often found in discussions of the causes of growth which were produced by the neolithic, or agricultural, revolution; in particular, arguments about the effect of better nutrition have been suggested. However, if we examine the nature of geometric growth, it is clear that the average rates of growth were so low (e.g. $r < 0.001$) that the differences in age-specific vital rates before and after the cultural change are miniscule and do not admit to direct causal "explanation" (e.g. how does better nutrition allow an average woman to bear an extra 1/100th of a child per year?). Sporadic sociocultural adjustment may be more useful than average rate changes in explanation (6b, 47).

In the absence of quantitative demographic theory, these discussions have been, in my opinion, essentially vacuous; the realities of population ecological dynamics over very long time periods demand more sophisticated treatment in the future. As has repeatedly been argued, feedback relations between human beings, their physical environment, and their culture must be considered as primary factors, and we must also remember that many discussions of small changes in average demographic rates are difficult to model in terms of the actual life experiences of real people in small populations, where "rates" have somewhat unclear meaning in any case.

BIODEMOGRAPHIC ASPECTS OF HUMAN SOCIAL BEHAVIOR

In the case of human beings, the feedback relations between demographic variables and the environment include culture and social behavior; one must assume that such behavior has some biological advantage, for otherwise it would not have evolved in the first place. Most anthropologists would immediately recognize demographic reflections of sociocultural behavior through its effects on fertility (e.g. intercourse taboos, contraception, age sets, bride price), and mortality (e.g. gerontocide, infanticide, murder, warfare); in fact, several authors have recently argued that warfare has had a central place in molding human biological evolution (3, 16, 70a, 95, 101, 247; but see 150). In addition, we have dealt earlier with the demographic genetic importance of mate-exchange patterns, aspects of human culture which have long been central to anthropological theory. A recent collection deals with some of these problems (193b).

Physical anthropologists have recently undertaken numerous field studies of monkey and ape societies, largely to provide data upon which inference about early hominid behavior could be based. Some ecological and sociodemographic results have followed from these studies. Schaller & Lowther (214) examined the possibilities of various kinds of predatory behavior which early hominids might have engaged in, directly related to their group structure (also see 239a). The social aspects of savannah primate societies as they relate to dominance hierarchies, territoriality, the heritability of status, or the ecological determinants of population size and structure have all been dealt with extensively (6, 70, 116, 122, 124, 125a, 133, 134, 208, 209, 239a). In general it has been found to be difficult to make rigid connections between primate populations and hominid populations of the early Pleistocene (but see 125a). One finding of great importance has been largely overlooked. Whereas primate societies' social behavior allows occasional immigration of males and often ostracizes young adult males, primitive human societies are generally characterized by the systematic exchange of females, rarely seen in nonhuman primates. This fundamental transition is currently unexplained.

Much of the widely published effort to use primate models of behavior has dealt with male aggression and dominance (Ardrey, Tiger, Fox, Morris, Lorenz), though such extrapolation has remained largely at the superficial and melodramatic level. The stress on dominance and aggression has diverted attention from the fact that the drive to associate must be of evolutionarily prior importance or there would not be social groups in the first place. Further, it has not been shown that unchecked dominance leads to higher reproductive fitness. If it is of evolutionary importance to be dominant, it must be of equal importance to be successfully subordinate, since the average human (or any animal) is subordinate to roughly half the population. This is a fundamental aspect of social behavior which must be taken into account in attempts to derive principles of human group structure.

Some recent work by biologists has tried to put these field studies into place in an evolutionary science of sociocultural behavior. This work is led by Richard Alexander (3–5), E. O. Wilson (268), and others (77, 240). As Alexander points out, most of anthropologists' efforts to explain the evolutionary reason for the existence of culture have relied on the concept of group selection, that is, that culture arose because groups which bore it out-competed those which did not. Most (but not all) biologists disagree with this argument, and support instead a classical Darwinian view that social behavior can only be understood as it affects the reproductive fitness of the individual or its immediate kin. This debate is related in particular to the evolution of altruistic behavior (95a, 240, 261, 262, 265, 266, 272).

We do not wish to get into this controversy here, except to note that whether or not group selection was important in the initial evolution of culture, a form of it does now take place (e.g. how else to explain biologically the fate of Tasmanians, whose mistake was simply not to have invented weapons equal to those of Europeans?). It is important to us to note the demographic theoretical ramifications of the controversy. If group selection is important, then demographic differences between groups become critical to an understanding of human evolution. On the other hand, if individual selection is primary, then it is the demographic differentiation within groups which predominates. In either case, what is the effect of the high intergroup migration? Were there "groups" long-lived enough to make these arguments demographically sensible? Certainly sociocultural behavior distributes death and reproduction nonuniformly within groups—it remains to be determined, however, to what extent this is related to genes. As Wilson points out in his landmark book (268), and as was central to its direct intellectual progenitors (43a, 132, 272), much of social behavior is directly related to the ecological determinants of population size and to the schedule of vital rates of the executors of social behavior. To the extent that such behavior is genetic, whether within or between groups, the evolution of those genes may be analyzed along lines already established (7, 51–56, 119, 194, 195) once the vital rate schedules have been determined—which is no mean task.

It should be pointed out here that the surge of new research in the evolutionary biology of social behavior, now called sociobiology, is taking on many aspects of a scientific vogue, with anthropologists forcing the rhetoric of sociobiology inappropriately onto their studies. An understanding of the population theory underlying their assertions is usually missing. Thus a discussion of some characteristics of that theory and its weaknesses for anthropological inference is in order.

Sociobiological theory is based on highly deterministic, purely "selectionist" foundations. That is, all of the social structure in a population is to be explained in terms of genetic differences mediated by natural selection in a deterministic way. The stochastic aspects of small population processes and the results of long-term selection in small groups are almost totally ignored. Thus a dominant male is said to carry the best genes for dominance, and his excess fertility to be nature's way of purifying the gene pool. Every helpful social act must be explained in terms of some competitive selective advantage for the actor; usually this advantage is explained in terms of reciprocal altruism in small stable groups (240), or in terms of the theory of *kin-selection* and *inclusive fitness* (95a): an individual will aid one of its genetic kin, and then only if the risk to itself in being helpful is offset by a gain in fitness to the recipient which is in an amount related to the degree of kinship between them.

This deterministic selectionist view will not stand up to recent progress in population theory. Space does not allow an extensive discussion of the reasons for this, but it will suffice to say that *either* natural selection for socially stratifying behavior in a population is very weak *or* genetic variability for the behavior will be minimal. If selection for alleles controlling some aspect of social behavior is strong, then in a relatively few generations only alleles producing that behavior will exist in significant number. Genetic variation for the trait will be rapidly exhausted and behavioral differences which remain in the group will acquire a predominantly nongenetic basis. If selection for such differences is weak, then stochastic factors, developmental differences, social inheritance, and so on will largely determine the social påttern of specific individuals, and, again, this pattern will not be based on genetic differences. In a small group of primates whose maximum lifetime fertility is about 10, how can two individuals differ in fitness by 1%? Such fitness differences for genes have meaning only in the long term, and fertility of the individuals in any given cohort will be determined by the over-riding power of stochastic factors. If selection favors not specific genes but the best whole genotypes (genomes), then in each generation there will be different genotypes competing for social (and hence demographic) advantage, since genes segregate and recombine during reproduction. Here again we cannot say that social differentiation in vital rates is due to specific selective forces which would be manifest in the short term.

We thus cannot consider social rank in a hunting band to be the product of different genes for head-manliness, nor dominance in monkey troops nor human social classes to be based on genetic selection. In sum, it is likely that we are much more genetically alike than our degree of social and demographic differentiation; our social patterns must have theoretical explanation, not in standard individual selection terms alone, but in relation to stochastic factors and the necessity for group living.

The overdeterministic approach of sociobiology as given by Wilson (268) and Alexander (3–5) leads directly to the accusation that their work, when applied to contemporary human societies, is an apology for the status quo regarding social differentiation, and that racial and social differences in a population have a genetic basis mandated by natural selection. This has been debated thoroughly recently (see *BioScience*, 1976, 3:182–90). The sociobiological approach is rightly accused of ad hoc determinism; however, it would seem that at this rudimentary stage in our knowledge of social evolution and its demographic representation, *any* position can be argued in terms having a spurious similarity to modern biological theory. Thus those advocating social change can also concoct sociobiological reasons why a different social structure would be "more fit." Neither Wilson nor his critics can be said to be immune from this, and it seems that our present theoretical genetic demography cannot lead us to a critical understanding of complex cultural organization; the biological processes are overwhelmed by stochastic factors and by the *sui generis* nature of cultural evolution.

It is nonetheless certain that demographic theory bears directly on an understanding of human cultural behavior. The analysis of that behavior and its evolutionary meaning must be sought primarily in demographic variables such as mortality, fertility, migration patterns, and the definition of population. Since the lead in this work has been taken by biologists, and culture has been somewhat poorly accommodated, there is clearly room for anthropologists to contribute. For example, observations on nonhuman animals are unlikely to explain such sociocultural phenomena as suicide, which since it occurs often among the young can hardly be related directly to an effort to maximize reproductive fitness, and which is too clearly social to be related to aberrant or diseased genetic states. There are many other examples. This is a fundamental aspect of our biodemographic existence, and yet it has been almost completely ignored by population scientists. Asking the evolutionary question with a valid understanding of population genetic processes will soon lead to progress in this area.

CONCLUSION

In perceiving human demography as a means of measuring elements of our biocultural evolution, and accordingly developing a sound biodemographic theory, anthropologists may be able to stem the tide of untrammeled speculation which has long beset us. The adapting of theory developed by demography gives short rein to such speculation and provides population anthropology with an infusion of much needed discipline.

Based on the preceding discussion of the current status of demographic anthropology, it is possible to list several problems which can successfully be examined in the near future. These are: 1. further modeling of the nature of the forces of mortality and their effect on the age distribution, and in particular an examination of the relative genetic and social importance of steady versus sporadic mortality forces; 2. the estimation of male fertility in primitive societies, and the consequent development of sound two-sex demographic and gentic models; 3. the parameterization and study of the demographic manifestations of social behavior, a fertile area so new that specific suggestions are elusive at present; 4. the better understanding of the way in which culture changes, such as the neolithic revolution, produced larger populations with different locational relationships, as measured in available archeological evidence; 5. the epidemiology of diseases and the nature of aging as manifest in aboriginal human populations; 6. the demography of wild primate populations, their vital rate schedules, aging processes, fertility and population size determinants, and their means of population regulation; 7. refinements in methods for the demographic study of genetic microdifferentiation, such as studies of village differences within tribes; 8. the aging and sexing of skeletal materials, and better recovery of juveniles; 9. improved understanding of the biologic importance of the regular marriage patterns, and elaborate kinship systems, on which primative culture is centered; and finally 10. stochastic study of the life table.

These issues all involve the use of demographic theory for making anthropological inference. Our gestalt on matters demographic must, however, be basically different from that of our demographer colleagues, a point they may fail to see (190). We can aspire to far less mathematical accuracy, and must instead by concerned with questions of grander scope than the study of national political statistics; indeed, ours is the study of the fundamental biological processes of human evolution and diversity. This process orientation means that we should concentrate on building a unified theory relating evolutionary biology to sociocultural behavior, with the understanding that biologically relevant aspects of human populations are reflected in demographic variables. If we can succeed in building such a theory, we will no longer be restricted to the study of primitive societies, and will then be able to understand human evolution through its manifestations in the behavior of present large nations. Then will our knowledge of primitive societies shed light on the serious biodemographic predicament which we all now face, one phenomenon which we must not leave to the laws of chance. And that is the yet unfulfilled promise of the anthropological perspective.

ACKNOWLEDGMENTS

I would like to acknowledge with thanks those of my peers who, equally qualified to have written this paper themselves, have volunteered assistance in finding literature and critically reading the manuscript. Their help has made the final product, at the very least, better than it was: Drs. Alan C. Swedlund, Richard H. Ward, Ezra B. W. Zubrow, H. Martin Wobst, Jane H. Underwood, Susan L. Norton, and David L. Rossmann. Financial support from NIH Research Grant GM 19513 is gratefully acknowledged.

Literature Cited

1. Acsádi, G., Nemeskéri, J. 1970. *History of Human Life Span and Mortality.* Budapest: Akademei Kiadó
2. Adlakha, A. 1972. Model life tables: An empirical test of their applicability to less developed countries. *Demography* 9:589–601
3. Alexander, R. D. 1972. The search for an evolutionary philosophy of man. *Proc. R. Soc. Victoria* 84: 99–120
4. Alexander, R. D. 1974. The evolution of social behavior. *Ann. Rev. Ecol. Syst.* 5:325–83
5. Alexander, R. D. 1975. The search for a general theory of behavior. *Behav. Sci.* 20:77–100
6. Altmann, S. A., Altmann, J. 1970. *Baboon Ecology: African Field Research.* Univ. Chicago Press
6a. Ammerman, A. J. 1975. Late Pleistocene population dynamics: An alternative view. *Hum. Ecol.* 3:219–33
6b. Ammerman, A. J., Cavalli-Sforza, L. L., Wagener, D. K. 1976. Towards the estimation of population growth in Old World prehistory. See Ref. 277
7. Anderson, W. W., King, C. E. 1970. Age-specific selection. *Proc. Natl. Acad. Sci. USA* 66:780–86
8. Angel, J. L. 1969. The bases of paleodemography. *Am. J. Phys. Anthropol.* 30:427–38
9. Armelagos, G. J., McArdle, A. 1975. Population, disease, and evolution. See Ref. 234, 1–10
10. Arriaga, E. E. 1968. New life tables for Latin American populations. *Population Monogr. Ser. 3.* Univ. California, Berkeley
11. Baker, P. T., Sanders, W. T. 1972. Demographic studies in anthropology. *Ann. Rev. Anthropol.* 1:151–78
12. Barclay, G. W. 1958. *Techniques of Population Analysis.* New York: Wiley
13. Barrett, J. C. 1971. A Monte-Carlo simulation of reproduction. See Ref. 31, 11–30
14. Benjamin, B., Haycocks, H. W. 1970. *The Analysis of Mortality and Other Actuarial Statistics.* Cambridge Univ. Press
15. Bennett, K. A. 1973. On the estimation of some demographic characteristics on a prehistoric population from the American Southwest. *Am. J. Phys. Anthropol.* 39:223–31
16. Bigelow, R. 1969. *The Dawn Warriors: Man's Evolution Toward Peace.* New York: Little, Brown
17. Binford, L. R. 1968. Post-Pleistocene adaptations. In *New Perspectives in Archeology,* ed. S. A. Binford, L. R. Binford, 313–41. Chicago: Aldine
18. Birdsell, J. B. 1950. Some implications of the genetical concept of race in terms of spatial analysis. *Cold Spring Harbor Symp.* 15:259–314
19. Birdsell, J. B. 1953. Some environmental and cultural factors influencing the structuring of Australian aboriginal populations. *Am. Nat.* 87:171–207
20. Birdsell, J. B. 1958. On population structure in generalized hunting and collecting populations. *Evolution* 12:189–205
21. Birdsell, J. B. 1968. Some predictions for the Pleistocene based on equilibrium systems among recent hunter-gatherers. See Ref. 143, 229–49
22. Birdsell, J. B. 1972. The problem of the evolution of human races: Classification or clines? *Soc. Biol.* 19:136–62
23. Birdsell, J. B. 1973. *Human Evolution.* Chicago: Rand McNally
23a. Birdsell, J. B. 1972. A basic demographic unit. *Curr. Anthropol.* 14:337–56
24. Black, F. L. 1975. Infectious diseases in primitive societies. *Science* 187:515–18
25. Blanton, R. E. 1975. The cybernetic analysis of human population growth. See Ref. 234, 116–26

26. Bodmer, W. F. 1968. Demographic approaches to the measurement of differential selection in human populations. *Proc. Natl. Acad. Sci. USA* 59:41–50

27. Boserup, E. 1965. *The Conditions of Agricultural Growth: The Economics of Agrarian Change under Population Pressure.* Chicago: Aldine

28. Bourgeois-Pichat, J. 1968. *The Concept of a Stable Population.* New York: United Nations

29. Boyce, A. J., Kuchemann, C. F., Harrison, G. A. 1967. Neighborhood knowledge and the distribution of marriage distances. *Ann. Hum. Genet.* 30:335–38

30. Brass, W. 1958. The distribution of births in human populations. *Popul. Stud.* 12:51–72

31. Brass, W. Ed. 1971. *Biological Aspects of Demography.* London: Taylor & Francis

32. Ibid. On the scale of mortality, 69–110

33. Brass, W., Coale, A. J. 1968. Methods of analysis and estimation. See Ref. 34, 88–150

34. Brass, W., Coale, A. J., Demeny, P., Heisel, D. F., Lorimer, F., Romaniuk, A., van de Walle, E. 1968. *The Demography of Tropical Africa.* Princeton Univ. Press

35. Bronte-Stewart, B., Butdz-Olsen, O. E., Hinckley, J. M., Brock, J. F. 1960. The health and nutritional status of the Kung Bushmen of southwest Africa. *S. Afr. J. Lab. Clin. Med.* 6:187–216

36. Brothwell, D. R. 1971. Paleodemography. See Ref. 31, 111–30

37. Brues, A. M. 1972. Models of clines and races. *Am. J. Phys. Anthropol.* 37:389–99

38. Brues, A. M. 1973. Models applicable to geographic variation in man. See Ref. 76, 129–41

39. Buchanan, R. 1975. Breast feeding —aid to infant health and fertility control. *Population Reports: Family Planning Programs, Ser. j, No. 4*

40. Burnet, M., White, D. O. 1972. *Natural History of Infectious Disease.* Cambridge Univ. Press

41. Caldwell, J. C., Okonjo, C., Eds. 1968. *The Population of Tropical Africa.* New York: Columbia Univ. Press

42. Cannings, C. C., Cavalli-Sforza, L. L. 1973. Human population structure. *Adv. Hum. Genet.* 4:105–71

43. Cannings, C. C., Skolnick, M. H. 1975. Genetic drift in exogamous marriage systems. *Theor. Popul. Biol.* 7:39–54

43a. Carr-Saunders, A. M. 1922. *The Population Problem: A Study in Human Evolution.* Oxford: Clarendon

44. Carrier, N. H. 1958. A note on the estimation of mortality and other population characteristics given deaths by age. *Popul. Stud.* 12:149–63

45. Carrier, N. H., Goh, T-J. 1972. The validation of Brass's model life table system. *Popul. Stud.* 26:29–51

46. Carrier, N. H., Hobcraft, J. 1971. *Demographic Estimation for Developing Societies.* London: Popul. Invest. Comm.

47. Cavalli-Sforza, L. L. 1972. Pygmies, an example of hunters-gatherers, and genetic consequences for man of domestication of plants and animals. In *Human Genetics,* ed. J. de Grouchy, F. Ebling, I. Henderson. Amsterdam: Excerpta Medica

48. Cavalli-Sforza, L. L., Bodmer, W. F. 1971. *The Genetics of Human Populations.* San Francisco: Freeman

49. Cavalli-Sforza, L. L., Kimura, M., Barrai, I. 1966. The probability of consanguineous marriages. *Genetics* 54:37–60

50. Cavalli-Sforza, L. L., Zei, G. 1967. Experiments with an artificial population. In *Proc. Third Int. Congr. Hum. Genet.,* ed. J. F. Crow, J. V. Neel, 473–78. Baltimore: Johns Hopkins

50a. Chagnon, N. A. 1974. *Studying the Yanomamö.* New York: Holt, Rinehart & Winston

51. Charlesworth, B. 1970. Selection in populations with overlapping generations. I. The use of Malthusian parameters in population genetics. *Theor. Popul. Biol.* 1:352–70

52. Ibid 1972. Selection in populations with overlapping generations. III. Conditions for genetic equilibrium. 3:377–95

53. Charlesworth, B. 1973. Selection in populations with overlapping generations. V. Natural selection and life histories. *Am. Nat.* 107:303–11

54. Charlesworth, B. 1974. Selection in populations with overlapping generations. VI. Rates of change of gene frequency and population growth rate. *Theor. Popul. Biol.* 6:108–33

374   WEISS

55. Charlesworth, B., Giesel, J. T. 1972. Selection in populations with overlapping generations. II. Relations between gene frequency and demographic variables. *Am. Nat.* 106:388–401
56. Ibid. Selection in populations with overlapping generations. IV. Fluctuations in gene frequency with density-dependent selection, 402–11
57. Coale, A. J. 1972. *The Growth and Structure of Human Populations: A Mathematical Investigation.* Princeton Univ. Press
58. Coale, A. J., Demeny, P. 1966. *Regional Model Life Tables and Stable Populations.* Princeton Univ. Press
59. Cohen, J. E. 1969. Natural primate troops and a stochastic population model. *Am. Nat.* 103:455–77
60. Cohen, J. E. 1971. *Casual Groups of Monkeys and Men.* Cambridge: Harvard Univ. Press
61. Cohen, J. E. 1972. Markov population processes as models of primate social and population dynamics. *Theor. Popul. Biol.* 3:119–34
62. Cook, S. F. 1972. Prehistoric demography. *McCaleb Modules Anthropol.* 16:1–42
63. Cowgill, G. L. 1975. On causes and consequences of ancient and modern population changes. *Am. Anthropol.* 77:505–25
64. Cowgill, G. L. 1975. Population pressure as a non-explanation. See Ref. 234, 127–31
65. Crawford, M., Workman, P., Eds. 1973. *Methods and Theories of Anthropological Genetics.* Albuquerque: Univ. New Mexico Press
66. Crow, J. F. 1958. Some possibilities for measuring selection intensities in man. *Hum. Biol.* 30:1–13
67. Crow, J. F., Kimura, M. 1970. *An Introduction to Population Genetics Theory.* New York: Harper & Row
68. Crow, J. F., Kimura, M. 1972. The effective number of a population with overlapping generations: A correction and further discussion. *Am. J. Genet.* 24:1–10
68a. Cutler, R. G. 1975. Evolution of human longevity and the genetic complexity governing aging rate. *Proc. Natl. Acad. Sci. USA* 72:4664–68
69. Demetrius, L. 1975. Natural selection and age-structured populations. *Genetics* 79:535–44
69a. Denham, W. W. 1974. Population structure, infant transport, and infanticide among Pleistocene and modern hunter-gatherers. *J. Anthropol. Res.* 30:191–98
70. DeVore, I., Ed. 1965. *Primate Behavior.* New York: Holt, Rinehart & Winston
70a. DiVale, W. T. 1972. Systematic population control in the Middle and Upper Paleolithic: Inferences based on contemporary hunter-gatherers. *World Archaeol.* 4:222–43
71. Dumond, D. E. 1972. Population growth and political centralization. See Ref. 226, 286–310
72. Dumond, D. E. 1975. The limitation of human population: A natural history. *Science* 187:713–21
73. Dunn, F. L. 1968. Epidemiological factors: Health and disease in hunter-gatherers. See Ref. 143, 221–28
74. Dyke, B. 1971. Potential mates in a small human population. *Soc. Biol.* 18:28–39
75. Dyke, B., MacCluer, J. W. 1973. Estimation of vital rates by means of Monte Carlo simulation. *Demography* 10:383–403
76. Dyke, B., MacCluer, J. W. 1974. *Computer Simulation in Human Population Studies.* New York: Academic
77. Etkin, W. 1967. *Social Behavior from Fish to Man.* Univ. Chicago Press
78. Felsenstein, J. 1971. Inbreeding and variance effective number in populations with overlapping generations. *Genetics* 68:581–97
79. Fraser, G. R. 1972. The implications of prevention and treatment of inherited disease for the genetic future of mankind. *J. Genet. Hum.* 20:185–205
80. Friedlaender, J. S. 1972. The population structure of South-Central Bougainville. *Am. J. Phys. Anthropol.* 35:13–26
80a. Frisch, R. E., Hegsted, D. M., Yoshinaga, K. 1975. Body weight and food intake at early estrus of rats on a high-fat diet. *Proc. Natl. Acad. Sci. USA* 72:4172–76
81. Genovés, S. 1969. Estimation of age and mortality. In *Science in Archaeology,* ed. D. Brothwell, E. Higgs, 342–52. New York: Praeger
82. Ibid. Sex determination in earlier man, 429–39
82a. Giesel, J. T. 1971. The relations between population structure and rate of inbreeding. *Evolution* 25:491–96

83. Gilbert, J. P., Hammel, E. A. 1966. Computer simulation and analysis of problems in kinship and social structure. *Am. Anthropol.* 68:71–93

84. Ginneken, J. K. van 1974. Prolonged breastfeeding as a birth spacing method. *Stud. Fam. Plann.* 5:201–6

85. Ginsburg, R. B. 1972. A class of doubly stochastic processes: With an application to the effects of lactation on the postpartum anovulatory period. See Ref. 92, 297–331

86. Ginsburg, R. B. 1973. The effect of lactation on the length of the postpartum anovulatory period: An application of a bivariate stochastic model. *Theor. Popul. Biol.* 4:276–99

87. Goldschmidt, E., Ed. 1963. *The Genetics of Migrant and Isolate Populations.* Baltimore: Williams & Wilkins

88. Golubitsky, M., Keeler, E. B., Rothschild, M. 1975. Convergence of the age structure: Applications of the projective method. *Theor. Popul. Biol.* 7:84–93

89. Goodman, L. A. 1967. On the age-sex composition of the population that would result from given fertility and mortality conditions. *Demography* 4:423–41

90. Goodman, L. A. 1971. On the sensitivity of the intrinsic growth rate to changes in the age-specific birth and death rates. *Theor. Popul. Biol.* 2:339–54

91. Goodman, L. A., Keyfitz, N., Pullum, T. W. 1974. Family formation and the frequency of various kinship relations. *Theor. Popul. Biol.* 5:1–27

92. Greville, T. N. E., Ed. 1972. *Population Dynamics.* New York: Academic

93. Hainline, J. 1966. Population genetic (serological) variability in Micronesia. *Ann. NY Acad. Sci.* 134:639–54

94. Hajnal, J. 1963. Random mating and the frequency of consanguineous marriages. *Proc. R. Soc. B* 159:125–77

95. Halberstein, R. A., Crawford, M. H. 1972. Human biology in Tlaxcala, Mexico: Demography. *Am. J. Phys. Anthropol.* 36:199–212

95a. Hamilton, W. D. 1972. Altruism and related phenomena, mainly in social insects. *Ann. Rev. Ecol. Syst.* 3:193–232

95b. Hammel, E. A., Hutchinson, D.

1973. Two tests of computer microsimulation: The effect of an incest tabu on population viability, and the effect of age differences between spouses on the skewing of consanguineal relationships between them. See Ref. 76, 1–14

96. Harpending, H. 1974. Genetic structure of small populations. *Ann. Rev. Anthropol.* 3:229–43

97. Harpending, H., Bertram, J. B. 1975. Human population dynamics in archaeological time: Some simple methods. See Ref. 234, 82–91

98. Harpending, H. C., Yellen, J. 1972. Hunter-gatherer populations and archeological inference. *World Archeol.* 4:244–53

99. Harrison, G. A., Boyce, A. J., Eds. 1972. *The Structure of Human Populations.* Oxford: Clarendon

100. Ibid. Migration, exchange, and the genetic structure of populations, 128–45

101. Harrison, R. 1973. *Warfare.* Minneapolis: Burgess

102. Hayden, B. 1972. Population control among hunter-gatherers. *World Archeol.* 4:205–21

103. Hayden, B. 1975. The carrying capacity dilemma: An alternative approach. *Am. Antiq.* 40:11–21

104. Henneberg, M. 1976. On the estimation of demographic variables from prehistoric populations. See Ref. 252, 41–48

105. Henry, L. 1969. Schemas de nuptialité: déséquilibre des sexes et célibat. *Population* 24:457–86

106. Hill, W. G. 1972. Effective size of populations with overlapping generations. *Theor. Popul. Biol.* 3:278–89

107. Hiorns, R. W. 1965. The fitting of growth and allied curves of the asymptotic regression type by Stevens' method. In *Tracts for Computers,* XXVII. Cambridge Univ. Press

108. Holloway, S. M., Smith, C. 1975. Effects of various medical and social practices on the frequency of genetic disorders. *Am. J. Hum. Genet.* 27:614–27

109. Howell, N. 1973. An empirical perspective on simulation models of human populations. See Ref. 76, 43–57

110. Howell, N. 1973. The feasibility of demographic studies in "anthropological" populations. See Ref. 65, 249–62

111. Howell, N. 1976. The population of

Dobe area !Kung. In *Kalahari Hunter-Gatherers*, ed. I. DeVore. Cambridge: Harvard Univ. Press. In press

112. Howell, N. 1976. Toward a uniformitarian theory of human paleodemography. See Ref. 252, 25–40

113. Howells, W. W. 1960. Estimating population numbers through archaeological and skeletal remains. In *The Application of Quantitative Methods in Archaeology*, ed. R. F. Heizer, S. F. Cook, 158–80. New York: Viking

114. Hunt, E. E., Teleki, G. 1975 The fertility of wild chimpanzees in the Gombe National Park, Tanzania, 1964–1973: its relevance to the demographic evolution of man. Presented at 1975 Meet. Am. Assoc. Adv. Sci., Washington DC

115. Imaizumi, Y., Nei, M., Furusho, T. 1970. Variability and heritability of human fertility. *Ann. Hum. Genet.* 33:251–59

116. Imanishi, K. 1960. Social organization of subhuman primates in their natural habitat. *Curr. Anthropol.* 1:393–407

117. Jacquard, A. 1967. La reproduction humaine en régime Malthusien. Un modèle de simulation par la méthode de Monte-Carlo. *Population* 22:897–920

118. Ibid 1970. Panmixie et structure des familles. 25:69–76

119. Jacquard, A. 1974. *The Genetic Structure of Populations*. New York: Springer-Verlag

120. Jacquard, A. 1975. Inbreeding: One word, several meanings. *Theor. Popul. Biol.* 7:338–63

121. Jacquard, A., Ward, R. H. 1976. The genetic consequences of changing reproductive behavior. See Ref. 252, 139–54

122. Jay, P. 1968. *Primates: Studies in Adaptation and Variability*. New York: Holt, Rinehart & Winston

122a. Johnston, F. E., Albers, M. E. 1973. Computer simulation of demographic processes. See Ref. 65, 201–17

123. Johnston, F. E., Kensinger, K. M., Jantz, R. L., Walker, G. F. 1969. The population structure of the Peruvian Cashinahua: Demographic, genetic, and cultural interrelationships. *Hum. Biol.* 41:29–41

124. Jolly, A. 1972. *The Evolution of Primate Behavior*. New York: Macmillan

125. Jorde, L. B., Harpending, H. C. 1976. Cross-spectral analysis of rainfall and human birth rate: An empirical test of linear model. See Ref. 252, 129–38

125a. Jorde, L. B., Spuhler, J. N. 1974. A statistical analysis of selected aspects of primate demography, ecology, and social behavior. *J. Anthropol. Res.* 30:199–224

126. Keyfitz, N. 1968. *Introduction to the Mathematics of Population*. Reading: Addison-Wesley

127. Keyfitz, N. 1972. Population waves. See Ref. 92, 1–38

128. Keyfitz, N., Flieger, W. 1971. *Population: Facts and Methods of Demography*. San Francisco: Freeman

129. King, C. E., Anderson, W. W. 1971. Age-specific selection. II. The interaction between r and K during population growth. *Am. Nat.* 105:137–56

130. Kobayashi, K. 1967. Trend in the length of life based on human skeletons from prehistoric to modern times in Japan. *J. Fac. Sci., Univ. Tokyo, Sec. V: Anthropology, Vol. 3*

131. Kojima, K-I., Kelleher, T. M. 1962. Survival of mutant genes. *Am. Nat.* 96:328–46

132. Krzywicki, L. 1934. *Primitive Society and its Vital Statistics*. London: Macmillan

133. Kummer, H. 1968. *Social Organization of Hamadryas Baboons*. Univ. Chicago Press

134. Kummer, H. 1971. *Primate Societies: Group Techniques of Ecological Adaptation*. Chicago: Aldine-Atherton

134a. Kunstadter, P. 1972. Demography, ecology, social structure, and settlement patterns. See Ref. 99, 313–51

135. Kunstadter, P., Buhler, R., Stephan, F. F., Westoff, C. F. 1963. Demographic variability and preferential marriage patterns. *Am. J. Phys. Anthropol.* 21:511–19

136. Lasker, G. W. 1960. Migration, isolation, and ongoing human evolution. *Hum. Biol.* 32:80–88

137. Lasker, G. W. 1973. Human genetic distances and human mating distances. See Ref. 65, 151–57

138. Lasker, G. W., Chiarelli, B., Masali, M., Fedele, F., Kaplan, B. A. 1972. Degree of human genetic isolation measured by isonymy and marital distances in two commu-

nities in an Italian Alpine Valley. *Hum. Biol.* 44:351–60

139. Lasker, G. W., Kaplan, B. 1964. The coefficient of breeding isolation: Population size, migration rates, and the possibilities for random genetic drift in six human communities in northern Peru. *Hum. Biol.* 36:327–38

140. Lee, R. B. 1972. !Kung spatial organization: An ecological and historical perspective. *Hum. Ecol.* 1:125–47

141. Lee, R. B. 1972. Population growth and the beginning of sedentary life among the !Kung bushmen. See Ref. 226, 329–42

142. Lee, R. 1974. The formal dynamics of controlled populations and the echo, the boom, and the bust. *Demography* 11:563–86

143. Lee, R. B., DeVore, I. 1968. *Man the Hunter.* Chicago: Aldine

144. Leslie, P. H. 1945. On the use of matrices in certain population mathematics. *Biometrika* 33:183–212

145. Ibid 1948. Some further notes on the use of matrices in population mathematics. 35:213–45

146. Lewis, E. G. 1942. On the generation and growth of a population. *Sankhya* 6:93–96

147. Lewis, H. E., Roberts, D. F., Edwards, A. W. F. 1972. Biological problems, and opportunities, of isolation among the islanders of Tristan de Cunha. In *Population and Social Change,* ed. D. Glass, R. Revelle, 383–417. London: Arnold

148. Li, F. H. F., Neel, J. V. 1973. A simulation of the fate of a mutant gene of neutral selective value in a primitive population. See Ref. 76, 221–40

149. Livingstone, F. B. 1965. Mathematical models of marriage systems. *Man* 146:149–52

150. Livingstone, F. B. 1967. The effects of warfare on the biology of the human species. *Nat. Hist.* 76:61–65. See also other papers in this issue

151. Livingstone, F. B. 1969. Genetics, ecology and the origins of incest and exogamy. *Curr. Anthropol.* 10:45–62

152. Lombardi, J. R. 1974. The effects of exogamy on demographic stability. In *Genealogical Mathematics,* ed. P. A. Ballonoff, 237–55. Paris: Mouton

153. Lombardi, J. 1974. Demographic stability of preferential marriage systems. In *Mathematical Models of Social and Cognitive Structures,* ed. P. A. Ballonoff, 70–80. Urbana: Univ. Illinois Press

154. Lotka, A. J. 1907. Relation between birth rates and death rates. *Science* 26:21–22

155. Lotka, A. J. 1931. Orphanhood in relation to demographic factors. *Metron* 9:37–109

156. Lotka, A. J. 1938. *Théorie Analytique des Associations Biologiques.* Paris: Hermann et Cie

157. Lovejoy, C. O. 1971. Methods for the detection of census error in paleodemography. *Am. Anthropol.* 73:101–9

158. MacCluer, J. W. 1973. Computer simulation in anthropology and human genetics. See Ref. 65, 219–48

159. MacCluer, J. W. 1974. Monte Carlo simulation: The effects of migration on some measures of genetic distance. In *Genetic Distance,* ed. J. F. Crow, C. Denniston, 77–96. New York: Plenum

160. MacCluer, J. W., Dyke, B. 1976. On the minimum size of endogamous populations. *Demography.* In press

161. MacCluer, J. W., Neel, J. V., Chagnon, N. A. 1971. Demographic structure of a primitive population: A simulation. *Am. J. Phys. Anthropol.* 35:193–208

162. MacCluer, J. W., Schull, W. J. 1970. Frequencies of consanguineous marriage and accumulation of inbreeding in an artificial population. *Am. J. Hum. Genet.* 22:160–75

163. Mann, A. E. 1975. Paleodemographic aspects of the South African Australopithecines. *Univ. Pennsylvania Publ. Anthropol. No. 1*

164. Martin, P. S. 1973. The discovery of America. *Science* 179:969–74

165a. Masset, C. 1971. Erreurs systematiques dans la determination de l'age par les sutures craniennes. *Bull. Mem. Soc. Anthropol. Paris* 7, ser. 12:85–105

165b. Masset, C. 1973. Influence du sexe et de l'age sur la conservation des os humains. In *L'homme, Hier et Aujourd'hui: recueil d'etudes en hommage a Andre Leroi-Gourhan,* ed. anon., 333–43. Paris: Editions Cujas

165c. Masset, C. 1973. La démographie des populations inhumées: Essai de paléodémographie. *L'Homme* 13:-95–131

166. Matsunaga, E. 1969. Some reflections on the biological consequences of family planning. *J. Med. Educ.* 44 (Suppl):87–90

167. Mayo, O., Nelson, M. M., Forfar, J. O. 1973. Variation in human fertility. *Hum. Hered.* 23:401–13

168. McArthur, N. 1967. *Island Populations of the Pacific.* Canberra: Aust. Natl. Univ. Press

169. McArthur, N. 1970. The demography of primitive populations. *Science* 167:1097–1101

170. McFarland, D. D. 1970. Effects of group size on the availability of marriage partners. *Demography* 7:411–15

171. McFarland, D. D. 1972. Comparison of alternative marriage models. See Ref. 92, 89–106

172. McKinley, K. R. 1971. Survivorship in Gracile and Robust Australopithecines: A demographic comparison and a proposed birth model. *Am. J. Phys. Anthropol.* 34:417–26

173. Miller, M. D. 1949. Elements of graduation. *Actuarial Monogr. No. 1.* Chicago: Soc. Actuaries

174. Mitra, S. 1973. On the efficiency of the estimates of life table functions. *Demography* 10:421–26

175. Moore, J. A., Swedlund, A. C., Armelagos, G. J. 1975. The use of life tables in paleodemography. See Ref. 234, 57–70

176. Morton, N. E. 1969. Human population structure. *Ann. Rev. Genet.* 3:53–74

177. Morton, N. E., Ed. 1973. *Genetic Structure of Populations.* Honolulu: Univ. Hawaii Press

178. Morton, N. E., Imaizumi, Y., Harris, D. E. 1971. Clans as genetic barriers. *Am. Anthropol.* 73:1005–10

179. Neel, J. V. 1971. Genetic aspects of the ecology of disease in the American Indian. In *The Ongoing Evolution of Latin American Populations,* ed. F. M. Salzano, 561–90. Springfield: Thomas

180. Neel, J. V., Centerwall, W. R., Chagnon, N. A., Casey, H. L. 1970. Notes on the effect of measles and measles vaccine in a virgin-soil population of South American Indians. *Am. J. Epidemiol.* 91:418–29

181. Neel, J. V., Salzano, F. M. 1967. Further studies on the Xavante Indians. X. Some hypotheses—generalizations resulting from these studies. *Am. J. Hum. Genet.* 19:554–74

182. Neel, J. V., Schull, W. J. 1972. Differential fertility and human evolution. *Evol. Biol.* 6:363–78

183. Neel, J. V., Ward, R. H. 1970. Village and tribal genetic distances among American Indians, and the possible implications for human evolution. *Proc. Natl. Acad. Sci. USA* 65:323–30

184. Neel, J. V., Weiss, K. M. 1975. The genetic structure of a tribal population, the Yanomama Indians. XII. Biodemographic studies. *Am. J. Phys. Anthropol.* 42:25–51

185. Nei, M., Imaizumi, Y. 1966. Genetic structure of human populations. *Heredity* 21:183–90

186. Nortman, D. 1974. Parental age as a factor in pregnancy outcome and child development. *Rep. Popul./ Fam. Plann. No. 16*

187. Norton, S. L. 1971. Population growth in Colonial America: A study of Ipswich, Massachusetts. *Popul. Studies* 25:433–52

188. Parlett, B. 1970. Ergodic properties of populations. I. The one sex model. *Theor. Popul. Biol.* 1:191–207

189. Parlett, B. 1972. Can there be a marriage function? See Ref. 92, 107–35

190. Petersen, W. 1975. A demographer's view of prehistoric demography. *Curr. Anthropol.* 16:227–45

191. Peterson, N. 1975. Hunter-gatherer territoriality: The perspective from Australia. *Am. Anthropol.* 77:53–68

192. Pielou, E. C. 1969. *An Introduction to Mathematical Ecology.* New York: Wiley

193. Polgar, S., Ed. 1971. *Culture and Population: A Collection of Current Studies.* Cambridge: Schenkman

193a. Polgar, S. 1972. Population history and population policies from an anthropological perspective. *Curr. Anthropol.* 13:203–11

193b. Polgar, S., Ed. 1975. *Population, Ecology and Social Evolution.* Chicago: Aldine.

194. Pollak, E., Kempthorne, O. 1970. Malthusian parameters in genetic populations. I. Haploid and selfing models. *Theor. Popul. Biol.* 1:315–45

195. Ibid 1971. Malthusian parameters in

genetic populations. II. Random mating populations in infinite habitats. 2:357–90

196. Pollard, J. H. 1966. On the use of the direct matrix product in analyzing certain stochastic population models. *Biometrika* 53:397–415

197. Pollard, J. H. 1973. *Mathematical Models for the Growth of Human Populations*. Cambridge Univ. Press

198. Preston, S. H. 1972. Influence of cause of death structure on age-patterns of mortality. See Ref. 92, 201–50

199. Preston, S. H. 1972. Interrelations between death rates and birth rates. *Theor. Popul. Biol.* 3:162–85

200. Preston, S. H., Keyfitz, N., Schoen, R. 1972. *Causes of Death: Life Tables for National Populations*. New York: Seminar

201. Preston, S. H., Nelson, V. E. 1974. Structure and change in causes of death: An international summary. *Popul. Stud.* 28:19–51

202. Rao, B. R., Mazumdar, S., Waller, J. H., Li, C. C. 1973. Correlation between the numbers of two types of children in a family. *Biometrics* 29:271–79

203. Reid, R. M. 1973. Inbreeding in human populations. See Ref. 65, 83–116

204. Roberts, D. F. 1964. Assumption and fact in anthropological genetics. *J. R. Anthropol. Inst.* 1964:87–102

205. Roberts, D. F. 1967. The development of inbreeding in an island population. *Cienc. Cult.* 19:78–84

206. Roberts, D. F. 1968. Genetic effects of population size reduction. *Nature* 220:1084–88

207. Roberts, D. F., Mohan, M. 1976. History, demography and genetics: The Fiji experience and its evolutionary implications. See Ref. 252, 117–28

208. Rowell, T. E. 1966. Forest-living baboons in Uganda. *J. Zool.* 149:344–64

209. Rowell, T. 1972. *The Social Behaviour of Monkeys*. Baltimore: Penguin

210. Salzano, F. M. 1963. Some genetic aspects of the demography of American Indians. See Ref. 229, 23–39

211. Salzano, F. M. 1972. Genetic aspects of the demography of American Indians and Eskimos. See Ref. 99, 234–51

212. Sanders, W. T. 1972. Population, agricultural history, and societal evolution in Mesoamerica. See Ref. 226, 101–53

213. Sanders, W. T., Price, B. J. 1968. *Mesoamerica: The Evolution of a Civilization*. New York: Random House

214. Schaller, G. B., Lowther, G. R. 1969. The relevance of carnivore behavior to the study of early hominids. *Southwest, J. Anthropol.* 25:307–41

215. Schull, W. J. 1972. Primitive populations—some contributions to the understanding of human population genetics. See Ref. 47, 112–23

216. Schull, W. J. 1972. Genetic implications of population breeding structure. See Ref. 99, 146–64

217. Schull, W. J., MacCluer, J. W. 1968. Human genetics: Structure of human populations. *Ann. Rev. Genet.* 2:279–304

218. Schwidetzky, I. 1965. Sonder bestattung und ihre paläodemographische bedeutung. *Homo* 18:230–47

219. Sharpe, F. R., Lotka, A. J. 1911. A problem in age-distribution. *Philos. Mag.* 21:435–38

220. Sheps, M. C., Menken, J. A. 1973. *Mathematical Models of Conception and Birth*. Univ. Chicago Press

221. Shryock, H. S., Siegel, J. S. 1971. *The Methods and Materials of Demography*. Washington DC: GPO

222. Skolnick, M. H., Cannings, C. C. 1972. Natural regulation of numbers in primitive human populations. *Nature* 239:287–88

223. Skolnick, M. H., Cannings, C. C. 1973. Simulation of small human populations. See Ref. 76, 167–96

224. Smith, C., Falconer, D. S., Duncan, L. J. P. 1972. A statistical and genetical study of diabetes. II. Heritability of liability. *Ann. Hum. Genet.* 35:281–99

225. Smouse, P. E., Weiss, K. M. 1975. Discrete demographic models with density-dependent vital rates. *Oecologia* 21:205–18

226. Spooner, B. 1972. *Population Growth: Anthropological Implications*. Cambridge: MIT Press

226a. Spuhler, J. N. 1976. Index of natural selection in human populations. See Ref. 277

227. Stott, D. H. 1962. Cultural and natural checks on population growth.

In *Culture and the Evolution of Man,* ed. M. F. Ashley-Montague, 355–76. Oxford Univ. Press

228. Sussman, R. W. 1972. Child transport, family size, and increase in human population during the Neolithic. *Curr. Anthropol.* 13:258–59

229. Sutter, J., Ed. 1962. *Human Displacements.* Entretiens de Monaco en Sciences Humaines

230. Sutter, J. 1963. The relationship between human population genetics and demography. In *The Genetics of Migrant and Isolate Populations,* ed. E. Goldschmidt, 160–68. Baltimore: Williams & Wilkins

231. Sutter, J., Toan, T-N. 1957. The problem of the structure of isolates and of their evolution among human populations. *Cold Spring Harbor Symp.* 22:379–83

232. Swedlund, A. C. 1971. The genetic structure of an historical population: A study of marriage and fertility in Old Deerfield, Massachusetts. *Univ. Mass. Dep. Anthropol. Res. Rep. No. 7*

233. Swedlund, A. C. 1972. Observations on the concept of neighborhood knowledge and the distribution of marriage distances. *Ann. Hum. Genet.* 35:327–30

234. Swedlund, A., Ed. 1975. *Population studies in archaeology and biological anthropology: A symposium.* Soc. Am. Archaeol. Mem. 30

235. Swedlund, A. C., Armelagos, G. J. 1969. Une recherche en paléodémographie: La Nubie soudanaise. *Ann. Econ. Soc. Civilis.* 6:1287–98

236. Swedlund, A., Armelagos, G. J. 1975. *Demographic Anthropology.* Dubuque: Brown

237. Sykes, Z. M. 1969. Some stochastic versions of the matrix model for population dynamics. *J. Am. Stat. Assoc.* 64:111–30

238. Sykes, Z. M. 1969. On discrete stable population theory. *Biometrics* 25:285–93

239. Talwar, P. P. 1970. Age patterns of fertility. *Univ. North Carolina Inst. Stat., Mimeo Ser. No. 656*

239a. Teleki, G. 1975. Primate subsistence patterns: Collector-predators and gatherer-hunters. *J. Hum. Evol.* 4:125–84

240. Trivers, R. L. 1971. The evolution of reciprocal altruism. *Q. Rev. Biol.* 46:35–57

241. Ubelaker, D. H. 1974. Reconstruction of demographic profiles from ossuary skeletal samples: A case study from the tidewater Potomac. *Smithsonian Contrib. Anthropol. No. 18*

242. Underwood, J. H. 1969. Preliminary investigations of demographic features and ecological variables of a Micronesian island population. *Micronesia* 5:1–14

243. Underwood, J. H. 1973. The demography of a myth: Abortion in Yap. *Hum. Biol. Oceania* 2:115–27

244. Underwood, J. H. 1973. Population history of Guam: Context of human microevolution. *Micronesia* 19:11–44

245. United Nations 1955. Age and sex patterns of mortality: Model life tables for underdeveloped countries. *Popul. Stud. No. 22*

246. United Nations 1956. Methods for population projections by sex and age. *Popul. Stud. No. 25*

247. Vayda, A. P. 1974. Warfare in ecological perspective. *Ann. Rev. Ecol. Syst.* 5:183–93

248. Ward, R. H. 1972. The genetic structure of a tribal population, the Yanomama Indians. V. Comparisons of a series of genetic networks. *Ann. Hum. Genet.* 36:21–43

249. Ward, R. H. 1973. Some aspects of genetic structure in the Yanomama and Makiritare: Two tribes of Southern Venezuela. See Ref. 65, 367–88

250. Ward, R. H., Neel, J. V. 1970. Gene frequencies and microdifferentiation among the Makiritare Indians. IV. A comparison of a genetic network with ethnohistory and migration matrices; a new index of genetic isolation. *Am. J. Hum. Genet.* 22:538–61

251. Ward, R. H., Neel, J. V. 1976. The genetic structure of a tribal population, the Yanomama Indians. XVII. Clines and their interpretation. *Genetics.* In press

252. Ward, R. H., Weiss, K. M. 1976. *The Demographic Evolution of Human Populations.* London: Academic [also *J. Hum. Evol.* 5(1)]

253. Weiss, K. M. 1972. On the systematic bias in skeletal sexing. *Am. J. Phys. Anthropol.* 37:239–50

254. Ibid. A general measure of human population growth regulation, 337–44

255. Weiss, K. M. 1973. *Demographic models for anthropology.* Soc. Am. Archaeol. Mem. 27

256. Weiss, K. M. 1975. The application of demographic methods to anthropological data. *Hum. Ecol.* 3:87–103

257. Weiss, K. M. 1975. Demographic disturbance and the use of life tables in anthropology. See Ref. 234, 46–56

258. Weiss, K. M., Ballonoff, P. A. 1975. *Demographic Genetics.* Stroudsburg, Pa.: Dowden, Hutchinson, Ross

259. Weiss, K. M., Maruyama, T. 1976. Archaeology, population genetics, and studies of human racial ancestry. *Am. J. Phys. Anthropol.* In press

260. Weiss, K. M., Smouse, P. E. 1976. The demographic stability of small human populations. See Ref. 252, 59–73

261. West, M. J. 1967. Foundress associations in polistine wasps. Dominance hierarchies and the evolution of social behavior. *Science* 157:1584–85

262. West-Eberhard, M. J. 1975. The evolution of social behavior by kin selection. *Q. Rev. Biol.* 50:1–33

263. Williams, B. J. 1974. *A model of band society. Soc. Am. Archaeol. Mem. 29*

264. Williams, B. J. 1975. Age differentials between spouses and Australian marriage systems. See. Ref. 234, 38–43

265. Williams, G. C. 1966. *Adaptation and Natural Selection. A Critique of Some Current Evolutionary Thought.* Princeton Univ. Press

266. Williams, G. C., Ed. 1971. *Group Selection.* Chicago: Aldine-Atherton

267. Wilmsen, E. N. 1973. Interaction, spacing behavior and the organization of hunting bands. *J. Anthropol. Res.* 29:1–31

268. Wilson, E. O. 1975. *Sociobiology: The New Synthesis.* Cambridge: Harvard Univ. Press

269. Wobst, H. M. 1974. Boundary conditions for Paleolithic social systems: A simulation approach. *Am. Antiq.* 29:147–78

270. Wobst, H. M. 1975. The demography of finite populations and the origins of the incest taboo. See Ref. 234, 75–81

271. Wobst, H. M. 1976. Locational relationships in Paleolithic society. See Ref. 252, 49–58

272. Wynne-Edwards, V. C. 1962. *Animal Dispersion in Relation to Social Behavior.* New York: Hafner

273. Yasuda, N., Cavalli-Sforza, L. L., Skolnick, M., Moroni, A. 1974. The evolution of surnames: An analysis of their distribution and extinction. *Theor. Popul. Biol.* 5:123–42

274. Yengoyan, A. A. 1968. Demographic and ecological influences on aboriginal Australian marriage sections. See Ref. 143, 185–99

275. Yengoyan, A. A. 1971. Demographic factors in Pitjandjara social organization. In *Australian Aboriginal Anthropology,* ed. R. M. Berndt, 70–91. Univ. Western Australia Press

276. Zubrow, E. B. W. 1971. Carrying capacity and dynamic equilibrium in the pre-historic southwest. *Am. Antiq.* 36:127–38

276a. Zubrow, E. B. W. 1973. Adequacy criteria and prediction in archaeological models. In *Research and Theory in Current Archaeology,* ed. C. Redman, 239–60. New York: Wiley

276b. Zubrow, E. B. W. 1975. *Prehistoric Carrying Capacity: A Model.* Menlo Park, Ca.: Cummings

277. Zubrow, E. B. W. 1976. *Demographic Anthropology: Quantitative Approaches.* Albuquerque: Univ. New Mexico Press

277a. Ibid. Stability and instability: A problem in long-term regional growth.

AUTHOR INDEX

SUBJECT INDEX

introduction, 169-71
origins, 173-75
sociolinguistics, 184-85
summary and forecast,
188
universals, 175-78
variability, 178-82
Crime
criminal behavior types, 9
Cross-cultural studies
of children's play, 295-97
computer citations in, 25
definition of cities, 250-52,
255, 261
and emic/etic distinction,
341-42
Cultural
anthropology
indexes of, 18-19
materialism
and the emic/etic distinction, 329-48
transmission
and child ethology, 271-72
content of, 204-5
interactive mode of, 202-
3
participants in, 203
theory work in, 195-208
Curiosity
comparative studies of,
267
Cytochrome c
in protein evolution, 73

D

Dakar
see Senegal
Daribi
of New Guinea
and descent ideology, 120
Deaf
sign language
implicational patterns in,
102
Demographic theory, 351-72
and anthropological genetics,
361-63
computer simulation, 362-
63
and anthropological inference, 351-61
age patterns of birth and
death, 352-61
demographic status and
evolution, 360-61
fertility, 358-60
introduction, 351-52
mortality, 357-58
paleodemography, 356-57
sample size, 355
ecological demography, 363-
67
hunter-gatherer popula-
tions, 363-65
population growth and size,

365-67
and social behavior
biodemographic aspects
of, 367-70
Dependency theory
and authority
in Indian culture, 223
and social stratification,
235
Dermatoglyphics
of African populations, 149,
151-54
Descent
groups and categories, 123-
36
ideology and behavior, 117-
20
see Kin groups
Developmental studies
of children's play, 310-12
Diseases
and demographic theory,
354, 358, 360, 371
Djuka
comparative word list for
and creole studies, 187
DNA
controller
in protein evolution, 80-
85
translation into amino acids,
71
Dominance
in young children, 270, 273
Dominance hierarchies
social aspects of
and demographic theory,
367-68
Dreams
evolutionary theory of, 270-
71
and imitation in childhood,
310
Duau
children's play, 309

E

Ecological demography, 363-
67
hunter-gatherer populations,
363-65
population growth and size,
365-67
Ecological studies
of children's play, 305-7
Economics
bibliography of, 19
Education
cultural theory of, 206-7
and culture
and children's play, 289
and mobility
in East Africa, 237
and social stratification,
244
in Taleland

social and psychological
aspects of, 298
Educational technology
sociocultural relevance of
in India, 223
Egypt
children's play in
comparative studies of,
296
roving palaces of
and city studies, 258
and Upper Palaeolithic
archaeology, 136-37
Electrophoresis
in amino acid sequencing,
74-75, 84-85
El Salvador
archaeological sites
and origins of Mesoameri-
can writing, 55-56
Emic/etic distinction
history and significance of,
329-48
behavioral and mental vs
etic and emic, 340-41
behavior stream events,
337-38
Burling's critique, 334-
35
cognitive rules, 336-37
cross-cultural compari-
sons, 341-44
emics and consciousness,
338-39
emics, meaning, and
purpose, 333-34
etics as observable, 339-
40
materialist epistemology,
330-31
mind vs behavior stream,
329-30
origins of terms, 331-32
Pike's behavioremes, 332-
33
and speech acts, 344-48
use of informants, 341
Emotions
comparative studies of,
271
Enculturation
and children's play, 297-
301
Endogamy
and microdifferentiation
studies, 161
Enga
of New Guinea
descent ideology among,
120
England
children's games in, 294,
305-6
comparative studies of,
296
English
Black

H

Hadza
  physical studies of, 152,
    157
Haitian Creole
  and pidgin studies, 169, 182,
    187
Hawaiian pidgin-creole
  studies of, 169, 171, 175-78,
    180-81
Hemoglobin
  and amino acid substitutions,
    74
  studies
    of African populations,
      160
Heredity
  early works on, 9
Hindu
  caste system
    and ideology, 238-39,
      244
  and social-cultural anthro-
    pology, 218
Histone IV
  lack of variation
    among species, 77
Holland (Michigan) Dutch
  children
    height-weight tables for,
      9
Holocene industry
  in India and Egypt, 136,
    138
Honduras
  origins of Classic Maya
    writing in, 56
Hottentots
  physical studies of, 159
Human relations area files,
    26-27
Humor
  and children's play
    communication studies of,
      302
Hunting and gathering
  in demographic theory, 357,
    363-65
  and social stratification
    theories, 228, 230, 245
Hyaturu
  physical studies of, 158
Hybridization
  early views of, 8-9

I

Iberia
  roving palaces of
    and city studies, 258
Ideology
  and experience
    in social stratification,
      237-38, 243-45
  see also Kin groups
Imitation

as socialization process,
    291, 297-301
Immune response
  in amino acid comparisons,
    74-75, 78
Incest taboo
  in comparative ethology,
    269-70
  in hunter-gatherer societies
    and demographic theory,
      364
India
  anthropological survey of,
    211
  ethnography
    and descent theory, 109
  household formation in
    and emic/etic destinction,
      339
  pidgin and creole studies in,
    172
  social-cultural anthropology
    in, 209-23
    focus, 209-13
    influence and perspectives,
      213-18
    interests and trends, 218-
      23
  and Upper Palaeolithic
    archaeology, 136-37, 141
Indians
  North American
    games of, 289, 309-10,
      314-15, 319
Indo-European language
  as parent of pidgin, 170
Indonesia
  ethnography
    and descent theory,
      109
Industry
  in India
    studies of, 222-23
Infant
  behavior studies
    in child ethology, 273-74
  and child-care patterns
    in comparative ethology,
      268-69, 274
  psychomotor development
    comparative studies of,
      150
Intellectual output
  and growth and maturation
    factors, 150
Ireland
  peoples of
    survey of, 9
Isoglossic theory
  and non-state linguistics,
    94-99
Israel
  children's games in, 296,
    299
  Mousterian industry in, 138-
    39
Italo-Spanish language

in pidgin studies, 171

J

Jamaica
  politics and language in,
    170
  race crossing in, 8
Jamaican Creole
  and pidgin studies, 169-70,
    179
Japan
  and Upper Palaeolithic
    archaeology, 136-37
Japanese
  children's play
    compared to Americans',
      296
Jermanovician industry
  of Poland, 140
Juba Arabic
  in pidgin and creole studies,
    186
Jugoslavia
  Upper Palaeolithic archae-
    ology in, 138-39
  burial cave, 143

K

Kachin
  social stratification
    and ideology, 244
Kadar
  of India
    restudy of, 220
Kannada
  and pidgin and creole studies,
    172
Kel Kummer
  demography and genealogies
    among, 161
Khasi
  of India
    restudy of, 220
Khoikhoi
  physical studies of, 154,
    159
Khoisan
  physical studies of, 159
Khormusan industry
  as Upper Palaeolithic, 137
Kibbutz children
  and incest avoidance, 270
Kikuyu
  physical studies of, 150,
    156
Kin groups
  and behavior study, 107-28
    conclusion, 126-28
    descent groups and catego-
      ries, 123-26
    descent ideology and behav-
      ior, 117-20
    local and kin groups, 115-
      17
    natives' and anthropologists'

CUMULATIVE INDEXES

CONTRIBUTING AUTHORS VOLUMES 1-5